P9-BJB-058

THE MAKING OF MODERN EUROPE 1648–1780

Geoffrey Treasure

THE MAKING OF MODERN EUROPE 1648–1780

Methuen · London & New York

First published in 1985 by
Methuen & Co. Ltd
11 New Fetter Lane
London EC4P 4EE

Published in the USA by
Methuen & Co.
in association with Methuen, Inc.
29 West 35th Street
New York, NY 10001

Typeset in Great Britain by
Northumberland Press Ltd
Gateshead, Tyne & Wear
and printed by
Richard Clay (The Chaucer Press) Ltd
Bungay, Suffolk

British Library Cataloguing in Publication Data

Treasure, G. R. R.
The making of modern Europe 1648–1780.
1. Europe – History – 1648–1780
I. Title
940.2′5 D273

ISBN 0-416-72360-8
ISBN 0-416-72370-5 Pbk

Library of Congress Cataloging in Publication Data

Treasure, G. R. R. (Geoffrey, Russell Richard)
The making of modern Europe, 1648–1780.
Bibliography: p.
Includes index.
1. Europe – History – 17th century.
2. Europe – History – 18th century.
I. Title.
D246.T74 1985 940.2′5 85-255

ISBN 0-416-72360-8
ISBN 0-416-72370-5 (pbk.)

TO ALEXANDRA

CONTENTS

LIST OF MAPS

PREFACE

Around the middle of the seventeenth century European life was transformed in many areas. In 1640 revolts in Catalonia and Portugal shook the stability of the Spanish state in a way which was to alter the balance of power in Europe. In the decade that followed there were disturbances, conflicts or rebellions in most states. In 1648 the last shots were fired, in Prague, of a war which had started there thirty years before and which had subsumed other conflicts to become the most damaging of European wars, at least until the twentieth century. Revolts caused primarily by the pressures of war mark this book's point of departure. The recovery and subsequent growth of states in a manner largely determined by their military needs provides its central theme.

'The making of modern Europe' is no empty phrase. In those years, out of the ferment of ideas that characterized the seventeenth century, European man emerged in some ways recognizably 'modern', and with him, the leading states which, to an increasing extent, controlled his life. The intellectual revolution, which engendered a critical attitude towards traditional authority, was responsible also for the confident assertion of a new kind of authority. Essentially secular, it derived its strength from faith in reason and research: from the scientists' methods, which could guide men towards a better understanding of the material universe and of their place in it, and from statesmen who sought a more humane and efficient use of power for the good of their peoples. Some consciously adopted the role of enlightened autocrat. Sovereigns like Frederick the

Great of Prussia, Joseph II of Austria, Catherine the Great of Russia, Charles III of Spain, Stanislaus of Poland and Leopold of Tuscany, and statesmen like Pombal of Portugal, Struensee of Denmark and Tanucci of Naples carried out reforms whose range is no more remarkable than the apparent unanimity of aim, method, even style which earned for the last decades of the *ancien régime* the title 'enlightened despotism'. I think it more appropriate to speak of 'enlightened absolutism': it conveys both the vitality of an aristocratic culture which affected most rulers in one way or another, and also the culmination of the prevailing trend towards the concentration of authority in the person of the ruler, embodying as he did the ever-increasing powers of the state. Even then it can be misleading as a concept, though not without value, if it be assumed to represent an ideology and if the record of the reforming sovereigns is judged outside the context of the history of their states. I have chosen to stress continuity, as for example within the Hohenzollern lands from the Great Elector to Frederick the Great, rather than to isolate one group of rulers for comparative treatment. I believe that history presented as the story of particular states, each with its distinctive traditions and institutions, has an essential part to play in complementing analysis of society and institutions: it provides a manageable framework within which the student can discover how statesmen ruled, and how their rule affected their subjects.

The author of a general history of Europe covering 140 years is faced with painful choices. Readers will find little here about art or music, except where, as in the case of Holland or Austria, a particularly rich achievement offers essential clues to the nature of the parent society. I urge the reader who wishes to know and understand Europe in the age of the baroque to listen to its music, look at its works of art and then perhaps to read the books of those who know more than I do about their technical aspects. Though I believe that another interesting history of Europe could be compiled from the experience of those peoples – Belgians, Swiss, the inhabitants of the smaller German and Italian states and of the Balkan lands under the Turks – where there was lacking (perhaps fortunately for them) the independence, unity or weight to count for much in diplomacy or war, I have reluctantly left them out of the reckoning in what is, in the main, a study of the major powers. At the same time I have sought to convey something of the spirit of the age in chapters about the orders of society, about people's faith and knowledge and the activities which reveal so much about their life: agriculture or trade, diplomacy or war.

This book has been long in the making. What it has lost to the diverse occupations of the schoolmaster it may have gained in the continuing experience of teaching: in years of trying to meet the needs of students, who naturally want things to be clear and orderly; and in having to restrain my own inclination to pursue what is curious and exceptional, which can so easily lead to a blurring of the outlines. I am grateful too for the delights of exploring the work of the many talented writers whose books are mentioned in the lists of recommended reading at the end of each chapter, and for the patience and helpfulness of those at Methuen and at home who made it all possible.

In particular I thank Peter Brooks, who first asked me to write this book; my colleagues in the Harrow School history department, especially Howard Shaw and Tony Beadles, for their interest and help over many years; Anna Fedden, Mary Cusack and Judith Ravenscroft of Methuen; L.C.B. Seaman for his constructive criticisms of the manuscript; Charlotte Park, Heather Beadles and Carolyne Darley who have wrestled with its typing; and at home my wife Melisa, who has shared in so much of the work, and Alexandra, Magdalen and Georgiana for their shiftwork on the index.

Harrow, May Day, 1984

Acknowledgement

The author and publisher would like to thank the copyright-holders for permission to base our Maps 2.2, 4.1 and 7.1 on maps in the *Hamlyn Historical Atlas* (1981), ed. R. Moore. © Newnes Books, a division of The Hamlyn Publishing Group Limited and Creative Cartography Limited, 1981, 1983.

I

THE EUROPEAN WORLD

The Bounds

In 1600, 'Europe' was still a term without precise political significance, an area without recognized external frontiers, except where seas provided them. During the century, as frontiers were delineated in diplomatic encounters of an increasingly sophisticated kind, the idea of Europe came to mean more. A cosmopolitan civilization was evolving. Though they may distinguish between eastern and western Europe, historians who write about this or that 'revolution', military, scientific or commercial, envisage the continent as a whole rather than a single state. By 1700 statesmen like the Anglo-Dutch William III had begun to talk about Europe as an interest to be defended against the ambition of a particular state. Louis XIV, with 20 million subjects, sovereign of about a fifth of the people of Europe, spoke confidently of 'giving peace to Europe'. Congresses assembled periodically after the peace of Westphalia (1648), itself the product of the first of such diplomatic gatherings, to settle European questions of peace and war, boundaries, commercial and political rights.

The western state system had broadened by 1600 to include all the continent from the Hebrides to the Dardanelles, but there remained a fringe area, from Norway to the Caspian sea, of states moving in their own orbits, absorbed in questions which mattered little to the Atlantic and Mediterranean powers. Commercial interests drew England, France and Holland to the Baltic and diplomacy had created certain links: Henry Valois became

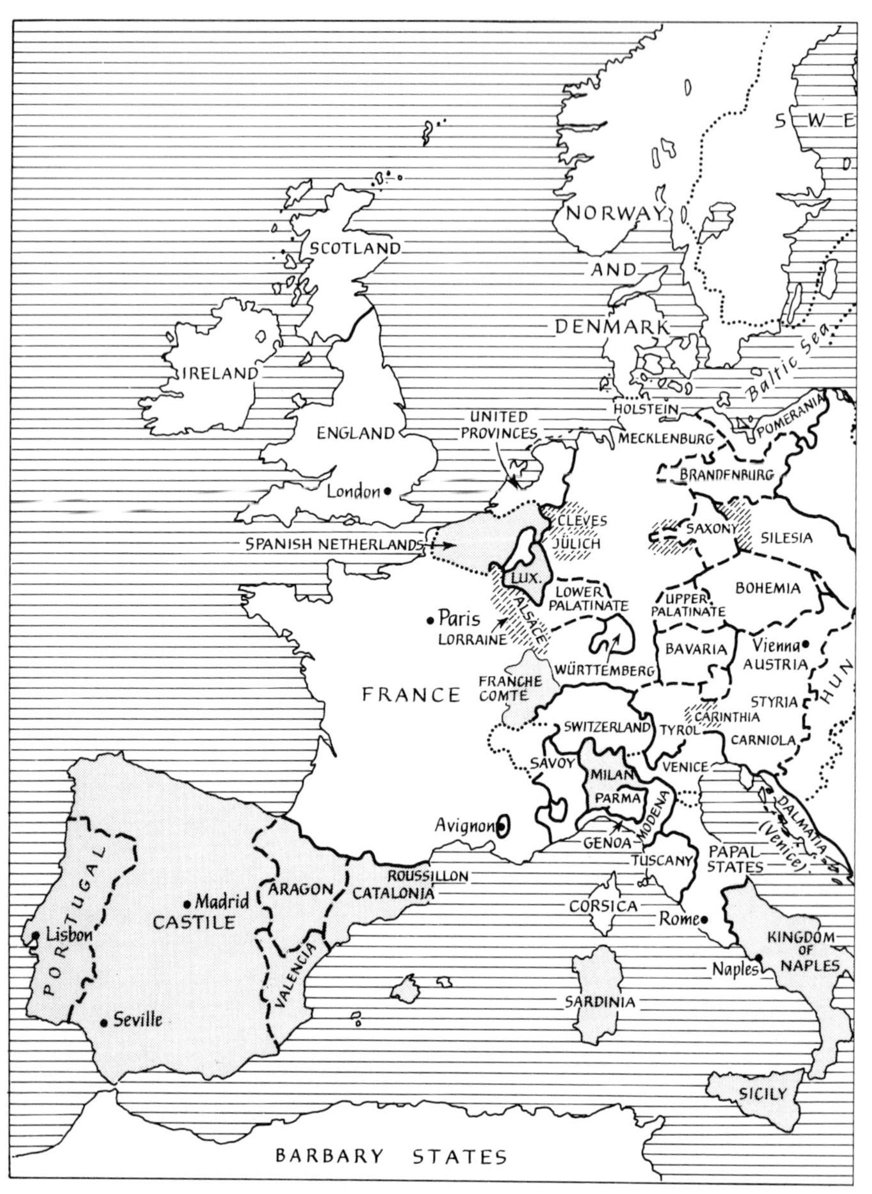

Map 1.1 *European frontiers in 1640*

Stable frontiers
Uncertain frontiers and regions of conflict
Boundaries within larger political units
Regions of broken frontiers and 'islands' of territory
Spanish possessions
DEN
INGRIA
ESTONIA
LIVONIA
Moscow
RUSSIA
KALMUKS
LITHUANIA
E. PRUSSIA
POLAND
DON COSSACKS
Caspian Sea
ZAPAROZHIAN COSSACKS
GARY
JEDISAN
MOLDAVIA
KHANATE OF THE CRIMEA
TRANSYLVANIA
Black Sea
SLAVONIA
WALLACHIA
ARMENIA
SERBIA
BOSNIA
BULGARIA
TREBIZOND
OTTOMAN
Constantinople
Ragusa
EMPIRE
KURDISTAN
ALBANIA
ANATOLIA
MOREA
CYPRUS
CRETE
0
400 km

king of Poland, James I of England married Anne of Denmark. But it was still usual for western statesmen to treat the Baltic states as belonging to a separate northern system, governed by its own interests and its own power balance. While the states appeared to be spending much of their energy upon fighting each other, political experience, economic progress and certain common cultural trends were binding them more closely together. Warfare, after 1648, was conducted on a grand scale but was limited both in objectives and, except indirectly, in its effect upon civilians: a deadly sport for professionals, the soldiers and their political masters.

Awareness of allegiance to a country, even where, as in France or Spain, there was an honoured tradition and a political reality behind the idea, seems to have been confined to quite small groups who had rights, responsibilities and an educated vision of this transcendent idea. It was beyond the ken of the ordinary villager or townsman for whom 'the political nation' only existed in the shape of the tax collector. The last century and a half of Europe's *ancien régime* was to see a general growth in the powers of the states; only Poland failed entirely in this respect and eventually paid the price. Yet the common features of government and societies remained more important than their differences. This book traces the separate course of particular states, but first examines the characteristics of the whole society. What lies before us is a whole culture and a continent still in equipoise, before the disruption and fragmentation that were to come with the rise of nationalism and the industrial democracies of modern times.

Turkey was in Europe but scarcely of it. The outposts of Ottoman power, and its satellites, defined the long eastern boundary from Moldavia to Dalmatia and across the Mediterranean. The line between Orthodox Russia and the rest of Christian Europe was never so sharp as that which divided Christendom and Islam. Northwards, Europe simply petered out, as it were, in the immensity of the steppes, the Pripet marshes, and forests of birch and alder. Except among those immediately affected, such as Swedes, Lithuanians and Poles, there was vagueness and lack of interest more than hostility. During the seventeenth century, however, Russia was drawn into the European orbit. The peace of Andrussovo (1667), giving Tsar Alexis the formerly Polish lands east of the Dnieper, with the city of Kiev, was a milestone as notable as the peace of Carlowitz (1699) which secured Hungary for the Habsburgs. The stormy reign of Tsar Peter I saw a deliberate effort to force the western powers to take Russia seriously. By his death, in 1725, Russia was a European state: still colonizing rather than assimilating her eastern lands and relatively little affected by the process; interlocked, however, with the diplomatic system of the west; western in forms, if not spirit, of government. Renaissance men had drawn the north-eastern boundary of Europe not at the Urals, but at the Don. Now a larger Europe began to take shape as the Christian Balkan peoples, who had preserved their identities and traditions under a tolerant Turkish rule

– Magyars, Croats, Serbs and Bulgars – began to lift their heads again. By 1700 the Dardanelles and the Bosphorus, the Black Sea, Caucasus and Urals marked the eastern limits. Still, however, the fringe lands remained indeterminate. Men were only starting to think, even in the west, of linear frontiers which defined the whole state rather than particular estates.

Racial differences were not yet being exploited for political ends, but they were important since they corresponded to characteristic cultures. Tall Teutons north of the Rhineland, round-headed Celts of the west, dark long-headed Mediterranean men and women provide some obvious contrasts. The high-cheekboned Slavs, originally the westward-migrating tribes checked by Charlemagne along the boundary which has ever since been one of the continent's crucial lines of demarcation, were becoming less distinctive as German colonists and speech spread into Slav areas, but Slavonic dialects persisted. In Russia the eastern Slavs absorbed their Tartar neighbours; the southern Slavs of the Balkans lost their identity neither to Ottoman conquerors nor to Habsburg liberators. The development of national languages was pointing meanwhile towards one of the potent forces of the future; it was part of the process by which states extended their control over their subjects. In France, under the scrutiny of the Academy, founded in 1635, the refinement of the language prepared the way for its civilizing role; French was soon to displace Latin as the common language of Europe's diplomats and savants. The Austrian bureaucracy, which had most to fear from racial and linguistic differences, used German wherever possible, so emphasizing its supremacy over Czech and Magyar. Everywhere the accepted usage of government and court was driving out the languages of minorities; everywhere provincial dialects were being abandoned by the educated: Provençal or Breton French would raise a smile at Versailles. The survival in Poland of the languages of several minorities, notably Ukrainian and German and the use of Latin for government business, was a mark of that country's weakness.

A vital element in Europe yet not part of Christendom were the Jews, an alien people of great value to the parent society. Within Jewry were two strains: the Sephardim, who had fled from Spain to other parts of Europe, and the Ashkenazim, the poorer Jews of the north and east. Whether rich merchants and money lenders, or poor artisans, the Jews did more than survive. They were strengthened by the isolated conditions in which they were forced to live, and united in respect for their rabbis, ordained guardians of cherished laws and history. In 1655 Cromwell re-admitted them to England. From France and Spain they were still officially excluded, to the detriment of those countries, as the experience of Holland suggests. There Jews were able to live and work in peace. The career of Spinoza, for example, would have been unthinkable in any other land; indeed it was his own congregation of Jews that condemned him for his radical views. More tolerant attitudes gained ground elsewhere in the eighteenth century:

'enlightened' statesmen, like Pombal of Portugal, preferred Jews to Jesuits, but popular prejudice remained strong.

The Jews had ever to bear the guilt of the crucifixion – as Christians were often reminded by their priests. At a time when it was generally accepted that morality depended upon religion, the Jews were presumed to be immoral. They were usually despised even where, as in parts of Germany and in Poland, they were relatively numerous. Some four-fifths of all European Jews were living in Poland by 1772. Of these Jews at the time of the Cossack raids, drawing upon a communal tradition which exile had little devalued, the Yiddish writer Isaac Bashevis Singer has written powerfully in his novel *The Slave* (1962), describing the antagonisms roused by a vulnerable, alien culture. In Poland are encountered the extremes in Jewry: the immensely rich capitalists, often corrupt in the pursuit of money and office; the numerous poor, tenacious of life and faith amid urban squalor; the ultra-conservatives; the mystical devotees of the cult of Hasidinism. Elsewhere greater social disabilities rarely weakened their economic position. They were persistently successful in adapting their methods to the changing rhythms and patterns of international trade, resourceful in finance, especially in the enlarging fields of banking and maritime brokerage, and they benefited from the exchange of information and capital with trusted co-religionists in other centres. At the same time they managed to remain, though scattered, and often living in ghetto conditions, a distinct civilization: in Braudel's words, 'a kind of confessional nation'.

A Human Scale

The exceptional situation of the Jews serves to emphasize the prime fact: Europe was Christendom. That was a significant term at a time when men almost universally accepted, in and over the animist world where magic still held many of them in thrall, the sovereignty of God and his laws, and when, at the start of the period, princes still believed that it might be their duty to defend Christianity against the infidel – and their own version of the faith against their fellow Christians. The churches which embodied the various interpretations of Christian truth were, as institutions, the grandest expression of the corporate ideal that shaped life at all levels. It can also be seen in institutions as distinctive in style and purpose as the *cofradías* of Spain or the *scuole* of Venice; or as universal as the guilds that everywhere controlled both conditions of employment and the production and marketing of goods. The order, college, guild or fraternity provided for nobles, churchmen, professional men, merchants and craftsmen alike the framework of social discipline; with it went that civilizing sense of belonging to a family of common interests which had been the positive aspect of 'feudalism' and which still characterized attitudes and institutions.

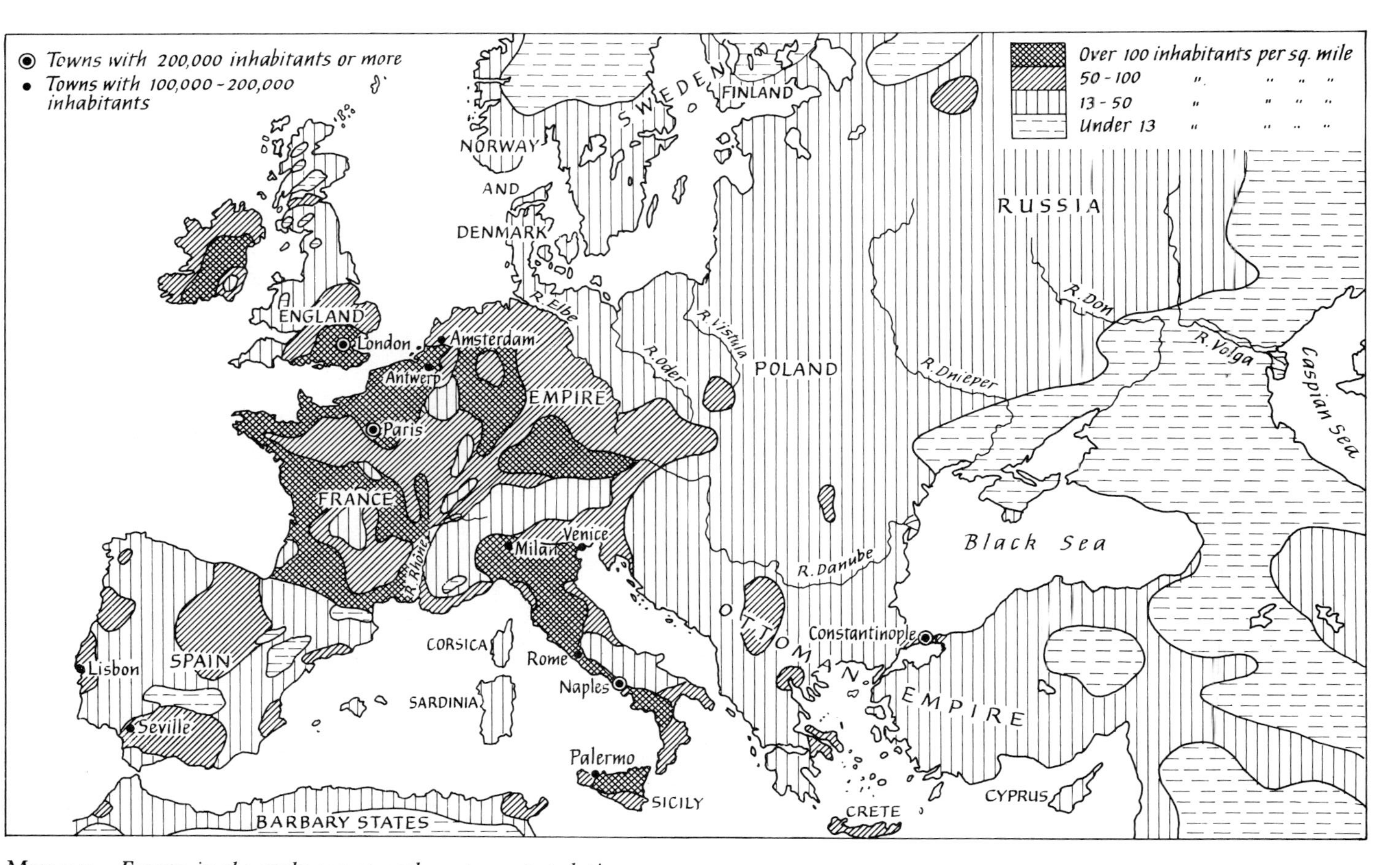

Map 1.2 *Europe in the early seventeenth century: population*

Certain 'feudal' characteristics persisted: notably in the countryside, in the shape of varying forms of personal service and dues owed by peasant to landowner; also in armies and courts where conditions of service still reflected the arrangements of earlier times when all power stemmed from the ownership of land. Europeans today are not only inheritors of the individualist ethic based upon 'natural' rights, but are also members of the systems, in some degree socialist or collectivist, which have arisen in response to the need to protect the individual from the abuse of those rights in a capitalist economy. It is hard therefore for them to grasp the character of an earlier society in which a man belonged to a mystical body, his church (the Reformation only increased for Protestants the sense of belonging); to a political authority, his prince; and to his local community, town or village, in which all were known and placed in accepted hierarchy: there his rights depended on the rank to which he was born, or the body to which he belonged by reason of his craft or profession. Citizens today, in a world which has experienced so much uprooting, such rupture or, at best, progressive departure from old ways, may find strange the values and insights of men who lived according to immemorial rhythms and at a pace which had hardly quickened in fifteen hundred years. Marlborough's men moved at the pace of the Roman legionaries.

Those who can cross the Atlantic in four hours have to adjust to the mentality of men for whom 40 kilometres a day was a good average journey on horseback, who would not expect to reach Antwerp, travelling from Venice by land or sea, in under fourteen days. Used to the rule of accurate clocks and watches they have to imagine daily living within a framework of light and darkness, not precise time. Accustomed to nearly universal literacy they have to make an imaginative effort to recall the people of an oral culture, who were attuned to ancestral voices and presences and who taught and learned more by precept than by reason's law. In the seventeenth century only about one in five of the adult population was able to read and write. The proportion, which rose significantly only in the second half of the eighteenth century, was lower among women than among men; higher in towns than in the countryside where, in many villages, even in western Europe, it might be only a handful beside the priest who could read a document or sign their names. Nothing in the records more poignantly suggests the powerlessness of the ordinary man, or the gulf that separated his world of custom and precedent from that of the lawyer or official, than the cross or token of calling, such as a roughly drawn pitchfork or hammer, appended to a register or deed upon which his livelihood might depend, but which he could not read. Braced, in the demonstrably unstable world of today, for constant change in all the relationships of life, the reader is asked to think about a life which had the stability of the patriarchal family and about an economy which was still based almost entirely on the domestic enterprise.

The family was the characteristic unit of the whole of life. Man today is taught, works and, in important respects, may virtually live in large concerns; he can hardly avoid to some extent deriving his values and tastes from mass markets and media. For the people of early modern Europe the big organization was exceptional: soldiers in an army, sailors on a big ship were out of the mainstream. Crowds were a rare and alarming experience; a popular rising was a departure from known, safe ways, and then all the more volatile and savage. To point to that humane and natural pattern of human activity, to stress the modest and intimate scale of existence, revolving round the family, extended as it might be by servants, apprentices or journeymen, is not to sentimentalize the past, but to provide a firm base for understanding it. In physical ways life was hazardous and death was a familiar guest, treated with perhaps less reserve and more resignation than in today's more guarded and more private families. A bare three-quarters of children who survived childbirth would live for more than a year; a scratch or graze might bring death from blood poisoning. Epidemics served only to dramatize the normal condition of helplessness before the mysteries of contagion. Average life expectancy was around 25. Those few who grew old could expect an honoured position within three-generation families in a society which did not willingly reject or isolate the old.

In western Europe the Roman Church no longer enjoyed a monopoly. The seamless robe, the concept of universality, had been torn apart by the Reformation and the religious wars. There certainly existed various philosophic notions and moral codes that were classical, pagan or at least not specifically Christian. But the few among the élite of educated men who came under such influences still lived in a society which knew no sanctions as effective as those of Christianity. Among such people too, the vaguer but still potent sense of belonging to a common civilization lived on. The *philosophe* of the eighteenth century was as cosmopolitan in his outlook as the Christian humanist of the Renaissance period. For Voltaire, as it had been for Erasmus, Europe was the parish. Two giant cities, London and Paris, approaching half a million inhabitants by 1700, dominated the attitudes and tastes of the educated minority. They were exceeded only by Constantinople, its 800,000 feeding on the wealth of tributary lands, and otherwise approached only by Naples, with perhaps 400,000 living in its teeming streets. Other great cities, Rome, Warsaw, Dresden, Venice, Amsterdam, Madrid, soon significantly to be joined by St Petersburg as it rose from the swamps of the Neva, whatever the local variations, visibly belonged to the same high urban culture in which architecture, music and painting conformed to universal standards. At the level of the nobility, accepted conventions about dress, manners, ways of waging war, for instance, were more important than national differences. The nobility and gentry of Europe, together with those professional men and merchants who might be described as belonging to the political community, because they were in a position to make, influence or at least obstruct public policy, constituted groups that might vary in status, yet can be described collectively as a class, in the sense in which that word is now applied to 'working' or 'middle' class: a section of the community having a recognizable style of living, appearing to have certain common interests, and being capable of collective action in defence of those interests. In the case of the upper class of pre-industrial Europe, it is possible to identify and to analyse its position and values because they were affirmed with an unquestioning confidence in God-ordained rank and rights. Noble or bourgeois, they made 'the history of events' that provides the main themes of this book.

An Aristocratic Age

The continuing vitality of the aristocratic order, notwithstanding the advance of government, is an outstanding feature of the age. The master principle of government was the assertion of a single overriding authority above particular loyalties. Those tended to focus upon territorial magnates with rights and duties derived originally from the delegation of authority which had characterized the feudal state. Everywhere agents of the state had to contend with owners of fiefs and franchises who claimed as of right to be custodians of the rural masses. Acting corporately in estates and diets, those landowners strove to maintain their privileges. They were inclined to respect the principle of hierarchy, but not the demands of an impersonal state. They could be sure that the sovereign depended as much on them as they on him. On the one hand aspirants and creditors were pressing hard upon a class whose traditions left little room for development within the confines of a static rural economy: if it were to survive, the feudal nobility had to adapt. The state on the other hand had to work through the men who had the authority and means to enforce the law. For then, as now, it was impossible to control a society without the acquiescence of a ruling class.

What constituted nobility? It was a question much debated at the time. Men used words meaning broadly 'noble' or 'gentleman', besides terms to convey a specially lofty status, like the Spanish 'grandee', in a loose way that absolves us from the effort to define more precisely. Between countries there were huge differences. The class structure was generally simpler in the north and east than in the west. Bohemian, Prussian or Polish squires, exacting four days of demesne labour from peasants who were bound to the soil, lived in a different world from those of Sweden, whose lands were leased to tenant farmers, or even France, where rents, in one form or other, were more important than feudal services. The nobles of Sweden, hungry for employment and promotion in army and government, had little in common with those of Italy, who had for the most part no significant function. Russia was unique in this, as in most other respects. As a consequence of the dreadfully effective assault of Ivan IV (1547–84) upon the old landowning class and Peter I's deliberate attempt to establish an aristocracy of service, culminating in his Table of Ranks (1722), there were no historic connections between particular families and estates, and no territorial titles. Even those two countries which seem to have had most in common, namely weak sovereigns, correspondingly influential magnates, and a numerous class of gentry richer in pride than in purse, afford extreme contrasts: the town-dwelling hidalgos of Spain were far removed from the 'barefoot' *szlachta*, whose white wooden farmhouses dotted the endless Polish plains.

Within countries moreover there was a broad distinction between higher and lower levels within the caste: not only between those who were titled and the rest, but also, as in Spain, between the *títulos* and the grandees. The latter were truly a caste apart. As the head of the Lemos family observed to Philip V: 'the grandeeship of the counts of Lemos was made by God and time.' It is not uncommon to find in Spain an extreme example of situations or ideas that are to be found elsewhere on the continent but in less dramatic form. For example, in the middle of the eighteenth century a third of the land of Spain was held by members of four great houses. But there was a tendency everywhere towards the aggrandizement of a few estates: through the principle of entail, through marriage, planned on the same dynastic principles as those which sustained the great royal families, sometimes through the favour of a sovereign, or as in Sweden or Bohemia, because of wartime opportunities for soldiers and courtiers to make their fortunes. Only 15 per cent of the nobility of Bohemia in 1700, whether Czech or German, were 'old families'. Where the conquest of new lands was not matched by restraining powers of central government, the results could be staggering. No one in eighteenth-century Hungary could match the Esterhazys, who could call so much of the country their own, but a number there held upwards of 100,000 acres. In Russia, where wealth was measured by serfs, Prince Cherkanskii was reckoned in 1690 to have 9000 peasant households.

Status increasingly, though not solely, signified economic circumstances, the substance behind the show. In France, where fine distinctions of title and sophisticated nuances of interpretation are the product of centuries of social experience, one trend is specially revealing. The old and main distinction among noblesse, between *épee* and *robe*, lost importance during the period. Apparently age of title came to count for more – but for antiquarians and purists, not for men of affairs and fashion. When in a regulation of 1760, the year 1400 was made a deadline, less than a thousand families, perhaps 1 in 50, passed the test. At the top of the hierarchy a class of magnates can be identified, a hundred or so families: *enfants de France*, the children and grandchildren of the reigning sovereign, and *pairs*, some fifty *ducs* who were entitled to play a part in the coronation. Below that élite ranged those *ducs*

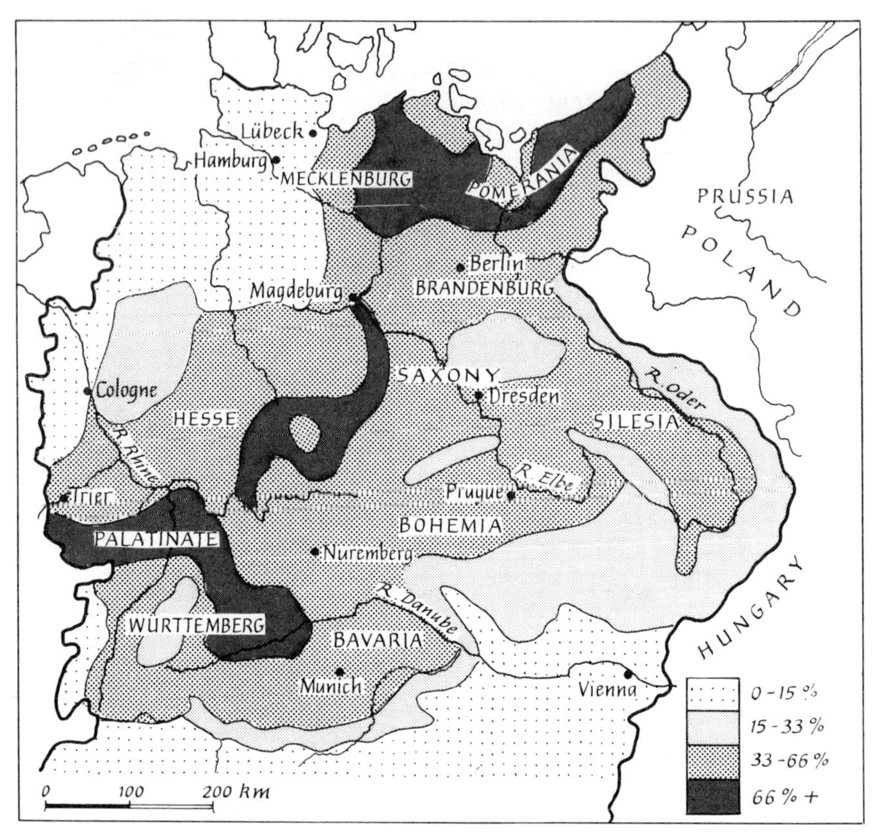

Map 1.3 *Germany: loss of population in the Thirty Years War*

who were not *pairs*, marquises and counts. The distinctions and marks of each grade were known and cherished. But the unmistakeable tendency was towards the formation of a plutocracy of nobles with a claim upon the king's generosity, or in a position to exploit his financial weakness. The process was not usually so blatant as the royal edict of 1695, empowering the king to create 500 new titles to reward subjects 'who, in acquiring them for a modest sum, will contribute to furnishing us the aid which we need to repel the obstinate efforts of our enemies'. In one way or another however, money could usually buy title, or office which would eventually lead to title.

The strenuous rearguard action fought by the old French nobility to defend their rights only emphasizes the trend. There was still a sharp line between noble and commoner. Crested coats of arms, the right to wear a sword, to have a reserved pew in the parish church and to have the church draped in black for a family funeral, privileged forms of trial – all were redolent of ancient honour. No less important a frontier, though harder to define, was that which divided the country nobles of modest means or ambition from the establishment of court and capital: ancient names, *grands seigneurs*, aristocratic bishops, lawyers secure in hereditary and lucrative office, indispensable financiers, perhaps some 4000 families in all. Even among the *noblesse campagnard* the degree of influence a nobleman could exert depended largely on the province and the constitution. In Brittany as many as 3000 gentlemen had the right to attend meetings of the Estates; in Languedoc only 23 of the wealthiest were so privileged.

Nowhere did aristocrats take themselves so seriously as in Vienna, where boxes at the theatre were reserved for their sole use; where, like their counterparts in Prague and Budapest, they prided themselves on their patronage of architects and musicians. From the foundation of the Sternkreusordern in 1668 to Maria Theresa's new academy for nobles in Vienna, the Theresianum (founded in 1749), nobles and their sovereigns showed a keen concern for the spiritual and material well-being of their sons and daughters. As can be seen elsewhere the cosmopolitan culture of Vienna was sustained by serf labour in an agrarian regime of brutal simplicity. The good Count Spork (1662–1738), 'father of the poor', who founded schools and hospitals and moderated labour dues, was famous partly because he was exceptional. Manorial rents and dues rose steeply in the period 1650–1740. If a lord introduced a new crop on the demesne, additional labour dues were exacted. If a crop was abandoned, the services required for cultivation were not; instead they were commuted for cash payment. Joseph II's assault on aristocratic privileges was inspired by more than the prejudices of a wilful autocrat. He wished to induce realism in a state which might well appear to be run for the benefit of the aristocracy. Nowhere was the proliferation of the court so striking, answering to the ceremonious instincts of sovereigns and the needs of their well-born subjects. The court under Joseph's grandfather Charles VI, most formal of monarchs, provided for noble clients to the extent of some 40,000 jobs. Joseph's mother Maria Theresa was concerned about economies: at her death there were 1500 chamberlains. The church also had an important role to play in the complacent world of Austrian landowners and courtiers. Kaunitz, one of fifteen children, received a prebend of Münster before he was 14.

So it was not only the efforts of magnates to find compensation for the reduction of their political role or, as in Poland, to justify its preservation, but simply the existence of large numbers of poor gentry that put weight behind efforts to preserve the privileges of what was legally a single order. In Russia, at the height of the bitter conservative reaction, in 1770, it was reckoned that three-fifths of all landowners owned less than twenty serfs. The census of 1687 showed that there were half a million 'nobles' in Spain. *Hidalguía* might mean little more than a Spaniard's estimation of himself and what he could impose on others. Unless he had a substantial estate or *señorío*, the hidalgo, individually, was insignificant. Nevertheless the very existence of such a class, committed to 'living nobly', in however meagre a style, had a profound effect on Spain: where noble privilege meant, effectively, not working, many hidalgos attached themselves to a great house for a coat and a loaf. The idea that gainful employment, as in farming or business, was demeaning, also lay behind the French notion of *dérogeance*, loss of status incurred when a man engaged in occupations thought to be unfitting to a gentleman. The principle was being progressively weakened. In 1620 it had been laid down that shipowning and participation in overseas commerce did not constitute *dérogeance*. Retail trade was still forbidden. It was probably lack of capital as much as concern about status that prevented some from engaging in commerce or manufactures. Certainly, in the eighteenth century, the higher in the social scale, the more likely is to be found a relaxed view of status: individuals were then to be found engaged in financial enterprises, in mines and iron on their own land, but also in the coffee and sugar trades.

The value of *dérogeance* to the French nobleman is at best debatable. Even the right not to pay taxes was not all that it might seem. For a start there were exceptions, notably those nobles in the *pays d'état* who held land that was not designated noble and had to pay the tax assessed on land. Then all nobles were taxed in some way: for example by the *arrière-ban*, the feudal summons to military service (or payment in lieu of service), or more effectively by special taxes like the capitation and the *dixième*. The nobility preserved their right not to pay the *taille* until the Revolution, but that should not divert students of the *ancien régime* from the true predicament of the French nobility. They lost by having to live, in the main, off the proceeds of a backward agriculture, and being excluded from the areas of growth and opportunity. It was their common complaint in the eighteenth century that they were thus disadvantaged; indeed they were doubly taxed: directly, after Machault's reforms of 1749, indirectly because peasants paid so much *taille* that they had correspondingly less to give in rents and services.

Elsewhere, as in Poland and Hungary, exemption from direct tax was complete and correspondingly more valuable; it represented the complete and unchallengeable control of landlords over life in the countryside. Till 1768 the Polish lord had powers of life and death over his serfs. Sicily represents another extreme case of landowner dominance though there, in the 1730s and 1740s, Charles VI managed to reduce their powers: he made decisions of the feudal courts subject to appeal in royal courts and limited the number of armed followers a nobleman might have.

Another aspect of privilege was the monopoly of posts in army and government. The demands of needy squires lent weight to the aristocratic reaction in eighteenth-century Sweden, where nobles were a numerous class: in 1718 some 10,000 out of a population of 1.5 million. The 'Age of Liberty' saw the reassertion of the traditional Swedish principle that the nobility were guardians of the country's liberties. Most of the functions of government passed into the hands of committees of estates which were able to enforce the principle of ministerial responsibility. With the crowd of nobles that attended the diet, as many as a thousand on critical matters, came the development of party government and with it pressure to secure a monopoly of jobs. In 1720, 85 per cent of the officials in central government, all the lords lieutenant, many sheriffs and most provincial judges were gentry. It was doubtless the prospect of state employment in the expanding bureaucratic machine that reconciled the nobility of Austria and Bohemia to Maria Theresa's reforms, aimed at making them pay more for the armed forces. The reforms may have been conceived by Haugwitz in the name of 'God-pleasing equality' but Maria Theresa ensured that the nobility take full advantage of a new field of opportunity. No one, she decreed, below the stature of knight should be eligible for the new district captaincies. Seigneurial land was assessed at a lower rate than that of peasants.

The trend can be seen most strikingly in Frederick the Great's Prussia. Estates there were mainly modest in size, at least compared to those of neighbouring Poland and Bohemia. The *Junkers* moreover had been contained by the loss, in the second half of the seventeenth century, of their main political rights, and by the large amount of royal land (in 1740 about a third of the total arable area). The bitter conflicts of the Great Elector's reign had left the *Junkers* with their social and fiscal privileges intact, rights of jurisdiction over their feudal tenants and a secure hold over the day-to-day administration of country districts. King Frederick William I's novel approach to the management of the royal estates, notably the allocation of short leases to commoners, led to the parallel growth of middle-class estate managers. At the end of his reign however (1740), the political problem of reconciling the nobility to the absolutist military state remained unsolved. Under the pressure of events after his attack on Silesia, also in accord with his own temperamental sympathy towards aristocratic manners, Frederick II (1740–86) adopted another approach. Regarding the nobility as 'foundations and pillars of the state', he taught them to regard the army as a permanent career. In the civil administration too Frederick deliberately altered the balance between middle and upper class in favour of the latter. The consequence of his preferential treatment of the *Junker* was that little could be done to control his dealings, or to advance the interests of peasantry and the towns which were so vital to the health of the economy. The nobles were fortified, becoming the strongest and most cohesive group in Europe, with the most favourable combination of useful role and social elevation. But they were not without their problems. Frederick created twice as many nobles as his father. Having been discouraged from losing status by entering trade, many were miserably poor on the pittance of army or official pay. So resulted a steady process of sale of noble possessions to pay for the perpetuation of a way of life that was anachronistically rigid. The creation of a working aristocracy was Frederick the Great's enduring masterpiece.

The way it was achieved, and the price that was paid, indicates both the strength of aristocracy at this time and the difficulties inherent in any effort to reconcile the interests of the class with those of society as a whole.

Civilizing trends were most apparent in those countries where as in England and Holland there was an open intellectual life, or where, as in Sweden in the eighteenth century, nobility was open to men of talent; where a Linnaeus or a Swedenborg could become noble, and nobles were freely marrying commoners; least so where, as in Spain, there was an enforced cultural isolation, or in the deepest countryside of Europe's eastern marches. Visitors to Spain were dismayed by the ignorance of the men, the withdrawn behaviour of the women, the longueurs of the *tertulia*, or evening gathering, the endless lounging in town squares. Life in Poland resolved itself for many of the *szlachta* into a simple round of hunting and carousing. In both Spain and Poland clerical influence, narrowly nationalistic, was a prime factor in the stunting of the class, its cultural outlook and its political evolution. In France the humanizing influence of the salons provided a milieu for the free discussion of moral and political matters, as well as those of social concern, among different sorts of people and talents in a way that might not otherwise have been possible in a caste-ridden society. The salons, where the rationalism of Descartes and his followers found its way into the thinking of the fashionable world, also opened the way to those feminine insights which were a feature of French upper-class culture, with its idealization of love, its concern with manners and motives, and refinement of language. All found characteristic expression in the Fronde, when the French aristocracy had a unique opportunity to express their values and pursue their ambitions, but unfortunately within a framework which gave little scope for responsible conduct. The failure of the Fronde opened the way for the final stage in the domestication of the nobility. A resplendent court became the setting for an aristocratic way of life that appealed to the vain, supported the idle and confirmed their privileges in a way that compensated for the loss of a political and administrative role.

For the nobleman fighting was not so much a professional function as a way of life, symbolized by his exclusive right to wear a sword. The princes of the early modern period required larger and more reliable armies, officered by men who would fight in the manner born but under direction. They needed the personal service of the feudal tradition but without its dangerously narrow concept of honour and of loyalty to the immediate superior. Armies expanded during the seventeenth century, usually beyond the country's means in response to the competitive policies of rulers. They also drew in the poorer nobles, younger sons, men richer in pride than in purse. As sovereigns gained control of the national purse and refined techniques of filling it, as courts, diplomatic missions and other agencies of government grew in splendour, the challenge of the great magnates to the growing state faded away. More intractable was the problem of the large numbers of poor gentry who were trapped between the conventions of their class and the expense of maintaining a minimum of service and ceremony, especially where, as in France, the personal status of nobility, though not the estate, was inherited by all sons; or, as in Russia, where the nobles were successful in resisting the principle of entail upon a single heir (Peter I's entail law of 1714 was repudiated in 1731). The Norman gentleman who wrote in 1656 that the nobility had been ruined by 'facility in finding money, luxury and war' was exaggerating, but not wildly. Yet war, with commissioned service in the expanding ranks of the new armies, provided a regular activity and livelihood for many active young gentlemen: energy that might have gone to the service of some magnate, to brawling and duelling, or to leading local revolts against tax officials, was canalized into the service of the crown. Where that was not achieved, as in Poland, or Hungary, the crown was certain to face disorder at home and be vulnerable to pressure from more successful rival states.

Towns: a Civilized Security

The European economy was one of innumerable self-sufficient units, each centring upon the market which it was the prime function of the town to provide. Where there was no specialized industry, like the silk of Lyons or porcelain of Dresden, or a centre of government, such as was to be found at Berlin, Copenhagen or Turin, in the deep country within France, Spain, Germany and Italy, away from the great ports which accounted for much of the urban growth of the period, the town stood at best for a civilized security rather than for material progress. The emphasis was on preserving existing rights. In all Europe in 1700 there were only forty-eight towns boasting a population of more than 40,000; most were under 10,000, many were but a thousand or two. Yet all but the very smallest and most decayed had their corporate pride. Dignified by at least one large church, very likely an abbey, a law court, guildhall, school and, of course, a market, the town was a little walled world apart, with its bourgeois crust of clerics, lawyers, officials and merchants, shopkeepers and master craftsmen, who provided the services or did the jobs for which a single village would have insufficient need, or which were suited to the more elaborate needs of richer citizens who might want wigs, spectacles, engravings or silverware. And so alongside the cobbled streets, with the butchers and bakers, would be the workshops and booths of tallow chandlers, cutlers, pewterers, coopers, saddle makers, drapers, glove makers, locksmiths, and many other specialist craftsmen. Each one had its guild. With 30,000 inhabitants Amiens was a relatively large city, and since Picardy was a textile district, the thirty-six guilds included bleachers, dyers and finishers of the cloth that was mostly woven in the villages around. The merchants who controlled the textile manufacture, from the provision of raw materials to the marketing of the finished product, might be aware of the needs of a wider market but even they were largely contained within the local economy, trading under the conditions that regulated life in the outlying villages.

In a straggling suburban lane might be found the malodorous tannery, or a cluster of the hovels of the poorer workers, or a whole quarter where the rougher, more independent ones, like the Roman boatmen and porters of the Trastevere district, pursued their occupation. The well-to-do might build houses beyond the walls, away from the stench and congestion. Typically, however, with its surrounding gardens and orchards, fields for the citizens' horses, cows and pigs, maybe vineyards, the town was in many respects a larger village. In all but the largest cities, where the poor occupied every inch of space, there would be tenements, often tall, animals on every patch of grass or waste, besides the ubiquitous hens, and the pigs that were invaluable for scavenging in the filthy streets. A German, writing in 1722, bewailed the fact that artisans were taking a hand in farming: 'it would be better if everyone kept his station', and the towns would be 'cleaner and healthier if they were cleared of livestock and large stores of manure'. Even where town business was brisk and townsmen 'kept their station', the relationship between the town and the orbital villages was to some extent one of mutual dependence. Needing local food, fresh, its price not weighted by transport costs, the town provided the essential market. The immemorial features persisted, along with the traditional mentalities. The townsman feared fire, which could be devastating: in Brussels in 1695, 3830 houses were burnt in a single outbreak. He feared the intrusion of beggars and refugees, whether from armies or the plague. Above all he feared the passage of troops: friendly or hostile, it made little difference to their demands for billets and supplies. As a consumer he suspected the peasant on whom ultimately he depended. He was perforce a hoarder, defensive even in the more peaceful districts, inward-looking. The town might house some of the specialists of rural life, drovers, wine growers and shepherds. But to the ordinary peasant, as the gates closed at curfew time and he trudged home, it was an alien, inhospitable place where lived the merchant clothier or ironmaster who exploited his labour; where he could expect to be cheated; where he could only gaze at the fine goods that were made for the merchants and the professional gentlemen: the latter a class which he might rightly believe to be the most rapidly growing in the community.

In the nineteenth century the bourgeois came to represent social mobility; even in pre-revolutionary Europe his was a rising class, thrusting upwards. But towards what goals? There was a general tendency to turn wealth made from trade into land, office, professional occupation or interest-bearing loans. Though it is broadly true that the bourgeoisie were advancing during this period, development was limited by the prolonged recession and it was in any case uneven. For most bourgeois, opportunity took the form of service in some official capacity rather than in trade or manufactures, though, as is shown by the example of Brandenburg, where the nobility dominated public office, there is no automatic correlation between the rise of the state and that of the bourgeoisie. In other countries nobility maintained their privileges, and absorbed ambitious bourgeois into their world. When allowance is made for certain dynamic areas in the European economy, those most affected by the growth of international trade, the picture superficially is one of stability and balance. In some areas, notably in eastern Europe where the landowner's power was greatest, and the Mediterranean lands where the recession was most damaging, but also throughout Germany, the situation was worse than that. Many towns were decaying, losing independence – whether to the state or, as commonly in Spain, to private landowners – and taxed more heavily: they were alienated and resentful, but powerless. Not only were such towns locked in the agrarian economy, but they were losing traditional business, with the growth of rural manufactures and the tendency of great landowners to set up their own breweries, brickworks and tanneries, and even to provide their own facilities for transport and trading. Even within the middle-sized and larger towns there were trends which suggest the weakening, if not disintegration, of the old urban regime and point to the alignments of a new order.

Distinctions between the landed nobles and the urban aristocrats of law and office were being gradually blurred, as the townsmen bought their landed estates and the landowners, becoming more urbanized (as they had long been in Spain and Italy), built their own town houses as a base for seasons of culture and more 'polite' entertainment than the countryside could provide. When only the richest or grandest could attend court, the provincial capital provided an acceptable alternative. Within the towns, popular forms of government were being abandoned as power came to be monopolized by small interrelated groups of wealthy men. The élites were often composed of men who took no active part in business. Though the structure of office, whether venal or hereditary, varied with each country, reflecting distinctive political conditions, there was a general expansion, in line with that of central government, and it usually meant the superimposing of new layers, rather than the destruction of the original layer of officialdom. In eighteenth-century Bayeux there were as many lawyers as shopkeepers: over 100. Generally there were more lawyers than work for them. Trained to contend, responsive to new ideas, the lawyer who was cheated of expectations might well become a dissident element.

At a lower level, the guilds showed a similar tendency towards oligarchy. The status of master, once the realistic aim of every guild member, now came as often by heredity as by effort. Guilds controlled admission by charging a fee (in Brussels for example it doubled between 1650 and 1720) and by requiring a 'masterpiece' from the aspiring member; this is the other point in the urban community where discontent could breed radicalism. Because of guild restrictions and the resulting cost of production, town industries, particularly textiles, were tending to move back into the countryside: it is the main reason why cities like Leyden, Rouen, Cologne and Nuremberg were actually losing population. At the same time, within an almost static total urban population, the number of large towns was growing. Between 1600 and 1750 the number over 100,000 grew from 8 to 13; those between 40,000 and 100,000, from 25 to 34. While 4 per cent of northern Europeans lived in cities of over 20,000 in 1600, nearly 8 per cent did so in 1750. Within the more substantial towns meanwhile the number of those who could accurately be called proletarian was growing: they were those who had nothing but their labour to offer. The urban journeyman was equivalent to the landless peasant in the countryside. It was his typical complaint that the masters used guild regulations to depress wages and restrict numbers in the trade. Out of such grievances arose the associations, which sought, occasionally through strikes, sometimes by violent means, to improve their lot; the building trade particularly was notorious for its secret societies. Related to this phenomenon and becoming steadily more serious as the eighteenth century proceeded, with the accelerating rise in population, the pressure of consumers on resources, and consequent price rises, was the increase in urban poverty, with larger pockets of unfortunates who had no regular work or visible means of support. In Berlin, at the end of the century, the meticulous Hohenzollern bureaucracy estimated the number to be about a third of a total population of 190,000. At the same time the rich were getting richer, or appeared to be when judged by the conspicuous expenditure of the age of dress, food and all the comforts, adornments and services required to sustain the fashionable life. The numerous craftsmen, shopkeepers and lackeys providing for the rich gave the larger towns an air of bustle and prosperity which was not entirely illusory. The craving for ever more beautiful objects stimulated demand and provided work. But in conjunction with the relentless increase in rural poverty which provided a flow of immigrants to reinforce the numbers of those who tried to work, or who begged or stole to survive, the blatant extremes of affluence and want could not fail to encourage crime and increase the danger of destructive riots. Leader in this, as in other respects, London served as warning: the terrifying Gordon riots of 1780 were an orgy of drunkenness, arson and looting. The squalor and tensions of cities induced city authorities to instigate schemes of street lighting and to look favourably upon the schemes of development in which private enterprise and public interest worked together to create the great squares and crescents of the baroque city; they provided further incentive, if it was needed after the example of Louis XIV's Versailles, for rulers to build palaces in glorious isolation from the city, like the Hohenzollerns' Charlottenburg and the Habsburgs' Schönbrunn.

The Peasant's World

The physical imperatives and Christian teaching and rituals, working on older strata of pagan customs and beliefs, formed a peasant culture as distinctive as that of the nobility or bourgeoisie. Passivity, tenacity, conservatism are among the traits that spring to mind of the townsmen who then, as now, might incline to the view ascribed to Gorky: 'peasants are all alike'. But the peasants cannot properly be described as a class. Their struggle to tame nature and to use her gifts, to meet or thwart their masters' demands, was fought in innumerable little pockets, usually in isolation. Only occasionally did they come together in general risings, and then they expressed a common interest only in negative terms of protest against oppression by state or landowner: frightening, and usually futile. Their chance of success in the less dramatic daily battle to survive was conditioned by soil, altitude and climate; communications and site in relation to river, sea, frontier or strategic route; rights of church, sovereign and landowner; form of tenure and, most important, whether the land was owned or in some way rented, the size of the holding. Essentially a peasant was a labourer on the land who sought to hold on to his own, to feed himself and his family, against all comers and all odds. There were few deserted villages in France, or even in Germany: refugees returned, the survivors of plague and fire clung on. By 1700 however, in Spain, 932 *despoblados* were recorded; from the start the upland sites were vulnerable, even without adverse economic or political conditions. Wherever he lived, the peasant's was a small world. The radius of his economy was that of a day's ride away from his village; its focus was the market town which would not usually be more than a dozen miles away. His life was virtually self-sufficient.

Four out of five Europeans were peasants, farmers or in one way or another dependent upon farming. This overall figure conceals extremes: in 1700 barely 3 per cent of Russians lived in towns, in England nearer 30 per cent; in France by the Revolution the figure had risen to 16 per cent. Europe's was still primarily a rural economy. It is therefore the work and ways of villages that provide materials for a picture of the life of ordinary people: the clothes and diet of the urban poor did not differ from those of their country cousins. The material environment of the village was created of animal or vegetable products, gathered and hand-worked on the spot. Fields and beasts provided food and clothing; wood came from the fringe of wasteland. Except in districts where stone was available and easy to work, houses were usually of wood or a sort of cob of clay and straw. The humble purpose of the house was to provide protection against cold and damp. It was primarily a shelter, at its simplest merely a refinement of the farm shed, with certain amenities for its human occupants, hearth, table, benches and mats or rushes strewn on the earthen floor; several, perhaps all the children of the house would share one bed. The roof was probably thatched, window apertures were small, usually unglazed and protected, if at all, by shutters. Glazing was one test of affluence. In relatively prosperous west Germany, Montaigne had noted as early as 1580 that village houses were glazed. But two travellers from Flanders to Spain in 1633 observed that glass disappeared from windows after they crossed the Loire at Saumur; a hundred years later it was still the case. The poorest cabins were one-storied, others had an attic for storing grain or a raised area for beds. For warmth the peasant lived as near as possible to his animals. In the wretched earth cabins of Brittany the animals actually shared the peasants' single room. Outside the hovel might be stacked dung, acorns or vegetable scraps for animal swill.

Meals were prepared and eaten off earthenware and wood, more rarely pewter. Though it was becoming scarce in the more intensively cultivated areas, fuel was normally wood; peat and dried dung were also used, occasionally coal in districts where the seams lay close to the surface. Corn was ground at the village mill, usually the lord's, though cottages might have ovens for baking. Women spun wool and flax for their men's breeches, linen shirts and woollen tunics, their own linen smocks and woollen gowns. The pictures of French peasant life by the brothers Le Nain illustrate what seems to have been the typical dress of ordinary people throughout western Europe. The clothes of the poor, like their house, served elemental needs: they were thick, to give protection against damp and cold, loose-fitting for ease of movement for working. While their women spun the wool, men might tan a skin into leather for boots or harness for horse, ox or mule; in most districts the horse was a rare and expensive animal. Farm implements, ploughs (except for the share), carts, rollers and harrows, as well as many of the craftsman's tools, were again made of wood, seasoned, split or rough-hewn. Few would possess saws; in Russia they were unknown before 1700. Iron was little used and likely to be of poor quality, made by local forges; the products of specialist foundries went to rich men's houses or to the armies.

The rural economy was austere but it did not lack variety. Millers, smiths, potters, wheelwrights, cobblers and clog makers, tanners and weavers plied their crafts for their communities: the last also for itinerant merchants. Craftsmen usually worked on a part-time basis, being specialists only in a limited sense, farming their own land as well. Except in districts where, as in Brittany, or Lucania, the poverty of the soil and lack of resources had enfeebled the human stock, craftsmanship was fostered by man's instinct to make well, out of the most suitable materials, the implements and utensils of everyday life. Leather jugs, wooden bowls, horn mugs, wicker baskets, rakes of willow or ash, and ox yokes might be fashioned in the long winter evenings, while women plaited straw, stitched sheepskin bags, wove halters from hemp or straw or peeled rushes for the precious candles by which they worked. More intricate skills, in metal working for example, could be provided by travelling tinkers. Masons, plasterers, glazers coming to work on church or manor house might bring with them knowledge of more advanced techniques. Villages on or around the main routes saw and heard something of the great world through merchants, students, pilgrims visiting shrines, officials of government. They might be able to buy broadsheets, almanacs and romances produced by enterprising printers at centres like Troyes in France, to be hawked around wherever there were a few who could read. Surviving copies now provide fascinating insights into popular superstitions and interests, with astrology, magical remedies and tales of legendary heroes prominent among them. They might be entertained by travelling troupes of jugglers and actors; they might benefit from the cash of thirsty and hungry wayfarers; they were certainly more vulnerable to the dreaded passage of armies and to billeting. Few villages were so remote as not to be served by the ubiquitous pedlars, the humblest but not the least important link in the chain of supply and demand; nor so poor as not to be affected by vagabonds and beggars, drawn from the layer of people who had insufficient land or none, and no savings. Driven perhaps to take to the road by some calamity, depending upon casual jobs, fencing, ditching or rat-catching, some looked for seasonal labour or new work in towns; some had been beggars since earliest childhood; some were derelicts addicted to cheap cider and home-distilled spirits; some crippled or sick or half-witted: all were in some degree dependent upon alms.

A brief sketch can only hint at the infinite diversity of types, skills and manners of peasant Europe. But the cardinal feature emerges plainly: it was an economy of innumerable self-sufficient units. It follows that little demand was generated for the development of large-scale manufactures for the home market. The rural community of villages and small towns was isolated within its own market economy – self-sustaining to a degree that is hard for us to conceive – rooted in its own soil and customs, distinctive and proud of it, and suspicious of change and of outsiders. Such a community tended to be passively resistant to pressures of government and local magnates where they did not conform to old custom; it was often effective in preserving privileges that gave, at least to its more substantial members, a pride in belonging to a community characterized both by order and by mutual dependence. It was less effective, tending rather to fatalism, when it came to dealing collectively with external threats or finding original solutions to age-old problems, because of the empirical conservatism of men who lived so close to nature, and because of their overriding concern with their land and rights. They feared change as they feared the night, for its unknown terrors. The possessing classes were mainly concerned with holding on against the clutching hands of the great mass below them; the mass was locked in the prison of ignorance. Customs and attitudes were those of people aware that they lived on a brink: more babies might be born but there was no increase in the food supply. It is what Le Roy Ladurie has called 'the implacable logic of the Malthusian equation', and today historians turn to the theories of Malthus with new respect, knowing, as they do, more about the background to his thinking. Mental attitudes apart, agriculture was all important, the universal industry and provider.

The village land of lowland Europe, where the majority lived and worked, was usually, not always, coterminous with the parish. In the village there were a number of holdings: house, yard, farm buildings, garden, orchards, whose owner was virtual master of all he surveyed, free of tithe, and liable only to light feudal dues. Around stretched the arable land in great fields, marked off by stone walls, hedges or deep furrow, farmed in two-year rotation in southern countries, with the fields lying fallow every other year; elsewhere in three-year rotation, typically of winter corn, spring corn and fallow. The fields were subdivided, often minutely, into strips and parcels. They were being consolidated steadily, and some large segments might belong to the same man; but they were not for the most part 'enclosed' at the start of the period, even in the Netherlands, where the situation was more volatile, feudalism virtually extinct and farming practice more enterprising than elsewhere. Round the nucleus or straggling line of the village one might see, according to the season, an expanse of plough or of grain, and the dun hue of fallow land. Beyond were meadows, rough pasture, scrub, marsh, heath and woodland: they provided grazing for the livestock; wood for building, firing, tool making; litter for animals; rushes for floors and candles; berries and nuts, which could be a staple part of the human diet, as in the chestnut districts of France. The exploitation and protection of these marginal tracts, so vital to the village economy, were among the collective responsibilities of the landowning peasants who met regularly, in many villages after church on Sunday.

Private and collective ownership thus went hand in hand. There were agreed restraints upon private property for the benefit of the inhabitants, such as the compulsory rotation of crops, rights of usage over woods and fields, pasturing on the fallow and gleaning off the stubble. The dates of the farming calendar, the allocation of tasks, were decided in this fashion. Nature disposes, man proposes: the agrarian strategy was planned by the individuals most concerned in the interests of the whole community. In the pre-mechanical age, peasants, men, women and children, had to work together to accomplish their seasonal tasks: the band of peasants, hoeing, sowing, reaping, is the archetypal scene. Within the bounds of law and custom there was, however, constant rivalry and pressure: the weak fell into debt, lost their land, took to casual labour for their more fortunate fellows; some abandoned their families and took to the road to beg, went to the nearest big town for work or enlisted in the army. The thrifty, efficient, skilful, and those who were fortunate in health or in the marriage stakes, increased their holdings.

As under a microscope, what is thought to be static is revealed by examination to be a scene of constant motion. The movement everywhere in Europe, even in conservative France or those parts of Germany, Saxony for example, where it was the prince's policy to foster an independent peasantry, was towards fewer and larger holdings, even though the majority remained tiny. Indeed, capitalist development was inherent in the village, subject as it was to the fluctuations of the market economy, sensitive as prices and demand in that economy were to the vagaries of climate and the ravages of war. As Marc Bloch observed of France, villages always displayed, 'with inevitable fluctuations in the line of cleavage, fairly well marked social divisions'. In his France it was the *coq de paroisse*, the village capitalist, who ruled the roost, hiring out his horses at monopoly rates and lending money to his less fortunate neighbours at rates of interest that ensured that he would one day foreclose and take the land. It is the process that Le Roy Ladurie has chronicled in his study of Languedoc, where often the capitalist would be an outsider, bourgeois or clerical proprietor. In the absence of lucrative alternative uses for capital, given the supreme status and value of land, it was inevitable that capital would play an increasing role.

Serfdom

Well-established rights, the tenacity of peasants, the density of population, acted as brakes upon the advance of capitalism in the west. In eastern Europe the population was more sparse; the ravages of the Thirty Years War were particularly severe in the thinly populated areas like Brandenburg; peasant rights were correspondingly hard to defend; landlords were already well placed to exploit plentiful land, cheap labour and the growing demand for grain from more populous southern Europe. The usual system of landownership in the west was that of *Grundherrschaft*, where the management of properties was entrusted by the owner to others, in exchange for leases, rents, payments in kind or some kind of share cropping, when stock, implements and seed were loaned in return for a share in proceeds. In eastern and much of central Europe *Gutherrschaft* was prevalent: there the overlord administered his property directly, and at his own risk. The river Elbe serves as a rough line of demarcation, though both systems could be found in an intermediary area running from Mecklenburg to Bavaria. In a rural ride eastwards across Germany, a man would see the different systems reflected in the changing landscape, the housing and conditions of the peasant. In the more intimate, diversified landscape of a country like Würzburg or Bamberg, what he would see might still correspond to the characteristic scene of the lowland west. He might indeed note, as did the Englishman Crabb Robinson, travelling towards the end of the eighteenth century, both the subservience of the men, which Robinson attributed to their feudal burdens, and the amount of field work done by women. As he came, however, to the open, flattish country around and beyond the Elbe, he would see tiny settlements of wooden cabins, standing in an expanse of ploughland or corn, enveloped sometimes by the forest from which the land had been recently cleared, fringed by waste or swamp. He would appreciate the importance of the great rivers as he saw the long barges of the Vistula, immense rafts of tree trunks, and the timber and above all the grain piled on the wharves of Thorn and Danzig. Land was plentiful and now worth the reclamation; the people were thinly spread. The landowner's mansion, perhaps recently rebuilt, with its great stables, barns and dovecotes, represented the formidable concentration of rights and powers that was spelt out in the daily burdens and humiliation of *Leibeigenschaft*: the peasants in that situation belonged to their *Junker*, who could buy and sell them like a chattel; they could not marry or leave the village without his consent. Eviction and buying out of peasants – *Bauernlegen* – was steadily increasing the size of the demesne. Their diet and physique may not have been bad – for strong workers were a valuable property – but the traveller may have noted, like Hardy in nineteenth-century Dorset, 'the desultory shamble of the general labourer', the proletarian who works mindlessly for a remote master. Tributary labour in Brandenburg was normally 4 to 5 days a week; in East Prussia as in Poland it could be 6 days. The prevailing Lutheranism provided a devout moral climate which ran counter to the worst excesses of a regime of exploitation. But it was a Lutheran pastor who wrote in 1684 that 'the peasants have that in common with the stockfish. They are best when well beaten and soft.' Some were shocked by what they saw. Goethe's mentor, J. M. von Loen, wrote in 1768 of this 'most wretched of all creatures' that he was

> like a mere animal. . . . From morning till night he must be digging the fields, whether scorched by the sun or numbed by the cold. At night he lies in the field . . . to keep the beasts from stealing his seed, and what he saves from their jaws is taken soon afterwards by a harsh official for arrears of rent and taxes.

Serfdom was sanctioned by rulers because they were generally in no position to offend the dominant landowning class but also because, for fiscal and military purposes, it was essential to hold the people down. In Poland the king was virtually a puppet, in Russia the tsar was an autocrat; in both countries the social system was moulded by fundamental demands and pressures. In the background were the great colonizing movements. In southern and eastern Russia there was no fixed frontier; behind the soldier–settlers came farmers and tradesmen; by the fourth decade of the eighteenth century, Russians had reached the Black Sea, controlled the mouths of the Don and Dnieper, and were moving over the Ural mountains into Siberia. Meanwhile, in old Muscovy, thousands of deserted villages witnessed to past anarchy and to the urge of peasants to escape their bonds: enshrined in the great code of 1649, the rights of landowners were everywhere supported by the state and used to reduce the peasants to mere chattels. And so in Russia was revived a type of natural economy, that which had long disappeared from western Europe. Of 4.4 million Russian serfs in 1730, 70 per cent were dependants of the nobility. The land reserved by the lord for his direct use absorbed most of that inhabited by the village communities; the peasants were expected not only to do farmwork but anything else the lord might require. In Poland the extraordinary wealth of the greatest landowners was part of a complex situation of royal weakness, aristocratic dominance and economic backwardness. Here again the size of the country in relation to its population, and the existence of a more or less open frontier on the east, at least until the treaty of Andrussovo in 1667, were crucial factors. By then the class of substantial landowners, *volniki*, who were not compelled to do manual work for an overlord, had already declined to insignificance, while the classes of the poorer peasants, *zagrodniki* and *chalnyniki* had swelled. Profits from the export of grain went to increase the size of the huge estates run by wretched gangs and managed by bailiffs, who were drawn often from the class of the lesser gentry, sometimes Jews. It was a monstrously unbalanced society, without significant economic advantages, except from the narrow viewpoint of the magnates, for labour was so cheap, land so plentiful that there was no incentive to improve the land or methods of farming.

The inefficiencies of the system, as much as its demoralizing effects upon the peasantry, were the cause of attempts by 'enlightened' rulers of the eighteenth century to relieve or reduce serfdom. In Prussia Frederick II found that he could make little headway against the landowners: too much had been ceded by his predecessors. In Catherine the Great's Russia serfdom actually increased in extent and severity. Maria Theresa of Austria was sensitive to the suffering and injustice, as well as to the political danger from oppressed Bohemia where, since the Habsburg reconquest in the 1620s, German-style labour service, the hated *Robot*, had been imposed on the large estates. The system named after her councillor, Anton von Raab, featuring the abolition of serfdom, the commutation of *Robot* and the division of a lord's demesnes into smallholdings to be rented by the peasants for cash, was introduced into some crown estates. In her own cautious way Maria Theresa accepted the principle that the state had to find a solution to an intolerable problem. For a more radical approach to the difficulty the peasants had to wait for the uncompromising Joseph II. The Danish experience is interesting. There King Christian VI extended serfdom until nearly all the Danish peasantry were subject to German-style obligations. In 1733 he decreed that no peasant between the ages of 14 and 36 (later extended to between 4 and 40) was to leave the estate on which he was born; the nobility were given the right of selecting those peasants who would serve in the army for an eight-year term. Individual reformers like von Bernstorff, followed by a land commission under Reventlow (1786) ended that system; in its place was set up, with the thoroughness that was possible only in a small country inured to paternalist government, a system of state-supported freehold farming. The new breed of smallholder, many specializing in dairy farming, developed the skills and found the markets which have since served them well. As in England, after enclosures, there were victims: the more numerous landless labourers became a rural proletariat.

The Mediterranean Lands

Behind the expansion of grain farming in northern Europe lay the serious recession in the Mediterranean lands. Again there is a diversity here which defies neat summary. It has been observed even of temperate England that there were forty-one distinct farming 'countries'. But in no other agricultural area of Europe may be found such differences in method and product between one country district and another a few miles away as there were in the Mediterranean bowl: there the lands around the northern shores and the Italian peninsula which reaches into the bowl had developed in different ways in response to local stimuli. A useful, if broad distinction can however be made between the mountain and lowland areas. In the Alps, Apennines, Pyrenees and the sierras of Spain, there was little advance beyond a system based on natural forests and carefully tended pastures. The rearing of cattle and sheep does not require a large labour force; a characteristic of these regions was therefore a steady emigration of men looking for work in valleys, cities and armies. Corresponding to this human movement was the seasonal migration of flocks and herds to the plain. This 'transhumance' or grazing change occurred between the Italian Alps and the Po valley, and between the Castilian plateaux and the Andalusian plains. In the latter movement about 2 million sheep of the privileged Mesta organization made the great trek every September and April. The encroachment upon the commons, cutting of trees and the erosion of the thin top soil by regular nibbling of the young grass shoots contributed to the greatest ecological disaster of the time, the impoverishment of the Castilian tablelands. The decline of Castilian wheat farming turned Spain after 1600 into a regular importer of grain.

The main concentrations of population were to be found in the lower hill slopes and valleys, and the irrigated levels of the coast. In such apparently favoured regions, for example the coastlands of Calabria or Catalonia, the hillsides above Lake Garda, the vineyards and olive groves of Languedoc, the typical Mediterranean agriculture was, and still is, to be found, with its combination of fertility and frugality. Methods of farming were dictated by several considerations: the soil lies for the most part thin over underlying rock; even where there is rich alluvial soil the long summer drought that can be expected in a normal year means that the soil will be dry and dusty for most of the summer. Rainfall tends to come in torrential downfalls. There is always therefore a short growing season; a regular risk of flooding adds to the regular problem of soil erosion and impoverishment.

So the farmer grew vines, olives, mulberries, oranges and lemons, since their roots reach deep down to the moisture while the fruit ripens in the sun. He employed a light plough to scratch the top soil, keeping it free from weeds, conserving moisture below. He only required two oxen, as opposed to the six needed for the heavy ploughs of the north; it follows that more peasants were able to survive independently on very little capital and tiny plots of land. The existence of innumerable smallholdings made for stability but not for enterprise; it was a factor in the reluctance of even the more enlightened landowners to invest in expensive schemes of irrigation and other improvements. Because of the short growing season, the staples of Mediterranean farming remained what they had been in classical times: winter-sown wheat, olives and vines. Recent introductions had lent variety: oranges, lemons, peaches and apricots were all introduced by the Arabs; so was the systematic irrigation which turned arid lands into fertile gardens, which could be seen at its most effective in Valencia, where it was controlled by a special Council of the Waters. The Po valley had long been the home of improvements which had been influential in the Netherlands and Britain. Here could be seen the flooding of water meadows to provide early grass; also rice fields where 'the corn of the marshes' was being steadily improved till the point at which, in the mid-eighteenth century, it gave yields up to fifteen times the seed sown. Drainage work was turning some of the malarial Pontine marshes into fertile ground; the embankment of part of the river Tiber was completed in 1678.

In 1600 it might have seemed as if the Mediterranean countries could remain self-sufficient. But the population had increased dramatically (in sixteenth-century Sicily from 600,000 to 1.1 million). Recent studies indicate that already low cereal yields, in the ratio of crop to seed, were falling. As the seventeenth century proceeded clouds gathered. As a whole the region entered a prolonged depression. Commercial causes cannot be overlooked, though recent research suggests that the decline in the volume of trade was neither so sudden nor so steep as has been supposed. The slow decline of Venice, its well-established dominance in the Levantine trade now threatened by the Dutch, provides one of several examples of a phenomenon whose most serious aspect was that the Mediterranean countries depended increasingly on the outside world for their basic needs. War played a part: indirectly in Castile, having ruinous effects upon an economy overburdened by war taxation; directly in Catalonia, after the revolt there of 1640, and in north Italy, where the Mantuan war (1628–31) was particularly destructive. One minute piece of research, into the accounts of Ambrogio d'Adda, a Milanese nobleman and large landowner, has shed light upon the plight of a whole region. His Lombard lands showed the healthy margin of profit that might be expected of that fertile region where farming techniques were as advanced as anywhere in Europe: in 1608–15, it was 47 per cent; in 1616–23, 42.8; in 1624–31, 10.8; in 1632–9, 4.9. Not too much should be built on this isolated example, though it is supported by others. Yet it does show the way in which scholars, working in depth on small areas or on individual merchants and landowners, are gradually piecing together a picture of the past, at least approaching in accuracy what we can know of the present. Ladurie shows on a larger canvas the extent of the change in Languedoc from an overall prosperity in the first half of the seventeenth century to a decline in the last decades, characterized by what he calls the 'shipwreck of the tenant farmers'. It was caused by lack of profit, reflecting a decline in the gross agricultural product and of prices, exacerbated by unfavourable climatic conditions (culminating in the great frost of 1708–9 which killed olive trees and blackened the vines), leading to a fall in population and the engrossing of estates, and lending fierce overtones to the Huguenot rebellion in the Cevennes (1702–5). The rising there of the Camisards with its attendant phenomena of religious revelation and ecstasy was the product in part of social despair. One of its leaders, the visionary Brousson, saw 'a people defeated and dispirited, towns almost ruined for want of trade, and highways filled with poor folk who importuned travellers for half a league'.

That, however, was a special situation. Apart from other factors, one cause of Languedoc's malaise was excessively high royal taxation. To return to the whole Mediterranean theatre, however, is to see the same depression of prices, plight of tenant farmers, collapse of enterprise. The record of Spain from the expulsion of the Moriscoes from Valencia (1609) to the prolongation of the war with Portugal (1641–63) long after it had ceased to offer hope of victory points to the effect of mistaken policies upon the economic well-being of the people. The Papal States and Sicily have records of public mismanagement nearly as calamitous. Most important throughout the region was the deficiency of capital and of investment. As elsewhere, the surplus was being drained away in conspicuous expenditure: baroque profusion alongside agrarian squalor. Some of the southern landowners were as bad as any in Europe: extravagant, neglectful of their estates, caring only for regular rents. Estates were growing larger, dependence on the landowner greater: in 1660 half of the Roman *campagna* was owned by six families. The great increase in short leases in Sicily encouraged tenants to farm for a quick profit, exhausting the soil in the process. The ignorant conservatism of the peasants made matters worse. It was peasants and fishermen, fearful of their livelihood, who, in 1707, broke the dykes in the recently drained Pontine marshes.

The Feudal Regime: France and Spain

A feature of the period, in Italy and elsewhere, was the revival of feudal pretensions and dues. It was equally effect and cause of the agrarian depression which hit landowners as well as tenants and spurred them to look for new ways of making a profit out of their lands. In Germany after the Thirty Years War landowners generally increased dues just as, and for the same reason as, their counterparts in the east were increasing the bonds of serfdom. The extent to which 'the seigneurial reaction', as it has been called, affected France, and the significance of the feudal regime among the causes of the Revolution that caused its destruction, not only in France but in other countries thereafter, are still in dispute. Meanwhile France, for all its many variations, provides ample material for understanding the regime within which more than half of Europe's inhabitants had lived since the Middle Ages.

The feudal seigneury was a group of estates which constituted the property and area of jurisdiction of an individual or a corporate body such as a monastery; it could be vast or tiny, part of a village or a whole district; often, perhaps even typically, it was identical in extent with the village. The seigneur might be layman or churchman, nobleman or commoner. Seigneuries could be bought; they did not confer nobility but some of its dignity, and could be a first step towards that coveted status. The seigneury had two parts. The domain usually comprised the dwelling, which might be an imposing château but was more commonly modest in scale, 'the home farm' and a park, the seigneurial court, a chapel and a mill; around the institutional nucleus there were the lands and woods which were directly subject to the seigneur though they might be farmed out to tenants. The other, larger half of the seigneury was composed of the *censives*, tenures. The peasants who worked these lands with little if any supervision paid a variety of dues, of which the *cens* was the most significant, not because it was large but because its payment, at a fixed annual date, meant recognition of the authority of the seigneur and corresponding limits upon the freedom of the peasants.

Around this core of law, tradition and usage ranged specific rights and dues as diverse as the mosaic of provinces and *pays* that constituted old France. They included *banalités*, monopoly rights, over mill (often leased), winepress and oven; *saisine* and *lods et ventes*, respectively a posthumous levy upon assets and a sort of purchase tax on property sold, exchanged or bartered, which was payable in cash and varied between a tenth and a third; *champart*, a seigneurial tithe, payable in kind, again up to a third of the crop, on part of the land granted (usually the most recent part, which illustrates the economic dependence of the peasant where land is scarce); seigneurial monopolies of hunting, fishing, river use, pigeon rearing; the privilege of the first harvest, for example the *droit de banvin*, by which the seigneur gathered his grapes first and sold his wine first; and, not least, the *corvées*, obligatory labour services. The bare summary conveys the potentiality, but also the problems involved, in control and exploitation. Evidence from the *terriers*, the charters of rights and dues which were usually drawn up when seigneuries changed hands, suggests that bourgeois purchasers, aided by new surveying and mapping techniques, were usually keen to secure the maximum return on their investment. The seigneur had probably renounced his right of criminal jurisdiction because it was too costly but retained the crucial right to judge disputes over boundaries and inheritances.

In some parts of southern and central France, there persisted 'allodial' tenures embodying the principle of absolute tenure, free of feudal obligations, upon the Roman principle which was to become the basis of Napoleonic property law. Recent studies have shown how widespread were such tenures – in Basse-Auvergne for example around 30 per cent of the land – and how tough was the resistance to the pressures of government, its tax officers and the great seigneurs. The allodial position eventually crumbled before the assaults of the crown lawyers. But the south remained relatively immune from seigneurial claims and exactions. 'No lord without title' seems to have been something more than a piece of legal chauvinism. Manorial rights were usually insignificant. Very different was the situation in backward Brittany, and Burgundy, both so long remote from the control of central government. The Breton seigneurs, more commonly resident than in other parts, contrived to live largely off peasant labour and dues. In Burgundy the language and approach was more openly feudal than elsewhere: the seigneury was a fief, the tenant always a vassal. Here, as in Franche Comté and other eastern provinces under the influence of Germany, were to be found the last serfs of France, *mainmortables*: tied to the soil, unable to marry without the lord's consent, they owed the seigneur special *tailles* and *corvées*, regulated by statute but more onerous than elsewhere. Barely one in ten of French peasants were serfs; yet serfdom, uncomplicated by the rights which even the lowliest of free peasants could claim, was probably the only landowner–peasant relationship that was truly profitable to the landowner. It is not surprising, though stridently out of tune with the chorus of enlightened opinion, that some eighteenth-century Burgundians, like the future *contrôleur-général* Joly de Fleury, praised the system, for they were concerned with the mobility of labour and that efficient use of land which was thwarted by the communal system of agriculture. The fortunes of landowner and peasant were equally in the last resort dependent on the productivity of the soil.

There was undoubtedly a change in the nature of the seigneurial regime in the last century before the Revolution.[1] In the popular risings of Richelieu's time, like that of the Croquants (1636–7), there are signs of solidarity between peasants and their lords: action was directed against the detested agents of central government, while the abolition of feudal dues did not feature in their manifestoes. In 1789 the situation was different. As Lefebvre explained, the peasants in that infinitely complex society had as many divergent interests as differences of status and occupation, but they

[1] For the so-called 'feudal reaction', see also pp. 316–17 and bibliography, p. 330.

were united in their hatred of seigneurial rights. So they turned in many districts upon the seigneurs and their agents, burned châteaux and destroyed the muniment rooms where lay the records of their servitude. They were affected no doubt by the propaganda of the *philosophes* and some were at least dimly aware of their 'natural rights'. They were resentful of the application of business methods and legal sanctions to a relationship which had grown out of common interest and had been ruled by custom. *Terriers* had been rewritten, common rights exploited, obsolete judicial powers revived. Law was apparently what the seigneur willed. A Breton monastery, in order to get a few more bushels from its holdings, simply adjusted the volume of the bushel. A duc de Rohan, turning corn merchant on his Breton estates, secured the sanction of the *parlement* of Rennes to extend a particular *corvée*: the peasant who was obliged to cart his corn to de Rohan's mill now had to cart it to the seaport.

The process was analogous to the early development of industrialism. Where the estate was sufficiently large and the people inured to dependence, the landowner enjoyed, like the early industrialist, sufficient bargaining power to enable him to exploit the situation to his own advantage. As in the industrial revolution, too, there was a beneficial side: Rohan's corn farming cut costs; but he was exceptional. Most seigneurs appeared to be concerned more with dues than improvements. They were short of capital and committed, all too often, to excessive expenditure. Some despised the work and the hands that fed them; they might have agreed with the author of *Les Inconvenients de droits féodaux* (1776) who argued that the mediocre sums raised by all the dues were eaten up by the costs of enforcing them, keeping records and financing law suits; some simply abdicated their responsibilities in the face of what seemed to be insuperable problems. Some again simply capitalized on old sources of revenue, and searched for new ones through agents whose livelihoood depended upon their zeal. From new bourgeois landowners who might have acquired a seigneury for prestige but expected it to yield some material return came an increasingly urban, *rentier* approach to the management of the feudal regime; they were matched by the stubbornness of peasants, owners by 1789 of 30 per cent of the land, in defence of their meagre incomes. The seigneurial regime was plainly doomed: it was inefficient and anachronistic. Significant improvements in agriculture depended upon the accumulation of profit in the hands of individual farmers and landowners; the dues, along with the greater weight of the royal taxes, were a drain upon the surplus. The surplus was in any case too small. That was the essential weakness, the source of the general poverty.

The revival of the feudal regime can also be seen in the experience of Valencia on the Mediterranean coast of Spain. There, agricultural production had been affected by the expulsion of the Moriscoes in 1609. The loss of about a quarter of Valencia's 450,000 inhabitants also damaged the feudal aristocracy and their creditors, investors in banks and other institutions which provided the capital for mortgages. There was therefore a strong vested interest behind the reconstruction of the province on terms that favoured the landowner. Since there was also no rush of immigrants (for Spain's population was falling) the peasant should have found himself in a strong bargaining position. As in north Germany however, the facts of territorial sovereignty counted for more than the laws of supply and demand. The tenant of the count of Cocentaina or of the marquis of Denia endured a servitude more extreme than anything known in Spain before. He could not move without his lord's leave; he owed him tithe and first-fruits; he forfeited his rights to common land; he had no property rights except by grace of the lord who monopolized bakeries, mills and taverns; if he manufactured anything he had to pay 10 per cent on each article; on wines 25 per cent, on sugar half of the canes cut. He was trapped within a feudal relationship which lacked its only conceivable justification: some form of mutual benefit. All was weighted in the landlord's favour. Agreements were interpreted to his advantage, petitions summarily dismissed; with lawyers in the *señor*'s pocket legal redress was impossible.

Harrassed by debts, abjectly poor, providing for rich men's tables in a society of cruel extremes, goaded by all the ills that man or nature could contrive, conscription, taxes, bandits, plague, locusts, even an earthquake, the peasants eventually rebelled. In the summer of 1693, with impressive organization, they assembled under Francisco García, a peasant farmer, and José Navarro, a surgeon, marched upon the viceregal capital and pleaded for aid and justice. Inevitably they were defeated. Such protests could only be futile when the most powerful forces of society acted together. No less striking is the weakness of the Habsburg monarchy and its neglect of social responsibility when the survival of the regime seemed to depend upon securing the support of the grandees, and upon strengthening rather than challenging the existing social structure. The Bourbon kings of the eighteenth century have a better record, notably the humane Charles III, who was specially interested in agricultural reform. Economic circumstances, the increase of population, the advance of a sounder money economy and the growth of manufactures did more, however, for the peasant than the edicts of that sensible king.

Rural Depression and Recovery

The seigneurial regime is only one of the elements in the poverty of 'the underdeveloped society' of rural Europe. Fundamental was insufficient capital investment. To that shortage feudal dues contributed, appropriating part of the surplus of the working peasant to the incomes of those who were unlikely to spend anything on the improvement of the soil. Tithe was a further imposition, as it had been ever since the capitularies of Charlemagne had defined its principles and terms. In France it was a widely varying amount by 1700, averaging around 8 per cent, returning upwards of 100 million *livres* altogether. That did not, however, greatly benefit the *curé* or *vicaire* since it went mainly to the big tithe owners, bishops, canons, monks and seigneurs; it was a constant source of discontent therefore, as the *cahiers* of 1789 were to show. Again, strictly 'feudal dues' have to be considered in the context of a wide variety of agricultural rents. One common form in France was that of *métayage*: in the regions of *métayage* proper, the landowner's share was half, that being the proportion advanced to the tenant for seed and stock. Where there were leases, the levy was certainly heavier than the tithe, amounting for example in the Beauvaisis to a fifth of the harvest, which meant about half the gross yield after the farmer's costs were taken into account. It was barely supportable in the good years; during a run of bad years it caused debts and bankruptcies. Landowners, many of them permanent absentees, rarely spent untaxed rentals on improving estates.

Between 1660 and 1700 prices and incomes were stable, tending, if anything, to fall. It was a reflection of the modest level of demand generated by a virtually static population, and consequently depressed levels of trade except in those areas where, as in Holland, there were exceptionally favourable factors at work. The recession was most severe in the inland regions and those where little, if any, extra income was earned by manufactures. After the end of the war against Sweden (1655–60) there was a striking decline in Poland: in the province of Masovia the population was reduced by 40 per cent, sowings were down by a third – harvests were less than a fifth of those of 1560; only 15 per cent of the land was being sowed by rotation, the rest being left fallow. Though less calamitous, the pattern is the same in Hungary, where too the peasant class was being gradually impoverished and subjected. Manufacturers shared in the general decline owing to, and contributing to, a loss of purchasing power. In this situation, relief could come mainly from a lightening of the fiscal demands of the state. What usually happened can be seen from the case of France. The main tax, the *taille*, was the fourth part in the French peasant's burdens, more important than the indirect taxes, tithe or feudal dues. Figures from one province, the Agenais, tell their own tale: the *taille* there was 123,000 *livres* in 1635, the year of France's entry into the Thirty Years War; in 1659 it was 474,000. It was reduced under Colbert and settled, up to the Dutch War (1672), at around 440,000; by 1693, when there was a capital tax to pay as well, it had climbed to 562,000. Because of the rising cost of war, the load of royal taxation and the administration required to collect it was mounting everywhere just at the time when the depression was entering its severest phase; the point had been reached when the only limit was the capacity of communities to pay. Under these conditions, there could be no significant agricultural improvement. Because of the pressure of population upon resources, more land was being cultivated. It might be waste pasture or scrub. In any case it meant that there was less manure to put back on the fields. With declining yields came further pressure upon the 'marginal' land. This was the poverty trap, with its trend towards monoculture of cereals, and accompanying malnutrition. As the gap widened between those peasants who were able to increase their holdings or to farm land for prosperous bourgeois or clerical landowners, and the great mass of small-holders and landless peasants, the rich few were acquiring greater status and independence: more than ever they had a vested interest in preserving the old regime.

During the early 1700s widespread warfare and several disastrous harvests produced sharp but irregular price rises. There ensued a fairly stable period of some thirty years, when the population was starting to rise again, fast enough to promote demand but not so fast as to fuel inflation; there were few bad harvests during this period and food was relatively cheap; in retrospect it appeared to have been the golden age of the consumer. During this time there were no general famines, even in the more backward countries, but there were also no fundamental economic changes: there was a measure of relief rather than real progress. From the middle of the century, as population began to rise more sharply, so did the prices of nearly all commodities. Wages, moreover, failed to keep up with prices. In Spain the population rose during the century by 43 per cent but prices almost doubled. Worst affected everywhere were the poorer peasants, partly or wholly dependent on wages, and the increasing number of town workers, competing for jobs without the bargaining power to protect them against the harsh conditions of an overcrowded labour market. In France where, between the 1730s and 1780s, the population rose by about 20 per cent and prices by 60 per cent, poverty became once again a political factor of crucial importance. Besides population, the supply of precious metals was a factor, as it had been during the long sixteenth-century inflation. Since, however, the increase in the supply, with new mines coming into operation in Mexico and Brazil around 1700, did not immediately lead to an increase in prices, it can be inferred that the larger inflow of bullion sustained rather than caused the eventual rise. A more immediate influence on prices was that of the harvest, plentiful or otherwise. A few bad years, such as occurred at regular intervals during the second half of the century, brought an immediate jump in bread prices. The average grain price did not fall thereafter to the same level as before; grain, moreover, established the price of other food prices, and eventually other commodities, though in less volatile fashion, followed the rising course.

Agricultural distress was to be one of the immediate causes of the French Revolution: the failure of the harvest of 1788 brought a sharp increase in the price of bread (on which urban workers were now spending about half their income) while the drop in demand for industrial goods reduced production and employment. A century before, a similar conjunction had produced local risings. In 1789, the vast city of Paris was to erupt in a fashion far more dangerous to the survival of the regime, sensitive as it was to any worsening in the economic condition; the city was stirred to action by demagogues against the privileged classes who themselves had been so shortsighted in their assaults upon the king's ministers, and so resistant to measures of reform. The edifice that collapsed in 1789 was grounded upon a regime of rural exploitation. That there was no such collapse and no revolution in Britain, even though London contained several elements of a revolutionary situation, is to some extent due to the relative prosperity of agriculture. We are reminded that there had been progress in other states in Europe which had a beneficial effect on the stability and resilience of their political systems.

Pioneers and Improvers

The progress of the Netherlands, seriously short of land, and long used to adapting to the problems of a difficult environment, shows the way in which the contraction or development of farming depended on the general level of incomes. Holland in particular was rich in private capital, open to international trade and not much affected by economic dogmatism. Pre-eminence in the commercial world and the advance of farming techniques here went hand in hand. Already some parts were acquiring the man-made appearance of today, with neat quadrilateral polders, intersected by canals and dikes, overlooked by the ubiquitous windmills with their scoop wheels and screw pumps, capable of lifting water up to 16 feet. Netherlands farmers seemed to be specially good at responding to the challenge of changing patterns of demand or to those accidents of politics and war that did so much damage to agriculture elsewhere. In Harlingerland in East Friesland the peasants changed from animal to arable husbandry because of the war levy of the years 1637–48, based on head of cattle; around Liège a ban on the export of cereals by the authorities concerned was enough to persuade farmers to concentrate upon livestock. Different indeed were the slow reflexes of French peasants in the Auvergne for example, who persisted in corn farming, with diminishing yields, on hill land that was ideal for livestock. Lack of cash, ingrained conservatism or the timidity of men inured to exploitation? Perhaps it is fruitless to distinguish between cause and effect.

The effects of balanced husbandry are not however difficult to appreciate. Larger animal herds meant more manure, and were reflected in the highest crop yields in Europe. Using beds and rows for sowing instead of scattering broadcast, the Netherlanders cultivated industrial textile plants, hemp and flax, madder and woad for dyestuffs; hops were grown alongside barley and vegetables for the towns; potatoes, so stubbornly resisted by the

French who preferred to grow Jerusalem artichokes (indeed the knobbly tuber of those days, with its deep sunk eyes, lacked culinary appeal), became a valuable supplement to eighteenth-century diet; tomatoes were grown, even tobacco, while 'turkeys' appeared in the fowl yard. Innovations in crop rotation enabled the Dutchman to make the best use of his precious land while drainage schemes added to its area. In Friesland cereals were usually grown in alternation with fodder crops like turnips and lucerne. In places sheep were folded, their dung then carted on to the land. In 1756 in the district of Klundert, whose records have been exhaustively examined, 58.3 per cent of the soil was sown with eight different types of cereal; 41.7 per cent carried pulses, industrial crops or potatoes. The Dutch brought to their farming the same inventiveness and rationality that informed all their affairs: the entrepreneurial spirit encouraged specialization. In the preparation of flax, for example, there were five separate processes. The 'tulip bloom' of de Witt's Holland with the accompanying mania of collecting and speculation, shows the way in which the grower responded to the acquisitive spirit of the town. And so Dutch agriculture supported the best-fed people in Europe and brought wealth into the economy. The Dutchman was renowned for his fine physique: it was attributed to his great eating of cheese; yet by 1700 the Dutch were exporting nine-tenths of their cheese.

Even where there was 'progressive' farming the peasant could not escape the afflictions of nature in the pre-scientific age, like rinderpest, the cattle disease which reached the Netherlands from Russia in 1713–20. The 'miracle crop', maize, brought more plentiful food to parts of Spain and north Italy, but even that was not an unmixed blessing as over-reliance on maize brought a disease of vitamin deficiency, pellagra. War also took its toll. During the French wars the Dutch were one of the most highly taxed people in Europe, and taxes bore most heavily upon the peasants, hard put to it to finance the waterworks to maintain precarious defences against flood. With some of the same factors in play that had brought prosperity to the Dutch, the British took over in the eighteenth century the pioneering role. Again we find the interaction of farming and manufactures: it has been estimated that the increasing use of iron for ploughs and horseshoes accounted for nearly half the total demand for iron in 1750. But in Britain the 'improving' country gentleman was the chief agent in the agricultural revolution, unrestrained by social taboos and assisted by relatively free land and labour markets. Enclosures, crop rotations and the scientific breeding which was transforming, as in the Netherlands, the appearance and utility of cattle and sheep, made it possible to sustain a steadily growing population.

The importance in both England and Holland of the relatively free markets in land and labour is underlined by the example of Spain where entirely different conditions prevailed. So much land was out of the market because of the system of entail and mortmain, which perpetuated great lay and ecclesiastical estates respectively, that the land which did come up for sale was correspondingly expensive; so much capital was tied up in one way or another that too little was available for improvements and there was a great temptation to adopt short-term methods. There was indeed a startling contrast to be observed in Spain: on the one hand the vast tracts of grassland, underused, devoted to the pasturing of sheep and bulls, which if used for mixed farming could have sustained twice the population, and on the other the tiny holdings of peasants unable to make a living because they had too little land.

The advance of population in the eighteenth century may have stimulated more efficient methods of food production. It also played its part in convincing rulers that they must take farming seriously. After the Seven Years War, the resettlement and more intensive use of the ravaged land of Prussia was a prime need. Frederick II formed and subsidized a land bank to lend money to landowners at low rates of interest. Altogether during his reign 0.25 million acres were reclaimed, 300,000 colonists resettled. Elsewhere agricultural societies were formed: there was much talk of reform, and some action, as when the elector of Saxony imported merino sheep. But Germany as a whole remained backward. Where the peasants were strong, holdings were generally small; they resisted change even where they were in a position to achieve it. Landowners blamed peasants for inertia, peasants denounced landowners for their exactions. The German townsman traditionally despised the countryman – 'der dumme Bauer'. Even Frederick's admirable edict of 1763, providing for six hours schooling for all children between the ages of 6 and 13, failed to produce the desired result. Few teachers were trained; they were desperately poor; in the summer the schools were empty. But it was a beginning; by the end of the eighteenth century many Prussian peasants could read and write, and with literacy, attitudes began to change. Where landowners were strong, as in Mecklenburg, large estates made possible extensive grain farming, Prussian-style. But the serf labour which supported this style of farming was unsuited to the requirements of efficient mixed farming.

After the middle of the eighteenth century, traditionalists were on the defensive against the physiocrats and their disciples, who argued against the impositions of feudalism and the restrictive customs of village communities. Partition of commons, leasing out of heathlands and enclosures characterized the whole of the 1760s. Some French noblemen studied, and praised, the new techniques; a few, like the enterprising viscountess du Pont, much praised by Arthur Young for her lucerne crops, took effective action. But the gathering depression of the 1770s meant an unfavourable climate for reformers. Much was heard of the 'disgrace of the fallows' but Arthur Young, travelling just before the Revolution, found that three-course rotation was prevalent in many districts. Landowners tended to prefer immediate benefits, whether from pasture rents or feudal dues, to long-term improvements which would require capital, patience and moral courage to withstand the suspicion and resentment aroused by any sort of change. Ironically it was the improving landowners who bore the brunt of opposition bred of centuries of neglect and exploitation. The crown gave no lead. It is hard to imagine Louis XV or Louis XVI writing articles for a farming journal, like their English contemporary George III.

Population and War

Most countries therefore exhibited some of the features of a pre-industrial or 'underdeveloped' economy. With the exception of the maritime and commercial powers, the relatively dynamic Britain and Holland, the scene is one of limited development within an inelastic frame: man was contained by his inability to produce more than a certain amount of food, or to make goods except by laborious hand production. In such an economy, population plays a fundamental part in determining the level of demand and production, through the amount of labour available for field and workshop, and through the number of consumers. It was common ground among economic theorists that men, in Bodin's words, were 'the only strength and wealth'. The sixteenth century had seen the last phase of the long recovery from the demographic calamity of the fourteenth century – the Black Death. In some areas the increase was spectacular: Braudel estimates that the population of the Mediterranean countries rose from 30–35 to 60–65 million. But around 1600 a natural ceiling seems to have been reached. Congested cities like Seville suffered terrible mortalities: a quarter of its people died in the plague of 1599. In Italy, where they 'cultivated their mountains', the familiar terrace formation can still be seen, evidence of the chronic land hunger. That there were too many people to be employed and fed became a standard argument for colonization, even for war. In the seventeenth century, as war was fought on an ever larger scale, it proved with its concomitants of famine and disease an all too effective check.

Within the period there are two distinct phases. From the end of the Thirty Years War in 1648 to around 1720 there were recurring demographic crises. There ensued what historians have called 'the vital revolution' when, for the first time, the population of Europe made a prolonged and steady advance without being pulled back by some violent episode. Allowing for an error of around 10 per cent, which reflects the use of partial or indirect data, Roger Mols estimates 104.7 million in 1600, 115.3 million in 1700, 144 million in 1750: the rate of increase advanced as the century wore on. Among the causes may be reckoned the ending of a particularly intense and destructive phase of war (in 1714 in the west, 1718 in the east, 1721 in the north), the retreat of the bubonic plague, local improvements in agriculture and a natural expansion in the still sparsely inhabited regions of eastern Europe. In 1750 Europe was approaching the end of its old biological regime, and was about to enter an era in which advances in knowledge actually affected the way people lived; the future was to lie with more efficient methods of production and with continuous progress by scientists in the war against disease. It is important, however, to stress that in continental Europe the necessary conditions for significant industrial advance had yet to be achieved. The population of 1750 was coming up to the peak of what could be achieved under the still prevailing conditions of the pre-industrial economy. The spectacular rise in the populations of Ireland and Norway during the next hundred years might indeed be used to show that industrial advance was not an essential pre-condition: so might the great Irish potato blight and subsequent famine (1846–8), when 1 million died out of 8 million, to show how vulnerable was a society dependent upon agriculture – in that case upon one crop.

At the start of the period the shadows of the Thirty Years War lay heavy over all those countries most involved: Sweden, Holland and Spanish Flanders, France, Spain, north Italy, the Habsburg family lands, above all Germany. The discrepancy between lofty aspirations, usually expressed in religious terms, and the atrocious realities of war waged largely by mercenary soldiers who lived in a self-contained world of their own, contemptuous of civilian rights, contributes to a certain nightmarish character which makes it no easier to be precise about the effects of the war. A case can be made for a revision of the more drastic conclusions. To secure remission of tax or higher compensations, rulers tended to exaggerate their losses; there is a propaganda element in some accounts; refugee movements, with all their dislocation and misery, do not necessarily constitute an overall loss. There is evidence for the continued prosperity of certain places, like Hamburg, the virtual immunity of others, like Oldenburg or Lippe, and for the recovery even of such embattled cities as Leipzig. It remains hard however to resist the conclusion that the war was a demographic disaster for Germany, surely a valid description, even if one takes the most cautious of views – that the population fell by about a quarter. In some parts, Brandenburg, Württemberg, for example, it fell by more than half. Nor was the war confined to Germany. There was widespread depopulation in Burgundy after the fighting there between French and Spanish; the southern Netherlands sustained lasting damage to economic life; in Italy, Mantua provided a spectacular case: after siege, sack and plague, in 1630–1, it lost 70 per cent of its inhabitants. During the conflicts of 1618–48 it became clear that the increase in the size of armies was not matched by tighter political control. It was the random and undisciplined nature of operations, more than death in battle, that caused such damage. The Thirty Years War was exceptional.

How important then was war, after 1648, among the factors affecting population? It should be noted that the rest of the century saw a further increase in the scale of operations and the size of armies. There was nothing comparable to the slaughter of the modern war of nations, with its conscript armies, and advanced technology, long-range artillery and machine guns, indiscriminate agents of casualties so great as to affect the birth rate of whole generations: in the world war of 1914–18 the combatant powers lost altogether 13 million men. In wars up to 1870, sickness in armies exceeded death in action in the proportion of 5 to 1 (in the next century the opposite was the case). On the battlefields the majority of those wounded might expect to die of blood poisoning or other infection, or be incapacitated for life. Casualties in the great, though rare, set-piece battles such as Seneffe (1674), Blenheim (1704) or Poltava (1709) were high in proportion to the numbers engaged and to the size of the waning states. Sweden during the reign of Charles XII, Prussia during the Seven Years War, provide two examples of particularly severe blood-letting; in both cases the population fell sharply. The effect upon a particular country was always modified by the fact that some, if not the majority, of soldiers were foreigners. It has been estimated that there were 50,000 Swiss soldiers in European armies at any given time in the first half of the eighteenth century. It was a human export trade which enabled that Arcadian country, so much admired by travellers, to maintain a balanced economy and a stable population without itself suffering from the incidental ravages of war. For war was chiefly damaging through the mere presence of an army in communities which had nothing to spare. The French commissioner for war in 1744 wrote that an army of 100,000 would require a delivery from the supply lines every four days, involving 600 carriages, with 2400 horses harnessed in fours. The average size of armies during the Thirty Years War was around 20,000. But these did not have the elaborate, home-based commissariat of later French armies, and they were expected to live off the land. The Swedes operated at relatively little cost to the mother country because they lived and fought in Germany or Poland. The passage of armies, with their scavenging patrols, placed a burden upon food supplies and disrupted agriculture when crops and barns were destroyed, horses, bullocks and mules impounded, and fields left unsown. Routes and systems of trade were also disrupted. The armies themselves, with their numerous camp followers, provided ideal conditions for the spread of diseases. Even in peacetime normal billeting was a grievous burden, which is why it was such an effective weapon when used by Louis XIV to coerce the Huguenots.

In general, by distorting the natural economy, by diverting towards destructive ends an excessive proportion of government funds, and through heavier taxes, war sapped the wealth of the community and reduced the ability of governments and individuals alike to plan and invest for greater production. The work of Colbert, for example, would have been unthinkable in the 1640s; it was checked by the war of 1672–8 and largely undone by the wars of 1689–1714. Peter I of Russia until after he had repelled Charles XII and made peace with the Turks, and Frederick II of Prussia until the end of the Seven Years War, are two prime examples of monarchs who were unable till peacetime to tackle seriously the economic problems to which war had so greatly contributed. Certain sectors of the economy benefited from war, notably metallurgy, textiles and shipbuilding. Technological advances might have wider application. The examples of the Dutch during the Spanish war that ended in 1648 and of the British in the wars of 1688–1714 show that, under favourable conditions, war could foster capitalist enterprise and promote the techniques of banking and investment. Conversely, the effect upon a backward country could be specially severe. Poland's economic decline was due largely to the devastation of Swedish or Russian armies occupying or employing scorched-earth tactics to achieve their strategic ends. The devastation of the Palatinate by Tessé in 1688–9 and that of parts of Bavaria by Marlborough in 1704 show that such tactics were still regarded as legitimate. In general, however, the tighter control of armies and their restricted use in textbook campaigns and battles limited the damage of war in the eighteenth century: it is not the least among that century's claims to a higher civilization.

Climate and Famine

In the natural economy, when the average life expectancy was so low, the risk of death in war may have been more lightly regarded. War's ravages were only, as it were, the presentation in high relief of 'normal' features of life. In France at this time the overall population fluctuated between the years of the great mortalities, when several millions went to premature graves, and the subsequent peaks of recovery. In a rural community, a wet summer or frosty spring could be as disastrous as the passage of an army. There is evidence that the second half of the century witnessed several phases of exceptionally unfavourable weather. Those who wish to investigate the 'little ice age' of the seventeenth century, must be prepared to examine some highly technical arguments, besides the more familiar evidence of parish registers, tax yields, trade returns and price indices. Using the telescopes that were available after 1610 astronomers noted that the sunspots which their predecessors had observed at intervals up till 1645 were notable for their absence. Aurora borealis, the Northern Lights, caused by particles from the sun entering the earth's atmosphere, was observed so rarely after 1640 that when it appeared it alarmed the superstitious. The evidence provided by measurement of the rings of trees, which are relatively thin in poor years, and then also reveal heavy deposits of the radioactive carbon 14 which is associated with the decline of solar energy, brings the authority of modern science to the support of the seventeenth-century observers. Snow lines were observed to be lower, glaciers advanced into Alpine valleys reaching their furthest point around 1670; some remarkable frosts were recorded. All the evidence points to a century of unfavourable climate, characterized by very cold winters and wet summers. The changes overall were probably small, a fall of about 1 per cent in solar radiation, of 1 degree centigrade in mean summer temperatures, but that was enough to tilt the precarious balance against the peasant producer. More than four-fifths of the population depended on cereal crops for sustenance. A fall of 1 degree in summer temperatures restricts the growing season by three weeks and the maximum altitude at which crops will ripen by 510 feet. The effect, in terms of declining yields, upon farmers and therefore upon the whole economy, in a period when even the bare sufficiency of food was only produced by widespread use of marginal land, was severe. A harsher climate meant more crop failures, lighter bread prices and, for some, starvation.

In this somewhat grey picture it is possible to identify three particularly black patches. Wet summers and a series of poor harvests affected all countries in the postwar years 1648–52. The disastrous harvest of the previous year was a direct cause of the revolt of the Sicilians in 1648. The Fronde which started in that year was only in part the result of grain scarcity and high prices, but successive bad years added much to the misery and violence of the civil war. Queen Christina of Sweden's crisis of 1650 was exacerbated again by harvest failure. Louis XIV's personal reign began in 1661 with a disastrous harvest and subsequent famine. These experiences were, however, relatively mild compared to the prolonged misery of the years 1691–6 when cold wet summers spoiled spring sowings throughout western and northern Europe. The effect of freakish climatic conditions can be studied in the Spanish experience of 1683. The account by Francisco Godoy of an African-style drought in Andalusia shows man absolutely at the mercy of nature when, during the whole of 1683, until the end of November, there was not a drop of rain:

> Almost the whole of Andalusia was in absolute drought. The crops were parched with heat, the trees burnt up, ... bread became so scarce and expensive that many people perished of hunger.... A stock farmer's 1,600 head of cattle was reduced to 200 because of drought and lack of fodder.

That drought was followed by monsoon-like rains bringing destructive floods; in the city of Granada alone 6000 houses were damaged. Then came the plague, endemic in southern Spain in this period, bringing about a quarter of a million deaths to Castile in one decade.

In the essay on history and climate in which he summarizes the arguments of climatologists, Le Roy Ladurie concludes that, while the great crises of the century may be attributed to 'successions of climatically and ecologically unfavourable years', the prolonged depression during which these 'short term crises' occurred 'cannot possibly be explained in terms of climate'. So he asserts the supremacy of social and economic conditions, 'proper human history', over climatological factors which, in the long term, may well cancel each other out. The arbitrary deals of nature, like the thunderbolts of war, serve only to highlight the essential characteristics of the economy: inelastic market forces, bad communications, lack of investment and of diversified production. Trapped in this primitive market situation, the peasant might find that even favourable runs of weather were a mixed blessing. During most of the period covered by Colbert's ministry in France (1661–83) harvests were abundant and cereal prices correspondingly low. The large class of small farmers found it more difficult than usual to pay their taxes and dues, so that many fell into debt. Against that background, a crop failure struck with immediate force, since such peasants had been reduced to relying largely on what they could produce for themselves. Gilbert Burnet wrote of a journey in September 1685: 'on the way from Paris to Lyon I was astonished by such great misery ... everywhere one meets nothing but wretched hovels, torn clothes and emaciated faces ... even the towns are terribly affected'. There he points to the way in which the condition of the peasant affected the whole community because of the effect of failing demand upon the manufacture of goods, already depressed by the monetary famine of the second half of the seventeenth century. And so it is necessary to look beyond such exceptional phenomena as the campaign of the Fronde that made desolate much of the country round Paris, or the notorious great frost of 1708–9 that blackened the vines and olives of Languedoc, as today the effects of an earthquake might be discounted in analysing the chronic poverty of a backward country. The constant factor throughout, during price inflation and recession, through war and peace, in seasons fair and foul was the defenceless condition of the peasant in the natural economy, in which supply always tended to exceed demand.

How common was famine? Examples are not hard to find. In Finland in 1697, a third of the population died; in 1698 Sweden suffered a famine not much less severe. All Scandinavia had a serious subsistence crisis in 1737–43. In 1662 the tax officials of Burgundy informed the king that 'famine this year has put an end to over seventy thousand families in your province and forced a third of the inhabitants, even in the good towns, to eat wild plants'. There were widespread famines in France in 1691–6 and 1709, the latter coming after the worst winter of which records exist. The *curé* of the parish of Vincelles in the Yonne wrote of that year:

> one sees men, women and children ... scratching the earth with their nails, searching for roots which they devour when they find them. Others less industrious scrabble the grass along with their animals, others completely broken lie along the roads waiting for death.

Of contemporary estimates there is no lack. A report from Tuscany in 1767 declared that of 316 preceding years, 111 had been marked by famine in some degree. That could be a special case, because it was hilly land of olive trees and vines which usually relied on purchases of Sicilian grain. When eighteenth-century reformers tackled agrarian problems they tended to rely on this sort of statistical exercise, a blend of science and folk memory, liable perhaps to be coloured by a sentimental view of the past. Famines could still be entirely local phenomena because of physical and fiscal barriers to marketing, transport and government measures of relief.

A composite picture leads to certain inescapable conclusions. Leaving on one side favoured areas like England and the Netherlands, it is clear that famine was endemic in Europe in the seventeenth century: worse in the eastern half than in the west; and in the west, most common in France and the drier parts of Spain and Italy. Despite some good years in mid-century, famines still occurred in the eighteenth century. Severe famine has a threefold impact on population. Women are rendered infertile; the death of young adults has an effect on the birth rate of the ensuing decade; young couples may defer marriage or take care not to have children. The absence of major checks and drops in the overall population suggests therefore that famines were becoming less widespread and severe. They would have been worse if it had not been for the maize, in Italy and the south of France, and potatoes, mainly in Germany; also important were the improvements in international and domestic trading facilities and more effective action by governments to relieve distress.

Poverty, Charity and Crime

Famine was the occasional collective crisis in the life of the poor; nature's way of restoring the precarious balance between people and resources. Poverty was the normal condition of at least half the people of Europe. Of this mass the more fortunate did certainly live in a reasonably secure way: they were those who had sufficient land, perhaps 15 acres or more, or a regular living wage; a well-balanced family, with more earners than dependents, and good health. Whatever the variants, the essence of the situation was that enough was earned to provide the daily bread. Below those fortunate ones ranged a great many who could slide into the pit of destitution at any time. Because of the lack of realizable assets, debt was a familiar condition everywhere: once incurred, unlikely to be repaid, usually the start of a progressive decline. In the words of Condorcet: 'he who possesses neither goods nor chattels is destined to fall into misery at the least accident'. It might be illness or injury to a breadwinner; an extra tax or billeting demand; the death or bankruptcy of an employer; the failure of a crop or the death of a cow – any one such event could be fatal. There was generally no understanding of birth control, though in desperation a couple might practise some voluntary abstinence. There was a tendency to marry later, while a surprisingly high proportion of western European girls, between 10 and 15 per cent, did not marry at all. Among the rest almost half married after the age of 25. This was the key to the rate of child-bearing: as P. Chaunu wrote, 'the real contraceptive weapon of classical Europe'. The poor had no reserves. For many young families disaster was the birth of a third or fourth child. The prevalence of infanticide has a grim significance. A drain opened in Rennes in the course of rebuilding in 1721 revealed the skeletons of eighty babies suffocated in the first hours of life. It was usual to regard the pathetic bundle on church steps, perhaps with a Christian name on a scrap of paper, or a pinch of salt to signify that it had not been baptized, as the offspring of an illicit union; but often married couples must have abandoned a baby rather than acquire another mouth to feed. In Brussels over 2000 babies were abandoned annually to be looked after by some charitable organization.

Even in the twentieth century when, in the west at least, poverty appears to be confined to relatively small minorities, it is hard to define precisely. The word 'relatively' suggests the importance of attitudes: material expectations vary when one generation's luxury is the next generation's necessity. There is a psychological factor: self-respect is involved. Poverty is often a hidden condition and has always been easier to describe than to quantify. For the *ancien régime* there is no lack of description. The parish priest of Les Bondons, in the Massif Central, saw unmistakeable poverty when, in 1760, he described parishioners whose nakedness and weakness allowed them to do little more than huddle together on rotting straw in their wretched hovels, some of them too weak to stand. The English traveller John Locke experienced it in the form of a Sunday dinner in a peasant's house in Provence that consisted of 'slices of congealed blood fried in oile'. A woman recognized poverty when she looked at the few beads or scrap of lace that were all she could add to her working clothes on festival days. The woman who made the lace knew it, losing her eyesight after twenty years of doing fine work in a bad light. Respectable congregations sought to avoid noticing it by commissioning new churches so that they would not have to travel to church through the poor sections of the town.

La Bruyère put a literary gloss upon poverty when he wrote:

> one sees certain wild animals, male and female, scattered about the countryside, black, livid and cracked with sun, bound to the soil that they till with invincible obstinacy; they have an articulate voice, and when they get up they reveal a human face, and in fact they are human. They retire to hovels where they live on black bread, water and roots.

The more the conditions of the poorest groups are investigated, the more it becomes apparent that La Bruyère was scarcely exaggerating. The traveller through the Auvergne, through high Castile, through the bare hills of southern Italy, might well see such sights. Arthur Young, an objective writer who had seen much that impressed him during his travels in France, wrote of Combourg, a Breton town, 'one of the most brutal, filthy places that can be seen, mud houses, no windows, and a pavement so broken as to impede all passengers but ease none'. He saw the château and asked: 'Who is this Monsieur de Chateaubriant, the owner, that has nerves strung for such a residence amidst such filth and poverty?' Travelling on the other side of France, through Champagne and Burgundy, Young went 80 miles before he was able to purchase any milk. Nearly every type of economic system was to be found in France. Because of its size it necessarily occupies a central position in any view of European society, providing standards against which exceptions, such as relatively well-off, meat-eating Englishmen, or Dutchmen, even poorer Mediterranean peasants, can be judged. Regional studies indicate that most French peasants were unable to live on their land alone because their holdings were too small, often under 15 acres; they therefore depended on some ancillary form of income from spinning or weaving, or from work elsewhere as seasonal migrants. Their diet was almost entirely meatless and fatless, 90 per cent cereal, either in the form of bread or some sort of gruel, often with vegetables, occasionally a little offal; except in the wine-growing districts wine was rarely drunk. There existed a numerous class who lived a life of makeshifts and scavenging. At least 10 per cent of the population normally depended on charity to survive, whether through institutions or more commonly through begging. As conditions worsened after 1760, and the price of bread rose beyond the earning capacity of the poor, the numbers of the itinerants and beggars increased and with them pressure on already inadequate provision of relief.

The seventeenth century was the heroic age of charitable work for the poor. The most influential figure in the movement was Vincent de Paul (1596–1660). His instructions to the order of well-born ladies which he founded to help 'our lords the poor' were compassionate and practical: 'For your monastery use the houses of the sick, for your chapel the parish church, for your cloister the streets of towns or the rooms of hospitals.' Witnessing, in their grey dresses and white *cornettes*, to the belief that charity was a Christian duty, the *Filles de Charité* founded hospitals for incurables, looked after stray children and sent nurses to the troops; in the Fronde they set up soup kitchens, nursed the sick and buried the dead. St Vincent's idea of the *hôpital général*, an institution in which the aged, destitute, crippled and orphaned could voluntarily find refuge, and which the rich would support as their consciences directed, was taken over by the French state and merged with older institutions in 1662, when, two years after Vincent's death, an edict commended the institution of *hôpitaux* throughout the land. The object was grand: to cater for the deserving poor on a nation-wide scale. Legislation for the poor was pervaded by concern for their moral and spiritual well-being. Beggars and prostitutes were carefully segregated. The day of *les enfants bleus* began with the children prostrating themselves on the floor and reciting the commandments. Idealism and utilitarianism in fine balance: the hand of Colbert is to be seen in the arrangement. There was little expense to the state, the streets would be tidied up, and a pool of cheap, disciplined child labour would be available for new manufacturers. It is fair to add that Colbert also directed subsidies to the poor parishes in times of dearth and that the policy as a whole went far to meet the stock criticism of ecclesiastical charity – that it simply encouraged idleness and improvidence.

In France by 1789, there were over 2000 *hôpitaux* and the idea had been taken up all over Catholic Europe: in effect the problem of the poor was left to private enterprise and Christian charity. It was believed no less strongly in Protestant countries that the poor should be aided by the Church. But important differences marked the Protestant from the Catholic approach. The Reformation had been accompanied by the secularization of Church property and in some countries by the establishment of churches under state control. It was a principle of canon law that part of Church revenue was intended for the maintenance of the poor. The state took over obligations of poor relief with the revenues of the Church. Protestant countries can be seen moving towards more systematic, if not more radical forms of relief. In Holland Church elders and in England parish overseers were empowered to raise poor-rates. In Brandenburg, a law of 1696 authorized parishes to provide work for the deserving poor, and punishment for others. In all these countries relief depended on the efficiency of the agent, and the concern of local people: neither could be taken for granted. In Denmark however, in 1683, the government enunciated the important principle that paupers had the legal right to relief: pauperism was defined so as to include both the unemployed and those who could not afford to support a family. The pauper lost freedom: he could be given work in land reclamation or road-building far from home. But supervised by salaried state officials, the system ensured work and food.

It might have been expected that the problem of poverty would be attacked vigorously by 'enlightened' reformers: anti-clerical, impatient with the past and concerned for efficiency, they tended, on the contrary, to be unenthusiastic. Rationalists deplored indiscriminate charity saying it perpetuated the poverty it sought to prevent. Administrators were concerned about being tricked by false pretences; the new breed of economists were opposed to any interference with the laws of nature – not least to any form of support which did not show a productive return. Taking their tone from prevailing attitudes, ecclesiastics themselves often become slack or sceptical. That, however, there must be public works was generally agreed. In Pombal's Portugal some of the confiscated property of the Jesuits was used to finance poor relief. In parts of France, the *corvée*, commuted into a money tax, subsidized *ateliers de charité*. More was done for children, and charity schools were founded everywhere. The emphasis tended to be on religious and practical instruction. There was a general fear of educating children 'beyond their station' which, considering the state of the labour market, was no more than realistic. There was undoubtedly, however, an element of alarm among the upper classes. In England the movement for elementary education was to find more favour after the French Revolution. Thorough in this as in so much else, Joseph II represents the 'enlightened' idea of charity at its best. Of the money raised by the dissolution of monasteries and lay brotherhoods, much was devoted to welfare services: orphanages, hospitals, medical schools, special institutions for the deaf, blind and lunatic were set up under the aegis of a special commission. By 1785, the Vienna General Hospital had 2000 beds. District commissioners were instructed in 1784 to make provision for deprived children of all sorts. Graduated charges and free medical care for paupers were among the features of a policy to deal with poverty, which was to remain without equal, in some countries, till the twentieth century: a model of humanity and commonsense.

It has always been notoriously difficult to quantify crime. Besides the obvious difficulty that it can only be measured by rates of detection, there is the fundamental problem of definition. With the enlargement of the role of the state and its laws there is new scope for the criminal. Thus cautioned the reader may not expect helpful guidance to this largely hidden area of life. But it is too important to ignore. In this period in which states became stronger and society more regulated, crime is easier to identify. There had formerly been little to distinguish the overtly treasonous acts of leaders of revolts like those of 1636–7 in France from the persistent banditry that preceded and followed them. How many of those responsible for the regular deaths of tax collectors were ever brought to justice? The conduct of nobles, raping, robbing, taking hostages and murdering, that was exposed by the *Jours d'Auvergne* in 1665 sounded shocking in the courtrooms of an ordered society, but was commonplace in war, when whole districts were reduced to the level where the only law was that of survival. Armies were brought under stricter discipline but warfare was still endemic and men who were licensed to kill and loot did not take readily to gentler modes of life, even if they could find civilian employment. The large number of deserters from every European army compounded the problem: *ipso facto* outlaws, they were a significant element in petty brigandage and in the occasional great risings of the rural poor. There persisted large areas, like the Cossack lands, beyond the scope of law, where crime was part of the way of life. Between the official foray and the unofficial cattle raid the distinction was blurred, as indeed it could become between the privateering licensed by the maritime power and piracy. Lawlessness was not merely a condition of Europe's marches or a by-product of war. In periods of extreme hardship, bringing the demoralization of entire communities (which was the situation of parts of France in the 1690s and 1700s), the grey area between the legitimate and the criminal could only expand. Neither begging nor prostitution were in themselves illegal but when they became the occupation of large groups they created an amoral ambience in which criminals could expect tolerance and protection. By 1789 there were 20,000 prostitutes in Paris. Perhaps more significantly, in relatively staid and well-governed Mainz it was estimated that a third of the women in the poorer districts were prostitutes.

Beggary took many forms. The most familiar, licensed, as it were, by a public accustomed in Catholic communities to the mendicant friar and taught that it was blessed to give, was that of the old or crippled, in some strategic position round the market square or at the church door. Then there were the hordes of children, clutching at coat tails, whining importunities, recounting well-rehearsed tales of misfortune: those were often real enough, as was the hunger in young faces pressed against the shutters of the baker's shop. They were eager trainees in the school of crime, learning to pick pockets or aid smugglers. Beggars in the countryside were notorious for starting fires and spreading disease. The French authorities recognized the criminal aspect when they classified *vagabonds* separately from *errants*, as being definitely on the wrong side of the law. They often acted in gangs and in lonely districts where householders would give more from fear than from compassion. With the acquiescence, if not approval, of their fellow poor who had nothing to fear because they had nothing to give, and might be rewarded with a share of the spoils, the beggar gang could easily evolve into regular banditry. Classic bandit country was a poor district near a trade route, ideally where there were woods and hills to shelter. Smollett recounted meeting a follower of the famous Mandrin, native of Valence, of common origin, who had served as a soldier and then as tax collector. He used his knowledge of the system to build up a regime of extortion and protection, and a gang of some 500, with 300 mules for the carriage of stolen or smuggled goods. He was eventually betrayed and broken on the wheel. But he remained a local hero. He had made good in the common struggle: where ordinary men hoped only to survive, he had robbed the rich, aped the manners of his betters, lived flamboyantly and died boldly. The Breton Marion de Fouet, child of a beggar, lived continuously in and out of prison and died eventually on the gallows, after being broken on the wheel for theft and murder. In life her main occupation when free, and when not producing bastard children, was robbing farmhouses. Her exploits usually ended in the death of the victim; she was neither a pretty nor an admirable figure. But she harmed only those who had something to lose. For those who had nothing, living in a province where thousands of children engaged as a matter of course in smuggling salt and so in a continuous war against the authorities, she could not fail to be a romantic figure.

By the imposition of tariffs and customs and by internal taxes which, like the French *gabelle*, might vary between provinces, the state encouraged the smuggling which became the largest single field of criminal activity. Large numbers were involved and others, as blind eyes or contented customers, became accomplices. It was the source of further crime as agents of government and smugglers waged their vicious war respectively to contain and exploit the profitable trade. Often yearly amounts of goods smuggled across national borders exceeded the volume of those products imported in a legal way. A man could make more by a single trip with illicit salt from Brittany to Mainz than he could by months of labouring; a sailor more by a Channel crossing with illicit brandy than he could by a year's fishing. As men found when they joined smuggling syndicates, ambushed the customs men, or simply knocked an inspector on the head, the response of government was pathetically inadequate. The occasional brutal and public punishments were no deterrent. The most thoughtful men of the age turned instead to considering the benefits of free trade or of a more rational legal code.

The Old Biological Regime

One aspect of the prevailing poverty was the high incidence of disease, what Mandrou calls 'the chronic morbidity' of the entire population. Difficulties of definition and interpretation hamper the study of disease in a prescientific culture. There is plenty to go on but the language and the ideas behind it are vague. We have little to guide us as to what people regarded as normal 'good health' or how common were various deformities. There are, for a start, no reliable statistics about height and weight, though it appears from the evidence of clothes, shoes and contemporary descriptions that the average height was smaller than that of today. That was clearly the result of malnutrition. Englishmen in 1914 were startled to discover from the measurements of recruiting boards that the poor of the larger towns were much shorter and thinner than their better-off contemporaries and that many were simply unfit for 'active service'. That condition may have reflected poor urban housing conditions, factory employment, social conditions and attitudes; it was also the consequence of generations of poverty and malnutrition. It would be a reasonable guess that the average height of the adult male in the seventeenth century was around five foot three. 'Men of quality' tended, because better fed, to be taller than their social inferiors. Frenchmen and Spaniards tended to be smaller than Germans, Scandinavians or Dutchmen, though it was surely flattery that led courtiers to describe Louis XIV, at five foot four, as tall. The peasant of France, Spain or Italy, was short of proteins and by twentieth-century standards gravely undernourished, with scant resistance to infection or the ailments of nutritional deficiency.

Unable to say much about what was regarded as good health or sound hygiene, the historian has to be content with a negative statement: a healthy person was one who suffered from no particular disease and was capable of a hard day's work. Description of ailments is obscured by current medical attitudes, even though science was enlarging its frontiers. The work of

Harvey, leading to a new understanding of the circulation of blood, and of Leeuwenhoek, looking through his microscopes at the blood circulating in the minute capillaries, or at spermatozoa in water, reveals how much scope existed for the advance of knowledge and understanding. A striking example of progress in practical medicine was the efficacy of vaccine against smallpox after the discoveries of Jenner and others – but vaccination was not much used till the end of the eighteenth century. There were other pools of light in the darkness. The anatomical theatre at Leyden was the first place after Padua where students could learn from the public dissection of human bodies. Dr Herman Boerhaave (1666–1738), professor simultaneously of chemistry, medicine and botany, made the place internationally famous. Students crowded to his lectures (given in Latin). Even more influential was his clinical teaching from the hospital ward. The pupils of this medical polymath founded or improved schools of medicine elsewhere; among them were Alexander Munro at Edinburgh and Van Swieten at Vienna. Empirically the practice of medicine made gains, as for example from the work of Francesco Redi, the Florentine physician, who was the first to develop by experiment (in a book of 1668) Harvey's principle that 'All living things come from an egg'. By proving the connection between meat, flies, eggs and maggots, he demolished the theory of spontaneous generation and opened the way for further studies of gallflies, fleas and lice. Doubtless, too, there were gifted healers who used their imagination and followed their instincts. But the benefits of new discoveries were limited to the better off. How limited they were may be inferred from the way in which Louis XIV's grandson and his family were treated – by regular bleeding – as they sank to death from what appears to have been measles; or the potions and spells that failed to heal the dying Charles II of Spain.

Behind the experimental forays of a few pioneers lagged the bulk of the medical profession, trained by book. Knowledge of the human body was morphological – confined that is to the discovery of forms, culminating in the superficial anatomy lesson. Organic life was of no account. Medical treatises still dwelt on conjunction and conflict inside the body, of the elements, air, fire and water whose action determined all. Illness was a foreign element lodged in the sick person's body which had to be expelled. One can see the concept and role of exorcism in this, and how the idea of diabolical possession fitted the medical notions of the time. Passions of the soul gave rise to particular ailments: envy caused insomnia and jaundice. Disease and illness were readily identifiable with sin and the devil; or with God's punishment upon the wrongdoer. Medical practice was thus a mixture of pedantic scholarship deriving from revered tradition, primitive but not always contemptible psychology, traditional and often worthless prescriptions; it was pseudo-scientific, deriving more from faith than experience, for all the Latin that bemused the patient. Doctors continued to apply the sovereign remedy of bleeding by leech in defiance surely of the evidence of their senses. In any case the common people continued to rely, perhaps sensibly, upon time-honoured potions and remedies, herbs and spells. They were not so far removed, in the prescientific age, from the professional men, for therapy was concerned with moderating symptoms. For this purpose doctors had some useful drugs: mercury, digitalis, the ipecacuanha root and opium, widely prescribed and used as a pain-killer, partial addictive but blessed relief for intolerable pain. But the wisest doctors knew the limitations of their craft. William Cullen (1710–90), the great Edinburgh physician, put it plainly: 'We know nothing of the nature of contagion that can lead us to any measures for removing or correcting it. We know only its effects.'

It is possible against this background to identify certain diseases – but because of variations of terminology, inadequate diagnosis and frightened secrecy there is a large area of vagueness. The fevers and agues, 'quartan, double quartan, triple quartan'; the swellings and ulcers, so precisely enumerated; 'worms' and 'gripes' – what were they all? It may not matter except to the specialist. From a miasma of suffering certain features emerge with appalling clarity. Because they were ignorant of the elementary principles of hygiene, lacked means to feed themselves properly and had little understanding of the causes of infection, the whole population was vulnerable. In towns where overcrowding within old walls created ideal conditions for disease, even though poverty induced people to reduce waste to a minimum, constantly re-using durable goods, there was a serious problem of waste disposal. The streets were public latrines, water was polluted, wells were unsafe. In town and country, ordinary folk lived in one or two rooms, under the same roof as their beasts, slept on straw which was infrequently changed, and ate with their fingers, or with unwashed knives and wooden spoons. Light and air were less important than warmth. Unventilated, heavy with the reek of damp clothes, sweat and urine, the conditions in such hovels in damp, cold spells can be imagined: rheumatic and arthritic ailments must have been usual. Peasants, all but the better off among them, wore the same clothes, winter and summer; lice and fleas abounded. They rarely washed. Indeed, children were often sewn into their clothes for the winter. Outside, dung and decaying vegetable scraps for animal food, often piled against the house, attracted flies. Doctors peered into the squalid hovels and noted with dismay that the sick and the healthy shared the same bed; a child might even lie against a corpse awaiting burial.

A deficient diet in childhood meant rickety legs, rare today but common even fifty years ago. Stunted, scarred maybe, or marked with skin disease, scorbutic from vitamin deficiency or weeping with impetigo, many of the poor would make less pleasing studies for the painter than those sturdy, comely peasants chosen by Louis Le Nain for his plain, unsentimental studies, faithful as they were to material detail and texture. A great deal of deformity must have been caused by crude methods of midwifery. The child who survived the process, perhaps having been brought into the world by means of some farm implement in the hands of the grimy old village *accoucheur*, was launched upon a hazardous voyage indeed. How hazardous can be seen on many a churchyard tombstone. There was little room for sentiment about the death of an infant. Those who did survive to adulthood might well have acquired a certain immunity. One can imagine the veneration with which the occasional ancient, the over-sixty, was regarded: not cast out but treated as an oracle, a link with the living past. The survivor might be held to exemplify the process of natural selection – the survival under ideal conditions of the fittest, maintaining the balance of population and the virility of the breed. But when were conditions conducive to the operation of this scientific theory? Not among mountain dwelling Savoyards suffering from goitre; nor among the inhabitants of the mosquito-infested swamps of the Roman *campagna* or the French Camargue where malaria reduced men to shivering weaklings, unlikely to benefit from the bark-derived quinine, first used in 1650. Not for the blind child born to syphilitic parents; nor for the mental defective, the 'village idiot' born to related parents, victims of the inbreeding that was the bane of many isolated communities.

Some diseases, like scarlet fever or measles, not regarded as deadly today, seem then to have been more serious. Typhus, spread by fleas and lice, was a big killer among the poor. It is estimated that between 10,000 and 12,000 people perished annually in eighteenth-century Sweden of typhus and smallpox, out of a population of 2 million. Typhoid was also common, spread by infected water. Tuberculosis, the prime disease of the Romantic Europe of *La Bohème* and the Brontës, seems to have been less common than it was to become. Cancer was certainly less so, though particularly hard to recognize from contemporary accounts. That is to be expected since there was little atmospheric pollution and relatively little smoking. Alcoholism was not the curse that it is today, despite an increase in the drinking of spirits, often home-distilled. There were also fewer stress-induced illnesses, mental or physical, as may be observed in the less materially advanced countries of the world today. Syphilis had been a growing menace since its introduction from America in the sixteenth century but it was less virulent in effect than when it first arrived. Again it is impossible to quantify because of the moral disgrace and consequent concealment; what the English called the pox, and doctors strove to cure by various medicines with a mercury base, was however a leading preoccupation of medical textbooks. Smallpox, disfiguring, often fatal, was very widespread till the development of vaccines in the late eighteenth century. Scrofula, honoured by tradition as the 'king's evil', curable supposedly by the royal touch, and the subject of an elaborate and regular ceremony in France and Britain, was a dangerous tubercular condition of the lymph glands caused by dietary deficiency.

In a category of its own for a different reason was the plague. It was chiefly an urban disease, most deadly in hot weather, in close-confined places. Its dreadful hold upon men's imagination is not surprising. A man who caught the plague died, whether it was the Black Death, the pulmonary variety, or the older, more common bubonic (buboes form in the groin and become gangrenous). Alexander Kinglake, visiting Cairo during a plague in 1835, noticed that 'the city was *silenced*'. He later observed that 'most of the people with whom I had anything to do during my stay at Cairo were seized with plague; and all these died' – nor did he hear of any instance in which a plague-stricken patient recovered. By the nineteenth century, plague had retreated from Europe though it remained endemic in certain hot countries: the plague of 1942 described by Albert Camus, was in Oran, uncomfortably near to Europe. The plague was widespread throughout Europe in the seventeenth century. It played a large part in reducing the population of Germany during the Thirty Years War. Seville, Paris and London all had serious outbreaks. But it was on the retreat. In the sixteenth century it had been a regular scourge (there were forty outbreaks in Besançon between 1439 and 1640). The famous plague, laconically recorded by Pepys, retrospectively and with more embroidery by Daniel Defoe, was also London's last; the outbreak in Paris in 1668 was the last of the six it suffered in that century. It made its last appearance in France in Marseille in 1720 when the streets were full, according to one source, of putrid bodies, gnawed by dogs. The last outbreak in western Europe was in Messina in 1743. There was a severe epidemic in Moscow in 1770, another in Odessa in 1814.

Was this a case, similar to that of leprosy in the Middle Ages, of the defeat of a germ by intelligent communal action? Leprosy had been dealt with by ruthless isolation of the afflicted. Oddly, however, lepers today do not seem to spread infection. It may be that the reasons for the diminution of the plague lie in the life cycle of the virus itself. Diseases seem to fluctuate in their force. The flea-infested black rat was losing its favoured habitat in the congested towns as stone replaced wood, and tiles replaced thatch. Whatever the reason, the retreat of the plague was the end of one of Europe's recurring nightmares. Authorities dealt with the plague with a battery of special measures: quarantine, road blocks, close confinement of the sick, fumigation, health certificates, burning of clothes. Individuals burnt aromatics, said their prayers and, if they had the means, fled. Plague created conditions in which the great gulf between rich and poor, normally bridged by the mutual dependence of labour and capital, governor and governed, or by the common belief and allegiances, yawned open. How, we may wonder, did the ordinary people feel as they watched the carriages trundling out of town, taking with them to fresh air and safety those whom they were accustomed to think of as their masters? There was no business done in the courts of London in the autumn of 1665: the lawyers were out of town. Sudden death and social disintegration: it was an image of hell.

Further Reading

W.G. East, *An Historical Geography of Europe* (4th edn, London, 1950), covers many aspects of the subject. H. Kinder and W. Hilgemann, *The Penguin Atlas of World History*, 1: *From the Beginning to the French Revolution*, trans. E.A. Menze; maps by H. and R. Bukar (Harmondsworth, 1974), has useful summaries of events besides its maps and diagrams. A historical atlas is an essential aid: the student can still do worse than use R. Muir's *Historical Atlas* (most recent edition, London, 1952). A good recent one, with accompanying essays, is R.I. Moore (ed.), *Hamlyn Historical Atlas* (London, 1981). W.Z. Ripley, *The Races of Europe* (1900), is still useful. For the question of definition, see H.D. Schmidt, 'The establishment of Europe as a political expression', *Historical Journal*, 9 (1966). Economic history conceived in such a generous way that it is also a rich and evocative account of society is the trilogy of F. Braudel, *Civilisation matérielle et capitalisme*. The first volume, *Capitalism and Material Life* (1966), trans. by M. Kochan (New York, 1973), is specially relevant to the themes of this chapter. Other wide-ranging books likely to stand the test of time are: G.N. Clark, *The Seventeenth Century* (Oxford, 1929), M.S. Anderson, *Europe in the Eighteenth Century, 1713–83* (Harlow, 1976), and two briefer volumes, R. Hatton, *Europe in the Age of Louis XIV* (London, 1969), and C.B.A. Behrens, *The Ancien Régime* (London, 1967), both profusely illustrated, both pointing to the findings of modern research. A solid textbook in the traditional manner is D.H. Pennington, *Seventeenth Century Europe* (Longman, 1972). An older book (first published in 1931) which has vigour and erudition beyond what can usually be found in a textbook is D. Ogg, *Europe in the Seventeenth Century* (London, 1971). E.N. Williams, *The Ancien Régime in Europe* (London, 1970), is a study of government and society in seven states, each examined in turn. Magnificently illustrated and containing some excellent short essays, *The Eighteenth Century: Europe in the Age of Enlightenment*, ed. A. Cobban (London, 1969), is well worth finding. Among French books in the new style, more concerned with analysis of society than with events, and excitingly catholic in their range of evidence, perhaps the best are: R. Mousnier, *Les XVIe et XVIIe Siècles* (1961), P. Chaunu, *La Civilisation de l'Europe classique* (1966), and *La Civilisation de l'Europe des Lumières* (1971). A.L. Moote, *The Seventeenth Century: Europe in Ferment* (Farnborough, 1970), is an American textbook by a specialist on the Fronde. The American series, *The Rise of Modern Europe*, can still be commended as full of useful detail, though inevitably somewhat dated: it is best perhaps where the material is least controversial, as in W.L. Dorn, *Competition for Empire, 1740–63* (New York, 1940). Up to date, but also suffering inevitably from the fragmented treatment of the big topics, are the volumes in the Fontana series. They do, however, have room for interesting detail. For this period, see J.W. Stoye, *Europe Unfolding, 1648–1688* (London, 1969), particularly good on eastern Europe; Olwen Hufton, *Europe: Privilege and Protest, 1730–89* (Brighton, 1980); the intervening volume (*1688–1730*) has still to appear. By contrast, a virtue of the volume in the *Short Oxford History of Modern Europe*, J. Doyle, *The Old European Order, 1660–1800* (London, 1978), is that it provides an overall view, including the revolutionary epoch. There are of course many individual contributions of impeccable scholarship to the *New Cambridge Modern History* (1957–70) of which the relevant volumes are 5, 6 and 7, with some parts of 4 and 8. Again discontinuity is a drawback, but they remain an invaluable source of reference, and sometimes a synoptic chapter provides the kind of introduction a student needs: for example, G.N. Clark, 'Social foundations of states', in vol. 5; J.O. Lindsay, 'The social classes and the foundations of states', in vol. 7; and, defining the themes for the seventeenth century, J.P. Cooper's fine introduction to vol. 4.

The treatment of more specific social and demographic questions has given rise to such a vast literature that the student needs pointing to particularly valuable or interesting work. The title of E. Le Roy Ladurie's work, *Times of Feast, Times of Famine: A History of Climate since the Year 1000* (London, 1972) speaks for itself. Questions of population may be approached through D.V. Glass and D.E.C. Eversley (eds), *Population in History* (London, 1965), and E.A. Wrigley, *Population and History* (New York, 1969). In the *Pelican Economic History*, vol. 2 (Harmondsworth, 1964), there is a good chapter on the subject by R. Mols; and others by K.F. Helleiner in *The Economic History of Europe*, vols 4 and 5 (Cambridge, 1967, 1969). See also O.A. and P. Ranum (eds), *Popular Attitudes toward Birth Control in Pre-Industrial France and England* (New York, 1972).

The more important of the now numerous studies of regions, towns and even villages from which a complete picture of European society is beginning to emerge are mentioned after chapters devoted to particular countries: see mainly chapter 7. An introduction is provided by J. Potter *et al.* (eds) *Peasant Society* (Boston, Mass., 1973). A good foundation book is M. Bloch, *French Rural History*, trans. J. Sondheimer (London, 1966). P. Goubert, whose great work on Beauvais (see chapter 7) is a mine of information on peasant life, presents a detailed picture of French society (see, for example, his account of feudalism) in *The Ancien Régime* (1969, trans. London, 1973).

Other books on particular countries which throw light on common social conditions are: H. Holborn, *Germany*, vol. 2 (London, 1964); J. Vicens Vives, *An Economic History of Spain* (Princeton, 1969); C.R. Boxer, *The Portuguese Seaborne Empire, 1425–1825* (London, 1969), which like his *The Dutch Seaborne Empire, 1600–1800* (London, 1965) contains a lot of material about the home country. D. Mack Smith, *A History of Sicily*, vols 2 and 3 (London, 1968–9), contains a lot of material for the study of southern Europe. For the Habsburg lands, see the early chapters of C.A. Macartney, *The Habsburg Empire, 1700–1918* (London, 1968); for Sweden, E. Hecksher, *Economic History of Sweden* (Cambridge, Mass., 1954); and for Russia (now well served), M.T. Florinsky, *Russia: a History and an Interpretation*, 2 vols (London, 1953). There is wider interest in the following books than their titles may suggest: W.E. Wright, *Serf, Seigneur and Sovereign: Agrarian Reform in Eighteenth Century Bohemia* (Minneapolis, 1966); O.H. Hufton, *The Poor of Eighteenth Century France* (Oxford, 1974); J. Blum, *Lord and Peasant in Russia from the Ninth to the Nineteenth Century* (1961); D. Sella, *Crisis and Continuity: The Economy of Spanish Lombardy in the Seventeenth Century* (Cambridge, Mass., 1979).

A. Goodwin (ed.), *The European Nobility in the Eighteenth Century* (London, 1953), provides, through different contributors, a comparative view of great interest. A fuller picture, though less concerned with government, is presented by P. Erlanger, *The Age of Courts and Kings* (London, 1966: expanded version of the original French edition). More penetrating are: J. Meyer, *Nobles et ses pouvoirs dans l'Europe d'ancien régime* (1973), and G. Chaussinand-Nogaret, *La Noblesse au XVIIIe siècle* (1976). Among particular studies, specially valuable are: R. Forster, *The House of Saulx-Tavanes, Versailles and Burgundy, 1700–1830* (Baltimore, 1971); R. Jones, *The Emancipation of the Russian Nobility, 1762–1785* (London, 1973); F.L. Carsten, 'The origins of the Junkers', *English Historical Review*, 62 (1947); J.C. Davies, *The Decline of the Venetian Nobility as a Ruling Class* (Oxford, 1962). Contemporary memoirs should not be neglected. In a class of its own is Saint-Simon's journal of life at Versailles. There are several editions, the most recent that of Lucy Norton. He may be approached through her selection, *Saint-Simon at Versailles* (1958). The comte de Ségur's *Memoirs* are valuable for the years before the Revolution: there is a fine Folio Society edition (London, 1961), ed. E. Cruickshanks. For the northern courts, see N.W. Wraxall, *Memoirs of the Courts of Berlin, Dresden, Warsaw and Vienna* (2 vols, Dublin, 1799). For Vienna especially, Lady Mary Wortley Montagu's *Letters* are available in an Everyman edition (London, 1907). *La Vie quotidienne* series includes a volume on *Les Cours allemands au XVIIIe siècle*, by P. Lafue (1963).

A good starting point for the history of towns is still the classic work of H. Pirenne, *Mediaeval Cities* (trans. Princeton, 1952). Urban history has been reinforced recently by some impressive studies in a field long dominated by G. Roupnel's admirable account of Dijon, *La Ville et la campagne au XVIIe siècle* (1922). A brief selection should include: J.C. Perrot, *Genèse d'une ville moderne: Caen au XVIIIe siècle* (1975); T.C.W. Blanning, *Reform and Revolution in Mainz, 1743–1803* (Cambridge, 1974); F.L. Ford, *Strasbourg in Transition, 1648–1789* (Cambridge, Mass., 1965); G.L. Burke, *The Making of Dutch Towns* (New York, 1960); Olwen Hufton, *Bayeux in the Late Eighteenth Century* (London, 1967). Social mobility is the theme of E.G. Barber, *The Bourgeoisie in Eighteenth Century France* (London, 1968). R. Mousnier, *Paris, capitale au temps de Richelieu et de Mazarin* (1978), O. Ranum, *Paris in the Age of Absolutism* (New York, 1968), and G. Rudé, *The Crowd in the French Revolution* (London, 1959), all provide insights into the lives of the *menu peuple* whom legislators ignored at their peril.

The work of the *Annales* school of writers, who use quantification, demography, sociology, anthropology, biology, linguistics and group psychology to bring to life the people of the past 'who have left no memorial', can be sampled in the series of volumes edited by Robert Forster and Orest Ranum, appearing from 1975: vol. 1, *Biology of Man in History* (Baltimore, 1975); vol. 2, *Family and Society* (Baltimore, 1977); vol. 3, *Rural Society in France* (Baltimore, 1977); vol. 4, *Deviants and the Abandoned in French Society* (Baltimore, 1978). Though his studies are centred upon the Renaissance period, the writing of Lucien Febvre, who with Marc Bloch was co-founder of *Annales* in 1929, introduces the reader to this 'wider and more human history': a good selection from his work, containing for example his essay on 'Sensibility and history', is to be found in P. Burke (ed.), *A New Kind of History* (London, 1973). The latter's own book, *Popular Culture in Early Modern Europe* (M.T. Smith, 1978), should not be overlooked. W. Beck, 'Searching for popular culture in early modern France', *Journal of Modern History*, 49 (1977) is a valuable review article.

The interest and significance of P. Laslett's pioneering study of changing mentalities, *The World We Have Lost* (London, 1965), is not confined to England which supplies him with most of his evidence; no more is that of R. Mandrou's

De la culture populaire au XVIIe et XVIIIe siècles confined to France. To those books, one by R. Ariès, exploring territory long neglected by historians, should be added: *Centuries of Childhood: A Social History of Family Life* (1960, trans. London, 1962). Also see J.L. Flanrin, *Families in Former Times: Kinship, Household and Sexuality* (Cambridge, 1979). Also important is the collection *Women and Society in Eighteenth Century France: Essays in honour of S.S. Spink*, ed. E. Jacobs *et al.* (London, 1979). Two books by Keith Thomas, again drawing almost entirely on the English evidence should be cited for what they tell us of European man: *Religion and the Decline of Magic* (London, 1971) and *Man and the Natural World* (London, 1983). The elusive subject of crime may be approached through M.R. Weisser, *Crime and Punishment in Early Modern Europe* (Brighton, 1979). Particularly good on policing is I.A. Cameron, *Crime and Repression in the Auvergne and the Guyenne, 1720–1790* (Cambridge, 1981). The conditions which produced much of the crime can be studied in C. Lis and H. Soly, *Poverty and Capitalism in Pre-Industrial Europe* (Brighton, 1979); also in O. Hufton, *The Poor of Eighteenth Century France* (Oxford, 1974). One form of punishment is studied by Paul Bamford, *Fighting Ships and Prisons: The Mediterranean Galleys of France in the Age of Louis XIV* (Minneapolis, 1973). One form of crime is studied by E. Hobsbawm, *Bandits* (New York, 1964). The most thorough investigation of the worst of the diseases that threatened life is J.F.D. Shrewsbury, *A History of Bubonic Plague in the British Isles* (Cambridge, 1970). The subject can be pursued in wider context in W.H. McNeill, *Plagues and Peoples* (Oxford, 1976), and in a particular case study, J.T. Alexander, *Bubonic Plague in Early Modern Russia: Public Health and Urban Disaster* (Baltimore, 1980).

2

EARLY CAPITALISM

A Slow Growth

It is likely that the foregoing survey of European society in this period will have left the reader more keenly aware of checks and obstacles than of factors favourable to economic progress. Inertia may well be his prevailing impression, all the stronger if he should wonder why, given the pioneering experience of Britain in the eighteenth century, continental Europe should have lagged so far behind in industrial development. That is an important question. But it should not be allowed to dominate an account of the world of early capitalism, in which significant changes were taking place affecting the demand for goods which is the main determinant of economic activity; in which there were technological developments, though not on a scale to match scientific progress; and in which resources and skills were accumulating for the impending breakthrough.

In the subsistence economy which contained the lives of most people, little if any income was available for purchases beyond basic needs. Food, clothes, furnishings and most necessary implements were produced locally and with local materials. Most production was for personal consumption without the intervention of any price mechanism: within communities there was also much giving in kind and barter. Closer inspection reveals, however, an economy of innumerable local variations. Vernacular building, for example, largely reflects the availability of building material, whether stone, brick or timber. It imposed limitations, but there was a positive side too;

the steep-gabled houses of Germany, in which fancy and utility are matched in satisfying harmony, are but one outstanding example of the hereditary skills that created distinctive styles of building. Demand was restrained generally by the absence of, or slow rate of improvement in, agricultural productivity, at least until the middle of the eighteenth century. In this, the basic industry of Europe, a large part of the harvest was required for next year's harvest because the ratio of seed to crop was so persistently low, and a third of all farmland was used each year for bread grains. Trapped within the subsistence economy, oppressed by the demands of landowner and state, the peasant had little to spend on goods. So the chronic weakness of the agricultural sector set limits to the diversification and specialization needed for the accumulation of capital, without which there could be little natural growth in towns; it followed that the workforce was tied to agriculture in numbers which depressed wage rates and encouraged conservatism. In eastern Europe this led to an intensification of the serf regime which the reformers of the eighteenth century were to see as a prime obstacle to economic progress. At the other extreme, in the relatively dynamic economies of western Europe, notably in Britain and Holland, capital was accumulated through trade, and some of it was put to work on the land. In most other areas during this period, which ends before the transforming impact of industrialization was felt to any extent, a persistently low level of demand was reflected in a paucity of private investment. Where there was real progress, it was often because of action by the state to improve communications or to foster and protect manufactures by subsidy, monopoly and tariff. The main obstacles to progress were being identified and sometimes effective action was taken.

By the third decade of the eighteenth century the rate of capital accumulation was starting to rise; so also was population. By mid-century, prices were rising, a sign of increasing demand. Britain was uniquely favoured by a combination of agricultural progress, surplus capital for investment coming from expanding commerce and the exploitation of overseas colonies, the possession of plentiful coal and iron ore, and fast-flowing streams for water power. By the end of the period, inventions in the textile and iron industries were lending impetus to industrialization. Meanwhile on the continent the development of manufactures within certain districts, while still dispersed and largely manual in operation, had reached a point at which it can be characterized as proto-industrialization. Though this did not mean that such districts would necessarily experience the industrial revolution that was transforming sectors of the British economy, the amassing of capital and development of wider markets was extending the base for eventual 'take-off'. In the period as a whole, though there were notable improvements and new techniques in both extractive and manufacturing industries, there were no inventions of the kind which transform the mode and scale of operations. For this reason, and because of the lack of market opportunities, levels of productivity and income remained low and the growth of wealth from this source was correspondingly slow. According to one estimate for the period 1500–1750 in western Europe, during which population rose by about 60 per cent, output, at 0.2 per cent a year, rose by only 65 per cent.

Attitudes were important. The prevailing economic theory, which was later misleadingly to be called 'mercantilism', was grounded on the assumption that markets were static: to increase trade, new markets had to be added to existing ones. Inevitably foreign trade seemed to be a kind of warfare. Where there was evidence of mobility and expansion, with lavish expenditure by common folk aping their social superiors, it was treated as a symptom of disorder. It was argued that the state would be stripped of its treasure and proper distinctions of status would be undermined. The moral context is important. Productive activity was not necessarily assumed to be a good in itself. One does not have to venture too far into the great debate about religion and the rise of capitalism to see that where the acquisitive spirit was lacking it was due in part to the traditional teaching of the Roman Church, close in this respect to that of Christ. It was a short step from asserting that it is blessed to be poor and to give to the poor to accepting the condition of poverty as part of God's plan for man. It helps to explain the apparently complacent world of the German ecclesiastical states in which, it was estimated in the early eighteenth century, there were 50 clergy and 260 beggars in each 1000 of the population. It was because of religious festivals, not because of shortage of fuel, that the iron industry of Carinthia operated only a hundred eight-hour shifts a year. In what some craftsmen may have regarded as the golden era before the advent of Colbert, Parisians celebrated 103 holidays a year. Yet mentalities were changing, not only in Protestant countries. The eighteenth-century statesmen who adopted utilitarian criteria for political and economic management took a sterner view of the obligations of workers. Arguments for the abolition of serfdom were based on practical as well as humane considerations. This phase in the development of capitalism was characterized too by a progressive shift in the distribution of income. Even in those parts of Europe where labour services were not increased, the gap between rich and poor tended to widen. In the developing areas, greater activity in commerce and finance led to the concentration in the hands of a relatively small number of most of the purchasing power, displayed by lavish spending in a manner hitherto associated with the nobility. As the same time, though it is impossible to calculate exactly, it is clear that a higher proportion of the total income was being spent by the state, most obviously during prolonged periods of war when governments had to raise more in taxes and loans. From all this it follows that the growth of towns, where it did occur, was a crucial factor in the development of the capitalist economy.

Capitals, centres of court and government, were specially important in the smaller or poorer states. The population of Paris was never more than 2.5 per cent of the French population; 8 per cent of Dutchmen, however, lived in Amsterdam in 1700. Like that of Stockholm, the growth of Amsterdam followed sturdily from activity in commerce. In Berlin too, the rise, from 8000 in 1648 to 170,000 in 1790, was the result of an increase in manufactures, starting with the influx of Huguenots in 1685, as well as that of the military and bureaucratic establishment of ambitious Hohenzollern rulers. But capitals had a momentum of their own, which had little to do with the workings of the economy: they prospered in line with the political tendency towards centralization because of the proliferation of courts of law, administrative offices and not least the court. There congregated, with all their clients and lackeys, those who served the prince, or served those who served him, or wished to be seen by him. The power and wealth of Denmark did not increase between 1660 and 1760 but the population of Copenhagen did, from 23,000 to 93,000. Though Sweden under Charles XI, and Brandenburg under Frederick William I, where the sovereign deliberately reduced the establishment and its cost, can be cited as exceptions, it is broadly true that the richer the country, the poorer was the court. In relatively backward Austria and Spain reformers pointed to swollen courts as prime targets for economy. Capitals too were usually seen as parasitic by critics who pointed to the one-way flow of goods, the sucking in of rents from the countryside, or the spirit of emulation which led to the wasteful spending of money derived from more productive sectors of the economy. Less appreciated, but important none the less, was the stimulus to the manufacture of luxury goods, which figured largely, for instance, in Colbert's plans for the regeneration of the French economy.[1] Great cities were also a source of lucrative employment through building and allied crafts. In Paris in 1630 there were 4000 carriages to raise their fortunate occupants above the filth of the streets; in 1700, there were 20,000. Where social conditions allowed, further benefits accrued from the return to the land, through purchase of estates, with some of the money made in law, government and finance.

Few provincial towns experienced sustained growth. Overall the percentage of the population living in cities was about the same in 1750 as it had been in 1500. The majority of German and Italian towns, for example, stayed at the same level, while most Polish and many Spanish towns decayed. In some cases, such as Leipzig, there was a sharp recovery from the exceptional losses sustained in the Thirty Years War. Sometimes a town sustained an old reputation for manufacture, like Augsburg for gold and silver ware; or acquired a new one, like Venice for inlaid furniture or Dresden for porcelain. But in the all-important textile industries, the trend was to rural production, at least in the primary stages. To this shift is due

[1] As by far the most important exponent of current theories of economic manipulation and control, Colbert is treated separately on pp. 254–61.

the decline of such great cities as Florence and Cologne. Larger towns were exceptionally vulnerable too to the plague and other diseases: Marseilles and Palermo might offer a way of life to the desperately poor immigrants from the impoverished hinterland of the Midi and Sicily; they also offered a way out. A Prussian army chaplain, Süssmilch, studied the records of parish ministers around 1740 to obtain comparative figures and discovered that the average annual death rate in villages was 26 per 1000 inhabitants, in small cities it was 30, in large cities over 40. If such places still grew it was as much a reflection of rural poverty, as in some Latin American cities today, as of exceptional opportunities: they were comfortable places only for their prospering bourgeoisie. At Lyons, by contrast, growth was resumed with steady immigration from the Dauphiné, after the check caused by the emigration of Huguenots in the 1680s, because of the activity of the silk industry and the role of the city as a centre of exchange. More commonly the population of towns rose or was sustained because of some special function. Toulouse was an administrative and legal centre; Cadiz was the main colonial *entrepôt*, with the Casa de Contratación, after 1717; Brest was an important naval base.

The expansion of overseas trade provided a healthy base for the prosperity of the cities of the Atlantic seaboard, like Bordeaux, Nantes, Lisbon and Cadiz, with the accompanying growth in ship-building, and such essential services as chandlering, insurance and brokerage. In such places especially can be studied the dynamism of the money economy which was beginning to make 'mercantilism' look inappropriate to the needs of the maritime powers. The growth of credit trading in the form of merchants' drafts, letters of credit and bills of exchange was making a vital contribution to the creation of national, even international markets, and to the accumulation of capital which was an essential precondition for industrial growth. Fairs had long provided a way of opening up the self-sufficient regional economies. Well-placed cities, Lyons on the Rhône, Hamburg commanding the Elbe, and Danzig the Vistula, had become by 1660 permanent centres of exchange where the sale of commodities was facilitated by the maintenance of price lists, sales of samples, holding of regular auctions and specialization in such commodities as coal, cotton, tea and tobacco. Retailing too was starting to acquire a modern look in the specialist shops of the larger cities, where men could buy their coffee from Brazil, their porcelain from Dresden, or their wigs, made on the premises, from hair bought from peasant girls. For the majority of farmer's wives the itinerant pedlar was still milliner, jeweller and purveyor of news. At the same time more formal channels of communication were becoming safer and more regular. By 1753 it was estimated that the sale of newspapers in Europe exceeded 7 million; provincial newspapers, like the early *Strassburg Zeitung*, founded in 1609, carried news of a wider world and, in places like Amsterdam, where such information was valuable, carried news of production and prices, along with the events, battles, treaties, earthquakes or epidemics, which might affect business. There were notable improvements in physical means of transport. From Dutch ports there were regular sailings for passengers to the main European ports.

The seaman was assisted by dredged harbours and improved dock facilities, as well as by the production of more accurate navigational instruments and charts. In 1600 there were 18 lighthouses on or off the shores of Europe; in 1750, 82: it is just one indicator of the ways in which science and technology could be harnessed by the state for the economic benefit of its subjects. It could also improve roads and make them safer for travellers, and it could encourage the building of canals. By 1660 nearly every Dutch city was linked in this way. Even in the Netherlands, guilds were obstructive and tolls were levied but the value of the service ensured adequate private funds for the improvement of transport. Elsewhere the general survival of internal tolls and the resistance of vested interests to their removal in the face of powerful economic arguments reminds us of the constraints under which governments operated. Because of the decline in the emperor's authority, there was nothing to restrain Germany's many princes from imposing the tolls which strangled internal trade. Though power and plenty were not necessarily incompatible goals, the 'mercantilist' tendency to subordinate the interests of commerce to short-term fiscal or diplomatic considerations can be seen also in the external tariffs which were such a formidable obstacle to the growth of trade.

Needs and Wants

It is easier to identify the factors affecting demand, and therefore the condition of the economy, than to assess the relative importance of the different needs which, en masse, constitute that demand: an abstraction but representing what was necessary or desirable to a hundred million individuals. Estimates can only be impressions, confirmed by specific cases such as one based on the study of wage rates in England and France, which suggests that 80 per cent of the income of the poor was spent on food, 10 per cent on clothing, and the rest on housing, furnishing and other necessities. Food supplies varied, over time, between areas and, conspicuously, between classes. Because of the overall pressure of population, the lack of progress in agriculture and the deterioration in climatic conditions already noted, there was undoubtedly a decline in what was already predominantly a cereal-based diet: compared to the sixteenth century, the seventeenth showed a decrease per head of about a third in food consumption; it was partly made up in the first half of the eighteenth century but recovery was halted in the second half. It is possible to be more specific. The inhabitants of Britain, Scandinavia and the Netherlands, enjoying a diet relatively high in proteins, and low in the proportion of cereal foods, continued to fare better than those of southern and eastern Europe, where little meat was eaten. In central Europe the increasing cultivation of potatoes helped to keep famine at bay. Generally more vegetables were consumed, notably beans, peas and root vegetables. There was an increase in the consumption of beer, wine and more dramatically spirits, with brandy being distilled from wine in France, and geneva (gin) becoming in the eighteenth century a major industry in Holland, finding an all too eager market in Britain. Schiedam, which produced geneva, was the only Dutch industrial city to grow in the eighteenth century. Tea, coffee and chocolate became more common and much cheaper. Even more spectacular was the rise in the consumption of sugar: in 1770, 200,000 tons a year were leaving America for the refineries of Europe. Whether chewed, as by Breton peasants, to ward off hunger, taken in the form of snuff, or more commonly smoked in clay pipes, tobacco, which had first been grown in 'physical gardens' in the first half of the sixteenth century, became an important article of Atlantic trade: by 1750, 55 million pounds a year were coming into Europe from North America.

The poor had only modest needs for clothing: men, women and children alike wore coarse, durable garments, mostly of thick wool or linen, with some leather and latterly increasing use of fustians. Though there was little specialization of dress for particular occupations, there was greater use of protective clothing: leather aprons for example by smiths, tanners and coopers. Fashion undoubtedly influenced the better-off men as well as women. As always, those who had least to do cared most about being *à la mode*. Servants might be better dressed than others of their class as became the dignity of the house. The introduction of new fabrics diversified clothing, stimulated manufactures in Europe and accounted for an increasing proportion of foreign trade, as delicately printed cotton from Egypt and India and silk fabrics from Persia and Syria were imported to delight the women and stimulate the European manufacturers to produce finer materials and more imaginative designs.

Two French developments influenced fashion. In 1633 Louis XIII lost his hair in an illness and wigs became fashionable, to remain so till the Revolution. In 1644 a Parisian jeweller discovered a process for colouring crystal to imitate jewels; these and the pastestones invented in Strasbourg at the end of the century brought such adornments within the reach of the less wealthy. Hats, buttons, shoes could all be mentioned to show the impact of fashion on the market and on employment. More expenditure on such articles was a sure sign of prosperity. In Friesland for example the average number of linen shirts owned by a farmer rose from 4 around 1600 to over 10 by 1700. There also women started to wear ornamented head dresses and their formal costumes had silver buttons.

Of all influences on demand, that of the expanding state was by far the most important, generally through the trend towards larger and uniformed armies; in particular cases through subsidies to particular industries, like the silk manufacture in France, and through regulation and insistence on quality – the last a vital element in Colbert's plan for making France the leader of fashion.

During this period the homes of the poor remained for the most part wretched hovels, commonly without windows, adequate partitions or even chimneys. In the housing of the rich there were important innovations, leading to what will by many be considered the golden age of domestic architecture, demonstrating at its best splendour without grossness, proportion without dullness, elegance without frivolity. As the great rebuilding of the sixteenth and seventeenth centuries fanned out northwards and westwards from Italy, it also came, wherever there was wealth to support it, within the reach of the middling classes in the community. For some reason, it is just those relatively modest houses of town and country that are the most pleasing, as evocative as the paintings of Vermeer, whose luminous interiors portray its virtues in the Dutch idiom, gracious but homely. Across the range, from the Parisian *hôtel*, grand, roomy but functional, providing for the needs of the extended household of the nobleman, to the simple burgher's house, making the most in height of its narrow frontage, the essential feature was the enhancement of privacy. The boudoir, the study, and the private bedrooms along a connecting passage represent that part of civilized life. Sanitation might still be little improved from the medieval standard and Harington's water closet, invented in 1707, was slow to be adopted, but furnishings were more ambitious and decorative, reaching standards of craftsmanship that increased their appeal and created work for specialist craftsmen, therefore increasing the circulation of money and stimulating further demand. A quick view of the eighteenth-century house, very likely brick-built, with sash windows, might include the use in furniture of fine woods, increasingly such imported woods as mahogany inlays; upholstered and padded chairs for greater comfort; the innovations of glass drinking vessels from about 1650, and of forks and table knives, fashionable by 1750; feather beds in place of the blanket over straw; the new 'china', table linen and wallpaper: all were designed to please the eye, but to be comfortable too.

Nowhere was the progress of civilization more evident than in the library, where theology no longer dominated the shelves, and practical manuals, on such important matters as estate management, joined the volumes of history, philosophy, travel, which might border on fiction, and fiction too, as the eighteenth century discovered the pleasures of the novel. Like the commissioning of paintings and the purchase of engravings, the creation of a fine library was still primarily a patrician ideal. It was also part of the spread of literacy whose effect in one country can be judged from the gain in the value of the postal monopoly in France: in 1673 it was 1.2 million *livres*, in 1777 it had risen to 8.8 million.

The ballet whose modern history can be traced to the foundation in 1661 by Louis XIV, himself an accomplished dancer, of L'Académie National de la Danse, represented the classical ideal: more stately than athletic, creating its poetry out of new combinations of music and choreography, it seemed to subdue the agility of the acrobat to the poise of the courtier. Though its greatest age was still to come, well before the transforming genius of Mozart gave it a wider appeal, the opera, which had its true beginnings in the work of Monteverdi (whose *Orfeo* was performed in Mantua in 1607), spread and captivated polite society. With its cultivation of the grand and heroic, creating as it were a universe of musical make-believe half-way between the worlds of mortals and gods, opera is, *par excellence*, the aristocratic art, emphasizing dramatically the gulf that was separating literate from illiterate. The theatre bridged the gulf, where the unlettered could still identify with the themes and appreciate the humour of pathos. That is, however, markedly less true of Racine than of Calderón. Here too refinement, the aristocratic ideal, was imposing its forbidding standards. People might gaze at the painting and sculptures of the new baroque churches, everyman's art gallery. In them they might also hear fine music; but for the most part the poor had to be content with simpler pleasures. At fairs and carnivals they could dance and sing, watch jugglers, puppet shows and enthralling works of magic. Little less enjoyable apparently were public executions. More edifying were the religious processions which gave Catholic communities a chance to pay homage to their special relic or patron saint. Though deprived of some of the more elevated aesthetic experiences, ordinary men benefited indirectly from the proliferation of the performing arts; for often these were presented with a sumptuousness which made them an important component in the budgets of courts and private patrons, creating demands on musicians, dancers, actors and craftsmen and a need for new structures and costumes.

The Money Economy

Because labour was cheap in relation to the cost of most commodities, it was a prominent factor of production. Most concerns were 'labour-intensive': that holds good for the household, from the very great to the comparatively humble, where the number of servants was a mark of status, for the farm where crops and animals were tended in time-honoured, time-consuming ways; and for the industrial enterprise, mine, quarry, mill or workshop, where output was closely related to the numbers involved. It was not only in agriculture that the hours of daylight affected the working day, for artificial lighting was expensive. Millstreams that froze, or dried up in summer, were an unreliable source of power. Hunger may have been a hard master, but men were not compelled to work within fixed times, or at the regular rhythm imposed by the machine. The more developed the manufacture, the more vulnerable were the workers to the cyclical nature of demand, particularly in textiles; the consequent unemployment was specially serious in places like Leyden where a high proportion of the inhabitants worked in the industry. Industrial training was largely gained through apprenticeship, and skills laboriously acquired were jealously guarded against outsiders and new techniques. Migration therefore played an important part in the transference of skills: it could be involuntary, like the dispersion of the Huguenots from France in the 1680s, or it could be state-sponsored, like Colbert's recruitment of silk workers and glass blowers. Workers were tempted by such favours as tax exemption, governments by the prospect of winning a share of markets in which they would otherwise be merely buyers. All the time a larger proportion of the labour force was being employed as wage labour.

One aspect of the growth of the money economy was an increase in the range of services provided. There was more recourse to doctors, though professional treatment remained the perhaps doubtful privilege of townspeople for the most part, and those not the poorest. In education, enrolment at universities fell away in the seventeenth century and barely returned to its sixteenth-century level, despite the creation of new universities, like Halle in Prussia, in the eighteenth century. There were many more schools in 1800 than there had been in 1600, but unevenly distributed. To provide more extensive education was the aim of all 'enlightened' statesmen. But when the Jesuits lost control of their 669 schools their staff was scattered and they could not all be replaced. Catherine the Great's hopes were grander than her achievement: in all Russia by 1800 there were only 1000 schools. Frederick II's emphasis on higher education was severely utilitarian and primary education in Prussia was simple and Bible-based. In economic terms such trends as the orientation of much of higher education towards 'the useful subjects' and the tendency of universities, particularly in Germany, to become training schools for bureaucrats, do not lend themselves to precise measurement. But the higher level of literacy, especially in northern and western Europe, as a result of the expansion of elementary education, was clearly important. So was the growth of specialist schools to teach navigation, commerce and military science. So was the foundation of institutions to promote learning and science, from famous bodies like Britain's influential Royal Society or France's Académie des Sciences to the numerous local societies which sprang up in the eighteenth century. Associated with the spread of educational opportunity and also with the growth of commerce, with its new emphasis upon contract and more sophisticated needs, was the demand for specialist services, some new, like those offered by insurance brokers (who later pioneered life insurance), some more specialized in function, such as surveyors, auctioneers, accountants; some, like the ubiquitous lawyers, simply more numerous. It was the justifiable complaint of cameralists and other reformers that universities turned out too many lawyers. There was indeed a depressed, resentful fringe among those whose opportunities did not match their qualifications. But it was a litigious age and the scope of law was being constantly expanded. There again, the state, with its edicts and codes, was the prime agent in the expansion of demand.

We have seen that the majority of the population had no reason to raise capital on any scale. For those who had, and could provide the investment needed for commercial and industrial growth to gain momentum, there were hindrances and counter-attractions which, together, had a disincentive effect. Even where the climate was favourable and rewards might be held to justify the risks, facilities did not always match the opportunities. The hindrances fall into two main categories, institutional and psychological. Among the former the strength of the guilds, the privileges of other corporate bodies, churches, municipalities and companies, the ubiquitous tolls all featured prominently in the programmes of reformers. Harder to evaluate, but no less significant, are the traditions, prejudices and preferences which supported, for example, the principle of *dérogeance* in France, according to which a nobleman not only demeaned himself but actually lost status if he became involved in most forms of productive enterprise. (Exceptions were mining and metallurgy which could be represented as extension of land use.) Justifiable caution played a part too. The experience of losses in civil and foreign wars reinforced everywhere the middle-class craving for security which can be seen in the preference for land and office as receptacles for surplus funds. Preoccupation with status was also important, with its corollary that it was the fact of possession, as much as the potential revenue that counted. There was a notable disparity in France between the amount of money available for the purchase of land and that spent on its improvement; the yield, as a result, was a mere 2.4 per cent a year, with correspondingly little to spare for re-investment – under half that in Britain. A similar disparity can be seen between the financial return on venal offices and their capital value, estimated in 1789, when such offices were abolished, at 1000 million *livres*: most represented less than a full-time job, many were wholly unnecessary, having been created by successive finance ministers to raise money.

Money raised thus by states might be put to use which would stimulate investment, and this should be borne in mind when considering other forms of financial dealings between individuals or consortia and the state which, on the face of it, diverted capital from manufactures or commerce. There were of course attractive speculations in the world of high finance, where public need and private enterprise met to deal and deliver. Tax farming could also make spectacular fortunes. During the years 1709 to 1715, when the French government was desperate for funds, tax farmers took nearly 100 million *livres* from the 350 levied. The risk was that the government, capitalizing on moral indignation, might turn on the successful financier: Bourvallon, son of a Breton peasant, whose name appeared in transactions of many kinds, was forced to disgorge 4.5 million *livres* in 1710. So long as there was no means of raising funds on a regular basis, as provided by the banks of England and Amsterdam, government and financiers were mutually dependent. The French system, if a web of official and private contracts can be so called, was both a weakness in government and a contributory factor in the paucity of private investment in business. Beneath the imperialists of high finance, the great risk-takers, was a host of lesser men who preferred a safe home for their savings to the risks of commerce. That this was not confined to countries like France and Spain can be seen from the trend in Holland where, in the eighteenth century, there was a big shift in investment from business to funds, with large amounts of capital being directed to whatever country offered the best return. Dutchmen held half the British public debt by 1780. The Dutch experience points to weaknesses in the argument of the physiocrats, who wanted less government intervention (and therefore expenditure), and advocated giving free play to the 'natural' instinct of businessmen to invest in trade. There is insufficient evidence that they would have so invested.

The 'artificial' measures of Colbert and other *dirigistes*, though sometimes failing because they ignored the working of the market, did promote employment and technological progress. Where there was insufficient incentive to individuals the state could 'prime the pump'. In countries like Austria and Brandenburg a degree of state initiative and regulation was the essential precondition of economic growth. The state enterprise was not necessarily less efficient than the private. Following Peter the Great's initiative there was a remarkable build up of iron production until by 1760 a belt along the Ural mountains was the largest industrial area in Europe. Despite appalling problems of transport much of it was for export. But before the end of the seventeenth century a growing proportion was privately managed: the growth in the private sector coincided with the end of supremacy and the industry was left behind by superior technology elsewhere. More typical was the tale of Guadalajara in Spain where a state factory was set up with the assistance of skilled Dutch weavers in 1718. Because of the lack of a guaranteed market for its high-quality, expensive cloth, it could only be kept afloat by large, regular subsidies.

The bill of exchange had long been known: it was a document accepted by the purchaser of a commodity which stipulated the payment and the date due. In the seventeenth century, because of longer trade routes and the strength of a buyer's market, payment dates were extended; up to twelve months was not uncommon. This tied up circulating capital and prevented the development of trade. The next stage in development, the adoption in western Europe of the existing Italian practice of using bills as negotiable instruments, was therefore crucial. The practice was legalized first in Holland (1651), then in England (1704) and in Spain (1737): bankers who bought bills, at a discount to cover their cost and risk, thereby released credit which would otherwise have been immobilized and expanded the numbers willing to risk money in this potentially profitable business. The foundations of a modern financial system were completed by the establishment of public banks.

Though not invariably, private investment is generally more realistic and cost-effective than that of governments. Where the individual's money is at stake, it is improbable that political or social arguments will be allowed to outweigh the strictly economic considerations. It follows that whereas Britain, whose canal building for example was financed by private enterprise, experienced exceptional growth, with success in one field of investment encouraging venture into other fields, in continental Europe as a whole it was the reluctance of the wealthy to invest a significant proportion of their revenues that accounts for the slow rate of growth. Besides the others already noticed, there are two related technical factors, the limited use of instruments of credit and the lack of reliable banking facilities. Improvements here were so important that together they constitute what has been termed a 'financial revolution'. In 1660 banks were few and far between. There had been little advance in 150 years, since princes and magnates, raising money too easily, spending it recklessly, accumulating debts and reneging upon them, had damaged the fragile apparatus upon which they relied. Great houses like the Fuggers had been ruined, interest rates had been raised by the survivors to unrealistic levels. In 1660 there were some municipal institutions like the bank of Hamburg and the great bank of Amsterdam. The latter played a crucial part in the growth of the Dutch economy by bringing order to the currency and facilitating transfers. It provided the model for the Bank of England, founded in 1694 as a private company, and soon to have a relationship of mutual dependence with the state. The first state bank, however, was that founded in Sweden in 1656; to provide a substitute for Sweden's copper currency, it issued the first notes. They were overproduced, not properly secured and lost their value precipitously. The crash should have been, but was not, heeded by imitators. Law's ambitious scheme for a 'royal bank' foundered because it was linked to his Louisiana company and its absurdly inflated prospects.[1] After 1720 the financiers who had done their best to ruin Law, resumed their hold over crown finance. Their good business was France's bad. The raising of taxes, servicing of loans, were more wasteful and expensive. Interest rates were higher because there was no attractive, secure, central agency of investment. Annuities continued to be more attractive than productive investment. Law's opponents were shortsighted, even in terms of their own financial interest: it was in Britain, where a state bank was most successful, that the largest expansion of private banking took place. The expanding money supply of Britain was one of its advantages, a significant exception in a general shortage.

[1] See also pp. 302–4.

Silver was everywhere the basic unit of value, and everywhere in short supply. One reason was that trade with the east was so one-sided. Eastern countries required few goods and the imbalance of trade had to be made up in silver. Governments tried to prevent the clipping of coins, and so they revalued. The deficiency remained; negotiable paper in the form of bank notes and bills of exchange went some way to meet it. The stock exchanges, commercial in their original function, dealt increasingly in government stocks. Business in such stocks encouraged other forms of investment; in particular joint-stock companies became a common device for attracting money and spreading risk. The collapse of speculative investments, most spectacularly in London and Paris in 1720, not only shook the credit of government but affected private companies floated to take advantage of the postwar boom in investment. Such setbacks checked the development of mechanisms of credit but did not affect the long-term trend. By the middle of the eighteenth century the operations of commerce, manufactures and public finance were plainly linked in one general system of credit. A military defeat or the failure of a harvest, which affected credit in one area, might also undermine confidence throughout the investing community. When credit failed in France in 1787, after several years of rising prices in the stock market, the selling and unease induced by fear of a repetition of the Law crisis, shook the entire regime.

The Old Industrial Regime

In 1750 the economy of Europe was still largely pre-industrial. It was nearer in most respects to the Middle Ages than to the nineteenth century. Midland and northern England, a belt along the Urals, Catalonia and Flanders were the scene of exceptionally large-scale operations which only emphasized, by contrast, the primitive conditions of most manufacturing enterprise. Technology still relied on a limited range of equipment. The power-driven fulling mills and paper mills, the mechanical bellows and tilt hammers suggested the shape of things to come. In the slitting mills of Liège the iron sheet passed under a grooved cylinder and was cut into rods of equal thickness: manned by 2 men it was said to do the jobs of 200. Water-driven silk looms in the Po valley, their secrets closely guarded until the Lombe brothers discovered them in 1717 and introduced them to England, anticipated the future mechanization of the textile industry. But in general, at loom and anvil, and on the building site, manual labour was the order of the day. To see the old industrial regime at its most impressive a Dutch shipyard might be visited, as by Peter the Great in 1697. There he saw, in the villages strung along the Zaan river, lumber saws powered by over 500 windmills, yards equipped with cranes and stacked with timber cut to set lengths to build the *fluitschip* to a standard design.

For most purposes, however, the typical unit of production was the small

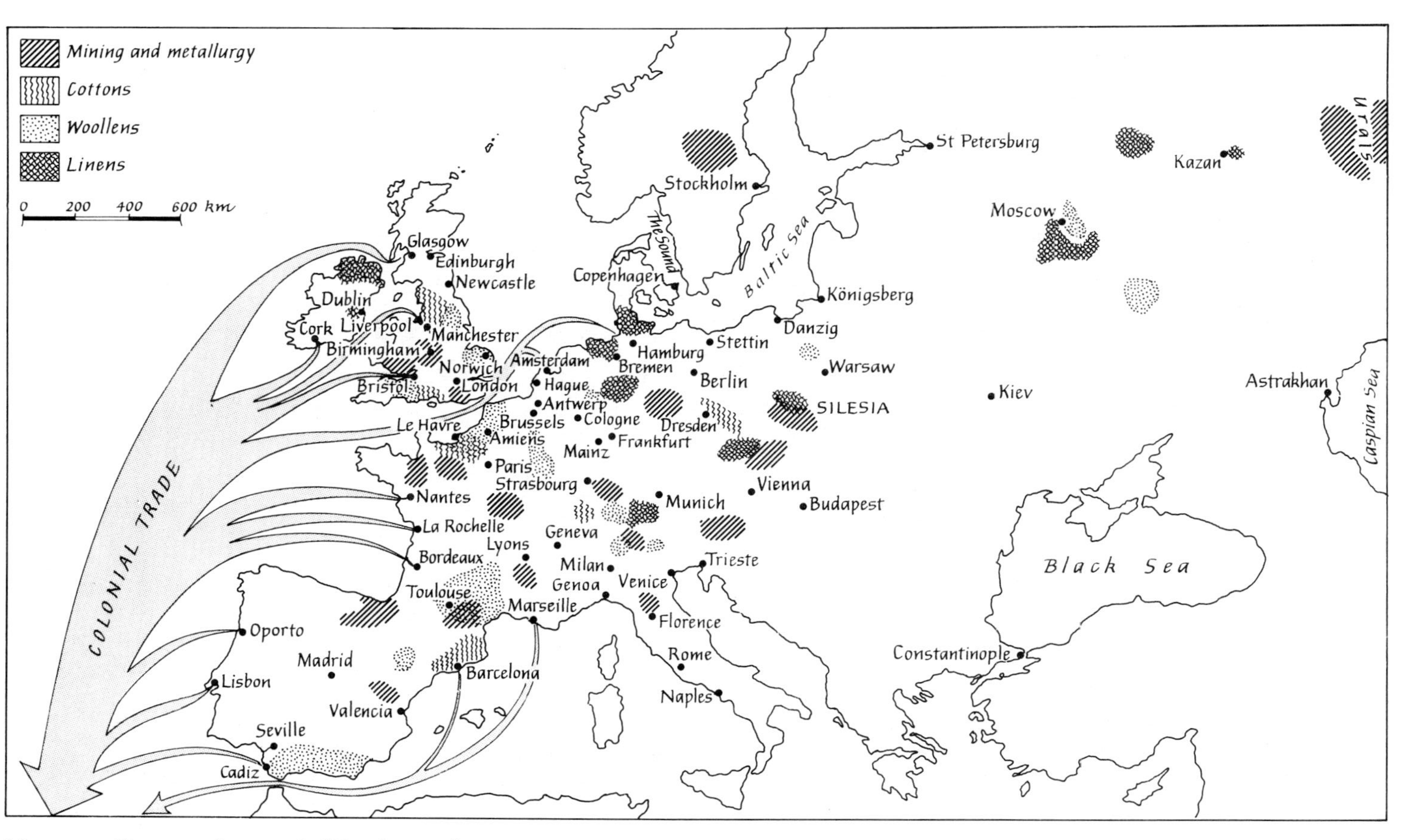

Map 2.1 *Towns and economic life, 1640–1780*

workshop, supplying a limited range of needs; for most people, in most communities, were still self-sufficient. Much of the work done was part-time. Even where it was a full-time occupation, the plant required was simple and inexpensive. Capital was represented in the main by tiny, dispersed parcels, the tools and equipment that could be housed in a modest workshop or a single room in the house. The merchant played an increasingly important part in the provision of capital, even for domestic industry. When, for example, the metal workers of Normandy made their knives, needles and locks for the local market, they were able to remain their own masters. But when in the seventeenth century they found new outlets in France and abroad, and had to draw on new supplies of iron, they came to rely on local businessmen for raw materials, wages and the marketing of their wares. In the textile industries, where imported or expensive fibres were required and there was a time-lag between the delivery of the raw materials and the sale of the finished product, the capital and marketing skills of the urban entrepreneur were essential to the cottage workers. Though concentrated round certain established centres, like Abbeville, Aachen and Leyden, this 'putting-out' system was established all over Europe, as merchants saw the advantages of evading guild control. Round Sedan, in eastern France, 25 merchants provided work for 15,000 peasants in the manufacture of woollen cloth. When the cotton industry was developed round Rouen and Barcelona, it was organized along the same lines. The system was capable of increasing output considerably, but only in measure roughly proportionate to the number of workers involved. Catalan cotton production was in the hands of 10,000 workers in 1760; by 1800 there were 100,000 organized in 3000 workshops.

Sometimes the need to produce as economically as possible could mean a complete change in the structure and location of an industry, as in Brabant, where peasant capitalists first moved into the weaving side of the linen trade, then established rural bleaching works which cut out, and ruined, the craftsmen of Haarlem, who had traditionally dominated the industry. Sometimes it altered the social balance, as in Electoral Saxony, where between 1550 and 1750, while the population doubled, the proportion of farmers fell, and that of the peasants who made most of their living by industry rose from 5 to 30 per cent of the population. It could have a significant demographic effect, as land became less important and couples married earlier, rather than wait, in the traditional peasant way, till they had sufficient land. In districts where the cottage textile manufacture spread, as in the uplands round Zürich, the population grew disproportionately fast: the resulting poverty there only increased the peasants' need to secure a second income from manufactures and weakened their bargaining position in an overcrowded labour market. In this dependence on the merchant's capital, which could be withdrawn whenever market conditions were adverse, can be seen an important feature of later industrial society.

Inevitably too the expansion of domestic manufactures brought with it problems of communication and control, not only of the rate of production but also of its quality, which were eventually to be resolved by concentration in factories, and by technical advances large enough to justify investment in machinery. Starting with Lombe's silk mills (1717) and Kaye's flying shuttle (1733), British successes in these respects set their textile production, that of cotton especially, on a dizzy path of growth. Steam engines were made, mainly at first for pumping, while advances in metallurgy contributed to Britain's commanding lead. Abraham Darby's process of coke smelting was perhaps the most important single improvement since it liberated the iron founder from dependence on diminishing supplies of timber for charcoal. Technical development on the continent was much less remarkable. The nine volumes of *Theatrum Machinarum* (1724), Jakob Leupold's description of engineering, is a record in general of steady development, reflecting the craftsman's empirical outlook. Improvement could be modest indeed. It is estimated that a miller could grind 17 kilograms of flour an hour in the twelfth century; by 1700 it might be as much as 25 kilograms. Sometimes it was an apparently small change which had important consequences: for example the shift in harness attachment from the horse's neck to his shoulders which was adopted in the early seventeenth century, significantly increasing his drawing power.

Typical of the kind of progress that was made was the way in which problems of vaulting were being overcome in the eighteenth century to make possible more ambitious bridge building. Mining was already well advanced and held back chiefly by the difficulty of drainage. In the Röhrerbuhel copper mines in the Tyrol, the Heiliger Geist shaft, at 886 metres, remained the deepest in the world until 1872; a third of its labour force was employed on draining. In engineering as a whole the main features, viewed from our standpoint, are the long intervals which elapsed between each tentative advance and the slowness with which scientific discoveries were translated into improved technology. For example Galileo, Torricelli, Guericke and Pascal were working on the vacuum in the first half of the seventeenth century; Papin was then experimenting on steam engines; but it was not till 1711 that Newcomen produced a model that had any practical use. Where there was a large increase in productivity, it was generally to be found in those manufactures where, as in the part-time production of linen, adopted by peasant householders in areas like Silesia and Brittany, the skills required were modest and the raw material, as in the case of flax, could be produced locally; or where there was an exceptional demand for an improved product, as there was for cotton; or in one of those specialized manufactures required to meet the rising demand being generated by the enrichment of the upper classes. For these the term 'luxuries' may be used, though they included some articles which would not seem so today. All were labour-intensive and most called for patience, precision and dexterity.

When technical ingenuity was challenged by the needs of the market the results could be impressive. Printing was of seminal importance because the advance of knowledge depended on it. Improved type-moulds, specialization in type-founding, leading to standardization and the invention of a printing press, were together largely responsible for a threefold increase between 1600 and 1700 in the number of pages that could be printed in a day. More spectacular was the effect of the 'Hollander' or pulverizing machine (*c.* 1670) whose daily output of pulp for paper exceeded the weekly output of eight stamping mills. The connection between technical innovation and style, in this case that of domestic architecture, is illustrated by the improvements in glass making which made possible not only the casting of large, clear sheets for mirrors, but also the larger panes required for the sash windows that were everywhere, by 1700, replacing the leaded panes of casements. A new product was sometimes made possible by a single discovery, as for example when the Saxons Tschirnhaus and Bottger successfully imitated the hard paste of Chinese ware which was to be used for the porcelain of Meissen. A way of life could be affected by one invention. When Huygens perfected his pendulum clock he introduced a new age of accurate, reliable timekeeping: error could be measured in seconds rather than minutes. Many more were produced, Geneva's 5000 pieces a year being overtaken by 1680 by the clock-makers of both London and Paris. Clock making also involved the skills of several groups of workers, each responsible for a particular task, such as the making of wheels or coil and the decoration of the dial. Specialization led to enhanced production: one of the characteristics of modern industry can here be seen in embryonic form.

Overseas Trade

Growth in manufactures was slow and uneven. Surer and larger profits were to be made in trade which, accordingly, attracted more investment. Merchant capitalism was favoured in this period by developments in financial services: the limitations upon the exchange of goods were overcome by new financial devices, while the costs of transactions were reduced by improvements in communications and transport. To sustain trade on a regular basis and to ensure that manufactures matched markets, merchants began to enter more directly into the process of production. European trade in the seventeenth and eighteenth centuries developed few new routes, nor was it stimulated, until towards the end of the period, by a rise in population. Growth came rather through the evolution of a new kind of trading system, in which existing contracts were strengthened and new areas and products were found to provide for, sometimes to create, demand. In all these ways the Dutch pioneered, showing Europe the way out of recession.[1] They had long been specialists in the bulk trades, carrying grain, timber and salt; with their *fluitships* they provided an economical service, undercutting their rivals by as much as a third. They introduced many new commodities into the trading areas; they amassed capital for more ambitious enterprises. Inevitably success brought rivalry and emulation as they built up a monopoly in the Baltic trade and a strong position in the Mediterranean, and thrust outwards into the lucrative markets first developed by the Portuguese. Their aggression invited retaliation; they were hated for their aggression; they were flattered by imitation.

By 1640 the first, spectacular phase of European expansion was virtually complete. The continent had become the centre of a world economy, and those countries, led by Spain, which had most successfully exploited the resources of new lands overseas had gained correspondingly in wealth and power. The Spanish had created in Central and South America a huge territorial empire, with half a million Europeans, but it was moving from dependence on the mother country towards self-sufficiency. Since the flow of precious metals from its mines, which had reached its peak about the turn of the century, was now decreasing, the colonists were earning less to pay for European goods. While less bullion entered the monetary system of Europe, more silver left it to pay for the goods of the east. As Europe entered the recession which was the inevitable consequence of this contraction of the money supply, ideas which were later to be called 'mercantilist' emerged as the guiding principles of economic policy. At a time when states were becoming sufficiently powerful to impose central direction, it was assumed that they should act to attract the largest possible amount of the precious metals which were held to be the measure of the wealth of the state. It seemed to contemporary analysts, not without reason, that states must compete more vigorously for trade and colonies. Prizes would go to those who were most successful in enlarging their share of what was held to be a fixed volume of trade; the problems of those who failed would be correspondingly acute. As was the case with England and Holland in 1654, 1664 and 1672, and with France in the last year, the issues might be sufficiently important to justify going to war. By its wide-ranging enterprise Holland exposed fallacies in the more rigid 'mercantilist' outlook which was conditioned, as in Colbert's case, by the combination of a strong administration and a vulnerable economy. Subsequently Britain forged ahead, benefiting from Holland's damaging involvement in wars (which can be judged by an increase in the national debt, from 30,000 *guilders* in 1688 to 148,000 by 1714), and establishing a clear ascendancy in the more favourable conditions of the eighteenth century. Spain, the greatest beneficiary of the first age of discoveries, had been the prime victim of the recession and subsequently

[1] See also pp. 466–9.

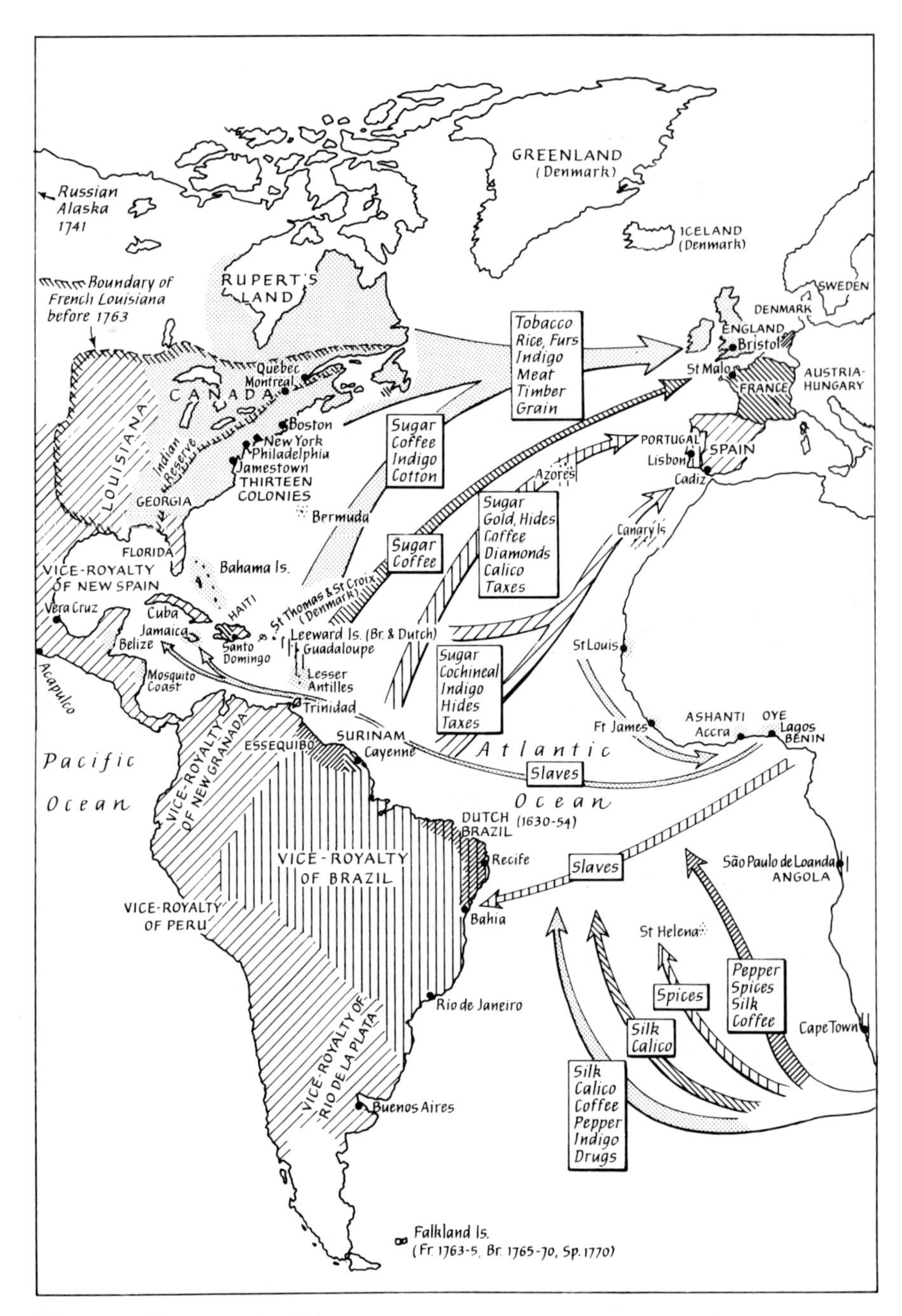

Map 2.2 *Europeans in Asia*

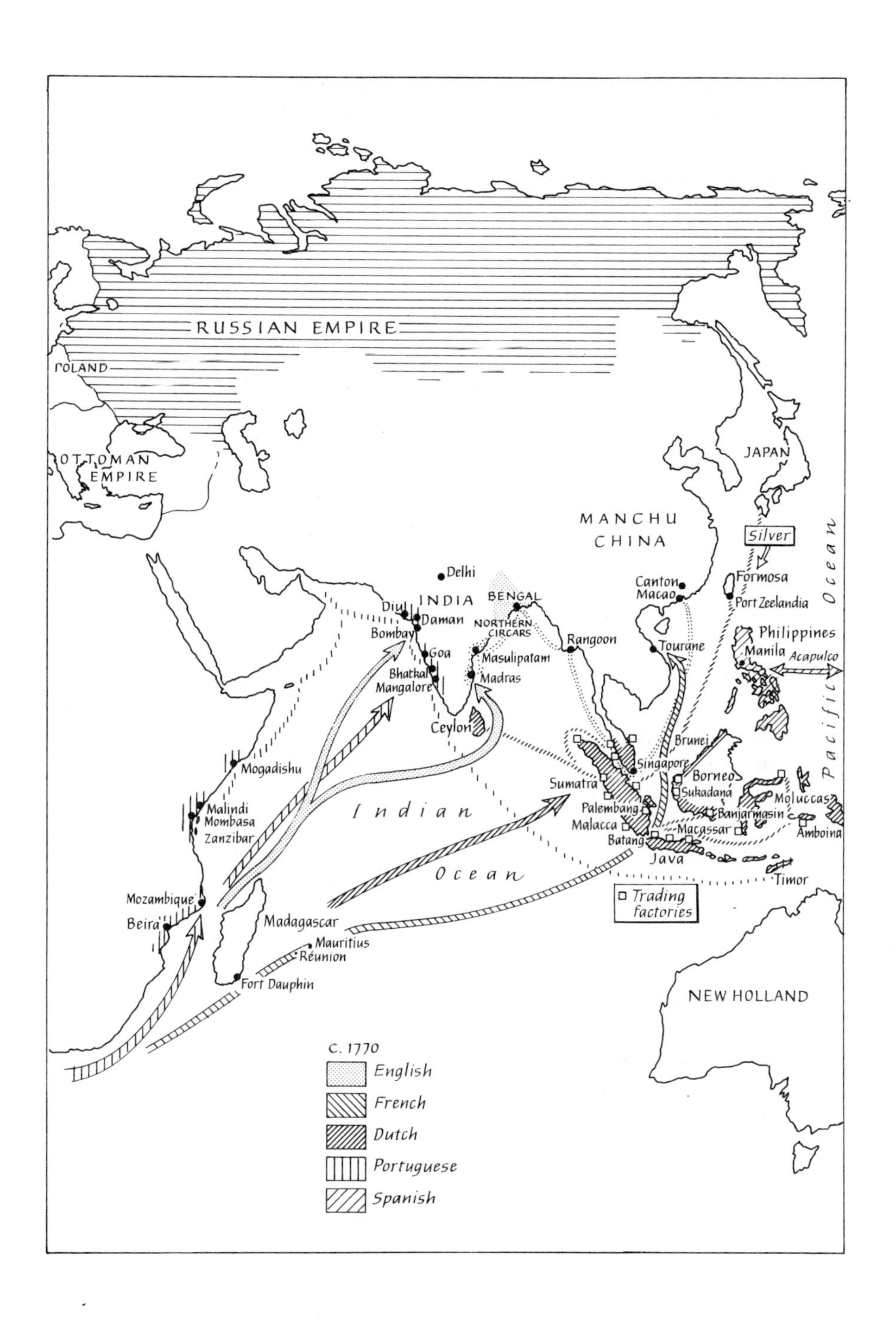

RUSSIAN EMPIRE
POLAND
OTTOMAN EMPIRE
MANCHU CHINA
JAPAN
Silver
Delhi
INDIA
BENGAL
NORTHERN CIRCARS
Diu
Daman
Bombay
Goa
Bhatkal
Mangalore
Masulipatam
Madras
Ceylon
Rangoon
Canton
Macao
Tourane
Formosa
Port Zeelandia
Philippines
Manila
Acapulco
Pacific Ocean
Brunei
Singapore
Borneo
Sukadana
Banjarmasin
Moluccas
Amboina
Sumatra
Palembang
Malacca
Batang
Macassar
Java
Timor
Trading factories
Mogadishu
Malindi
Mombasa
Zanzibar
Mozambique
Beira
Madagascar
Mauritius
Réunion
Fort Dauphin
Indian Ocean
NEW HOLLAND
c. 1770
English
French
Dutch
Portuguese
Spanish

made but a modest recovery. The Thirty Years War had much to do with it; social and political factors also contributed to the decay of her industries and the decline in her trade. No country's economy seemed able to generate from its own resources the growth in manufacturing that was later to come with advances in technology and the application of capital to mass production. Overseas trade and the ancillary development of colonies offered the surest means of progress.

Europe was already coming to depend on overseas sources, whether settled colonies or trading agencies, for those goods which could not be produced at home: spices, such as cinnamon, cloves, nutmeg, ginger; pepper, the prime example of a commodity of high value in relation to bulk; cottons and dyestuffs; the hardwoods, teak and mahogany; and, just being introduced, tea, coffee and chocolate. The continent was exporting, in exchange, relatively little. Either the native market was too poor, its facilities for exchange too limited; or the European goods, woollens or hardware, for the most part, were unsuitable. A substantial export trade could only be built up where there was a settled colony of Europeans. Overall the balance was made up in silver, mined in America and dispatched to Europe, finding its way thence to the east. The role of middleman at the busy centres of the trading network was a profitable one. A few trading companies and their host cities, principally the Dutch companies and Amsterdam, benefited hugely. But the picture of Europe as a whole was that of a consumer on a vast scale, indulging itself, but at a high cost: for the outflow of silver reduced demand for home-produced goods and discouraged investment.

In the second half of the seventeenth century there were some important developments which thereafter gained momentum. By the last quarter of the eighteenth century, which saw the successful revolt of the British American colonies but also the extension of the British *raj* in India, the situation had been transformed. The age of cheap sugar dawned with the intensive cultivation of Brazilian and West Indian plantations by a labour force of slaves: the Portuguese used native Indians until the supply ran dangerously low, then they and the Dutch, followed by the British and French, turned to the vast human reservoir of West Africa. Monoculture threatened the prosperity of the Barbadoes, where between 1643 and 1680 the black slave population increased from 6000 to 35,000; there were temporary slumps in demand and prices, usually after overproduction, as in the 1730s; but demand increased generally in line with the growing prosperity of sweet-toothed Europeans. By 1767 West Indian sugar production, mainly British and French, was 144,000 tons a year, twenty times that of 1655. For the home countries the 'sugar islands' had become valuable assets, worth the deployment of large amphibious forces. In 1763, after the Seven Years War, they were one of the main counters in negotiations: when Guadeloupe was returned to the French, many on the British side were disgruntled because they thought that it was worth more than Canada.

Without plentiful slave labour the sugar boom would have been impossible. The statistics of the trade which provided the slaves are eloquent: by 1780 there were 900,000 in the West Indian islands, 800,000 in Brazil, 400,000 in the mainland American colonies. The transported communities could not maintain themselves. There was an insistent call for more hands, as first tobacco, then cotton growing was expanded to supply the growing European market. There was also keen competition among shipowners to cater for the demand, and profit margins were narrow, at best about 10 per cent on a voyage. About the same percentage died in the crowded holds of the Dutch, English and French slavers. The casualty rate among the crews who transported them there was even higher. It was costly too to maintain the slaving posts. Most of the slaves were bought, not captured, from conniving chieftains. In some years the companies made a loss. In any case slaving was never more than a small part of the Atlantic colonial trade. It contributed, but only marginally, to the prosperity of Atlantic ports, like Nantes, Bristol and Liverpool. The homelands suffered a shocking, debilitating loss: 8 million were transported altogether in the eighteenth century. But the catchment area was sufficiently large to mitigate the effect on a particular community. On the other side the plantation economy was unbalanced and inherently unstable. The planters lived with the fear of violence from escaped slaves. The system was never fully restored in the French West Indies after the bloody uprising of Saint Domingue in 1791. The British slave trade was abolished in 1806; others soon followed suit. In retrospect it seems that more lost than gained by the trade. The chief beneficiaries were the luckier plantation owners, many of them absentee, the European consumers, who enjoyed inexpensive sugar and tobacco, the manufacturers who could expand their cotton production because of the plentiful raw material, and the governments whose rising income from import duties enabled them to reduce other forms of taxation.

A growing number of Europeans emigrated to the mainland of America. Spain's colonies grew steadily till 1800, when their combined population approached 15 million: of that number, however, only about 2 million were white. Between 1700 and 1760, 200,000 Portuguese emigrated to Brazil: perhaps more than that small country could afford to lose, but only a fifth of the number of black slaves transported there during that period. In 1660 there were around 60,000 Dutch and English colonists in the raw and struggling communities of North America, of whom about two-thirds had been born in Europe. The Dutch colonists of New Amsterdam became English by the treaty of Breda in 1667 and a more dynamic phase of colonization began. A hundred years later, on the eve of revolt, there were thirteen colonies with a population of 2.5 million.

The immigration of French Huguenots after 1685, and, between 1700 and 1770, that of a quarter of a million Germans, pointed to the cosmopolitan future of the United States. Europeans did not come only on religious grounds; many were attracted by the openness and diversity of the colonies, and their relative freedom from government supervision. Most European colonies were treated as provinces of the mother country. French Canada provides an extreme contrast. Its climate was unsuitable for plantation crops such as tobacco and cotton and conditions were rigorous. But the main reason why it had only 70,000 inhabitants when it was ceded to Britain in 1763 was that it was essentially a state enterprise. Colbert's sponsorship and regulation of the early settlements at Quebec and Montreal had been designed to produce in 'New France' a limb of the mother country, capable of playing a part in the overall economic plan, as a market for French goods and a source of raw material. Under *intendant* and bishop, barred to Huguenots and unwelcoming to adventurers, it was not fulfilling the potential recognized by Pitt when he made his triple attack on French Canada, the centrepiece of his imperial strategy. Louisiana, where a fort was founded at the mouth of the Mississippi in 1699, was even less successful. Till Law puffed up its prospects there were more transported criminals than voluntary settlers. After the collapse, in 1720, of Law's plan to make the Mississippi company and its trade the commercial wing of an integrated financial system, the colony stagnated in its unhealthy swamps.

The Spaniards had been the first to envisage their American colonies as provinces of the mother country. They were governed by a Council of the Indies sitting in Madrid. The prime function of the viceroys was to ensure that the *corregidores*, local representatives of the king, enforced the Spanish law and system. The enterprise of missionaries helped further to provide an orderly, protective structure for what were essentially colonies of exploitation. Greed, opportunism and religious idealism: the paradoxes implicit in the actions of the conquistadores persisted. At the Spanish end, the noble ideal of civilized, legal rule conflicted with the pressing claims of finance. The sale of office and grants of *encomienda* induced cynicism and corruption. The reforming ministers of the eighteenth century introduced home-trained *intendants* who, like their French counterparts, enjoyed wide powers. Their attempts to tighten up the system only fuelled the resentment of the American-born creole aristocracy and brought nearer the day when they, like the North American colonists, would fight for their independence. The same pattern can be seen in Portuguese Brazil, where again the dynamism, and chief cause of contention, was provided by the discovery of precious metals. Civil war broke out between the prospectors who had found gold in Minas Gerais in 1708 and the immigrants from the coast, followed by a second wave from Portugal. The governor, not unwillingly, enforced a military system of rule. Pombal, who came to power in 1755, wanted to make a coherent profitable business out of the pieces of the far-flung empire; inevitably that meant an extension of central control. The Jesuits put up a tough resistance to the alliance of government and church authorities, seeking to bring their settlements in Paraguay under secular control. The government succeeded, to the discomfiture of the Jesuits and the native Indians whom they were protecting and educating. But for Portugal, as for other colonial powers, the larger question remained: how long could a European state properly manage the affairs of a distant land? The more assets a colony possessed, the more incentive the home government had to bring it under control; the more rapidly the colony grew and generated spending power, the more it approached self-sufficiency and aspired to independence. By contrast it was a strength of the British in India that there was such a small white presence. There, as was the case of the Portuguese in Goa, the issues were simpler, for economy and society were affected only indirectly at the trading level; it was therefore largely a question of the commercial and military authorities being able to maintain an amicable relationship with the native community, usually through an amenable ruler. Between merchant and politician there might be conflicts of interest, but there was also an essential will to act together to survive and prosper. The problem, as ever, was to enjoy the benefits of trade without incurring too much of the costs and responsibilities of power.

The Portuguese and Dutch built extensive and profitable empires out of strings of trading posts. The voyages were risky and costly. But the profit was sufficient to make them worthwhile, even if they never managed to establish a complete monopoly. Pepper and spices were the mainstay of the Dutch eastern trade, until the establishment of coffee plantations in Java in the late eighteenth century. The fine cottons and silks, together with saltpetre, required for gunpowder, attracted European traders to India and made it the most important region in the east. Once established in their factories, traders became involved in local trade, and so in politics. A flourishing re-export trade grew up in trading stations all over the east, sending back to Europe the goods of Japan and China. In 1684 foreign traders were allowed to settle and trade outside Canton. The silk and porcelain that attracted them there in the first place were soon dwarfed in importance by the growth of the tea trade. Between 1730 and 1785 tea exports rose by over 600 per cent. Directly or indirectly all eastern trade was controlled by the state. The Spanish and Portuguese governments organized shipments. The Dutch, English and French trade was managed by companies whose charters granted a monopoly on terms variously beneficial to the state.

Most successful at first, and the model for the rest, was the Dutch East India Company, a state enterprise, formed in 1602, for which each of the United Provinces provided capital, from which each shared the dividends; its directors were elected by their nominees. Through its operations the state acquired a stake in a lucrative trade while the company came to have an influence on the policy of the state even greater than that of its British equivalent. By 1720 the East India Company was the largest trading concern in Britain. In the wars of 1740–63 the political and commercial interests at stake were so important that the state could not fail to be involved. In the Seven Years War Pitt made virtue out of necessity and supported the operations of Clive, 'the heaven born general' and victor of Plassey. In truth the commercial empire was by then too important to lose, could not stand still and had to grow; growth meant taking over the lands of princes who could not be relied upon simply to be allies. Some remarkable Englishmen, Clive himself, Hastings and Wellesley, showed that territorial expansion was not incompatible with commercial advantage, so long as government was prepared to give support. They also taught generations to come to accept responsibly the burden of power and the duties of civilized rule. Generally the British and Dutch companies flourished because commercial considerations normally predominated over political. The Compagnie des Indes, like other French trading companies, suffered by contrast from subordination, at first to the state's overall economic policy and second to strategic aims which were dominated by traditional concerns; the government listened to diplomats and soldiers, not to sailors, and merchants; it looked to the Rhine rather than to the Atlantic. The French colonies were strong in controls, weak in funds. Not till 1730, when it was released from government management, did the company mount a serious challenge to the Dutch and British companies, already benefiting from their freedom to operate and invest according to strictly commercial criteria. But as each trading empire became more ambitious and complicated, problems of control became more acute: for the government over the companies, and for the companies over their individual servants. A colonial governor might enjoy powers comparable to those of the greatest statesman at home: to make wars and treaties, command armies and fleets. The company servant was paid little but was able to make a fortune by private dealing. When it could take a year or more to contact and transmit instructions, the authorities at home could only state principles and rules and trust to their men on the spot to act with discretion. In practice that might mean a Maetsuyker (governor of the Dutch East Indies, 1653–78) or a Clive making decisions about peace and war, in a situation where he might well believe himself to be best placed to assess the balance of risk and gain. Thus the Dutch company became master of Java by intervening in the power struggle of native princes. It was not exactly what Maetsuyker expected when he first espoused the cause of the dispossessed Susuhunan in 1677; nor what the *Heeren* of Amsterdam wanted. It was a slow process, over a century, but in retrospect almost inevitable. As another Dutchman, Laurens Reael, had written in 1614: 'we have begun to pull on a chain and one link drags the other'.

The most dramatic conflict, however, was that of the British and French in India where both sought to capitalize on the anarchic conditions that followed the collapse of the Mogul empire with the death of Aurangzeb in 1707. The British eventually came out on top in the conflict that began in

1744 when they refused the non-aggression pact offered by Dupleix, governor of French Pondicherry. Thereafter strategic decisions at home, accidents in India, notably the inconstancy and incompetence of the French client Suraj-ud-Dowlah and the genius of Clive, played a part in the defeat of Dupleix's plan to build a French empire on the backs of a compliant native prince. Between 1689 and 1789, French trade as a whole grew fivefold: the European sector fourfold and the colonial sector no less than tenfold, largely through re-export business: rates unmatched by any other country. If the French had secured their position in India, their future would have been bright indeed.

Further Reading

The works listed here are in addition to those cited after chapter 1 which have a particular bearing on social history. For a clear, readable account the student may need to look no further than J. de Vries, *The Economy of Europe in an Age of Crisis, 1600–1750* (Cambridge, 1976), and C.M. Cipolla (ed.), *Fontana Economic History of Europe*, vol. 2 (London, 1973). Helpful is C.H. Wilson and G. Parker (eds), *An Introduction to the Sources of European Economic History, 1500–1800* (London, 1978). Much detail about particular aspects is to be found in the *Cambridge Economic History of Europe*. It is arranged by subjects but most useful for this period is vol. 4, ed. C.H. Wilson and R.R. Rich; it contains for instance F. Braudel and F.C. Spooner, 'Prices in Europe from 1450 to 1750'. Price history is inevitably technical. For a lucid explanation, see J. Sperling, 'The internal payments mechanism in the seventeenth and eighteenth centuries', *Economic History Review*, 15 (1962). The work of one of the most influential historians in the field may be sampled in J. Meuvret, 'Monetary circulation and use of coinage in sixteenth and seventeenth century France', in P. Earle (ed.), *Essays in European Economic History* (Oxford, 1974). The specialist with stamina may wish to read F.C. Spooner, *The International Economy and Monetary Movements in France, 1493–1725* (Cambridge, 1973). A wider survey is P. Vilar, *A History of Gold and Money, 1450–1920* (trans., London, 1976). For a summary of the view of two other masters, E.J. Hamilton and P. Chaunu, see the latter's article 'Atlantic economy and world economy', in P. Earle (ed.), cited above. For banking, see R. de Roover, 'New interpretations of the history of banking', *Journal of World History*, 4 (1954). A detailed study with wide ramifications is H. Luthy, *La Banque protestante en France de la révocation de l'Edit de Nantes à la Révolution*, 2 vols (1956, 1961). His conclusions are helpfully summarized in J. Bouvier's review article on the book in *Annales*, 18, 4 (1963).

The standard introduction to agriculture is B.H. Slicher van Bath, *The Agrarian History of Western Europe, A.D. 500–1850* (1962). Important is E. Boserup, *The Conditions of Agricultural Growth* (London, 1965). See also 'The transformation of European agriculture' in M. Postan and H.J. Habbakuk (eds), *Cambridge Economic History*, vol. 6, Part 2. Besides some of the regional studies cited after chapter 1, see particularly: J. de Vries, *The Dutch Rural Economy in the Golden Age* (New Haven, 1974); R. Forster, 'Obstacles to agricultural growth in 18th century France', *American Historical Review*, 75 (1970); F. Huggett, *The Land Question and European Society* (London, 1975); E.L. Jones and S.J. Woolf (eds), *Agrarian*

Change and Economic Development: the Historical Problems (London, 1970); A. Mayhew, *Rural Settlement and Farming in Germany* (London, 1973).

The manufactures and trade of pre-industrial Europe can best be studied in C. Cipolla, *Before the Industrial Revolution* (London, 1976), and F. Braudel, *The Wheels of Commerce*, vol. 2 of *Civilisation and Capitalism* (London, 1983). For the transitional period, see W.W. Rostow, *The Stages of Economic Growth* (Cambridge, 1960), D.S. Landes, *The Unbound Prometheus: Technological Change in Europe since 1750* (Cambridge, 1969), and C. Kennedy and A.P. Thirlwall, 'Technical progress: a survey', *Journal of Economic History*, 32 (1972). The opening chapters of A.S. Milward and S.B. Saul, *The Economic Development of Continental Europe*, (London, 1973) convey the picture before 'take-off'; it was already starting in Britain in the years covered by R.M. Hartwell (ed.), *Causes of the Industrial Revolution in England* (London, 1967), which contains an interesting comparison of French and English growth in an article by P. Crouzet. For particular aspects, see W.O. Henderson, *Studies in the Economic Policy of Frederick the Great* (London, 1963); C. Cipolla, 'The decline of Italy: the case of a fully matured economy', *Economic History Review*, series 2, 5 (1952); and for a specially revealing study of the importance of one of the most skilled of industries, C. Cipolla, *Clocks and Culture* (1967). In the same category comes G.N. Clark, *Science and Social Welfare in the Age of Newton* (1949), particularly for the connection between science and technology. For the way in which rural industries functioned, Herman Kellenbenz, 'Rural industries in the west from the end of the middle ages to the eighteenth century', in P. Earle (ed.), *Essays* (Oxford, 1974); also F. Mendels, 'Agriculture and peasant industry in eighteenth century Flanders', in W.N. Parker and E.L. Jones (eds), *European Peasants and their Markets* (Princeton, 1975); and for the most important of those industries, Charles Wilson, 'Cloth production and international competition in the seventeenth century', *Economic History Review*, 13 (1960).

Mercantilism has been a subject of controversy ever since the term was first used to describe the evolution of economic life between the sixteenth and eighteenth centuries. I have not used the term as an organizing concept; rather as a convenient way of describing certain principles behind the policies of governments. But there is room for different interpretations of the motives behind those policies and for different assessments of their validity. The debate has been a lively one and may be traced back to a major source, E. Hecksher, *Mercantilism*, 2 vols (1935), or followed through the writings of Charles Wilson, an economic historian who also writes vividly, as in 'Treasure and the trade balance: the mercantilist problem', *Economic History Review*, 2 (1949); 'The other face of mercantilism', *Transactions of the Royal Historical Society*, 9 (1959); or *Mercantilism*, Historical Association pamphlet, no. G.37 (1958). See also D.C. Coleman (ed.), *Revisions in Mercantilism* (1969), and W.E. Minchinton (ed.), *Mercantilism, System or Expedient* (Lexington, 1969). Dealing with the main body of ideas critical of mercantilism, R.L. Meek, *The Economics of Physiocracy* (1962), analyses extracts from the French economists; see also his *Precursors of Adam Smith 1750–1775* (London, 1973).

There is no shortage of books on Europe overseas. Ralph Davis, *The Rise of the Atlantic Economies* (London, 1973), and G. Williams, *The Expansion of Europe in the Eighteenth Century* (1966), provide good introductions. The pattern is incomplete without knowledge of the English experience, so R. Davis, *A Commercial Revolution. English Overseas Trade in the Seventeenth and Eighteenth Centuries*

(London, 1967), should not be overlooked. See also J.H. Parry, *Trade and Dominion: the European Overseas Empires in the Eighteenth Century* (London, 1971). J.H. Parry, *The Spanish Seaborne Empire* (1966), and C.R. Boxer, *The Dutch Seaborne Empire, 1600–1800* (London, 1965) and *The Portuguese Seaborne Empire, 1415–1825* (London, 1969), are not only highly readable; they offer an extra dimension to the study of the home country. A valuable comparative study is F. Mauro, 'Towards an intercontinental model: European overseas expansion between 1500 and 1800', *Economic History Review*, 14 (1961). For particular experiences, see W.J. Eccles, *Canada under Louis XIV, 1663–1701* (Oxford, 1964) (difficult except for specialists); J. Clark, *La Rochelle and the Atlantic Economy during the Eighteenth Century* (Baltimore, 1982); M. Savelle, *Empires to Nations: Expansion in America, 1713–1824* (London, 1975); K.G. Davies, *The North Atlantic World in the Seventeenth Century* (London, 1975); and N. Steensgard, *The Asian Trade Revolution of the Seventeenth Century* (Chicago, 1975). R. Anstey, *The Atlantic Slave Trade and British Abolition, 1760–1810* (London, 1975), provides a clear analysis of some controversial material. See also R.L. Stein, *The French Slave Trade in the Eighteenth Century: an Old Regime Business* (Madison, Wisconsin, 1979).

3

GOD AND MAN

Faith and Doubt

The language, values and conduct of the men and women of seventeenth-century Europe expressed an unquestioning belief in God. There still existed a coherent view of the world as the scene of a constant struggle between good and evil forces, as personified by God and the devil. The personal God, a loving but stern father, was the unseen but all-seeing witness of the acts and thoughts of every day. Kings were God's lieutenants; indeed all authority was God-given. For king and peasant, kingdom or village, the idea of divine retribution had a sobering power. 'Our nation was insolent and unruly,' wrote Mme de Maintenon in 1710, after defeats in war and a harsh winter; 'God wishes to punish it and enlighten it.' From baptism to extreme unction, or whatever consoling rite a Protestant might practise, men lived under the sign of the cross. The afterlife was still portrayed in the traditional way. Though baroque artists came to pay more attention to the joys of heaven than to the pains of hell, both were still envisaged as physical states and were correspondingly vivid in the popular mind. Those who feared damnation feared unending physical torment. Grace and redemption may have been words of imprecise meaning to the ordinary Christian but they conveyed awesome possibilities. When theologians sought to define them and to catch their essence they were assured of a large audience. Theology was more than an intellectual game, profoundly affected though it was in methods and style by the current rationalism.

There might well be political and worldly implications, as in the controversy between Jesuits and Jansenists, or that between relatively liberal Arminians and orthodox Calvinists. But the eager attention given to the issues suggests that they were a central concern of the educated world. With wider opportunities for education came not, at first, a greater detachment but a more earnest quest for the truth.

When some enlightened thinkers came to equate Christianity with superstition there was sufficient evidence to give credence to their jibes. Clergy were usually better educated than in the past. By 1700 most Catholic priests had been trained in seminaries and most Protestant ministers had attended universities. But they ministered in the main to illiterate people, living simple lives, close to nature, trusting and literal in their response; prompted more by instinct than by reason and more readily influenced by signs than by doctrines. The Church still had to accommodate the survivals of paganism. Christian rites and festivals overlay but did not replace the older magic of an animist universe: wells and wishing stones were sanctified, dubious saints were venerated for their miraculous powers. The credulous faith that Dr Levi found in 1935, in the south Italian countryside beyond Eboli, 'where Christ stopped', preserved by its exceptional isolation, would have been commonplace in the towns and villages of Europe in 1700. When priest and people were at one in assuming that God played an active part in the functioning of His universe, the priest was expected to be the mediator, in the recurring miracle of the Mass or through interpretation of the Holy Book in which all truth and wisdom were contained. God and His saints were invoked to aid the farmer and to cure the sick. For the lives of some of the saints, the authenticity of their relics or their efficacy, history could offer little evidence. But that did not diminish their appeal to men who craved their intervention to redress the harsh laws of nature, and who might echo the words of the mathematician Gassendi in 1640: 'Men would no longer feel any admiration or veneration for God if He did not surpass them, and if they could boast that they were as clever as He.'

Everywhere people appear to have accepted religious ideas that did not conflict with their reading of the material world. Men like François de Sales (1567–1622), author of popular manuals of devotion, canonized unusually soon after his death, and John Bunyan (1628–88), the English shoemaker and author of *Pilgrim's Progress*, influenced succeeding generations by their writings because they stood on common ground with their readers. In matters of belief there was still no significant gap between the cultures of the learned and the illiterate. It was, moreover, because they agreed in their acceptance of fundamental articles of faith that educated Christians fought so vehemently over details of interpretation, and simple folk could be roused to fight against rival communities and households whose errors could only mean that Antichrist was at work. There was still no lack of believers who could respond to the call of Calvin (it might as well have been Ignatius) to have such ardour for the honour of God that when it was wounded they should feel anguish that burnt inside. 1648 was indeed a significant date: the treaty of Westphalia marked the end of the confessional wars and the bankruptcy of the time-stained principle that it was right for Christians to fight for the church that embodied their understanding of spiritual truth. But its significance would surely have been less clear to contemporaries than it was to become with the growth of scientific materialism and the corresponding search, among educated Christians, for new ground on which to base a reasonable faith.

God guided man on his precarious course through the world, which was but one stage in an eternal journey. The devil sought to waylay and divert him. Belief in witchcraft was losing its hold upon educated men in the seventeenth century, but less evidently so among the masses, who continued to reflect the view of so many educated men of the Renaissance period that there existed a complete alternative religion, a deadly menace to the Christian. There was indeed nothing comparable, after about 1640, to the witch holocaust of south Germany and the Rhineland in the early decades of the century. The prince bishop of Bamburg (1623–33), Johann von Dornheim, had found 600 witches to burn in his modest estate. Just as the earlier purges followed the recovery of Catholicism during the early years of the Thirty Years War, so the outbreak of witch-burning in Sweden coincided with the postwar return to rigorous orthodoxy in the Lutheran churches. By then, however, the intellectual climate was altering. Why there should have been a falling off in the persecution of poor people, sometimes beggars, usually women, for alleged complicity with Satan and the powers of darkness, is still a matter for debate, as is the extent to which the prevalence of persecution in the previous century reflects conflicts over religious doctrine or the oppressive poverty of rural communities, further distressed by war; its causes lie in a dark area of collective psychology upon which the historian must hesitate to pronounce. It is notable however that the decline coincided with the general imposition of stricter discipline at the parish level, with firmer leadership from educated clergy. It is interesting too that the witch craze never affected Spain or Italy where extensive monastic charity alleviated the plight of the poor and heresy was controlled by the Inquisition. Most important surely was the scrutiny of magistrates and the revulsion of educated men. It found legislative expression in the French edict of 1682 which defined magic and witchcraft as crimes, but crimes only of deception. By the eighteenth century everywhere, trials were rare and executions isolated, bizarre events.

The Reformation had torn apart the 'seamless robe' of institutional Christianity. For many Protestants the fabric of a Church-ordered society had gone beyond recall. For the Catholic majority, however, the supremacy of the Pope, the hierarchy of saints, the cult of the Virgin Mary, the necessity of seven sacraments, the doctrines of transubstantiation and the real presence, the practice of Communion in one kind, together with the expectation of purgatory, the efficacy of relics and benefits of pilgrimage, were more clearly known and more cherished than ever. For the Catholic, faith seems to have consisted less in a personal sense of God's mercy; rather in acceptance of the truth as revealed by God and as presented and interpreted by the Church. By 1660 the dividing lines between the confessions had become permanent and were to change remarkably little thereafter. They had come to represent more than different interpretations of Christian doctrine and practice. There were now clearer lines, as if the war of movement had given way to a phase of entrenchment in which the process of attrition was only tempered by the indifference of one commander or a rare switch of allegiance in another. At the level of parish and congregation differences could bear fruit in communal zeal and personal devotion. But at more rarified levels, where new perceptions in science and philosophy were beginning to affect modes of belief, the continued failure of Christians to agree about what appeared to be fundamental articles of faith could not fail to be damaging.[1]

The prolonged efforts of Christian apologists, like Jacques-Bénigne Bossuet (1627–1704) and Gottfried Wilhelm von Leibnitz (1646–1716), to find a basis for reunion were unsuccessful. Leibnitz believed that the Lutheran church should negotiate reunion as a body and managed to persuade some Lutherans in Hanover to sign articles of reconciliation which began by recognizing the Pope's claim to be head of the Church. Bossuet with whom he corresponded did not share the common Catholic assumption that Protestant heresy sprang from human malice or the devil's machinations and his *Exposition de la doctrine catholique* was so moderate that he was charged with watering down Roman doctrines to appeal to heretics. But he would not give way on the issue of papal authority. Each man stood for much that was good in his respective position. The way in which the world of ideas was changing is reflected in the bishop's experience. Court preacher and tutor, historian, political theorist and theologian, Bossuet expounded, notably in his *Politique tirée de l'écriture sainte* and *Discours sur l'histoire universelle*, a view of the world and its history that was based upon his reading of the Old Testament: he regarded it as verbally inspired, the laws, prophets and patriarchs there described evincing God's purpose, as did the subsequent experience of the Christian centuries. He believed in the unity of knowledge, as so many branches from the one tree of Christian truth; therefore, in the unity of history. The theme of his *Histoire des variations* was that the Protestant churches were discredited by their differences, severed branches from the tree, and so cut off from the truth in unity. The compelling logic and magisterial writing had a profound

[1] For further discussion of changing religious and philosophical views in the context of the Enlightenment, see also pp. 123ff.

influence upon his contemporaries. But their shakiness became apparent as men began to test the hypotheses and find them wanting.

Scholarly criticism of the Bible, notably by the Oratorian Richard Simon (1638–1712), author of *Histoire critique du vieux testament* (1678), attempts of Christian rationalists like Nicholas Malebranche (1638–1715) to create a new synthesis to combat the pantheism of Spinoza, and the quest of Fénelon and others for a religion of the heart sapped the traditional theology. From outside the theologian's world, travellers' accounts of other civilizations which apparently owed nothing to Judaism or Christianity, and the evidence of the geologist's trowel for a much older world than that supposed by Bossuet to have been created in 4004 BC posed more questions than they answered. Perhaps most damaging in the long run was the sensationalist psychology of John Locke for whom there were no innate ideas, so that *all* religion could have had its origin in the early experience of man. Locke was influential upon his correspondent Pierre Bayle (1647–1706), the exiled Huguenot, who found such a wide audience for his two great undertakings, the *Nouvelles de la république des lettres* and the *Dictionnaire historique et critique*. In the controversy with his dogmatic fellow Huguenot, Pierre Jurieu, he did lasting damage to the accepted procedure, that of argument from texts, when he asserted that no isolated statement could be valid against the general sense of the Gospels and natural decency. His *Pensées diverses sur la comète* (1683) scrutinized the superstitious belief that comets were divine warnings of disasters to come. Was there good reason to rely upon tradition when there was no historical or scientific evidence to support it? Why should men suppose that God should concern Himself directly, immediately, in man's affairs? The questions were baffling to Bossuet, a lonely giant at the centre of this 'crisis of the European conscience' which was really a crisis *within* Christianity. He ended his days fighting his 'great battle' for the Church with untiring pen, but with a rancour which betrays, perhaps, his awareness of the disintegration of a system.

Mathematician, jurist and philosopher, encyclopedic in his knowledge and interests in the world of ideas, surely the most influential German between Luther and Goethe, Leibnitz fashioned out of his own struggle between the requirements of rational method and the prompting of his Lutheran conscience a coherent system of belief in which God remained pre-eminent and still a free agent, presiding over a harmonious world in which there was no necessity for doctrinal conflict. In Leibnitz can be seen the benevolence that characterizes the new theology, liberated as it was from dogma and tradition. 'You are right,' he wrote in 1691, 'to call me a Catholic at heart; I am even one openly.... But the essence of Catholicity is not external communion with Rome. The true and essential communion, which makes us members of Jesus Christ, is charity.' There was also the optimistic assurance that a loving God had created the best possible world whose inherent goodness could even be demonstrated, through contrast, by the existence of evil. Leibnitz's thought was subtle, constantly evolving, never summarized in a comprehensive work; known therefore only to his correspondents and disciples among whom Christian Wolff (1674–1754), the leading rationalist of his generation of German intellectuals, was most influential. He made a system out of Leibnitz's random writings and in the process altered their spirit. Wolff, rather than Leibnitz, whom he misrepresented as a cool and bland logician, was responsible for the complacent message, so acceptable to those in authority, but ridiculed by Voltaire, that 'all was for the best in the best of all possible worlds'.

The efforts of Bossuet to shore up the old, those of Leibnitz to provide the foundations for a new building, might sustain and inspire men of like spirit. But by 1700, some of the more daring or merely fashionable of the educated world, while continuing to live off the inherited capital of the Christian centuries, were beginning to doubt the worth of their inheritance. There may have been reassurance to men troubled by intellectual doubts but there was little to inspire devotion, in the formulations of the English 'latitudinarian' school, for example, who sought to reduce theological differences to insignificance by applying to faith the sole test of reasonableness. For subscribers to the undemanding, undogmatic faith of *Christianity not Mysterious* (the title of John Toland's work of 1696), emotional certainty was suspect, 'enthusiasm' was positively dangerous. But the critical spirit was not thus easily contained; the doubt which had been the Cartesians' point of departure was not to be stilled by the process of reduction to an uncontroversial minimum. From seeing God as the creator of a mechanistic universe which thereafter, because it embodied His perfection, could, indeed should, function without His further intervention, it was but a short step to doubting His existence altogether. For all the efforts of the synthesizers, science and philosophy became detached from theology; the religious spirit became perceptibly less influential in the small but dominant world of intellect, power and fashion which prided itself on being 'enlightened'.

There was, however, a time-lag in the transmission of new ideas, which was neither so sudden nor so dramatic as is conveyed by Paul Hazard's celebrated aphorism: 'one day the French were thinking like Bossuet; all of a sudden they began to think like Voltaire'. Paradoxes and inconsistencies abounded, showing something of the agonized reluctance with which the most thoughtful and sensitive abandoned old ideas and their yearning for a true understanding of God. Simon believed, perhaps rightly, that he was strengthening true religion by his scholarly perusal of texts. Locke denied toleration to the atheists. Bayle believed that his elimination of the possibility of miracles led to an enhanced view of 'God's infinite greatness' in the maintenance of laws which He himself established.

Schooling was still limited, and relatively few, even among the literate, were at first exposed to the new ideas. Only in Lutheran Sweden did the ideal of a school in every parish approximate to the reality. The masses of Europe continued to be illiterate, but the vitality of Christian belief was not confined to the less privileged areas of society. The persistent conservatism of this family-based culture should not be overlooked. Christians held on everywhere to what they learned at the fireside. If they went to school they were likely to be taught by clerics, more firmly than ever under ecclesiastical control. Most of the tasks carried out today by secular authorities, starting with registration, were then the responsibility of the Church. When men went to church they probably heard orthodox doctrine with an emphasis on the duty of obedience. The reforms of the previous century had their effect in tighter parochial discipline, more efficient clergy, more devoted pastoral care. Everywhere the evidence of the eighteenth century tells of a more active church life; more regular communions in Catholic parishes, the growing influence of Pietism in Germany and Scandinavia, more Bibles, breviaries and pious works distributed and read; less superstition and more faithful rendering of Christian doctrine. Nor should music, conveying awe and joy to many whom words might not reach, be forgotten. Much of the finest baroque music, especially in Germany, where the tradition of the chorale was particularly strong, was composed for singing in churches. The seventeenth may have been the last Christian century, the last that is when the Christian faith commanded the intellectual heights, unchallenged in essentials: when to be sceptical was to be eccentric. The eighteenth century was above all the age of popular piety, before the development of an industrial society, with concurrent shifts of population and the appearance of a new popular culture whose materialism reflected some of the cruder and more negative aspects of 'advanced' science and philosophy. Before that transformation of society, even in the most sophisticated circles, there were always influential voices to remind men of the uncompromising standards of Christianity. Meanwhile, among those for whom reason proved a barren guide to life's complexities, 'enthusiasm' appeared in a series of movements, like that of Pietism in Germany and Methodism in England, which showed that men were still hungry for an authentic Christian message. The most notable effect of the Enlightenment was upon that ground where Church leaders met the 'philosophers' and gave an inadequate account of themselves, where the traditional clerical position was exposed to destructive criticism. In this new climate, so favourable to the growth of one species or another of the genus 'natural religion', the Church was coming to look more like a man-made institution, less like the body of Christ. Locke saw it as 'a voluntary society of men, joining together of their own accord to the publick worshipping of God'. Where the leadership of the Church was blind or unresponsive to the need to adapt, where it was excessively privileged, there can be seen most clearly the nature of that crisis of authority which threatened to destroy the traditional structure entirely; during the French

Revolution, in France at least, it did so. Everywhere in the eighteenth century the churches were losing their influence on politics. Nowhere is that to be seen more plainly than in the condition of the papacy which embodied a single authority, unique and sanctioned by God.

The Papacy

Queen Christina of Sweden was one of a number of prominent Protestants who led a trend to Roman Catholicism in the middle years of the seventeenth century. Better-educated clergy, expanding missionary work, resplendent churches, witnessed to the vitality of the Church. Yet it is beyond question that the authority of the popes was already declining. 'Who now fears the Pope?' wrote Rome's most distinguished convert in her copy of Machiavelli's *Prince*. 'Here are statues, obelisks and palaces, but of men there are none.' The papacy entered the eighteenth century ill-equipped to meet the intellectual or political challenges of an increasingly secular age. It would have needed an exceptional man and a long period of office to have arrested the decline. The institution lacked continuity as each pope came to serve out the last dozen years or so of a life spent most probably in diplomacy and administration.

If we look at the promotion of cardinals we find that there are interests to be satisfied that had little to do with the well-being of the Church. Louis XIV, for example, insisted upon the elevation of Forbes Jansen, whose main achievement had been to persuade the Turks to go to war with the Emperor. Cardinals, whatever their background, tended to range themselves in parties, Italian, Spanish or French, and to respond to political pressures. When they came to elect a pope they looked usually for a safe man, acceptable to the majority, ageing, preferably with an understanding of the complex machinery of papal government and experience of the Curia or diplomacy; amiable manners, literary and artistic interests would weigh more than a record of radical reforms or profound theology. A pope elected on these terms sought to survive without yielding too much to rulers who wanted virtual independence for their churches, or to doctrinal pressure groups, like the Jansenists, who sought his support for their cause. The man might grow with the office. Clement XI (1700–21), canon lawyer and administrator, was not ordained priest until 1700 and celebrated his first Mass two days before the opening of the conclave that elected him. The pope of *Unigenitus* (1713) and the pitiless campaign against the Jansenists showed that he was ready to fall in with the wishes of a strong ruler. He was a better man, however, than is suggested by the famous remark of Victor Amadeus, that he would always have been esteemed worthy of the papacy if he had never obtained it. He showed a special interest in the training of priests for the mission field.

To adjust to a changing world, to keep on terms with Erastian princes, to embellish the churches and squares of the Eternal City, to live without scandal and to make necessary reforms in the government of the Papal States, were more typical aims of the popes in an age which began with a pope vainly condemning the peace of Westphalia and ended with the suppression of the Jesuit order in 1774 at the behest of the Catholic powers. Innocent X (1644–55) was among the weakest of them, dominated in practical affairs by his sister-in-law Olympia Maidalchini, who dispensed patronage more generously than wisely. Innocent XI (1676–89), reformer of monasteries, zealous crusader, patron of schemes of reunion and conversion (but not of Louis XIV's onslaught upon the Huguenots) would by contrast be impressive in any company. With an austere and proud manner that recalls the great medieval popes went sufficient toughness and skill to stand up to Louis XIV at his most formidable. The struggle over Gallicanism brought out his combative spirit but diverted his energies from more fruitful business.

The history of two eighteenth-century popes reveals problems of a different sort. Benedict XIII (1724–30) had been a Dominican friar. He was too unworldly to prevent government from falling into the hands of a clique who left an unsavoury reputation for corruption. His successor, Clement XII, from the Curia, began by imprisoning Benedict's aide, Cardinal Coscio, but could not maintain the impetus of reform.

In 1648 Nuncio Chigi could do no more than protest against the Westphalia peace settlements. Thirteen years later, at the Pyrenees negotiations, the same Chigi, now Alexander VII (1655–67), mathematician and patron of Bernini and other baroque artists, was not even represented. At the treaty of Utrecht, the papal fiefs of Sicily and Sardinia were disposed of as if the papacy had not existed. At a time when power was measured by the size of a prince's army, the Pope was being treated as a territorial prince of no greater significance, for all the traditions of his office, than any other of comparable wealth and lands: more than Lorraine, but perhaps less than Venice. The advance of the Protestant states, England, Holland and Brandenburg, was partly responsible for this. Equally significant in this process of devaluation was the aggressive conduct of the greatest Catholic sovereign, Louis XIV.

Established churches were also political agencies. It was not only in Lutheran Sweden or nominally Calvinist Brandenburg for example that the clergyman was a necessary link in the chain of government: without his voice and his practical services, not least as registrar, it would be difficult to bring the masses to accept the state and to pay its dues. But that clergyman, even in those countries, like England, where the sovereign was head of the church, belonged to an organization in some degree separate and independent. The fact that bishoprics, deaneries, abbacies were commonly in the gift of the state provided a means of influence. In Catholic countries papal confirmation was required; their rulers were as keen as Lutherans to keep control of appointments and so to reinforce the official body while ensuring that it remained theirs to command. The close identification of Church and state in Spain is exemplified by the fact that the Inquisition, that effective instrument of censorship and surveillance, was under royal rather than under papal control. 'What could exist without a dominant religion?' asked the devout Maria Theresa. It is a moot question whether France would have remained officially Catholic if Francis I had not gained the powers he required by the concordat of Bologna in 1516, the year before Luther posted his fateful theses, or if he had been blocked, as Henry VIII was over his divorce question, in some equally vital matter of state. Behind the sovereign's rights over the appointment of bishops lay the potent principles of absolute sovereignty: that kings had their authority direct from God and had all property at their disposal. Even in its most extreme form absolutism was not in theory incompatible with the spiritual claims of the Church. 'Render unto Caesar the things that are Caesar's and unto God the things that are God's'; the text was not neglected. But in practice there was ground for conflict when it came to deciding what, among the endowments of the Church, did belong to Caesar. The possibility of schism continued to cast a shadow over the calculations of the Vatican, whether it was dealing with the traditional Gallicanism of Louis XIV or the radical anticlericalism of the Emperor Joseph II.

To secure the independence of the French church and to fortify his own authority Louis XIV did not shrink from damaging the papacy. The affair of the Corsican Guards (1662–4), when a quarrel over the rights of the French ambassador at Rome was used by Louis to win a well-publicized diplomatic victory, was but the opening cannonade before the serious battle over the *régale*: that issue was extended until the whole relationship of king and pope was involved. The *régale* was an old right of the French monarchy, in respect of its original lands, by which, during the vacancy of a see, the king could appoint to benefices within its gift and receive its revenue. In 1673 Louis issued an edict extending the right, which had been understood to pertain only to the original provinces of the kingdom, to the whole of France. Innocent XI stood firm while dioceses fell vacant and were left unfilled (thirty by the end of his life) and a stream of propaganda washed about, publicizing the feud.

The king looked to the Assembly of Clergy for support against the Pope, and a committee of the Assembly produced the Four Articles affirming the king's independence in temporal matters (1682). The Pope protested; and the Assembly retorted: 'The Gallican church governs itself by its own laws.' When Louis bid for the leadership of Catholic Europe by revoking the edict of Nantes (1685) and thereby irreparably damaged the schemes of reunion in which Innocent was interested, the latter was not impressed. He confirmed the appointment of Clement of Bavaria to the archbishopric of Cologne, at the expense of Louis's candidate; in 1688 Louis seized Avignon, the Pope's possession in the south of France, while his foreign minister issued a manifesto stating his grievances against the Pope as a 'Jansenist, Quietist and supporter of the heretic William of Orange'. Catholicism presented anything but the united front to which Bossuet attached such importance in controversy with the Huguenots. By the time a settlement was patched up by the rigidly orthodox Innocent XII (1691–1700), upon the basis of acceptance of the Gallican Articles coupled with an understanding that they would not be enforced, the damage had been done. Nor was it repaired by the entente of Louis's last years, as he returned to orthodoxy and sought papal aid against the Jansenists. The Curia may, however, have derived a wry satisfaction from the difficulties in which Louis then found himself when he tried to win from *parlement* approval, and registration, of the bull *Unigenitus* and was confronted by those very Gallican principles which he had formerly espoused.

The Gallican quarrel illustrates a trend which is noticeable before the full impact of 'enlightened' ideas and secular notions of sovereignty made itself felt. Spain, where the Inquisition came under royal and not papal control, had what amounted to a state church long before the severe concordat of 1753. The Emperor would sometimes treat Rome as an Italian principality in league with his enemies; the nuncio was expelled from Vienna in 1705 and imperial troops later violated Roman territories. When they expelled the Jesuits in 1759 the Portuguese precipitated a crisis in the Vatican which was not finally to be resolved until the abolition of the Society in 1773. Elections exposed the prevailing attitude. There was bargaining like that which preceded the election of a king of Poland. At the conclave of 1700, the French cardinals agreed to the election of Albani (Clement XI) only after sounding the views of their ambassador. The great sovereigns still behaved as if Catholic Christendom needed the Pope; but even such an able and enlightened pope as Benedict XIV (1675–1758) had to make concessions which weakened his authority.

The most constructive challenge to that authority came from the ideas of von Hontheim, an official of the elector of Trier, who wrote under the pseudonym Febronius. He proposed in his book *Concerning the Condition of the Church and the Legitimate Power of the Pope* (1763) that the Pope, being fallible, should be subordinate to the Church; appeals from his decisions should be carried to a general council. The Church should be decentralized and the Pope be merely primate among bishops. In every country, authority should be exercised by national or provincial synods. It is striking that these ideas, essentially a new version of ideas current in the fourteenth and fifteenth centuries, should have emanated from a Catholic stronghold and that they attracted widespread support. The radical assault of the Emperor Joseph II upon the Church, its lands, monasteries, schools and rites, culminating in the patent of toleration (1781) demonstrates how vulnerable the papacy had become even before the Revolution came to pose problems of a new and larger dimension. In 1782 Pope Pius VI took the unprecedented step of travelling to Vienna to recall the Emperor to his Catholic duty. He was received with cold formality and came away with no concessions. Joseph made it plain that he intended nothing less than personal control of the Church in his lands, and he used it to reorganize dioceses, to reform seminaries and to endow hospitals. The peasants, who loved their painted churches, relics and pilgrimages, resented the interference of Joseph and his bureaucrats, and greeted the Pope rapturously. In their devotion, Pius may have seen what was to be the true strength of the papacy in the future. His successor Pius VII underwent another chastening experience when he went to Paris (1804) to seal the concordat and crown Napoleon. It was the beginning of a struggle during the course of which he was bullied, deprived of power, actually imprisoned. But he contributed, by his staunch resistance, to the downfall of the Emperor and to the revival of clerical influence in Europe. The papacy survived its crisis.

Jansenism

Further tensions and other challenges to authority arose from the differences between those religious attitudes which were in some way absolute, intense or demanding – or, as the eighteenth-century Englishman might call them, 'enthusiastic' – and those which were more formal, reflecting one or other of the compromises which most Christians found it necessary to make with the world they lived in. The history of Jansenism in France provides an example of Christians who set themselves the highest standards, rejected compromise, and attracted, like the Huguenots, though for different reasons, the unfriendly attention of the government.

Several strands went into the making of the Jansenist movement. Puritan, legalistic, exclusive and perfectionist, they were disciples in the first place of Cornelius Jansen (1583–1638), the Flemish bishop, scholar and anti-French propagandist, and St Cyran (1581–1643), mystic, experienced confessor and a *dévôt* of the most extreme kind. They saw themselves variously as reformers in a corrupt society, pioneers seeking to rediscover the vitality of the early Church, rationalists, seeking truth by adherence to the rules of Descartes, and guardians of true doctrine against the lax standards and moral compromises of churchmen who were so intent upon winning souls that they became cynical about the methods they employed. Their conspiratorial airs, the connections with those *dévôts* who opposed his foreign policy, had aroused Richelieu's suspicion. He may have seen in St Cyran another Calvin, a threat to orthodoxy and a source of schism. Theologically, notably in their view of God's grace, Jansenists were close to Calvin: they held that the majority whom grace did not touch were irrevocably damned. In their attitudes towards the Church they inclined towards an extreme Gallicanism. Their condemnation of dancing and gambling offended Richelieu, patron of music and ballet, as it did Louis XIV, the master of a sumptuous court. Not all Jansenists followed St Cyran in his morbid extravagance of language, but strains of hysteria did persist. Pierre Nicole (1625–95) illustrates what could come from a pessimistic temperament dwelling on the consequences of the Fall in a world where man was denied free will. Writing in his *Crainte de Dieu* of the justice of God which 'plunges men into the abyss of eternal torture', he went on: 'We pass our days in this spiritual carnage .... The world by which we are carried along is a river of blood; to perish one merely has to allow oneself to be carried along.' Happily Jansenism had a nobler, less negative character than such words would suggest.

The home of Jansenism was Port Royal: two institutions but one in spirit. Both the Paris convent in the Faubourg Saint-Jacques, where Jacqueline and Agnes Arnauld reformed the discipline according to the precepts of their confessor St Cyran, and the male community of Port Royal des Champs, a house of retreat for devout laymen, were dominated by a few families. Six Arnauld girls had entered the convent by 1640; one, Mme de Maître, was a widow; with her were her four daughters. Three of her sons were solitaries; a younger brother, Antoine, kept closely in touch. When he wrote *De la fréquente Communion* he was not merely presenting the Jansenist case to his own world of the sophisticated bourgeoisie and that in a year, 1643, when the whole political structure of France was in jeopardy after the deaths of Richelieu and Louis XIII. He was also following a family tradition in attacking the Jesuits for his father had led the opposition in *parlement* to the return of the Jesuits to France in Henry IV's reign. The argument of the book was that the Jesuits debased the sacraments by allowing easy penance and encouraged the idea of salvation on cheap terms; in the Jansenist view that was the natural consequence of a mistaken view of divine grace. The Jesuits attacked the book as an indictment of their methods and a threat to their existence. The battle, so evidently fascinating to contemporaries, centred on five propositions, alleged by the syndic of the Sorbonne to be contained in Jansen's *Augustinus* and to be heretical, and condemned as such by bull of Pope Innocent X in 1653. The Jansenist defence was based upon questioning the *fact* that the propositions were contained in the original work; thus they hoped to avoid questioning the *right* of the Church to condemn them.

The quarrel was raised to a higher level by the intervention of the mathematician Blaise Pascal on behalf of Antoine. His *Lettres provinciales*, the first of which appeared in January 1656, the month in which his friend was formally censured by the Sorbonne, were printed anonymously by different presses; they purported to be letters from a country gentleman, staying in Paris, to a friend. Pascal's weapons were intimate knowledge of the doctrinal issues and of the character of the Jesuit order, a sharp understanding of the power of ridicule and, above all, a mastery of style which makes the *Lettres* a landmark in the development of French literature. Though scrupulous about facts, Pascal did not hesitate to play on bourgeois xenophobia. His view of the Jesuits is a distorted one because he concentrated upon their methods in this domestic affair, in particular upon their use of moral case law. Yet the merit of the Jansenist position, their scorn for any form of intellectual chicanery, was never more finely expressed. The combativeness and exclusive pride of Port Royal can also be discerned. Pascal wrote in the confidence of his new-found faith and did not stop to think of the damage he was doing to the Church. No wonder that Voltaire enjoyed the letters. He said that the early ones were as witty as Molière, the latter as grand as Bossuet. Pascal helped to create the climate of public opinion in which, after protracted negotiations, the conscience-saving formulary of 1669 was devised and the Jansenist nuns who accepted it were left to enjoy the 'Peace of the Church': they signed 'purely and simply' instead of 'sincerely'. The true significance of the affair lies in the attitudes: extreme, dramatic, but authentic expressions of contrasting Christian values. The Church would have been less active as a force for good in the world if the crusading Jesuit order had been denied scope for its work in missions and schools; the world would have been poorer without the Jansenists' single-minded affirmation of Christian standards. The argument, like the attitudes, was perpetual. It did not need the support of notorious *frondeurs*, like the duchesse de Longueville, to keep Port Royal on the government's agenda. Pascal and Arnauld had ensured that the Jesuits would return to the attack.

Jansenism made significant converts, with some ardent sympathizers, like Pavillon and Caulet among the bishops, and acquired a certain respectability, losing in the process some of its air of unworldliness. The movement remained a small one, if judged by the number of avowed supporters of Port Royal and exponents of Augustinian theology. But it became increasingly influential through the Oratory, with its seminaries for the training of priests upon the fashionable Cartesian principles, as adopted notably by Pierre Nicole (1625–95), author of a book on logic for Jansenist schools. Jansenists of his generation were busy, practical men, concerned with teaching, converting Huguenots, translating for their Bible of Mons, working on reform of the liturgy, looking for salvation from lives of practical goodness. Persecution was resumed under Harlay, archbishop of Paris; the disgrace of Pomponne, the Jansenist foreign minister in 1679, removed a powerful protector. The truculence of their foremost protagonist, Pasquier Quesnel, and his challenging work, *Réflexions morales sur le Nouveau Testament* (1678), invited aggression. Harlay's successor, Noailles, elected in 1695, tried to protect them, but the Jesuits found support at Versailles and at Rome. At court, Mme de Maintenon was the embodiment of pious conformity while Pope Clement XI (1700–21), having secured a settlement of the Gallican question, was anxious to sustain the orthodoxy of the king.

Louis XIV could not, however, look so easily to Rome for support. His *volte face* invited opposition from *parlement*, where Gallican and antipapal sentiments had hitherto been encouraged; his drive against the Huguenots was visibly failing; meanwhile the quietist affair presented the disturbing spectacle of the two most famous churchmen in the country, Bossuet and Fénelon, in public dispute.

Louis paid dearly for condemnation of the Jansenists – an indication of how seriously he took them.[1] Port Royal refused to accept a bull cancelling the compromise solution of 1669, and in 1710 the two houses were suppressed; the remaining nineteen nuns were sent to other houses. Jansenist doctrines, however, remained intact; indeed, persecution strengthened their influence. In 1713 the bull *Unigenitus* anathematized 101 propositions extracted from Quesnel's book. Gallicans lined up in the Sorbonne and *parlement* to fight under the leadership of Noailles, and with the support of several ministers. Louis, who had already been concerned about the democratic character of some Jansenist ideas, now faced a general resistance for the first time. He accepted the bull on behalf of the nation – but *parlement* did not register it until 1720, five years after his death. In the later history of the movement, the excesses of some of its wilder supporters, like the convulsionaries who claimed miracles and danced around the tomb of the saintly deacon Paris at St Medard, and the apocalyptic tendencies of those who began 'to look for a sign', should be distinguished from the persistent underground of resistance: a demoralizing factor in Church life that was nourished by Jansenist-minded priests and lawyers. A constant irritant was provided by the *billets de confession* which bishops required before a man might attend the sacrements, testifying to his having confessed to an orthodox priest. Eventually, in 1756 Pope Benedict XIV disallowed them.

It is easy to see how Jansenist ideas merged in this situation with the growing resentment of the lower clergy, usually, after the middle of the seventeenth century, seminary-trained, more open to the cultural influences of the Enlightenment and more critical of the wealth and privileges of aristocratic bishops and abbots. The 'Jansenism' of the eighteenth century, significant in its contribution to the Enlightenment, and so to the Revolution, was for *parlement* a new version of Gallicanism, while the continuing struggle provided its leaders with practice in the techniques of resistance, taking advantage of procedure gambits, drafting pleas and speeches in a carefully orchestrated campaign. The effect was to damage the institutional support for faith which the Jansenists desired to save from the ungodly.

Jansenism had originated in the Netherlands and there alone had kept its early theological character. When the Dutch Catholics refused to accept the bull *Unigenitus*, the Pope refused to invest their bishops and pronounced

[1] See also pp. 291–5 and pp. 315–19 for the political significance of Jansenism in Louis XIV's and Louis XV's reigns.

them schismatical. Venice, where the antipapal tradition was strong, also refused the bull. Even in the southern Netherlands draconian measures against the Louvain theological faculty were withdrawn before they could be imposed in 1730. In Spain Jansenism provided precedents and arguments for anticlericals and opponents of Jesuits and the Inquisition. German Jansenism illustrates another aspect of this wide-ranging movement; there it took name and colour from Febronius, a pupil of the Flemish jurist van Espen and author of *The Present State of the Church and the Legitimate Power of the Roman Pontiff* (1763). Febronians advocated the elevation of the ruler's authority above that of the Church and looked forward to the accession of Joseph to the Habsburg empire where the power of the Church was so strong, so well endowed through its schools, so influential in society. Jansenism, contributing everywhere to the anticlericalism of the Enlightenment, had altered almost beyond recognition from the earlier movement of the pioneers of Port Royal. But one feature remained constant: hostility to the Jesuits. The downfall of the Jesuits and the progressive policies of Catholic sovereigns in the late eighteenth century meant that theological Jansenism faded away everywhere, except in France, where it continued to be influential at parish level. Even there, however, it was in the main a revival of the teaching of Edmond Richer who had claimed that the government of the Church belonged to its own pastors. The radical *curé* of the *cahiers* of 1789 cared more about his fair share of tithe and a say in the running of his church than about rival doctrines of grace and will. He came into his inheritance with the Civil Constitution of the Clergy of 1790, providing for a state-controlled and salaried church, with elective bishops: a radical departure indeed from Catholic tradition.

Quietism

Jansenism, in its theological character, was a harking back to the spirit of the sixteenth-century reformers: a revulsion from the conservative definitions of the council of Trent (ended in 1564). The same process can be seen in the devotional sphere. Reformers had protested against the emptiness of institutional religion and insisted upon the right of every individual to seek a direct way to his God. The Church, after Trent, frowned upon enthusiasm and sought to insure against future aberrations of thought and devotion. No effort should be spared, no adornment of art or architecture was superfluous in the enhancement of worship. Spreading from Rome, its spiritual home, the baroque style celebrated the victory of Rome and the dogmatic certainties of the Tridentine decrees. Figures of the saints, reliquaries, reredoses and baldachinos witnessed, with the poetry of movement that was the special feature of the style, to the efficacy of prayers to the dead, the mediation of saints and the mystery of transubstantiation. Intellectual acceptance is assumed; passion, awe and mystery are the more confidently evoked.

The Jesuits were leading patrons of the baroque: the *Gesù* in Rome is a sublime expression of their outward-looking, adventurous spirit, grounded as it was upon a stern inner discipline. Like a sermon by Bossuet, or a composition by Vivaldi, the exuberant flourishes of the great baroque artists carry conviction because they embellish structures that are strictly classical in design.

Aids to devotion alone could not satisfy those ardent few who, as in all ages, looked for a mystical experience of the reality of God. The Church was always on its guard against those who claimed that it was possible to find a private way, by some exercise of mind or imagination. The dangers were plain: mystics might feel that they had no need of the ministrations of the Church, they might even hold themselves absolved from normal restraints upon conduct. It was hard to draw the line between the authentic mystical experience that is the aspiration of the saint, and self-delusion. Validity was best judged in the context of the person's whole life and friends. St Theresa and St John of the Cross, the greatest of the Spanish school of mystics, had been accepted and canonized. The Illuminists of Seville and Cadiz, 7000 of them, who claimed that mental prayer alone was necessary for salvation and that they could thus be perfected, were condemned by the Inquisition in 1623. The case alarmed the orthodox, and suited the authoritarian. (It helps explain Richelieu's wary attitude towards Bérulle and the Oratory, Spanish in Christo-centric theology, as in political sympathy.) St Ignatius, founder of the Jesuits, author of the *Exercitia spiritualia*, had taught that the soul, by psychological effort, could be trained to see itself in the light of eternity. Some mystics thought that this methodical approach was unnecessary since they were called by divine voice to the 'prayer of quiet' in which God required the subject to adhere to Him. One such was Miguel Molinos, Spanish priest, condemned by the Inquisition in 1687. Judgement of such a man, holy man, charlatan, whatever he may have been, is necessarily subjective, now as then. Groups of quietists in Italy, Spain and France regarded him as their leader. When he was arrested he had 12,000 letters from devotees. The most famous of them was Mme Guyon, though she came to her own 'peace of God' in eccentric fashion. Her fame derives largely from the support of archbishop Fénelon (1651–1715) and from the battle he fought, against Bishop Bossuet, for the validity of her sort of mystical experience.

The problem that Mme Guyon posed to those who had to examine her was formidable. Bossuet, rational and orthodox, for whom mysticism was 'essentially a lamentable extravagance, a kind of spiritual failing tempting the odder saints', noted that she sat opposite her friends in complete silence, acting as a reservoir through which grace flowed into them. In her writing she seems to relate herself in a literal and sensuous way to God. In Fénelon's sympathy there was no doubt much of his own longing for a richer spiritual life than his duties at Versailles allowed. His brave partisanship should be set in the context of a more far-reaching protest – against what he and his friends saw as the perversion by a militarist and despotic regime of the proper role of the king: the defence of the interests of Church and people. Unfortunately Fénelon became so entangled in the affair as to become politically ineffective at a time when his voice should have been heard. In 1695 the Articles of Issy defined the limits beyond which the mystic must not go, disallowing any claim that extraordinary states of prayer were the only way to perfection. In 1699 Fénelon's *Maximes*, setting out what he held to be the authentic tradition of Christian mysticism, were condemned by the Pope. Ultimately, after long controversy, Fénelon was censured, though in mild terms. Bossuet had fought to save Church (and state) from what he saw as one insidious element in a general challenge to authority. Fénelon – more narrowly, or more imaginatively, according to one's point of view – had fought for the purity of faith.

Pietism

The movement of Pietism in Germany provides another example of the search for a religion of the heart. The aftermath of the Thirty Years War found the German Lutheran and Calvinist churches in disarray. Changes of prince and creed had induced bewilderment; political solutions to problems of spiritual allegiance had been discredited. The formula *cuius regio, eius religio* suited the constitution of a country minutely divided into over 300 sovereign units but it did little for the development of an active spiritual life. Catholicism retained the initiative. One notable conversion was that of Augustus the Strong of Saxony, though his Lutheran subjects were generally left in peace. However, in the Palatinate, 'Catholic' with the accession of Philip William in 1697, the largely Protestant population was subjected to intensive missionary work by the Jesuits. Everywhere the church was dependent on the ruler. Lutheran theology, with its notion of the 'Godly prince', tended to produce oppressive conditions. The Saxon system, in which the church was run by 'superintendents', instead of bishops, under the ruler operating as 'high magistrate', was widely imitated. In effect, ministers were subservient, laymen were allowed little part in church life and the ruler was encouraged to play the pope. Von Herder remarked of Prussia: 'A minister is only entitled to exist now, under state control, and by authority of the prince, as a moral teacher, a farmer, a list-maker, a secret agent of the police.' Von Herder was typical, however, of the better sort of minister, often university-trained. As in England, Holland and Scandinavia, there were devout and learned men to be found in the poorest parishes. The system rendered such men less effective than they might have been. Fear of witchcraft, and antisemitism kept their hold on the peasants; thought was contained in rigid patterns, teaching was often pedantic. More was heard of the civil advantages of a well-regulated clergy than of the unpredictable working of the Holy Spirit. The *Landeskirchen* (state churches) 'resembled a series of inland pools, stagnant save for exceptional inundations' (Drummond). Some refreshing dew came, however, from the movement of Pietism.

Pietism was not wholly new. There had been influential mystics, like Jacob Boehme, to keep alive the spirit of Luther. It was to the founding principles of the latter that P.J. Spener, author of *Pia desidera* (1675), appealed. He declared that the aim of true religion must be the transformation of personality. He urged pastors to preach the gospel and abandon controversy. To disseminate the word of God he set up *collegia pietatis*, centres where ministers and laymen could work together in fellowship. In 1694 the University of Halle was founded to serve as the centre of the rapidly growing movement. It was surrounded by a cluster of useful institutions: an orphanage, a printing press and a hospital; there were associated schools. The heart of the place was the theological faculty through which, at the height of its fame, over a thousand students passed every year. The flourishing life of Halle shows an unfamiliar side of the age of reason, and another, vital, Germany apart from the princes and their petty courts. One function of the University was indeed to supply the Prussian state with a flow of well-trained officials; but its hallmark was Christian philanthropy. Lutherans became more active in missionary work: Spener's successor, A.H. Franke, sponsored a mission to south India and sent Mühlenberg to America to organize Lutheran churches there. J.A. Bengel, a biblical scholar, of Württemberg saw the danger of pietists shrinking from corporate responsibility and taught that Christians must be active in their communities.

The challenge of rationalism nevertheless remained strong. Halle, for example, was also the home of Christian Wolff, professor of mathematics, who expounded a 'natural religion'. Frederick II of Prussia, imbued with the secular spirit of the Enlightenment, despised the values of the Christian gospel. For him the Pietists were 'protestant Jansenists'. In Scandinavia, notably in Denmark under King Christian VI (1730–46), Sabbatarianism and censorship were indeed the keynotes of an austere regime. But there was a generosity of spirit about German Pietists which challenges Frederick's assessment. Their teaching of the gospel reached the neglected poor. They strengthened the popular tradition of church music. They contributed to the revival of the German language and with it a degree of patriotic awareness, an influence whose importance becomes clearer in the age of Napoleon.

Where Pietists failed was in providing for future growth in church and cultural life by keeping a balance between spiritual ardour and intellectual vitality. There was a recurring mystical strain in German religion, prominent after times of prolonged misfortune, such as the Black Death or the Thirty Years War. 'Love may reach God but not knowing.' The spirit of *The Cloud of Unknowing* was reanimated in the extraordinary life and teaching of Count Lewis von Zinzendorf. He was a pupil of Franke at Halle but no system or training can account for his vision and style. Committed from childhood to Christian evangelism, influenced by the Bohemian Brethren for whom, in 1722, he provided a sanctuary on his Saxon estates, he devoted his life to the communities of brethren, Moravians, as they were called, through whose efforts he hoped to regenerate, and ultimately to unite, the churches of the world. He preached, and practised, a religion of love. Zinzendorf was apparently sincere in his plea for a childlike faith, and both practical and tough in his direction of a movement which could easily have degenerated into anarchy. The ideal of *Hernhut* (the name means 'Lord's protection'), and the Moravian settlements which were established elsewhere, was that of a disciplined, self-supporting fellowship in which men might come to a deeper experience of Christian love. He guarded it severely against lapses into hysteria, though he could not prevent – indeed perhaps contributed to – a cloyingly sentimental tone. Both the earnestness and the mawkishness anticipate the style of nineteenth-century evangelism.

Zinzendorf stood firmly against those who wanted to found a new church. Personal mission was what he held important, and the Moravians were the greatest Protestant missionaries of their time. In Greenland and Labrador they organized their native converts into Christian communities similar to those of the Jesuits in Paraguay. Like the Jesuits they encountered the hostility of established bodies in church and state. As it seemed to one Prussian cleric: 'Their leaders are gradually sapping the foundation of the civil government of any country they may settle in, and establishing an Empire within an Empire.' Moravians were to be important in the melting pot of the New World. But the most important contact was undoubtedly that with John Wesley, which changed Wesley's life and inspired his evangelical mission. The defence of individual rights, the example of men of gentle spirit, above all perhaps the concern for the poor and outcasts, were more significant than the infantile tendencies of some Moravians. But Zinzendorf limited the ground he worked on, and the prospects of his movement, by placing the main emphasis upon feeling as thus: 'He who wishes to comprehend God with his mind becomes an atheist.'

Intolerance: the Huguenot Case

When Louis XIV revoked his grandfather's edict of Nantes in October 1685 he embarked on the last stage of a policy of coercion which appears in retrospect to have been wholly misguided. Occupying a uniquely strong position he had allowed himself to be swayed by the vehemence of his Catholic subjects, represented by activists in the Church: devout, ambitious or simply conventional, they were not, as he was, in a position to judge the political consequences. His policy represented a fateful departure from the *politique* tradition epitomized in Richelieu's comment after the fall of La Rochelle in 1628: 'the conversion of the Reformed is a work we must await from heaven'. Unless the large reduction in the number of Protestants living in France be counted a gain, the policy must be judged a failure. The *intendant* Daguesseau may well have voiced the misgivings of many officials when he wrote that 'both Catholicism and the state will feel the consequences of this more keenly in the future than either has yet experienced'.[1] The central issue was one of authority and Louis's assertion of the rights of a ruler to dictate his subjects' religion stimulated debate wherever men pondered the issues of belief and freedom. Some 200,000 exiles were a powerful, far from silent witness for the case for toleration: as presented by Locke and his correspondent, the Huguenot exile Pierre Bayle, the case was better founded, intellectually and empirically, than at any time since the time of Erasmus, before the era of religious wars. There is substance therefore in the traditional idea that 1685 was a turning point in the history of Europe, whether it be seen from the standpoint of diplomacy, religion or political philosophy. But to go from there to assert that Louis was merely bigoted or blind is to misrepresent the case.

The peace of Westphalia had left Protestants and Roman Catholics in rough equilibrium in Germany. In the first decades after the war rulers seemed to be more realistic, shocked by losses and aware of limited resources. The Emperor Ferdinand III was more moderate than his father or his son. Louis XIV publically acknowledged the loyalty of Huguenots after the Fronde and at first adopted a conciliatory tone towards them. But old attitudes died hard and even then there were few signs of a positive spirit of toleration. Milton's *Areopagitica*, that fine defence of freedom of speech, specifically excluded popery from such freedom. It was a Huguenot, Benoît, who wrote that 'differences of religion disfigure a state'. It was normally assumed that the existence of a dissident minority was a cause of weakness. France was the only country in western Europe to have constitutionally guaranteed toleration of a religious minority. The tendency everywhere towards an Erastian submission of the church to the authority of the state and its God-ordained ruler, together with the movement in Catholic countries towards semi-independent national churches, were actually strengthening pressures for conformity. At the same time there was evidence that Rome was gaining ground again, the Protestant confessions were faltering and introspective. Queen Christina of Sweden, though she was notably eccentric and had already decided to abdicate, was perhaps the most celebrated among individual converts to Rome. The Emperor Ferdinand II had failed to win for Rome and Austria the triumphs for which he had prayed and schemed; but Bohemia at least had been recovered for the faith, the Jesuits completing what the soldiers had begun. In 1685 the accession of Philip of Neuburg, Catholic and father-in-law of the Emperor Leopold,

[1] See also pp. 291–2 for the revocation in the context of Louis XIV's government.

to the Palatinate, together with that of James II to the English throne, suggested a significant shift in the balance as Louis pondered the feasibility of the final solution. A series of measures had already sapped the strength of the Huguenots and, it seemed, the will of the remnant to hold out. In 1679 the *chambres de l'édit* had been abolished; in 1680 all marriages between Huguenots and Catholics were declared invalid. Between 1679 and 1683 Huguenots were debarred from one public profession after another. Their 'temples' were being closed. The promulgation, in 1682, of the Gallican articles, reaffirming the crown's rights in and over the church in France had clarified the issue of authority. At the end of 1684 a jury of theologians informed the scrupulous king that he could legitimately revoke his grandfather's 'perpetual and irrevocable' edict. The misgivings of Protestants had already been seen in timid declarations of submissiveness to the secular ruler or, in the case of the Lutherans, in a new interest in schemes of reunion.

There was a positive ideal and honourable tradition stretching back to the early years of the century, to Comenius, Althusius and Grotius, behind the ecumenical efforts of these years. Bishop Bossuet took seriously the ideas about reunion put forward by Paul Ferry, Lutheran pastor of Metz. Bishop Rojas y Spinola, who was also concerned, at the Pope's behest, with rallying support for the Emperor against the Turks, was travelling round Europe between 1678 and 1683 seeking backing for a fresh approach to the Lutheran question; he envisaged the meeting of a general council and a dialogue starting, at least, from the premise that Lutherans were not heretical. After the revocation such budding schemes were checked before they could bear fruit. It is likely, however, that Catholic insistence on the validity of the doctrines defined by the council of Trent would in any case have prevented reunion, even between Lutheran and Catholic. Leibnitz came to see them as an impassable obstacle even though he went so far towards the Catholic position that he was suspected of a secret conversion. Looking back from the present position in the unceasing quest for reunion, not entirely unlike that of the 1680s, we may be more surprised at the optimism of the ecumenical pioneers of 300 years ago than at the dogmatic attitudes of those who then sought not to compromise but to coerce. Daniel Jablonski (1660–1741) laboured in the congenial climate of Berlin to effect a union of Calvinist and Lutheran on the basis of common acceptance of a German translation of the English prayer book. In the short term greater weight was attached to those who, like Samuel Pufendorf (1632–94), the German jurist, argued for liberty of belief on the ground that the magistrate should have no authority over faith and opinion: 'it is no part of a prince's duty to prosecute those who differ from him in religion.' By 1660, wrote W.K. Jordan, summarizing the work of the liberal Calvinists of Holland, the Latitudinarians of England and the colonial pioneers of America, 'the theory of religious toleration stood substantially complete'. The theory had now been further tested in the times of persecution to such effect that the princes were ready to follow where philosophers pointed the way.

There was a strident conflict within Calvinism, as purists fought a rearguard action, for Calvin's own view of predestination for example, against the liberalism which they thought was fatally weakening the church. For orthodox Dutch Calvinists the problem was compounded by the pervasive influence of rationalist and Erastian ideas in a free society which attracted dissidents from stricter or alien regimes. Some like the émigré Pierre Jurieu held that it was such views that had weakened Huguenotism to the point at which Louis XIV felt that it was safe to attack it. Others however had come to Holland in anticipation of finding the religious freedom they had been denied in France. They might find, as Temple wrote of the years immediately preceding the war against France, that no man could complain 'of pressure in his conscience, of being forced to any public profession of his private faith; of being restrained from his own manner of worship in his house, or obliged to any other abroad'. But against the background of war and the recent Huguenot immigration theological debate became acrimonious. As always there were political influences. Orthodox zealots looked to the house of Orange for support against ministers who, like Koelman of Sluis, dismissed by the states-general in 1675, appeared to place a higher value on personal religious experience than on the authorized forms of service, or like the rationalist Bekker who was deposed by his synod for writing sceptically about the interpretation of comets as messengers of God. William III, embattled against Louis XIV, took the authoritarian view and did nothing to help the unfortunate Van Walten, who had supported Bekker and who died in prison, three years after being first charged with blasphemy. His case fulfilled the prediction of Bayle who had written in 1686: 'God preserve us from the Protestant inquisition! Another five or six years and it will have become so terrible that people will be longing to have the Roman one back again!' In Charles II's England a similar trend can be seen, as the exclusive character of the Church of England was fortified by repressive legislation against dissenters. Ironically it was not the lax and sceptical Charles but his brother James II, the Roman Catholic, who was committed to the principle of toleration, in which, however, his enemies saw only his designs for undermining the Church of England and promoting his own faith. The vicious anti-popery mobs, their exploitation for political ends and the murderous injustice of the 'Plot' trials of 1679–80 played an important part in preparing French Catholic opinion for the repression of the Huguenots. Meanwhile on the other side of Europe, after the relief of Vienna in 1683, the Emperor Leopold was advancing into Hungary and imposing his faith on the Calvinist nobles. The century ended there with the banning of all Protestant public worship; the religion of peasants henceforward depended on their lords.

It does not seem therefore that Louis XIV was exceptional in his concern for uniformity nor in his willingness to act to enforce it. His was not the world of Leibnitz or Locke but of Bishop Bossuet, who was to acclaim the revocation as 'the miracle of our times', and of Fénelon, for whom unity was 'the sacred bond which alone can hold the allegiance of souls'. Unity was a key word in the vocabulary of French absolutism, denoting the essential alternative to the separatism and disorder which had produced such bitterness in communities throughout the land. It was not confined to churchmen. Transcending matters of theology and law it expressed the *politique* conviction that religious differences sapped the vitality of the state. Gallican bishops, anxious to prove their doctrinal orthodoxy, officials who wanted to impress the king, and the king himself, in whom *dévôt* and *politique* were uneasily balanced, all subscribed to the ideal. Numbering about 1.5 million, the Huguenots were a small part of the population in 1660 and had been loyal since 1629; but their contentious past mattered more than their present condition. To seek rational grounds for Louis's policy of repression is unprofitable: his pronouncements and actions were inconsistent; his attitudes, like those of his subjects, were formed by ancestral memories of religious war. Characteristic of such wars is the alternation in times of weakness between concession and rigour: the resolve to have the last word in the argument hardens throughout the whole frustrating process. Now church and state were strong as never before. The ex-Huguenot Henry IV, for whom conversion had been a political necessity, had again been merely realistic when in 1598, by his edict of Nantes, he conceded to the Huguenots the right of public worship in their existing 'temples' and complete civil rights, together with special privileges, such as representation on the *chambres de l'édit* which were added to some *parlements*, the right to hold assemblies, even to fortify certain towns. There was no active spirit of toleration. The edict, like other diplomatic 'solutions', had reflected the military situation: in 1598 it was one of stalemate. After further risings Richelieu acted with decisive force. After the successful siege of La Rochelle, his treaty of Alais (1629) deprived the Huguenots of their military privileges, but it offended the *dévôts* because he conceded freedom of worship.

The Huguenots had made no attempt to exploit the crown's difficulties during the Fronde. Should the state then accept the loyalty and overlook the heresy? To Mazarin, most diplomatic, least dogmatic of men, that was the politic way. But as the reign of Louis XIV proceeded an alternative policy took shape. Ascendancy in war and diplomacy added a touch of chauvinism to conventional preaching about conformity. The mere existence of the Huguenots was a sort of *lèse-majesté*: it was the duty of the good subject to conform. In 1668 France's most admired soldier, the Huguenots' natural leader, Turenne bowed before the logic of politics and found theology to support his painful decision to renounce Protestantism 'in which every individual wishes to found a faith after his own inclinations'. With the defection of many of the nobles, protectors of Huguenot communities in more turbulent times, leadership devolved upon bourgeois. In spirit, as in structure, Huguenotism had been a revolutionary movement, radical and missionary; since 1598, more obviously since 1629, it had become conservative and introspective; its seminaries were not immune from the general European crisis of Calvinism.

Calvinism's intellectual appeal lay in its compelling logic, its spiritual strength largely in stress on the individual, his rights and responsibilities. Followers of Arminius (1550–1609), Remonstrants as they were called in Holland, gave up predestination and accepted the right of the state to control religion, so modifying Calvin's essential tenet of the single and absolute nature of God's sovereignty. While theologians compromised, pastors tended to preach submission: remote indeed from Calvin was Basnage de Beauval, who in 1684, in his *Tolérances des Réligions*, defended the principle of toleration on the grounds that men cannot be so sure of the whole truth that they can persecute others for their views; or Pastor Merlat who declared in the year of the revocation that 'sovereigns have no other law but their own will'. Such teaching might have had a less damaging effect on Huguenot morale if there had existed a great French Bible, such as that which nourished English Protestantism. A dry and unpoetic translation was no substitute for the rich literary inheritance of Catholics. The church in France exhibited moreover an inspiring range of intellect and achievement: from the didactic talent of Bishop Bossuet, one of whose chief concerns was the reunion of the Lutheran and Catholic churches, to the subtle genius of Fénelon, sympathetic to mysticism and to the religion of the heart, to the pastoral zeal of Le Camus who, after 1685, was leader among the bishops who denounced the persecution of the Huguenots for its degrading effect upon worship. Such men were worthy successors to the spiritual leadership of a previous generation, Bérulle, founder of the Oratory, François de Sales, author of moving devotional works and most popular of French saints, and Vincent de Paul, who had done more than any man to rouse Christian consciences to the needs of 'our lords the poor' and whose charitable order, the *Filles de Charité*, was a living advertisement of the virtues of French Catholicism.

The Jesuits too contributed to the vitality of the church in this age, through their missionary work and their successful schools: at their college at Clermont there were 2000 pupils in 1651, nearly 3000 in 1675. Their damaging battle with the Jansenists was important to Huguenots because it revealed how little separated them on the questions of divine grace and human will when Dominican friars, Jansenists and Calvinists could all interpret St Augustine in similar fashion. So Jansenism, the puritan pressure group that remained obstinately Catholic, offered a bridge to uneasy Huguenots. Pellisson, author of the imaginative plan to 'compensate' Huguenot converts in the 1670s, was himself a former Huguenot; so was

Mme de Maintenon. Jansenist efforts to instruct the *nouveaux convertis* in the faith by the distribution of prayer books in French were helpfully broad-minded. But the members of Port Royal and their sympathizers were a tiny majority – and predominantly Parisian. The average French Catholic saw the Huguenot problem in the light of his own community and its inherited grievances over schools, burial grounds and belfries – commonly too over land and jobs. He welcomed the successive edicts which stripped the Huguenot of his rights and debarred him from the professions. He expected his leaders to find means of destroying them altogether. From hungry peasants and militant priests, especially in the south, welled up resentments that gave credibility to episcopal rhetoric. Bishops at the church assembly were traditionally outspoken about these 'rebellious slaves' in their 'synagogues of Satan'. Theology provided more subtle support to the advocates of repression. The view of St Augustine was widely quoted in the 1680s: that since error was a tyrannical oppression of feeble souls it was legitimate to appeal to the civil authority to free those souls. In 1682 the saint's letter to a Donatist bishop, justifying the use of force, was specially published, with royal approval. Bossuet pointed out that the Protestants had accepted the same principle in their dealings with the Anabaptists.

When in October 1685, by the edict of Fontainebleau, Louis XIV revoked his grandfather's edict, the issues had become relatively simple. The argument was mainly about timing, cost, particularly of Pellisson's *fund*, administrative convenience and diplomatic relations. The chief difficulty Louis had to overcome in the end was that of honour: how could he renege on his grandfather's pledge? For that his Jesuit confessor La Chaise, who alone, as Bayle pointed out, 'could inform the King of what he could answer for in his conduct', could offer the argument of the greater good. That the cause was good few doubted, though some might have misgivings about feasibility or scruples about the use of force. Louis had called a halt in 1681 to the first *dragonnades*, billeting of troops on Huguenot households, because of reports of atrocities and their effect on foreign opinion. But when in 1685 his *intendants* reported conversions in droves, it was easy to believe that the sect was disintegrating. Louis could not doubt 'but that it is the Divine Will that I should be His instrument in bringing back to His ways all those who are subject to me'. He was conscientiously aware of his responsibility as one who sat on 'the throne of God', that God who, in Bossuet's words, 'established kings as His ministers and reigns by them'. Those who resisted were simply 'bad subjects'. Another glimpse into a world of exalted, self-deceiving idealism is afforded by Mme de Maintenon, since 1683 the king's wife in all but public recognition, and her master's voice on matters of conscience: 'I well believe that many of these conversions are insincere but God avails Himself of all ways to bring heretics to Him.' On the fringe of that world, Mme de Sévigné expressed her sense of the achievement in phrases that leave the reader wondering how much was irony or mere naivete, or indeed the delight of the natural writer at having such momentous matters to record.

> Many people have been converted without knowing why. He [Père Bourdalue] will explain it to them and make them good Catholics. Up till now the dragoons have been good missionaries. The preachers that are being sent out will complete the work.

It turned out to be harder than that.

Besides the waverers and those who made what public accommodation was required of them, there was left a hard core of resisters, perhaps half a million. Government, committed to a tidy and final solution, saw it differently from churchmen, themselves far from unanimous: some were content to accept the implications of clause 12 of the edict which stated: 'on condition that they do not practise their religion Huguenots may live in the realm without abjuring until it pleases God to enlighten them.' The fact that the Pope was unimpressed by the whole operation and was sceptical about the motives of the king, who was still defying him over the Gallican question, made it harder for priests to decide upon right courses of action. Bishop Le Camus, who characteristically laid stress upon penitence and humility, produced a daring formula for the remaining Huguenots of his diocese, was challenged by the Jesuit Robert, denounced at Rome for his indifference to images and relics, and at once vindicated by the Pope. The limits of what could be achieved can be seen in the work of Fénelon in the Saintonge, where he found unhappy consequences of the use of force. The typical Huguenot, he believed, was bound to his faith less by conviction than by habit; rather than arouse his spirit by argument or prod him with the bayonet, the priest should 'explain the gospel'. One third of the ministers in his area were converted and it remained peaceful during the revolt in the Cevennes. Another approach was that of Bâville, *intendant* in Languedoc, where Huguenot communities were traditionally resolute: with the support of the local bishops he mounted an operation which made large numbers of 'converts' in such ways as to harden the resistance of the rest. Within months of the edict of Fontainebleau all semblance of unity had gone. The Jansenists, who had taken issue with the Jesuits over the mechanical treatment of the sacraments, revived old prejudices about their Huguenot sympathies when they denounced *dragonnades*; Archbishop Harlay responded by banning Le Tourneau's translation of the service book. Such protests and quarrels were excellent ammunition for Huguenot apologists, already well supplied with tales of cruelty and living evidence in the shape of the Huguenot émigrés, 65,000 of them in the United Provinces alone.

As early as 1685 Le Camus complained about the entry into France of Jurieu's *Pastorales* that they undid 'in a day the work of months'. Jurieu, who operated a spy ring and sustained the morale of his fellow Huguenots by prophecies foretelling the end of the reign of Antichrist and the victory of the true church, set the tone for propaganda that found avid readers, not only in France. Echoes of his apocalyptic style can be detected in the frenzied outpourings of the *illuminés* of the Cevennes, where the revolt of the Camisards (1702–5) was provoked mainly by militant *curés*; they could not, said Villars, the general entrusted with the major task of repressing it, 'lose their habit of browbeating their parishes'. The fires lit in the wooded mountains and valleys of the Cevennes warmed the hearts of Huguenots everywhere. As in other resistance movements, it was less a matter of achievement than example. The government had destroyed the institutional framework of French Calvinism, and with it respect, in the persecuted remnant, for the authority of the king which they had hitherto shown. It had hardened the resolve to remain intact and separate, to have nothing to do with reunion. It had revived the consciousness of special mission: Huguenots had been punished by God for their backslidings; now purged and stripped, a leaner body, they stood for the right of the individual, with his Bible, to reach his God direct, without aid of priest or sacrament. They hoped that they would be given new status, on the insistence of the English and Dutch at the treaties of 1713 and 1714. They were disappointed, but not for long. In March 1715 Louis XIV accepted the facts in an edict whose bland words failed to conceal the defeat of a policy and of an ideal: 'The Huguenots' long stay in France was sufficient proof that they had embraced the Catholic religion, without which they would have been neither suffered nor tolerated.' In August of that year Antoine Court presided over a provincial synod, the first for thirty years.

The Jesuits: Originality, Heroism and Disaster

The downfall of the Jesuits in the eighteenth century, leading to their expulsion from one Catholic country after another, and to their eventual dissolution by Clement XIV in 1773, illustrates further aspects of religion in the age of reason. It may appear strange that the Society of Jesus, the modernists of the Counter-Reformation, its most disciplined apologists and effective teachers, so notable for their readiness to enter the world and to use its methods, should be the chief victims of the Enlightenment. But old prejudices, as well as valid principles, were now fortified by new fashions of thought. The Jesuits, who were trained theologically to go further than other Catholics in a liberal view of man's efforts to attain salvation, had always offended puritan defenders of 'single-standard' Christianity by their compromising methods. To catch many fish they had spread their net wide, using tempting bait. Beyond doubt they had been successful. Successive Bourbon and Habsburg princes had been guided by Jesuit confessors. They had a near monopoly of education in provincial France. At the end of the sixteenth century they had won Poland for Rome; they had been the chief agents in the imposition of Catholic orthodoxy in Bohemia after the revolt of 1618. In those countries, however, critics would say that their dominance was unhealthy, that they worked too deferentially within the social system and taught men to be good Catholics rather than useful citizens. They became obnoxious to a pragmatic generation of rulers determined to extend secular authority over every area of life. While it was the Jesuits' apparent independence that made them unpopular both at Rome and in the Catholic countries, paradoxically it was their dependence in the last resort upon the secular power that made them vulnerable. They were allegedly too powerful and ambiguous in loyalty for a man like Pombal, the commercially minded and radical dictator of Portugal (1750–77). They were too papal for the Bourbon autocrats. They suffered moreover for their efforts to touch the hearts of plain men. *The History of the People of God* (1753) by Berruyer, a popular interpretation of the Bible, was placed on the Index: it was alleged 'to have overthrown morality and discipline to accommodate the passions of men'. The Jesuits were too daring for the Church authorities while at the same time accused of being too conservative by the Enlightenment. For anticlerical forces everywhere they served as a cheap sacrifice to the god of reason. They had already been weakened by the factious and unimaginative bureaucracy of Rome. In their hour of need they were abandoned by the Pope himself.

In France, Jansenism, by principles and by force of circumstances anti-Jesuit and Gallican, had won supporters in *parlement* and in the *salons*. The Jesuits were associated with those ultramontane policies which, it was urged, had damaged the country; with the harrying of the Jansenists upon minute points of theology; with the court camarilla responsible for Louis XIV's assault upon the Huguenots. They had never recovered the middle ground of intellectual opinion which they had lost under the assault of Pascal, and which was their reputation in the world of the *salons*, where *bien-peasants* considered the works of Montesquieu and Voltaire. In the *Lettres provinciales* (1656), Pascal had criticized their moral theology, their casuistry and their 'easy devotion', with exquisite skill and without compassion, and the charges had stuck: intellectually they cheated, spiritually they bent the rules! The Jesuit missionary operations in South America and the Far East, so heroic and optimistic, looked very different to the theologians of the Sorbonne and the Vatican; and different again to sceptics who doubted whether it was necessary or right to convert men of another civilization.

Ironically, it was Jesuit missionaries in the Far East and their accounts of the inhabitants, their culture and morals, that encouraged the idea that the Christian civilization did not have the monopoly of wisdom. At a time when discoveries in geology and the physical sciences were throwing doubt upon the traditional Christian account of creation and the evolution of man, it was unsettling to be assured by the Jesuits that the morality of the Chinese was in many respects superior to that of the westerner! Idealized types begin to appear: 'the noble savage', 'the Chinese philosopher'. In the hands of the encyclopedist Bayle, travellers' observations became ammunition for his gospel of doubt. We can see how theologians' minds worked when we read in La Bruyère, usually a faithful reporter of trends: 'some complete their demoralization by extensive travel and lose whatever shreds of religion remain to them. Every day they see a new religion, new customs, new rites.' Truth to the Catholic theologian was not relative but absolute. It was dangerous to introduce the idea that practices thought to be grounded upon reason and revelation had no higher authority than that of custom.

To the handful of Jesuits working in China, the issues were more local; but the stakes were large. They made encouraging progress and had won the confidence of the Emperor Kang-Hsi (1661–1721), who valued their knowledge of geography and astronomy. The Jesuit fathers believed that they could so preach Christianity as to make it acceptable to the intellectual élite, the mandarins, and so to the nation. But there needed to be some compromise. Language made no barrier, for Chinese terms could be 'baptized' for Christian use: conversions in the pagan Europe of the Dark Ages provided precedents for that. Confucius could be accepted for the great ethical teacher he undoubtedly was. It was possible to claim that the Confucian rites which were so dear to the Chinese were social rather than religious in character. Since the Emperor himself avowed that the veneration of ancestors was only a civil custom, it was surely unwise to condemn the Jesuits for allowing it to their converts. In all there was nothing specifically anti-Christian about Chinese culture. The Jesuits were working on the frontier, far from the hothouses of western theology in which the devout were engaged upon disputes over grace and free will, or over what was or was not valid in the way of meditation. A few concessions, they argued, might win many souls. The Dominicans held a stricter view. After intense study and fierce controversy at the Vatican and Sorbonne, fuelled by the jealous reports of rival orders in the missionary field, Rome spoke unequivocally. In a series of verdicts, the last of them in 1715, Clement XIII condemned the Jesuit concessions in China and Malabar. Two successive legates, sent to conciliate and define, succeeded only in antagonizing the Jesuit fathers. The latter may have been too optimistic in their assessment: undoubtedly the papal policy spoiled what chance existed of converting China. The Emperor felt that he had been betrayed; the handful of converts was now persecuted. Either a bubble of self-deception had been pricked, and truth had prevailed; or a momentous opportunity to extend Christ's kingdom had been lost.

The Portuguese were strongest in denunciation of Jesuit practices since they were held to be contravening Portuguese colonial rights. In 1750 a boundary treaty between Spain and Portugal delivered a large area of Paraguay to Portuguese rule. It was here that the Jesuits had their most famous mission. In land hitherto unclaimed, where Indians had voluntarily submitted to Spanish rule, the Jesuits had created self-sufficient communities from which outsiders were excluded. Each of these 'reductions' as they were called, about forty in number, was a model township, built round a square, with the homes and gardens of the Indians on three sides and on the fourth the church, school and infirmary. The town planning is interesting but more important was the system of race relations. Every aspect of the community's life was meticulously controlled by the two resident priests. The Jesuits' enemies said that they exploited the Indians who made the commodities by which the work was financed. Modern critics might condemn an excessive paternalism, but admit that there was also a fine concern for the natives' well-being. The Jesuits tried to stop their Indians from trading on their own behalf; but they also defended them against wholesale eviction at the hands of the Portuguese. A native revolt was attributed to the Jesuits. Pombal made capital out of the situation and his *Brief Relation* (1758) presented the Jesuits as tyrants, aiming at world domination. Benedict XIV invested Saldanda, archbishop of Lisbon, with powers of visitation and reform. It was unfortunate for the Jesuits that their great preacher, Malagrida, should have chosen the disaster of the Lisbon earthquake as a pretext for a sermon upon the iniquities of the Portuguese government. His name was mentioned, with other Jesuits, in connection with the attempted assassination of Joseph I. Pombal demanded that suspects be tried by a state court; but Pope Clement XII demurred at such an invasion of clerical prerogative.

On 3 September 1759, a year to the day after the alleged attempt on Joseph I, Pombal expelled the Jesuits from Portugal. As it was, in 1764 Louis XV, not without embarrassment, bowed to the clamour in *parlement*. Three years later Charles III of Spain followed suit. Secular-minded absolutists could claim a victory for statecraft; others might think that it was a blow to religion. They contributed to their own downfall. Lavallette, superior of the Jesuit mission in French Martinique, having incurred debts in the course of unwise business dealings, appealed for justice to *parlement*, guardian of the anti-clerical tradition. In France Ricci, general of the Society might have saved the Order by conceding that his authority could be exercised by a vicar-general resident there, so meeting the Gallican objection to a foreign body. Of all the Christian bodies, the Jesuits were best qualified to find a means of reconciling traditional authority with eighteenth-century thinking. Their suppression was damaging to Catholic missionary enterprise, and to those whom missionaries served.

In 1750 there were altogether 273 Jesuit missions overseas. The subsequent unhappy history of the Indians throughout the American continent puts the Jesuits' originality and humanitarian enterprise into their true perspective. Meanwhile the Jesuit example continued to have a powerful indirect influence on the life of the Church. Devotions, such as that of the Sacred Heart which they had encouraged, but which their critics disliked because of its emotional character, remained popular. Orders like the Passionists and Redemptionists continued intact, and strong for a future when the Church was able to shake off state controls and the Jesuits were to come into their own again.

Further Reading

An excellent general survey is that of G.R. Cragg, *The Church and the Age of Reason, 1648–1789* (Harmondsworth, 1960). Essential background is provided by the works of A.G. Dickens: *Reformation and Society in Sixteenth Century Europe* (London, 1966), and *The Counter-Reformation* (London, 1969). P. Janelle, *The Counter-Reformation* (Milwaukee, 1949), H. Daniel-Rops, *The Catholic Reformation* (trans. London, 1962), and H.O. Evenett, ed. J. Bossy, *The Spirit of the Counter-Reformation* (Cambridge, 1968), all in different ways go beyond the traditional idea of the Counter-Reformation as simply Rome's counter-attack against Protestantism. See also J. Bossy, 'The Counter-Reformation and the people of Catholic Europe', *Past and Present*, 47 (1970). For a summary of the main issues, some of them still contentious, M. Mullett's *The Counter-Reformation* (London, 1984) is helpful. J. Delumeau, *Catholicism between Luther and Voltaire* (Tunbridge Wells, 1977), is a balanced, modern account. The standard history of missions in this period is K.S. Latourette, *A History of the Expansion of Christianity*, vol. 3 (Exeter, 1971). A good general book on Protestantism is that of E.G. Léonard, *Protestantism* (English trans. 1964). Pietism is well described in K.S. Pinson, *Pietism as a Factor in the Rise of German Nationalism* (1934). For Orthodoxy and the Old Believers in particular, see R.O. Crummey, *The Old Believers and the World of Anti-Christ* (London, 1970). J. McManners, *French Ecclesiastical Society under the Ancien Régime* (Manchester, 1960), a study of Angers, is masterly and entertaining. Though most of his evidence is drawn from England, K. Thomas's *Religion and the Decline of Magic* (Harmondsworth, 1973) is essential reading for mentalities in general, the decline of witchcraft in particular. See also R. Mandrou, *Magistrats et sorciers en France au XVIIe siècle* (1968).

Many aspects of Church life are surveyed in the series *Histoire de l'Eglise*, ed. A. Fliche and V. Martin; vol. 19, by E. Préclin and E. Jarry, *Les Luttes politiques et doctrinales aux XVIIe et XVIIIe siècles* (1955), is helpful towards understanding the conflicts that overshadow Church life in the period. For the one conflict, see particularly J. Orcibal, *Louis XIV et les Protestants* (1951). For another, *Gallicanism*, see A.G. Martimort, 'Comment les Français voyaient le Pape', *Bulletin de la Societé d'Etudes au XVIIe siècle*, 24 (1955). A good concise survey of Jansenism is that of L. Cognet, *Le Jansénisme* (1961). N. Abercrombie, *The Origins of Jansenism* (1936), will help those who wish to master a subject of far-reaching importance which they can also pursue in D. van Kley, *The Jansenists and the Expulsion of the Jesuits from France 1757–65* (London, 1975). Jansenism is a major topic in R. A. Knox's *Enthusiasm* (1950) – subjective, entertaining, full of insights; another is quietism, the subject also of Michael Bedoyère, *The Archbishop and the Lady* (1956), a more serious study than the title would suggest. There is a good selection, in translation, of Fénelon's letters, ed. J. McEuen (1960). For Gallicanism, see A.G. Martimort, *Le Gallicanisme de Bossuet* (1927). The life of another great churchman is the subject of H. Daniel-Rops, *Monsieur Vincent* (1966).

The Jesuits' principal chronicler is J. Broderick, in *The Origin of the Jesuits* (London, 1947) and *The Progress of the Jesuits* (1957). See also R. Fulop-Miller, *The Power and Secret of the Jesuits* (1957). H. Graef, *The Story of Mysticism* (1966), gives an introduction to an important subject. H. Kamen's *Spanish Inquisition* (New York, 1977) is a standard work on that much misunderstood organization. By contrast, he is also the author of *The Rise of Toleration* (1967). The subject of P. Hazard's stimulating study of changing ideas at the turn of the century is better conveyed by the French title, *La Crise de la conscience européenne, 1680–1715*, than by the title of the English translation, *The European Mind* (1953). R.R. Palmer, *Catholics and Unbelievers in Eighteenth Century France* (1939), deals with some of its effects.

4

ADVENTURES OF MIND AND IMAGINATION

Prologue. All in Doubt

It is not only by contrast with the economic growth and the expansive spirit of the Renaissance that the seventeenth century can seem, as it did to contemporaries, a time of retreats and calamities. Intolerance, oppression and the inhumanity of man to man were more evident than the gentler fruits of the spirit or the wiser voices of reason. Even where the general economic recession was least harmful, little was done to counter disease and famine. It is not surprising that the dominant theme in the life of the time was the search for order. One undisputed achievement was the growth of states and of the resources that they could command. Another was the development of the technology of war. The main result of the former was to increase the resources available for the latter. In one field of human activity, however, there was outstanding progress, affecting all areas of life. In the Renaissance period some of the barriers which stood between man and his understanding of the material universe had been identified and probed. In the seventeenth century they were overthrown. Seeking new answers to new questions, man came to an entirely new conception of the ideal as well as of the real world. The scientific revolution was in the first place an intellectual revolution.

Medieval men had envisaged a world of things arranged according to their ideal nature. Their questions about truth were part of one great and comprehensive enquiry. What, they asked, was the enduring and intelligible reality behind or within the world of change, growth and decay that they actually experienced. In any class of things they looked for the innate and essential quality beneath all variations: its substantial forms. The properties of any object of study followed from the substance whose form made it what it was. The natural universe consisted of an infinite number of such elemental forms: irreducible realities. Given that any object had latent tendencies, a change in nature could be traced to the effort in particular things to achieve their proper forms. In a fundamentally purposive nature, responding always to God's will, change occurs as the relatively unformed becomes formed, each element having a will of its own which drives it to find means of fulfilling its essence. Medieval and Renaissance man pursued his enquiries within this limiting conceptual framework, seeking in any object the substantial form. Literary men at the beginning of the seventeenth century, confronted by accelerating changes within society, were preoccupied with the notions of order, degree, priority and place. Let them be upset and what discord followed: it is a recurring theme in the plays of Shakespeare. They believed in a chain of being, linked gradations of substantial forms stretching from the elements to the angelic hosts. Still a step behind the pioneering scientists, they lacked two vital conceptions which were to provide the key to a new world of ideas: that of forces which could act on the elements, as Newton was to envisage the force of gravity, and that of a planet's being composed of the same matter as an earthly object. When Nikolaus Copernicus (1475–1543) suggested that men think of the earth as moving round the sun and on its own axis, he disturbed the profound medieval sense of the universe as an affair between God and men, as the Bible pictured it on the sixth day of the Creation.

Through mathematics and observation men were able to find ways out of the enclosed intellectual world of the Middle Ages and direct science upon its twin paths: the empirical and the rational. Like Copernicus, Johann Kepler (1571–1630) was carried away by the mystery of mathematics. Nature, he said, loved simplicity. His first law was that each planet moved on an ellipse, with the sun lying at one focus of this ellipse. But his second and third laws describing the varying speed at which a line from a planet travels along its ellipse, and the movement of one planet from another, broke finally with the tradition of movement within a circle which had been cherished from the time of the Greeks. Galileo Galilei (1564–1642) found evidence for Copernicus's hypothesis that earth and planets revolved round the sun and the moon about the earth when his perspective glasses revealed scars on the moon and blemishes on the sun's surface. Now the firm association that existed so long between religious beliefs, moral principles and the traditional scheme of nature was truly shaken. 'The new philosophy puts all in doubt,' wrote Donne. Poetry and drama abounded with notes of unhappy confusion about God's universe and man's place in it. The outraged reaction of conservatives came from something deeper and more positive than scholasticism defending vested interests. The emotional commitment to the old world view was analogous to the commitment of so many to Rome and the torn, no longer seamless robe of Catholic Christendom. Inexorably, as in the realm of theology, the unsettling scientific views gained a hold. In the new physics there was no attempt to relate objects and processes to their intrinsic nature, or to the attainment of ends, or to a hierarchy of status. The new naturalists asked: how can the qualities and changes of things be related to an exact system of material properties? The properties providing this new conceptual framework were those that could be treated mathematically; those that were merely accessible to the senses were excluded; but not speed which was measurable in terms of time and distance, not size, shape or density.

The Century of Mathematics

Mathematics had long been a higher academic game, pursued by its devotees for its own sake, without the ulterior motives that underlay theology or philosophy. In the seventeenth century it assumed the central position, influencing knowledge in other spheres, and therefore life, as never before. The various branches of enquiry were pursued by one brilliant man after another. The 'century of genius' might well be called 'the century of mathematics'. At the start of the century logarithms had been introduced, a calculating device which can be used without understanding the principles on which it depends. The slide rule was invented. Notation, the language of mathematics, was both simplified and developed, with the signs that are still familiar. It was Simon Stevin (1548–1620), the military engineer, who first used decimals. Galileo urged a mathematical approach to the problems of the universe since its book was written in mathematical language and its alphabet consisted of triangle, circles and geometrical figures. The pioneers of the new science were more often than not to be found outside the official centres of learning and indeed the learned professions. Often it was immediate practical problems, how to measure a tun of wine, how to discover at what angle a gun would fire furthest, which stimulated study. It was, however, the study of mathematics that led to the most important advances and enabled its practitioners to bridge some gaps between bold speculation and reasonable certainty. So it was that Johann Kepler proceeded from the study of conic sections to the laws of planetary motion. Mathematics was indeed the 'general science', in the words of Descartes, 'which should explain all that can be known about quantity and measure, considered independently of any application to a particular subject'. René Descartes (1596–1650) gave to mathematics the idea of the property of a curve and its use, in relation to fixed lines at right angles, and in equations which expressed that relationship. From this idea, following the previous application of algebra to geometry, came coordinate geometry and the use of the graph which became the stock in trade of the statistician, and then, completing earlier discoveries, invented separately by Newton and Leibnitz, the calculus.

'Sometimes one man gives the tone to a whole century,' wrote Fontenelle of Descartes. It was not simply of his mathematics that Fontenelle would have been thinking but of the method, philosophy and system which followed from the application of mathematical reasoning to the mysteries of the universe, and man's place in it. Within ten years of the master's death, Cartesianism commanded the intellectual heights; by the end of the century it had become the prevailing orthodoxy. The method as expounded in his *Discours de la méthode* (1637) was one of *doubt*: all was uncertain until established by reasoning from self-evident propositions, on principles analogous to those of geometry. Starting from the bedrock of the incontrovertible 'I think, therefore I am', and proceeding eventually to the existence of God and of everything material, the philosophy made room for God as the ordainer of a mechanistic, ordered universe; man was envisaged as belonging to the two worlds, having a mechanical body and an immortal soul, implanted at birth with certain basic notions. The system of physics was based on matter's primary qualities of motion, weight and extension. It explained celestial mechanics in terms of a complex series of vortices in whirlpools of matter. It was applicable to all branches of enquiry. There was a mechanistic model for all living things. 'I want you to consider', wrote Descartes in his *Traité de l'homme* (published posthumously) 'that all these functions follow naturally in this machine simply from the arrangement of its parts, no more or less than do the movements of a clock, or other automaton, from that of its weights and wheels'.

In order to introduce a new philosophy 'it will first be necessary to new-mould the brains of men and make them apt to distinguish truth from falsehood'. Not only did scientifically minded contemporaries agree with Galileo's dramatic challenge; they also believed they had a method, reliable and self-correcting: if not the Cartesian, it was the empirical, associated with the name of Francis Bacon (1561–1626), the great English lawyer, whose influence was to prove in the long run as great as that of Descartes. Bacon called confidently for 'a new science'. He insisted upon the prime role of organized experiment, with the systematic recording of results and co-operation between scientists in allied fields. When a sufficient number of phenomena had been investigated general laws could be established by the method of inductive reasoning which, as he described it in his *Novum Organum* (1620), 'derives from ... particulars, rising by a gradual and unbroken ascent, so that it arrives at the most general axioms last of all'. Those axioms should then be tested and verified by further experiments. Bacon's method could lead to cumulative growth in knowledge; it was also self-correcting. Behind it lay the vision that his method would advance 'the true and lawful goal of the sciences ... that human life be endowed with new powers and inventions'; they would make men more prosperous and contented. Here was the dream of modern man in embryo: material prosperity through scientific progress.

It was this empirical method which Descartes held to be inadequate when he maintained that philosophy must proceed from what is clear and definable to what is complex and uncertain by a process of *deductive* reasoning. In his *Discours*, as if to emphasize the novelty of his approach and to reach the uncommitted intelligent readership, the product of such schools as the Jesuit academy which he had attended, he exchanged the normal Latin for French and exploited to the full its value as a vehicle for clear and logical expression. When he declared that learning might impede reason, and therefore discovery, by implanting prejudice, he was thinking particularly of the study of ancient languages and of history. But it was his rejection of the empirical method that led him to his odder aberrations, like his idea that animals were mere automata: 'doubtless when the swallows come in spring they act like clocks'. Scientists in the eighteenth century returned to Bacon. But too much must not be made of schools of thought. The most creative among scientists had always held to the idea that knowledge must be derived from experience; it was the work of the mathematicians to give them the technical means to evaluate and to prove.

In 1687 Newton published the *Philosophiae naturalis principia mathematica*; it matches the *Discours* in power and influence as the other supreme peak in seventeenth-century man's intellectual quest. Astronomer, physicist, chemist, Isaac Newton (1642–1727) was, like Descartes and Pascal, a remarkable mathematician; he was also the resourceful, observant scientist of the Baconian ideal; it was the combination of polymath, disciplined experimenter and problem-solver of rare facility that made him the supreme genius of the scientific revolution. He did not break so completely with Descartes as might be supposed from the controversy that engaged the attention of all who sought to keep abreast of new trends and discoveries; indeed he remained faithful to the Frenchman's fundamental idea of the universe as machine. But Newton's machine operated according to a series of laws, the gist of which was that the principle of gravitation was everywhere present and everywhere efficient. The Cartesian had to show not only that his mechanics gave a truer explanation of the facts but also that his methods were sounder. For him science was a deductive exercise. He would not allow the right to use a principle the cause of which was unknown; he might concede that Newton's conclusions followed from his assumptions, but he questioned those assumptions. The Dutchman Christiaan Huygens (1629–95) was the devoted disciple of Descartes; he was also a formidable mathematician and inventor in his own right, who worked out the first tenable theory of centrifugal force and invented the balance spring for watches. When, in 1688, he put the case for those who called for a mechanical explanation, he acknowledged that Newton's assumption of forces acting between members of the solar system was justified by the correct

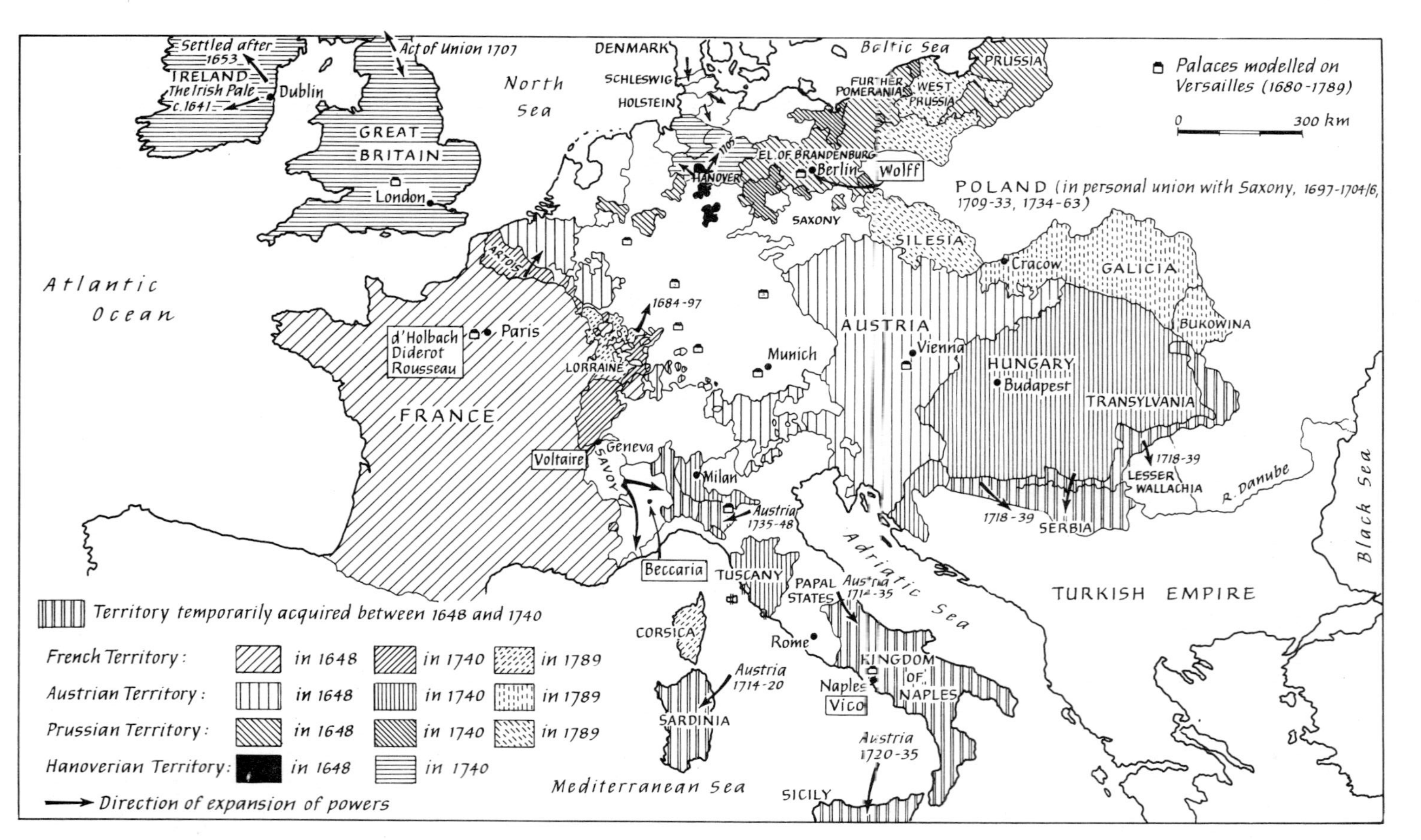

Map 4.1 *Changing frontiers in Enlightened Europe*

conclusions that followed from it; he accepted that Descartes's explanation of the motion of planets and comets was inadequate. But he refused to go on to accept that attraction was affecting nor merely pairs of heavenly bodies but every pair of particles, however minute. In other words, in so far as Newton had explained the mathematical pattern underlying the solar system, he was acceptable; what the Cartesian must still think most important was to identify the mechanical causes. Newton made gravitation, by which he explained all aspects of the motion of bodies, 'a property inherent in corporeal matter'. Huygens thought that to be absurd and looked for 'an agent acting constantly according to certain laws'. It was held by some that Newton, in rejecting the idea of a mechanical explanation of the universe, was returning to 'occult qualities' reminiscent of Aristotle, a view to which his voluminous writing about theology and alchemy gave some support. Some eminent thinkers, notably Leibnitz and Berkeley, believed that he was unsound on natural religion. Those few moreover who actually read the *Principia* found it a dry and difficult mathematical treatise. Not surprisingly therefore Cartesian views maintained their hold into the eighteenth century.

Gradually, however, Newton's work won understanding and support. One medium paradoxically was the outstanding textbook of Cartesian physics, Rohault's *Traité de physique*, which was successively brought up to date with detailed notes putting Newton's case. In 1732 Mauperthuis put the Cartesians on the defensive by a penetrating analysis in which he defended Newton's right to use a principle the *cause* of which was yet unknown. Voltaire, playing the part of Bayle a generation before, used his authority in the literary world to sway the scientific debate. In his *Lettres philosophiques* (1734) he introduced Newton as 'the destroyer of the system of Descartes'. Meanwhile Newton's physics were being justified by their successful application in different fields of science. The return of Halley's comet was accurately predicted. Coulomb's torsion balance, used to verify the laws of magnetic attraction, proved that Newton's law of inverse squares holds good for electric magnetic attraction.

Cartesianism reduced nature to a system, a set of habits within a world of rules. The new attitude had to take account of accidents and circumstances. Observation and experiment showed nature to be untidy and unpredictable, a mass of conflicting forces. Reason was supposed in classical theory to be common to all men, its laws immutable; now there was everywhere a quickening urge to discover, an impatience with general abstractions and logical systems. It is hard to believe that scientific research inspired by such pioneering figures as Boyle, Harvey and Leeuwenhoek would not have had sufficient momentum to break through at some point or other on the scientific front line. It is wrong to ascribe too much to one man. But it was Newton, more than any other, who was responsible for the great shift in European thought, round about the turn of the century: from an inclination towards the strictly rational approach, with a view to attaining order and certainty, to the outward-looking mood of the traveller who does not need to be sure of his route before he sets out to find new lands.

Enquiring Minds

To what extent is it correct to talk about a scientific movement? That there was some unity of outlook is certain: that questions should now be resolved by both observation and reason was agreed. This approach was not confined to the physical sciences. John Locke, well described by Voltaire as the anatomist of the soul, admirably representative of the new spirit, can be seen tackling what today would be studied as separate subjects, in his pursuit of truth. Psychology and epistemology, ethics, social and political theory and economics all interested him and were subjected to his empirical, statistical method. The sciences came to depend more upon exact measurement. Instruments of precision, microscopes, telescopes, balances and barometers, were invented or improved. Social and political problems were tackled quantitatively. The increasing use of statistics may be noted. The population of England was estimated by Gregory King in 1688; soon afterwards Vauban tried to do the same in France. The first official census in Europe was in 1703 in Iceland, a conveniently small unit. Mathematical possibilities were demonstrated by Pascal and Huygens, calculating chances in the game of hazard. In 1671 the Dutch statesman Johan de Witt, a trained mathematician who had written a book on geometry, decided to raise money for the state by an offer of state annuities. For the figures of life-expectancy he had to rely on conjecture – and on the methods of Huygens. William Petty's *Political Arithmetic* was perhaps more ambitious than reliable. But statistics of trade and prices were already proving their value to governments.

While, however, there was agreement on outlook and to some extent on methods, scientific progress was less concerted than may appear in the use of words like movement or revolution. The reality is harder to define but no less significant: a qualitative change within European culture, with science and its methods taking the place of traditional metaphysics as an intellectual discipline. There were many different activities, generating their own energy. Links were forged by the personal relationships of talented and enterprising individuals in the tiny cultural élite of the western world. P. Mersenne (1588–1648) had built up a network of researchers including Galileo and Hobbes, besides the most important of French scientists. His correspondence and conferences had been largely responsible for the primacy of Paris in the intellectual world of the middle of the seventeenth century. Very different from the learned friar, but no less influential in his time, was Bernard de Fontenelle (1657–1757). He was a new phenomenon, the popular scientist. In method he was Cartesian, advocating order and precision in all things.

> The geometric spirit is not so attached to geometry that it cannot be disentangled and carried over to other areas of knowledge. A work on politics, on criticism, perhaps even on eloquence, will be better, all other things being equal, if it is written by the hand of a Geometer.

His philosophy was based on two things: 'one, that we have enquiring minds; two, that we have very short sight'. Modest in pretension as ambitious in scope, he excelled in the valuable art of making the work of specialists available to ordinary men and women. His *Entretiens sur la pluralité des mondes* (1686) was designed to bring the new astronomy 'within the grasp of the feminine intelligence'. It appears that his patronizing approach succeeded: in that year *Mercure Galante* reported that a young lady refused an eligible suitor on the grounds that he would not give her any plausible ideas about 'the squaring of the circle'. More important of course than the reduction of science to the level of polite conversation, was the stimulus to new ideas and the corrosive effect of regular exposure of the old ideas to the test of evidence and the discipline of logic. 'Make sure of the facts before you bother about their cause': Fontenelle's law supplies a motto for the age of Voltaire and the *Encyclopédie*. Related sciences made contact at obvious points: mechanics with astronomy, chemistry with physiology. But there were sciences too whose methods remained distinct. The naturalist for example needed little mathematics; the observations of the astronomer were different from those of the chemist. Technology and science had to be studied together. But some important inventions, in the field of agriculture for example, owed little to scientific research, more to the craftsman's approach of trial and error, looking for more convenient and efficient ways of making things. The scientific spirit left its mark on political theory and theology in this period. But those studies, we have seen, have their own *raison d'être*, their own inspirations.

An important role in the advance of science was played by the learned societies. The Royal Society of London and the Académie des Sciences were pioneers in the 1660s. The Académie acquired a new constitution in 1700 which increased its membership from 20 to 70 and provided for a special record, the *Histoires et mémoires*. In the same year the Societas Regis Scientiarum of Berlin, which owed its inception to Leibnitz, began to take shape; it was his plan to cover Europe with a network of scientific institutions. In 1754 a comparable institution was set up in Moscow. Learning in the eighteenth century knew no frontiers, though makeshift barriers were set up by vested interests. The Inquisition in Spain for example, with little dissent to worry about, turned its attention to the exclusion of secular works from abroad that might make the Spaniards think for themselves. Though there was professional jealousy then as always, there was a remarkable degree of sharing between scholars and inventors engaged upon interlocking studies. The learned society provided a means of exchange, of recording and disseminating ideas and discoveries: a useful community of civilized men.

In England the coffee houses provided a sociable extension of more formal studies. John Harris, author of one of the technical encyclopedias, the *Lexicon Technicon* (1704), and the Huguenot émigré Abraham de Moivre, author of a textbook on *Probability, the Doctrine of Chance* (1716), both lectured at the Marine Coffee House in London to navigators, insurance brokers and other interested persons. The job of such men was all the more important since the universities made at first little provision for scientific research or education. Since the Middle Ages scientific education had been contained within the faculties of arts and medicine; advanced scientific studies depended naturally on the latter and most university-trained scientists till the nineteenth century had a medical training. Leyden was the pioneer in bringing the new science into medicine. There worked Herman Boerhaave (1668–1738), the outstanding clinical teacher of his time. More typical, however, of the attitude of the academic establishment, directed by men who were dogmatically faithful to the methods in which they had been trained, was the University of Paris, which admitted the Cartesian physics about the same time as the French scientific world recognized that Newton had proved it false.

The societies were founded, like literary societies before them, as homes for the new learning outside the conservative university system. The Académie des Sciences shows what was achieved. It was the model, far more than the Royal Society, for the other foundations of Europe. Newton was the glory of the Royal Society but, as Voltaire said, it did not produce him – and the same could be said of Stephen Hales or the geologist Ray. It was short of money and it could never carry out a large-scale project of research. From the start, however, the Académie was an official organ of government, reflecting Colbert's scientific approach to problems of society and government. After 1683 Louvois was responsible and characteristically placed most emphasis upon problems of war and public works. As in Holland during the time of the war against Spain, war was ever a fertile mother of invention, especially in such areas as mining and ballistics. Aquaducts, hydraulic problems and the properties of metals also took up the academicians' time. Fortunately Pontchartrain, who took over supervision in 1692 and placed it under his nephew Bignon, took a loftier view. Transferred to spacious quarters in the Louvre, equipped with a library, and apparatus and collections of specimens, with a corps of twenty stipendiary members, with a permanent secretary whose job was to co-ordinate their activities, working in the disciplined framework of a department of state, the academicians became the scientific élite of Europe. There the astronomer La Hire, the anatomist Duverney, the botanist Tournefourt, specialists in different fields, worked together in fruitful association. Chemistry, physics and physiology went forward together. Associated members spread the Académie's influence; student members were trained to preserve continuity. Practical applications were not neglected. In 1695 a comprehensive survey of technical appliances and manufacturing processes was begun under the young physician Ferchault de Réaumur (1683–1757). Fifty years later, four years after his death, appeared the first of 121 parts of his survey, *Description et perfection des arts et métiers*. (It had been anticipated, to Réaumur's chagrin, by the *Encyclopédie*, no less complete and impressive in technical details.) Expeditions were financed: to Lapland in 1736–7, to Peru in 1735–44. Their object was to check Newton's theory of the shape of the earth and provide maps; but they brought back valuable information and specimens.

High standards spread outwards. The Paris Observatory, under Cassini, became the best in Europe. The Jardin du Roi, which had been established by Louis XIII as a garden of medicinal plants, began to play a large part in the development of botanical science. The heyday of the Jardin was under the directorship of Antoine Jussieu (1686–1758). One of his two brothers refined Linnaeus's sexual classification of plants and introduced the cedar of Lebanon to the Jardin; another introduced heliotrope; a nephew, Antoine-Laurent de Jussieu published *Genera plantorum*, which carried the evolutionary theory some way forward. With this extraordinary dynasty the Jardin grew around its hot-houses; an amphitheatre and laboratories were built. Here Georges Buffon (1707–88) was appointed superintendent in 1739. An energetic administrator as well as a writer, it was his achievement to bring together in one history of the earth (in thirty-six volumes) the knowledge of astronomers, mathematicians, geologists and naturalists. In the chemical department of the Jardin G.F. Rouelle (1703–70) was the first to perceive that salts were produced by the combination of acids and bases. Diderot, the encyclopedist, was one of his admirers; among his pupils was A. Lavoisier; another was Sage, who later set up a chair of mineralogical chemistry and persuaded the government to set up the École des Mines. There was nothing remote or impracticable about the studies or interests of such men.

Research and Invention

A good example of the zig-zag but far from random way in which scientific advances were made is afforded by the experiments of Torricelli and Pascal on the vacuum, and their sequels. In 1644 Galileo's pupil, Evangelista Torricelli showed by his experiments with tubes filled with mercury, placed in a basin also filled with mercury, that there could be a vacuum in the tube and that the surrounding atmosphere had weight which exerted pressure on the mercury in the basin. Prompted by Mersenne, who observed the experiment, Blaise Pascal,[1] from childhood a prodigious mathematician, confirmed and extended the theory that air had weight. His experiments proved that the height of the mercury depended upon the weight and

[1] For Pascal as Jansenist and writer, see also pp. 102–3.

pressure of the atmosphere. In 1648 his brother-in-law Florian Perier climbed the Puy de Dôme, 3500 feet above the town of Clermont, to compare the height of a tube of mercury with another that he had left below in the town. Pascal was convinced by the result of the agency of atmospheric pressure. He went on to complete his work on 'the equilibrium of fluids' and the 'weight of the mass of the air' which are the basis of modern hydrostatics and aerostatics. Perier meanwhile had kept records of variations in the rise and fall of mercury in his tubes. The duke of Tuscany sponsored a similar scheme to secure comparative readings in Italian cities: so the barometer was born. The question remained: how could a vacuum be created except by using mercury? Perier posed the question in his edition of Pascal's work. In 1658 Robert Guericke of Magdeburg gave his celebrated demonstration before the members of the Imperial Diet at Regensburg of the pressures which surrounded a copper sphere after the air had been expelled by a pump: teams of horses, pulling in opposite directions, failed to pull apart the halves of the sphere. Meanwhile the English 'chymist' Robert Boyle (1627–91) was engaged upon the seminal work which was to bring chemical theory within the mechanical philosophy, so lifting the subject from its frame of alchemy into a respected part of physics. He read of Guericke's experiment, improved the mechanism of the pump which he and Hooke were then making, and enlarged the size of the vacuum. They were soon able to tabulate the inverse proportions of pressures and expansions and to distinguish between the air's compressibility and elasticity. So the air pump joined the barometer and another step was taken along the road that was to lead to the steam engine.

As early as 1615 the German engineer de Caus had described an engine in which the steam issuing from pipes struck the paddles on a wheel, rotating the wheel which drove a gear system. In 1655 the marquis of Worcester described a steam engine which he used to throw a jet of water to a height of 40 feet and was granted a patent for his design. In 1666 Huygens suggested to Colbert tests to compare the power of gunpowder and of steam. Huygens knew of Guericke's experiments, showing the working capacity of a piston driven by air pressure into a cylinder which had been exhausted by means of the air pump. Among those who were inspired to go further along that path was a Huguenot refugee from Blois who became professor of mathematics at Marburg University. A plaque in the theatre at Cassel records an event to which great significance was later to be attached: 'Denis Papin, discoverer of the steam engine, successfully demonstrated the first large-scale application of steam on this spot, in June 1706, in the presence of Karl Landgrave of Hesse.' In 1690 Papin had published his first design for an engine based on evacuating the cylinder by condensation of the steam. Whatever may be thought of the claim that he was 'the discoverer' it is certain that his steam engine, capable of pumping water to a height of more than 100 feet, was a great improvement on that of Thomas

Savory, who showed a working model to the Royal Society in 1699. But Papin took (from Leibnitz's drawing of Savory's machine) the idea of using separate containers for raising steam and for useful power: the prototypes respectively of the boiler and the cylinder. Papin suffered from the misunderstanding and ridicule so often the lot of the man who is ahead of his time. Rebuffed by the landgrave, he set out to travel down the Elbe to Britain in his paddle driven boat; it was pushed ashore by the bargees of Minden and smashed up by a jeering mob. Without his ship he was coolly received in England; after 1712 no more was heard of him. The lead in steam technology was taken by Britain and it was there that Newcomen and Watt were to make the decisive improvements that made it a viable commercial proposition.

Even in Britain where commercial needs were so pressing, where inventive genius abounded and capital was available, the progress of technology was remarkably slow. More than fifty years were to elapse between Newcomen's atmospheric machine of 1722 and the production of Watt's improved model of 1774, the true beginning of the age of steam. That gives some idea of the obstacles to progress in the previous century, when the theoretical advances in different branches of science were only beginning to change a climate of scepticism into one of hope. Recurring economic and political crises sapped initiative among the potential patrons of uncertain ventures. The academic and the artisan occupied different worlds. Indeed the immediate effect of the 'scientific revolution' was to complete the separation of a distinctive intellectual élite from the rest: the more advanced the ideas, the more rare and difficult their transmission and application. Schools were inadequate and, like universities, wedded to the traditional subjects of humanist culture. Where necessary an astronomer like Galileo might grind his own lenses, construct his own telescope. A wealthy patron might direct craftsmen in the search for mechanical improvement. But in general the exploitation of new discoveries was delayed by the lack of necessary instruments. It had taken Galileo only ten months to construct his own telescope to view the stars in an entirely new clarity and proximity and to announce his dramatic discoveries to a suspicious world: the moon's mountains, the Milky Way's innumerable stars and Jupiter's satellite moons. It was not till the end of the century, with the work of John Flamsteed and others in making further technical improvements that the telescope became a serious scientific tool. Galileo had made a thermometer, but it was not until 1724 that the Prussian Gabriel Fahrenheit (1686–1724) was able to give the world a reliable thermometer, calibrated to an accepted system of measurement. There was no overall direction, no programme, little co-operation except at the local level: if there was understanding of the need for agreed quantitative standards, action still came slowly. That is why, although there was undoubtedly a movement of scientific *ideas*, it is misleading to talk of a 'scientific movement'.

One device of measurement was everywhere the same and was steadily improved. In 1657 the first true pendulum clock was made at the Hague to the design of Christiaan Huygens. By inventing the balance spring he also made possible efficient pocket watches. The age of precise time keeping had arrived. With the pendulum clock, error expectation, formerly around 500 seconds a day, fell at once to a mere 10. Clock making, which was the first industry to put into practice the laws of the new dynamics, was also to facilitate the solution of further problems in those fields. Clock-makers also played a vital part in the development of scientific precision instruments, researching the properties of copper and steel, the thermal expansion of metals and the elasticity of springs. The special skills required of the clock-maker ensured him a uniquely respected place in society. In the Netherlands at the end of the century professions were ranked in fourteen classes: clock-makers were in the second. It is not hard to see why, fitting so aptly into the Cartesian picture of the world, the clock was the mechanism *par excellence* to the exponents of the new science; nor why Lewis Mumford could write that 'the clock not the steam engine, is the key machine of the modern industrial world'.

With the more general use of clocks and watches that is reflected in the rapid growth of centres of specialized manufacture, of which London and Geneva were by 1700 the most celebrated, went a more disciplined tempo of living, affecting in particular the mentality of the business world. With it too went a stronger awareness of the need for accuracy in the making of maps and charts. Soldiers needed reliable campaign maps, seamen charts showing reefs and currents. Landowners required precise evidence of their rights, statesmen began to think in terms of linear frontiers. The treaty of 1718 between the Emperor and Holland was the first in which a boundary was delineated on the map. With the aid of new mathematical techniques the art of surveying made rapid strides. By the end of the seventeenth century the best of the maps and charts were comparable in accuracy with those which we use today. In 1665 the Jesuit Athanasius Kircher marked sea currents on a map for the first time. Lighthouses were built (Eddystone was finished in 1699) and buoys were placed along channels. Roads were measured accurately. Ogilby's road surveys made use of the hodometer or waywiser. His *Britannia*, a folio volume of maps, was published in 1675. While maps, charts and clocks represent the search for accuracy it is typical of the age that they were also works of art. A clock by Tompion or a map by Blaeu is now cherished by its owner for its beauty as it was then valued for its utility.

Heaven and Earth

The most advanced science of the period and the one to which mathematics was most applicable was astronomy. In 1500 the Aristotelian idea of a universe of concentric crystalline spheres, with the earth at the centre, together with the linked idea of the motion of bodies as being constant and dependent on contact with a mover, was still a vital part of the mental world of European men. Upon it rested the notion, no less sensible and reassuring, that men had their place in a 'great chain of being', God's favoured creatures in a hierarchy which stretched from the archangels at the throne of God to the humblest forms of life on earth. Two hundred years later nothing was left of that world picture but art and anachronism. The shock of such a revolution needs no stress. It implied so much about the world, man's place in it and his relationship to God, that it touched life at every point. It affected so many branches of knowledge that it should properly be seen as the central process of 'the scientific revolution'. It is unlikely, however, that Copernicus thought that he was contributing to such a revolution when he published his *De revolutionibus* (1543) in which by setting the earth moving among the other planets he abolished Aristotle's basic distinction between the motion of bodies on a stationary earth and those of heavenly bodies. He hoped more modestly that his work might make possible a new calendar. Tycho Brahe, aloof and absorbed in his Danish island observatory, set a new standard for star gazers with twenty years of systematic observations starting in 1577. Johann Kepler (1571–1630) worked out laws of planetary motions, notably their elliptical orbit, in the course of long painstaking calculations as he sought to understand the world in terms of mathematical harmonies.

The importance of Galileo may lie chiefly in his contribution to modern scientific method and in his work on mechanics, yielding rich rewards in the shape of his idea of inertia (that a state of uniform motion is as 'natural' as a state of rest) and his studies of acceleration. It was however his astronomical findings that had the greatest impact on contemporaries: the four satellites of Jupiter, the multitudinous stars that form the Milky Way, and the mountains and valleys that feature on what had seemed the smooth surface of the moon. The Holy Office, guardian of the Aristotelian cosmology and the theology which rested now so insecurely upon it, censured the aged Galileo for upholding the Copernican view (1633). The sentence, to recite the seven penitential psalms once a week for three years, was as light as the process was futile. Plainly the inquisitors were trapped within a comprehensive system whose interlocking parts were now being dismantled in such a way as to threaten the collapse of the whole. In its place and no less comprehensive, Newton presented his 'frame of the system of the world'.

Newton's *Principia* was certainly founded on the work of his predecessors, notably Descartes, Kepler and Galileo. Moreover he owed a lot to Huygens and his theory of centrifugal force. It was Newton's universal application of the law of gravitation that was uniquely important, together with the fact that he alone was capable of the intricate mathematical calculation required to support the practical working of the law. It was the product of 'seventeen to eighteen months' by his own account, finished in the spring of 1686, a time of obsessive, sustained mental toil with insights and subtleties which ensure it a special place in the history of science. In the Newtonian universe physics and astronomy complemented each other. The sun and the planets comprised a self-contained system whose movements were determined by the interaction of its components. The stars were sprinkled through a space that was vast beyond the possibility of calculation: too remote to influence earth, but still subject to, and exercising, the force of gravity. The picture has been modified but it is still recognizable today. In its time, though not at once, everywhere or without opposition, the belief spread that Newton had explained for ever how the universe worked. Systematic observations, like those of Flamsteed, whose findings were presented in his *Historia coelistis Britannica* (1712), with some notable discoveries such as that of the aberration of light and the mutation of the earth's axis (Bradley) and that of the secular aberration of the moon (Malfey), confirmed the soundness of Newton's all powerful idea. More than any other man, this devout Christian and cautious empiricist was responsible for what he would surely never have endorsed: the optimism that was to inform science and the views of all whom it touched until the twentieth century. Stripped of its more facile aspects, it was essentially a belief in the capacity of man, guided by the light of reason, to explain all natural phenomena and so to improve his situation progressively in a world that was no longer inherently hostile, inviolate or mysterious.

Newton was active in another field of physical science which, though it offered less scope for mathematics, encouraged experiment and brought results. Optics was the first subject in his lectures and research. There had already been many experiments and theories. Descartes, who held that light was a pressure transmitted through his plenum of space, had investigated rainbows and calculated successfully the angle of the bow. In 1666 Newton procured a 'triangular glass prism to try the celebrated phenomena of colours'. By pressing a glass prism on to a lens of known curvature he made the colours into circles, since called Newton's rings. These were then measured and compared with estimates of the thickness of the air film from point to point. The experiments were repeated, using light of one colour only, when alternate light and dark rings were visible. Newton decided that light of each definite colour was subject to fits of easy transmission and easy reflection. He inferred that some of the colours of natural objects are due to their minute structure and calculated the dimensions needed to give these effects. After observation, reasoning and calculation, a further factor can be seen in Newton's work: the rare ability to make an imaginative projection beyond the limits of the evidence. In the queries at the end of his *Opticks* (1704), which contains the account of all his experiments, he suggests in the most guarded way, and as an invitation to further research, a corpuscular theory of light (as opposed to Huygens's idea of a complex of waves). His intuition is fascinatingly close to the ideas of those modern physicists for whom the structure of light is essentially atomic.

The first glass electrical machine was made and described by Francis Hawksbee, whose mechanical skills, also demonstrated by his air pumps, made an important contribution in the electrical field. Hawksbee's *Physico-Mechanical Experiments* of 1709 showed how a weak charge of electricity could be generated by rotating a glass globe against the hands or some material. It was not until 1746 that von Kleist of Pomerania and Musschenbrock of Leyden, working independently, simultaneously produced the condenser, a glass bottle coated outside and inside with tinfoil. The difference between conductors and insulators was made clear by other investigators. Most famous in this field was Benjamin Franklin (1706–90) who advanced the theory that lightning was actually electricity. The action of sharp points in discharging electrical bodies suggested the idea of the lightning conductor to d'Alibard and other Frenchmen. In 1752 a 40-foot rod was erected at Marly by the *curé* to 'determine the question whether the clouds that contain lightning are electrified or not'. The answer came swiftly: sparks were drawn from the lower end of the rod but the *curé* escaped with an injured arm. Less fortunate was Professor Rechman who was killed by a shock from an iron rod erected on his house in St Petersburg. Franklin had carried out a similar experiment with a kite which proved to be safe. The lightning conductor was the practical result. In his *History and Present State of Electricity* (1767) Joseph Priestley (1733–1804) recorded the 'side flash' and the oscillatory discharge of electricity; he was also the first to suggest that the law of electrical attraction was like that of gravitational attraction, an inverse square law. The Coulomb 'torsion balance', using two pith balls within a closed chamber, equally charged and therefore equally repellent, made it possible to investigate the distribution of electricity on surfaces and the laws of electricity and magnetism. Experiments were also made on the electrification which resulted from heating certain minerals and crystals, and into the shock-producing capabilities of the torpedo fish and the electric eel. Luigi Galvani (1737–98) of Bologna studied the susceptibility of nerves to such discharges and showed that contraction of the muscles could be produced by electrical action, and vice versa. Working on his results, Alessandro Volta (1745–1827) was to discover further that not only muscular contraction but also sensations were thus caused, and went on to demonstrate that the animal source of 'galvanism' was not essential. Galvani's famous frogs, in other words, were merely registering the electricity produced by the contact of the metals attached to them. Volta's instruments for producing electric current (*c.* 1800) were the foundation of modern electrochemistry.

The microscope was to biology and botany what the telescope was to astronomy: it revealed new worlds. Robert Hooke in his *Micrographia*

(1665), with its copper-plate engravings, publicized what could be done by combining glasses in a 'compound' instrument. Add the improvements in surgical instruments and it will be seen what opportunities there were for the study and dissection of plants and bodies. Of its nature biology was a field of diverse and empirical exploration. The complexity of living things and their processes did not make for the precise formulation of laws. For all that it was not untouched by the values of the age of rationalism. There were two broad ideas which inspired research. The first was that a principle of order must exist and a 'natural' classification ought therefore to be determined. The second was that the nature of living things could be analysed and processes discovered which would explain their functioning in their environment. Purposeful travel led to the discovery of specimens and to speculation about their relationships. Naturalists like Pierre de Tournefort (1656–1708) travelled widely and collected, corresponded and exchanged specimens; scientific curiosity, the charm of novelty, the thrill of the chase and the kudos that attached to the discoverer of the unusual all played a part. It was while climbing Mount Ararat that Tournefort discovered that altitude has the same effect as latitude upon the distribution of plant species. Medicinal needs and delight in beautiful flowers and rare plants were catered for by botanical gardens; the herbarium of the Jardin des Plantes was only the most important of many such collections, some of them private. As so often in this age, art and science served each other in botanical illustrations and the *chef d'oeuvres* of the great flower painters. Of the hundreds of Dutchmen who specialized in this genre, Jan van Huysum (1682–1749) could be selected to represent their virtuosity: 'with a skill never surpassed he fills his canvasses with great tumbled sprays of blossom tricked out with trompe l'oeil dewdrops, with gleaming leaves bearing insects so life-like that one is perplexed by their immobility' (Wilfrid Blunt).

Zoology was handicapped by the problem of preserving animal specimens. Stuffed bodies, dried parts and skeletons were brought back; menageries were started; systematic dissection brought advances by the comparative method. Duverney explained the anatomy of an elephant provided by the menagerie of Versailles to a fashionable Paris audience. Edward Tyson (d. 1708), by his work on the porpoise and the chimpanzee which he dubbed *Orangoutang, sive homo silvestris* (1699), began the comparative study of man and the apes that was to lead to the idea of evolution. Anthony van Leeuwenhoek (1632–1723) excelled even the ingenious Hooke in his explorations with the microscope: red blood corpuscles, muscle fibres, bacteria, the spermatozoa of man and other mammals, and of fish, oysters and snails were all examined and recorded. A minor coup was achieved in 1725 by Peysonnel, a Marseilles doctor, when he discovered that corals were not plants but animals. The giant among biologists, with whose work the science moved into new and fruitful territory, was Réaumur (1683–1757). He was trained in law and mathematics and practised as an engineer before government patronage gave him the opportunity to settle in a Paris suburb with his laboratory and collections. His memorial was the massive *Mémoires pour servir a l'histoire des insectes* (six volumes, 1734–42). His great contribution was to realize that biology must move on to the investigation of physiology and behaviour in relation to environments.

The greatest name among naturalists is that of the Swede Carl Linnaeus (1707–78). The publication of his *Systema natura* in 1735 provided a satisfactory system of cataloguing and indexing. John Ray had witnessed to the spirit of order in his vast *Historia plantarum* (1686–1704) when he based a classification of 18,000 plants on the constitution of their flowers and fruits. In the process he made some fundamental distinctions between species, and used the old logical term for the first time in its modern biological sense. Tournefort gave botanical classification further refinements: many of his natural groupings or *genera* survive today. Linnaeus seemed to be less concerned with natural classification than with arbitrary characteristics, such as the number of stamens or pistils selected to achieve a comprehensive means of identifying all organisms. His methodical skill contributed to the lasting success of his other innovation, the consistent binomial naming of species: genus followed by species. Linnaeus held that the same species had existed from the day of the Creation and that any differences between parents and offspring were aberrations of nature, not to be attributed to the great creative force, the divine wisdom that had fashioned the species. Examination of the rogue form of the toadflax, a mutant, as he thought produced by fertilization with foreign pollen, led him to concede, however, that new species and hybrids could suddenly occur in some such means.

'Everything happens by degrees in nature, nothing by jumps' Leibnitz declared in his magisterial manner. His 'law of continuity' reinforced the idea of a scale of nature: linear in the eighteenth century it was later to branch like a tree. The more complex the progression the more challenging to those who were to study the question of evolution. For the time being it could be held that nature represented a mighty harmony, divine in origin, created complete in form and perfect in the adaptation of species to environment and to other species. In Linnaeus's neat picture, the plants fed on the soil, insects on plants, birds on insects, larger birds on smaller birds, and so on; a view plainly reassuring to man, at the apex of the hierarchy of dependent life, but as rigid in its way as the medieval view of the terrestrial world under God. The optimism engendered by this view of a harmonious world was soon to be dispelled by the mordant criticism of the second generation of sceptical philosophers, led by Hume and Helvétius. It was firmly based however on the conviction that research was revealing, piece by piece, the perfect wholeness of God's creation so that the study of nature was a pious duty. This was a culture whose greatest secular parable was man in a natural garden, like Foigny's hermaphroditic deists enjoying perfect freedom and equality in his imaginary *Terre Australe Connue* (1676); whose religious outlook was coloured by what rationalist theologians, explaining to their gratified readers that nature had been rescued from Satan and restored to God, termed 'natural light'; and whose most talented philosopher, Spinoza, so far from the atheist he was alleged by some of his contemporaries to be, could declare: 'omnia existentia est perfectio.'

Such a position could not be expected to last for ever when active minds were still asking fundamental questions. Existing schemes of nature were being constantly added to provide the data for theories of evolution. The *Nouveaux Essais* of the polymath Leibnitz which were written and known to the cognoscenti in 1703 though not published till 1765, stimulated thinking about the transformation of species. His *Protogea* (1693) postulated a series of geological changes produced by the earth's cooling and the action of fire, wind and water, the biblical flood among those caused by the latter. One of his connections was the Dane Niels Stensen, who had described the formation of the strata by marine sedimentation and called fossils to witness before the end of the seventeenth century. Observers of the earth, like Lluyd and Woodward in England, saw that fossils could be used to discover the stages of the earth's history, if not to establish an exact chronology. Vallisnieri studied Italy and concluded that much of the land had once been covered by the sea. Inspired by Réaumur's explanation of the presence inland of marine shells, Fontenelle instigated the first geological map: it is a good example of the value of this clear-sighted, objective popularizer of other men's research. Fossils, he realized, were historical documents. And so geologists, slow though they were to depart from biblical stories and to give up trying to match them with the evidence of eye, pick and trowel, joined other scientists for whom the idea of a static universe ran counter to instinct and observation, and animal and plant breeders (like the tulip fanciers of Holland) who were discovering what selective breeding could do in challenging the Leibnitzian view of the harmonious order created by God, whole and self-regulating.

The French mathematician and geneticist Pierre-Louis de Maupertuis (1698–1759), in essays written in the 1740s, made the first sharp break, offering a mechanistic conception, in which species were produced by the selection for survival of individuals best suited to their environment. Infinite variety, he held, was possible from the combination of 'seminal molecules' from each parent. Those species that had survived out of the chance production of 'an innumerable multitude of individuals' were those in which 'order and adaptation were found, and those species which we see today are only the smallest part of those which a blind destiny has produced'. His fellow countryman, the naturalist Georges Buffon (1707–88), did not accept anything like this general idea of evolution, but criticized

Linnaeus for the artificiality of his scheme. He returned to the method best suited to the biologist, that of observation as a means to discovering causal laws. In nature he held that there were only individuals belonging to species, defined in terms of genetic continuity. His approach was to lead to the study of artificial selection, the geographical distribution of species, the extinction of some and variations in others. Lamarck was to follow him on the way to evolution, Darwin to acknowledge his inspiration.

The Mighty Light

'The candle that is set up in us shines bright enough for all our purposes.' The confidence, expressed here by Locke and shared by most of the secular philosophers of what the French called the *siècle des lumières*, is the most striking feature of this phase in Europe's intellectual history. The product of the scientific revolution, it was based on the conviction that scientific method had given to thinking men the right keys to use in the search for truth in all areas of life. It followed, not only that they felt justified in rejecting traditional methods and authorities, but also that they could formulate, in the light of reason (a word which came to mean little more than 'commonsense'), universal principles which would be valid equally for human behaviour as for political organization. They could look forward therefore to continual progress within a perfectible world. The blandly smiling faces of the *philosophes* painted by de la Tour reflect their belief in themselves and in mankind; how different from the stern countenances of the age of religious war! They could now think more of physics than of metaphysics. The same light that illuminated the way forward exposed the follies and fallacies of the world around them. And so they defined and selected targets for attack: the abuse of arbitrary power, injustice, intolerance, censorship and superstitition, which, for many, included orthodox religious observance. The French Enlightenment was anticlerical, even when not wholly anti-Christian. But it was a European, not exclusively a French experience. There was a significant difference between the Catholic countries, where the Church presented a large and vulnerable target and where, for example, its monopoly of education or right of censorship made it objectionable, and Protestant countries where the intellectual giants, Newton, Johnson, Leibnitz, Wolff, did not find that rationality and piety were necessarily incongruous. Even among Catholic countries there were profound differences: as between France and Austria where neo-Jansenism brought an earnest, puritan concern for pragmatic reforms which were more anti-Papal than anti-Catholic. A distinction should also be made between countries where the court dominated where, as in Charles III's Spain, the impulse and direction could only come from the sovereign; and those, like Holland, where an educated bourgeoisie called the tune and where ideas and inventions emerged as the product of a relatively free society: where perhaps the life of a capital city, Amsterdam, Edinburgh or Milan, provided a lively forum for the interchange of opinions. Again the country, like Germany, where university life was strong, may be contrasted with those like England, where some of the most important work, even in science, was done outside formal academic institutions. Pietist Denmark, where enlightenment came in the form of emancipation from some irksome restraints upon conduct, was a different world from post-partition Poland where the main impetus came from the struggle to survive as an independent nation. Leopold of Tuscany was able to draw on the heritage of a rich humanist tradition and civic pride; Pombal in Portugal was inspired chiefly by the need to restore vitality to a country with a pioneering commercial and maritime past. Whether one looks at the intellectual and social milieu of the various countries or at the individual responses and policies of the statesmen of the second half of the century, that generation of enlightened absolutists who recognized that they had a responsibility to initiate rational and useful reforms, the first impression is of an underlying unity. As Rousseau said: 'There is no longer a France, a Germany, a Spain; not even English. There are only Europeans. All have the same tastes, the same passions, the same way of life.' Certainly all Europeans were affected to some extent by 'the mighty light which spreads itself over the world', as the Deist Lord Shaftesbury described it. But they responded in different ways.

Viewed more closely this Europe appears still to be fragmented, its intellectual leadership individual, even idiosyncratic. Even in France, where the *philosophes* did constitute a movement with clearly defined objectives, there were conflicts of principle as well as of personalities. Yet it was French leadership which lent a kind of coherence to the Enlightenment which, without it, would have been no more than a general disposition to act upon rational principles. The intellectual power, the wit and above all the versatility of such men as Montesquieu, Voltaire and Diderot are not the only reasons for the process of cultural colonization which numbered Frederick the Great and Catherine the Great among its willing agents. In a period when political frontiers mattered little in intellectual circles and nationalist sentiment was hardly stirring, French writers were able to reach an appreciative audience far beyond the *salons*. It was there that they acquired their characteristic *esprit de corps*; there, in the socially acceptable and stimulating milieu which attracted d'Holbach from Germany and Hume from Scotland, they could identify objectives and plan campaigns; they could replenish their inkwells and sharpen their quills. The French language is specially well suited to the clear expression of complex ideas. It was easier for Germans, Poles and Russians to read the originals than to translate and adapt. What they found was a seductively complete and reasonable view of life. At its centre was the idea of man as master of his destiny: in Kant's words 'he had come of age'. But the process should not be seen in simple terms of emancipation from traditional constraints.

Fundamentally it was the rejection of the old and the continuing search for a new kind of authority.

Challenges to Authority

Standing sentinel over the world of educated Europeans in 1600, the twin sources of authority, Scripture and the classics, each embodied the idea that civilization had degenerated from a former golden age, be it in Eden or in Athens.[1] Man was therefore drawn to look back at the sources of Jewish and classical history to discover higher values or more significant truths than he could see in his own society. After the example of the humanists of the Renaissance, studying the literature of Greece and Rome, reformers and counter-reformers sought to buttress their theological arguments by renewed study of the Bible and the early fathers. The scene had then been set for potential conflict between the ecclesiastical defenders of the traditional view of Christian revelation and those who were repelled by its harsher aspects; further disillusioned by the outcome of the 'religious wars', like Montaigne, they might lean towards the classical conception of human dignity and virtue in a secular context. But for most of the seventeenth century the crucial struggle was postponed. The churches maintained and extended their hold over education, and classical studies remained under their wing. There was yet no authority convincing enough to be set against that of the Scriptures. In particular there was little to encourage men to believe in their own reasoning powers or in the possibilities of systematic experimentation. The experience of Blaise Pascal (1632–62) epitomizes the dilemma of this transitional period. Mathematician of genius, rationalist and devout Jansenist, torn apart by the conflicting demands of faith and reason, he found peace in a mystical experience and confirmation, in 'certitude, joy, peace, forgetfulness of the world and of everything except God', of the idea that God's grace must work independently of the intellect.

In the sphere of political thought the one radical challenge was more or less contained. Thomas Hobbes (1588–1679) had composed in his *Leviathan* (1651) a secular defence of absolute monarchy, grounded on the premise that man was impelled in all his action by his instinct for self-preservation. Yet for the first three-quarters of the seventeenth century the Bible still appeared to command the field and the idea of the divine right of kings enjoyed after 1660 a brief ascendancy. It appears in full splendour in the writing of Bossuet who derived his view of proper political authority from the history of the Jews; their experience was of unique importance since it embodied all that could be learnt about the will of God before the advent of Christ. By comparison, 'whatever was wisest in Sparta, in Athens, in Rome; or to go back to the very beginning, in Egypt and the best governed

[1] The ensuing pages should be read in conjunction with pp. 125–7 and 186–8, where, for example, Hobbes, Bossuet and Descartes appear in different, though related contexts.

of all states, is as nothing compared to the wisdom that is contained in the law of God'. To men brought up in this tradition, philosophy, history, even science, should be studied in the light of God's revelation of the truth about men, and strictly within the limits of the divine scheme as it is unfolded in the Bible. The attack upon this tradition was well under way before the end of the century; 'enlightened' men assumed it to have succeeded.

Bossuet believed that he could accommodate Cartesianism within his scheme. Descartes himself declared, at the conclusion of his *Principia Philosophiae*: 'Above all, we will observe as an infallible rule, that what God has said is incomparably more certain than all the rest.' But he had forged a lethal weapon for others to use against that idea of revealed truth. As Huygens wrote: 'What has above all commended his philosophy is not that he has debunked the old ideas but that he has dared to substitute for them causes for which one can comprehend all that there is in nature.' Descartes's follower, Baruch Spinoza (1632–77), saw nature as God, its physical laws being what we know of the divine mind. At the same time the human mind acts according to the same divine law. For him the highest good was the intellectual love of God, a part of the infinite love of God himself. He was a pantheist for whom 'whatsoever is, is in God, and without God nothing can be, or be conceived'. He was not of course an atheist, but it is not hard to see why his detractors said that his determinism diminished the role of God: to say He was everything came very near to saying He was nothing.

Spinoza was in some respects an isolated figure, not influential till the next century. But in the hands of others among Descartes's disciples reasoned faith was to become reasoned humanism. Whatever his special interest, even if it was primarily biblical criticism, the logician could not work in isolation, immune from other influences, suspicious though he might be of knowledge which, in Descartes's view, prejudiced argument. Pascal exactly characterized such an inward-looking frame of mind, being reluctant to travel: 'All the ills that affect a man proceed from one cause, namely that he has not learnt to sit quietly and contentedly in a room.' With travellers' tales introducing new and potent concepts, sentiment and curiosity could not be so confined. 'Some,' said la Bruyère, 'complete their demoralisation by extensive travel and lose whatever shreds of religion remain to them. Every day they see a new religion, new customs, new rites.' It was disturbing, though stimulating, to learn from the Jesuits that the morality of the Chinese, who had not the benefit of Christian teaching, was in its own way honourable and humane. The mandarins, who had acquired by ability the foremost position in the hierarchy, seemed to be models of philosophy in power; China's laws were correspondingly 'enlightened'. Lahontan introduced in 1703 the notion of the 'noble savage' who could lead a moral life by the light of natural religion. Cultivated Europeans learnt to think in relative terms; as they began to lose confidence in the uniquely God-given character of European laws and values, and in the theology and history that sustained them, they were provided, through the device of *voyages imaginaires*, with new insights and standards of reference. As Fénelon was to show in *Télemaque*, the visionary Utopia can provide a most convenient setting for criticisms of contemporary institutions.

In the age of Newton, as we have seen, the frontiers of science were shifting fast. Research revealed discrepancies between classical theory and nature, between a system governed by immutable laws, and life, as they observed it, unpredictable, a mass of conflicting forces, above all elusive and resistant to definitions. Paris towards the *fin de siècle* was full of foreigners who came to observe experiments and demonstrations: it was all too easy for the *beau monde*, as Fontenelle called his readership, to conclude that science could tell all. Not only science, but learning in general flourished in the cultural common market that served the needs of those who wanted to learn, and those who wanted just to keep up with the exciting game. Some of the best minds in Paris met at the Entresol Club in the 1720s, to drink tea and discuss public concerns; significantly it was dissolved by the government in 1731. If England was still influenced by French fashion, there was also a noticeable current starting to flow in the opposite direction. Even before Voltaire's patronage and the eventual victory of empiricism over Cartesianism, the names of Newton and Locke were familiar to Frenchmen. The latter spent six years, 1683–9, in Holland, in the years of royalist reaction in England; there he associated with other literary exiles who shared a bond in their abhorrence of Louis XIV's religious policies; there he wrote the influential *Essay on Toleration*. The Huguenot ministers, Jurieu and Claude, revolted against the mandates of the Roman Church and the ideal of the unified state as it was epitomized in the king. The coincidence of the Huguenot dispersion and the English revolution of 1688–9 brought about a significant cross-fertilization. The avante-garde of the Huguenots came to accept naturally Locke's idea that the people had a sovereign power and that the prince was merely a delegate. The central figure in debate and the dissemination of ideas was Pierre Bayle (1647–1706).

Voltaire called Bayle 'the first of the sceptical philosophers'. He might also be called the first of the encyclopedists, for he was a publicist by instinct, interested primarily in the collection of facts and the dissemination of ideas. The very name, *Nouvelles de la République des Lettres*, which appeared between 1684 and 1687, suggests the method of this higher form of journalism, the philosophy behind it and the people for whom it was intended. His great *Dictionnaire Historique* (1695) exposed the distortions and fallacies of the past by the plausible means of factual articles. Bayle came to believe that nothing was certain and his dictionary, which ran into many editions during the eighteenth century, became the sceptics' bible. His articles were informed throughout by hatred of dogma and the belief that in an imperfect world no person has a monopoly of truth of virtue. Bayle, whose brother died in a French prison in 1685, continued to profess belief in royal authority, seeking to enlighten rather than to overturn the French king. He appears too to have been as much concerned to expose the limitations of human reason as to attack superstition. But the effect of his work, and that of others less scrupulous pouring from the printing presses of the Netherlands and Rhineland, easily penetrating the nervous censorship of the French authorities and finding a ready market elsewhere in Europe, could not fail to be broadly subversive.

Yet moles within the citadel of faith may have done more damage than those who skirmished around its walls. The work of the earnest Malebranche, priest and disciple of Descartes, provides a useful corrective, if still needed, to the idea of science and philosophy as somehow distinct activities. For it was Malebranche, though he had little mathematical knowledge or scientific training, who came nearest, working from the analogy with sound, to the idea that was to evade the great Newton, that light has a measurable wavelength. His *Récherche de la Verité* has been called 'the last essay in Christian philosophy'. By making God subservient to the all powerful reason, he deprived Him no less surely than did the pantheist Spinoza, of His prerogatives and of the *raison d'être* with which Descartes had provided Him. So it was that Malebranche earned Fénelon's rebuke: 'you did not see that what you were really doing was subordinating religion to philosophy'.

By the 1680s the Jesuits were backing the efforts of the French government to enforce the teaching of traditional Aristotelian theories in universities, to counter the Cartesian bias of the Oratorians. There could already be seen what was to prove a recurring source of weakness in the government as in the church during the next century: sponsorship of the losing, or at least unfashionable side in the current intellectual debate. The danger of the close association of church and state is illustrated by the case of Bossuet, who was to the classical age and the baroque court what Voltaire was to the Enlightenment and the *salons*: oracle and seer. Bossuet encouraged Richard Simon when he set out to refute Protestantism through historical study of the Bible, but he was appalled when he saw where it led. Inevitably scholarship revealed the inconsistent and unreliable nature of many parts of the Bible. Simon's works were banned in 1678 but the Dutch printers saw to it that they remained in circulation. Historical method was starting to assume its place in the comprehensive search for truth. In the hands of Gibbon for example, himself following the pioneering search of the seventeenth-century giants, Mabillon and Tillemont, history was to become, if not more objective, at least more scrupulous and thorough in the use of documents. The physiocrat Turgot was to suggest that it be added to 'the physical sciences'. But the *philosophes* characteristically believed that history was becoming a science because like other intellectual activities it was subject to philosophic method. It was also subject to the prevailing materialist bias which is the reason why, scholarly though individual writers, like Hume, might be, the Enlightenment was in some aspects limited and vulnerable to fresh insights about man and to further research into the past which, for Helvétius, was simply rubbish: 'the stupid veneration of peoples for ancient laws and customs'. Such a reversal of values could not have been foreseen a hundred years earlier when Bossuet, increasingly strident in the polemics of his old age, as if he realized that the traditional defences were starting to give way, began at the same time to make concessions. In the third edition of his *Universal History* he accepted the view of Fr Perron that a difference between the Vulgate and Septuagint editions of the Bible made 5500 BC a possible date for the creation, thus accommodating his work to recent discoveries about early Egyptian and Chinese history. Theology, science, history – in each area of the old world picture traditional authority was being questioned, and minds and imaginations attracted to new possibilities.

A New World of Ideas

It was not so much that certainties were being established. Indeed the conflict between Cartesian and Newtonian physics, not resolved in favour of the latter till the 1730s, was actually confusing the picture in one area where certainty might have been anticipated. Men might not know what to believe or how to establish the truth; they were learning what not to believe. This first phase of the Enlightenment was above all an unsettling experience in a period of intellectual history. The dilemmas that faced thoughtful men are epitomized in the ultimate scepticism of Bayle: 'the grounds of doubting are themselves doubtful; we must therefore doubt whether we ought to doubt'. To Bayle then there appeared still to be lacking a criterion of truth, a system by which the reliability of evidence could be checked and a new model of the universe be constructed from parts which satisfied the new tests of credibility. Gradually, however, science appeared, in one department after another, to be established on an unassailable base of experimentally verifiable facts. With a new set of criteria upon which to judge between truth and error, came the confidence that characterizes the second phase of the Enlightenment. It is even possible to trace it to a single year, 1734, when the publication of Pope's *Essay on Man* – with its bland affirmation in polished, quote-worthy couplets of a deism that could be reduced to the comfortable formula, 'whatever is, is right', of Montesquieu's seminal work, *Considérations sur les causes de la grandeur de Romains et leur decadence*, with its empirical view of history, and of Voltaire's *Lettres philosophiques*, observations on the relative freedom of British thought, writing and institutions – may be taken as the sign that the forces were gathering for assault. They did not operate under a single command, nor did they adopt a common tactic; but they were animated by the conviction that truth was unfolding before their eyes; they were being 'enlightened'.

Of course the evolution of ideas and the response of men are never so orderly or predictable as is suggested by attempts to distinguish between periods, to place bounds and attach labels. The state of mind of Newton himself illustrates the point. Years after he had published his *Principia* he was searching for the precise plan of Solomon's temple which he believed to offer the surest guide to the topography of heaven. That was the preoccupation of the man who had done as much as anyone to bring about the second phase of the intellectual revolution. The elegant simplicity of a single law which could explain all movement, terrestrial and celestial, offered men the hope of comprehending the workings of a world in which they had hitherto dwelt, in uncertainty and apprehension, only trusting to familiar authority, like children in the night. Newton, who once memorably described himself as like a small boy playing with pebbles by the shore of a great unknown sea, was not, however, dismayed to find that his law did not provide the basis for a self-regulating universe. Motion, he calculated was 'much more apt to be lost than got and is always upon the decay'; the earth's axis was slipping and such defects could only be redressed by the direct intervention of God. So Newton's God was not, as Leibnitz implied, the prisoner of his own created universe and its laws. On the contrary he was a free agent whose regular intervention was necessary if 'the laws of nature' were to be envisaged as a God closer to the omniscient, active God of the Bible than to the 'supreme being' of the deists.

Nature in the post-Newtonian world, from being a mass of phenomena which men were unwise to investigate, became a system of intelligible forces: in Newton's words 'exceedingly simple and comfortable to herself'. It is no accident that this was a great age of garden-making, as men came to delight in imposing order upon a natural environment or, as in *le jardin anglais*, exploiting nature according to well-defined principles. The very word 'nature' was changing, to become, along with reason, a cult word of the new faith. How could men not be optimistic when what had appeared threatening or hostile now became an ally, when man himself was offered keys to discovering what was still unknown to him? – when suddenly, above all, instead of the swirl of ideas of the years of transition, all currents of the new thinking seemed to flow together?

Newton's counterpart as philosopher of empiricism, was John Locke (1632–1704). His *Second Treatise on Civil Government* (1690) offered a theoretical justification for a contractual view of monarchy as a limited and revocable agreement between ruler and ruled. His works on education, toleration and the rational basis for Christian belief were more influential among the *bien-pensants* of the continent, where his political theories could only be of academic interest. They convey the versatility of a man of affairs who was also a scientist and philosopher. The journal of his travels in France (1675–9) is studded with notes on botany, zoology, weather, instruments of all kinds, statistics, particularly those concerning prices and taxes, and recurring through all, his two prime interests, medicine and metaphysics; it is the perfect introduction to the world of the scientific revolution as well as to one of its liveliest minds. Locke was the first to regard philosophy as purely critical enquiry, with its own problems, not above but essentially similar to other sciences. What he called his 'historical plain method' was admired by Voltaire who regarded him as specially wise because he had not written 'a romance of the soul' but modestly offered 'a history of it'. The object of his *Essay Concerning Human Understanding* (1690), as he stated it, was 'to inquire into the original, certainty, and extent of human knowledge; together with the grounds and degrees of belief, opinion, and assent'. Whence, he asked, came the mind 'by that vast store which the busy and boundless fancy of man has painted on it with an almost endless variety. Whence has it all the materials of reason and knowledge? To this, I answer, in one word, from experience.' He refuted Descartes's view that men could have any innate ideas and, making use of anthropological evidence from different countries, presented a radical alternative view: that knowledge consisted of ideas imprinted on the mind through observation of external objects and reflection on the evidence provided by the senses. Moral values, Locke maintained, were derived from sensations of pleasure or of pain, the mind calling good what experience shows to produce pleasure.

Though he dared to suggest that souls were born without the idea of God, Locke deemed himself Christian. He held that sensationalism was a God-given principle which, correctly followed, would lead to conduct that was ethically sound. For Morelly, author of the *Code de la nature* (1755), the natural *bienfaisance* of man was the basis of his religion as well as the regulator of his behaviour. As in the case of Descartes and Newton, however, Locke had opened a way to disciples who took up the challenge and drove on to logical conclusions which might be far removed from the intention and spirit of the master. One such was the Irishman and bishop, George Berkeley, who suggested that the observer has no more proof of the independent existence of primary qualities than of secondary ones. There was no proof that matter existed beyond the idea of it in the mind. Most philosophers after Descartes resolved the problem of the dualism of mind and matter by becoming materialists, eliminating mind: Berkeley eliminated matter. He was not taken seriously. Locke was perhaps more scientific, certainly better attuned than the Bishop to the intellectual preoccupations and practical needs of the age. After he had been discovered by Voltaire, simplified and presented to the French world of letters, his posthumous influence, as advocate of toleration, of a rational basis for Christianity, above all of the sensationalist psychology, was assured. In the debate about moral values Locke offered a new argument for toleration, and indeed for potential equality: beliefs, like other differences among men, were largely the product of environment. It followed too that society could and should be responsible for the moral improvement of its members. Finally, since human irrationality was the product of erroneous ideas implanted by misguided schooling, education acquired a new importance. Its improvement, which was usually held to entail release from the control of the Church, became a desirable objective. Disclosing scientific laws applicable to man, his mind and social relations, Locke pointed the way along the road on which some 'enlightened' rulers were to travel.

After the victory of empirical methods, experiment was generally seen not as an aid, brought in to confirm the product of deductive reasoning, but as the point of departure. All knowledge was held to be subjective and relative to the sense perception of man. In his influential work *Traité des sensations* (1754), Étienne de Condillac (1715–80) concluded that all knowledge had to be reduced to probability. Voltaire, always faithfully reflecting the changes in intellectual climate, had clearly absorbed the message when he wrote, 'We see appearances only; we are in a dream.' Enlightenment science examined *how*, but renounced *why*. There was a general mistrust, even animosity towards 'systems'. The naturalist Buffon wrote, in his introduction to the first volume of his *Histoire naturelle* (1749): 'We must, therefore, resign ourselves to describing as cause what is a general effect, and abandon the attempt to push our knowledge any further. These general effects are for us the true laws of nature.'

Man needed to be reassured in this unfamiliar world that he was entering. Along with the Newtonian revolution in physics went the growth of belief in the idea of a benign providence on which man could rely since it could be shown to be active in the world around him. Writers earnestly plied their readers with examples of God's benevolent intention as it was manifest in his creatures. Pluche, for example, wrote of domestic animals that they 'are not merely docile, but they naturally love us and come to us spontaneously to offer their various services'. Voltaire observed of mountain ranges that they were 'a chain of high and continuous aqueducts, which by their apertures allow the rivers and the arms of the sea the space which they need to irrigate the land'. There were dangers in this attractive view of the universe and of God's role in it. The idea of Providence could degenerate into a fatuous complacency. It was a wholly unscientific assumption in an age in which for the first time scientists, if not at peace with men of religion, at least enjoyed a truce and had a free hand to pursue researches which were showing them a less comforting, more complicated world.

Mauperthuis had repudiated the genetic theory of pre-existence since it could not explain the known facts of heredity, nor the existence of hybrid or deformed creatures; in its place he put a theory of spontaneous generation. It had important consequences. Scientists began to attribute to matter a form of life. Buffon wrote: 'life and movement, instead of being a metaphysical degree of existence, are physical properties of matter'. It was no longer necessary to assume the fixity of species; instead there was a new conception of life as a constant, shapeless, flux. A blow to the idea of nature as regulated by universal laws was dealt by observations of particular species. Even more damaging was the solution of particular problems in the realm of astronomy which proved that Newton was wrong to assume that gravitation would not keep the solar system working regularly without divine intervention. Irregularities in the orbit of planets, for example, were found by d'Alembert to be self-correcting. No less unsettling, though incomplete and, of their nature, less susceptible to proof, were the observations of geologists. Guettard for example, in the volcanic hills of the Puy de Dôme area, found that evidence of fossils and rocks conflicted with the time-span allowed for in the Old Testament. Whether they were stressing the complexity of matter, with the suggestion that it could generate life, or the equally revolutionary conception of a world and life in it that had been evolving over an immense period of time, scientists were dispensing with God, if not as an extra factor, belonging to a separate world of intuitive understanding, certainly as a necessary factor in their explanation of the universe. Scepticism advanced boldly into the middle ground of opinion where some theologians were still seeking compromise, rallying round the standard of providence, others in full retreat, looking for old ground and trusted weapons. Julien La Mettrie (1709–51), in *L'Homme machine* (1747), asked: 'who knows if the reason for the existence of man is not his existence itself?' and articulated a new version of the doubters' gospel: 'We know nothing about nature: causes hidden within nature itself may have produced everything.' The way was open for the avowed atheism of baron d'Holbach (1723–89) who declared, in his *Système de la nature* (1770) that there was no divine purpose, no master plan: 'the whole cannot have an object for outside itself there is nothing towards which it can tend'. Those, like Voltaire, who rejected d'Holbach's bleak conception of a universe of matter in motion, in which everything happened of necessity and the answer to all questions was that 'it cannot be otherwise', but still allowed themselves to remain conceptually prisoners of scientific method, could in any case find no comfort in the teaching of an established church which insisted still on the literal truth of revelation. It might seem to them that there was no alternative but to go with David Hume (1711–76), for whom the idea of miracles was repugnant to reason, and religion was 'a riddle, an aenigma, an inexplicable mystery': to be, as it were, a sceptic about scepticism and to deny that man could reach objective knowledge of any kind.

The French Ascendancy

It is possible of course to say that these were intellectual games for the few. It is probable that the mass of the people, even in relatively advanced England and France were untouched by philosophical speculation and untroubled by doubts about revealed religion. For them the Bible was literally true, morality was based on the commandments. Even among the literate classes in the countries most affected by the new thinking, those who actively participated in the debate or could follow the reasoning were to be counted in hundreds rather than thousands. But delayed and diminished though it may have been, the impact was eventually considerable, especially in France, where there was a ready sale for writers who sought to apply the rational and experimental methods to what Hume called the science of man. Foremost among them was Charles de Secondat de Montesquieu (1689–1755), whose *De l'esprit des lois* appeared in twenty-two editions within eighteen months of its publication in 1748. Born a nobleman, though of a family of relatively modest standing, he had inherited from an uncle a presidency in the *parlement* of Bordeaux; his magistracy was a support and an income; his career was essentially that of a man of letters, more scholarly than most of the *philosophes* but a shrewd judge of men. This work of Montesquieu cannot be defined within a single category. He had already won fame with a youthful *jeu d'esprit*, the *Lettres persanes* (1721), in which he used the supposed correspondence of a Persian visitor to Paris to satirize the Church, under that 'magician' the Pope; the society upon which it appeared, to the disinterested Uzbek, as to his secular-minded creator, to impose so fraudulently; and, by implication, the political system which supported it.

Politics is 'a science which teaches princes to what lengths they may carry the violation of justice without injuring their own interests'. This sprightly judgement typified the sharp humour of Montesquieu's attempt, in his words, 'to mix philosophy, politics and ethics into a novel and to bind the whole together by a secret and so to speak, obscure chain'. Its importance lay in its being derived from his experience of the events of the Regency when accepted institutions and beliefs were being questioned as never before. The 'obscure chain', the logic that lies hidden behind what appears to be arbitrary appearances, emerged as a theory of laws of political decline in *L'Esprit*, when he turned a life's reading to good account in a wide-ranging enquiry into political systems as the product of custom and circumstances. Laws for this historically minded lawyer were not abstract rules but 'the necessary relationships which derive from the nature of things'. Accepting completely Locke's psychological theory of sense impressions, he went further, following the line of the Sicilian Giambattista Vico (1688–1744), the highly original author of *Scienza nuova* (1725), and proceeded, arguing always from example, towards the idea that human values are the evolving product of society itself. Among the factors governing society, he listed 'climate, religion, laws, the principles of government, the example of the past, social practices and manners', and concluded: 'from these a general spirit is formed'. Montesquieu's belief in knowledge as a factor in the shaping of society is characteristic of his age; so also is his interest in precedents and examples from ancient Greece and Rome; so indeed is the

Anglophil tendency – which did not however prevent him from misinterpreting the English constitution as being based on 'the separation of the powers'. Moral freedom was realizable, he argued, only under a government whose laws were enacted by an elected legislature, administered by a separate executive and enforced by an independent judiciary. The doctrine, with the ideal of mixed government, was at first to be more influential in the New World than in the Old. Modelled on a Newtonian view of the static equilibrium of forces in the universe, it was conceived essentially as a safeguard against despotism, rather than as an instrument of progress. It did not therefore appeal to those for whom the chief obstacle to progress was privilege, who looked to an 'enlightened autocrat' to reform society and who feared, like Claude Helvétius (1715–71), that his ideas would please 'our aristocrats and petty despots of all grades'. Financier, amateur philosopher, whose influential work, *De l'esprit* (1759), argued that each individual, in seeking his own good, contributed to the general good, Helvétius urged that laws, being man-made, 'should be changed by men so as to be more useful to them'. He believed that 'the art of forming men is in all countries so closely linked to the form of government, that it is perhaps not possible to make any considerable change in public education without making one in the constitution of states'. And the spirit of the Enlightenment is well conveyed in his suggestion that 'one must construct experimental ethics in the same way as experimental physics'. Montesquieu's political conservatism belonged to a different world from that of the younger generation of *philosophes*, disenchanted, utilitarian and convinced of the need for social engineering. In any case it was the sensibility and method of this most urbane of writers that counted for most. With his insight into the reasons for human diversity went a great toleration for the resulting variations of laws and systems. His vision of society as an integrated whole served as a warning, which might well have been heeded by the more dogmatic sovereigns, against any attempt to regulate society by the precepts of a universal principle of reason. At the same time the dispassionate manner of his enquiry, scientific at least in the way he argued from the evidence of the past, strengthened belief in the ability of reason to find solutions for human problems. Along that road he could not travel, for he saw the problem of right conduct as one of adapting to circumstances. It was left to Voltaire and those like him, who saw enlightenment more in terms of campaign, to advocate the power to change.

The political education of François Arouet (1694–1778), whose pen name Voltaire was to become, for innumerable readers, synonymous with the Enlightenment, was begun in the Jesuit college of Louis le Grand, continued in the sceptical, emancipated society of Regency Paris, and was completed first in the Bastille, then in England. From the Paris fortress to which he was consigned by *lettre de cachet* for a public insult to the duc de Rohan, he was released after eleven months on condition that he went to

England. For a precociously fluent writer, who liked to impress, amuse but also to play with ideas, such experiences might have been contrived to turn critic into combatant, ideas into obsessions. Epitomized in such personal encounters, hurtful and more than a little absurd, the failings of bureaucratic absolutism, compounded by concessions to privileged groups, were heightened for him by contrast with the tolerance (though it was not secured by law), the political freedom and the open society which he found in agreeable exile among the wits and writers of London. Thenceforward, in all his writings, there can be seen the commitment, explicit or inferred, of a man who believed that he lived in 'curious times and amid astonishing contrasts: reason on the one hand, the most absurd fanaticism on the other'. The fanatics were those who were attached, with a faith impervious to argument, to the old regime in church and state. The reasonable were those who believed in progress and thought that it was feasible. But through what agency? When Voltaire wrote of 'a civil war in every soul' he meant the conflict between the general preference of intellectuals for a strong government, *étât policé*, which experience told them was the necessary alternative to anarchy, and the growing conviction among such people that the old order was not working.

Of all the advocates of toleration and reason, Voltaire became the best known, the most admired and feared. It was not that he was particularly original: he was essentially a popularizer and publicist; generally, he followed rather than led advanced opinion. Nor can his influence be measured simply in practical results. Though he might play, at different times the role of adviser and confidant of princes, notably Frederick the Great with whom he stayed at Potsdam from 1757 to 1759, he learnt then, as in his activities with France, that it was easier to criticize than to change society and its laws. For that a revolution was required. It would take forms of which Voltaire, who condemned the resistance of *parlements* to Maupeou in 1771, would surely not have approved. It is not surprising that he was no politician: he grew up under a regime which denied political opportunity. It is more significant that he was not, in the true sense, a philosopher, as were Vico, Hume, Rousseau, even Montesquieu. He dwelt mainly on the surface of life, probing, evaluating and transmitting what he found. It is that which makes him seem so inconsistent; it is also that which made it possible for him to represent the changing mood and opinion of his age. He was not a man to sacrifice safety or comfort. He became wealthy, not only from his books but from investments in the Nantes slave trade. He tried to evade taxes on his estate at Ferney, a miniature kingdom with a staff of fifty before his death; but he was rigorous there in the extraction of feudal dues. He could be both vain and vindictive. He was generous chiefly in imaginative energy, in the indignation expressed in the celebrated war cry 'écrasez l'infame', and in the time he devoted to the causes of those who were wronged by those whom he opposed.

What then was Voltaire's importance? First and foremost it was as a promoter of particular causes, Newtonian science, the reform of archaic laws. In his *Lettres philosophiques* (1734) he effectively delivered the *coup de grâce* to the system of Descartes and promoted Newton as the supreme authority. He could be devastating in argument because he was a master of the French language, whose polemical potential Pascal's *Lettres provinciales* had so powerfully demonstrated a century before. There was more than the technical mastery of the subtleties of syntax and the precision of words which caused French to replace Latin as the language of scholarship, diplomacy and the self-elected club of Europe's enlightened. There was also the astute judgement which enabled him to play on his readers' sensibilities. As he wrote: 'the most useful books are those to which the readers themselves contribute half; they develop the idea of which the author has presented the seed'. And so he made causes out of cases, lifting an episode – the execution of Admiral Byng (1757), for failing to win a battle; of Jean Calas, apparently for being a Huguenot (1762); of the chevalier de la Barre, for alleged blasphemy (1764) – to the level where they could be judged as examples of the follies and crimes of which humanity was capable when it did not listen to the voice of reason or when it was imprisoned within unjust or archaic systems. By his own insatiable curiosity he stimulated curiosity in others: an effective solvent of established institutions.

As in his lifetime, judgements of Voltaire have continued to be subjective. Some stress the negative side and regret the damage caused by his relentless war against the church in the name of reason. It is fair to say that his assaults were often crude and ill-informed, going beyond the institutions to the beliefs and practices, not only of Catholics, but of Jews as well. Even those who are sympathetic towards his iconoclasm may concede that he had little to put in the place of religion, that he offered no alternative vision, outlined no ideal society. But that is no weakness in the eyes of such a devoted admirer as Theodore Besterman, for whom Voltaire was the supreme liberator, the writer who most effectively taught men to realize their powers. 'This catalytic instant in man's long struggles to become himself, for man simply *sapiens* to become *philosophicus*, this movement in the history of humanity is called Voltaire.' To an exceptional degree Voltaire had the gift of making men think about important questions, indeed his questions were usually clearer than his answers. His views were sometimes affected profoundly by personal experiences, such as the death of his beloved mistress, Étienne, another man's wife, while giving birth to Voltaire's child, or some event, like the Lisbon earthquake of 1755, which cast doubt upon the idea of a providential order within a harmonious universe. Then it is instructive to see how he, as interpreter-in-chief to his age, responded, belatedly and ambiguously, to the challenge of one of the most profound among questioners of that complacent orthodoxy, Hume.

David Hume (1711–76) was endowed with the clearest, least sentimental of minds and the most equable of temperaments, as much at home in the *salons* of Paris as in his native Edinburgh. In his *Inquiry into Human Understanding*, he rejected the inference of a just God from the workings of nature as a craven compromise between the claims of traditional Christianity and those of the scientists. Starting from the idea of cause as the necessary foundation of knowledge, he postulated that since causality could not be demonstrated, the validity of knowledge is itself questionable. He saw experience as showing only the succession of events, not any intrinsic connection between events. He believed that habit leads men to expect certain sequences and consequences: the rational structure of the universe was only such a presupposition. He concluded that the uniformity of nature is an axiom, not a proof of the validity of scientific statements. And so Hume helped to change the course of thinking in and about science. Had science simply substituted for religion a new metaphysics? Was the rational order anything more than a premise? Of course science still had the advantage over religion in philosophical terms in that it recognized a premise to be just that, and no more: not an absolute truth, revealed, beyond question. The emphasis in science was moving moreover, in these middle years of the century, to the experimental; the main interest was in origin and evolution: in the particular rather than in synthesis and system. The scientist was reluctant to be convinced except by irrefutable evidence; but his doubt was more creative than the philosopher's because it was inherently capable of adding to the stock of knowledge. The *philosophe* could not find the antidote to smallpox. What he could do was to analyse the conflict and express the shift of ideas in ways that could both entertain and also clarify, for those who would have been lost in the abstract reasoning of Hume. In *Candide* (1759) Voltaire's ingenuous hero stands between the optimist Dr Pangloss, with his 'worthless bliss', and Martin who believes in the reality of evil in a world torn between the supernatural forces of good and evil. He is disillusioned by the dreadful misfortunes that mock his simple humanity. The author's conclusion is one of pessimistic resignation, positive only in its advice that the wise man, wishing to avoid pain, should not worry about problems which are of their nature insoluble, but should 'cultivate his garden'. Work, says the wise Turk, 'keeps at bay three great evils: boredom, vice and need'. It is typical of Voltaire that he should ascribe this eminently practical, if unelevated philosophy, to a Turk.

The marquis de Condorcet (1743–94), mathematician and one of the more radical of the *philosophes*, described them as 'a class of men less concerned with discovering truth than with propagating it', who 'find their glory rather in destroying popular error than in pushing back the frontiers of knowledge'. That was the spirit which animated the greatest publishing enterprise of the century, the *Encyclopédie*, which appeared in seventeen volumes between 1751 and 1765, after checks and attacks which would have discouraged any one less tough and committed than its publisher, André-

François Le Breton (1708–79), and its chief editor, Denis Diderot (1713–84), who saw it through to a triumphant, and profitable, conclusion. The critical point was reached when the publication of Helvétius's *De l'esprit*, together with controversy over the orthodoxy of another contributor, the abbé de Prades, and increasing concern about the growth and influence of freemasonry, convinced some ministers that they faced a general conspiracy to undermine authority. If they had been as united and determined as the church authorities the *Encyclopédie* would have been throttled. In 1759 it was placed on the Index and a ban of excommunication was pronounced on any who should read it. The knowledge that Pope Benedict XIV was privately sympathetic lessened the impact of the ban; a change of heart on the part of government made it irrelevant; a new chief of police, de Sartine, was friendly; and so production continued, though without d'Alembert, or Rousseau, an early contributor who was now moving into a world of his own, detached and hostile to the encyclopedists and their utilitarian philosophy. The *Encyclopédie* was completed with the publication of the last ten volumes together in 1765.

Diderot's co-editor, the mathematician Jean le Rond d'Alembert (1717–83), who took his first name from the parish church where he was found abandoned on the steps, had set the tone for the work in the masterly preface in which he described how history showed knowledge accumulating, offering always the means of improvement. The title page of the first volume proclaimed the authors' intention to outline the current state of knowledge about the sciences, arts and crafts. Among its 160 contributors were working craftsmen who provided the accurate detail which characterizes the numerous technical articles. Pervading all was the idea of knowledge as a social function, providing the means by which, in Diderot's words, 'our children, better instructed than we, may at the same time become more virtuous and happy'. Embodying the idea that man was naturally good and capable of perfection through the acquisition of knowledge, it was a magnificent witness to the spirit of improvement. That kind of utilitarianism, tinged with Locke's doctrine of environmentalism, was one aspect of what d'Alembert called 'the philosophic spirit'. If it had been no more it would have been as useful as the *Cyclopaedia* of Ephraim Chambers which it was originally intended to copy; it would not have been the prime textbook for young intellectuals, those who shared Diderot's vision of the *Encyclopédie* as a means through which he could 'change the common way of thinking'. Diderot had paid his due to the select club of those who could call themselves martyrs for Enlightenment: he had been imprisoned in Vincennes gaol (1749); he had seen one of his works, *Pensées philosophiques*, condemned and burned by the authorities. In his more important work, *Sur l'interprétation de la nature* (1755), he contributed to thinking on that theme the idea of nature as a great creative process of which man was an integral part. But his most important achievement was the production of the *Encyclopédie*. Nearly every important thinker contributed to what was, in essence, a summary of what had been achieved in the scientific revolution. There was sufficient unanimity of approach to endow the new faith of scientific empiricism with the authority that Scripture and its interpreters had so long enjoyed, but which they now had to defend against the more deadly and sophisticated weapons with which the *Encyclopédie* armed their assailants.

Self-indulgence and energy, idealism and worldliness characterized the many-sided personality of Diderot who needed the challenge of the *Encyclopédie* to bring out his courageous spirit. For Diderot anticipated the style, Bohemian it may be called for want of a better word, which was to find its archetype in Jean Jacques Rousseau (1712–78) and to evoke a response in thousands of eager disciples for whom the stark materialism of d'Holbach, for example, might have been, as indeed it was for Voltaire, a disillusioning end to the liberating process of the Enlightenment with men being forced, it seemed, to choose between complete scepticism and rigorous determinism. 'It came upon us so grey, so cimmerian, so corpse-like that we could hardly endure its ghost': so Goethe spoke for the Romantic generation. In his novel of the 1760s *Le Neveu de Rameau*, Diderot's hero, eccentric and nonconformist, persuades his orthodox bourgeois uncle, who professes, and praises, virtue, to confess to actions so cynical as to stand conventional values on their head. It is easy to see that such disillusion was Rousseau's point of departure, though it is harder to see where he was travelling. His questions were, in any case, more important than his answers. Ridiculing those who derived right action from right thinking, he exposed a salient question: if virtue were dependent on culture, and culture were the prerogative of a privileged minority, then what was the prospect for the rest? 'We have physicists, geometricians, chemists, astronomers, poets, musicians and painters in plenty; but we no longer have a citizen among us.'

His own self-absorbed, self-analytical personality and feckless, dissatisfied life made Rousseau a suitable representative for those who felt estranged from a cultural élite, the 'learned society in which Diderot had such faith, which appeared content to remain a protected species within society, readier to criticize its external faults than to challenge its essential form. Diderot wrote only 'for those with whom I should enjoy conversing. I address my words to the philosophers; so far as I am concerned there is no one else in the world': *de haut en bas*. With Rousseau, such confidence in the inherent value of a culture which was inevitably the possession of a privileged, literate minority, to which had been added the assurance of unlimited progress, came to an abrupt end. He questioned its premises and principles. His *Confessions* were to portray a man of good instincts and intentions forced to become a rogue and an outcast by the artificiality of society. His first essay, *Discours sur les arts et sciences*, had expressed his perplexity at what he held to be the contradiction between the exterior world of appearances and the inner realm of feeling. In it appears the seminal idea of nature as a primal condition of innocence in which man was whole, not torn apart by conflict between inner promptings and external sanctions; not perfect, but transparent, incapable of successful deception. Now 'we no longer dare seem what we really are but lie under a perpetual constraint'. With Rousseau's view of culture went a new emphasis upon the value of emotions. And with him the key eighteenth-century word nature, already so serviceable, whether to the exponents of an undogmatic religion, of universal principles of law or of the market economy, acquires a new meaning and resonance. In his *Discours sur les origines d'inegalité* (1755) he wrote: 'We cannot desire or fear anything, except from the idea we have of it, or from the simple impulse of nature.' Speaking for those whom the knowledge-mongers, the encyclopedists, saw as hopeless stragglers in the long march of civilization, Rousseau turned to the basic relations of life, love and friendship and introduced an uncomfortable, prophetic note, precursor of much democratic rhetoric: 'Money, though it buys everything else, cannot buy morals and citizens.' Nor could the *philosophes* expect to achieve much so long as they shared, with the princes whom they sought to sway, in the moral corruption of man by his culture: 'So long as power alone is on one side, and knowledge and understanding on the other, the learned will seldom make great objects their study, princes will still more rarely perform great actions and the peoples will continue as they are, mean, corrupt and miserable.' It was a far cry indeed from the ideal of the *philosophes* when they counselled autocrats on the beneficent use of their power. How far it was from the reality the reader of the ensuing chapters may judge for himself.

Though Rousseau thought that civilization was rotten in inception and in all its forms, he did not believe that a return to nature was either possible or desirable. For him the state of nature was mainly hypothetical. It was potentially a revolutionary hypothesis, but Rousseau was no revolutionary. He believed that man must seek to recover his lost wholeness at a higher level of existence. To this end the individual needed a new education; and humanity a new political constitution. *Emile* (1762) proposed an education which would foster in the individual 'natural' growth. His *Discours sur l'économie politique* (1755) and *Contrat social* (1762) contained proposals for a constitution to enable the individual to develop his personality without impairing the principle of social equality. The *Contrat social* was banned; the author prudently left the country, his book attracted all the more attention and readers. In it Rousseau addressed himself to the crucial question of authority. He rejected both natural law and force as the basis of legitimate authority. What form of association then will allow both security and the freedom which is natural to man? It is one in which 'each man, giving himself to all, gives himself to nobody'. It is to be realized through his conception of the general will which is expressed in a system of laws, to which all freely submit. It is more, however, than the sum of individual wills, which is no more than public opinion. It is general because its object is general; it is public spirit seeking the common good, which Rousseau defines as 'liberty and equality': equality 'because liberty cannot exist without it'. He advocated the total sovereignty of the state, a sovereignty which presupposes that the state would be guided by the general will. His good society was a democratic, egalitarian republic: if not exactly Geneva, yet clearly influenced by his upbringing in the city state as Aristotle had been by his experience of Athens.

Even so brief a resumé of the ideas of a subtle, paradoxical thinker, whose ideas are often as elusive as his personality, is enough to suggest that in his lifetime Rousseau's influence on men and events was slight. Already some, however, had been inspired by him. When the *illuministo* Italian nobleman Giambattista Biffi heard of Rousseau's death he wrote: 'The greatest genius of our age is dead.... My father, my guide, my master, my idol.... His enemies were all fanatics, asses, priests, charlatans, traitors, liars. His friends are all good men, sensitive spirits.' Such adulation was a foretaste of what was to come. The eloquence with which his ideas were expressed was matched by their intrinsic appeal, transcending logic, speaking to the condition of radicals and of men of sensibility on both sides of the Atlantic. That the bourgeois might fear for social consequences, like the draughtsmen of the Declaration of Rights of 1789, careful to proclaim the sacred right of property, did not diminish its impact. Rousseau's idea of the loss of nature and his picture of 'de-natured' man who 'knows only how to live in the opinion of others' was as potent for the generation which was to witness the overturning of the *ancien régime* as the idea of the loss of God under the worldly leadership of the Catholic Church had been for the generation of Luther and Ignatius. In Rousseau's case the appeal was especially to the young and dispossessed who might identify with his self-estrangement and equate artificiality with the privilege that thwarted talent: to men like the young lawyer of Arras, Maximilien Robespierre; to Italians, like the members of the Milanese Società dei Pugni (Society of Fists) who wanted to stir up Lombard society under Austrian rule; or to Germans who resented alike the lack of opportunity under their own regimes and the cultural influence of the French. On the one hand the severe rationalism of Kant, on the other hand the emotional idealism of *Sturm und Drang* found their inspiration in Rousseau. Yet with both, with the author of the *Critique of Pure Reason* (1781), as with the romantic hero portrayed by Johann Wolfgang von Goethe (1749–1832) in his *Sorrows of Young Werther*, we seem to take leave of the Enlightenment. It died with the harsh authoritarianism of Robespierre and the Jacobins: symbolically, we might say, with the execution of Condorcet, sanguine to the end about the prospect for humanity, on the guillotine which represented, for the Jacobins, the justice of the people.

Germany and Italy

Everywhere the influence of French ideas had been a stimulus to reforms. But the way in which these reforms were carried out and their underlying philosophy reflected the local situation. In both Germany and Italy, for example, circumstances favoured an emphasis on the kind of practical reforms which the philosophes, operating, as N. Hampson describes them, 'in a kind of void', could only recommend to foreign rulers.

In no other country were universities so important as in Germany. By 1800 there were nearly 50; France at the time had 22, England but 2. Between 1600 and 1800 there were 24 new foundations reflecting usually the concern of a prince for the training of his subjects rather than private benefactors' zeal for higher learning. Not all were as vigorous as Halle (1694) or Gottingen (1737), but with the best Protestant universities leading the way in the humanities, mathematics, natural sciences and medicine, and young men being drawn from the Catholic south, some of the universities there responded to the challenge. After drastic reforms of the curriculum Vienna came to the fore in the last quarter of the century, attracting students from all over Europe. In general universities dominated intellectual and cultural life to a unique degree. Rulers valued them, and their teachers were influential because they served the state by educating those who too would serve. In the Lutheran countries, not only lawyers and administrators but teachers and clergy were in effect civil servants since education and religion were under the direction of the state. Most courses were to some degree vocational. The British king George II, visiting Göttingen, noted with satisfaction (and implied criticism of Oxford and Cambridge) that 'they are not satisfied here with a bare dry theory: the scholars are brought up in the practice of the sciences, to the end that they may prove more useful hereafter'. Some of the leading academic figures also held posts which enabled them to influence government; Joseph von Sonnenfels, for example, the notably humane political economist, was adviser to the Habsburgs on the serf question.

The subservience of church to state has led historians to emphasize the importance of Lutheranism in the evolution of the distinctive German attitude towards authority. In the eighteenth century moreover it was given a new flavour through the pervasive influence of Pietism, essentially a devotional movement but imbued with an active reforming spirit. But the earnest religious spirit, which affected life at all levels, was not confined to the Protestant confessions. Anti-clericalism tended to be an issue in the larger Catholic states because of the prominent role of the church as landowners and educators: in Joseph II's Austria Jansenism was an important factor in disputes with the papacy as well as in the struggle to free education from the grip of the Jesuits. But there was nothing comparable anywhere in Germany to the revolt of western intellectuals against traditional dogma. To be a philosopher, in Germany, was not to be a sceptic; rather the reverse. Amid all his speculations Leibnitz who, more than any other, influenced the way thoughtful Germans felt about life, held to the idea of a personal God, existing apart from, not subject to the limitations of a materialist universe. It was devotion, not indifference that led him to search for grounds for Christian reunion. His disciple Wolff, the leading figure of the *Aufklärung*, whom even Frederick the Great respected, believed that reason and revelation could be reconciled. Fundamentally opposed though he was to the Pietists, who secured his expulsion from Halle in 1723, the rational philosopher and the emotional revivalists shared essential Christian tenets. In Halle there evolved, out of the fusion of Pietism and Wolffism, a new 'scientific' theology which was both orthodox in such doctrines as the Trinity and 'progressive' in the spirit of the *Aufklärung*.

There may be differences of opinion about the reasons for the uncompromisingly Christian character of the *Aufklärung*. One factor, beyond doubt, is the acceptance of the principle of *cuius regio, eius religio*, with mostly opened frontiers for those who wished to migrate to another state where the prince was of their religious persuasion. It enhanced the role of the prince in ecclesiastical matters and reduced the scope for the conflicts which did so much, in western Europe, to foster doubt about authority. The religious spirit of the time may also have been an aspect of a general conservatism and respect for authority. In this the role of the lawyers and the nature of the law they taught was crucial. As expounded by the three most influential, Samuel Pufendorf (1632–94), Christian Tomasius (1655–1728) and Christian Wolff (1679–1754), natural law endorsed absolutism. They believed that the state had its origin in a contract and that there were certain civil rights; they advocated religious toleration and humane justice; they were opposed to torture, to the persecution of those alleged to be witches and of unmarried mothers. But they did not affirm the need for any constitutional safeguards; the subjects' liberties were to be enjoyed only at the discretion of the prince. Wolff, echoing Tomasius, declared that 'he who exercises the civil power has the right to establish everything that appears to him to serve the public good'. For him there could be no separation of powers. His sovereign was legislature, executive and judicature all in one. As defined in Wolff's *Rational Thoughts on the Social Life of Mankind* (1756), he was also to be a positive force in the land, benevolent in every sphere covered by modern government: as it were Luther's 'godly prince' in eighteenth-century dress, serving his people's needs, intellectual and artistic as well as material. It is the Enlightenment view about progress but home-grown, owing little to French thought. Wolff envisaged progress being achieved under direction of the sovereign who would create the schools, orphanages and hospitals and provide for the officials to run them: the *Wohlfahrtstaat* as he termed it. Wolff was only one among numerous writers in this vein, making their contribution to the ideal of enlightened bureaucratic absolutism. Chairs of natural law and cameralism (the science of administration) sprang up all over Germany. In Catholic as well as Protestant states it was coming to be accepted that the state should intervene and direct in every sphere of life. Though influenced too by the local school of cameralists, going back to seventeenth-century writers like Hörnigk and Becher, the emperor Joseph II exemplified the ideal. By his time, however, there was already a vigorous reaction against the rationality and practicality of the natural law school, with its emphasis upon regimentation.

The generation of Goethe, Schiller and Fichte valued above all feeling and spontaneity. The *Weltanschauung* of the literary revival appeared to be favourable to political liberalism. But unlike writers of 'Romantic' persuasion elsewhere in Europe the eloquent Germans did not at first effect a significant change in the way their countrymen saw political authority. There was one significant dissident, Johann Gottfried von Herder (1744–1803), the scholarly, detached superintendent of the clergy of Weimar. His ideal *Volk*-state would have had a republican form of constitution, indeed no rulers, since 'their existence is regarded as a denial of the rule of law'. But he had little impact until later generations explored his dense, difficult works, and then used only the conservative and nationalist elements: his experience illustrates the way in which the heavy paternalism of a small German state could muffle controversial views. Even Kant, who was opposed to cameralism and advocated the separation of powers, with the political participation of a large part of the population, the man who might have seemed most likely to have stirred up a radical movement, would not allow even the theoretical right of revolution. In his influential work, *Was ist Aufklärung?*, Kant drew a distinction which was to prove serviceable to future generations of German intellectuals, between the public and private use of one's reason. With Frederick the Great in mind he advanced the no less typical German paradox: the ruler with 'a well-disciplined and numerous army' could provide more liberty than a republic. In words which provide a significant text for modern German history he elaborated on the theme: 'a high degree of civil freedom seems advantageous to a people's intellectual freedom, yet it also sets up insuperable barriers to it. Conversely, a lesser degree of civil freedom gives intellectual freedom enough room to expand to its fullest extent.'

It is easy to overlook the affairs of the Italian states of the *ancien régime*, divided as they were by geography, history and politics. Independence, precarious or sterile, or foreign rule: neither condition suggests vitality. In the unsentimental reckoning of diplomacy the states represented, at least until the peace of Aix-la-Chapelle (1748), which created a state of equilibrium in which rulers could preserve neutrality, pawns to be moved about a board dominated by more important pieces. The general economic decline witnessed to the effects of the shift from Mediterranean to Atlantic lands of the most important activities in trade and manufactures: traditional urban industries proved unable to compete effectively against the products of Britain, Holland and France. Some luxury industries survived; silk became an important export. But the cities stagnated; if they grew, like Naples, it was as a parasitical centre of government. A backward agararian economy proved incapable of providing for any but the bare needs of most of the people. Most of the land in the plains was owned by nobility or church. Italy presented startling contrasts, between high art and the pomp of aristocratic living, and a general, demoralizing poverty: a land, it seemed to visitors, of monuments and beggars. They came to see the monuments, perhaps to listen to the music in which they might recognize the source and inspiration of some of the best of their own. But they usually returned convinced that Italy was backward. Its intellectual life would have remained a closed book to most of them. As elsewhere the Italian Enlightenment consisted of small, isolated groups, nobles, clerics, professors, bound perhaps by little more than love of talk and dislike for the local authority, be it church or state. Measured by impact on their governments they had relatively little effect. Where there was significant change it was usually the work of an enlightened ruler, like Leopold of Tuscany (1765–90), or a minister like Bernardo Tanucci, who would have achieved little in Naples without the intelligent support of his master, the future Charles III of Spain. Even in Savoy, the very success of the reforms of Victor Amadeus (1675–1730) and Charles Emanuel III (1730–73), which strengthened the state, blocked the way to the development of an independent critical intelligentsia. But the genius of Italians could not everywhere be so contained.

It may simply be that the spirit of the Renaissance was not dead. The heavy hand of the church, symbolized by the presence of Galileo on the Index of forbidden books; the survival, not only in the south, of a kind of feudal power which provided startling examples of servitude and degradation; or even at the mundane level of daily living, the vexations caused by the petty dues and taxes which, with the restrictive power of the guilds, hampered the development of the economy, were among the obvious targets for liberals and humanitarians. Universities, like those of Bologna, Padua or Naples, had preserved the tradition of scholarship and could still provide a stimulating home for such original thinkers as Giambattista Vico, author of *Scienza nuova* (1725), and Antonio Genovesi, another Neapolitan, who became professor of philosophy in 1741, at the age of 28, later turned his mind to ethics and finally, as a branch of ethics, to economic theory. An unusual feature of Genovesi's work was that he remained, while assaulting all established authorities, the church among them, a devout priest. He rose too above particular Neapolitan concerns to those of Italy as a whole, even to hint at the possibility of its future unification. But the distinguishing characteristic of Italians enlightened, as befits the land which produced such great scientists as Luigi Galvani and Alexander Volta, is their tendency to be severely practical. They introduced to political philosophy the slogan of utilitarianism, 'the greatest happiness of the greatest number'. They dealt with economics, government and education from the sober standpoint of men who realized that their country had fallen behind, with the passion of patriots who felt that it must be roused. These qualities can be seen in the work of Cesare Beccaria (1783–94), the Milanese nobleman.

Beccaria's most important work, *Of Crimes and Punishments*, was published in 1764. Within his lifetime it was translated into twenty-two languages. His pupils and imitators included Catherine the Great, who used his ideas extensively in her instruction to the commission for the reform of Russian laws, and Jeremy Bentham, perhaps the most influential single figure in the reform of English law. 'Newtoncino', as Beccaria was called by his admirers in the Society of Fists, sought to apply 'the geometric spirit' to the study of criminal law. By justice he understood 'nothing more than that bond which is necessary to keep the interest of individuals united; without which men would return to their original state of barbarity'. Punishments which 'exceed the necessity of preserving this bond, are in their nature unjust'. And so Beccaria condemned torture and capital punishment, questioned the treatment of sins as crimes, urged the importance of equality before the law and of prevention being given priority over punishment, and advocated the separation of the judicial and administrative powers. So much of the best in enlightened thought comes together in the work of this good man. Some of the most important reforms of the last years of the *ancien régime* and many more to follow in the revolutionary decade constitute a memorial to Beccaria and those like him who dared to articulate their faith in human reason into words. In the work of Beccaria, the link between philosophy and reform is plain to see. The Enlightenment was indeed, in Kant's words, 'man's escape from self-incurred tutelage'.

Further Reading

There is no shortage of books on the scientific revolution. H. Butterfield, *The Origins of Modern Science* (London, 1970), is a stimulating introduction. The arrangement of E.J. Dijksterhuis, *The Mechanisation of the World Picture* (trans. Oxford, 1961), makes it a specially helpful work of reference. A.R. Hall, *The Scientific Revolution, 1500–1800* (1954), is authoritative. His volume in 'The Rise of Modern Science' series, *From Galileo to Newton, 1630–1720* (New York, 1982), is less technical. Hugh Kearney, *Origins of the Scientific Revolution* (1964), is a collation of views on the subject up to that date. A Lancaster Pamphlet, P.M. Harman, *The Scientific Revolution* (London, 1983), provides a useful synoptic view. The connection between science and social and economic change is the theme of articles, by Christopher Hill, Hugh Kearney and T.K. Rabb, among others, in *Past and Present*, 27–32 (1964–5). A comprehensive study is A. Wolf, *A History of Science, Philosophy and Technology in the Eighteenth Century* (2nd edn, 1952). Links with technology are also considered in A.E. Musson (ed.), *Science, Technology and Economic Growth in the Eighteenth Century* (London, 1972); with intellectual trends, in J.E. King, *Science and Rationalism in the Government of Louis XIV, 1661–83* (Baltimore, 1949); and with society, in G.N. Clark, *Science and Social Welfare in the Age of Newton* (Oxford, 1946). S. Drake, *Discoveries and Opinions of Galileo* (New York, 1957), uses the astronomer's own writing. For his life and contribution to science, A. Kenny, *Descartes* (New York, 1968), may be best; for his philosophy, Bernard Williams, *Descartes* (Harmondsworth, 1978), is as clear as the abstruse nature of his subject's thinking will allow. Two other important biographical studies are: R. Lenoble, *Mersenne, ou la naissance du mechanism* (Paris, 1943), and L. Chauvois, *William Harvey* (1957). Though his prime concern, as in his subsequent volume, *The Eighteenth Century Background* (1940), is the intellectual climate as it affected literature, Basil Willey's *The Seventeenth Century Background* (London, 1979) offers a full treatment of Descartes. There is an excellent short book on Newton (1961) by C. Andrade. Another useful account for the non-scientist is F. Manuel, *A Portrait of Isaac Newton* (London, 1980). Also helpful and stimulating is Charles Singer, *A Short History of Scientific Ideas to 1900* (Oxford, 1962). The diffusion of scientific ideas can be studied in M. Ornstein, *The Role of the Scientific Societies in the Seventeenth Century* (1913). There are two particularly interesting case studies: E. Cochrane, *Tradition and Enlightenment in the Tuscan Academies, 1690–1800* (1961), and R. Hahn, *The Anatomy of a Scientific Institution, the Paris Academy of Sciences, 1666–1803* (Berkeley, 1971).

The student of the Enlightenment is now faced by an array of books. If he wishes to start with the originals, he will find no shortage of editions of the works of Locke, Montesquieu or Voltaire. The best recent biography of Locke is by Maurice Cranston, *John Locke* (Harlow, 1957). Another good introduction to the world of the Enlightenment is John Lough (ed.), *Locke, Travels in France, 1675–9* (1959). F. Neumann's introduction to Montesquieu's *Spirit of the Laws* (1945) is good. A fine and readable account of the intellectual revolution is that of P. Hazard, *The European Mind, 1680–1715* (1935, trans. 1953); see also the same author's *European Thought in the Eighteenth Century* (1946, trans. 1954). Perhaps the best, certainly the fullest general account is that of P. Gay, *The Enlightenment: an Interpretation* (2 vols, 1966, 1969). His vast bibliography witnesses to the sheer quantity of writing on the subject as well as to his own erudition. Shorter, elegant, not easy but skilfully founded on an analysis of society, is N. Hampson, *The Enlightenment* (Harmondsworth, 1968). An interesting approach, specially valuable for the light shed on countries, like Italy and Switzerland, which tend to escape attention, is that of Roy Porter and M. Teich (eds), *The Enlightenment in National Context* (Cambridge, 1981), in which each contributor deals with a different country. A clear and succinct summary of the ideas of the leading thinkers is provided by Robert Anchor, *The Enlightenment Tradition* (Berkeley, 1967). Among them, important studies of individual thinkers are those of E. Labrousse, *Pierre Bayle* (2 vols, 1963, 1964); R. Shackleton, *Montesquieu, A Critical Biography* (Oxford, 1961); A.M. Wilson,

Diderot (New York, 1972); and H.T. Mason, *Voltaire* (London, 1981). For the latter, see also I.O. Wade, *The Intellectual Development of Voltaire* (1975). *The Encyclopédie* (London, 1971) is the scholarly work of an always readable writer, J. Lough; see also his general books on France listed after chapter 8. On French cultural influence a standard work is L. Réau, *L'Europe française au siècle des lumières* (Paris, 1933). A. Cobban, *In Search of Humanity in the Eighteenth Century* (1960), covers many aspects of intellectual life in the eighteenth century; see also his other books, listed after chapter 8. R.N. Stromberg, 'History in the eighteenth century', *Journal of the History of Ideas*, 12 (1951), sees the Enlightenment as lacking in historical sense or any concept of organic growth. G. Boas, 'In search of the Age of Reason', in E.R. Wasserman (ed.), *Aspects of the Eighteenth Century* (Baltimore, 1966), discusses difficulties of interpretation of an age which used words like 'nature' and 'reason' to support quite different points of view. P. Gay enters highly debatable ground in his article, 'The Enlightenment in the history of political theory', *Political Science Quarterly*, 69 (1954). The reader may wish to explore the wide range of possible assessments of the Enlightenment: as for example between Gay's judgement that 'its essence was freedom, in a word, of moral man to make his own way in the world' and the view of J.L. Talmon, expressed in his *Origins of Totalitarian Democracy* (1952), that it was hostile to the idea of freedom as dependent on the natural conflict of ideas and interests because it thought in terms of a 'preordained, harmonious and perfect scheme of things, to which men are irresistibly driven, and at which they are bound to arrive', and the no less iconoclastic L.G. Crocker's *An Age of Crisis: Man and World in Eighteenth-Century French Thought* (Baltimore, 1959). If so, he is urged to read M.S. Anderson's fascinating essay on the historiography of the Enlightenment in *Historians and Eighteenth Century Europe* (Oxford, 1979). He will find there quoted Crocker's sobering judgement: 'By affirming what they perceived to be man's true place in the universe, they loosed the metaphysical moorings and set him adrift.'

Judgements of the Enlightenment as a whole are necessarily coloured by authors' views, whether conservative or radical, religious or sceptical; so it may help the student to try to identify the different kinds of Enlightenment within Europe. Particularly helpful in this respect are: H. Brunschwig, *Enlightenment and Romanticism in Prussia* (Chicago, 1977), I. Berlin, 'Herder and the Enlightenment', in E.R. Wasserman (ed.), *Aspects of the Eighteenth Century* (Baltimore, 1966), for one of the great original thinkers, particularly hard to classify; another, Vico, is among the subjects of F. Venturi, *Italy and the Enlightenment: Studies in a Cosmopolitan Century* (London, 1972). Like Hampson, Venturi is careful to place the Enlightenment against the background of political and social history: he urges that the historian of ideas should 'seek to understand what the terms, words, concepts and myths really mean'. An excellent account of Italian society and of the place in it of the Illuminismo is S. Woolf, *A History of Italy, 1700–1860* (London, 1979). The influence of German ideas on Russia can be traced in M. Raeff, 'The Enlightenment in Russia and Russian thought in the Enlightenment', in J.G. Garrard (ed.), *The Eighteenth Century in Russia* (Oxford, 1973). Returning to France, and the flight from rationalism at the end of the century, R. Darnton's *Mesmerism and the End of the Enlightenment in France* (Cambridge, Mass., 1968), and, specifically on 'gutter Rousseauism', his 'The high Enlightenment and the low-life of literature in pre-revolutionary France', *Past and Present*, 51 (1971), should be noted. Finally, lest early conditioning be neglected: the state of schools and universities in the period is the subject of J.W. Adamson, *A Short History of Education* (Cambridge, 1969). See also two volumes edited by L. Stone, *The University in Society*, 2 vols (Princeton, 1974) and *Schooling and Society* (Baltimore, 1976).

5

QUESTIONS OF AUTHORITY

Estates in Decline

The modern world was slow to take shape out of the disintegration of medieval society which followed the calamities of the fourteenth century, the century of plague, peasant revolts and papal schism. But in one dramatic period of transformation, from the end of the fifteenth century to the middle of the sixteenth, some of the main features of the new order began to emerge. Overseas discoveries and settlements enlarged the scope of commerce and finance and contributed to what was to prove a permanent shift in the volume of business from the Mediterranean to western Europe. Price inflation, which was occurring in response to a steady rise in population and consequent pressure on resources even before bullion imports made much impact on the money supply, was radically altering the economic base. New opportunities for enrichment and less inhibited attitudes towards money affected the traditional structure of society. As cities grew, urban values became more influential. Money made in finance, commerce and office went to buying land; existing landowners, reduced in circumstances or ousted by newcomers, became, in an altogether more fluid society, a force for disorder. Their aspirations could not be satisfied completely by the burgeoning of courts and agencies of government. With the increasing centralization of authority and the assumption of new responsibilities and rights in finance and justice, sovereigns tested their powers and enlarged their patronage. They went out to fight as lightly as ever but with more men and more deadly weapons. Ominously for the future, the 'Italian wars', which began with Charles VIII's invasion of Italy, became a broader conflict. Princes could make war and peace upon their own initiative: it was to be as true of Frederick the Great in 1740 as it was of Charles VIII in 1494. The consequences might be far-reaching, even beyond the countries involved. It was likely to be the most important decision the ruler would make. But outside this traditional sphere, to what extent was the ruler free to act?

During this period the normal form of European government was monarchy, ruling over a society dominated by orders, corporations, colleges and societies, each having clearly understood duties and privileges. It was held, as by St Paul, that such bodies were mutually dependent: like parts of living tissue, the vitality of each was important to the whole. It was further accepted as a truth, self-evident, hallowed by tradition and grounded in Christian doctrine, all the more emphatically stated therefore on occasions when sovereigns were pressing the superior rights of the crown, that in this hierarchical society men had rights not as individuals but by virtue of membership of their order or corporate body. Orders or 'Estates' were first the clergy; second the nobility, divided in practice, sometimes formally, into upper and lower; third the bourgeoisie, organized in boroughs with rights defined by charter; in companies of merchants or guilds of craftsmen; in chambers of advocates, attorneys and legal officials; in societies of doctors, surgeons and apothecaries; in academies of artists and men of learning. With variations of form but surprising consistency in spirit, it was the kind of society which German historians have labelled the *Ständestaat*: the term serves neatly to denote the corporate structures and mentality which survived until the articulation, first in America, then in France, of the revolutionary idea that all citizens of one indivisible country should enjoy equal and inalienable rights simply by virtue of belonging to that country.

In the face of the gradual, uneven but inexorable advance of rulers' authority, men had banded in their orders to promote their own interests: churchmen, concerned to stress the responsibilities of princes under law, of which they believed they were the natural guardians, nobles, drawing instinctively together to defend privileges acquired by the sword and held as of right, and townsmen seeking corporate privileges to protect economic activities that were mistrusted in a society increasingly dominated by clerical and noble values. It was often politic for the ruler too to obtain sanction from leading members of the orders if his rule were to be effective over wider areas. Hence had arisen the assemblies of one kind or another, usually representing orders, called Estates and acquiring the look of permanence: their set forms and traditional procedures evolved from the tendency in the *Ständestaat* to treat yesterday's custom as today's law. In the fifteenth and sixteenth centuries, when institutions of this type flourished everywhere in the Europe of the Latin tradition, from Sicily to Scandinavia, and Scotland to Hungary, Estates were conceived as representing, if not the whole population of the state, certainly those elements that were important in politics. The claim was not weakened by limited membership. The *cortes* of Castile for example represented only eighteen towns but claimed to stand for all the regions of Castile. Even at that stage the nobility tended to assume the dominant position that befitted their standing in society. But their claim to represent all who dwelt on their estates was sounder in law and in the understanding of those people, conditioned as they were to respect territorial rights, than we can readily understand. Nor were powers lacking to match the strength of the representative idea.

At one extreme were the estates or *cortes* of eastern Spain, reflecting the weak position of the sovereign in relation to the governing social groups, who used the *cortes* to guard local interests and class immunities. In particular the *cortes* of Aragon had been able to bargain successfully with rulers whose ambitions exceeded their resources. At the other extreme was the Estates-General of France where the size of the country meant that rulers preferred to deal with the smaller assemblies of the outlying provinces, where some estates met regularly and acquired strong traditions and a permanent staff for the assessment of taxes and administering their affairs. In France the crown was able to exploit the divisions between provinces as well as between classes. Its crucial advantage however was that it could levy tax, notably the *taille* (in the *pays d'élection*, which were the original provinces of the realm) without reference to any assembly. By contrast, in the German empire, the estates were influential because they controlled the purse: *Landtage sind Geldtage*. Throughout Europe in 1500 there were rulers who found it hard to manage their estates, yet accepted them as part of the constitution of their realms and used them in government, especially to raise taxes.

It might then have seemed to an informed observer that the new power accruing to the state from the rise in population, expansion of commerce, improvements in communication and financial facilities, the spread of literacy and, in particular, that formidable new resource, printing, might be shared between the princes and representative bodies which had also been increasing their authority, for the most part, without serious conflict. However, by 1600, after conflicts over constitutional and fiscal differences, exacerbated by the new quarrels over religion, which in particular had also stimulated debate about the nature and proper use of authority, thoughtful, practical men were coming generally to see the best hope for an efficient government to lie in an autocratic regime. The middle of the century witnessed a number of constitutional conflicts in which the representative principle was put to the trial. There could be little doubt about the outcome.

By 1700, Estates, where they still existed, were in decay. The few exceptions, Holland, Poland, Würtemburg, by their eccentricity, serve only in different ways to confirm that absolutism had gained the day.

The Search for Security

Luther's challenge of 1517 had not only shattered the long-precarious notion of a unified Christendom. It had introduced an age of 'religious war', as princes found new justification for fighting and evoked a response tinged with religious fervour. The subsequent Reformation provided rulers who were sympathetic towards its aims, or merely opportunistic, with the opportunity to increase their assets and powers. A less tangible gain than church lands, one not confined to Protestant states, was the new view of royal authority worked out by Lutheran theologians. To answer the question left by the elimination of papal authority and to safeguard a church that was grounded on the rights of individual conscience, Luther advocated trust in the 'godly prince' who derived his authority direct from God. The principle of divine right was already well founded upon medieval notions of the sanctity of kingship and was expressed in the sacramental rites within the ceremony of coronation and in the practice of healing for the king's evil. Now the principle of divine right was to be adopted by Catholics. In logic, if not in language, it was no great leap from Luther's 'godly prince' to Bossuet's 'lieutenant of God'.

Even before the Reformation new ways were being explored in the spheres of politics and religion. The ideas of Machiavelli, Erasmus and Copernicus reached a larger audience through the new technique of printing. Political scientist, humanist and astronomer, they shared alike the qualities of radicalism and pragmatism that were typical of the new culture. Meanwhile the High Renaissance of the arts in the work of men like Michelangelo, Van Eyck and Holbein was marked by the search for perfection in the optimistic spirit which is another of the hallmarks of the age. But such optimism could not be sustained. In the last phase of economic growth, the inflation which was so rewarding to the merchants and manufacturers, financiers and high officials so placed that they could accumulate office, make short-term contracts and leases, trade and loan money on their own terms, was eroding the position of those who could not exploit it but were still committed to the high expenditure characteristic of an ostentatious age. And so great princes and landowners accumulated debts. Only by severe economies could Elizabeth of England remain solvent. Even Philip II's vast resources were unequal to his several commitments, notably that of reducing the revolt of his Netherlands subjects. In France civil wars followed the death of Henry II and the accession of a minor, the first of three weak sovereigns. The experience of France between the massacre of Vassy in 1562 and the edict of Nantes in 1598 was profoundly disturbing.

Crucial questions were posed about authority, spiritual and secular; answers were confused. As in the Netherlands a determined minority showed that it could defy the prince. The edict was far from a definitive settlement, a mere truce.

Another truce, in 1609, brought an end to the fighting in the Netherlands. Again both sides regarded it not as the final solution but as a necessary breathing space. A pope, seeming to authorize political murder, set the tone for an age of assassination. The religious parties were apparently irreconcilable. The Catholicism of the Counter-Reformation was traditional, clearly defined and intolerant. The spirit of the Inquisition and the Index was defensive, suspicious of novelty, profoundly illiberal. In Calvinism, so effective as an ideology of revolution, can be seen the same narrowness, exclusiveness, ruthless logic: wonderfully elevated – but flying from commonsense. By contrast with the boldness of the great spirits of the High Renaissance, embracing novelties in the confident expectation of progress, like the first sailors who dared open seas rather than hug the land, the prevailing mood among intellectuals and artists was now one of confusion and pessimism. At best, in the writings of one of the wisest, Montaigne (1533–92), it is stoical. It is instructive to contrast his mordant scepticism with the optimistic voice of Leibnitz, the accommodating metaphysician: a century on, he sought to reconcile the principles of Christianity to those of rationalism, and by this means, Lutherans to Catholics, on the basis of a new authority, acceptable to men of reason. Meanwhile Bacon, most learned of English savants, turned to a cautious empiricism, reaching for knowledge by induction, from the amassing of facts. The opposite approach was that of Descartes, who sought by deductive method to present a materialist view of the external world; but again he was imbued with a melancholy conviction that all received standards were problematical, all traditional ideas valueless.[1] History was discarded. 'There was no such wisdom in the world as I had previously hoped to find,' wrote Descartes. By strictly logical method he sought to establish certainty. The paradox is that in seeking to resolve doubt he provided method and precedent for a universal scepticism which bleakly reflected the disorder of society.

The sequence of wars which began with the revolt of Bohemia and became known as the Thirty Years War was a resumption of the unfinished business of previous wars. At the outset there were long-cherished designs of religious conversion and territorial acquisition. There was dogmatic faith, epitomized by the Emperor Ferdinand II (1619–37). There was the relentless search for security and the persistent illusion that it could be won by force of arms. There was all too much scope for greedy adventurers, like Wallenstein, chief among entrepreneurs in the profitable business of warfare. In all there was confirmation for doubters, as religious idealism was

[1] See also pp. 125–30 for a further examination of the role of Bacon and Descartes in the scientific context.

discredited by political failures, notably that of the Emperor's scheme for the restitution of church land, which was the crux of the German war. Out of the aimlessness and atrocities of years in which Germany alone lost more than a quarter of her inhabitants came a paralysing sense of incoherence; some saw the gap between ideal and reality which Cervantes captures in his study of Don Quixote, archaic gentleman of Castile; others only the hopelessness of Grimmelshausen's Simplicissimus, poor lunatic wandering round the wasted lands. Where there was strong purpose, translated into effective action, it was likely to be secular in inspiration. The success of Richelieu, limited and costly though it was, was based on his uncompromising pursuit of French interests, on his clear-sighted choice of Sweden as an ally, and the moral courage with which he stood up to outraged fellow Catholics. He was aided by the equally secular policy of Pope Urban VIII who seemed more interested in curtailing Habsburg power in Italy than he was in furthering the Catholic crusade. It was in that spirit that the treaties of Westphalia (1648) were eventually fashioned, a magnificent exercise in restoring balance and security.[1]

Westphalia represented the idea that was taking hold of men's minds in the 1640s and 1650s, that a new order was feasible. In a negative way it expressed the inclination to accept that matters of religion could not be settled by force alone. After years of bargaining, a set of answers was found to various claims for satisfaction, compensation, adjustment and arbitration: solutions dictated by might or right to problems of dislocation and imbalance. The same forces and motives can be seen at work in individual states. The Thirty Years War had been a crucible in which the main ingredients of the old polities had been tested: privileged estates and corporations, systems of patronage. Out of the intensification of war came some of the characteristic features of the new order: larger bureaucracies, more exacting and efficient systems of taxation, more direct control of subjects. They were not achieved without struggle. The same forces and motives can be seen at work in individual states. The collapse of the Fronde in France and of the opposition to Queen Christina in Sweden, and the restoration of Charles II in England, that elegant compromise between apparently irreconcilable elements, all appear to stem from a conviction among those who belonged to the political nation, the small number of men in each country who understood the workings of the system, who were articulate and had the political interest, resources and status to act effectively, that resolution of problems was possible. In other words, they had come to believe in the possibility of establishing order. The preferred way was acceptance of the authority of the prince: absolutism. The alternative had been experienced in different situations – in conflicts and revolts, in one grand case (England), in revolution – and, to some degree, everywhere in Europe.

[1] For the 'Great Settlement', see also pp. 198–201.

A General Crisis?

It is not surprising that some historians have refused to be content with coincidence to account for the similiarities of particular episodes but have sought common causes for what has seemed to them to be a 'general crisis'. Others deny that the term 'crisis' has validity in this context, or assert that it is wrong to apply it particularly to this period, the middle years of the century. Others again, preferring to think of a succession of small crises, have found it impossible to fit all into a single scheme. Even among protagonists of the idea of a general crisis there are divisions reflecting ideological positions which affect the methods, and even the scope, of enquiry; broadly, however, they can be divided between those who conceive of it mainly in political terms and those, not necessarily Marxists, for whom it stems from fundamental economic and social conditions.

In characteristic Marxist thinking, as represented notably by Hobsbawm, the general crisis represents a decisive phase in the evolution of society from feudalism to capitalism: it is essentially, in origin, a crisis of production. For Trevor-Roper it is chiefly a consequence of the growth of the state, with swollen courts and bureaucracies offering benefits to the fortunate few and arousing corresponding resentment among outsiders, 'the country', who therefore rebel. Offering a somewhat different interpretation, Mousnier believes that such revolts were caused by the excessive tax burden and other intrusions of central government upon the province and its interests. He sees the contradictory tendencies in society and government, which had long coexisted, now coming to the surface in bitter confrontation. Nobility and bourgeoisie fight to defend their positions in a world of constricted economic opportunity. The masses of the people are trapped in their poverty: widespread popular revolts express their fury and despair. The records of his own country support Mousnier's thesis, but he may be thought to take too French a view of Europe as a whole and to go beyond what the evidence can sustain when he extends his thesis to the whole century and to every sphere of life and thought:

> The State, the social group and the individual were all struggling ceaselessly to restore, in their environment and in themselves, order and unity as represented by authoritarian forms of government, the clarity of Cartesian thinking, the restraint and proportion of classical art and architecture, the humane precepts of international law.

His conclusion is sombre: 'The struggle is vain. The period ends with further distress and conflict, and questioning of the fundamental ideas.' To support his argument, Mousnier calls to witness the turbulence of the baroque as well as the restless empiricism of the new science and the growing scepticism in matters of faith. The reader may judge for himself how well this accords with events and trends in seventeenth-century France, but before he tests the concept of a general crisis which affected the whole of Europe, he needs at least a brief resumé of the economic evidence. Fortunately, from research and debate certain facts and trends are emerging with sufficient clarity to make possible an informed approach to the whole question.

Population in Europe was reaching its peak at around 100 million before the seventeenth century began. The check came earlier in the Mediterranean regions than in the rest of Europe, where growth had been less spectacular. There was little, if any, overall growth during the century. In France large fluctuations indicated the severe effects of famine, while in Spain the population actually declined. In Germany the Thirty Years War reduced the population by at least a quarter. Besides an increase in the death rate, there is some evidence for deliberate family planning; certainly there was a tendency to later marriage. A depression in prices set in from the late 1630s; thereafter they were generally, if not uniformly, low for a hundred years. Cereal yield ratios, that is of grain to seed, were static, even slightly declining during this period. From around 1650 there was a big reduction in the export of grain from the vital Baltic region. However, increasing cultivation of alternative crops, maize, buckwheat and rice in southern and western Europe, may be allowed to qualify assumptions about falling levels in the international grain trade which, for example, are used to support Marxist views of the 'general crisis'. Studies of other areas of economic activity again provide inconclusive evidence: in the ubiquitous manufacture of woollen textiles, for example, there was a shift away from guild control to production in the countryside. Given competition, new processes and the dislocation caused by wars, inevitably there were local slumps; but there is no evidence of a general decline in production. Figures for the trade between Seville and Spanish America show a decline in the first half of the century being checked in the second half, while there was a rapid increase in trade with the 'other Americas' in such commodities as sugar and coffee, notably with Brazil. Trade with Asia, when measured by the number of ships sent from European to Asian harbours, shows contraction in the years 1621 to 1650, coinciding with the Thirty Years War and with the difficulties in the Baltic trade at that time, but a notable expansion between 1651 and 1670. Finally the violent fluctuations which might be expected in wartime are absent from the registers of the Baltic Sound tolls, with more consistent signs of a real depression in the 1650s and 1660s, followed by recovery in the next two decades. It is clear that new, if temporary, limitations upon economic growth led to greater competitiveness and fostered 'mercantilist' theories about the role the state should assume in fostering and protecting merchants and manufacturers. The well-documented growth in the English trade in the last four decades of the seventeenth century was partly at the expense of Holland. Enterprising investment and vigorous commercial policies make both countries exceptions, however, in any judgement about Europe as a whole. Overall in any case the evidence from trade and manufactures does not support an extreme version of the theory of 'general crisis'. There was a fall in the rate of growth, but not actual retrogression.

There is, however, no doubt about the plight of the peasant farmer, whether measured by the grim statistics of crop yields, population or rural indebtedness. Contemporaries naturally held the weather responsible; recently historians have given serious attention to the adverse affects of what has been termed the 'little ice age', caused by a fall of 1 degree centigrade in overall temperatures, which was sufficient to reduce the growing season of plants by several weeks and the maximum altitude for cultivation by 500 feet. The sixteenth-century growth in population had led to the cultivation of marginal land, especially in hill country. Enforced retreat from those terraces and pastures was a step nearer starvation. There were more migrants trying to find work and food in congested towns, themselves breeding grounds for disease. Famines after bad summers were exacerbated by associated diseases, like dysentery and typhus. Vagrancy, banditry and begging increased everywhere; revolts became more frequent.[1]

The experience of Castile and France in these years was particularly cruel. In the former, parish registers showed a fall in baptisms and marriages; whole villages and hamlets were sometimes abandoned. The distinctive feature of France in those years was the popular revolt. The revolts of the Croquants (1636–7) and the Bretons (1675) were only the most serious of provincial disorders which affected towns as well as countryside, and expressed the desperation and lawlessness of men who had nothing to lose. There was nothing new about such revolts and they often followed traditional patterns. But it is significant that the early modern revolt was directed, unlike the medieval *jacquerie*, not against seigneurs or local officials (who might well be conniving, if not actually leading it), but against the state and its tax collectors. In that respect they complement the more avowedly political revolts and confrontations of the period, and their cause was the same: it is to be found in the related phenomena of economic recession and the expansion of the state. The innovating, encroaching, centralizing policies of government were resented by all who did not directly benefit. In particular it was the new destructiveness of war, both cause and effect of the increase in the powers of government, that turned so many subjects into rebels and created, in conditions of unprecedented wretchedness, the resolve to find a better, more settled way. Inevitably, to those who had most cause to be alarmed by the alternative of anarchy, that meant acceptance of a stronger government.

The early modern state existed above all by virtue of its armed forces and at least half its revenues were spent in preparations for, or fighting in, wars.

[1] For development of this topic, see pp. 43–4.

In every major country except Spain and Poland, the army, by 1700, was more than twice the size it had been in 1600. In the case of the Dutch, for example, it grew from 30,000 to 100,000: in that of Sweden from 20,000 to 100,000; the combined armies of Holland, France, England, Sweden and Russia exceeded 0.75 million by the end of the century. That is why war is a central concern of historians of the *ancien régime*, of interest in itself for the development of tactics, and changes in organization and style; and crucial in its impact on society and government. Between 1530 and 1630, the cost of raising armies had risen fivefold, well in advance of the general rate of inflation. Thereafter the great increase in the size of armies was not matched, except in Holland, by growth in the economy. It was not only that war was becoming more intensive. Because of the spread of alliances, it involved several states at once. Unless his lands were isolated or well away from the main strategic routes, a prince could not be sure that he would not be drawn in; in any case prestige and diplomatic weight required that an army be maintained. It was the lesson so well learnt by the Elector Frederick William of Brandenburg (1640–88) from his father's bitter experience of futile diplomacy and ravaged lands.

Religious differences had become a major factor in international relations. The right accorded to the territorial prince by the treaty of Augsburg (1555) to enforce his own religion among his subjects made the religious policy of rulers a determining factor in the lives of millions. Not only was there persecution and hardship, as for Protestants in Styria and Bohemia under the rule of Ferdinand II. There was also a perceptible widening of the cultural gap between courts and the mass of the people, together with their local leaders; for it was inevitable that many of the territorial magnates should stand aloof, from penury, principle or mere distaste, from the codes and manners of such courts as those of Ferdinand II, Louis XIII or Charles I, with their esoteric ballets, masques and modish conversation. It is at that point that religious militancy enters the pattern of protests. Whether characterized by puritanism in England, the opposed parties of Huguenot and *devôt* in France or *predikant* dogmatism in Holland, it was a potent force for the revival of spiritual life, but also for the unrest that princes feared in a climate that increasingly saw a general contagion of subjects. The latter, no less naturally, judged the growth of government by what they saw in courts and officialdom: to them, the soaring taxes were evidence of usurpation and exploitation, but to hard-pressed ministers they were the inevitable price to be paid for security. A spectacular case was that of Richelieu's ministry in France (1624–42), when a fourfold increase in the *taille* was accompanied by the wholesale creation of offices for sale; along with attempts to raise money from tax-exempt nobles through revival of the obsolete *arrière-ban*. Typically, as in Charles I's England, government *in extremis* was prepared to adapt old methods as well as to experiment in new. Altogether it was a formula for revolution. Paradoxically it was also the precondition of absolutism, bred, as it was, by war, out of financial necessity.

Absolutism

The term 'absolutism' is both grand and imprecise, therefore, open to widely differing and subjective interpretation. Men of the seventeenth century also ranged widely in their theories about the origins and nature of *imperium*, while accepting it was best that it should be *absolutum*. The commotions of the middle of the seventeenth century did not cause men to abandon the old principle of Aristotle that, in the best states, laws rule, not men. For Spinoza, absolute sovereignty, if any such thing exists, is really the sovereignty held by the whole people. Besides the problem of definition, there are further reasons for approaching absolutism with caution. The term implies a preoccupation of sovereigns and ministers with theory; yet all political experience suggests that they would be mainly concerned with mundane questions of security and solvency. For the mass of subjects, even those capable of thinking in abstract terms about rule, rights and law, or indeed about the interests of any community larger than that in which they lived, the form of government mattered only to the extent that they felt its impact on purse or person. Meaning the ultimate in authority because released from all constraints, absolutism is particularly seductive when it implies the static and definite character that fits theoretical models. Very different in reality was the dynamic relationship of rulers and ruled, the former striving to maintain freedom of manoeuvre, the latter defending, as best they could, their rights and immunities against royal trespass. No less misleading is the picture of a ruler who could deliver more than was in fact possible in the conditions of the time. By definition, it is an abstraction, tinged with the intellectual's pride, and wishful thinking hardening into dogma. Historians have reacted to such ingenuous views so that it is becoming normal to see absolutism in terms of resistance and limitations; or, with some justification, as a plausible but fraudulent cover for what, politics being as ever the art of the possible, amounted to connivance between sovereigns and their leading subjects.

It can, therefore, be urged that absolutism has become a cliché, so wide in meaning as to be meaningless. But the term should not for that reason be abandoned. In that it embraces the trends towards central regulation, particularly in economic affairs, it is more readily recognizable by the modern reader than it would have been by previous generations who had less experience of those trends. It belongs to the realm of historical myths when it is used as a label for a political system. But properly used, to describe a general tendency in both the theory and exercise of power, it takes us into a long-vanished political world which had grown around a hierarchy of orders, and into an aristocratic European culture, whose common assumptions were more important than differences of country, language, even religion. It belongs to a period when monarchy was not popular, or national, or constitutional; to states in the transitional stage between the feudal and the bureaucratic. It also belongs to a new intellectual order emerging from the ferment of ideas that has been labelled the 'scientific revolution'. It was the first system to benefit from the great advance in printing technology and it was expounded in a host of dissertations, pamphlets and sermons. In France, for example, Richelieu's propaganda system was at its service, with such skilful writers as Lebret to make an intellectually satisfying system out of the wheeling and dealing that was the reality of seventeenth-century government, and to familiarize subjects with the still novel concept of an impersonal state, which could make prior claim on their allegiance.

However far removed from reality, absolutism characterizes a phase of political thought which is notable for a virtual consensus, emerging from a medley of ideas about origins, sanctions and forms, upon the need for more effective sovereignty and for obedience in subjects. When allowance has been made for the extremism that is the privilege of intellectuals who do not have to implement their ideas, and for the artifices that give an air of unreality to such arguments as that about the original contract that was alleged to have been made between ruler and subjects, there remains a significant degree of harmony between the philosophers and the practitioners of government, even when it did not, as in the case of Bossuet, arise from shared experience and convictions in the intimate world of the court.

It is always dangerous to associate a system too closely with cultural development. Philosophies, fashionable modes of thinking, and styles of living change more rapidly than forms of government. Absolutism was embedded in the culture of the Renaissance and achieved its highest expression in the baroque. As can be seen in the courts of the Hofburg and Versailles, the two greatest showpieces of the cult, it was heavily dependent on symbolism; intellectually it owed much to the Catholic revival and to adaptation of classical philosophy. It was prescientific and something of its necessarily ephemeral character can be seen as the process of liberation from the biblical and Aristotelian framework. It could be supported by Cartesian logic, but it was vulnerable to the advance of empirical science. It was always restricted, and was eventually undermined by the contradiction within 'divine right' monarchy which is exposed when one turns from theory to practice. If it was God's purpose to invest absolute rulers with powers to establish a harmonious and hierarchical political universe, they must recognize the rights and status of their Christian subjects, deriving from their own place in the hierarchy. Even that concern, which can be observed in Louis XIV's essentially conservative government, was bound to fail to draw the king close to the social organization he was committed to protect. Given the legislative sovereignty which is the cardinal feature of absolutism, the king was endowed with a creative power. Given the blank cheque and the king's signature upon it, his ministers would inevitably seek to extend their power, and that of the state they served. When obstructed they would by-pass constitutional checkpoints and, when necessary, create new agencies for direct action. Thus even when the aims of government were lofty and its conduct responsible, at least in terms of the interest of the state, they were exposed and opposed as 'ambitious', their policies 'unnatural'; in short the regime was one of 'usurpation'. That was always the concern and theme of the privileged groups who manned the checkpoints. They were able at times to block or deflect innovating policies. But they did not hold the commanding heights of opinion. Those were seized, entrenched and embellished, in the seventeenth century, by the absolutists.

Among the writers who accepted the challenge of developing ideas into a system and who left work of permanent value, Grotius, Hobbes, Spinoza and Bossuet all displayed a realistic appreciation of the facts of political life, together with the wisdom to comprehend specifically political ideas within a larger view of the universe and of human behaviour. Neither specialist nor academic in their pursuit of truth, they represented a still unified culture in which the search for order, the classical ideal, can be seen to have inspired alike philosopher, mathematician, lawyer and artist. Behind the several facets of this culture can be discerned certain dominant ideas which seemed to men of the time to represent the pillars of a civilized security. There was a moral order in the universe, which men rarely called by any name but God; and all government was under that God. The creator of thinking man, God was himself the epitome of the rational principle. It was therefore a duty of the Christian philosopher to use his mind and eyes to arrive at scientific certainty, in the new confidence that the same cause will always produce the same effect. In the same spirit men studied the rights and obligations of rulers and subjects and it is in this age that the idea of a science of politics first appears, whose first principle was that it was necessary for men to owe allegiance to a state. It was not inevitable that they should think in that way. That it was the product as much of their experience of civil war as of their understanding of the laws of science can be seen from the work of those earlier philosophers, such as Johannes Althusius (1557–1638), who sought to justify civil disobedience.

At the time when Althusius, a German Calvinist and author of *Politica methodica digesta*, propounded his antimonarchical views the argument about sovereignty was still open, the course and outcome, in terms of rulers and their powers, uncertain. He envisaged the social contract as being made between small groups and then between those groups and the ruler. The rights of the component groups of the state were derived from the people. The state was therefore under the constraints imposed by the existence of intermediaries. The awkward gap that existed in effect between the people and their supposed delegates did not lessen the attraction of the theory to advocates of greater power for representative institutions. The idea of an obligation resting on a solemn agreement was familiar to lawyers; it also fitted in with the feudal notion of conditional loyalty which had so often been used to justify the withdrawal of allegiance and which was still alive and useful in the seventeenth century. Althusius might deny the validity of the contract as a theory to justify revolutionary opposition, as it had been adopted by Calvinists, and set it up as a positive doctrine of the foundations of the state. But he defended the idea, essential to those who supported the revolt in the Netherlands, that a representative body had the right to resist a despotic prince; and he further defined sovereignty as essentially popular, allowing for the right of representatives of the people to withdraw it from a ruler who exercised power illegally. For him sovereignty was the power to resist illegitimate exercise of power, not an instrument to unify and strengthen the state.

But there had already been formulated a theory of sovereignty which in the short term, matching the need of the hour, was to prove more influential. Indeed if one had to select one man, one book and one assertion as prophet, foundation and text of absolutism, then it must be Jean Bodin (1530–96), author of the *République* and its chief postulate, that there has to be a single supreme authority in the state in which are united the legislative, executive and judicial powers. 'The principal mark of sovereign majesty and absolute power is essentially the right to impose laws on subjects generally without their consent.' Bodin held law to be 'nothing other than the command of the sovereign in the exercise of his power'. But that did not mean that absolute sovereignty was also arbitrary. 'It is not within the competence of any prince in the world to levy taxes at will on his people, or sieze the goods of another arbitrarily.' The way in which Bodin qualified the ruler's mandate is significant because it represented, not merely an ideal view of the rights of subjects, as individuals and also as members of estates and corporations, but also the realities of government which sovereigns were bound to acknowledge. 'Since the sovereign prince has no power to transgress the laws of nature which God, whose image he is on earth, has ordained, he cannot take the property of another without a just and reasonable cause.' He went on to affirm the value of estates to a king, for 'his majesty is the greater, more illustrious, when his people acknowledge him as sovereign'. Bodin's qualified endorsement of absolutism provided a basis for extensions of his ideas in ways which he might not have approved. Using the keys that he provided, royalist writers put finishing touches to the theory of the divine right of kings. Kings were established on their thrones by the command of God. Like the Pope, the ruler was commissioned by God. Neither Pope nor subjects, acting in the name of the law, people, contract or any other postulated authority, could interrupt the hereditary royal succession which, like the office itself, was ordained by God.

Political theory soared to a rarified level. But the realities which Bodin had grasped did not change. The estates represented the great fief-holders. With a few exceptions they lost their function in the seventeenth century. But the landed interest remained important even though its allegiance changed. Absolute monarchy throughout the west (though scarcely at all in Russia) continued to be doubly limited: by the survival of traditional political entities below it; by the moral law above it. It necessarily operated within the bounds set by those orders in the state whose interests it protected. When it stepped beyond those bounds it incurred the risk of rebellion.

From the notion of a single sovereignty to that of its being completely independent of external powers was a natural progression. Theory evolved in the field of international law to meet the requirements of sovereigns who were already starting to act on that assumption. Activities previously emanating from several centres, feudal, ecclesiastical and civic, were now coming under the control of the state. It is likely that Richelieu would have acted as he did to secure Sedan, or the Great Elector, Prussia, which he had held till then only as vassal of the king of Poland, even if there had been no informed opinion to support them. The idea of the fief still had its uses, as Louis XIV was to show when he exploited it to prove claims to 'dependencies' in the course of the reunions. But it was losing validity in the face of new claims for sovereigns with armies and diplomats at their service. In 1713 the papal fiefs of Sicily and Sardinia were disposed of as if the papacy did not exist. Little was left by then of the political structure in which the medieval dream of a united Christendom had been embodied. But instead of a moral vacuum in which the single reality and deciding factor were the power of the individual ruler, there had come to exist a body of law whose strength lay, not only in proven principles of private law, applied to public issues, but also in the Christian spirit which appealed to princes of sensitive conscience. Above all it was realistic. It was the first principle of Hugo Grotius (1583–1645), author of *De jure belli et pacis* (1625), that a sovereign state was subject to no human authority outside itself.

Grotius was forced to live all his later life in exile from his native Holland because, as a leading theologian of the moderate Remonstrants, he was involved in the downfall of Oldenbarneveldt and narrowly escaped his patron's death. From embattled Holland, temporarily dominated by orthodox Calvinism, Grotius escaped to life in Paris and diplomatic service to the king of Sweden. So he came to adopt a role for which he was well qualified: that of objective analysis and exposition of the affairs of nations. Specially significant was his use of natural law, already an overworked term, with a long history and uses both religious and political. Grotius adopted it as a convenient source of principles governing relations between the states, where there could be no existing sovereign authority to which to appeal. In the process he completed the separation of natural law from its religious aspects. How revolutionary his assertion of the independence of natural law from revealed religion was held to be can be gauged from the fact that in the Austrian Netherlands of the eighteenth century his work was banned. Grotius was interested in the way in which men and communities actually behave and how, in their own interests, they ought to behave. His supreme ideal is that of justice. His work is also, however, informed by a humanitarian spirit which may have been roused by what he saw of the dealings of statesmen like Ferdinand II, Richelieu and Gustavus Adolphus: the distance between their ideals and moral claims in general and their actions over particular instances, not to mention the appalling results, the apparently uncontrollable nature, of the forces they unleashed. The Thirty Years War also revealed the illusory nature of military powers. The preponderance of the Emperor, in military terms, between 1620 and 1631 did not enable him to implement the edict of restitution. As the war dragged on it became increasingly obvious that the armies were virtually out of control. At the end the Emperor could point to a repressed, officially Catholic Bohemia; Counter-Reformation Catholicism was riding high, while Lutheranism emerged politically defeatist and even Calvinism was affected by Erastian tendencies: that is to say that some of their leaders accepted the subordination of ecclesiastical to secular authority. But the prime lesson of the war was that religious differences could not be resolved by force alone. The war also prepared the way for further accessions of power by those princes sufficiently well established or bold enough to grasp their opportunities. It weakened the will of the estates, particularly in Germany. The constitutional quarrels and civil wars which followed in the later stages or aftermath of war brought a further discrediting of the representative principle and reinforcement of the rights of the sovereign. Men were then ready to listen to the bold voice of Thomas Hobbes (1588–1679) proclaiming the futility of man's imagining that he could establish a sound order while preserving his individual rights. Hobbes expressed the political disillusionment of his time and provided the basis for a new, untrammelled version of absolutism.

As a young man Hobbes had assisted Bacon during the period when he was engaged upon the research which led to the publication of the *Novum organum* in 1620, with its outline of the new experimental method. To Bacon's influence may be ascribed Hobbes's characteristic beliefs that scientific method counted more than reverence for tradition, and that knowledge meant power to use nature for human purposes. He also spent many years in the study of classics, choosing Thucydides for translation, he who 'least of all liked democracy'. He became familiar with the principles of the new rationalism in discussions with its leading figures, Mersenne, Gassendi, Descartes. Like Descartes he was stimulated by the idea of a universal system of philosophy. In his detachment, self-sufficiency and devotion to exact truth, he has something in common with Spinoza, whose *Ethics* was explicitly written to guide rational beings to the good life. It was the method of geometry that fascinated Hobbes as it did Spinoza. 'Wisdom' he saw as the 'product of reason which alone gives knowledge of general, eternal and immutable truths'. The method offered a means of working out a solution to the problems of his own country, in the grip of forces which were all the more destructive because, as he saw them, Englishmen were stupid and prone to the excesses of individualism which could only lead to anarchy: they were 'boiling with questions concerning the rights of dominion and the obedience due from subjects'. If divergent opinions lay at the root of civil wars, there was great appeal in the method which could establish conclusions with demonstrative certainty. In brief he argued that the only hope for permanent peace was an absolute sovereign, whose commands were laws, enforced by judges, bishops and military, all responsible to him and appointed by him alone. His *Leviathan* (published in England in 1651) represents the work of one decade, but the thinking of several. Its importance lies not in its conclusions but in the way in which they were reached. Uninfluential as a political tract it was of the highest importance as an innovation in political philosophy. Its originality lay in the way in which he proceeded from two fundamental ideas, both familiar in his intellectual circle but now brought together to provide the foundations for a complete philosophy of man and civil society. First, nature had an underlying mathematical structure which was not apparent to the senses but which could be revealed by the techniques of the geometer. Second, representing both the powerful influence of Galileo and the absolute rejection of the Aristotelian world view of the earth at the centre of a universe in which everything had due place in a hierarchical system under God, Hobbes conceived a world of bodies composed of particles and moved by other bodies and particles. Thus physics and psychology came together in one compelling view of social life permeated by motion. Life is a race with no goal other than being foremost and there can be 'no contentment but in proceeding'. Liberty is 'an absence of the lets and hindrances of motion'. In his materialist view self-interest could be the only operative motive. Men go to war because of their desire for power, and from war proceed 'slaughter, solitude and the want of all things'. In the condition of war 'nothing can be unjust.... Force and fraud are the two cardinal virtues. Justice and injustice ... relate to men in Society, not in Solitude.'

For Hobbes, the theory of social contract was a valuable device for denying the claims of increasingly arbitrary sovereigns: first that authority was divinely sanctioned and second that patriarchy was the natural order of society, as in the Old Testament. The latter view, by contrast, was the foundation of the political theory of Jacques-Bénigne Bossuet[1] (1627–1704) who is important more for what he represents in the French situation (the exalted absolutism of Versailles) than for his originality as a political theorist. With an array of quotations from the Bible, he set out in a logical

[1] See also pp. 93–4, 106–7.

series of 'propositions' (in the approved manner of Descartes whose disciple he was) to show that absolute hereditary monarchy was ordained by God as the best of all forms of government. It was his justification for a level of interference by the state in the rights of subjects beyond that which would have been conceived of a century before. It mapped the road along which Louis XIV travelled to the revocation of the edict of Nantes.

Political theory in any age tends to be the interpretation of the existing political situation: the ideal system reflects real fears and needs. For all his rhetoric, Bossuet, no less than Hobbes and Spinoza, was influenced by the overriding problem of the age: security. Writing from the relative calm of the German and Scandinavian principalities, Bossuet's contemporary, Samuel von Pufendorf (1632–94), was another Cartesian system-builder who had to come to terms with reality. Along with Grotius with whom, oddly, he shared the experience of having spent some time in prison for purely political reasons, he was the most respected and influential legal theorist of his day. The work which established his reputation was published in 1672, under the title of *De jure naturae et gentium*, when he was at Lund. He had been summoned there by the king of Sweden. He ended his days as historiographer to the elector of Brandenburg. He was as much a political philosopher as an academic lawyer. The rationalist and the empiricist in him came into conflict over the question of the origin of law: he came to see it in the helplessness, or *imbecillitas*, which forces individuals into society. He was inevitably led on to consider the connection between natural law and the state, as it existed in history. He conceived of the state, like others of his time, as the repository of unlimited sovereignty, free from any political or ecclesiastical authority. But he was a German, concerned with the Empire, embracing numerous principalities. He was primarily concerned with the creation of a framework within which the states and the Empire could enjoy a constructive relationship, and with rules derived from natural law which could provide a code of behaviour for ruler and ruled alike. Perceiving that the Empire could never achieve the structure of a single state, he saw the future of Germany as lying with the development within a federation of the particular states. That is not surprising in a protégé of the Great Elector. He was less of an 'imperial patriot' than Leibnitz for whom the Empire was the political counterpart of the 'harmony' which was his philosophical ideal and his religious quest. But he was perhaps more realistic and, certainly in this respect, more influential than Leibnitz. Even if some of the reforms which Pufendorf advocated, such as a common currency and internal free trade, had to wait for the nineteenth century, and even though he qualified his endorsement of absolutism by stressing the idea that the state was more important than the prince, he can be seen, as he was by his many readers, as providing academic credentials for the natural course of political development.

If Pufendorf was the philosopher of German 'enlightened despotism',

John Locke (1632–1704) was the philosopher of the revolution of 1688 which confirmed England's divergence from the political pattern of the continent. For this most practical and observant of philosophers, much travelled, a physician, involved in political life through his connection with Shaftesbury and specially interested in economic questions, there was no moral justification for state authority beyond a certain limit, however it was authorized and wielded. Like other theorists, Locke had his own useful fiction: in his case it was that the English Commons were a true representation of the people who were heirs to those original dwellers in a state of nature who had agreed conditionally to establish a government 'for the regulating and preserving of Property'. The condition was that they only owed allegiance to a government that would not enslave them or rule them in an arbitrary fashion. Representative government was the best form because an elected legislature 'cannot possibly be arbitrary' and is 'bound' to rule justly. Writing from his experience of what preceded and followed the 'glorious revolution' and of a form of government in which the executive was subordinate to the legislature in a distinctly English way, Locke was none the less influential in Europe in the century that separated the publication of his *Treatise on Civil Government* (1689) from the revolution. Critics of the kind of arbitrary power then overthrown found in him a humane and liberal tutor.

It is arguable, however, that of all the factors involved in the change from the 'divine right' to utilitarian, Frederick-the-Great-style absolutism, such as the decline of traditional modes of religious belief, the progress of rationalism and of empirical science, the most important were to be found within the increasingly mobile societies of the day. Change was generated by the ambition of individuals to make money and to be powerful, and by the need of the state to resolve the resulting tensions and conflicts while pursuing the twin goals of economic self-sufficiency and military success. It was the common experience of each state that men were ceasing to be content with a status ordained by accident of birth in a society under patriarchal authority and were coming to regard themselves as responsible for the institutions which shaped their lives. With greater economic opportunity and the accompanying development of commercial values and methods, with different kinds of expertise and the tendency to specialize which is one of the characteristics of a 'modern' society, a new view of political authority can be seen emerging together with new patterns of control. They can be seen in Louis XIV's France where real power was exercised by men of proven ability who created their own empires; symbolically, the force of change can be seen by looking from Condé to Colbert, from the great feudatory to the great functionary. The authority which the new class of manager–ministers helped to create, and which they, as successful meritocrats, respected, was what Max Weber called 'legal-rational'. Obedience was less to the person than to the legally established authority. At the very time when Bossuet was expressing the mystique of monarchy in religious terms, the king's servants were devoting themselves to the work of constructing the bureaucratic absolutism which is the characteristic form of the last hundred years of the *ancien régime*. It was what the great Hohenzollerns and Habsburgs grasped when they wrote of service to the state. The state was impersonal and the king, embodying its absolute authority, was still as much bound to serve it as the least of his subjects. Frederick the Great's, or indeed Joseph II's, interpretation of duty was necessarily, however, a subjective one. In effect expedience ruled: absolutism was morally bankrupt, ready to be wound up under the influence of the revolution which occurred in that country, France, where the gap between official ideologies and the intellectual world was widest.

Further Reading

Stimulating introductory books are T.K. Rabb, *The Struggle for Stability in Early Modern Europe* (New York, 1976) (making use of a wide range of evidence, including art), and J.H. Shennan, *The Origins of the Modern European State, 1450–1725* (London, 1974), usefully stressing the continuity, as well as the break, between Renaissance and later development. Though it seems to sacrifice some of what was irregular and accidental in the evolution of the state, P. Anderson, *Lineaments of the Absolutist State* (London, 1979), is also thought-provoking. The essays of H.G. Koenigsberger, *Estates and Revolutions* (Ithaca, 1971), contribute to understanding what actually happened in the early conflicts out of which states grew. Here the best general survey is A.R. Myers, *Parliaments and Estates in Europe to 1789* (London, 1975). Essential for Germany is F.C. Carsten, *Princes and Parliaments in Germany from the Fifteenth to Eighteenth Centuries* (1959). There is a valuable article by E.L. Petersen, 'From domain state to tax state: synthesis and interpretation', *Scandinavian Economic History Review*, 23 (1975). J.M. Hayden analyses the last manifestation of the representative ideal in France in *France and the Estates General of 1614*. M. Beloff, *The Age of Absolutism 1660–1815* (1954), a short comparative survey, wears well. There are a number of good essays in Ragnhild Hatton (ed.), *Louis XIV and Absolutism* (1976). Especially valuable in this context are the first two, E.H. Kossman, 'The singularity of absolutism', and G. Durand, 'What was absolutism?' See also works cited after chapter 7 for the French experience, which was so influential in the sphere of government. Specially important, and also cited there, is David Parker, *The Making of French Absolutism* (1983). The growth of the court is an important aspect of the rise of the state. It is given lavish and scholarly treatment in H. Trevor-Roper (ed.), *The Courts of Europe. Politics, Patronage and Royalty, 1400–1800* (London, 1977).

War in general, the Thirty Years War in particular, was the most important factor in the evolution of the modern state. Besides books cited after chapter 6 (for example, M. Roberts, *Military Revolution* (1956)), the following should be mentioned for the light they throw on the disordered Europe out of which governments emerged with, for the most part, greater powers. G. Benecke, *Germany in the Thirty Years War* (London, 1978), makes telling use of documents;

T.K. Rabb (cd.), *The Thirty Years War* (Boston, 1972) has selections from a number of writers; in the *Journal of Modern History*, 34 (1962), Rabb discusses one vital aspect, 'The economic effects of the Thirty Years War', as does H. Kamen in *Past and Present*, 39 (1968). The latter's *The Iron Century* (1971), though it only covers the period up to 1660, is excellent on the pre-conditions for the rise of absolutism.

Though its precise character is still a matter for debate, and there is no consensus about its duration or indeed exceptional status among the disordered periods in European history, there is enough recognition of the crucial character of the mid-century years to have drawn scholars into fruitful debate about the general crisis. Fortunately the principal contributions can be studied in collected volumes of essays: *Crisis in Europe 1560–1660* (London, 1970), ed. T. Aston, brings together the *Past and Present* articles of J.H. Elliot, Pierre Goubert, E.J. Hobsbawm, Michael Roberts and H.R. Trevor-Roper, among others. In G. Parker and L.M. Smith (eds), *The General Crisis of the Seventeenth Century* (London, 1978), there are important articles by Nils Steensgaard, whose balanced survey gives the reader perhaps the most helpful introduction to what has become a confusing topic, Elliot again, in 'Crisis and continuity' and A. Lloyd Moote, in 'Pre-conditions of revolution', providing helpful perspectives and cautioning against unduly dogmatic or schematic 'over-views' of what was, whatever else it was, a widely varying experience. In *Preconditions of Revolution in Early Modern Europe* (Baltimore, 1971), for example, the editors of another collection of essays, R. Forster and J. P. Greene, suggest that there are five distinct kinds of upheaval: great national revolutions, national revolts with the potential to become revolutions, a large-scale regional rebellion with limited potential to become a revolution, a secessionist *coup d'état* and urban *jacqueries*. Besides regional studies such as those listed after chapter 7, P. Zagorin, *Rebels and Rulers* (Cambridge 1982), and R. Mousnier, *Peasant Uprisings in Seventeenth Century France, Russia and China* (trans. London, 1971), enable the reader to assess the significance of popular risings, simultaneous in time but very different in circumstances. Finally the book which first explored the subject should not be overlooked: R.B. Merriman, *Six Contemporaneous Revolutions* (1938; rev. edn, New York, 1963).

The political philosophy which interpreted, prompted or rationalized political developments can be approached through Q. Skinner, *The Foundations of Modern Political Thought*, 2 vols, (Cambridge, 1978). A good introduction to the work of Jean Bodin is the long article of D. Parker, 'Law, society and the state in the thought of Jean Bodin', *Journal of History of Political Thought*, 2 (1981). A good short study of Hobbes's life and thought is Richard Peters, *Hobbes* (London, 1979). There are a number of editions of *Leviathan*, as of the works of Spinoza. There is a helpful introduction to the former in the edition edited by Michael Oakeshott (Oxford, 1951). The development of French absolutist theory may be followed in W.F. Church, *Richelieu and Reason of State* (Princeton, 1972), and N.O. Keohane, *Philosophy and the State in France from the Renaissance to the Enlightenment* (New York, 1980).

6

DIPLOMACY AND WAR

Theory and Practice

The growth in the power of states was accompanied by a greater professionalism among diplomats and more elaborate means of conducting international affairs. Modern diplomacy was the product of the insecure world of Renaissance Italy, with its constant changes within and between states and the consequent need of rulers for regular, reliable information from representatives on the spot. As in other aspects of political life Italy had been the laboratory of the western world. The words of Ermaloa Barbaro would have been appropriate for an ambassador of the age of Louis XIV, two centuries on: his first duty was 'the same as any other government servant's: to do, say, advise and think whatever may best serve the preservation and aggrandizement of his own state'. The Italian and German wars of the first half of the sixteenth century fostered the spread of resident diplomacy and of chanceries capable of supporting rulers in the execution of foreign policy. But the long period of religious and civil wars which followed the peace of Cateau-Cambrésis checked the process. The Reformation gave rise to intractable problems over diplomatic immunity, for an ambassador might demand the right to worship God after his master's manner. At the same time embassies were suspect as the centre of alien and subversive ideas. By the end of the sixteenth century only the Valois among the Catholic rulers of Europe held to the policy of exchanging ambassadors with Protestant powers. The virtual severance of diplomatic links between northern and southern Europe and the distortion of the envoy's role were significant casualties of this period of ideological conflict, reflecting the morality that condoned religious persecution and political assassination. By contrast the seventeenth century saw the fashioning of a new doctrine of international law and the development of conventions that enabled envoys to do their business in a secure environment. The practice of holding congresses for the settlement of matters arising out of wars which involved a number of states, whether judged by the manner or by the outcome of their negotiations, should take a place among the civilized practices of the age.

Representatives of seventeenth-century states worked in a world which had learnt to mistrust projects of general reform and which set little value upon the universality of the Middle Ages. That concept had left its trace in the use of Latin in diplomatic documents, but it was soon to go: at the peace of Rastadt, in 1714, French was used. Sully's *grand dessein* for a balanced federation of European states was the product of leisured years when he had no opportunity to influence affairs directly and it was, in any case, strongly tinged with ambition for France. It belonged moreover to the uneasy time before it was apparent that the revolt of Bohemia would develop into the series of related or overlapping conflicts which came to be known as the Thirty Years War. A fitting product of that war was Grimmelshausen's plea in his novel *Simplicissimus* for an international peace plan, put appropriately into the mouth of a wandering lunatic. The new realism was reflected in the prolonged negotiations that were to lead to the peace of Westphalia. The Emperor, important now chiefly as a ruler of his family lands, was forced to allow German states to treat for themselves, and after the peace they had the right to send their own representatives to foreign states. The Pope condemned the settlement as 'null and void' because it took so little account of his views, while at the peace of the Pyrenees, eleven years later, he was not even represented. In theory as in practice there was a keener awareness of what was possible, and a building upon actual powers. Professors of law, like Gentili and Grotius, assumed that the sovereign state was subject to no human authority whatever outside itself. In his *De jure belli et pacis* (1625) Grotius[1] postulated the existence of a fundamental law of nature, stemming from mankind's reserves of conscience and reason, and standing above the interests of dynasty and nation. Accepting that war was inevitable as the outlet for the passions of nations, he assigned to it a magisterial role, as judge and executioner in the international order. Wars of ambition, conquest and propaganda were unjust. Furthermore he asserted that no arrangement between powers to provide for a balanced stability could last unless rulers recognized that their acts must be governed by certain principles higher than mere expediency.

It would be wrong to exaggerate the influence of Grotius's book on the

[1] See also pp. 185–6.

politics of the times. Inevitably, as in later centuries, the main factor in the conduct of international affairs was the existence of jealous, separate sovereignties. There was progress, however; the body of rules of international law was enlarged. More treaties were subsequently concluded by which two or more powers agreed to observe certain rules; though that did not reduce the scope for disagreement about how those rules should be interpreted. International law did not make the relations of states more legal or more regular, but it did provide a body of experience in the regular, legal handling of disputes.

Inevitably too war figured more largely than peace in Grotius's treaties. There were agreed rules about its conduct. A country which was 'neutral' for instance might expect to be protected from the worst ravages, but it usually had to allow belligerent powers to cross its territory, as the French crossed Cologne and the Spanish Netherlands in their marches against Holland in 1672. The exchange of prisoners was usually arranged by exchange of equal ranks, an officer counting as several soldiers, those unclaimed to be sent to the gallows. Belligerents had the right to exact contributions from the inhabitants in a theatre of war. Naval practices proved more contentious and exercised the ingenuity of lawyers and pacifists. Grotius's doctrine of *mare liberum* was no general statement of principle but an attack upon the Portuguese claim to exclusive rights in the Indian Ocean. There was dispute about 'coastal waters' as distinct from high seas. Colbert's naval ordinance of 1681 defined the *mer littorale* as that 'which the sea covers and leaves bare during the new and full moons and up to where the great tides reach on the beaches'; the definition based on the range of cannon fire belonged to the next century. By far the most important question was that of the salute, the customary courtesies of salvo or dipping the flag, between the vessels of two different powers. It was a contributory cause of the mid-century wars between the English and the Dutch. Colbert wrote in 1677 that France claimed that 'all other nations must bow to her at sea as at the Court of Kings'; in the following year the Genoese learnt that it was no idle boast when a French squadron, sent to demand the first salute and being refused, bombarded the city. The English would never give way on this point, and so even when they and the French were allies, their ships had to avoid meeting at sea; when in 1685 a Spanish commander refused to salute the French colours Admiral Tourville attacked his fleet.

Such aggressiveness might be held to mark the coming of age of the states. It went along with the more precise definition of sovereign rights by political theorists and the more rigorous application of sovereign power within states. It reflected too the typical attitudes of this ceremonious age and the influence throughout society of a courtly culture in which the intricacies of Byzantium, the opulence of Burgundy and the gravity of Spain all contributed to the formation of a distinctive and pretentious style. At all levels where men aspired to live nobly, and in all countries, though most in Spain and in courts such as those of Vienna and Versailles where the Spanish influence was strong, honour and precedence were at a premium: men risked their lives in duels for points of honour; a man's status was judged by his clothes, his carriage and his servants; an impoverished nobleman had rather starve than give up his *maitre d'hôtel.* At the apex of society the presentation had to be very grand indeed. When Louis XIV went to meet his Spanish bride the procession was several miles long. Upon the same considerations of prestige an ambassador was expected to maintain great pomp. His first arrival was attended by elaborate ceremonial. Outside the city which housed court or government, a procession of several coaches, with soldiers, servants, liveried pages and musicians, would form. The ambassador proceeded in his carriage to a mansion reserved for such occasions, to the accompaniment of bells and cannon, to be received by the town authorities who could only hope to be repaid by years of ambassadorial spending for such display as they felt befitted their corporate dignity. A few days later another procession preceded the presentation of letters of credence and a first audience with the sovereign and his leaders. At Versailles or Vienna such an occasion was invariably splendid. Saint-Simon's memorable account of the elaborate reception of the sham Persian ambassador, with a full parade of the court establishment before Louis and his family, makes the reader wince for the duping of the old king in a matter so important to him.

It was in tune with the more pragmatic outlook of the eighteenth century, and necessary because of the crippling cost in ambassadors, that such ceremonies were modified, being reserved for those eminent ambassadors who demanded them. Usually an ambassador was simply received at court, as in Britain today. At the same time disputes over precedence became less common and acrimonious: an indication of more settled times and secure thrones. In the age of Louis XIV the incident that arose inevitably from disputes over place and order was sometimes deliberately magnified. In October 1661 a violent fracas in London between the rival households of the French and Spanish ambassadors, in which several people were killed, and the French worsted, gave Louis a chance to draw attention to the supremacy of France in general, and his claim to the Spanish Netherlands in particular. Ministers' memoirs show that he attached high importance to the incident. The Spanish ambassador was expelled, and an apology exacted from Madrid with recognition of the precedence of the French ambassadors in every court. The Emperor did not bend so easily. Because Louis XIV would not concede the right of precedence which the Austrians accorded to the Spanish ambassador, his representative at Vienna had to be content with the modest title and limited privileges of envoy extraordinary.

In 1660 the development of specialized foreign ministries was still far from complete. The ensuing century saw the emergence of larger departments and more regular bureaucratic procedures; but also the persistence of the traditional idea that the foreign policy was the special business of kings, a prerogative and a mystery. It is not surprising that this should be the case in countries like Russia or Prussia where the state evolved as the extension of the powers of the autocrat on whose will and personality all depended. And so the policy of Peter the Great's Russia or Frederick the Great's Prussia, was wholly and at times disconcertingly the policy of the ruler. In the France of Louis XIV the king's acute understanding and will to dominate were balanced by the expertise of foreign ministers to whom usually he had the sense to listen. But Louis XV's private diplomacy, *le sécret du roi*, crossed and confused the official policy, conducted by the secretary of state and his large and experienced department, a good instrument but poorly used: an ironic situation, for the French in the seventeenth century had led the way in the evolution of diplomatic method and provided a model for others to follow.

There was a more restrained, civilized and far-sighted aspect than is suggested by Louis XIV's sometimes aggressive tactics. There were precedents to guide him. Richelieu, who had come to office to find there were no copies available of his predecessor's instructions to ambassadors, had established the idea that negotiation must be a permanent activity, aiming at solid and lasting relationships. He regarded a treaty, once signed and ratified, as something to be observed 'with religious scruple'. He established important precedents too in his use of unofficial envoys, like Father Joseph, for negotiations over which he wished to maintain control. Following Richelieu's example rulers tended to withhold the grant of *plena potestas*, the full powers without which the negotiators could not arrive at a valid agreement, until an advanced stage, so as to prevent rash commitments by unwary envoys.

Under Louis XIV's foreign ministers, Lionne, Pomponne, Torcy, all experienced diplomats, there was no formal establishment, only a handful of cypher clerks and interpreters. But abroad the coverage was ambitious, far beyond the scale of other powers. By 1685 there were permanent embassies in all the more important capitals, together with special ministers resident in such places as Heidelberg, Hamburg and Genoa and consuls to represent French interests mostly in the Levant, where the French had always been to the fore, having established the first European embassy in Constantinople in 1535. By 1715 there were thirty-two permanent representatives. Where France led, others followed. Russia had twenty-one envoys by 1720. Even the relatively minor German state of Hamburg had sixteen. Since a large part of diplomacy has always been understanding of the conventions of polite society, nobles were preferred for Rome, Madrid or London. But a bourgeois served for Holland or Venice. The ambassador was expected to be fully cognizant of conditions in his destined country.

Before departure there was an elaborate briefing: with him went letters of introduction, instructions and the cypher table which was necessary because of the general custom of interception by postmasters who transcribed the more interesting parts for their masters. He might have to treat or bribe. His prime duty, however, was to gather and transmit information. He had to comply carefully with the customs of the court and take note of the prejudices of the ruler. Attendance at long and frequent religious ceremonies was the lot of the Catholic ambassador to the Emperor's court. The duc d'Aumont, appointed ambassador to London, was advised that the 'English constitution is such that it is not regarded as offensive by the court of King James to have relations with the opposition. The duke need not therefore reject the society of the Whigs.' An embassy might be the foundation of a different sort of reputation. William Temple's *Observations upon the United Provinces*, the fruit of his embassy at The Hague from 1668 to 1670 and the negotiations which led to the Triple Alliance, were a respected, much used source of information about the institutions and character of that country.

From the memoirs of François de Callières, Louis XIV's experienced representative at the negotiations which led to the peace of Ryswick, we can see what was expected of the men who served that exacting master. The ideal diplomat should be 'quick, resourceful, a good listener, courteous and agreeable'. By studying history and memoirs and by finding out about foreign institutions and habits he should be able 'to tell in any country where the real sovereignty lies'. Like a banker, the good diplomat should build up credit by inspiring trust. A lie 'may confer success today but will create an atmosphere of suspicion which will make further success tomorrow impossible' and 'the secret of negotiation is to harmonize the real interests of the powers concerned'. It could have been his master's voice. Louis XIV prided himself on meticulous attention to the letter of a treaty but added his own nuance: 'there is no agreement in any clause so watertight as not to allow some elasticity of interpretation'. He once went so far as to compare treaties to compliments, 'absolutely necessary for coexistence but of little significance beyond their sound'. Inevitably there were double standards in the fashioning of treaties between sovereigns who looked on diplomacy as the handmaid of war, indeed part of an incessant campaign: however punctilious in form it was inevitably dishonest in spirit. Louis XIV and William III put their seals to a treaty in 1697 which was to be 'a universal, perpetual peace to be inviolably, religiously and sincerely observed'. Within five years they were at war again. It was a war which William and the Emperor wanted and which Louis would have preferred not to fight. But it was the outcome of successive wars and negotiations in which Louis had enjoyed the initiative and set the standard.

The Great Settlement

At the concluding stages of the larger wars the issues were resolved by envoys coming together at a congress: there, frontiers were drawn, sovereignty defined, trading and other rights confirmed. Versailles (1919), Vienna (1815) stand in direct line of succession to Paris (1763), Aix-la-Chapelle (1748) and Utrecht (1713): the year in each case is that in which the business was concluded. Utrecht was the ninth from the congress of Westphalia (1648), the first and in some ways the greatest, which began to assemble in 1643 to consider the vast problems of law, religion, ethics and expediency created by all the conflicts which had merged in the Thirty Years War. It is easy to find fault with the procedures and tactics of these assemblies of diplomats, though to do so from the standpoint of the twentieth century and its diplomatic experience would be to invite retaliation. As always, what the diplomat could achieve, though some were markedly more competent than others, was affected by the counters at his disposal: his country's military record, its strategic location and economic condition; in the seventeenth century religious criteria were also important. The deliberations and results of the congresses are interesting in themselves. No one can claim to understand the seventeenth century, its values and modes of thought, who has not studied the peace of Westphalia. Its terms provide the essential map for the diplomacy of the old regime, even though subsequent wars led to adjustments in what continued to be regarded as the foundation of a secure European order.

The delegates of Westphalia met in two towns, Münster and Osnabrück, because it would have been impossible to settle the questions of precedence that would have arisen if they had all assembled together. In January 1648 the United Provinces and Spain made their peace which ended the Eighty Years War, confirmed the independence of the United Provinces and the division between north and south: the product of geography and strategy but now becoming a cultural line as well. Spanish Flanders remained, clearly vulnerable to French aggression, damaged economically by the closure of the river Scheldt which the Spanish were forced to concede. Antwerp was never to recover the importance which Amsterdam had gained, as a centre of commerce and finance. In October 1648, while the Swedes were attacking Prague, where the Bohemian revolt thirty years beforehand had set Europe alight with its religious war, after five years of wrestling about status and boundaries the remaining treaties were signed. The delays had been caused by conventional ideas and tactical manoeuvres. The papal mediator had announced that he would not sit in the same room as heretics, the duc de Longueville, nominally head of the French legation, refused to enter unless he were accorded the title of *Altesse*, and planted a garden to show that he was prepared to wait. None of the French agents were to treat with Volmar, the Emperor's personal agent, because he was only a lawyer. Time thus gained in 1644–5 benefited the French as the Catholic Austro-Bavarian position deteriorated sharply under the pressure of French and Swedish attacks. In 1648, however, Mazarin found himself pressed to settle, with the Dutch out of the war and incipient revolt in his capital.

During the period of active debate and negotiations, 1646–8, the complex issues had been clarified: the complaints of the imperial estates and cities which had been affected by the Habsburg policy of 'Restitution' to Catholicism; the position of the 'rebels', notably the Elector Palatine; the satisfaction of auxiliaries and outside powers, notably France; compensation for losses. The instructions of Mazarin to his envoys indicate the aims of France in this period. They were to recover the Low Countries for 'an impregnable barrier' to northern France, for only then would Paris be truly 'the heart of France'. The Fronde, bringing invasion from Spanish troops, was to underline the danger: Paris was under a week's march from the Spanish fortresses. It was a prime aim of Louis XIV in both the War of the Queen's Rights and the Dutch War, to annex Artois and Picardy and to establish and fortify a more distant frontier. To secure the old county of Burgundy and Luxembourg they should be prepared to sacrifice Roussillon and Catalonia (the French had established themselves there after the Catalan revolt in 1640). They were to reach for the Rhine by acquisitions in Alsace and Lorraine. Thus France would secure her position in relation to Holland and the Empire.

Apart from the Spanish succession, which became a leading determinant of policy in Louis XIV's reign, and the development of the aggressive trade policies which led to the assault on Holland in 1672, the instructions serve as a summary of France's aims for the rest of the century. France was in the strongest position in these negotiations and her overall gains were substantial, if less than Mazarin hoped for. With the possession of Metz, Toul, Verdun, Moyenvic, Breisach and the right to garrison Phillipsburg, the French were well placed to defend or to exploit the divisions of Germany. In the settlement of Alsace there was an ambiguity which left the field open for further action. France obtained the 'landgraviate' of Upper and Lower Alsace, in full sovereignty, and the 'provincial prefecture' of the 'ten Alsatian towns', which were, like the nobility of Lower Alsace, to be left in full possession of their privileges. Did the landgraviate bring territorial, or merely feudal rights? D'Avaux prophesied that these doubts contained the seeds of future wars. Eventually, in the reunions of the ages, the tangle was resolved, behind an imposing array of academic arguments about rights over 'dependencies', by straightforward annexation. The Austrian character of the Empire was strengthened by the consolidation of the family lands: Upper Austria regained and Bohemia held in full sovereignty. For Germany it was laid down that important matters should be referred to an assembly of all states of the Empire. The German princes were allowed to make alliances outside or among themselves without the Emperor's consent. Of course they had already been doing so. Bavaria had made an alliance with France. The Elector Frederick William of Brandenburg had given notice of a new independence of approach by making his separate peace with the Swedes (1643), so putting himself in a position to restore his country and present himself as a worthy recipient of French patronage. To the wasted Hohenzollern state was now added Eastern Pomerania, the bishoprics of Minden, Halberstadt and Cammin, and the reversion to Magdeburg; it was the nucleus of a middle power between Austria and Sweden – though it would have taken great prescience to have foretold that Brandenburg–Prussia would be a great power in less than a century.

Mazarin saw that a larger Brandenburg might usefully balance Sweden. The ally whom Richelieu had called in from the north to check the Habsburgs had proved to be uncomfortably demanding. Sweden now became an important German power by her acquisition of Western Pomerania, Bremen and Verden, with a secure hold upon the southern shore of the Baltic: it was to prove an overextended position and a big factor in the northern wars which were fought to decide control of the Baltic and its rivers. By contrast with the conspicuous winners, Maximilian of Bavaria, who had dealt so confidently from his strong and well-organized base in the earlier middle years of the war, emerged with nothing more than he had gained at the outset: the title of elector and the lands of the Upper Palatinate. Charles Lewis, heir to the Elector Frederick who had caused so much trouble in the first place by accepting the Bohemian crown, was restored to his title and the Lower Palatinate. It was no longer so difficult to alter the constitution of the Holy Roman Empire. Nor was it so difficult to find a solution for the religious questions that had formerly seemed so intractable. Rome denounced what seemed to be a surrender to expediency. But the lesson of the war was that the use of force had failed to resolve religious differences, besides devaluing the ideals of the champions of the rival creeds. The diplomats fell back upon the principle of *cuius regio, eius religio*: now, alongside Lutheranism, Calvinism was officially recognized.

Sensitive as they were to the material conditions which were forcing the rulers of Europe to reconsider traditional policies, the diplomats should not be credited perhaps with more than a rudimentary idea of the balance of power. Their awareness of an overriding common interest together with particular pressures which forced them to settle, the empirical approach followed by skilful drafting, together created a settlement which came to be regarded as a great instrument of public law: the starting point for later treaties was that they were adjustments to Westphalia. But it was a serious weakness in the old diplomacy that between the great congresses there was no permanent mechanism for arbitration and conciliation; instead the grouping of powers in formal alliances ensured that a single act of aggression became a general war. There is a glaring disproportion, for example, between the extent, duration and destructiveness of the War of the Austrian Succession (1740–8) and the importance of the original issues. In 1791, in the middle of the Revolution which was to remove in the name of human rights the restraints which characterized the old diplomacy of checks and balances, Burke was to hold it against the new generation of politicians that they regarded the treaty of Westphalia as an antiquated fable. He was right to perceive a change of spirit and to fear the force of nationalism. But it does not follow that the dynasts who planned the partitions of Poland were any less concerned than the demagogues of revolutionary France to put their country's interest before the good of Europe. Ultimately the fate of disputed provinces, a Lorraine, a Silesia, a Podolia, depended on one sovereign's assessment of the odds, of what he could get away with. The French of Louis XIV's day always maintained that their periodic aggressions were intended to maintain the provisions of Westphalia. Plainly there was an element of self-deception there. Because of his superior resources and his willingness to go to war to achieve his objectives, it was inevitable that Louis should set the pace and provide the tone.

War Aims and Values

In the seventeenth and eighteenth centuries the culture of the courts and dominant aristocracies was essentially militaristic in conceptions, aims and style. Among those who directed or influenced the affairs of states war was accepted as a normal condition. Periods of peace were indeed exceptional. There were only 7 calendar years in the seventeenth century without a war somewhere in the continent: 1610, 1669–71 and 1680–2. During Louis XIV's reign his country was at war for 46 out of 72 years, Holland during the same period for 38. The Empire, Poland and Sweden could show comparable figures. A period of relative quiescence during the twenties and thirties of the eighteenth century ended in 1740 with Frederick the Great's attack upon Silesia which introduced a further phase of dynastic warfare. Broadly speaking the period falls into halves. In the middle is the War of the Spanish Succession which saw the climax of a growth in armaments that had been too rapid to be sustained indefinitely and the extension of war to include overseas possessions. The drain upon resources, at a time when the ambitions of states and their political development were not matched by comparable economic growth, had been too damaging.

The second phase began with a relatively stable period in international relations after the treaties of Rastadt (1714), Carlowitz (1718) and Nystad (1721), which ended the Spanish Succession, Austro-Turkish and Northern wars respectively. By comparison with the spectacular advances of the previous century – the 'military revolution' – it was a period of consolidation. Monarchs like Frederick William I of Prussia cherished their armies as costly investments in security; generals tended, for sound, practical reasons, to fight by the rule book. In the west at least, eighteenth-century warfare, as practised for example on the fields of Flanders in the War of the Austrian Succession, looks like a formal game; the movement of armies is as deliberate and intricate as a composition by Bach. The civilized moderation and outward decorum of language and style can be misleading. The influential *Reveries on the Art of War* by Marshal Saxe, successful commander in those campaigns, reveals a cool professionalism, unsentimental and impatient with the formalities of dress and parade, which did not further the essential business of the commander: to kill more of his enemies than he could kill of yours. Casualties in the set-piece battle remained murderously high. Moreover, the conventions mattered little in northern and eastern Europe. 'Burn, destroy, rob, arrest' was how Poles saw Charles XII's 'protection' of their country in 1706–7. While among western states one can see that a plateau had been attained in the size of armies, the development of Russia and Prussia into military powers of the first rank pointed the way to the renewal of European war on the grand scale in mid-century.

European rulers still tended to regard states as personal property. Typical pretexts for going to war, not usually challenged in ethical terms, and normally accepted as being within the sovereign's rights and competence, were disputes about property, inheritance or dynastic interest: the latter might still include religion and was increasingly coming to mean trade. The causes of war did not normally concern its chroniclers; judgements were usually in narrow terms of legal right rather than those of morality. But there was a general abhorrence of civil war: it impaired the authority of the state and involved irregular forces. 'The greatest of all evils is civil war. The evil to be feared from a fool who succeeds by right of birth is not as considerable, nor as certain.' Pascal, who experienced the Fronde, was here stating a principle that had been less clearly understood a century before. But it was always hard to define a civil war. The vast mêlée that lasted from 1618 to 1648 was both a war between the states of Europe and a German civil war. After the peace of Westphalia, state interests were more clearly defined. Yet certain anomalies remained. Huguenots and Catalans were organized political communities and their leaders claimed corresponding rights when it came to fighting for survival. External war could, moreover, lead to civil war: Condé and Turenne returned in 1648 from fighting the Spaniard to fight each other.

Just as civil wars were specially wrong, so wars against the infidel had traditionally been seen as specially right; they could impose a claim, as at the times of Turkish invasion, when the security of a large region was also at stake, above narrow dynastic interest. It was held against Louis XIV, especially in Germany, that he did not lend his support to the league against the Turks when they threatened Vienna, or join the Holy League subsequently formed to exploit Christian victory. It weakened his own claim to be espousing the interests of the Church when he turned on the Huguenot minority in France. The failure of his attempt to impose conformity contributed to the increasingly secular outlook that was affecting statesmen in this, as in other spheres of policy. The wars of the League of Augsburg and the Grand Alliance still, however, had an ideological content, largely missing from later wars, since the expulsion of Huguenots lent a sharp anti-Catholic emphasis to the aims of the Dutch and British, hosts to so many exiles. Huguenot propaganda against Louis, feebly countered by the French, whose king remained obstinately old-fashioned in his view of what a king was entitled to do with his own, helped to stiffen opinion in the states-general and in parliament, among troops as well as tax payers. British persecution of Roman Catholics similarly antagonized the French. It was seen then that religious feeling could still be a force in public opinion, reinforcing a superficial and short-lived trend towards nationalism in the relations of the western powers and contributing, along with commercial rivalries and, in particular, growing interest in colonies, to an element of ferocity which is unusual in a period characterized generally by a pragmatic spirit.

One casualty of the new outlook was the crusade. Again the drive against the Turks was uncharacteristic. The language, at first, was that of crusade: John Sobieski, in the words of the Pope, was 'A man sent by God'. But the concerns, at least as seen from Paris, were dynastic. By reconquering Hungary the Emperor could fulfil his obligation to those who, by law, were already his subjects, and increase the power of his state without offending the other German states. It was a very different matter from the idea of an international crusade for religion's sake. It had been a favourite argument of the *dévôts* in France, when Richelieu was bent on using French strength to combat the Spanish, that the Catholic countries should combine against the Turk. The idea was revived by the Lutheran philosopher, Leibnitz, at the height of the war between France and Holland (1676). Author of one of the fashionable schemes of the time for Lutheran–Catholic reunion, representative of a generation of Germans who saw Germany as the victim of the quarrels of the great powers, Leibnitz proposed to Pomponne that the French should join the Emperor in 'chasing the Turk out of Europe'. Pomponne, the least chauvinistic of Louis XIV's ministers, merely observed that 'Holy Wars have been out of fashion since the time of St Louis'. Moreover, an action of this sort would bring its own problems, as the later history of the 'Eastern question' was to show. The territorial expansion of Austria and Russia in the Turkish Balkans only sharpened the appetite of these two powers, and led ultimately to the partitions of Poland. War at the circumference might distract the powers from local conflict; it was more likely to bring further tension and conflict at the centre.

Colonial ambitions and rivalries were another important element in the sequence of wars that involved, in one combination or another, Spain, France, Holland and England; incidental in 1688–97, crucial in 1740–63. Trade was at stake, and the struggle for a larger share of what was thought to be a limited volume of trade was, second only to dynastic ambition, a major cause of war. The wars between England and Holland fought between 1652 and 1674 were primarily about trade and were fought mainly at sea. In the series of continental wars which began with the invasion of Holland by France in 1672, naval campaigns assumed new importance. Commerce-raiding became a large factor, and peace terms were affected crucially by the economic condition of the belligerents. 'Now,' wrote Charles d'Avenant in 1695, 'the whole art of war is in a manner reduced to money; and nowadays that prince who can best find money to feed, clothe and pay his army, not he that hath the most valiant troops, is surest of success and conquest.' The Nine Years War (1688–97) and the War of the Spanish Succession (1701–14) approached in some respects the modern idea of 'total' war, in the impact upon society, not only of taxation but also of loans, the new state banks (in England and Holland) and the more ambitious operations of financiers and war contractors: men like Thomas Brydges in England or Samuel Bernard in France were as important as generals whom they helped to keep in the field.

Louis XIV was old-fashioned, even in the 1680s, in his attempts to impose conformity of faith and in the pronounced Catholic bias of his foreign policy. The consequences of the double failure – to eliminate Huguenotism and to defeat the coalition of his enemies – fostered a critical spirit which was not confined to the morality of war. In that area there was another influence at work: the spread of rationalism reinforced the lesson of successive 'religious wars', that creeds could not be imposed by force. But it was a devout, conservative priest who made the boldest stand against the militarist ideals of the French court. Archbishop Fénelon's advice to his pupil and the heir-apparent, the duke of Burgundy, was to put the well-being of citizens before such pagan ideals as glory or honour. He weighed the desolation of the French countryside against the acquisition of frontier towns and condemned the king's policy and the philosophy behind it: in his desire to be master of Europe, Louis XIV had forgotten his prime duty to the French people. Louis's grandson, Burgundy, the unsuccessful commander at the battle of Oudenaarde (1708), made a stand thereafter for peace at almost any price and was held by all except his intimates to be a coward. He was in fact conscientious, independent in his views, a man of moral courage. He did not live to be king and we are left to speculate on the course that French history might have taken had he done so. After the Seven Years War we can again see informed opinion, of which the economist Turgot is a good representative, turning against war. Yet the French were drawn into the American War (1778) which, with its legacy of debt, has a large place among the causes of the Revolution.

Such a positive reappraisal in high places was exceptional. Occasional incidents, like the ravaging of the Palatinate in 1688–9 by Tessé or that of Bavaria in 1704 by Marlborough, were reminders that strategic considerations might take priority over all else – even with a commander like Marlborough, epitome of the courtesy of the age. They also brought an outraged public reaction. Accounts of atrocities played a part in seventeenth-century war propaganda, particularly during the years of the Huguenot dispersion (1680–90). Radical thinking about the ethics of war can, however, only be found in a few isolated individuals like Grimmelshausen whose black humour has its artistic counterpart in the etchings of Jacques Callot, depicting the atrocities and waste of war in his series *Les Misères de guerre*. Plans for the peaceful realignment of the great powers were normally tinged with self-interest, like Sully's *grand dessein*. There was to be a significant change of emphasis when Saint-Pierre worked out, on Sully's basis, his own *Project de paix perpetuelle* (1719); the philosophical *abbé* questioned the value of war and planned constructively to prevent it.

The limitations as well as the strength of eighteenth-century opinion can be seen in the case of Voltaire. He admired Frederick the Great, who began his reign with an unprovoked attack in defiance of the conventional wisdom about 'limited war', introduced a new style of statecraft in which other 'enlightened' sovereigns, notably Joseph II of Austria, complacently followed him – and ushered in a period of warfare comparable with that of 1689–1714. As a historian, however, Voltaire's accounts of Charles XII and Louis XIV combine a taste for the heroic with a more sophisticated calculation of social cost. His is an ironic and, within limits, humane view, though tinged with pessimism about human nature. He pities the French during the Nine Years War, who 'perished of hunger to the music of *Te Deums*'. Writing of his sources for the life of Charles XII and of the journal of M. Alderfeld, he made a wry selection:

> Monday, April 3rd: So many thousand men slaughtered in such-and-such a place. Tuesday: Whole villages were reduced to ashes, women consumed by the flames with the children they held in their arms. Thursday: We annihilated with a thousand bombs the houses of a free and innocent town that failed to pay, money down, a thousand crowns to a foreign conqueror who passed its walls .... This is a theme, more or less, of four volumes.

He comments of the siege of Turin (1706): 'Assuredly what was spent on all these preparations for destruction would have sufficed to found and render flourishing the most populous colony.' About the quarrel of English and French over the boundaries of Canada he points out that 'a similar dispute between two simple merchants would have been settled in a couple of hours by arbitrators'.

For all his commonsense Voltaire recognized the force of state interest. The more efficiently men were organized in states, the more easily their natural competitiveness could be mobilized for war. He was unimpressed by the project of Saint-Pierre, for 'man was a carnivorous animal' and would always fight. The growth of strong states ensured that he would fight more efficiently. The most that informed opinion could do was to create a climate in which the operations of war would be limited, and the conduct of soldiers controlled by civilized rules. To some extent this climate did exist. It is a melancholy fact that the progress of civilization in Europe has at every stage been accompanied by an advance in the techniques of war. At least, however, war in the eighteenth century did not destroy the civilization that engendered it. The object of battle was to gain the field, not to destroy the enemy. The British government defined rules and conventions by putting the unfortunate Admiral Byng on trial for cowardice and dereliction of duty after the loss of Minorca (1757). It evoked a magnanimous response from his adversary the duc de Richelieu, who, 'distressed to hear of the charges', attributed the French victory to the better condition and equipment of their ships and to 'the fortune of war, which determine the outcome of all battles'. At the height of a war, traders carried on normally, not discriminating in their business between friend and foe: men could travel freely without passports. There might be 'an enemy of the crown' but there was no such thing as 'enemy country'.

War was treated as normal, but a long war might produce a reaction; as in Sweden after the death of Charles XII, or in Holland, after the peace of Rastadt. There was always in the latter country, and in England, a strong force of opinion against any war that did not appear beneficial to trading interests, but equally strong for war, as in the affair of Jenkins' Ear (1739), when it did so appear. After the Spanish Succession and Northern wars, the object of Dubois and Fleury in France was to preserve the balance achieved by the peace of Utrecht, to husband resources and to avoid any commitment that might lead to a general war. The Emperor Charles VI devoted his energies to finding diplomatic solutions for the problems of his daughter's inheritance. Walpole in England went to great lengths to avoid war. Yet though circumstances might dictate a pause, there was no fundamental change of attitudes. As the singularly futile War of the Polish Succession (1733–8) showed, behind the diplomatic manoeuvres lay always the assumption that armies were there to be used: *ultima ratio regum*. The ideal of balance among powers survived for want of a more positive incentive. It can be said too to represent the commonsense of the age, which shrank from extremes. The aims of states, the values of courts remained, however, competitively militaristic. Though statistics became more readily available (the work of Vauban and Boisguilebert, for example, had provided some sophisticated and detailed information about the economy of France at the end of the seventeenth century), statesmen continued to make decisions about peace and war without counting the cost to society. 'Enlightened' rulers were no less willing than their predecessors to go to war to achieve their ends. Frederick II set the example with his attack on Silesia in 1740, when political and economic arguments served to rationalize his craving for action and acclaim. Elizabeth and Catherine of Russia, Maria Theresa perforce and Joseph II without qualms, followed his example. They might find in diplomacy a means of gaining their ends without fighting. The partitions of Poland (the first was in 1772) can be defended on that ground; but they display a lack of scruple and a recklessness about consequences on the part of the principal executioners, Frederick, Catherine and Joseph, which is hard to envisage in Louis XIV or Leopold.

After 1740 France 'pursued its traditions rather than its interests'. There were few sound material reasons for entering the War of the Austrian Succession – and the French had accepted the Pragmatic Sanction, guaranteeing the rights of Maria Theresa. The decision represented, therefore, the victory of Belle-Isle and the war party at court over the aged Fleury; it could be viewed as a return to the natural order of things. The French army was the most aristocratic in Europe and was grossly top-heavy, with 1 officer to every 15 men on active service. Soldiering was the French nobleman's *métier*. He was obliged to be more professional than his forebears; warfare was a technical business and required a large permanent establishment. The rationale of feudalism had long been lost in the evolution of the bureaucratic state. But much of the older spirit survived. The king went to war to further the interests of his dynasty. The nobleman expected him to provide suitable occasions for the service that was an integral part of his privileged status. 'I have officers whom I do not need,' wrote Louis XV. 'But I am sure they need me.' For every 1 officer on duty with the troops in 1775 there were 5 paid but unemployed, 60,000 in all, with pay and pensions absorbing more than half the army's budget – an expensive luxury and a dangerous war lobby as well.

A prudent spirit characterized the warfare of the eighteenth century. By his initial rashness Frederick the Great endangered his state, and he later had to fight what became a war of survival (1756–63). He was too imaginative to remain entirely within the conventions in statecraft or strategy: he was a genius among competent, careful men. Yet none was more aware than he of the need to preserve society from the ravages of war; it was his ideal, when he engaged in war, that the civilian population should not be aware that a state of war existed. Campaigns were everywhere fought according to recognized rules about strategy, military honours, the treatment and exchange of prisoners, and the rights of civilians: billeting and foraging were normally controlled, though still a terrible imposition. Looting was less common than formerly, though no army could be relied upon, certainly not the Russian. If a town capitulated before the final assault, it was spared the sack; if not, soldiers could make free with the place for a stated period. Normally a besieged commander would surrender on terms when it became clear that further resistance was useless; he had lost the game, but preserved life and honour.

There was nothing comparable in later wars (except possibly in Poland during the Swedish occupation of 1701–9) to the widespread devastation of the Thirty Years War, when there was little to choose, in their conduct towards civilians, between the armies nominally under state control, like the Swedish or the French, and those of the great *condottieri*, like Wallenstein. An army of that time on the move tended to resemble a mass migration: with as many camp-followers as soldiers. The war taught a sobering lesson on the danger of unleashing armies without adequate control. Stricter regulation of armed forces was thereafter a priority among rulers for they consumed a large proportion of the state's resources. Commanders were, therefore, made more directly answerable to their governments. Their troops acquired some of the more disciplined attributes of professionals: regular pay, uniforms, promotion by merit, even perhaps the exposure to more humane attitudes, all contributed to the change. Soldiers did not live in a separate world; barracks were unusual and in the 'close season' of winter, men were spread around the billets. Officers attended court or retired to their estates. The spread of education and the compassionate ethics of Christianity, as interpreted in an age which wearied of dogmatic quarrels, may have had an effect on conduct. More important than such attributes was the concern of statesmen for the preservation of the highly developed structure of the state. Warfare came generally to be 'limited', paradoxically because of the advances of the 'military revolution' of the previous century. Armies were better armed and trained, correspondingly more destructive and expensive. Besides the concern for stable relationships, and the respect for convention which are to be seen in war, as in other aspects of eighteenth-century life, there was a rational self-interest at work. Unhappy was the fate of a country which, like Poland, could not keep up with the arms race. On the other hand the decline of Spain, the ordeal of France at the end of Louis XIV's wars, the eclipse of Sweden after the reign of Charles XII, were surely warnings against trusting too blindly in the god of war.

War then was the sport of kings, not a contest of the peoples. In this period, between the 'religious wars', when operations were conducted by relatively small semi-feudal or mercenary armies, accustomed to terrorize civilians, and the wars of nations that came after 1789, with conscript armies and weapons of mass destruction, it is arguable that war made less impact upon the lives of the people at large than at any time since the Middle Ages. It is significant that the greatest wars were fought, at least in name, over succession questions: in turn Spain, Poland, Austria and Bavaria provided problems which were too intractable or vital to the interests of the great dynasties for solution by diplomacy and its weapons, treaty, subsidy or marriage. Even then the combatants appeared to recognize a common interest in keeping hostilities within bounds. Wars were long drawn out but battles few and far between – and rarely decisive.

Between the battle of Rocroy in 1643 which marked the eclipse of Spain as a first-class power, and the peace of Versailles in 1783, which ended the last major war of our period, there were very few battles which decided more than the outcome of one campaign. The relief of Vienna, the battles of Blenheim and Poltava would be on any short list of significant actions. Whatever the choice, there is a far longer list of indecisive engagements, where the advantage of one side was not sufficient, or where casualties were too high, or there were other physical or psychological factors to prevent victory being fully exploited. Sometimes, for other than military reasons, a battle acquires great significance: Fehrbellin (1675), where the world was given a foretaste of Hohenzollern military might in a relatively small victory over the Swedes; or Rossbach (1757), where the rout of the French indicated a serious decline in the efficiency and morale of the French army and dealt a disproportionately heavy blow to French prestige, are in this category. But the typical battle of the period in western Europe was a grappling of two large masses; the winner might be whoever was able to comply most closely with the advice of Turpin de Crissé (1754): 'Battles are won not by numbers but by the manner of forming your troops together and their order and discipline.' When battle was joined, it was the commander's concern to preserve his battle order intact. But irregularity of ground and the accidents of battle would soon destroy the parade-ground effect. The unwieldy collisions and charges then produced a mêlée somewhat different from the colourful tableaux beloved of the artists. Three battles in Flanders fields, Seneffe (1674), Neerwinden (1693) and Laffeldt (1747), may be cited as examples of this type; none of them had much effect upon the overall war situation or upon subsequent negotiations.

Just as the aims of war were normally limited and concrete (not for the eighteenth century the crude demand for 'unconditional surrender') and therefore not conducive to the spirit of fighting to the death, so campaigns were conducted with a view to securing the maximum advantage compatible with the security of one's force. It was a maxim of Marshal Saxe that 'War should be made so as to leave nothing to chance.' Actions were bloody because of improvements in artillery, the use of the bayonet and the deployment of masses of infantry densely packed; but the great slaughter of Malplaquet (1709), when the casualties were more than 30,000 out of the 120,000 involved on both sides together, was to remain unmatched until Borodino (1812). In both cases, the reasons for the high casualties are similar – and revealing. The invading commanders were fighting for their reputation; both relied upon tactics that had served them well in the past, and perhaps underestimated their opponents. Marlborough and Napoleon, in different circumstances, both needed to impress their countrymen by a decisive victory. The French at Malplaquet and the Russians at Borodino were fighting for their homelands and resisted with exceptional stubbornness. More typical of eighteenth-century warfare was Fontenoy (1745). It was marked by skilful deployment of the French defence by Marshal Saxe who made his name in this battle, and by the good order and steadiness of both sides. Ligonier (veteran British commander who was born a French Huguenot) had the presence of mind, in the thick of battle, when ordered by Cumberland to retreat, to write a note to Marshal Saxe desiring him to take care of the dead and wounded. That was a small triumph of the human spirit, a gleam of chivalry upon a scene that was not wholly sordid.

The Army and the State

Throughout the seventeenth century the scale and range of war became larger as the European states became more successful in exploiting their manpower and materials. The armies of the War of the Spanish Succession were 3 to 4 times larger than those of the Thirty Years War. At the height of Louis XIV's reign the French army exceeded 1.5 per cent of the population, a figure never achieved again during the *ancien régime*. It placed an intolerable burden on the economy. It was indeed widely held that 1 in 100 was the largest that a state could be expected to raise. In Prussia, however, an efficient machinery of finance and recruitment, perfected over the previous century of state building and driven by Frederick the Great's fierce will to survive, produced by the end of the Seven Years War the astounding proportion of 4 in 100. Though Prussia's situation was exceptional, large armies were everywhere the rule, composed for the most part of peasant infantry and officered by the landed gentry. As well as large numbers there were significant changes in the way armies were used; also corresponding political changes. The state which could not raise or control a sufficient force, and find the means of maintaining it on a regular footing, could expect to be insignificant, or to succumb to aggression. Those states which remained in the forefront, or forced their way to it, experienced a challenge to existing structures, constitutional, administrative and economic which, however resolved, could only result in a larger role for the state and a more strictly ordered society, in which revolts could be repressed more ruthlessly, taxes collected more regularly, justice dispensed more fairly. More people came directly into state service; at both ends of the social scale, for disaffected nobleman or destitute vagrant, military service offered a satisfactory alternative to wastrel lives. It was not only such people that were drawn to serve for honour, bread or the chance of loot. Furthermore, society became more manageable when the potentially lawless were drawn into the machines of the competing powers. Many more were indirectly involved in providing for and administering to the armed forces. A few, contractors, financiers mostly, made great fortunes; at the humblest level many were harassed, even ruined, by the requirements of billeting and what was euphemistically termed 'contribution', otherwise simply a regulated version of the old system of living off the land. Through the relentless increase in taxes most of the community was affected. At the apex were governments which, for all the sophistication of diplomacy and the elegance of courts, were essentially machines for making war: France or Austria, no less than Prussia or Russia, even if the war motive was less stark and uncompromising in the older states. It should not be thought that the development was confined to the men under arms and the swelling empires of officialdom; nor that economic effects were negative. The state's activity as the largest purchaser of food, textiles, metalware, naval stores, and as the largest employer in construction, in harbours, fortresses and roads, had a largely beneficial effect on demand which was all the more important in the long recession, whose effects it did much to mitigate. The military concerns of the state could be, as in modern times, the basis for new technologies. Also, among economic effects should be included the evolution of credit finance and the refinement of management skills. Medicine, particularly surgery, was promoted by the pressing need to conserve manpower at a time when most of those wounded in battle died, and more died of disease in camp than on the battlefield. In the more backward countries, notably Russia, education was fostered largely as a means of providing a reliable corps of officers. Not only was the military revolution at the heart of the development of absolute government, it affected profoundly, at all levels and in all activities, the evolution of society.

In 1672, 100,000 French troops invaded the United Provinces, crossed the Rhine and threatened Amsterdam. A century before, the seizure of Brill by the 'sea beggars' had begun the revolt of the Netherlands and the war which, more than any other, wore down the Spanish strength. The years between saw the changes that justify the use of the term 'revolution'. Stimulus came from two great wars: that between Spain and the United Provinces, and the Thirty Years War with which it merged when, after the Bohemian revolt, the Spanish decided to renew war against their rebel subjects. The first true standing army was the Spanish, who had to keep an army continuously active in the Netherlands during the revolt. Improvement in fortification meant that sieges lasted longer: a larger besieging army was required to attack the town and to provide cover against relief operations. Meanwhile the recurring impact of Ottoman armies and fleets compelled the powers concerned, notably again the Spanish, to develop their armaments. The Thirty Years War was a gigantic laboratory of military science: experiments were random and reckless, the conventions were flouted; prizes went to the boldest in conditions which favoured the enterprising. When armies reverted to linear tactics in order to make the best use of improved fire power, there had to be an increase in numbers. The line of battle was strengthened by the provision of second and third lines to prevent penetration, and lengthened to prevent flank attack. A similar logic affected naval warfare. The addition of second and third tiers of guns to warships strengthened the line; further ships guarded against the line being 'doubled' by the enemy. As is the case in the twentieth century the only limiting factor was finance. Cost inflation, responding to inflexible patterns of demand, is always relatively severe in the armaments sector. Vast debts and successive bankruptcies marred the records of the leading powers of the sixteenth century, the Empire, France and Spain. That did little to restrain the ambitions of their rulers but they were forced to rely on the services of entrepreneurs to provide the supplies, even, as in the case of Wallenstein, a complete military outfit. In prospering, solvent Holland, even, finance for the war at sea and the expansion of trade, which was in itself a form of war, was provided by corporate overseas companies, armed, semi-independent organizations, all powerful in their sphere, even influencing issues of peace and war.

Over-mighty country or over-mighty subject: the essence of the problem was the same, whether measured in arrogant imperialism which evoked a no less forceful response from Holland's English rivals, or in the anarchy and distress of Germany in the 1630s and 1640s. Necessity was the mother of coercion. The entrepreneurs were brought under control, eventually cut out by professional forces under state control. By the end of the seventeenth century every important state controlled 'regular' armies: on a permanent footing, recruited, paid and managed by officials of the state. A clear distinction was established between soldiers and civilians. In the age of Louis XIV the pace was set by France, with a fifth of the total population of Europe, with correspondingly large resources to support an army of a quarter of a million and military goals which leaders of opinion and makers of policy, not least the king, regarded as legitimate but which rival states understandably were determined to resist. French aggression may have been the most significant factor but it was not the only cause of the great expansion of armaments in this period. The Empire's permanent confrontation with the Turks was another vital school of war. Montecuccoli, Charles of Lorraine and Eugène of Savoy were among its most distinguished students. Peter the Great could only see Russia achieve its strategic objectives through the creation of a western-style army: his military reforms were the most important element in the making of the new Russia. Under Charles XI and Charles XII Sweden made a prodigious effort to maintain the position established by Gustavus Adolphus. Prussia built the state round and for the army. England played a distinctive part after the accession of William of Orange (1689) and the wars with France that ensued. Charles II had 3500 soldiers in 1663; William III was at one time paying 90,000. Naval resources were used to excellent effect and the Mediterranean was opened to British ships after the acquisition of Gibraltar in 1704. A military tradition was forged by the genius of Marlborough who, with Turenne, may be accounted the ablest of the heirs of Maurice of Nassau (1566–1625), master of the fortification and siegecraft which the geography of his war called for, and of Gustavus Adolphus (died 1632) who had set himself, in Roberts's words, 'to liberate strategy from the tenacious mud of the Netherlands'. Marlborough's skilful use of resources and intelligent staff work, systematic training and single-minded commitment to the object of defeating the enemy recall the inventive Maurice who pioneered the use of small adaptable units, and the Swedish king–commander who took all Poland and Germany for his field of war. The tactical innovation of Maurice and Gustavus was the return to linear formations, with closely integrated divisions, ranged in two or three ranks and marshalled so as to exploit several types of weapon, serviceable equally for attack and defence. For Gustavus's semi-independent mobile brigades new methods of training and higher standards of leadership had been demanded. Backed by draconian punishments the drill schedules of the Prussian armies were designed to make the men rigid automata, more afraid of their officers than of the enemy. There were more officers; men were expected to show greater initiative, new means were discovered of raising morale. The psalm and sermon played their part. Cromwell's Ironsides, like Gustavus's Lutherans, believed in their cause, followed a leader with whom they could identify, and acquired a rare cohesion through self-discipline.

The prayers and preaching were exceptional, the messianic spirit a transitory phenomenon; and the righteous zeal turned rapidly into the callousness that led to such incidents as Cromwell's massacre at Drogheda, and to the aimless savagery that characterized the later operations of the Swedes in Germany. 'Young angels became old devils' but the new professionalism became part of the tradition. Armies were retained in winter; the close season was used for training – and grew shorter until the convention that armies did not fight in the winter died a natural death. The Habsburgs found that they enjoyed an advantage over the Turks in Hungary in winter when the Turkish camels could not stand the cold. Turenne demonstrated the possibilities of winter campaigning during his last and most brilliant operations in the Vosges mountains (1674–5). It remained usual, however, for armies to desist from active operations in the coldest months. Drill acquired an importance that it never subsequently lost. Armies began to march in step: following the Prussian example Saxe introduced this into the French army in the 1740s. The wearing of uniforms gradually replaced the token that could so easily be discarded by the soldier of fortune. They were adapted very slowly. The full splendour of military uniforms came with the eighteenth century when the scarlet, blue and gold cocked hats and grenadiers' mitre hats (designed to enable them to throw grenades unimpeded by the brim), besides more exotic costumes such as those of the Prussian Hussars, copied from Hungary, proclaimed the pride of belonging to a world apart from civilians. Senior officers were distinguished by increasing magnificence of ornament rather than by badges of rank. Officers took to wearing uniform off duty. Kings, following the example of Charles XII, wore uniform. The king, like his soldiers, thus showed himself to be a servant of the state. At all levels the new armies engendered a spirit of identification with the country. In Britain one can see the instinct for liberty at work in the assumption of parliament that armies were strictly for wars. Mean treatment in peacetime, refusal to provide adequate barracks, for example, led to inefficiency, and British wars normally began with defeats. Their officers were encouraged to regard themselves as amateurs, commissioned foxhunters. Despite the military proclivities of her Dutch and Hanoverian kings, the army was never allowed to influence, let alone control, the policy of the state. In Holland, too, the composition and operations of the army were jealously supervised. The exceptions illuminate the rule; elsewhere in Europe the major states were essentially military autocracies.

The greatest armies, the French and Imperial, as later the Prussian and Russian, continued to contain an important mercenary element. The commander, whose skills were in demand, could still change allegiance as a modern business executive changes his firm. The officer class could easily assimilate talented foreigners: with greater professionalism there remained the old freemasonry of the camp. The Dutch and British armies in the War of the Spanish Succession contained more Germans than their own nationals. At the top, French-born Eugène for the Austrians, English Jacobite Berwick and German Saxe for the French, and Scottish Keith for the Prussians enjoyed the highest commands. Young aspirants went to study war under acknowledged experts. Contemporaries would have seen little irony in the fact that John Churchill learned his soldiering under Turenne, for class counted for more than country. Social attitudes remained old-fashioned, but armies lost their feudal character. Nobles and gentry predominated among the officers. It was generally held that they were more responsive to the call of honour, more valiant than men of middle-class stock. But they had to accept administrative control.

In recruitment, pay and discipline, the state took over, from feudal lord or specialist contractor, the role of provider and controller. When Michel Le Tellier, who had been an *intendant* with the army in Richelieu's time, became war minister in 1643, the French army had proved itself capable of winning great battles; notably Condé's victories at Rocroy in 1643 and Lens in 1648. But it was a defective instrument of power in relation to the size of the country and its resources. Despite the efforts of Richelieu and Sublet de Noyers, there was chronic indiscipline. In the words of Le Tellier, the army was 'a republic, composed of as many provinces as there are lieutenant-generals'. His great work was to bring the forces absolutely under the control of the king. His son Louvois later presided over the expansion of the army and the development of specialist arms and made a distinctive contribution in the commissariat: he was the 'great victualler'. By the time he became minister the essential reforms had been carried out. All commissions were issued by the king, without intermediary. A new ladder of promotion was set up, with two new and unpurchasable ranks, lieutenant-colonel and major. A vital principle underlay these changes. In the typical army of the old sort, Wallenstein's for example, there was still no fixed corps of officers; the difference between officer and private was one of degree; the notion implied by the modern terminology, 'officers and *other ranks*', was missing. Not till the death of Turenne, the revered captain, doyen of the old type, veteran of the German war and despiser of bureaucrats, could the reforms be fully implemented (1675). Then the creation of the new ranks set up a new ladder of promotion by merit alongside the old, purchasable ranks. When in 1684 the king created twenty-seven new infantry regiments, all the new colonels had been either majors or lieutenant-colonels. A fair proportion rose to the top of the hierarchy in this fashion – more than in the eighteenth century, when there was a reaction against such social levelling.

The slogan '*carrière ouverte aux talents*' belongs to the men of 1789; but it was, at least in the army, the principle of Louvois. Inspectors were sent out to check abuses such as false musters: the strictness of one of them, Martinet, gave a new word to the English language. To facilitate rapid expansion of the army's peace establishment, a regular reserve of officers was set up. Although there were experiments with a militia system (the militia was integrated with the regular forces in the later stages of the War of the Spanish Succession), the prime aim was to create a truly professional army. Its status in the community was enhanced by practical measures: regular pay drew the foreigner, tax exemptions favoured the Frenchman. A few ex-soldiers found honourable retirement in the Hôtel des Invalides, the first regular establishment of its kind. The grandeur of the building reflects the values of the regime: the army was cherished by Louis and Louvois, the symbol and the instrument of France's dominance in Europe. It was kept under constant surveillance. *Intendants* became the regular means of a central control that became oppressively strict and detailed. In 1678 Louvois wrote to the *intendant* in Roussillon: 'Your first duty is to let me know everything that is said, projected and done in the army.' When the unsubtle policies of Louvois in the 1680s caused the European states to combine against France her military planning was exposed as conservative and pedantic; generals, at least after the death of Luxembourg in 1695, were discouraged from using their initiative. Towards the end of the reign Louis was taking on the functions of a chief of staff. Remote control, in a war of several fronts, against opponents who could muster equal numbers and had learned from the French experience, was one factor in the disappointing performance of the French armies in Flanders and Italy between 1702 and 1709. An instructive contrast is provided by the relatively successful performance of those armies in which there was no division of authority and whose general, like Frederick the Great, was also king. The risks were proportionately greater as well – as Charles XII's reign showed.

The French did not gain from the great inflation of armaments for where they had led, their opponents had perforce to follow. The crucial factors were the ability of the sovereign to tax at will and to marshal the resources of the country by more efficient government. Since that depended in the last resort upon his possessing a reliable army, the arrival of the standing army and the making of the absolute state went together. Prussia provides the best example of the reciprocal process. The *Intendantur der Armee* became the nucleus of the central government; the *Generalkriegskommissariat* was not just an army department but the main governing body of the state. In Russia, where, again, the building of the army was the building of the state, a crucial struggle was waged by Peter against the Zaporozhian Cossacks – fierce warriors, valuable allies, dangerous enemies. They were not finally assimilated until Catherine's suppression of the Pugachev revolt in 1775–83. Peter, who in 1718 divided Russia into regimental districts based his policy upon the assumption that the landowner was personally responsible for military service. The fact that Austria's army in 1740 was no greater than Prussia's though her population was eight times as large is a telling comment on her political and economic weakness. The heroic spirit of Empress Maria Theresa and the reforms of her minister Haugwitz enabled the Empire to overcome the worst of her problems. In Spain, the reluctance of hidalgos to serve in the army was a pointer to her decadence. Poland failed to provide even the base for modernization – and paid the penalty.

One of the lessons of the Thirty Years War had been that neutrality was no guarantee of immunity from war. No small state had suffered worse than Brandenburg–Prussia from invasion and occupation during a period when military necessity overrode political scruples. Not only rulers but also their subjects, who had to pay, could see greater advantages to be gained from security of property and trade than from constitutional rights. There were benefits to the privileged classes in an expansion of the army; a role in society as member of an officer corps was especially appealing to younger sons and to those who could otherwise only look forward to a narrow existence on a small estate. A new class of magnates was created in Germany and Scandinavia out of the senior officers who were rewarded by large estates, especially in lands which had been newly acquired or where old families could be turned out – such as Pomerania, Bohemia and Hungary. At a lower level a different sort of pressure can be seen. Armament industries stimulated economic activity in that period of the seventeenth century when there was a chronic lack of demand. Service in the armies provided employment too, and helped to relieve some of the pressures caused by surplus population in the poor margins of Europe. Swiss and

Croats, Scots, Irish and Finns enlisted for bread; the flow of recruits enabled states to expand their armies without having to resort to conscription, though various forms of selective service were devised. When one adds that armies drew for recruits, besides misfits and miscreants, on landless peasants and unemployed artisans, and provided employment in metal working, textiles and other industries, the expansion of armies is seen to have played a central and useful role in the economy of Europe.

Arms and the Men

The tactics of the time required large masses of infantry. But armies were subject to the law of diminishing returns; the greater the pressure of recruitment, the higher the rate of desertion. It was easy for the peasant soldier to slip away, discard his uniform and return to his village. After the mammoth engagements of Flanders, notably Malplaquet (1709), there was some questioning of the effectiveness of such large forces. Marshal Saxe used to say that 50,000 was the most that could be effectively controlled. The concentration of French troops in Flanders for the campaign of 1747 actually gave him 130,000. But at the battle of Roucoux in that year only half the opposing forces were engaged and casualties were correspondingly light.

The high rate of casualties (1 in 6 was the ratio at Malplaquet; at Zorndorf in 1758, the Russians lost 26,000 out of 80,000) reflected the slow-moving pace, the tightly packed formations of the eighteenth-century battlefield – and helps to explain why commanders were chary of committing their troops and tended to adopt a defensive strategy. Primarily that was due to improvements in weaponry. Artillery had been used to deadly effect by Gustavus, who attached field guns to each infantry battalion to give fire support. Eugène gave his cavalry 'galloper' guns. When guns were intelligently used, artillery anticipated its role as the great destroyer of the eighteenth-century firing grape or canister, with an effective range of about 500 yards. Marlborough frequently sited his guns himself, insisted on prepared powder charges and introduced a well-sprung cart for swifter movement of ammunition. At Malplaquet, however, he had a taste of his own medicine, when a well-concealed French battery cut swathes in the ranks of the Dutch Blue Guards. The capture of the enemy's artillery, when it was massed in one place, was usually the decisive stroke in a battle, as when the Prussians defeated the Saxons at Kesseldorf (1745). Prince Liechtenstein's three-pounders, easily manoeuvrable, rapid-firing as a musket, served by specially trained master gunners, were the showpiece of the revitalized Austrian army of the 1750s. Considering the potential killing power of artillery, commanders were surprisingly slow to effect further improvements. Lack of interest in technology is a recognizable aristocratic trait. Eventually, improvements in metallurgy (coke smelting, cheaper and sounder iron, new methods of boring giving more accurate calibre) were exploited – notably by Gribeauval, inspector-general of the French artillery after 1765. He shorted gun barrels, used horses instead of bullocks and improved gun carriages so that his artillery were able on occasion to keep up with the infantry and were more manoeuvrable in battle. Ironically it was the revolutionary armies that benefited most from these changes, as from those in tactics, notably the use of the column instead of the line.

Muskets were improved by the invention of the flintlock mechanism in the late seventeenth century. The firelock was discharged by sparks from a flint and steel, activated by a trigger which ignited a pinch of powder. The soldier could now dispense with the slow-burning fuse which he had to use to ignite the charge every time he fired. The long pike became obsolete at about the same time, with the introduction of the 'needle' bayonet, which could be fitted into a socket below the muzzle without interrupting fire. Pikemen had formerly been used to protect the musketeers against cavalry. The bayonet was used wirh deadly effect in battles like Narva and Denain. Frederick, who regarded the bayonet as the main offensive weapon, was sceptical about the values of the flintlock except in defence. With its smooth bore, the muzzle-loading firelock was capable of more rapid, though not more accurate, fire than the old matchlock musket. Firing round bullets it could achieve three rounds a minute when aiming was dispensed with. It was most effective when infantry were formed into ranks: three became the norm, the front rank kneeling, the rear rank firing over the shoulder of the middle rank. The use of linear formations, with volley firing, dictated tactics and imposed serious limitations upon the commander.

Because of the improvements in weapons, infantry played the main part in most battles. Of the 120,000 with whom Louis XIV invaded the Netherlands in 1672, 75 per cent were infantry: it was to be the usual proportion. At Ramillies (1706) it was the cavalry charge which won the day for Marlborough. But at Mollwitz (1741), after Frederick the Great had seen the cavalry routed and had left the field, the Prussian infantry stood firm and won the battle for their absent king. At Malplaquet there were 60,000 horses altogether. Not surprisingly foraging for horses was one of the several factors which tied armies, for the most part, to the traditional seasonal pattern for campaigning. Turenne and Condé were admirers of *la charge sauvage*: the later tendency of the French to train cavalry to manoeuvre in parade-ground fashion, firing pistols or carbines at the halt, was one of several ways in which they deviated from the spirit and tactics of those great commanders of the school of Gustavus.

Both Marlborough and Charles XII favoured the shock of cold steel. The latter's cavalry were trained to ride in wedge formation, three ranks deep, 'knee behind knee'. Under Max of Baden and Eugène the cavalry were the best arm of the Austrian army. They also made use of 'hussar' regiments, light cavalry of Magyar origin, valuable for skirmishing and reconnaissance.

Variations such as these are a reminder that conditions of battle varied enormously in the different theatres, and tactics with them. The Austrian style was perfected in the Turkish wars. The Turks themselves lagged behind the western powers until the reforms of the Frenchman, Bonneval, in the 1730s. The Austrians found that they could normally withstand the ill-coordinated Turkish attacks by drawing up their line in the old rectangular formation of alternate infantry and cavalry. The French, by contrast, normally kept their cavalry on the flanks, employing them throughout the battle. The Swedes and English preferred to hold them in reserve, for a crisis or the *coup de grâce*.

The sixteenth century had seen the development of an entirely new kind of defensive system; the *trace italienne* was a circuit of thick, low walls, surmounted at intervals by quadrilateral bastions. Designed to meet the challenge of the artillery which had proved to be such a potent instrument against castles and curtain walls of the traditional type, the *trace* set limits upon the mobility of armies and compelled commanders to study the logistics of siege warfare; starvation was usually preferable to assault but long sieges devoured the besieger's resources, human as well as material – living in crowded camps, operating in wet trenches, men readily succumbed to sickness. Warfare became altogether more prosaic, more scientific and, even outpacing price rises in other sectors, far more costly. Operations in the open plains of Hungary, north Italy and Flanders, where the feudal hosts had galloped and fought for generations, came to revolve round commanding citadels such as a Gran, Mantua or Breda. There was still room for the skills of manoeuvre as practised by the great Turenne who advised his fellow-general Condé: 'make few sieges and fight plenty of battles. When you are masters of the countryside, the villages will give us the towns.' But the open battle might be less decisive than the capture of a strongpoint. In July 1708 at Oudenaarde, the French had left the field in rout. Marlborough's victory was complete but he could not advance into France till he had reduced Lille: it cost him a further 5 months and 14,000 casualties. The city was one of many fortified by Sebastien Vauban, part of the defensive line with which he hoped to secure France's vulnerable northern frontier.

The science of military engineering, pioneered by such men as Pagan, Maurice of Nassau and Spinola, was perfected by Vauban and his talented assistants. He was able to draw upon the improved surveying techniques and engineering and architectural skills of the time; he was ingenious, single-minded, devoted to his country and its defence. Nor was his a narrow patriotism. He incurred disgrace for his honest, thorough survey of France's poverty; ironically the huge programme of building, with thirty-three new fortresses and several hundred renovations between 1678 and 1698, was responsible for a large part of the tax burden on the people whose plight he described in *Dîme royale*. He was never starved of labour or resources.

He learned as he went along by conducting 53 sieges of enemy cities; even the most difficult, like that of Maastricht in 1673, became under his direction a formal spectacle, immaculate in staging and ready on the appointed day for the king and his court to watch the final surrender. Some parts of Vauban's work can be studied today, at Besançon for example. Before his death France was ringed by a defensive line of fortresses, each suited to the terrain stretching from Lille to Briançon. With its double or triple girdle of walls, its angled forts and central barbican, its massive doors gilt with fleur-de-lis opening upon works of severe utility, a Vauban fortress was a superb instrument of strategy, providing a secure base for garrison and supply, extending and protecting the field of manoeuvre. At the same time in its formality and precision it was typical of its age, a work of classical art, visibly related to the culture of Racine and Claude.

The core of the new armies was provided by long-service professionals, bachelors-at-arms for whom any civilian occupation would have been unthinkable. The perennial problem of governments was how to supplement these men. It was the more acute in the eighteenth century as economic conditions began to ease – even though population rose as well. Famine had always been the best recruiting sergeant. Disease, endemic in camp life, and desertion created a constant wastage. The latter problem was most severe where discipline was most strict. In 1711 Frederick I ordered that in future the deserter should have his nose and one ear cut off and be sent to hard labour for life. In his successor's reign, 1713–40, when there was hardly any fighting, the Prussian army lost 30,000 men by desertion. Every state adopted its own means of filling the ranks. One reason for the preference for foreigners in some armies, like the Prussian and Dutch, was that the rulers, imbued with mercantilist principles, wished to conserve native manpower for farming and manufactures. Preparing perhaps unconsciously for their future role as architects of German unity, Prussian kings provided military service for the inhabitants of the smaller German states. About half of Prussia's army was composed of non-Prussians but most of these were German. In Russia the greatest difficulty was the practical one of securing the men, so that landowners were made to provide contingents of serfs, few of whom ever returned to the land. Sometimes diplomacy was involved. The Dutch negotiated the peace of 1700 between Denmark and Sweden with a view to hiring Danish troops in the forthcoming year. Hesse-Cassel specialized in the troop trade: between 1677 and 1815 the rulers of this small German state negotiated thirty-seven treaties for the export of soldiers to other countries – mainly to Britain (Hessians helped to defeat Jacobite Scotland and lose America). Frederick the Great, ever keen to align himself with enlightened opinion, condemned the landgrave of Hesse in a letter to Voltaire for selling his subjects, 'comme on vend du bétail pour le faire égorger'. With the upsurge of nationalism came the myth of exploitation – and the idea that the British could not fight their enemies without

German troops. Embellished by the hands of nineteenth-century nationalist historians, the myth was to serve as anti-British propaganda in two world wars. In 1939 foreign minister Ribbentrop used it in talks with Molotov, seeking to convince him about British weakness, and in 1951 it was used for East German propaganda against NATO and West German rearmament.

When the home product was used, there was a preference for peasants over townsfolk; they were supposed to be tougher although they succumbed easily to unfamiliar infections in congested quarters. Louvois's militia system in France was intended to provide a reserve for home defence, but it came increasingly to be used as a source for recruits. Another revival of an old method of manning armies was less successful. When the government revived the *arrière-ban* in 1675, the result was unsatisfactory. Commanders were not impressed by the quality of the feudal array, with its surly squires armed with old swords and fowling-pieces. In Sweden, Charles XI devised an original solution to the problem of the peacetime army in the shape of the *indelningsverk*. Upon the principle of basing the army on the land, estates were assigned for the maintenance of troops who, since they lived in one district, could be regularly trained and swiftly mobilized.

Everywhere the old militia system fell into desuetude. In Spain, in 1692, there were nominally 495,000 militia men; but only 59,000 of those on the rolls were actually armed. Prussians came nearest to a regular system of conscription; the main object was to overcome the awkwardness of changing from peace to wartime conditions: no state could afford to keep large numbers permanently under arms in peacetime, nor wished to risk being caught unprepared at the outset of war. Louis XIV had begun the system of maintaining a standing reserve of officers. It was this reserve which enabled the French to mobilize so rapidly in 1667; in 1668 when the War of the Queen's Rights ended, the officers supposed to have been demobilized were absorbed secretly into permanent formations. The Prussian method was more suited to the conditions of that paternally governed state. In peacetime the conscripts were called up for two months training with their regiments each year. Troops were unoccupied for long periods even in wartime: boredom was demoralizing. In peacetime Prussian soldiers were allowed to work; barracks were turned into spinning mills, soldiers were allowed to assist with harvesting or take temporary jobs. In practice the typical peasant-infantryman was less cut off from society than the soldier of the nineteenth century. His officer was also a courtier, a landed gentleman or a farmer, for whom soldiering was but an extension of his other interests.

Tough conditions of service, and low pay, often in arrears, necessitated a discipline which was crudely harsh, especially in the Russian, German and British armies, and maintained by constant floggings, the wooden horse, the knout (a Russian speciality) and, ultimate deterrent, the firing squad. The French army, whose punishments were relatively mild, had a reputation too for lax discipline. When so little of patriotism or religious feeling enthused the troops, when the training consisted of parade-ground movements which reduced the individual to an automaton (in the Prussian army specially tight dress was devised to enable the men to be packed more closely together), there was apparently no way out of the dispiriting round of threats and punishments. Yet it was the very shortcomings of these armies, their clumsy weapons and their low morale, that imposed limits upon commanders and helped to ensure that slaughter and destruction were contained within reasonable bounds.

Navies

The expansion of navies, like that of armies, played an important part in the economic and political development of the countries concerned. Stricter state control followed from the need to ensure the means to build and maintain ships and to recruit and train their crews. Of course the majority of rulers were not concerned at all with fighting at sea: they included the Emperor and, apart from a brief experiment on the part of the Great Elector, Prussia. Peter the Great's navy was a *tour de force*; depending entirely on his interest and energy, it decayed rapidly after his death. All rulers who had more than a few miles of coastline and had hitherto neglected the provision of ships or had left it to private enterprise, now had to make the choice: to risk becoming increasingly vulnerable to sea attack and reliant on the goodwill of an ally, and to accept a large initial handicap in any struggle for commercial supremacy; or to allocate precious financial resources to the costly business of maintaining a regular navy. Alterations in the balance of naval power in this period provide a very accurate commentary on the economic condition of the maritime powers.

At the beginning of the seventeenth century the Spanish still maintained a large number of warships in the Atlantic and Mediterranean; until the battle of the Downs, in 1639, when the Dutch destroyed their main fleet, and the further loss of ships when the Portuguese rebelled in the following year, their navy was remarkably successful in its principal role, the convoying of the annual bullion fleet from America. For nearly a century thereafter, until the reforms of Patino under the Bourbon monarchy, the Spanish navy was negligible, reflecting the decline of the mother country. The Dutch could not have won independence from Spain by the efforts of their armies alone; sea power was crucial and remained the basis of their continued strength and prosperity from trade. They enjoyed certain advantages. Amsterdam supplied ships for commerce and war to other European countries. Dutch contractors controlled much of the supply of hemp for sails and of tar for caulking from the Baltic. A high proportion of the Dutch population were able to serve as warship crews. By the end of the century, however, the sequence of wars that began in 1654 with the first of three against England, all arising out of commercial rivalry, had taken its toll. Both in size and efficiency the navy of the United Provinces, which, in the 1660s, possessed an unrivalled 100 ships, carrying 4000 guns and 21,000 men, had lost its primacy to England, and was never to recover it. Even in Holland there had been debate about the proportion of money to be allotted between army and navy because of the vulnerable southern frontier and the ambition of William of Orange to construct a coalition strong enough to defeat Louis XIV. Only in insular Britain was the navy consistently regarded as more important than the army.

William III was suspect to his English subjects because he appeared not to grasp that 'the first article in an Englishman's political creed', in the words of his minister Halifax, 'must be that he believeth in the sea'. That could never have been written by a Frenchman, though Colbert, following the pioneering example of Richelieu, had already created such a formidable navy that it was to challenge the English for mastery for more than a century. Colbert showed what could be achieved when there were sufficient natural advantages, experienced seamen, administrative expertise and the financial resources. But when these resources proved insufficient for all needs and there was debate about priorities, the navy suffered. Vauban's argument for adopting 'the subtle and stealthy maritime war' was essentially that of the authors of German submarine warfare in the world wars of the twentieth century. Since Anglo-Dutch war capacity was sustained by the profits of trade, and a large navy was valueless unless it could control the seas, the French navy should be used to destroy the enemy's commerce or bring about their financial collapse from the expense of protecting it. To a hard-pressed administration the chief advantage of this *guerre de corse*, with royal ships leased to private syndicates, was economy; in the long term, however, it was to prove costly, for it was a game that two could play. British losses were severe but they had the will and resources to make them good. Colbert had demonstrated that France's colonial and commercial development depended on a strong navy; Admiral Tourville's victory at Beachy Head in 1690 showed what that navy could have achieved had the financial commitment been sustained, with the strong executive control and intelligent planning that typified the French approach to the problems of ship design, recruiting of seamen and dockyard facilities; and so the history of the eighteenth century might have been very different. As it was, the English, despite setbacks such as the loss of Minorca in 1757, consolidated their dominant position. The revival of the French navy under the devoted administration of Maurepas, minister under Fleury, and another period of reform and technological advance after 1763, further illustrate the potential that was wasted because of the continental bias in the overall direction of policy.

The pattern of future naval battles and evolution of fleets was formed during the Anglo-Dutch wars of 1654–74. The battles in 'line ahead' formation, which were essentially prolonged artillery duels, put a premium on short-range gunnery and on the construction of robust ships. The acceptance of that style of fighting and gun power made for standardization in the design of 'ships', those which were capable of performing in the line, as opposed to frigates, sloops and other light craft used for reconnaissance and communication. There was no place in the new battle formation for the converted merchantman which was relegated to auxiliary duties such as the transport of troops or commissioned as a privateer. In battle at sea, as on land, all was to be regular and precise. It is the mark of the age and is to be seen in such compilations as the mathematician Paul Hoste's *L'Art des armées navales* (1697). The main feature of the naval revolution, as in the case of armies, was, however, the size of the forces involved. Along with the intense rivalry of the English and Dutch, Colbert's determination to achieve parity provided stimulus. The appearance of Tourville at Beachy Head with 70 ships, including 7 of 80 guns or more, brought home to their enemies the dimensions of the challenge. The naval race continued, and each of the three powers built and fitted ships at an unprecedented rate: during the Nine Years War, with construction running roughly level in the three countries, 221 ships were constructed. The French effort fell off in the last years of the war: in 1695–8 when the English launched 44 of their total of 69 and the Dutch 24 out of 78, the French produced only 19. It is the measure of the superior resources of England and their more compelling motivation. Destructive as the *guerre de corse* was, the French policy represented a great waste of the administration, training, maintenance and support facilities so laboriously built up by Colbert. With the Dutch faltering at the same time, not only in the numbers but also in the quality of the ships constructed (their shipwrights had become notoriously conservative), the English were able to move into an unassailable position of supremacy. La Hogue (1692), where Tourville was defeated by a greatly superior English force, came to seem in retrospect one of the decisive battles of the age.

Everywhere there was conflict and jealousy between the gentlemen and the professional sailor; everywhere the same pressures to achieve a more regular and committed officer class. The Danes were the first to establish a training corps, in 1661, its members being sent for experience with foreign navies or ocean voyages on merchantmen. The English relied, in typically empirical fashion, on individual arrangements; common everywhere was the young man learning his craft under a relation or patron. The approach to training in France reflects the assumption there that science should lead to practical improvements. In 1669 special colleges for teaching navigation were set up for training *gardes de la marine*, of whom there were 700 by the end of the century. Undoubtedly practical problems stimulated research. But technical progress was generally of a limited, evolutionary sort, inhibited by the conservatism of seamen and shipwrights, working by rule of thumb. Innovation was usually through government initiative. Battle experience also dictated the bounds within which improvements took place. It was held that if a ship intended to fire broadsides its length could not be more than three times its width. The materials available also limited development, as in the extent of the beam that could be constructed in the traditional fashion: there was no way of joining the heaviest timbers end to end with sufficient strength. By the late seventeenth century the French were generally reckoned to be the best designers, and they sustained their reputation: the magnificent *États de Bourgogne*, launched in 1782, was still in service in 1848 and provided a model for construction until the end of the age of sail. British commanders of the eighteenth century frequently complained that their ships were inferior to the French, in sailing qualities and gun power. The British, characteristically it might be said, were handicapped by their neglect of theory and their reluctance or inability to develop sufficient facilities for research. The French were more receptive to new ideas, the work for example of mathematicians like Euler (1707–83) on fluid resistance and floating bodies. There was not in Britain a distinct class, such as existed in France, of naval engineers. But the British did pioneer two inventions of the highest importance and generally adopted, but not before they themselves had gained great advantage from them. First was copper sheathing which reduced the fouling of bottoms by weeds, barnacles and the destructive teredo worm; second the carronade, a short barrelled large-calibre gun with low muzzle velocity which was manufactured on a large scale from 1778.

It took more men and more expensive plant to keep ships at sea than to maintain regiments in fighting trim. To maintain all in good order governments had to be continually vigilant. Dockyard work and contracting afforded many opportunities for the profiteer. The record of naval administration in all countries is one of ceaseless struggle against abuses. Temptation to hard-pressed governments to economize on maintenance and supply was countered only by its unfortunate results. The statesmen of Britain and France at least had to take seriously their responsibilities to the navy: the development of colonies and the increasing importance of colonial trade, with the consequent extension of the theatre of war, culminated in the epic struggle for America and India between those countries from 1740 to 1763, resumed in 1778. A policy of retrenchment, like that of the last years of Louis XIV's reign, would have been unthinkable in the eighteenth century. In France, however, much still depended on the enthusiasm of particular ministers. The large sums spent on the improvement of Rochefort in Louis XIV's reign and on Cherbourg in Louis XVI's reign reflected a strong voice in council. Expenditure on navies was not wasted, even when it did not lead to victories. Even a brief list of requirements – anchors and blocks, guns and powder, sailcloth and ropes – suggests the way in which naval construction stimulated the relevant areas of the economy. As in the analogous case of railway building in the early nineteenth century heavy capital expenditure was required before there was any significant return of investment; in this way competitive spending on navies became a factor in the development of state finance. With navies absorbing a larger share of the available funds and with the fierce struggle for markets that characterized the period, it is not surprising that it was the protection of commerce that weighed most with ministers, and therefore with the admirals whose professional advancement depended on them; nor that commerce was extended in the process. A large part of international trade was in the raw materials required for navies. Only the Scandinavian countries were self-sufficient in this respect. England, France and Holland were all heavily reliant on imported materials which came in the main from the Baltic. The straight timber of pine and larch for masts, spars and planks, together with pitch and tar, came from Swedish and Norwegian forests; hemp for cables, and flax for sailcloth were imported from Russia. This dependence was a major factor in the foreign policy of the sea powers.

The growth of navies was more irregular than that of armies because they had special needs. Since they had to draw mainly from seafarers, fishermen and merchantseamen, they had to make the service attractive or use some form of compulsion. The French *inscription maritime*, established by Colbert, with its register of all classes of seamen, made the English press-gangs seem a very crude and haphazard method. But it was no less unpopular, resistance coming not only from fishermen, whose livelihood was threatened, or from naval officers, who were for the first time listed in order of seniority, but from the provincial *parlements*, jealous of yet another intrusion into their jurisdictions. The Swedes tried to base their recruitment of seamen on the landholding system established by Charles XI to supply soldiers; in the Danish navy seamen were reinforced by convicts; in Holland the use of embargo secured men from merchant vessels; in France sailors were supplemented by 'sea soldiers' up to a third of the total force. Recruitment everywhere was hampered by arrears of pay; at best it was meagre. The pay of the French sailor was unchanged between 1700 and 1789, though prices nearly doubled. But the chief factor was the general horror of naval service. The foetid, ill-ventilated quarters, the limitations of diet, with the inevitable mould, rot and contamination of longer voyages, meant sickness and mortality that were usually heavier than losses from shipwrecks in storm or battle. The Franco-Spanish fleet that sailed against Britain in 1779 was so afflicted by disease that the sea was full of corpses and Devon fishermen refused to eat fish for months. The Dutch were innovators in the use of naval physicians; the Spanish first used hospital ships; the English devoted more charitable effort to educating boys for sea than to caring for the casualties of that service, but the Royal Hospital at Greenwich was given over to disabled pensioners of the War of the Spanish Succession; the French were more generous, with Colbert's *caisse des invalides*, financed by a tax on imports and prizes, which provided half-pay for cripples and was open to all registered men.

The range of administration and the ingenuity of officials were also stretched by the navies' appetite for raw materials. Measures were taken to protect the forests with their precious oak, already denuded in some areas by the need of charcoal for iron forging. In France the development of the navy gave rise to a whole new area of law and administration. When Colbert's forest code of 1669 was supplemented by further decrees in 1700 the navy had full powers to survey and pre-empt in private forests and rivers. But it is significant that the bureaucratic and venal forestry service, the *Eaux et Forêts*, failed in its basic duty of replanting after overcutting. Despite the expertise of the French bureaucracy, the enterprise of particular *intendants* in the way they used their far-reaching powers, and the intelligent application in France of science, the interests of a navy were best served in a society whose economy was dominated by maritime trade and whose security depended entirely on sea power. It was in Britain that those conditions were to be found in the economy from around 1650, and were to be protected by the political system established after 1688.

Further Reading

War

Still the best work on the 'military revolution' is the influential essay by Michael Roberts which can be found, conveniently, in his collected *Essays on Swedish History* (1967). Since its first publication (1957), his ideas have been modified and extended, but his picture of a revolution in tactics and of a 'prodigious increase in the scale of warfare in Europe', having a corresponding impact on society and government, remains substantially intact, as Geoffrey Parker concludes in his searching examination, 'The military revolution, 1560–1660 – a myth?', in his *Spain and the Netherlands* (London, 1979). Also valuable is Michael Duffy's 'Military revolution and the state' in a collection of essays under that title (Exeter, 1980). The same collection (from Exeter University) has Colin Jones's 'The military revolution and the professionalism of the French army under the ancient regime', while there is an important article by the same author in *History*, 214 (1980): 'The welfare of the French foot-soldier from Richelieu to Napoleon'. Brief but stimulating, Michael Howard's *War in European History* (Oxford, 1976) puts the period in perspective. G.N. Clark's *War and Society in the 17th Century* (1958) is specially good on attitudes, and conveys the wider significance of subjects that might appear marginal, like duelling.

Major works for the specialist are A. Corvisier's *Armies and Societies in Europe, 1484–1785*, trans. G. Rothrock (Ann Arbor, 1968), and *The German Military Enterpriser and His Workforce* (2 vols, Wiesbaden, 1964–5). There is no modern work on the great Le Telliers, perhaps because of the stature of L. André's comprehensive work, *Michel Le Tellier et Louvois*, which was published, fittingly, in the middle of the Second World War (in 1942).

Another major work, mainly about an earlier period, has relevance to this one: Geoffrey Parker's *The Army of Flanders and the Spanish Road, 1567–1659* (Cambridge, 1972), builds up from minute research engrossing pictures of the organization and mentalities of long-service soldiers. On a smaller scale, among useful chapters in each volume of the *New Cambridge Modern History*, especially valuable, treating naval and other neglected aspects, is J.H. Bromley's chapter in vol. 7. Two works by modern military historians should be cited: D. Chandler, *The Art of Warfare in the Age of Marlborough* (London, 1976), and C. Duffy, *The Army of Frederick the Great* (Newton Abbot, 1974). The latter's ideas can be studied first-hand in J. Luvaas, *Frederick the Great on the Art of War* (New York, 1966). The principles of the master of siegecraft can be examined in S. de Vauban's *Manual of Siegecraft and Fortification*, trans. G. Rothrock (Ann Arbor, 1966), while extracts from Marshal Saxe's *Reveries on the Art of War* are printed, along with other interesting documents, in G. Simcox (ed.), *War, Diplomacy and Imperialism* (New York, 1973). J. Ehrman, *The Navy in the War of William III, 1689–97* (Cambridge, 1953), has much material on the French and Dutch navies.

Diplomacy

Though there is still scope for revision in particular cases, and though there is a chance of a return to diplomatic studies as a topic of interest to more than the handful of historians who at present specialize in them, the situation at present is that there exist magisterial works on the major diplomatic questions and that students can look with confidence, for the most part, both to such works and to more recent textbook summaries based upon them. All the older textbooks give full attention to diplomatic history, disproportionately so, it may now seem: a balance between the various topics which should prove helpful to the student will be found in D. Ogg, *Europe in the Seventeenth Century* (1936, new edn, London, 1971), M.S. Anderson, *Europe in the Eighteenth Century* (new edn, Harlow, 1976), G.R.R. Treasure, *Seventeenth Century France* (London, 1981). There are good chapters in G.N. Clark, *The Seventeenth Century* (Oxford, 1929), and a pleasing general study by a diplomat turned historian, H. Nicholson, *Diplomacy* (1930). In *Renaissance Diplomacy*, by H. Mattingley (1955), there is valuable material for the origins and character of early diplomacy. For a sound comprehensive view the best account is probably that of G. Zeller, *Les Temps modernes*, II: *De Louis XIV à 1789* (1955). The ideals of diplomacy are skilfully explained in the first volume of Albert Sorel's *L'Europe et la Révolution française* (1885, trans. A. Cobban and J.W. Hunt, 1969).

Two interesting general accounts are: L. Dehio, *The Precarious Balance: the Problem of Power in Europe, 1494–1945* (1963), and F.H. Hinsley, *Power and the Pursuit of Peace* (Cambridge, 1967). See also the article by Jacob Viner, 'Power versus plenty as objectives of foreign policy in the 17th and 18th centuries', in *World Politics*, 1 (1) (1948). Among the great questions and settlements there is particularly good writing on the Spanish Succession by M. Thompson: 'Louis XIV and William III', in *English Historical Review*, 298 (1961), and 'Louis XIV and the Grand Alliance', *Bulletin of the Institute of Historical Research*, 89 (1961); and, by D.B. Horn, *Great Britain and Europe in the Eighteenth Century* (1967); see also his excellent chapter on the 'diplomatic revolution' in the *New Cambridge Modern History* (vol. 7). Articles reprinted (with some new essays) in R. Hatton (ed.), *Louis XIV and Europe* (London, 1976) deal with important issues like the Dutch War at a time when France was dictating the course and pace of diplomacy.

7

LOUIS XIV's FRANCE

The Land and its People

France, according to Vauban's meticulous report of 1707, was then a country of some 19 million inhabitants of whom over 0.75 million lived in Paris. That is an acceptable figure within a margin of some 2 million either way, allowing not only for his errors (which seem roughly to cancel one another out) but also for the periodic sharp drops, following the great mortalities which contained a rising trend within bounds set by the conditions of a still primitive rural economy. France might be more accurately described as several countries united under one crown. The Englishman in particular should beware comparison between his shire and the French province and think rather of so many Irelands, Wales or Scotlands; at least when he looks beyond the central and northern parts of the mosaic of provinces of which France was composed. Throughout the centuries of accretion and consolidation through marriage, diplomacy and war, France had been influenced by the cultures both of the north and of the Mediterranean: Flemish and German, Italian and, recently and pervasively, through her soldiers, merchants and priests, Spanish. In the outcome Mediterranean France was wholly different in ecology, laws and culture from the rest. High hills, dense forests and sequestered valleys created, in the Massif Central, another world apart: favourable terrain for feudal bullying and tax evasion. In the eastern provinces laws and customs which strongly favoured the seigneurs reflected the lax rule of the dukes of

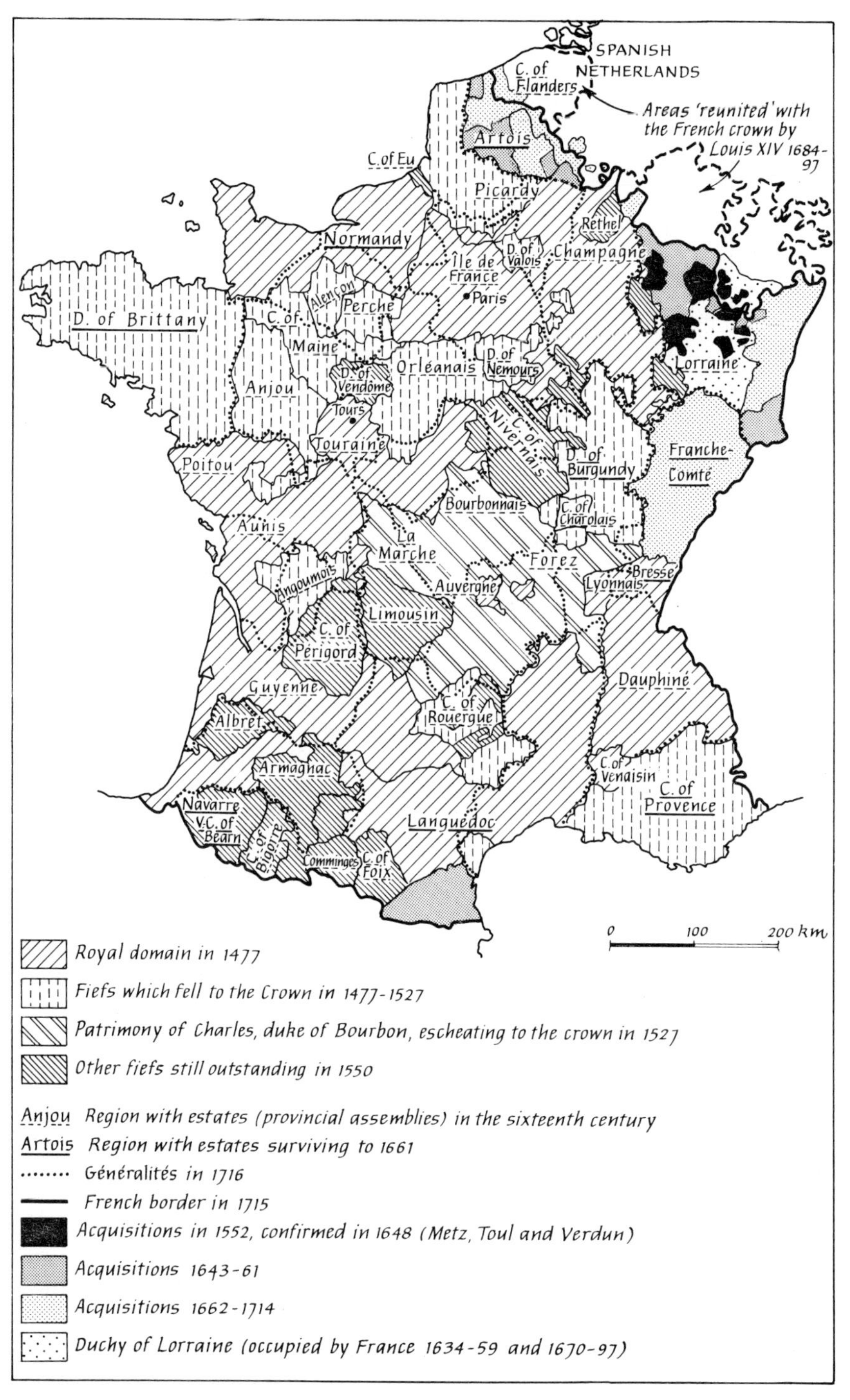

Map 7.1 *The* ancien régime *in France*

Burgundy. Even Normandy, relatively near the centre, exhibited a separatism that still recalled centuries of association with England. Celtic Brittany had not been finally secured until 1532. More than a million of Louis XIV's subjects were Frenchmen of even more recent standing when he assumed personal rule in 1661; half a million more were to be added during his reign, like the inhabitants of Franche-Comté and other frontier districts affected by the 'reunions'.

Along with relatively small regions of northern Italy, the southern Netherlands and southern England, France had the highest proportion in Europe of inhabitants to land: about 40 to the square kilometre. With extensive fertile areas and a climate which rarely ran to such extremes as those of the great winter of 1709, it might seem to have offered a fair field for self-sufficient peasants and improving landowners. The reality was different. Natural population increase was checked by periodic famines and epidemics, features of a rural economy lacking in the resources and techniques needed for higher production. The concentration of power in the hands of a few ministers, with agents in the provinces who had the right to act in the king's name, might seem to have presented unique opportunities to combat inertia and to overcome the physical barriers to progress. But that again is to misunderstand the nature of a society that was static, rooted and imprisoned within cherished traditions, thwarted by obstacles that villagers could not remove, and weighed down by impositions that they might resent but could not normally resist – and which in any case they had not yet been taught to see as 'unnatural'. It exaggerates the effectiveness of government, even the 'absolute' government of Louis XIV; it also implies an objective and unsentimental awareness of the problems that even the best informed were unlikely to possess. Marshal Vauban, for example, wrote penetratingly about the monetary famine and the consequent depression, at the end of a career spent in the expenditure of a large proportion of the royal revenue in directing expensive sieges and works of fortification. Colbert, whose principles of government were avowedly scientific and rational, patronized lavish building projects and subscribed warmly to a war against the Dutch that was shortsighted in conception and ruinously expensive in outcome. Archbishop Fénelon, outspoken critic of the militarism of Versailles, had been a fervent advocate of the policies which led to the revocation of the edict of Nantes and the loss of Huguenot citizens which so damaged both the economy and France's standing in Europe. Gifted as those men were, and though afforded exceptional scope for independent action, they were still men of their time and of a society that was less malleable than eighteenth-century physiocrats or nineteenth-century liberals were to assume.

It was a society imbued with the spirit of hierarchy and, among the upper orders to which a few belonged and many aspired, with a crippling disdain for commercial values. The very language men spoke defined the gulf that separated the articulate, propertied minority, about a tenth, from the mass of the population. French, as we know it, was the language of state, court, law, literature, the *beau monde* who might converse in *salons* or join learned societies. Away from Paris the traveller soon found himself in regions where country dwellers, even inhabitants of small towns, spoke the patois of their district, serviceable for their simple needs. If a Parisian went to Marseille or Rennes, he needed an interpreter. Nor was it a literate society. The large sample investigated by Maggiolo from the years 1686–90 reveals 71 per cent illiteracy among men and 86 per cent among women; comparable figures for a hundred years later were 53 per cent and 73 per cent.

The landscape was a stable one with unspectacular changes: a few villages were abandoned, a few towns grew in line with prosperity or shrank with depression. There were forest clearances, draining of swamps and enclosures, but the overall picture was one of equilibrium. Four out of five Frenchmen lived in the countryside, whether they owned land or not, and most of them were farmers. The majority of the producers in the manufacturing sector were peasants whose main employment was agricultural. Over a million were employed whole- or part-time in the weaving and spinning of wool and linen cloth. In Picardy, the main wool and textile area, workers living in the villages were more numerous than those of the towns where the more specialized activities, like bleaching and finishing, took place. In a few towns, often trading centres as well, like Lyon, Rouen, Amiens, there was a class of wage workers, embryo of the proletariat of future industrial society; but the total number of such wage earners did not exceed 100,000 before 1750. The population too was sedentary by modern standards. Most Frenchmen lived and died in the community in which they were born, though there was also a sizeable vagrant population: migrant workers, beggars and gypsies, were perhaps half a million in all, though the number would be swollen in bad times.

Transportation was slow and costly: there were only three important canals in 1700, the Briaire, Orléans and Midi. Wine would be four days in transit from Paris to Orléans, bales of cloth a month from Rouen to Lyon. A man took two weeks to travel from Paris to Bordeaux on roads that were mostly wider versions of the dirty tracks that ran from village to village, with innumerable tolls to pay and constant danger from brigandage, even as near to Paris as the forest of Fontainebleau. The favoured regions were those around navigable rivers where a boat of reasonable size, in good water, operated by 6 men and 4 tow-horses, could carry goods which on road would require 200 men and 400 horses or mules. Markets were local, within a 5-mile radius and inelastic; storage facilities were inadequate and as a result price movements were erratic. For a population living largely on grain, life was all the more precarious. Peasants were especially vulnerable in districts where alternative employment was limited. Everywhere coin was of low quality and scarce, growing scarcer between 1660 and 1726; then there was an improvement following the stabilization of the silver content which checked the speculation and hoarding that had driven out good money.

Everywhere the feudal regime persisted,[1] though in bewildering variety; in most of the south impositions were light, scarcely worth the trouble and expense of collecting; in Brittany and some of the Eastern provinces grievously heavy; in Burgundy and the Franche-Comté were still to be found the *mainmortables* or serfs tied to the land of the seigneur. They were not typical. Is there amongst all the types of landholding a typical peasant? At the higher end of the scale was the independent farmer with a hundred acres or more, teams of horses and oxen, a dozen cows or fifty sheep, big wheeled ploughs, rollers, carts with iron axles. He might also be farming the land of some wealthy family or abbey. He and his family were comfortably off, proof against hard times; as an employer of labour, he could exploit and expand; he was able to loan plough and horses, even provide seed; to lend money, and to foreclose, when it suited him. There were few such peasant capitalists in any village. At the other end of the scale were day labourers of country and town, owning no land, saddled probably with debts and earning below even the modest level at which the *taille* was levied. They are the *bas peuple* whom Vauban described, who 'seldom drink wine, eat meat not three times a year, and use little salt ... three-fourths of them are dressed in nothing but half-rotting, tattered linen and are shod throughout the year with *sabots* and no other covering for the foot'. From this class came the domestic servants, casual labourers, mowers, threshers, wood cutters, builders' labourers, vine dressers and grape pickers. With their families they may have numbered as many as six million; they may have been described in French official documents as the *lie du peuple* but, as Vauban pointed out, they were essential to society for 'It is they who provide all the soldiers and sailors.' He might have added that their existence kept wages down and prices low.

More numerous were the small proprietors or farmers of another man's land, 3 million heads of households, therefore the largest element in French society, normally, however, barely self-sufficient, vulnerable in bad years and liable then to sink to beggary. They were marginally better off in the south than in the north, especially wretched if they lived in the wheat lands, as in Picardy – there they were doubly dependent on the weather and the cycles of the textile manufacture since their families normally supplemented incomes by weaving – or in one of the districts where a system of sharecropping known as *métayage*, was the rule. Pressure of population kept holdings small and enabled the owner of the land to strike a hard bargain. A high proportion of *métayers* failed to serve out their contracts; they lapsed into debt, gave up their holdings or were evicted. By contrast the *haricotiers* of the country round Paris, able to exploit the needs of the city by market

[1] For further details, and for a wider picture of the agrarian regime, see pp. 21–5 and 30–3.

gardening, or the peasants of the enclosed meadows of Normandy, might be sufficiently well off to pay their taxes regularly.

The Fiscal Regime

How heavy was the burden of taxation? The chief direct tax was the *taille*, the legacy of a vital achievement in the evolution of royal government when, in 1439, Charles VII had successfully asserted the right to levy it annually without special consent. By 1648 it stood at over 50 million *livres*, having tripled since 1630. That was to represent a peak until the last two decades of Louis XIV's reign when it was raised further, with the addition of the *capitation* and the *dixième*, special taxes conceived in response to the needs of war. At its recurring peaks the level of taxation could be said to represent what the government considered the provinces could raise without actually revolting: passive or active resistance, evasion, corruption or plain inability to pay in times of dearth, meant that the government requirement was some way above what was actually paid. In the *pays d'élection*, the original provinces covering about two-thirds of the country, the *taille* was fixed arbitrarily by the finance ministers, who decided the total amount to be paid in the forthcoming year, after receiving reports from *trésoriers* assessing the taxable capacity of each province. In the province the *élu*, the man responsible for collection in the *élection* or tax district, had the right to call for troops to be billeted in defaulters' houses and to distrain their goods. A letter from Colbert to the *intendant* at Limoges suggests the tone of government:

> You can give publicity to the fact that the king keeps ready, 20 leagues from Paris, an army of 20,000 men, ready to march into any province where there is a suspicion of a rising in order to inflict exemplary punishment and to show the whole people the obedience they owe to His Majesty.

In the *pays d'état* of which the most important were Languedoc and Brittany, whose estates still had a say in the annual tax estimates, the direct tax was the *taille réelle* assessed on the value of property. It was a fairer and more stable system, not least because nobles had to pay if they held land that was not designated as noble. Elsewhere they enjoyed exemption from direct tax, along with the church (which paid corporately a relatively undemanding *don gratuit*), large numbers of office holders and all the inhabitants of a number of privileged towns. It is not surprising that many peasants saved, not to improve their land and so invite more tax, but to buy an office; nor that the government was forced, as in 1646, to decree that any peasant settling in a town must pay *taille* to his former village for the next ten years.

The indirect taxes should have been more equitable than the *taille* since they fell, in theory, on all. Again, however, there were exemptions and anomalies. The nobility and clergy had gained exemption in the fifteenth century for the products of their domaine lands. The *pays d'état* raised their own indirect taxes and paid a contribution to the crown. Customs duties were levied not only at the frontiers but also between certain provinces. The diversity of such customs duties, many of which were private, was a serious obstacle to trade. The *aides* were levied mainly on drink, but also on the sale of selected commodities such as fish and wood. The most important *aide*, a wine tax embracing the whole process of production and distribution from vineyard to tavern, suffered from the usual disadvantages: an army of officials struggled to prevent widespread evasion. In lean times, or when officials pressed too hard, there were riots, as at Bordeaux and Agen in 1635. It was the advantage of the *gabelle* that demand for salt was ubiquitous and steady. The way in which the tax had grown to the point at which it occupied, with the *taille*, a central place in the royal finances, reflected the piecemeal way, with coercion here, concession there, in which the kingdom had grown. By 1640 it had yielded 13 million *livres*, a quarter of the yield of the *taille*. The *pays de grandes gabelles* in the north and centre of France corresponded to the provinces unoccupied by the English when the tax was started in the fourteenth century: there the salt was collected in royal warehouses and sold at a price designed to give producer, merchant and the crown a reasonable profit. In the *pays de petites gabelles* collection was so difficult that government had to be content with a smaller duty, while certain areas, notably Brittany, were exempt altogether. Like the *aides*, the *gabelle* was farmed out to a consortium or to individual financiers. Contending with smuggling and evasion, armed with stringent royal decrees, their agents crossed the always blurred lines between the interests of state and private citizen and between the powers of executive, legislature and judiciary in a way that was characteristic of continental Europe at this time.

Everywhere royal taxes came on top of feudal dues, ecclesiastical tithes and whatever rent the peasant had to pay in cash or kind. The amount of tithe paid varied enormously, between 3 and 15 per cent with a mean of about 8 per cent: as in other areas the exceptions are so numerous that it is hard to establish what was normal. At 8 per cent, though levied only on the main cereal crops, and vines, it could amount to as much as one-fifth of the overall burden on the peasant. It was taken in kind, from the sheaves or grapes; before even the seigneur, the tithe collector had the first pick. Much or all of the product went often, not to the *curé*, whom the peasant might have been willing to support, but to agents acting for a cathedral chapter and abbey, even sometimes for a lay proprietor. It was hard enough even when a conscientious tithe-owner put money back into the village to repair the church, support the *curé* or relieve the poor. When it went to augment the revenues of remote, indifferent grandees then it took its place in the popular mind as one more odious aspect of the feudal regime under which they struggled to make their living. Faced by such diversity it is easier to see the impact of taxes and dues upon the economy as a whole than quantify burdens upon the individual. A *haricotier* might, for example, pay about 20 *livres* a year in *taille*, about 6 per cent of his income, or the price of a calf. He was relatively affluent. For many the price of a calf was the difference between survival and failure as an independent proprietor. It emerges from studies of the revolt of the *Nu-pieds* in Normandy (1639) that many villages were so far in arrears of tax payment that the dues of previous years had to be written off. The *taille*, we have seen, was only one of several royal taxes and the state only one of several masters competing for a share of the peasants' income. The overall burden rarely came to less than 20 per cent of that income and might be as high as 40 per cent. The chronic poverty of the mass of the peasantry was reflected in depressed prices and level of demand and so played a central role in the working of the economy as a whole. The picture is particularly bleak during Louis XIV's reign, which coincided with a phase of depressed prices in Europe as a whole. War expenditure, running consistently from 1672 at more than half the entire revenue of the state, made the situation worse. It was not primarily the shortcomings of the administration that imposed limits on the yield of the *taille*, certainly not moderation on the part of government, always desperate for revenue to meet the regular deficits, but the declining income of the peasants and the general shortage of coins.

By any standard of equity or commonsense, the government was taxing the wrong people: taking too much from the producer, too little from the *rentier*. The impact of taxation would have been less damaging, however, if the *rentier* class had invested more in trading and manufactures, or ploughed back more into the land from which almost all the clergy and nobility, the urban bourgeoisie, the lawyers and officials, received all or most of their income. Why did they not do so? There was no shortage of higher incomes or of concentrations of capital in private hands. In many provinces severe primogeniture laws preserved up to three-quarters of the inheritance for the eldest son. Following the example of the king and his court the greatest nobles, lay and ecclesiastical, felt compelled to keep up a princely style of life which was likely to be in excess of his income. Builders, decorators, craftsmen and artists found employment: so all was not loss. Even the large households of domestic servants provided for those who might otherwise have been beggars. But expenditure on coaches, horses, fine clothes of sumptuous materials like lace and satin, tapestries, precious objects of gold and silver and the newly fashionable porcelain of Sèvres and Limoges soaked up money derived from levies on the land – which was, as the physiocrats were later to argue, the primary source of wealth. Gambling was a particular vice of the rich, one cause of the depleted fortunes which caused so many nobleman to contract *mésalliances* with the daughters of commoners, in Mme de Sévigné's ironic phrase, 'to manure their fields'. The bourgeois was seldom reluctant to exchange wealth for a noble connection. Indeed the pursuit of title and aping of aristocratic manners were among the most powerful forces in French society. Nor is it difficult to see why.

The nobility might be losing their political influence. But they enjoyed valuable privileges and could bask in a self-esteem that was supported by solid material benefits, chief among which for most of them was exemption from direct tax. After 1695 the nobles had to pay the *capitation* instituted in that year, but typically they were soon granted a special lower rate. No less important were the special protected avenues to some of the most favoured occupations: commissions in the army and navy, the ranks and duties of squire and page at courts, leading to higher offices, the membership of prestigious bodies such as the Order of the Holy Spirit or the College of the Four Nations (founded by Mazarin). The major benefices of the Church, abbeys and bishoprics, were regarded by a number of noble families as their exclusive preserve. Most bishops were noblemen and most again held another benefice, an abbey *in commendam* for example, which they might seldom or never visit. Honorific privileges counted in an age that regarded highly such insignia of rank as the wearing of the sword, the crested coat of arms, the weathercock over the seigneurial mansion, the special pew and hatchments in the parish church. 'To live nobly', with the suggestion of valour at war and in the hunting field, generosity with one's own and other men's money, firmness upon points of honour and contempt for the commoner and his base occupations, remained a powerful ideal, despite the intrusion of moneyed interests and the poverty of country gentry, revealed by the records of the *arrière-ban*, a feudal summons to military service, which show that a high proportion of them had incomes of less than 300 *livres* a year. The conservative prejudices of the mass of gentry of limited means, who thought that they still had more to gain by clinging to noble status than from taking up common pursuits, sustained the firm rules of *dérogeance*, entailing loss of nobility for engaging in business, except certain designated activities: glass making, iron founding, eventually mining which counted as 'extending' the estate. On a conservative estimate this class numbered 250,000, rather over 1 per cent of the population (combining the total of nobles of every sort of creation with their families), but even in this number their restricted, protracted condition must have constituted a weakness in the state.

It was compounded by the anti-commercial spirit of the mass of the bourgeoisie. The equivalent to nobility for the aspirant bourgeois was high office, some of which, notably the great crown offices which might be mere sinecures, judicial and financial offices, and municipal posts in about fifteen towns, the latter somewhat of a laughing stock, carried noble status automatically but were being increasingly reserved for noblemen on a semi-hereditary basis. Indeed to look at a provincial *parlement*, like that of Rennes, is to see privilege and exclusiveness in its purest and most obdurate form. From 1660 no commoner was admitted to the *parlement*. In 1670 of 216 families of *parlementaire* nobility, 136 dated from before 1500. It was a tight and wealthy group: only about 60 married burghers' daughters; the rest of 412 known marriages were to daughters of nobles. By the eighteenth century a majority could reckon on 20,000 *livres* a year income, most of it drawn from seigneuries of which this oligarchy enjoyed the best in Brittany. They set the tone in exploitation of rights and legalistic concern for provincial privileges; in patrician values and conservative resistance to change: they were capitalists but indifferent towards commerce and manufactures. The Frenchman's love of office was fostered by the needs of government which, since the sixteenth century, had found the sale of offices a convenient way of raising money, and by the yearning of the bourgeois, affected undoubtedly by periods of civil war, for the security that office provided and the place, however humble, in the hierarchy of the town. Transmittable to heirs, offices usually carried exemption from the *taille*. They had come therefore to represent an important hereditary interest, in Richelieu's words, a disorder which 'is part of the order of the state'. Such order cost the country dear. The tax roll of the town of Beauvais, with a population of 13,000, in 1696, shows 57 exempt officials. Offices represented a steady haemorrhage of the capital accruing from the profits of trade.

The expansion of offices reflects, but does not by itself account for the timidity of the bourgeois, his reluctance to be an entrepreneur. Periods of political instability and civil war, with hazardous conditions on roads and at sea, with lawlessness and brigandage persisting long after the Fronde, contributed to the mentality. So too did education, dominated by the Church. As elsewhere in Catholic Europe, it was humanist, Latin-based, neglectful of the rudiments of technical knowledge, attuned naturally to the needs of the professions, particularly the law and the Church. In eighteenth-century Angers, with a population of 34,000, there were 53 full-scale courts or tribunals dispensing justice, and 30 religious houses. At Beauvais, among the tax-exempt were 460 ecclesiastics, secular and regular. At Bayeux the decay of the stocking industry left an ecclesiastical and legal establishment in a position of quite disproportionate strength and wealth in a town numbering, in 1740, some 10,000; but the important bishopric had a chapter of 12 great dignitaries and some 49 canons, the clerical population altogether numbered between 500 and 600. Those are extreme examples but it is arguable that the life lived by the bourgeois within such close-knit traditional communities was more typical than that of the few great towns such as Lyon, Marseille or Bordeaux, where the commercial spirit was more in evidence. There was a prevailing belief in self-sufficiency and a respect for the restrictive, exclusive control of guilds. A study of Amiens, a town of 30,000–40,000 inhabitants, the foremost producer of woollen fabrics throughout the old regime, has shown the very slow spread of the general use of bills and notes of exchange. Only in the last quarter of the seventeenth century did economic necessity gradually prevail over religious and legal scruples. Throughout society there was a preference for hard cash, even in transactions over farm leases. Not only was there no state bank but there was no really independent private bank. The failure successively of Colbert, Desmarets and Law to establish such a bank may be compared instructively with the development of such banks in Amsterdam and London. That particular defect in the financial structure was a consequence rather than a cause of the disorder and debility of the *ancien régime*, but it was to prove instrumental in bringing about the crisis of bankruptcy, which was to lead to its destruction. A hundred and fifty years before the Revolution monarchy faced a challenge which it survived but in a fashion which did much to determine its future character.

Revolt and Civil War

Deriving its name absurdly from the catapult with which street urchins slung stones at passing carriages, the Fronde was not a single movement but several distinct eruptions, leading to sporadic but destructive campaigns and to widespread disorder. In origin it was a revolt of magistrates and office holders. The royal officers of finance, led by the *trésoriers*, had come to the point of open defiance, ostensibly because of an increase in the *paulette*, the annual payment of which ensured heredity of office. More fundamentally they resented the invasion of their administrative and money-raising functions by tax farmers and *intendants*. Here they were on common ground with the magistrates of *parlement*, self-constituted guardians, not only of those particular rights which had been devalued by what they regarded as the usurping regime of over-powerful ministers, but also of the fundamental laws of the land. In May 1648 the magistrates had decided upon a union of the four sovereign courts, of which *parlement* was composed, to draw up a plan of reform. In August, Mazarin's clumsy attempt to arrest its leaders, Broussel and Blancmesnil, turned protest into rebellion and provided them with popular support. The mob came out into the streets, barricades were set up. Almost immediately the party of *parlement* was divided, between the minority of hotheads who looked for a permanent reduction in the powers of the crown and made novel and unhistorical claims, and the moderate majority who feared for their property, suspected the motives of their aristocratic patrons and sought a compromise solution with the crown. Their position was fundamentally a conservative one. But in the eyes of a man like Omer Talon, who spoke for *parlement* at the *lit de justice* of January 1648, held by the crown to force through the taxes which *parlement* had refused to register, or Matthieu Molé, *premier président* and chief negotiator at the peace of Rueil (March 1649) which effectively ended the *Fronde parlementaire*, it was based not on self-interest but concern for the condition of the land and its suffering poor. More specifically the oligarchy of magistrates represented that greater army of office holders in law, finance an administration who had seen the value of their offices reduced by wholesale creations.

The great nobles similarly could claim to represent broader interests. They had not been persuaded by the failure of past revolts, by exile, confiscations, even, as in the notorious case of Montmorency (1632), executions, to accept the claims of a monarchy which had clawed into its hands some of their powers and perquisites. Now, as in the years after Henry IV's death (1610) and the regency of Marie de Médicis, they saw in the minority of Louis XIV, 10 years old in 1648, the chance to recover lost ground. The plight of the *noblesse* as a whole strengthened their cause and spelt danger to the sovereign who depended on their loyalty to man his army and maintain order in the countryside. The crown's fiscal policies had been shaped by the necessities of war: in 1630 the French had gone to war against Spain in north Italy and made arrangements to subsidize the Swedes; in 1635 they had openly gone to war against the Habsburg sovereigns. The weight fell directly on the peasantry through an increase in the *taille*, but indirectly on the seigneurs who depended on the peasants' dues. The revolts of the Croquants of the central and south-western provinces in 1636–7 and of the *Nu-pieds* of Normandy in 1639 had been all the more dangerous because of the complicity of office holders and seigneurs. The nobility could also point to a sustained attack on the cherished principle of immunity from direct tax, notably from the exploitation of the *arrière-ban*, the feudal summons to military service, as a form of taxation.

Richelieu had surmounted his greatest challenge in 1630, when his foreign policy had roused the anger of the *dévôts*, those Catholics who believed that the interests of the Church should take precedence over all else, and specifically deplored war against Spain. But they found that Louis XIII was resolved to uphold his minister against all comers. In the Fronde Mazarin had to fight a more prolonged battle of survival against the same interests, in many cases the same men who, for different reasons, wanted to put the clock back. Though never defined in the form of a party programme, the threat to government, as the Fronde went on its erratic course, was just that combination which Richelieu had provoked of moral indignation and factious self-interest. Richelieu had been an efficient bishop, wrote manuals of devotion and befriended the zealous Capucin, Father Joseph; in the pursuit of a secular national policy he had retained much of the *dévôt* spirit. But Mazarin, who became a cardinal without becoming a priest, had no such credentials. To a man like Vincent de Paul, he was no true churchman but a mere politician – and an outsider at that. He could only rely on the fragile authority of a boy king, whose rights his opponents also claimed to defend. The Spanish queen mother, Anne of Austria, was, however, determined to sustain him in power. There was also a loyal group of ministers, whose prospects depended on the crown. On such men as the chancellor Séguier and war minister Le Tellier, convinced authoritarians, Richelieu's posthumous influence was very important.

In the welter of personal claims and corporate grievances that characterizes the Fronde there were features which were less disreputable than they might appear from the record of grandees like Longueville or Beaufort, bent on extracting as much as possible from the weakness of regency government; or from the plausible propaganda of Gondi, better known by his later title de Retz, clever, theatrical, and, as coadjutor to his uncle, the archbishop, well placed to manipulate the clergy; the moving spirit of the Fronde and, through his mendacious memoirs, chief recorder to its combinations and absurdities. There was the continuing *dévôt* mistrust of a secular foreign policy which had also led to wars and taxes beyond the capacity of the people to sustain. Associated with it, as it had been in earlier revolts against the crown, was the yearning for a largely mythical past when kings ruled moderately within the limits of their rightful revenue, with the counsel of their 'natural' advisers and the support of a loyal, brave nobility.

In disagreeable contrast was the present situation of a government which had been reduced for years to raising money in such arbitrary ways as to complete the alienation of the very men who should have been supporters of royal authority. In the correspondence of Séguier, the chancellor, can be seen the frustration of central government because of the inadequacy of officials and, as they saw it, their collusion in obstruction and revolt. Le Tellier, war minister, former *intendant*, well illustrates the administrative mind, impatient with tradition and status: to maintain the war effort he needed money and supplies, and the strong arm of *intendants* to secure them. With mounting deficits it was easier for *surintendants* to deal direct with financiers at court than to go through the formal procedures of money raising through the established officials. That negotiation with syndicates of financiers was profitable as well as convenient did not lessen the appeal of private-enterprise finance to *surintendants* like Particelli d'Emeri, the prime target for *frondeur* fury. Arrogant imperialists of high finance, moving in a secret world of high risks and high profits, the tax farmers enjoyed support and influence at court and even among some dignitaries in *parlement*. The *trésoriers*' failure to raise money efficiently had been a main reason for the use of *intendants* in the first place. There was substance, however, in the claim they made in July 1648 that 'the domain was entirely out of the king's control, through contracts and transfers, most of them fictitious'. When the financial officials made common cause with *parlement* and could expect at least the sympathy of the great nobles, the revolt of the magistrates could be seen for what it was: a general crisis of authority.

It may have appeared during the Fronde as if anarchy would become a chronic condition and that the crown's authority would be permanently impaired. Critical times were January 1649, when the princes pledged their support to *parlement*; the following January, when, following the arrest of

Condé, Conti and Longueville, civil war spread to the provinces; and February 1651, when the three were released and held a convention of princes and *parlement* which proceeded to discuss the summons of an estates-general, the establishment of a council of twenty representing the three estates, and the deprivation of Anne of Austria. If Mazarin and Anne had lost their nerve, even so far as to consent to the meeting of an estates-general, they would have created the conditions for the revolution that the Fronde never became: one that would have achieved an effective check upon the powers of the crown. But Mazarin's diplomatic experience had trained him to recognize and exploit the divisions which existed at all levels: within *parlement*, between the magistrates and the officers of finance; and, crucially, between the leaders of *parlement* and the great nobles. In this society of orders in temporary disarray there was neither dominant ideology nor acceptable leader to overcome the corporate rivalries. There lies the profound difference between the Fronde and the Puritan revolution in England. Rebels remained royalist. 'Vive le roi et les princes et point de Mazarin' was the cry of 1651: no more revolutionary than the traditional cry, 'Vive le roi sans taille et sans gabelle'. The dilemma of *parlement*'s leaders was succinctly put by a judge in 1652. 'If the Condéan armies win there will ensue the decline of monarchy; a royalist success will ensure tyranny.' For the most part the judges took refuge in neutrality, whenever possible making legality the criterion. Successive decrees denounced the raising of arms and collecting of taxes without express royal consent. Fortunately for Mazarin and Anne, the principle of monarchy, upon which all authority depended, was represented by the reassuringly normal personality of Louis XIV.

Every appearance of the sovereign evoked a response which testified to a general yearning for order. Fresh from republican England John Evelyn witnessed Louis's coming-of-age ceremony in September 1651 and declared that 'the French were the only people in Europe who idolise their sovereign'. He watched the ceremony with 'Mr. Hobbes, the famous philosopher of Malmesbury'. It is tempting to speculate on the thoughts of the author of *Leviathan*, that uncompromising statement of the necessity of absolute monarchy published in the same year: the contrast, he might have thought, between the uncertain future of Charles of England, whose attempt to recover his throne was about to end in disaster at the battle of Worcester, and the acclamation of Parisians for the young Louis, riding in the middle of 'a glorious cavalcade', a prince, as Evelyn saw him, of 'grave, yet sweet countenance'. 'Already,' wrote the Parisian Guy Patin, 'the bourgeois of Paris feel violent inclination beyond what they normally feel for their prince.' Between the rightful sovereign, and his irresolute uncle Gaston of Orléans, with his record of treachery, or the arrogant Condé, whose qualities did not include the ability to delegate or compromise, the choice was not hard – except for members of Condé's immediate circle, and those more numerous perhaps who had reason to fear the return of Mazarin and wanted Orléans, as lieutenant-general, to fight him.

In this situation, Gondi's return to loyalty, eased by the promise of a cardinal's hat, was an indication of the trend. The audacity of his schemes and the range of his contacts in Paris, in the *salons*, among the *dévôt* clergy and the *menu peuple*, had made him a dangerous enemy. Turenne by contrast had always been a reluctant *frondeur*. At the end of 1650, after his defeat at the battle of Rethel, he returned to his allegiance. He was Condé's equal as a soldier and Le Tellier saw to it that he did not lack money for his troops, while Mazarin negotiated for German mercenaries to support them. Condé contributed to his own defeat first by failing to follow up his victory at Bléneau in April 1652, then by calling in the Spanish. After Mazarin's second departure in August Condé managed the defence of Paris against the royalist troops and in October won the confused street battle of the Faubourg St Antoine, with the aid of Gaston's remarkable daughter, 'Mademoiselle'. But he could only hold the city by dictatorial methods that alienated even the rump of his supporters in *parlement*. The formation of an emergency government composed of nobles and judges had been humiliating to Condé. As one of his supporters wrote: 'See how miserable are [the princes of the blood] to be compelled to act deferentially towards men who are infinitely beneath their rank.' Condé was incapable of behaving like a subject; he could not act royally without giving offence.

Mazarin exploited Condé's unpopularity with a skill which went far to atone for earlier blunders. Just as he was in no hurry to conclude the war against Spain, so he was content to play a waiting game with the *frondeurs*. He took a long view – and he was little concerned about the sufferings of the people. In 1650, sensing that his presence on French soil only detracted from the credit of the court party, he had retreated to Cologne, whence he had governed by letter. In January 1652 he returned but when an army of Lorrainers and Spaniards approached the capital he again slipped away, leaving Anne free to negotiate without the embarrassing presence of the man who was generally believed to be her lover. The queen mother had contributed to earlier tensions by her haughty attitude towards the magistrates. But she had learned restraint in adversity and she never lacked dignity. She managed the son of whom she was justly proud, protectively and with unfailing tact.

Besides Anne, Mazarin and Turenne, the inner group of ministers, notably Le Tellier, Fouquet and Séguier, contributed to the success of the crown. Thinking in national terms, also concerned about their own careers, they could only envisage growth in their own responsibilities and clientele, and the power of the state as coming from an enhanced royal power. Nor for lesser men was there much attraction in constitutional novelties. The *Mazarinades* of the *frondeurs*' scurrilous lampoons and squibs were poor in political invention. There was nothing comparable to that outpouring of social and political ideas that characterized the two decades of the English revolution. The natural caution of venal bureaucrats whose offices depended ultimately on the crown, and the respect for authority instilled by the authoritarian principles of Roman law, left *parlementaires* neither precedent nor inspiration to build a stronger constitutional position. Significantly *parlement* early abandoned a general inquest into financial dealings, in favour of legal proceedings where individual magistrates had a grievance. They were lawyers, not politicians. Everywhere in the provinces, sectarian differences between one count and another prevented effective common action. The opposition of the officers was similar to that of the magistrates: they were not so much demanding a new system as competing for more privileged positions within the old one.

The encroachment of royal government upon the towns of France might have been expected to produce a concerted campaign for the recovery of municipal rights. But they were isolated, each within the orbit of its own area and market, and displayed no sense of solidarity. Some within the merchant community wanted restrictive tariffs, others suffered by them; again there was no unanimity, but a perennial tendency to seek protection, which could only mean reliance on authoritarian government. Special interests apart, the solid middle element of citizenry, *bons bourgeois*, early rallied to the crown; they feared for their property and they soon realized the danger of arousing the *menu peuple*. It is telling that even in Bordeaux the members of the *Ormée*, who there rebelled for a time successfully against both local *parlement* and municipality, showed a highly corporate sense of identity and saw the crown, not as enemy, but as ally against local aristocracy. The way in which Bordeaux was isolated in the last few months of the Fronde emphasizes, however, the lack of any kind of organic unity in the country. For the same reason that France was hard to govern, it was hard for opponents of government to concert their resistance. That did not mean that there was no damage. The cost of the Fronde became apparent as large tracts of France, notably in the north and east, and in Normandy, experienced the horrors of war. It was important that the *curés*, whose aversion to Mazarin had roused Parisian hostility towards him, were later among the strongest protagonists of the crown: they saw the sufferings of the common people at first hand. It was important too, that the Huguenots, who had recent experience of the effects of civil war, remained loyal. Last but not least, the weakness of Spain has to be reckoned with. Even in the 1590s Henry IV and the patriotic party had gained more than they had lost from the intrusion of Spanish troops. The country that was unable to suppress its own revolts in Catalonia and Portugal could now provide no more than a diversion.

A Partial Restoration

The king returned to Paris in October 1652, Mazarin was re-installed in February 1653 and Bordeaux fell in August. After the collapse of his attempted coalition of Bordeaux *parlementaires* and friendly nobles in the Guienne, Condé offered his sword to Spain. He did not come to terms till the Franco-Spanish peace of 1659: meanwhile he was of more use than danger to a government which could treat him as traitor rather than rebel. With the progressive ending of the fighting came recognition both of the scale of the damage and of the need for tough government. The restoration of royal authority was a slow, imperfect process, in the face of sullen resistance. *Intendants* were sent out, though prudently at first, under their old name, *maîtres des requêtes*, and with specific tasks, usually of a military nature. Le Tellier, former *intendant*, now immersed in the work of reforming the army, typifies the ministerial view; the Spanish had to be defeated, proper authority restored to the countryside. Reports to ministers spoke of peasants seeking the protection of local gentry, rendering dues and services in return for protection. The *surintendant* Fouquet was not alone in receiving signed professions of loyalty. Society was infected, as it had been after the religious wars, with the attitudes of decadent feudalism: when royal authority was in abeyance, a man must look after himself as best he could. To Séguier, who had already been chancellor at the time of the Normandy revolt of 1639 and had seen there what he now saw everywhere, the collusion of local men, *parlementaires*, gentry and peasants in revolt against central government, it was plain that officials had to be given a free hand, if necessary, to see to the collection of taxes by supervising the work of local *bureaux*. Since the *trésoriers* were unable to raise the cash for the extra funds required for the prosecution of war, the government had to resort again to tax farmers. That suited Fouquet, relative and partner of rich bankers, *procureur-général* of *parlement*, well placed therefore to command the summits of judiciary and finance. Nor did it trouble Mazarin.

Mazarin had learnt a few more tricks and a lot more caution: his mentality had not changed. With his genuine concern for the tuition of the young king went an almost obsessive desire to enrich himself. Besides his clientele, his books and works of art, he cared chiefly for the completion of the great exercise with which he had been entrusted by Richelieu. He was content for the peace of the Pyrenees to be his monument. In 1658 assemblies of local nobles in the west, a popular revolt in the Sologne, recurring troubles in the Saintonge and a faction struggle in Marseille pointed to the danger of a general rebellion; only then did he stir himself to make a conclusive demonstration of royal power. In January 1660, Louis XIV entered Provence at the head of his court and his troops. Aix and Arles had already been repressed by the energetic action of Governor Mercoeur and the *premier président* of the *parlement* of Aix, D'Oppède. Now Marseille was disarmed, its walls razed and a new citadel built. The elected magistrates were no longer allowed to call themselves *consuls* and their city lost its independent status. It was the first of several lessons in the realities of the new political order. Subjects were to be taught, in the words of Le Bret, who had written on behalf of Richelieu his *De la souvereignté du roy* in 1632, that sovereignty, though 'anchored to the common good' was a supreme power based upon an individual 'which gives him the right to command absolutely'. Richelieu, pleading *raison d'état*, confronted by a series of emergencies, supported by a harshly authoritarian king, had acted in the conviction that all institutions and customs could be changed by royal authority. When, on Mazarin's death in March 1661, Louis XIV decided to be his own *premier ministre*, he could bring to that role the mystical authority of sovereign and could therefore rely on a greater measure of co-operation. The independent and the obstreperous could be isolated and dealt with by royal justice.

The *frondeurs* had been defeated but not completely; the crown had emerged victorious but at the price of concession and compromise which left marks on the regime. *Parlement* had demanded, and by the declaration of St Germain (October 1648) secured, the regular payment of the *rentes*, the lowering of the *taille* and a special tribunal for the treatment of dishonest financial officers: all were to be implemented in the early reforms of Colbert, along with further and less palatable measures, like the reduction in interest rates on the *rentes* to the uniform rate of 5 per cent. Colbert was able to act arbitrarily, as when he set up a special chamber to try Fouquet, disregarding his right to trial by his colleagues of *parlement*, because he and his fellow ministers were sure of the support of the king. In the provinces the king's authority was once more to be exercised by *intendants*, whose withdrawal *parlement* had put among the forefront of their demands.

The pacification of the south, the trial of Fouquet, which began in 1661, the transportation of hundreds of peasants which followed the revolt of the Boulonnais in 1662 and the *Jours d'Auvergne*, the crown's inquest into the misconduct of the nobles of that unruly province (1665–6), informed the country in no uncertain terms that Louis XIV meant to be obeyed. The hallowed institution of monarchy was adorned by the professional skills and confident presence of the young king. If there was an underlying nervousness he concealed it remarkably well. Through the exertions of ministers enjoying his confidence the new regime was to show a capacity for decisive action. But it was marked indelibly by the concessions and compromises of the years in which Mazarin had striven to recover control for the crown and to bring the war against Spain to a successful conclusion. He had sought to inculcate realism and he should not be blamed if his royal pupil later forgot his precepts or overplayed his hand. Even in foreign affairs the hand was not as strong as it was made to seem at first by the weaknesses and divisions of his opponents. At home, from the start, Louis's power was limited by the very conditions on which he was allowed to enjoy the privilege of autocratic rule.

Abandoning their wider claims and grievances, the judges of *parlement* concentrated on their own interests, seeking to preserve the prestige and economic advantages of their offices. Ministers appealed to their traditional Gallican prejudices, directed their attention to the ever popular subject of corruption among tax farmers, asserted the sovereignty of the crown where it was necessary and, under the direction of Colbert, worked on methods of speeding up judicial procedure: the 1677 Civil Ordinance was welcomed by *parlementaires*. When, however, Louis XIV awakened old passions and fears by his ultramontane policies of the latter part of the reign, in particular his onslaught on the Jansenists, and began to act in arbitrary fashion, as for example in the legitimization of the royal bastards in 1714, *parlement* was to show by its opposition, continued in the following reign, that the spirit of the Fronde had been only lulled, not quenched. During the reign of Louis XIV *parlement*'s prestige grew to such a point that it was able to mount once again a serious challenge, over finance as well as over religion, to the authority of Louis XV. The rigid exclusion of the nobles from Louis XIV's councils seemed, correspondingly, to underline the failure of the magnates to recover the ground they had lost under Richelieu's regime. For the loss of political power they were, however, to be partly compensated by the consolidation of their rights in society and by new opportunities in an expanding court. There they might still influence in ways that were to affect the king's judgement and curb ministers' reforming efforts. Defended by great armies, sustained by loyal officials, adorned by the elevating notion of divine right, Louis XIV's kingship was still in essentials that of Henry IV and Louis XIII. Absolutism rested, apparently securely, upon the consensus of the king and his most influential subjects. It had been gained at the cost of concessions that were now part of the system: the tax exemptions of nobles and office holders, the privileged corporate structure in the towns and the feudal regime in the countryside. The Fronde had made clear the mutual dependence of crown and dominant groups within the community, in the provinces as in Paris. The crown had not emerged above, or independent of, the arrangements of patrons and clients which still counted for more than any formal bureaucratic structure. But it had secured a nominal advantage: because authoritarian rule was generally held to be necessary, it was easier to show that it was right. In practical terms, there was more room to manoeuvre, to improve existing agencies of government and to create new ones.

Louis XIV

Cardinal Mazarin died in March 1661, leaving a huge personal fortune, a great library and collection of pictures with suitable palaces to house them for the benefit of future generations, and a relatively stable country; but he left too deficits and debts of a size that called for urgent treatment. The next day ministers were summoned to hear the king's pleasure. Louis was 22, an assiduous student of policy but hitherto content to let Mazarin prescribe and direct. It was expected that he would name a new *premier ministre* to whom he should entrust the management of royal affairs. No doubt Fouquet was hopeful, together with his large following among officials, lawyers and financiers, the sort of clientele without which an ambitious politician could not hope to maintain his standing. Louis's words spelt the end of the old system:

> It is now time that I governed for myself; you will assist me with your counsels, when I ask for them ... and you Messieurs, my Secretaries of State, I order you not to sign anything, not even a passport ... without my command; to render account to me personally each day and to favour no one.

The words were firm and precise but his ministers must have wondered: how long would it last? Louis XIV's personal rule lasted for the rest of his long life.

Master of a court which was already responding enthusiastically to his desire to be entertained, Louis could be forgiven if he had contented himself with the pleasures of pre-eminence among courtiers who stood to gain by his extravagance and women who competed to attract his attention. He took his pleasures as his due. But he was too astute to mistake the show for the substance. He strove to perfect his exacting role in an increasingly elaborate ritual which was to culminate with the completion of the palace of Versailles in the 1680s: by then an unvarying routine, from *levée* to *couchée*, taught a daily lesson in royal dignity and devotion to duty. The public day began always with Mass. Religion played an important part. Close to his Spanish mother in this respect, he was steeped in the ritual and obligations of an unquestioning faith. Reinforcing his awareness of what was expected of him by churchmen this was to have significant consequences for Huguenot and Jansenist. Meanwhile, each Thursday, courtiers were edified by the sight of the young king with his queen washing the feet of thirteen poor people.

Attendance at councils was the central activity of each day. Louis gave priority from the start to the business of government and found fulfilment in exact and notably competent exercise of his *métier*. It was not surprising in the great-grandson of Philip II of Spain, most meticulous of sovereigns. Louis's graceful mastery in personal relations, together with the unerring eye for detail which commanded the respect of his courtiers, even when his subjects were learning to loathe his name, were all nearer, however, to his grandfather, Henry IV, 'the good king' associated in the minds of Frenchmen of Louis XIV's time with peace and prosperity. In the case of Henry IV, there was an element of nostalgia, engendered by the resentments of the cardinal's regime. Louis XIV's own legend grew around him in the euphoric mood of the court circle in the first two decades when France's diplomats and soldiers seemed to be irresistible. In *le roi soleil*, his admirers maintained, were combined the best qualities of Roman emperor and Christian king.

Led by the prolific Le Brun, the artists and craftsmen of Versailles embellished the myth in paint and plaster. Gazed on with rapture, or taken for granted as conventional exercises in the repertoire of flattery, the lofty depictions of Louis, in various guises but always triumphant over his foes, were so many hostages to fortune. When fortune turned contrary and courtiers talked of reverses and surrenders under those heavy ceilings, the theme of glory became a mockery, an invitation to scoffers and cynics. That was to come but, in its first emergence from the scaffolding, the vast palace of Le Vau and Mansard, started in 1668 after the peace of Aix and built mainly in the next two decades, evoked awe among Louis' fellow princes. Great and small they copied not only his architecture but also the style of his government in a way that conveyed their respect, not only for the institution but for his own professionalism. In his own words his role was 'to be informed about everything; listening to the least of my subjects'. After describing his military, diplomatic and financial responsibilities, Louis stressed the importance of being independent:

> keeping my business as secret as any other has done before me; distributing my favours by my own judgement and ... keeping those who serve me, although loaded with benefits for themselves and their families, in a modest station far removed from the rank and power of first ministers.

There was some self-deception: Louis relied on the views of ministers and *intendants*, and they learnt how to present matters in a way that he would approve. Yet it is evident that his ministers respected him for his judgement as well as his industry. Beneath the bland surface, the unhealed wounds of the Fronde continued to hurt in a way that manifested itself, for example, in his apparently irrational decision in 1671 to order that all records of that period should be destroyed. Suspicion of other men's motives and his determination to be self-sufficient were traits that could have developed in middle age into paranoia – that disease of the lonely great – had he not been temperamentally stable and, until the later years of the reign, successful in his undertakings. He was also endowed with an exceptionally strong physique and was blessed by the love of at least one good woman, in the person of his mistress Mademoiselle de la Vallière, and the devoted care of another who became his second wife in 1683, the sensible and reassuring Mme de Maintenon. The prejudices remained, however, and they led to several disastrous misjudgements in the fields of foreign policy and religion. He was shrewd and efficient rather than imaginative. Perhaps he did not travel enough. The palace that he dominated also circumscribed him, so that he seemed to be king of Versailles, not of Paris, certainly not of France. It became increasingly difficult to give honest and disinterested advice, as Vauban and Fénelon found to their cost. Louis's distinctive achievement was to create and fix the image of a monarchy that was grand and disinterested, superior to human failings. The coolness which came from years of learning to suppress spontaneous feeling did not preclude the formal courtesy for which he was famous. He could be magnanimous too, as when he received Marshal Villeroi with consoling words after his disgraceful defeat at Ramillies in 1706. He would doff his hat to servants around the palace, but he would also insist on women at court, even his mistresses, concealing their pregnancies, oblivious apparently to their discomfort and risk. Such callousness was of a piece with the stoicism and dignity he displayed during the public and personal misfortunes of the last years of his reign, when he was unbowed by the defeat of his armies and successive mortalities within his family. Then as always, it induced confidence and evoked loyalty in those who served him that he distinguished so clearly between his personal and public affairs and that he was never party to intrigue. It is on that criterion, more perhaps than on any other that he is to be judged a more responsible master, therefore a better king, than either Louis XV or the unfortunate Louis XVI.

Royal Government

One strength of Louis XIV's government can be seen in the small *conseil en haut*, a flexible instrument of policy making and execution, in which usually only the most important ministers would sit: those for foreign affairs, the army and navy and finance, not necessarily those holding secretaryships of state, which had to be bought when opportunity arose, but those whom, like Colbert and Lionne in 1661, Louis wanted to advise him. It represented the logical development of the trend under the guidance of the cardinals towards specialist councils. The *conseil des finances*, created in 1661 to replace Fouquet's office of *surintendant*, the *conseil des depêches*, supervising the machinery of government, dealing with dispatches from all parts of the kingdom, presided over usually by the chancellor, and later the *conseil de conscience*, revived to deal with religious affairs, were all extensions of the absolutist principle: the king governed, assisted by small groups of senior ministers. The heads of the greatest families, even those 'of the blood', were specifically excluded; government was a business for the professional and expert; the feudal right of counsel was irrelevant if not dead. 'Le règne de vile bourgeoisie' was how Saint-Simon in his *Mémoires* summed up the '*mécanique*'. Except from the view of the contemporary nobleman, it was not truly a bourgeois government – as that of de Witt's Holland might be said to be. Men like Colbert and Le Tellier, with the dynasties they created, and the élite of functionaries, *conseilleurs, secrétaires du roi*, *intendants*, were a new aristocracy of office concentrating ever more power into their hands, and guarding it more jealously. As the regime wore on the governing class came to look more aristocratic; the distinction between one sort of nobleman and another became increasingly blurred. What mattered was that all were essentially king's men. The days of divided loyalties, of the great feudatories jockeying for influence over the crown, and using it to advance interests which were often at variance with the professed aims of the crown, were over. At the apex, then, a decisive change was occurring in the complexion of authority. This was accompanied by more vigorous efforts to reform by central direction: the economy, law, police, army and navy. At the centre that meant a growing bureaucracy. The company of *fermiers-généraux*, the financiers who managed most of the indirect taxation, created a dependent empire of directors, controllers and receivers. The crown had to delegate. Could it, at the same time, control? Here the role of the *intendant* was all important.

Richelieu had used *intendants*, usually with temporary commissions, for specific tasks: the commissariat of an army in a frontier province or the settlement of disorders in town or countryside. The resentments among local officers, and *parlement*'s demand of 1648 that they should be withdrawn, indicates that they were effective. Richelieu did not apparently envisage the institution of permanent and resident officials: that was the development of Louis XIV's reign. 'The intendant gives constant intelligence of all things to the court': as Locke saw, he provided the information upon which the government decided its policy. He had to watch notables of his province and to arbitrate in disputes over justice or taxation. If his were a frontier province he had special responsibilities for billeting and supply. He supervised some aspects of town administration and police, the poor law, markets, the numerous problems arising out of communal debts; after 1691, he verified the municipal accounts. In a circular of 1670 Colbert told *intendants* that to see to the operation of the *taille* was the 'most important work entrusted to their hands'. In 1672 he wrote: 'It is vital that you should have a particular and detailed knowledge of all the *élections* of your *généralité*.' He expected much of the *intendants*, but he also knew that they had to tread carefully in the thickets of local officialdom: the rights of *élus* and of the *cours des aides* must be respected. He tried to restrict the practice of delegation. Inevitably, however, as duties mounted by that process of natural increase to which all administration is prone, the numbers of *subdélégués* grew. Even as the powers of government were being increased, compromises were made in a fashion typical of the *ancien régime*. An edict of 1692 enacted that towns had to accept mayors approved by the crown. Two months later the city of Dijon was allowed to pay 100,000 *livres* for the right to nominate its own mayor: it is the familiar story of government action to restrain a privilege being sacrificed to urgent financial demands. The government's drive against Huguenots provided further duties and opportunities. Men like Marillac and Foucault helped, by their initiatives, to shape the policy of Versailles, pioneering the use of troops and sending optimistic reports of the numbers thus converted. The record of Bâville, the 'king of Languedoc', co-operating with local bishops and the army, illustrates the power that an *intendant* could wield under such special circumstances. He could judge, with two counsellors, cases arising out of the Huguenot legislation and there was no appeal against his sentences, ranging from confiscation of goods to service in the galleys, even execution. Where there were Huguenots, or where there were famines calling for emergency measures, as in the southern provinces after the 'great winter' of 1708–9, the *intendant* was in the front line. He bore the brunt and could be made the scapegoat: *intendants* were quite often dismissed or transferred to another province.

In the eighteenth century the office acquired a greater stability. *Intendants* were normally recruited from the close, wealthy, official circle; they became grand local figures, like the royal governors before them. They could carry out great projects. Road building was perhaps the most important, vital to the economy but resented by the peasants who supplied the forced labour, the hated *corvée*. At Rochefort, de Muin supervised the new building of the new town and port. Turgot, later Louis XVI's first *contrôleur-général*, acquired the experience of administration that informed his radical plans for reform – free trade, fair taxation and the improvement of agriculture – in the notoriously difficult province of the Limousin. Many of the ministers of the *ancien régime* climbed by the same ladder. They were specially well equipped for the responsibilities of central government because they had experienced conditions in the field; they had seen the transformation that an edict underwent in the course of its journey from the minister's chamber to the people to whom it was supposed to apply. After the Revolution, which abolished the *intendants*, they were to reappear, as the prefects of the new departments. The Revolution made for a greater tidiness and more effective central control; the *intendants* and the *ancien régime* were always enmeshed in the network of the old officialdom. Sometimes they worked fruitfully with provincial governors who retained powers and patronage enough, to enable the more ambitious and conscientious among them to make their presence felt. *Parlements* and estates, where they existed, had to be bargained with. Officials, enjoying the security that came with the purchase of office, resisted innovation and fought for their share of the perquisites of government. Duties overlapped. The *subdélégués*, and increasingly the *intendant* himself, were entwined in the interests of the province. In the years up to the Revolution, the *intendant* was less effective than might have been expected in coping with the resistance of privileged interests, because of his own divided loyalties. It might be easier to compromise than to fight against the pedantry of the lawyer, the restrictive spirit of manufacturers, the intransigence of the country nobility and the suspicious conservatism of the peasant. The agent of the administrative revolution was less a free agent, and more a pillar of the structure of unreformed France, than a recital of his official duties would suggest.

Colbert

France was still a land of diminutive family enterprises: a smithy, mill or workshop run by a handful of people. The most important industry was weaving, wool and linen, mostly of modest quality and for local wear. The larger concern, like the textile factory of Van Robais at Abbeville, was a rare exception. France's largest industry was bound by restrictive guild regulations: before it reached the wearer, woollen cloth had been worked on by 8 or 9 men in succession, each a specialist belonging to a different craft or guild. The merchant in this widespread business, putting out work for craftsmen, often lacking precise techniques of accountancy, secure in the knowledge that wages could always be lowered because there was always an excess of needy workers, was the typical figure in a sluggish economy. Bad communications ensured the prevalence of small markets serving virtually self-sufficient local markets; the lack of a developed system of credit was further inhibiting. In this setting, in the face of the crippling handicap of a price depression which affected demand throughout the economy, with periodic agrarian crises, the resourcefulness of Jean-Baptiste Colbert (1619–83) rises to the level of statesmanship. For two decades, he laboured, his appetite for detail unsated, his vision of a country of productive workers undimmed.

Descended from a leading family of merchants and office holders in Rheims, Colbert received his early training under Le Tellier and Mazarin. For the management of his political and financial concerns the Cardinal relied upon ambitious, competent servants like Colbert who, following the grander example of Fouquet, had his own extensive clientele by the 1650s: some fifty functionaries and financiers in the sort of loose interdependent grouping that enabled the business of the state to be carried on, some fortunate clients to become rich and a few of those best placed or cleverest to establish in turn their own little empires. Mazarin's affairs were a comprehensive schooling in the resources and shortcomings of the French state and in the skills and abuses of political management. When the Cardinal took over the revenues of Montauban and Guienne to cover the cost of contracts to supply the army with bread, Colbert found that the *taille* was frequently remitted because powerful patrons were protecting the community. When he surveyed the property of Nivernais which Mazarin wished to buy, he took into account, as part of the price, the value of the powers that had accrued to the duke of Nevers as the king's commissary. The furthering of private interests in the king's name was a familiar feature of Colbert's world. When Mazarin died, Louis was furnished with memoranda proposing measures which amounted to a complete programme for the regeneration of the French economy. The young king was impressed. He entered into the spirit and approved the tactics of Colbert's attack on Fouquet, linchpin of the system by which he had risen but which he was resolved to change.

Joint *surintendant* since the age of 37, and the more active of the two, Fouquet was patron of a network of associates in the interlocking worlds of law, finance and Parisian society. He demonstrated his special kind of power by periodic exercises in money raising, notably that of 1658, when tax collection was interrupted by peasant risings in western France. Given a situation in which the king was unable to raise taxes without recourse to costly credits, advances, discounts and commissions, then it is likely that only Fouquet could have provided the means to carry on the war, and that only by methods that enriched the revenue officers at all levels. He alone could not be called to account at the audits of the *chambre des comptes* and could therefore negotiate privately, at rates of interest that reflected the current credit of the state rather than the legal maximum of 5 per cent; since the deals were secret, control was defective. Much depended upon the private credit of the minister who would not have been able to provide for the expenses of the state if, as he admitted, 'my wealth, my expenditure, my splendour of life and my liberality, had not given me credit'. Fouquet's magnificent palace at Vaux-le-Vicompte, his discerning patronage of artists, suggest that he was not the man to be satisfied by mere acquisition. After Fouquet's fellow *surintendant*, Abel Servien, died in 1659, Colbert pressed his own claims on Mazarin, while Fouquet planned to defend himself in ways which formed the basis of the subsequent charges of treason. He sought to enrol influential friends, governors of provinces and fortresses and he obtained signed statements of loyalty to himself that recall the feudal spirit of the Fronde. His arrest, in September 1661, was a sudden, theatrical coup rather in the Mazarin style: nothing in Louis's words or manner had prepared the *surintendant* for the blow. There were precedents, however, for the subsequent trial, which lasted nearly three years. The public condemnation of a financial officer was a valuable occasion for presenting the crown as pure in its intentions, oppressive only because of the wickedness of some of its agents. In December 1662, Lamoignon, attentive to legal niceties, was replaced by the chancellor Séguier, whose long career had been built on unwavering loyalty to the crown. The chamber of justice found Fouquet guilty on various financial and political counts. From then till his death in 1680 his solitary confinement reminded ambitious Frenchmen of the danger of challenging the crown. Though common folk might at times, notably after the Breton revolt of 1675, hang in their hundreds, executions among men of rank and substance were to be rare.

Another kind of political lesson was taught by Colbert's use of the chamber, which sat till 1669, to examine the claims of all who had lent money to the government during the past twenty-five years. The total amount taken from individuals, by fine or cancellation of debt, was around 70 million *livres*. The process also provided a threatening background for the reduction of interest in the *rentes*. Those in the legal and financial establishment who lost by the operation never forgave Colbert. But the system was not changed fundamentally. Profits and influence were transferred from one group to another, consisting of those who could be useful to the minister in finance, whether in the fiscal or commercial sphere. The influence of financiers as a class was not so much reduced as mobilized for Colbert's campaign to create wealth through higher production. He was simultaneously engaged in the recovery of demesne land and the reduction of offices. The Fronde had revealed how sensitive office holders were to what they deemed exploitation; but its failure indicates too the underlying force for stability created by those who owed their status to the crown. Colbert could prune but could not carry out wholesale abolitions even after a survey showed that 40,000 out of 46,000 offices in the departments of justice and finance were unnecessary. The case of offices illustrates the compromising spirit in which the edifice of absolutism was constructed. There was more of mend and make do about the method than of rebuilding on first principles; rationalist though he might be, in the identification and analysis of conditions and objectives, Colbert also proved himself capable of empirical wisdom in his pursuit of the larger goals.

First was the reduction of the *taille* and the shifting of a proportion of the burden on to indirect taxes. He realized that the *taille* must be fixed at an enforceable rate. He cancelled much of the arrears of tax that had so often proved to be a cause of local revolt among desperate communities: the birth of the dauphin in 1662 was a convenient pretext for him to wipe the slate. The more moderate rates, the return to the normal collection by *receveurs*, meticulous auditing, together with the greater vigilance of *intendants*, helped ensure regular payments for the future. In 1661 the entire revenue for 1662 was pledged in advance. After six years of tight control Colbert was able to show that 63 million *livres* were at the disposal of the king from all forms of tax, from an assessment of 91 million, as against 31 and 83 million respectively in the last year of Fouquet's management; the annual cost of interest rates had been reduced from 52 to 14 million a year. Tougher terms for the tax farmers meant a 60 per cent increase in the yield of the *gabelle*. The *taille* from the privileged *pays d'états*, where tax was assessed on property by officials of the estates, was increased by 50 per cent, but that for the bulk of the peasants who lived in *pays d'élection* was reduced by 15 per cent. The low grain prices that were to persist for most of Louis's reign reduced the benefit to the peasant. The elaborate controls which reflected Colbert's concern for self-sufficiency caused waste and loss by preventing the exports that would have dealt with the surplus in good years. The failure to remove local customs barriers outweighed any gains from new roads.

More broadly the whole economic strategy was undermined by the government's failure to tackle the crucial question of tax exemption. Inquests into false titles of nobility were pursued with rigour but only insignificant amounts of tax lost through exemption were recovered. For all that there can be no doubt about the magnitude of Colbert's achievement. During these years, with the doubling of 'free income' the crown regained solvency and control.

It is not only in the sphere of foreign policy that 1672 may be seen as a turning point. Because of the length and strain of the Dutch war a historical opportunity to make more radical reforms was lost. 1675 saw a tax revolt in Brittany which required an army to suppress. In 1679 Colbert was writing to suggest the use of troops to collect the *taille*; in the same year in Tours alone fifty village collectors were in prison because they had failed to collect their quota. By then he was having difficulty in holding his ground against the Le Telliers, the elder one chancellor since 1677, the younger marquis de Louvois, war minister in his father's place and devoted to his army of a quarter of a million which had been consuming 70 per cent of the revenue and which he now sought to maintain at peacetime strength. Louis had enjoyed his campaigning and was amenable to Louvois's arguments about the need to acquire territories on the eastern frontier and construct fortresses to defend it. The new financial situation was similar to that of 1661, only now there were larger commitments and the *contrôleur-général* had less room to manoeuvre. His commercial projects had apparently made little impression on the sluggish mass of the economy. Were they therefore faulty in principle or in execution?

Colbert did not lack vision, but it was of a conservative sort. The deteriorating condition of Spain affected his generation, serving notice of the danger of neglecting manufactures, debasing coin, allowing an adverse balance of trade and the drain of bullion. More positively the example of the Dutch was influential, with their merchant fleet, some twenty times larger than the French, and their valuable colonies. There the application of capital to business ventures was not thwarted by social taboos. Important too was the traditional argument, to be found in earlier writers like Montchrestien, that France was uniquely well endowed by nature with good harbours, fertile soil, and at least sufficient manufactures and skills: all ripe for development but needing protection and stimulus from the state. Colbert's assumption, a common one among economic theorists at the time, that there was a fixed volume of trade for which the nations had to contend, was out of date at a time when new areas and types of trade were being opened up in America and the east. It was to be the complaint of the merchants at the general council of 1701, to which representatives came from different towns, that Colbertism did not allow for the benefits that would come from free interchange of goods: only the delegate from Rouen defended the late minister's policy. But it was in part because of Colbert's work for French manufactures, through subsidies, the importation of skilled workers, even regulations to raise standards of workmanship, that the opportunities for enlarged trade existed by the end of the century. In 1664 there were only about 60 merchant ships of over 300 tons; by Colbert's death, over 700, to carry wine, olives, fine textiles, glass and porcelain to the growing market of wealth and taste, from Moscow to Palermo. French concerns were selling silk to the value of 2 million *livres* to Spain.

The society in which Colbert so greatly flourished, with the close-knit family interest and the noble titles that meant so much to him, was the corporate society. In his massive memoirs he merely elaborated upon conventional patterns of economic analysis. For Hauser, who compared him unfavourably with Richelieu as economic imperialist, it is 'the distance between the perfect clerk and the statesman'. But he was more interesting and his achievement was worth more than that judgement would suggest. In the financial field his work was supremely competent. As an administrator he did more than anyone to make the *intendants*, after 1666 one for each *généralité*, strong and reliable arms of the executive. To such men he communicated some of his methodical, resourceful approach. A true product of the age of Descartes, he accepted few limits to the ability of rational men to shape the human condition. Before action could be taken data must be collected and tabulated: thus armed the minister must think continually 'and with penetration'. The great inquest, launched in 1663, provided him with a social and economic map of the country. That such an inquest was necessary gives some idea of the darkness within which ministers had been groping, their reliance on local or prejudiced information. Colbert's mathematical spirit made him reluctant to base legislation upon guesswork. Under his orders the *Journal des Savants* published, from 1672, a monthly statement of baptisms and deaths in Paris. With him (and his Dutch contemporary and rival de Witt) we enter the age of statistics in the service of government.

Inevitably there was a gap between the rarefied world of his bureau, with its reports and memoranda, and the realities of life in the country. The glowing language of the prospectus for his new trading companies may be contrasted with their performance: the West Indies and Northern companies, the latter designed to move into Dutch preserves in the Baltic, had been wound up by 1678; the East Indies company had by then only an old base at Madagascar and a new base in Pondicherry. The same disillusioning effect can be gained by comparing the prospects with performance of his Royal Company of Mines and Foundries in Languedoc (1666): he required local businesses to exploit native mineral resources to reduce imports, and offered premiums; they did not respond and the concern failed. But initiatives of one sort or another, with direct subsidies, or tax concessions, did bring unexpected fruits. He did not live to see the success of the Languedoc drapery concerns which he had fostered against all discouragement. But the

Languedoc canal, product of local and central funds and initiatives, together with the skill and resource of Riquet, would not have been completed by 1682 without his backing. The royal workshop, the Gobelins, originated in the concentration of many small concerns to provide for the artistic needs of the court. It received a disproportionately large subsidy, 7 million *livres* in his lifetime, against only 11 million for all private industry. But it contributed to France's reputation for superlative craftsmanship: well founded, it was appreciated by connoisseurs all over Europe, for whom to have French furniture, tapestries or glass, was to be *à la mode*. The history of glass manufacture shows Colbert at his most enterprising. Skilled glass blowers were imported from Venice to instruct Parisians: by 1680 he was able to boast that the royal mirror factory was depriving Venice of 1 million *livres* a year.

The concept of trade as a form of war recurs constantly. It is here that Colbert is most vulnerable to criticism because most clearly affected by the values of the Versailles monarchy that he helped to create. From the outset he sought ways of exalting the king's glory in paint and sculpture, in medals and verses, above all in palaces. He would have preferred to extend the Louvre as the king's chief residence and was able to improve it and the Tuileries, but when Louis set his heart on Versailles Colbert mobilized teams of craftsmen and artists to construct and adorn a palace fit for *le roi soleil*. So far from grudging the expense he welcomed the chance to advertise the king's power in a palace of unprecedented size: 600 feet long in its final form. Colbert did not see the contradictions that others have seen in his various activities. Commissioned artists and regulating academies were weapons in his campaign for France no less than tariffs, ships and trading companies. Building and decoration on this scale helped French designers and craftsmen to establish themselves. When French architects were preferred to Bernini for the rebuilding of the Louvre they threw off the Italian influence, developed their distinctive style and entered upon an age of grand commissions. Colbert was always keenly aware of the economic value of grand projects: they provided employment and had beneficial side-effects. Also it was a form of state spending that was acceptable to the king. So was the building up of the navy, another essential part of Colbert's economic plan.

When it came to deciding on priorities, in the 1680s, Louis was to neglect the fleet for the army. But he backed Colbert's work for long enough to make France a maritime power for the first time in her history. Richelieu had made a beginning but the opportunities provided by the Atlantic seaboard were neglected till Colbert's day; meanwhile but a few rotten hulks remained from the regime of Mazarin. Progress among navies was stimulated by the commercial rivalry of England and Holland. Colbert saw too that a strong navy was necessary to give effective backing to his tariff war. A measure of rebuilding was inevitable in any case since with the appearance of sailing vessels in the Mediterranean the galley was rendered obsolete. Dockyards and arsenals were constructed at Toulon, Brest, Rochefort and Dunkirk. Urgently and thoroughly the resources of France were mobilized: forests were laid low, others planted. A regular system of conscription was introduced, with a register of all classes of seamen. Resistance to 'the maritime classes' came not only from local fishermen but also from provincial *parlements*. As ever the question of authority raised its head. Behind the ruthless efficiency of a new system local officials saw not so much the threat to the individual rights of a seaman as encroachment on their own area of authority. Skilled seamen could be found; experienced officers were a greater problem. A naval tradition could not be created overnight. But before the minister's death the new navy had won its first battles, like those of Duquesne over the Dutch off Sicily in January–April 1676. Colbert found 20 ships; he left 250. The ability and courage of de Tourville made the navy, for a brief but glorious time at the start of the Nine Years War, a real threat to Anglo-Dutch supremacy. After the death of Colbert's son Seignelay, the navy was allowed to run down and reduced to the subordinate role of commerce raiding. Even that, in the hands of adventurous seamen such as Jean Bart, was a large contribution to the war effort.

It is inescapable that economic planning based on the 'mercantilist' assumption that a favourable balance of trade could only be achieved at the expense of another country, and developed through tariffs, like that of 1667 which doubled the duty on imported cloth, pointed to war. Colbert welcomed the war against the Dutch, though he hoped it would be short-lived, and was to regret its extension and effects. If this was a weakness in Colbert's statesmanship and source of many of his disappointments, it was the fault of his contemporaries everywhere. 'Mercantilism' was not merely economic theory; it was a political approach to economic problems. Colbert was a statist who saw himself as the instrument of the king's glory. His bureaucratic background and training did not, however, help him to understand the world of merchants of seaports like Nantes and Bordeaux. He might consult them but they were allowed to have little effect on policy: 'they nearly always understand merely their own little commerce, and not the great forces which make commerce go'. His words reveal his limitations. In England it was the continual pressure of private interests that made governments adopt a mercantile policy culminating in the Navigation Laws – so that Adam Smith could later write of 'a conspiracy contrived by a minority for their own interests'. In France the impulse towards regulation came from the top. But the merchants, despite much passive resistance, did not emerge as a coherent hostile body, forcing government to change its policy, until the end of the century. It was the bitter experience of the cost of war, rather than any radical change in thinking, that brought about a reaction.

When the conceptual framework within which he worked, the psychological and physical obstacles, the special handicap of economic recession are all taken into account, there remains a record of significant achievements. It was not the fault of Colbert that future generations were to fail to capitalize on sound beginnings, in India for example; after ten years of Frontenac's governorship of 'little France' in Canada, there were some 10,000 Frenchmen settled in communities along the valley of the Saint Lawrence, principally at Montreal and Quebec (the latter was becoming a flourishing port). By the end of the reign foreign trade was worth 200 million *livres* a year, of which two-thirds represented exports. France was in a position to challenge Britain for overseas supremacy. At home future reformers were still to point to the diversity of laws and the existence of numerous internal customs and tolls, standing in the way of the political and economic unification of the country. But in both areas Colbert had made an important start. In successive codes of law, dealing, for example, with maritime law (1672) and commerce (1673), he sought to regularize practice. All codes and ordinances together fell short of his ideal, 'one whole and perfect body of laws', which had to wait for the Revolution and Napoleon. Success was incomplete too in the sphere of tolls and customs. At least, in the 'five great farms', the central provinces of France, roughly corresponding to the old Capetian domain, he did establish uniform rates. His *manufactures royales*, privileged to display the emblem of the fleur-de-lis, or private enterprises like that of Van Robais, subsidized and cherished, had a high casualty rate. It is easy to point to excessive controls: 150 edicts were issued for the cloth industry alone. But it is hard to see how large-scale operations, producing high-quality goods, with the experienced workmen and high capital outlay required, with raw materials in the right quality and quantity, and managers devoted to excellence, could have been achieved without Colbert. In the cloth trade he had found contraction: sales and quality were actually falling. If he had not supported Flemish or Dutch entrepreneurs and craftsmen, providing them with loans, subsidies and temporary monopolies, the guilds would have preserved their stranglehold, the high capital outlay would have deterred entrepreneurs, and the reputation for quality and the development of overseas markets would not have been gained. It was no mean achievement for him to be able to write (in 1681) 'that the king will no longer give the same privileges and exemptions as in the past because there are now enough manufactures for the whole kingdom'.

Louis XIV and Europe

Mazarin schooled Louis XIV in the conventions and procedures of diplomacy. The young king came to regard the conduct of foreign policy as his particular *métier* and thought himself sufficiently expert to decide matters for himself. But there was nothing casual or impulsive about his approach. Intense and self-disciplined, shrewd though prone to self-deception, Louis was ever conscious of the responsibilities of kingship. '*La gloire*', the phrase so often on his lips, should be interpreted in a wider sense than that of personal magnificence or triumph. It meant reputation, enhanced as it might be by the encounters of diplomacy or war. It embraced those chivalric values which had not yet begun to look old-fashioned. Rulers as different in style and circumstances, as the Emperor Leopold, William of Orange and the Elector Frederick William of Brandenburg thought in the same traditional way: the standing of the head of the family was crucially important. Ceremonies and titles were not superficial but of the essence; precedence could be worth fighting for; so could a royal pledge.

In October 1661 a fight in London between the rival households of the French and Spanish ambassadors gave Louis a chance to publicize his case in the matter of the Queen's dowry and to humiliate Spain before the courts of Europe. Besides public apology Louis required that Spain accept the precedence of his ambassadors in every court. In February 1662 he suddenly demanded payment of the dowry in the shape of Hainault, Cambrai and Franche-Comté. The Spanish ambassador hurriedly conceded the initial demand. Spain was so weak that bullying tactics were almost bound to succeed. Nor could Pope Alexander VII hope to stand up to Louis in the affair of the Corsican Guards of the Vatican who, under some provocation, in August 1662, attacked the French embassy in Rome and insulted the ambassador's wife. Avignon, the Pope's fief in the south of France was occupied and the Pope had to send his nephew Cardinal Chigi to apologize before the territory was restored. Before the eventual truce of 1664 Alexander had been made to disband his Corsican Guard and to erect an obelisk recording the insult to the king. Much can be read into this incident: the stern Gallican spirit of some of Louis's advisers, the waning political influence of the papacy. As in the London affair the original issue was comparatively petty even in an age when precedence was held to indicate precisely the status of a sovereign. The French were deliberately using small incidents to advertise their strength. The policy may have been Lionne's, but Louis's signature is unmistakeable; as in his insistence that the inscription on the obelisk should be of such a size that it should easily be read by the passer-by.

It was in that rigorous spirit that he went to war against the English in 1666, adhering to the terms of his treaty with the Dutch of 1662. In 1679 he insisted on the return of Western Pomerania from victorious Brandenburg to his ally Sweden. Without anything to gain from it, in a then hostile Europe, he saluted the young exile James Edward Stuart as James III. There his honour was directly involved. Honourable dealings satisfied the king's *amour propre*; they also added to the reputation of the country. For the concept of *gloire* included the *bienfait*, well-being, of the nation. That nation was not the abstract entity of later ages, a body of citizens enjoying natural rights, but the ruler's patrimony. Among dynasts it was assumed that the head of the family must defend, if possible extend, his inheritance. Given France's new-found strength, that could only mean war. Ministers were relieved, by Louis's decision to be his own *premier ministre*, of the wider responsibilities that had constrained Richelieu and Mazarin; their promptings matched the king's need to prove himself in an exacting sphere.

It may be that Louis felt less secure in his own position than his bland public manner and complacent memoirs would suggest. He still had misgivings about the security of the realm, in particular of the eastern provinces and the capital itself. Since 1659, Artois had been mainly French but the Spanish still had Flanders, Luxembourg and Franche-Comté. The frontier, which should be envisaged as an irregular sequence of estates and citadels rather than as a continuous line, lay just beyond the rivers Somme, Meuse and Aisne. Running through open country of plains, downs and gentle hills, those rivers were not so much barriers to an enemy as lines of advance. In 1636, the year of Corbie, imperialist forces had advanced to that town, 60 kilometres from Paris, and there had been talk of evacuating the capital. During the Fronde, reviving memories of the religious wars, Spanish troops were active in Picardy, Champagne and Burgundy. Since then the Spanish menace had receded but the many-sided nature of the country's decline may not have been so plain to French observers as it has been to historians. Moreover the third quarter of the century, which saw the Spanish regain Catalonia and abandon their claim to Portugal, also saw a modest recovery in Spain's ailing economy. Beyond dispute then and now was the weakness of Spanish arms, exposed by French victories at Rocroy and Lens (1643 and 1648). The other Habsburg ruler, the Emperor, was unable to gain satisfaction for his traditional claims on the loyalty of the German states in the shape of alliances, garrisons or cash.

At the peace of Westphalia (1648) the diplomacy of Richelieu and Mazarin, and the efforts of French soldiers in thirteen years of war, had been rewarded by the acquisition of strategic outposts: the three bishoprics, Metz, Toul and Verdun were transferred to French sovereignty, along with Franche-Comté and the Rhine crossing at Breisach. Ambiguous clauses that had been necessary if the French were to gain what they wanted and the Emperor save face left uncertainties, notably over the sovereignty of some Alsatian towns, which Louis and Leopold each subsequently strove to resolve in their own interest. The Emperor would not be reconciled to the loss of Alsace, Louis wished to consolidate his position. Another area in which the claims of the two dynasts was incompatible was defined by the peace of the Pyrenees with Spain in 1659, which brought territorial gains, notably Artois and Roussillon and with them the conviction among France's generals that more could be won whenever the king gave the order. Chiefly, however, there was the grand prospect of gaining the entire Spanish inheritance by virtue of that clause in the treaty in which Louis XIV's bride, Maria Theresa, renounced her claim, upon the condition, which Mazarin guessed rightly would not be fulfilled, that the Spanish paid the whole of her large dowry.

The War of Devolution began in May 1667 with a straightforward act of aggression. Philip IV of Spain had died in September 1665, leaving his lands to his frail and backward son Charles, aged 4, and specifically excluding Maria Theresa from all or part of the inheritance. Louis's response, after careful preparation, was the invasion of Spanish Flanders. There was also a parade of legal right based absurdly on a Brabant law, that property devolved on the children of the first marriage to the exclusion of those of the second. A French pamphlet asserted on Louis's behalf that, as king he ought to prevent injustice, as husband to oppose this usurpation, and as father to assure his patrimony to his son. Turenne met with no serious resistance in Flanders where fortress after fortress surrendered until the French came up to the gates of Brussels and Ghent. The Emperor could do little since the Rhineland states would not co-operate. Mazarin's patronage of the elector of Mainz's League of the Rhine, formed in 1658 to defend the interests of his bishopric, along with Cologne and Trier, against all comers, proved its worth. But England and Holland drew together in defensive union. The Dutch had not been alarmed by Louis XIV's purchase of Dunkirk from England in 1662 but they saw in the invasion of Flanders the possibility that Antwerp, if revived under French control, would become a competitor in trade. In January Louis made a private partition treaty with the Emperor which he described as 'a marvellous confirmation of the rights of the queen'. In the following month, February 1668, he launched his army into Franche-Comté to forestall an attack from Spain in that quarter and enable him to negotiate from strength. Sweden then joined the Dutch and English to make the Triple Alliance, in April. Since Louis had gained from Leopold the prospect of the Spanish Netherlands, Franche-Comté and Sicily, more than he could hope for by fighting, he was content to offer moderate terms. At Aix-la-Chapelle, in May 1668, his emissaries insisted on keeping only some isolated Flemish towns; Franche-Comté was restored. It was enough to enable Vauban to set about his life work of strengthening the frontier with a chain of fortresses. By his well-publicized generosity Louis soothed German fears. He did not expect the king of Spain to live long.

Versailles was still a building site: earthworks and scaffolding, mountains of stone, thousands of workmen, teams of craftsmen and artists meant clamour, confusion and discomfort before the elegant design of Le Vau could take shape and the grander frame of Mansard be superimposed to provide a complete, formal setting for court and government. The court meanwhile was itinerant; there were tensions among ministers. Aix was criticized as being weak and inconclusive. Louis was under pressure to restore unity and a sense of direction and to show himself as master. Diplomacy could do so much but only war could square the account. With the English alliance secured in 1670 by the treaty of Dover, the way was clear for the war of retribution which began with a massive two-pronged assault upon Holland in May 1672.

Calculated Aggression

The Dutch War was the logical continuation of the War of the Queen's Rights. Those rights had been denied, not by a military check but by the diplomats of England and Holland, interfering without warrant in the dynastic business of France and Spain. Louis did not sufficiently take into account the raw sensibilities of the Dutch. After seventy years of fighting to win their independence they were bound to be anxious about the southern provinces. It was not so much that they now wanted the provinces for themselves, more that they felt more secure with weak Spanish garrisons, or, as was to become the policy after the Dutch War, with some of their own garrisons forming a barrier in the south. They in turn had little idea of the intense feelings of jealousy and fear that their success in war and commerce had roused in others. Their opinions, voiced in the pamphlets and cartoons of the free press, were strident and provocative. In the ideal world statesmen ought not to be affected by prejudice and propaganda; history shows repeatedly that they are. The evidence of Louis's memoirs shows him to be acutely sensitive about imaginary slights to his person and country – one and the same in dealings at this level. His ministers shared his irritation and impatience. Lionne died in 1670, before he could see the diplomacy which had brought about the virtual isolation of Holland consummated by war.

There was no suggestion of conciliation in Lionne's words to his successor, Pomponne: 'It did not belong to merchants, themselves usurpers, to decide in sovereign manner the interests of the two greatest monarchs in Christendom.' The key word is 'usurpers'. Legitimacy had a high place in Louis's own thinking. It was one thing to use the Dutch, as Richelieu had used the Swedes, as a tactical weapon against the Habsburgs; another to submit to dictation from the seven provinces, to Louis's mind not a state because not a monarchy; only a federation governed by 'business men and cheese merchants'. The younger Le Tellier, marquis de Louvois, who moved into his father's job as war minister, brought to it his brusquely efficient talent for administration. Proud of his growing army, crudely single-minded in approach, he had opposed the peace of Aix because he wanted to test his troops while the Dutch were still unprepared. Militarism was in the ascendant at court and money did not seem to be short. The role of the *contrôleur-général* was far from negative. Fearing the rising star of Louvois, and anxious not to fall behind in zeal for his sovereign's interest,

Colbert positively welcomed trade war as the natural extension of his commercial policy of prohibitive tariffs. He had made plain in 1667 his determination to break the semi-monopoly of the Dutch in the world's carrying trade. 'As we have ruined Spain on land so we must ruin Holland at sea.' He saw Antwerp and the vital river Scheldt as the tactical objective. He spoke of war as 'the only means by which His Majesty can put an end to the insolence of this nation'.

No doubt Colbert hoped for another short war. The campaign began with triumph as the fall of Rheinberg and three other strongholds on the Rhine was followed by the crossing of the river and the fanning out of Louis's armies through Overyssel, Gelderland and Utrecht. Few would have guessed then that the war would have lasted for another six years. Louis attacked the Holland of de Witt; after the latter's murder it was the intransigent prince of Orange that he had to fight. The Dutch certainly offered great concessions in the late summer of 1672 but they may have been playing for time. Louis's insistence on a religious clause guaranteeing equal rights for the Roman Catholics and the dispatch of an annual envoy bearing a medallion in token of submission were in character. Even if he was serious in his peace terms he was happy to see the war continue. His instructions and memoranda during the succeeding years show him absorbed in the exercise of his métier, personally drawing up marching orders, consulting with the efficient and plausible Chamlay, who became his intimate military adviser.

The war ended satisfactorily but it brought shocks and setbacks like William's capture of Naarden in August 1673. It exposed strains, the old rivalry between Condé and Turenne, and a new antagonism between the generals and Louvois, who was intent on civilian control. Condé won a bloody victory at Senef in 1674 which brought no lasting advantage: he retired, disgruntled, in 1676. In July 1675 Turenne was killed by a stray bullet while out reconnoitring the lines of his formidable adversary Montecuccoli. His reputation had been enhanced by his skilful winter campaign in the Vosges; his death was mourned like Nelson's after Trafalgar. Neither his political nor his military record had been flawless but he had come to symbolize, even more than Condé, the new era of political stability and military prowess. In myth Condé and Turenne were the great captains, unique and irreplaceable. In fact there were competent successors, notably Luxembourg, but the age of easy victories was past. The defection of the English in 1674 and the intervention of the Emperor and Spain created new alignments which foreshadowed the pattern of later years. Louis finally found himself engaged in a European war to defend his gains against a coalition which contained at different times Lorraine, which he had occupied as a tactical move in 1667, and Brandenburg. He had already become in hostile propaganda 'the Christian Turk', but he found the experience of campaigning refreshing, and the French continued to win victories, like that of Cassel in April 1677, which were useful counters for the French diplomats in the long-delayed peace talks.

Much was sacrificed in the Dutch War: the impetus of Colbert's policies of fiscal reform and commercial expansion, goodwill in Germany, a strong basis for negotiations with the Emperor over the Spanish succession. The deterioration in relations with England, where the mounting opposition to Charles II had its origins in the secret treaty of Dover, by which Charles had pledged action on behalf of his Roman Catholic minority in return for a subsidy, and the marriage of Mary, his niece, to William of Orange (1677) were bad auguries for the future. The peace of Nijmegen (1678) brought the French precious gains of territory: notably Ypres, Cambrai and Valenciennes, among a line of strong places from Dunkirk to the Meuse. France now kept Franche-Comté which the Spanish had never been able to defend. Yet after 1679 Louis kept his armies on a war footing, at a size unprecedented in peacetime, of over 200,000.

He was not content with what had been achieved. The frontier was an unsatisfactory patchwork: enclaves of territory belonged to foreign princes in a way that was displeasing to the rational official mind. The creation of a linear frontier might be said to follow logically from the centralizing principle of the modern state. But a frontier that could be defended was the immediate and practical motive behind the annexations of 1679–84, known as the 'reunions'. They followed investigations, mostly in special courts, into the rights of the French crown to certain 'dependencies'. The term had been used in the treaties of Westphalia and Nijmegen to describe lands that owed, or had once owed, feudal allegiance to estates then ceded to France. It was of course the strategic value of particular dependencies, like Trarbach, commanding a loop of the Moselle, and Strasbourg, with its vital bridge over the Rhine, that caused most concern outside France. Altogether the reunions were a very large-scale operation. Annexations included the province of the Saare up to the Moselle, the principality of Montbéliard; the county of Chinon and most of Luxembourg; many places in Flanders and almost everything in Upper and Lower Alsace, providing sharp clarification of the hazy terms of Westphalia. Among the German princes the elector of Trier and the duke of Württemberg were dismayed to find themselves on the border of France. Great alarm was caused by the *coup de main*, neatly executed by Louvois, which brought French troops marching into Strasbourg. The proud city with its independent tradition, more like a Swiss canton than the imperial free city that it was supposed to be, was regarded by Germans like Maximilian of Baden, commander of the imperial army, as 'a guarantee of peace' whereas 'for France it is a door through which she can invade German soil as often as she wishes'. Louis made no bones about the strategic value of the city but he also rejoiced at a victory for the faith. The city was allowed to keep its reformed religion but Egon de Faustenbourg returned to his cathedral – and the cathedral to its Roman rites. By October 1681, when Louis made his solemn entry to hear the celebratory *Te Deum*, 400 barges had already arrived, laden with stone for Vauban's ambitious fortifications. His government's commemorative medal bore the proud inscription: *Clausa Germania Gallia.*

The case seems plain: Louis was acting in a way that was calculated to rouse the greatest suspicion and anger; he was therefore to some extent the author of his subsequent misfortunes. There is no doubt that one important part of the legacy of the cardinals, French prestige in Germany, was marred by repercussions from the invasion of Holland and the reunions. But the dangers were understood by Louis and his ministers. They thought that the game was worth the candle – and the game was played with skill. In October 1679 in the second treaty of St Germain, the Great Elector and John George II of Saxony promised their vote for Louis or the dauphin at the next imperial election. Bavaria was secured once more by the marriage of the dauphin to a sister of Maximilian Emmanuel. In England French money contributed to Charles II's successful efforts to master the opposition of the Whigs and to secure the succession of his Catholic brother James.

Louis had long been convinced that Leopold had settled into a steady intransigence, that he would fight for the whole Spanish succession and for the recovery of Alsace. Therefore he gave up earlier ideas of taking over the rest of the Spanish Netherlands, trying instead to secure as much land as possible to create an impregnable defensive position while the Emperor was otherwise engaged with the Turks. Undeniably he put France's territorial interests before those of Europe as a whole. The Austrians were not being altruistic in the conquest of Hungary which followed the relief of Vienna in 1683; there was more of narrow dynasticism than Christian brotherhood in Leopold's ungracious treatment of his Polish allies, fellow crusaders against the Turk. William risked all to win the English throne and strengthen his hand for the next round of war against his mortal enemy. Louis's militancy was at least matched by his rivals. Indeed he became more meticulous and moderate with age. There were tactical advantages to be gained from Leopold's embarrassment as he retreated before the Turkish onslaught. And so Louis did not send troops in response to the Emperor's appeal in 1683. His fastidious sense of what was proper prevented him, however, from what a Frederick the Great would surely have seen as the logical step from a policy of non-cooperation. However, Louis's sole consideration was not that of territorial gain, and so he did not attack the Emperor's lands in the west. In the event Louis lost both politically and morally. Already suspect to the German princes because of the reunions, he now appeared as aggressor across a widening gap. They looked with enhanced respect to the Emperor who had fulfilled his traditional role defending them against the Turks. Louis felt that moderation and prudence had been poorly rewarded and looked for another way to restore his position, at least among the Catholic princes.

'Grand designs' are usually myths created by elderly politicians in their memoirs, like Sully, or historians looking for some pattern to impose upon events. Even the Spanish succession, thought by Mignet to be the pivot of the reign, did not dominate Louis to the extent of stopping him from pursuing other objectives which were likely to weaken his claim or force him to fight for it. Similarly the view that Louis was obsessed during the 1680s with the idea that the electors of the Empire might be persuaded to elect a Frenchman is almost certainly mistaken. The master stroke, as he saw it, of revoking the edict of Nantes (October 1685) was the fulfilment of a heartfelt desire but not of a consistent policy; indeed it represented a change of policy, a step taken after much hesitation and in response to immediate tactical arguments. Louis always reacted empirically to opportunities and challenges. If there was a single theme throughout it was the quest for security, but that was overlaid at different times not only by concern for dynastic right and for prestige, but also by arguments of religion.

Even without skilful exploitation by Huguenots and sympathizers the revocation would have hardened Protestant opinion against Louis. It played an important part for example in the failure of James II and his efforts to promote the interests of Catholicism in England – with unfortunate effects for Louis. It strengthened the hand of the Orange party in Holland, representing as they did Calvinist rigour and the tradition of war. It also, however, increased the support of uncommitted German states for the Emperor. Persistent and expert attempts to build up a friendly party of princes in North Germany (1690–4) failed because of underlying suspicion of Louis's motives and because the Emperor was seen to have more to offer; to the duke of Hanover, for example, who was promised an electorate in return for promises of support. It further embarrassed the Pope and presented Christendom with the spectacle of Supreme Pontiff and Very Christian Majesty, already at loggerheads over the Gallican question, now further estranged by an act which Bossuet, inviting his congregation 'to dote on the piety of Louis', hailed as 'the miracle of our times'. Only four years later Louvois unleashed against the Emperor and Holland, joined now by England, a preventive war which was to last nearly nine years, in which some 20,000 trained soldiers and sailors served with the king's enemies. Within France a fifth column of Huguenots, in touch with the allies, forced the government to protect the coast against enemy landings. Against that background of deepening enmities Bossuet felt impelled to admit: 'Your so-called Reformation was never stronger. All the protestant peoples are now united in a single bloc.' The revocation emphasized the moral division of Europe. 'Today,' wrote Leibnitz in 1692, 'it is virtually the north that is ranged against the south, the Teuton races challenging the Latin.' By then the balance of power had altered dramatically in favour of the Emperor. Had Louis simply miscalculated?

However strong the political and administrative arguments for revocation, the evidence about Louis, his ministers and bishops, points to a mood of moral seriousness, with some agonizing soul-searching and much of the exaltation of men embarking on a crusade. It was Louis's decision, and he was proud to be breaking free from the vacillations of earlier years. Judgements of his statecraft have to take into account the likelihood that the action which can be seen as the turning point in his reign was viewed by the king as something right and good in itself, and which therefore had to be done, whatever the risk. He calculated that it would further France's reputation abroad and it is plain that he was wrong. But he is some way removed in spirit and action from the cynical power politics of the 'enlightened' rulers of the next century. In 1740 Frederick the Great would use the religious claims of a minority of Silesian Lutherans to justify naked aggression; Catherine of Russia, the grievances of Orthodox Christians in Poland to excuse the first partition of that unhappy country in 1772. Bigoted or complacent Louis XIV may appear to be, but unscrupulous he was not. It may have been his chief fault that he was too typical a Frenchman and Catholic of his times. What he lacked in statecraft was not competence nor even mental subtlety but that rare quality of imagination which would have enabled him to look outside the bounds of tradition, to penetrate the minds of foreigners. It was a quality that Richelieu possessed and Louis did not. He would have been an admirable staff officer but he would surely have failed as a general.

It must be remembered that Louis was not simply king in council, Olympian, detached, and immune from partisan pressure. He believed, like his great-grandfather Philip II of Spain whom he resembled perhaps more than his grandfather Henry IV, that he stood to gain from the jealous competition between ministers and their factions. Perhaps memories of the Fronde explain his concern to prevent a uniting of critics. Colbert, Le Tellier and their successors bid high for his attention and they were hardly disinterested advisers. The king was also the centre of a flattering court. The grand architecture of Versailles of which he was inordinately proud, and which became his settled residence in 1682, the art of painters and sculptors all working to a brief to extol the king's glory, the Byzantine rituals of the palace day and the values of courtiers who had to find some justification for a rootless, dependent existence altogether amounted to an insistent plea for fine gestures and heroic actions. Louis did not need the symbolism of the *salon de guerre* to convince him that conquest was a fitting ambition for a prince. At different times he heard many arguments for making war: for his legitimate rights, for the Catholic Church, for the economic well-being of France. Not until the last years of the century did he hear positive arguments for peace. In the shape of the numerous officers who thronged the court there was a permanent and persuasive lobby for war. To read Bossuet's majestic and passionate tributes to Turenne and Condé in his funeral sermons is to realize how deeply the French court was imbued with the spirit of militarism. It was in fighting that the French nobleman could express his manhood and loyalty. The man who was, in honoured theory, father of his country, was in practice and outlook more like the head of his nobility. The king who was so determined to reduce the independence of the nobility shared by and large its mentality.

Normally therefore he took pleasure in war, especially in sieges, under Vauban's direction orderly and exact operations; in summer jaunts for king and court which could be relied on, after the necessary trenching and sapping, to end with breach, entry and capitulation: a gratifying exercise for all concerned. Nor is it surprising that he sanctioned the use of force on several occasions when the situation seemed to require less drastic treatment. In 1683 Genoa was devastated by the new French bomb-ketches, or gun-ships, because the doge had allowed Spanish ships to be refitted in his harbours; the doge had to come to Versailles to ask the king's pardon. Italians, already roused by Louis's Gallican policy and his periodic sallies against the Pope, had been alerted by the occupation of Casale in 1681 to the possibility that he had planned to revive traditional pretensions in north Italy. Nor did his treatment of the young Duke Victor Amadeus of Savoy allay their fears. He was forced to receive several thousand French troops in his country and in 1685 ordered to help Louis deal with the heretic Vaudois on his side of the Alps. Victor Amadeus was to be a valuable member of later coalitions against Louis.

Though Louis was insensitive in his treatment of Italian affairs his injuries and insults were insignificant in scale and effect compared to the blunder of the devastation of the Palatinate in the early months of 1689. It was primarily defensive in conception, the creation of a neutral zone which could not sustain an enemy army in order to shorten the front. Chamlay's letter to Louvois in which he suggests that the action would 'make the king absolute master of the Rhine' suggests a more positive approach. Whatever the reasoning behind it there can be no doubt about the effect of the deliberate sacking of Heidelberg, Spier, Worms, Mannheim, fifty castles and hundreds of villages. Thousands of homeless were left to find shelter among fellow Germans: every refugee an argument against the king of France. After a period when armies had been brought under tighter control the devastation revived memories of the Thirty Years War: then it was random savagery, now a deliberate act of state policy. It made mockery of Louis's championship of the rights of his sister-in-law Elizabeth Charlotte to the Palatinate. Pamphlets and broadsheets, crudely illustrated, denouncing the new 'Huns' and their ruler who followed the principles of Machiavelli and sought the alliance of the Turk, were avidly read. Scorched earth had gained a strategic advantage but at a price that was only worth paying if war was inevitable. Louis thought that it was, and also that the balance of power had altered dramatically in favour of the Emperor. Events proved him right.

In August 1684 at Ratisbon, the Emperor, Spain and France agreed to a twenty years truce. Louis had undoubtedly hoped to convert it into a lasting peace for he had gained Strasbourg, Luxembourg and the substantial areas secured by the *réunions*. Since then his actions, each having its own practical purpose, had turned particular problems into a general crisis; limited, defensive operations into a general war. Louvois may have been right to plan for a defensive war, but his calculations were upset by the success of William in winning the English throne. In 1689 William was in a position to embark on the war for which he had been preparing since the previous summer when he set up camp at Nijmegen within reach of Cologne. He could rely, for the time being, on solid support from parliament. In May 1689 he entered into an alliance with the Emperor which had better prospects than that of the Dutch war. By promising to support Leopold over the Spanish succession he persuaded him to divert his main strength from Hungary to the Rhine. The two sovereigns formally engaged themselves to restore western Europe to the position of Westphalia and the Pyrenees, to restore Lorraine to its duke and Pinerolo to the duke of Savoy. Charles II of Spain, after the death of his French queen Marie-Louise and his subsequent marriage to Leopold's sister-in-law Mariana of Neuberg, was bound for the time being to the Emperor's party. When Louis sent an expedition to aid James II in Ireland, England declared war. Savoy joined the coalition in 1690. The German states, Brandenburg, Saxony, Hanover and Hesse-Cassel, were already pledged by their agreement at Magdeburg. Sweden later lent assistance to a coalition which, for all its divergences of aim, faced Louis with will and resources equal to his own.

The Nine Years War that began in effect with the devastation of the Palatinate was different in character from previous wars. Flanders, where Louis's generals played with skill the conventional military chess game, was only one front among several. Ireland, till James II's final defeat in 1691, was an important secondary front, occupying valuable British troops. When Savoy and Spain joined the Grand Alliance, Italy became a battleground and French troops crossed the Pyrenees into Spain. Simultaneously the Holy League was fighting the Turks in Greece, around the Dnieper and the Danube. Though there was no direct alliance, the fortunes of Louis's armies were closely linked to those of the Turks: Austrian victories, like that of Zalankhamen in 1691, were unwelcome at Versailles. The Flanders theatre remained the most important for Louis, and for William, who was worsted by the resourceful Luxembourg in two great battles, Steenkirke and Neerwinden (1692, 1693). Though William did manage to capture Namur in 1695, it was not the military record that determined the outcome of peace negotiations at Ryswick. By any reckoning Louis won the war in Flanders, though no single battle was decisive. He undoubtedly lost the peace. And so it was not merely in scale that the Nine Years War was different. The conflicts that took place in North America, the West Indies and India were minor affairs. But they pointed to a future when the rivalries of colonies would have a direct bearing on the fortunes of the mother countries and claim an increasing share of their resources. Meanwhile the leading nations were being affected by the more intensive and wide-ranging character of war. As armies and navies came more tightly under the control of the state, the state was affected more profoundly by the ever growing appetite of the military establishment: the vast armies, the magazines, the commissariat for men and horses, fortresses, more sophisticated in design to meet the challenge of more effective siege weapons, the costly infrastructure of dockyards, shipwrights, pilots and ordnance, all that was required to keep ships at sea.

The French may have suffered by giving precedence, as they did after Colbert, to military over naval expenditure. But they showed awareness of the changing demands of a war of resources by evolving a mature strategy of commerce-raiding. In 1690 Tourville had shown that the French navy was equal to the best when he defeated the English at Beachy Head. His defeat at La Hogue two years later at the hands of Admiral Russell was no disgrace for he was outnumbered rather than outfought. The French therefore adopted the *guerre de corse*, with privateers organized on the lines of a state company, money being found from private sources but ships provided, manned and disciplined by the state. Jean Bart and Duguay-Trouin were among the most successful sea captains of history. But theirs was the strategy of the weaker side, reflecting the shortage of cash. The wars that began in 1689 and ended in 1714, with but a short interval (1697–1701) for diplomatic exchanges that were overshadowed by the near certainty that war would soon be resumed, amount to virtually one war from the point of view of the military historian: it was a war of resources. Even more than the substantial war contribution of the imperial armies, under inspiring generalship, it was the capacity of the maritime powers to mobilize their resources that eventually carried the day. The French could not match the mechanisms, the Bank of England and the Treasury, that enriched individuals without impoverishing the state. Too greatly dependent on taxes, they were all the more severely affected by the dreadful sequence of harvest failures between 1691 and 1695: the people were afflicted, the tax base was eroded. By 1697 William needed peace because he was being harried in parliament, and was oppressed by the imminent prospect of the death of the king of Spain. For Louis, who had been putting out peace feelers since 1693, the need was more urgent as debt and deficit pointed the way to bankruptcy.

Concessions were inevitable in the Ryswick negotiations. They were made more willingly because the French negotiators were thinking of a larger prize. The foreign minister, Pomponne, long reputed a dove among hawks, was blamed for sacrificing the soldiers' gains. No one was better placed to understand the economic argument behind the peace than the much travelled Vauban who was soon to claim in his *Dîme royale*, an informal survey of the country, that 1 in 10 Frenchmen were reduced to begging. Yet in a letter to Racine he declared that the peace was 'more infamous than Cateau-Cambrésis'. Concerned about creating a defensible frontier Vauban was upset by the cession of so many fortress towns, Breisach and Freiburg among them. To Spain were returned Luxembourg, Charleroi and Courtrai. But Louis did not expect them to be lost for long. The future of Spain preoccupied William as much as Louis. The peace completed in October 1697 had brought William mitigation of commercial tariffs in favour of the Dutch, the right to garrison a line of 'barrier fortresses' in the Spanish Netherlands and the recognition as king of England 'by Grace of God' which Louis had so long withheld. It was said of him in parliament that 'he was given to England to hold the balance of Europe'. That balance was in question as Charles the Sufferer's tenuous hold on life began to slip at last and the succession question approached its crisis.

The Spanish Succession

After Ryswick no arrangement existed for the disposal of the great inheritance except the partition treaty of 1668, long obsolete, and a vague agreement of 1689 between the Emperor and Holland by which Holland promised to support the Emperor's claim. Like Louis, the Emperor claimed both as husband and as grandson. On those grounds Louis had the superior claim because his mother was the elder daughter of Philip III, Leopold's the younger; his wife was the elder sister of Charles II and Leopold's the younger. Leopold claimed that Louis had renounced the claim to succession on his wife's behalf, but Louis had already fought the War of Devolution on the principle that the conditions laid down for that renunciation had not been fulfilled. By his wife Margaret Theresa, Leopold only had a daughter, Marie-Antoinette: she had married the elector of Bavaria and had a son Ferdinand-Joseph. On this neutral candidate (he was 8 years old in 1698) William and Louis agreed on terms which show that Louis seriously looked for settlement rather than war, for the dauphin, representing the French claim, was only to have Sicily and the Presidi (fortified ports in Tuscany), the archduke Charles, Milan. But Ferdinand-Joseph died, unaware of the destiny planned for him, and in June 1699, with unusual haste, France and England agreed upon new lines of partition. Louis accepted a plan which gave the main part to the archduke Charles, reserving only Lorraine, whose duke was to be transferred to Milan, or Nice and Savoy if Milan were to be transferred to the duke of Savoy. William had acquired a throne on the principle that the people's representatives had the right to choose a sovereign; Louis stood for the principle of legitimacy, and was soon to reaffirm it on the death of the man whom William had supplanted. The two men now combined to impose upon the Spanish people a king who was neither evidently legitimate nor desired, to slice off part of the inheritance into the bargain, and to move minor princes about the board as if their subjects did not matter at all. Leopold was deeply suspicious of Louis and his motives. Encouraged by the war party at court he decided to wait on events, receive the whole succession by will and defend it if necessary; if not, fight for it anyway. So while Leopold gave out that it was improper to bestow the succession on a still living king, Louis, William and the states-general signed the second partition treaty, in March 1700.

The partition treaties represent an attempt by three of the strongest powers to avert general war by imposing their own solution of the succession problem. William's interest was clear. He wished to keep the French out of the Low Countries. Louis's motives are harder to fathom. When he subsequently declared for the will and the principle of legitimacy, he was naturally accused of bad faith. But such inconsistency arose inevitably from the conflict between the traditional values of the prince and the changing interests of the state. In accepting the conditions of the Grand Alliance, in particular in recognizing William, Leopold, who had been so strong for family right before the publication of the will, was similarly to defer to the claims of state interest. The partition treaties can be seen as an early example of great powers combining to enforce a system of collective security. Dynastic and feudal rights had long been the basis of the public law of Europe. Now economic factors had to be taken more seriously into account. The signatories of the Grand Alliance were not unaware of the special interests which served to divide them; but there was a common danger which enabled them temporarily to unite in the name of the peace and order of Europe. The same would be true of the Quadruple Alliance in 1718 when Britain, France, the Emperor and Holland closed ranks in the face of Spanish aggression, in that case threatening the Emperor's interest in north Italy. By then a long and expensive war had reinforced the case for collective action.

Before Charles II died in November 1700 he made a will leaving his lands entire to the duke of Anjou, Louis's second grandson. Harcourt, the French ambassador, had worked adroitly to build up a pro-French party at the Spanish court. Cardinal Portecarrero had argued persuasively that only the Bourbons had the resources to defend the Empire. Charles's German queen had alienated many by her over-zealous efforts on behalf of the Emperor. But the decision was Charles's alone, made in a spirit of resentment that heretical Dutch and English should plan the dismemberment of his empire, but also in the hope that the French would enable the young prince, in any war that he might have to fight, to defend his lands, vulnerable Flanders, Milan, Naples and the colonies.

Charles's decision forced Louis to make a choice between treaty and will.

Arguments of honour and profit were evenly balanced; in either course there were great risks. He chose the will. In retrospect it seems that he made the wrong choice but Torcy, his capable, realistic foreign minister thought it right; so did Burgundy, his eldest grandson and soon to be a severe critic of government policy. The will represented, as Louis said in his address to the court, a just claim, the will of the king and the wish of his people. It offered more than could have been gained by any war. To have stood by the treaty would have meant giving up any chance of advancing the French frontier in the direction of the Low Countries. With the Spanish Empire in the hands of a French prince great commercial advantages would acrue to French merchants. It is not hard to see what Colbert, Torcy's uncle, would have advised. Perhaps the clinching argument was that France would probably have to fight anyway. Even before the announcement of the will Leopold had moved troops into North Italy. There were of course far graver dangers in a war against a coalition than against the Emperor alone. But was it inevitable that England would fight? Could not Louis find means of keeping his enemies divided?

It is certain that Louis did not want war. Indeed he understood fully the likely consequences for his country: the experience of the previous wars pointed to a prospect of calamities, even if his soldiers continued to win their battles. In July 1698 he had written to Tallard, the man who was to lose the battle of Blenheim and the invincible reputation of the French army:

> nothing is more certain than the misfortunes which war would bring with it and the sufferings of peoples; and after having sacrificed such great advantages to give peace to my subjects, no interest appears to me more important than that of preserving the tranquility which they now enjoy.

The moderate, chastened diplomat of Ryswick and the partition treaties did not suddenly revert to thoughtless bellicosity. He did, however, remain determined to hold what he held to be his just inheritance and to stand by the principles to which he had now returned. He offered William and his minister Heinsius little hope of concessions, as if determined to extract the maximum benefit for France from the Bourbon succession. He supplied the material for hostile propaganda as if unable to imagine the cumulative effect of actions, each of which were justifiable from his angle, on foreign observers predisposed to mistrust him. He was right to suppose that William was bent on war but failed to exploit the difficulties that he faced in parliament which had paid off most of the army, demanded lower taxes, and was deeply suspicious about foreign commitments.

In February 1701 *parlement* registered letters patent reserving the right of Philip of Anjou to the French throne. It seems to have been Louis's intention not that France and Spain should be united but that Philip V should not be debarred from the French throne in the unlikely event of his becoming eligible. Twelve years and four royal deaths later he stood next in succession to a boy of 3: Louis could not have anticipated such mortalities in a healthy family. Then French troops suddenly entered the Netherlands, seized the barrier fortresses and imprisoned their Dutch garrisons, all in the name of the king of Spain whom the states-general had not recognized: they did so and the troops were released. The barrier was one of the main objectives of Dutch diplomacy, while in England Louis's coup was represented as the invasion of Flanders. Merchants' complaints there were substantiated by news that the French fleet had sailed to guard Cádiz and that the French Guinea Company had gained by treaty with Madrid the privilege of the *asiento*, that is of importing Negro slaves into South America, coveted (and later gained at Utrecht) by the English. The merchants did not know that Louis's instructions for Harcourt to the new king were that Dutch and English ships were to be excluded from the Indies and South America. Of course the Spanish needed help. Since the Emperor was planning to move against Milan it was a reasonable precaution of Louis to send troops under Catinat to defend the duchy. By September, when the Grand Alliance was made, he was already fighting Prince Eugène.

The contracting parties to the Grand Alliance, England, Holland and the Empire, stated their aims clearly: they would procure for the Emperor satisfaction of his claim to Spain; for the maritime powers 'particular and sufficient surety for their realms and for the navigation and commerce of their subjects'; they would restore the barrier; they undertook to prevent forever the union of the French and Spanish crowns; they would share between England and Holland any gains in the Spanish colonies. Louis was given two months to consider terms which amounted to a manifesto of war. Louis's chief hope was to exploit the discrepancy between the allies and their aims. The dynastic designs of Austria, the commercial imperialism of the English, the predominant wish of the Dutch for security, contained from the outset the seeds of disharmony. In particular there was no reason why an English parliament should be generous in support of an Austrian archduke. Nine days after the completion of the Grand Alliance, on 18 September, James II died at St Germain.

Louis XIV's decision to recognize James II's son as king of England was a considered act of policy as well as a generous salute to the principle of heredity and to a royal kinsman in need, *amende honorable* for what many at court regarded as the betrayal of James II at Ryswick. Anticipating a succession dispute on William's death Louis was anxious not to be caught backing the wrong horse (like Mazarin in 1660). But it is hard to defend his action on political grounds. Parliament had just ruled the succession after Anne to the Protestant house of Hanover by the Act of Settlement; now to hear that Louis was dictating his own settlement united English politicians as nothing else could. The tone of London opinion can be heard in the city of London's protest: 'our condition would be wretched indeed if we had to be governed at the behest of a prince who has used fire, sword and galleys to destroy the Protestants of his estates'. Parliament passed a measure attainting James of high treason for having assumed the title of king, which was largely the work of Bolingbroke, later architect of the Tory peace and exile for Jacobitism! William then dissolved parliament and secured a Whig majority which promptly voted for large armaments. In the following March he died but his spirit lived in the coalition that he bequeathed to his successor. Anne and her leading politicians were wholeheartedly for war against what their manifesto called Louis's aspiration to universal monarchy, and Marlborough assumed command of the army with sufficient money and authority to play a part worthy of his genius.

A War Too Many

The bare recital of diplomatic pledges and agreements shows that France started the war at a disadvantage. Hanover, Saxony, Brandenburg and the Palatinate were among the German princes who promised support to the Emperor. Exceptionally, Maximilian Emmanuel of Bavaria made a straight treaty of alliance with Louis by which he undertook to ban the passage of imperial troops and to raise 10,000 troops; in return Louis promised money and help in the event of an imperial election. But both Savoy and Portugal whose positions would significantly affect operations in north Italy and Spain respectively, after favouring France at first, changed sides in 1703; the Emperor outbid Louis by the offer of Montferrat to Victor Amadeus, while the Methuen treaty bound Portugal to England. Charles XII of Sweden, occupied with his own war against Poland and Russia, resisted French advances while Denmark, though nominally neutral, sold valuable contingents of troops to Marlborough's army. Leopold had Rakoczy's Hungarian revolt on his hands, the Dutch were increasingly defensive as the war went on, reluctant to let their troops fight outside the Netherlands, and the English Tories, though divided, became increasingly critical of Marlborough; yet Louis could hope neither for easy victory nor quick peace. After 1703, for three years, Huguenot insurgents, 'Camisards', kept an army pinned down in the Cevennes. The effect was seen when Villars was recalled after his victory against a German army at Hochstadt in 1703 to deal with the Camisards. The exposed French bridgehead into Bavaria tempted Marlborough and Eugène to make their historic marches from Flanders and north Italy to join forces and bring Marsin, Tallard and the elector of Bavaria to action. The resulting battle of Blenheim, on 13 August 1704, was decisive. The French and Bavarians lost 30,000 killed or captured. Tallard was himself captured. Bavaria was lost; France fought thereafter to save her own soil from invasion.

To emphasize the importance of Blenheim one has to imagine what would have happened in London if Marlborough had lost. His risky march would have been denounced, the expense and worse the relevance of the war would have been questioned. The fruitful partnership of Marlborough and Eugène would never have blossomed. Louis would have had something to play with in peace talks; but now he had his back to the wall. After Ramillies in May 1706, where Marlborough's masterly tactics and Villeroi's indifferent handling of his army brought more high casualties and an unseemly rout, the great towns of Flanders were taken in succession, until Marlborough captured Menin, Louvain, Ghent, Oudenaarde, Antwerp and Brussels and stood on French soil. Vendôme, who was holding the line of the Adige against Eugène, was transferred to threatened Flanders. The move would have made sense if Louis had ordered his commanders in Italy, La Feuillade and Marsin, to concentrate their troops, and then allowed them tactical freedom. La Feuillade, in Vauban's expert opinion, bungled the siege of Turin though he had lavish siege equipment. French troops were dispersed between Turin, the mountains of Savoy and the line of the Adige which Eugène pierced without difficulty. When he attacked the French at Turin in September he gained a victory easier than Ramillies, and no less important. The French lost 9000 troops, their defeatist general Marsin, all their siege equipment and, as it turned out, Italy.

Even before Ramillies Louis was putting out peace feelers. After the battle he was ready to give up the will and negotiate on the basis of the partition treaty. But his bargaining position was weaker than ever. With every misfortune he offered more; the allies, relishing their strength, stiffened their demands. 'Reasonable satisfaction' for Charles was now interpreted as the whole succession. The Dutch claimed French towns as well as Spanish for their 'security'. The whole basis of their policy was altered: the war, from being, ostensibly, one to preserve the balance of power, became one to impose upon the Spanish people a king whom a majority were soon to show they did not want. It was in Spain that Louis found hope to sustain him in a war of endurance. There was revulsion of feeling for Philip. Castilian hatred of Portugal and of the Catalans gave fierce life to a popular, priest-led movement which swept Charles out of Madrid, which he had occupied the year before, and harassed his armies in retreat. In April 1707 the Jacobite, Berwick, James II's illegitimate son, won the battle of Almanza over Galway (the former Huguenot Ruvigny) and Spain was saved for Philip V. From then on the preservation of his grandson's kingdom became Louis's chief aim.

In 1707 Vendôme ceded nothing to Marlborough while Villars, the most resourceful of French generals, carried the 'lines of Stolhofen' and captured Heidelberg, Stuttgart and Mannheim. In 1708, however, the Whigs received endorsement at the general election and Marlborough was encouraged to press on with his plan for invading France. On 11 July, he shattered the army of Vendôme and the duke of Burgundy at Oudenaarde in an audacious running battle which opened the road to France. While he settled down to besiege Lille, the French army and court joined in a bitter quarrel about responsibility for the misconduct of the battle. Boufflers defended Lille with inspiring determination, aided by old Vauban who had designed its fortification and now lent his services as simple volunteer. The allies were made to pay dearly for the city which did not capitulate till December.

The year 1709 began with the ordeal of the great frost. Rivers froze, even the swift-flowing Rhône. The fruit trees and early sowings were caught, wolves roamed the countryside and it was said at court that 'the common people were dying of cold like flies'. The harvest of 1708 had been poor, that of 1709 was worse. In Picardy the price of bread quadrupled in the year. In August 1709 the *contrôleur-général*, Desmarets, Chamillart's successor, wrote to the king: 'For four months now not a week has passed without there being some seditious outbreak. Troops have been needed in nearly every province to keep them under control.' The most common form of disorder was the bread riot. Risings were apparently spontaneous and expressed the people's suffering. It is significant that they were not concerted and that they seem to have been without political motive or inspiration. But the stability of the regime could no longer be taken for granted. Famine and riot were reflected in the revenue figures. From 1700 to 1706 the total expenses were 1100 million, the ordinary revenues 350 million: the figures for 1708 to 1715 were 1914 and 461 respectively. In 1709 Desmarets despaired of collecting taxes at all for 'it would be imprudent to exact the ordinary taxes from men who lack bread'. He feared 'a total breakdown' and 'the most terrible uprisings'. 'To all these evils no remedy can be found but prompt peace.'

Pessimistic ministers who received the reports from the provinces were joined by those who had long been critical of the militarist tendency. At court a party was forming round Burgundy, Beauvillier and Chevreuse which argued for peace at any price. Old arguments about the state's role in the economy were revived. *Dévôts* saw the hand of God and retribution for blasphemous alliances and unwarranted aggression. Mme de Maintenon expressed their mood of pious contrition. 'Our king was too glorious, He wishes to humble him in order to save him. France was overgrown and perhaps unjustly; He wishes to confine it within narrower bounds and perhaps more solid.' From his frontier diocese Archbishop Fénelon wrote that considerations of honour and prestige should not stand in the way: 'It would be better to sacrifice Franche-Comté and the Three Bishoprics than to risk the whole of France again.' In the same spirit Burgundy, with whom lay the hopes of reformers, argued about the loss of Lille: 'has not the state subsisted for whole centuries without this town, and indeed without Arras or Cambrai?' To show that he was in earnest about peace Louis sent Torcy himself to treat with the allies in May 1709. As Marlborough and Eugène began the summer campaign which they hoped would bring them to Paris their masters drew up articles of peace that were not only harsh but unrealistic. The new barrier required by the Dutch was to include the French towns Lille and Tournai; the Emperor required Strasbourg; Spain was to go to Charles with all the rights he ought to have possessed by the will of Philip IV, so that the French were threatened by the loss of Franche-Comté, Artois and Rousillon. Louis was to enforce these terms on his grandson. Whatever the intention, a guarantee of Louis's good faith or a deliberate move to ensure that he rejected the terms, the result was that Louis resolved to fight on: 'since I have to make war, I would rather fight against my own enemies than against my own children'.

Heinsius and the other negotiators might have taken more note of the patriotic demonstrations in Spain and Philip V's determination to die sword in hand rather than abandon his heritage. Marlborough, his eyes on Paris, was like a master composer who feared lest he should be interrupted in the composition of the last movement of a symphony. The Austrians were typically rigid. Louis was to blame for the undoubted mistrust his efforts at negotiation inspired. From the start of the war he had used agents, including both neutrals and Dutchmen, in a way that suggested either that he wanted peace desperately or that he was trying simply to split the allies. He blundered in his first choice of Rouillé, a man known to be unacceptable to the Dutch. Now instead of leaving negotiations in the capable hands of Torcy he allowed Chamillart to supervise simultaneous negotiations. In 1709 Louis may not however have felt that he was the loser by all his efforts. He believed that he had a clear moral justification for war. The open letter which he caused to be read in all the churches suggests that he saw with a new clarity what would have been far from obvious to a man nurtured in the patrimonial idea of kingship, that he should ask Frenchmen to understand what had happened and to fight for their homeland. He was convinced that Frenchmen would scorn to receive peace 'on conditions so contrary to justice and to the honour of the French name'.

In Villars, commander of the last effective French army in the west, reinforced now by large numbers of militiamen, guarding Artois, Picardy and the flat open lands that lie between the frontier and the capital, Louis had the right general for the fateful time. Flamboyant and boastful in manner and words but cautious in action and keenly aware of his awesome responsibility, he nursed his strength, constructed the formidable trench system of La Bassée and resisted all Marlborough's inducements to battle. His supply problem was grim and his troops were allowed bread only on marching days. In camp they fasted but may still have reckoned themselves better off than the peasants at home. Ragged, hungry, angry men responded to Villars's warm style of leadership. After the fall of Tournai, reputed the strongest fortress in Europe, he edged forwards and dug in to fight a defensive battle. In and between the woods of Sars and La Lanière, throughout a September day, 220,000 men, slightly less than half of them

French, fought the furious battle of Malplaquet. Eventually Villars withdrew but in good order. Efficient use of fire power at close range, the firm discipline of infantry and cavalry, the confident expectations of success on the allied side met by the resolution of men who knew they were fighting for the *patrie*, the consequent failure of either side to achieve a breakthrough, account for the carnage of this battle, unsurpassed till Borodino in 1812. 'I hope in God it may be the last battle I may ever see ... I do not believe they have lost as many as we. None alive ever saw such a battle.' The words of Orkney, one of Marlborough's generals, presage the political storm to come. Marlborough went on to take Mons in October but Paris was saved. When peace negotiations were resumed at Gertruydensberg in March 1710, the Dutch and English were stiffer than ever. The Austrians were firm for the Archduke Charles's claim to the Spanish throne but they did not favour the idea of a united Netherlands. By their rancorous obstinacy in what their historian Geyl described as 'one of the most disastrous and truly humiliating episodes of all Dutch history', the Dutch exposed themselves to the political reaction in England and to the narrow dynasticism of the Habsburgs. The allies never again negotiated from strength and unity.

In 1710 Marlborough was unable to deliver the decisive victory that he and his political supporters required. Costly sieges gave him Douai, Béthune and Aire but not Arras, his main objective. He was no longer prepared to risk frontal assault on prepared entrenchments while Villars did not make the fatal mistake for which Marlborough manoeuvred. In 1711 however, operating without the support of Prince Eugène, he pierced the *ne plus ultra* lines in an operation of bluff and surprise, with a long night march, that was acclaimed as a masterpiece of the military art. But his political base had been destroyed. In the previous October the Tories, representing all those who were discontented with high taxes and continental campaigning, defeated the Whigs who were encumbered by their pledges to the Dutch and Austrians. Everywhere the great war had brought to the fore internal dissensions. The Emperor had found that the Hungarians were more loyal to their constitution than to their king: taxes brought revolt that lasted till 1711. Only purposeful negotiation and large concessions made possible the act of union between England and Scotland and neutralized the forces of disruption. Louis learned the cost of his anti-Huguenot measures when the Camisards revolted in 1702, but he gained from the separatism of the Catalans. It was Catalan support for the archduke Charles as much as positive loyalty to unimpressive Philip that roused the Castilians to such fervour for their legitimate Bourbon sovereign. The victories of Vendôme and Berwick, notably Brihuega and Villaviciosa in December 1710, gave weight to the political verdict. The allies had lost the war for Spain when in April 1711 the emperor Joseph died, to be succeeded by the archduke as Charles VI. Bolingbroke could then argue the absurdity of fighting to prevent one union of powers only to sanction another.

While England carried out a phased withdrawal from the war, French diplomats recovered the initiative. Marlborough had to make do with a smaller army. Supplies were reduced and Eugène was recalled to Germany to meet French attacks timed to coincide with the imperial election. In September, after his capture of Bouchain, Marlborough was again poised to drive into France. But in December he was recalled to face charges of misconduct. For Bolingbroke it was a necessary part of the operation of making a separate peace with France. For Louis, resilient in all his troubles, it brought relief and hope for a new diplomatic alignment: in his words, 'the affair of the duke of Marlborough will do all we desire'. Between January 1712, when plenipotentiaries met at Utrecht, and April 1713 when Heinsius finally agreed 'to drink the chalice of peace', terms were cobbled together which were far from humiliating to the French. The revelation of the secret preliminaries of the previous year between Bolingbroke's emissary Prior and Torcy left the Dutch with no option but to negotiate if they were not to be isolated. Bolingbroke chose to treat the formal proceedings of the congress, delayed as much by Louis's insistence upon compensation for his allies as by Dutch obduracy, as a façade behind which the real business was done in straight parley with Torcy. Louis experienced the sadness of successive deaths in the family: after the dauphin in 1711, Burgundy and his wife and eldest son in one week of August 1712, leaving only the duc de Berry (to die in 1713), Philip of Spain (on whose exclusion the allies insisted) and Burgundy's second son, a frail child of 2, to stand between him and his detested nephew, Philip of Orléans. His cause was assisted, however, by the passive role of the British general Ormonde, Marlborough's successor, whose orders not to engage in battle were communicated to the French. In July 1712 Villars won the bold victory of Denain, severed Eugène's communications, wrecked his invasion plans, then followed up his success by recapturing Douai, Quesnoy and Bouchain. It required further victories on the Rhine, and the capture of Freiburg in 1713 before the Emperor would resign himself to peace and let Eugène make terms. Eventually, in March 1714, at Rastadt, significantly in French and not the customary Latin of diplomatic usage, the last treaty was made and peace restored to western Europe.

Louis had gone to war to defend legitimacy: in particular the rights of James Edward and of his grandson to the Spanish throne. He was compelled to abandon James and to recognize Anne. But Philip was confirmed as king: he stood secure in the approbation of his subjects, and their discomfiture. Separatist Catalans were confounded, and the central administration under the supervision of French advisers was stronger than it had ever been. Though for the present there was resentment in Madrid about the way in which the Empire was being dismembered, there was a prospect of future co-operation: it was to be fulfilled in the 'family compact'. France and Spain were to have one common interest from the outset, in opposing the extension of British sea power into the Mediterranean: for the British gained Gibraltar and Minorca. The acquisition by the Emperor of Naples and most of the Milanese and Sardinia (in 1720 exchanged with Savoy for Sicily) provided another motive for Bourbon counter-aggression in the future. The Emperor also secured the Spanish Netherlands where the Dutch were given their barrier of fortresses, but Lille remained to France, as did Strasbourg. A limit had been set to France's advance. In the words of Ranke she had not gained sovereignty over the world but was still the greatest power on the continent. It was a position that was consolidated under the moderate regimes of Dubois and Fleury and might have been maintained had not subsequent ministers succumbed to the lure of war in the fateful middle years of the century when France 'consulted her traditions rather than her interests'.

Alternative Voices

In 1684 Racine had told the Académie that Louis's enemies were 'forced to accept his law without having been able, for all their efforts, to move an inch beyond the close circle that he had traced around them'. *Contrôleur-général* Le Peletier, Colbert's successor, looked forward to a long peace, to reordering the finances, 'to taking sound measures concerning the Spanish succession, and to bringing to an end the excessive hostilities aroused by the enterprises of M. de Louvois'. But Le Pelletier did not have the authority of Colbert, whose death in 1683 left the ministerial body unbalanced. Louvois, the war minister, was allowed by Louis XIV to exert excessive influence on decisions, which he knew how to dress up so as to please the king. Louis was satisfied with his mastery of the little worlds of court and council where everything seemed to be working so well. It was the political and spiritual milieu in which the revocation of the edict of Nantes could appear to be an act of piety and of statesmanship. In 1685 Lamoignon, *premier président* and an author of the legal codes that represented royal government at its most constructive and enlightened, rejoiced before *parlement* that Louis had done 'in a single year what others have been unable to do in a whole century'. The first results of military aggression appeared to justify such confidence. When, however, checks were followed by defeats, debts mounted and credit waned, and when the mood of religious exhortation gave way to one of disillusion and recrimination, the king's policies appeared in a less favourable light. In 1689 France was at war again, against a determined coalition directed by a bitter enemy, William of Orange, now king of England. In 1693, before a French army had been defeated and before the worst of the famines of which Voltaire was to write that 'men perished of misery to the sound of *Te Deum*', Mme de Maintenon wrote, concerning moves to persuade the king of Sweden to mediate: 'the King will bring about peace as soon as he can, and wishes it as truly as we do'.

Later, in 1697, at the peace of Ryswick, Louis made unpopular concessions, not because his armies had been defeated but because his coffers were empty. In 1701 hostilities were resumed as Louis set himself to defend the Spanish inheritance of his grandson, Philip of Anjou. He was reluctant from the start; after 1708 he was desperate for peace. The war lasted till 1714: it was prolonged and intensive beyond all previous experience, and it was calamitous. Long before the end of his reign, when he is said to have confessed to 'loving war too much', Louis understood that war had imposed an excessive burden on his people. In years of victory, that may not have been apparent at Versailles. But when courtiers who walked about the state rooms, like the *salon de Mars*, an explicit celebration in paint and plaster of the glories of war and of the king, heard of Blenheim, Turin and Ramillies, defeat, surrender and rout, disillusion spread like dry rot. One reaction was to blame the generals, Villeroi, Tallard, Marsin, even Vendôme; another to criticize palace control which allegedly inhibited the commanders in the field; another to point to the excessive power in the hands of ministers, notably the unfortunate Chamillart, who for a time combined responsibility for both finance and war. After Ramillies (1706) it seems that Chamillart himself lost heart; but he was not relieved in his post till 1709. The ageing king wanted familiar faces about him.

The gossip among cliques began to acquire political overtones. Thoughts about the succession of the dauphin concentrated the minds of his circle, 'the cabal of Meudon'; the undoubted immorality and alleged ambition of Orléans caused some alarm. The idea that the royal bastards should be legitimized, as a further line of defence against the accession of Orléans, was mooted; more strongly after the death of Burgundy in 1712, a year after that of the dauphin, had brought nearer the possibility of an Orléans succession. That did not deter Saint-Simon, in whose *Mémoirs* can be found a yearning and a programme for the revival of aristocratic power: first Burgundy, then Orléans was to be its promoter. Tireless chronicler of court affairs, Saint-Simon brought consummate skill to the compiling of his saga of manners and manoeuvres. But the qualities that made him a great artist were precisely those that made him an unreliable judge of state affairs. He was well placed to describe alterations in the location of power and in the values of society, but his own privileged position in the hierarchy and his prejudiced cast of mind prevented him from seeing beyond factions to the deeper stresses within society. Very different was the case of the veteran marshal Vauban. When he put his experience of surveying and statistics to use in his comprehensive study of the realm, *Dîme royale*, he estimated that prices had fallen by about a third in the second half of the century. Copies of the book were printed in 1707, and distributed only among friends, but it was still banned and the author disgraced. Characteristically he went to serve as a volunteer under Boufflers, defending Lille.

Saint-Simon's was a secret voice, Vauban's a lonely one. If not exactly outsiders, they were somewhat isolated figures. But in the person of the young duke of Burgundy, disillusion touched the heart of the regime. Burgundy was 29 when his father's death, in 1711, made him heir to the throne. He had been given a secluded, intensive education under the duc de Beauvillier, high-minded and devout, subsequently the one nobleman to be accepted by the council, and Fénelon, another nobleman who remained his friend and mentor. François de Salignac de la Mothe-Fénelon (1651–1715), *abbé*, future archbishop of Cambrai, brought a rare sensibility to the task of educating a prince who might be king. The combination in him of spirituality and political awareness was exceptional, though recognizably in the *dévôt* tradition of those who in earlier generations had opposed the growth of royal power and the militant secular trend in foreign policy. Undoubtedly Fénelon saw the young prince as a means of putting into effect his ideas about state and society. In a fine passage in his *Dialogue des morts* he summarized his own view of the obligations of subjects: 'each individual owes incomparably more to the human race, which is the great fatherland, than to the particular country into which he is born'.

After the battle of Oudenaarde (1708), where he was co-commander, Burgundy adopted an open pacifism, reflecting that of Fénelon, by then in disgrace and exile in his frontier diocese. The mood was defeatist but there was a positive side to the thinking of Burgundy and his circle and it was more than the untimely suddenness of his death that made his friend Saint-Simon lament the occasion so eloquently: 'He seemed to have been born for the happiness of France and Europe.' Now 'in his death France suffered her final chastisement, for God showed her the prince she did not deserve'. He wrote to Beauvillier: 'You have come to bury the future.' With Burgundy faded the vision of an alternative form of government, so attractive to those who felt that they were excluded from their rightful place in government as well as to *parlementaires* who were uneasy about the increasingly arbitrary tendency of government. Should it be taken seriously? In *Télémaque*, which described the republic of Salente, where the population was engaged in farming, and the ruler, renouncing war, sought ways to increase the wealth of the land, readers could see a studied rebuke to the king. In Mentor's description of kings who 'recognize no laws other than their absolute wills' Louis might recognize himself and also the frustrations of his position: 'They can do everything, but by the extent to which they use their power they sap the foundations of that power.' Fénelon urged a policy attuned both to the aristocratic ideal and to the economic needs of France. The *Tables de Chaulnes*, drawn up for Burgundy, with the duc de Chevreuse, in 1711, when it was expected that Burgundy might become king, reveal the explicit intention of the author to destroy absolutism and the administrative machinery on which it rested – and which it supported. Nearly every reform was aimed at the restoration of the power of the *noblesse* and the upper clergy. Fénelon's view of the role of aristocracy in government was indeed a triumph of hope over experience. His view of the French economy was oversimplified to the point of naivety, though it was to reappear, in more developed form, in the arguments of the physiocrats. His programme was never fairly tested. The experience of the *polysynodie* suggests that the mechanism of government would have remained essentially the same under whatever superstructure of noble councils was erected. It is likely that Burgundy would have been conscientious and dutiful as king. It is possible that he would have had the strength to have risen above the lobbying of ministers and to have resisted the kind of pressures for war to which Louis XV yielded. It is easy to believe that he would have been a better king than Louis XV, but harder to see how he would have effected the radical changes in government that were required if the regime were to be permanently strengthened.

It was the distressing famines which followed the bad harvests of 1691–4 that had prompted Fénelon's famous letter of 1694, addressed to Mme de Maintenon, but undoubtedly meant for the king, 'like a man with a bandage over his eyes', and for ministers whom he accused of misleading the king and sacrificing everything to the royal authority; that at a time when 'your peoples are dying of famine. . . . all France is no more than a huge hospital, desolated and without provision. . . , there is sedition in all parts'. He was specific: 'You have destroyed part of the real resources within the country in order to defend empty conquests outside it.' The charge was justified by evidence of falling tax returns which compelled the government to introduce the *capitation* (1695), the first graduated tax on all classes. Again, in the latter half of the War of the Spanish Succession the demands of the tax collector weighed on the peasant producer so intolerably that many defaulted and some starved. Deficits mounted to the point at which the volume of debt threatened the stability of the regime, imposing a crippling burden for the future. In 1680 Colbert had been concerned about a deficit of 13 million *livres*. From 1708 to 1715, expenditure amounted to 1914 million, revenue to 461. The tax farms, which accurately reflect the economic conditions of the country and which brought in 66 million *livres* in an average Colbert budget, were down by 1715 to 47 million. Pontchartrain, Chamillart and Desmarets, successively *contrôleurs-généraux*, had recourse to expedients old and new: lotteries, the sale of offices and titles, the depreciation of coinage. To favour its own transactions the crown manipulated the exchange rate of the *louis d'or*. Loans could only be raised by offering high rates of interest, thus increasing the levy on next year's income, which could lead to bankruptcy.

As the state's credit declined, the role of the private banker or syndicate became more crucial. Government, never completely independent of the financial interest, now had to come to terms with the new plutocrats in a relationship of mutual dependence which was to last, in various forms, to the Revolution. The brothers Paris, sons of an innkeeper, pledged their private credit to supply the army for the campaign which culminated in the battle of Malplaquet (1709). Samuel Bernard made a fortune estimated at 60 million *livres* from grain dealings, munitions supply and exchange transactions. When he became bankrupt in 1709 he had to be propped up by the state, whose credit was inseparable from his own; he survived to make another fortune. At the height of the famine of that year after the severest winter of the century, Desmarets despaired of raising taxes at all for 'it would be imprudent to exact the ordinary taxes from men who lack bread'. In the following year the *dixième* was imposed, a more radical and punitive tax than the *capitation* which had first established the principle that a noble could pay direct tax. Desmarets was prepared to think flexibly and the crisis empowered him to act boldly. Like Pontchartrain, another minister of outstanding expertise and ingenuity, his work indicates what France's future might have been if a more moderate direction in earlier years had not created a situation of permanent emergency in which policy amounted to a series of reflexes to pressing demands for cash to pay the troops.

The French countryside had seen fearsome popular revolts, when peasant bands had ranged about, pillaging and killing, principally tax officials. The revolts of the Croquants (1636–7), the *Nu-pieds* of Normandy (1639) and the Bretons (1675), all in one way or another directed against the government and its taxes, had required an army to restore order. The eighteenth century saw no concerted revolts on the same scale, though there was widespread disorder. In the province of Quercy in the south-west in 1709, the *intendant* reported that there were 30,000 men under arms, Cahors was besieged for ten days, he himself was held by a detachment in his coach and 'escaped only by a miracle'. He knew the authors of the trouble but they are 'so many that it would be dangerous to make an example of them'. But the disorders of the eighteenth century did not show the same tendency of local officials and gentry to support the cause of the province. It is the stability of the regime even in the worst conditions that is impressive. There was no question, as in the 1630s, of the complicity of great magnates. In some measure it was due to the consolidation of royal government, the extension of its powers, the efficiency of the *intendants* and their *subdélégués*. It shows the extent to which Louis had secured the committed support of the majority of the privileged classes. It was in part a matter of patronage and employment, the continuing allure of the court, the size of the army. The king's own example also counted for much.

Louis was stoical in the face of calamities, and personal bereavement. Between 1711 and 1714, four heirs to his throne died; not to mention the much loved duchess of Burgundy. Since Philip of Anjou was debarred, having become king of Spain, only the little great grandson, the future Louis

XV was left, destined, like Louis XIV, to succeed to the throne at the age of 5. Much then depended on Louis, on his steady support of his ministers, his refusal to lose his nerve. To what extent did the unchanging routine of Versailles mask greater discontents? How firm was the absolutist consensus? It appears that the Burgundy–Fénelon circle was limited and to some extent discredited by the suggestion of eccentricity. Fénelon's quixotic support of Mme de Guyon and of quietism[1] gave his critics a stick to beat him with. Pacifism, moreover, required a degree of moral courage; it also ensured that there would be general disapproval. In another area of government there was a revolt against existing policies which did achieve a significant change.

In 1701, deputies of leading commercial towns criticized the government's protectionist policy before the *conseil de commerce*. They argued that agriculture had been sacrificed to manufactures, that too much had been conceded to monopolies, that the privileges given to particular companies had affected the spirit of enterprise; that the principle of the favourable balance had been adhered to too rigidly and that trade relations with other countries had suffered accordingly. The deputy from Languedoc declared that France must abandon the doctrine of Colbert that France could surpass the world in and by her trade. Such men represented local interests; they could not be expected to appreciate the wider issues and needs of the state. They had been injured by the government's efforts to secure control over the municipalities, where the expansion of the *intendant*'s role and the conversion of elected, municipal offices into hereditary, venal ones was destroying the vestiges of civic independence. They tested Colbert's policies by the evidence of their balance sheets. They were representative of a widespread revolt against Colbertism among the business community. Looking forward to a larger freedom of trade, they anticipated the arguments of the physiocrats of the eighteenth century. Before the end of the reign ministers began to make significant concessions. Freedom of trading was restored to certain ports, Marseille and Bordeaux among them. In 1712, Desmarets, Colbert's great-nephew, showed how far he had departed from Colbertism when he wrote to the head of the trade mission to England, that he did not fear free trade: 'My opinion is that the more facilities we give to foreigners to send their goods to us the more we will be able to sell of our own.' In that spirit the government made a commercial treaty with the Dutch; only the opposition of Whig merchants in London prevented a similar treaty with England; it was left to the Whig ministry to make one after the Hanoverian succession. Of course merchants were unfair in ascribing France's economic difficulties to Colbert's policies alone: they had been conceived in response to a severe monetary famine which would have been more acute without his measures. He and his successors had to meet the bills of war out of resources reduced by years of recession. Indeed the fact that merchants were able to think hopefully of the advantages that

[1] See also pp. 105–7.

would accrue from freedom of trade witnesses to the success of some of his efforts. But since Colbertism was an integral part of the growth in state power, such an onslaught upon its principles contributed to the general crisis of confidence.

The Cost of Conformity

Another important element in absolutist theory was represented by the drive for religious conformity which culminated in the revocation of the edict of Nantes.[1] The emigration of at least 200,000 Huguenots did material damage to the economy. The loss of capital and of men skilled in finance and business was even more serious than that of craftsmen. Abraham Valery of Languedoc was able to set up a factory as soon as he arrived in Halle. One Paris merchant took 600,000 *livres* with him to Holland. Ministers were aware of the potential damage. Writing to his brother, archbishop of Rheims, of his delight in hearing that 'all is Catholic' in the provinces of the Saintonge and Angoumois, Louvois added: 'His Majesty recommends that you be accommodating to the bankers and manufacturers.' Harder to assess, more insidious, is the effect upon opinion. 'My realm is being purged of bad and troublesome subjects,' wrote the king. For that imagined benefit, Louis paid a high price. It became easier for the Emperor to rally the uncommitted German states behind him. It became harder for the Catholic James II of England to help his co-religionists without rousing Protestant suspicion: the revocation contributed to his downfall and the coup of William of Orange, so unfortunate for France. Even the Pope was embarrassed by the action of a king who was still defying him over the question of Gallican rights and the appointment of bishops. Huguenots in exile were effective propagandists. The French censors were unable to prevent pamphlets and journals flooding in from the presses of Holland and Germany. Jurieu's *Pastorales* encouraged Huguenots to look forward to the end of the reign of Antichrist and the triumph of the true church. Bayle wrote: 'if people only knew the force and present significance of the expression, no one would envy France the distinction of "being wholly Catholic" under Louis the Great. The Roman church is nothing but a fury and a whore.' Besides the survival of a determined remnant in France, the harsh measures taken to overcome their resistance sowed doubts in the minds of devout Catholics. In letters of February 1686 to Louvois, published by Jurieu as evidence from within the French Catholic establishment, Montgaillard, Bishop of St Pons, exposed orders to drive all without exception to the altar, 'even those who spit and trample upon the Eucharist'. With Jansenists openly critical of Jesuit methods, in particular their apparently light use of the sacraments as a test of conversion, the dangerous feud between Jansenists and Jesuits was reanimated. As each party criticized

[1] See also pp. 109–17 for analysis of the causes of the revocation.

the methods of the other, it only made it worse that the crown came down so heavily on the Jesuit side and was drawn into a policy of persecution which was to have serious consequences. Catholic laymen began to express their doubts more openly. Vauban was characteristically blunt: 'Kings are master of the lives and goods of their subjects but never of their opinions.'

In his *Histoires des variations* Bossuet had sought to prove that the Protestant tendency to schism illustrated the essential weakness of any departure from revealed immutable truth. Now the Catholic ideal was discredited by the imposition of that truth by force upon a defenceless minority. Rome's critics could show that the Catholics too had their 'variations'. Revocation was an act of faith but it was also an act of state, and rejection of the idea led naturally to rejection of the authority behind it. In one remote area, the Cevennes, the hard line of local priests and officials provoked open revolt. The Camisards, so called because of their white shirts, went on to resist with such fanaticism that it took an army and one of France's most capable soldiers, Marshal Villars, three years (1702–5) to put down their revolt, and that not before the king had ordered the destruction of most of their villages. The prophesyings and ecstasies of those zealots, under their young leader Jean Cavalier, have their own place in the history of religious enthusiasm. More important in the long term was the stirring in the intellectual world of liberal ideas about the nature of political authority. The coincidence of the Huguenot dispersion and the English revolution (1688–9) gave rise to renewed speculation about the nature of faith and of sovereignty.

A few years before, leading Huguenots had loyally bowed before the absolute authority of the king, like the pastor Merlat who, in 1685, had declared that 'sovereigns have no other law but their will'. Now the *avant-garde* was coming to accept the idea that the people had a sovereign power and that the prince was merely a delegate. The royal authority in France was not to be overturned so readily or limited so severely as that of England. But after 1685 royal authority had need of other sanctions besides those of God and of the traditions that enshrined the majesty of the 'Very Christian King'. The philosophy of divine right was impaired, never to recover its hold. In the eighteenth century the alliance of Church and king was to be of little benefit to either party. Habits of loyalty did not change overnight. The French were still disposed to love their king. There lacked the representative body which might have provided the mechanism for constitutional resistance. Since Louis had assumed personal rule, *parlement* had registered every edict that came to them. But perversely, while the Huguenot policy was clearly failing, the government renewed the attack on Jansenism and so roused the latent spirit of defiance in the only body which could claim a share in sovereignty.

Since the 'peace of the Church' (1669) Jansenism[1] had spread, mainly

[1] See also pp. 101–5.

through the influence of Oratorians and the seminaries in which they taught, into the parishes of France. Even before the dispersal of the pitiful remnant of the nuns of Port Royal in 1709, it had so ramified that it could no longer be properly called a movement, let alone a party; the several distinct interests and attitudes only found a common focus in recurring conflicts, provoked by Jansenist enthusiasts or by their critics: by the Jesuits, over-zealous clerics like Christophe de Beaumont, archbishop of Paris. Richer, an early seventeenth-century theologian, whose radical views on Church authority were now revived by defenders of the rights of the lower clergy against bishops, had been passionately anti-Jesuit and that remained a lively prejudice in *parlement*. Critics of the Jesuits took heart from the Pope's repudiation of the Jesuit missionaries in China, accused by their enemies of condoning pagan rites. The renewal of the struggle should not be attributed solely to Louis's concern about the potentially treasonous character of Jansenism. The appointment of Cardinal Noailles, a known sympathizer, to be archbishop of Paris in 1695, was treated by the more militant Jansenists as a signal to take the offensive. When Quesnel was arrested in 1703 his correspondence revealed the existence of a web of sympathizers, throughout France, but also in Rome. Jesuits were not alone in fearing that Jansenism under such guides as Quesnel would become a limb of Protestantism, no less dangerous because within the Church. In 1705 the bull *Vineam Domini* confirmed the rigorist position and opened the way for the strict enforcement of a formulary which the nuns could not sign. Père Le Tellier, the king's confessor, was not satisfied with the destruction of Port Royal but pressed for a comprehensive bull. It is the point at which both Louis and the Pope would have done well to call a halt. For the Pope, and the Church, whose wider interests had already been damaged by Louis XIV's intransigence, the bull *Unigenitus*, which condemned 101 propositions extracted from Quesnel's book, was a fateful error. The character of Jansenism, the awful logic of predestination, its perfectionism, might have been expected to limit its appeal to an élite, like orthodox Calvinists, self-sufficient rather than missionary. But the bull defined as heretical a large area of Christian belief to which many subscribed who would not have called themselves Jansenists but who were now forced to take sides. It sought to clarify, beyond dispute, what might best have been left undefined. The educated layman was told that he must leave study of the Scriptures to the priest; must simply obey without question. The timing could not have been worse. For it was not only in the political sphere that men were starting to ask fundamental questions. Were they now to be deprived of the freedom of interpretation which went with the spirit, inherent in Jansenism, but not confined to it, of individual devotion? Through what became a bitter schism the impact and inspiration of the *dévôt* movement was weakened. Fénelon, protector of Mme Guyon, and Quesnel, heirs in their different ways and insights to the Bérullian tradition of Christ-centred devotion, became opponents just when they might have made common cause against materialism. The public quarrels of the godly further exposed the church to the gibes of its enemies, whether Huguenots or sceptics. It damaged the fragile unity that had once been described by Fénelon as 'the sacred bond which alone can hold the allegiance of souls, our heart-felt aspiration'.

Louis XIV's commitment to the Jesuit side helped to focus attention on other aspects of his government which caused disquiet. He could achieve his end only with *parlement*'s co-operation, but it was precisely there that concern about arbitrary trends in government could now be voiced: with the righteous indignation of men who believed that they stood for something more important than their own interests, the guardians of the fundamental laws could denounce the king's abandonment of those Gallican principles which, when it had suited him, as in 1682, through the bishops in the Church Assembly he had so stoutly affirmed. Jansenists aroused public sympathy because it seemed that they were being bullied. The argument proceeded along traditional lines but before a wider audience of literate Frenchmen, not merely Parisians now, many of them critical of the government, and some evidently aware of the political implications of the debate. *Parlement*'s position was that of the king in the 1680s: there was no ecclesiastical exception to the authority of the king, who 'depended on God and recognized no power above him' and who was, therefore, sovereign over the church which was, in its secular character, part of the royal estate. The claim which had been so powerful a weapon against the Pope, which was such an important element in the absolutist's notion of sovereignty, now became, by supreme irony the means through which *parlement*, defying the crown, earned public applause while asserting its constitutional rights. So the king's maladroit handling of the Jansenist affair led to the most powerful challenge of his reign – and he died before the issue was resolved: by then it had contributed significantly to the general crisis of authority. It had always been an important element in acceptance of the king's absolutism, to the point of adulation but not of mindless surrender, that his rule was not arbitrary, but exercised within a framework of fundamental law and accepted custom. The idea of the king cherished by so many subjects, a unifying force in a country which lacked organic unity, was that of a protector impartial and judicious. It was in that spirit that Louis appealed to his subjects in 1709 as Marlborough manoeuvred in Artois and planned to march on Paris. In an open letter to be read aloud in churches by the priest, he had confided his cause to his people:

> Although my affection is no less than I feel for my own children, although I share all the sufferings inflicted by war upon my faithful subjects, and have plainly shown all Europe that I wish sincerely that they should enjoy peace, I am convinced that they themselves would scorn to receive it on conditions so contrary to justice and to the honour of the French name.

Either his instincts were sound or he had been well advised. If it had all been so earlier he might not have had to make such an appeal.

The king had guaranteed acceptance of *Unigenitus*, as part of his deal with the Pope, contrary to the letter and spirit of the Gallican Articles which had stipulated that the Pope's judgement in matters of faith was mandatory only when it was unanimously backed by the French clergy. Even from a council of bishops, deliberately chosen from less than half of the episcopate, Louis could not secure this unanimity. So Jansenist sympathizers, led by Noailles, formed an alliance with the chief law officers, d'Aguesseau, a future chancellor, and Joly de Fleury, who affirmed that the king must have unanimous consent if the bull was to become the law of the church: till such time it could not be registered as the law of the land. In February 1714 the king sent the bull for registration. In the stormy debate that ensued old Gallican prejudices had a full airing. Particularly obnoxious was that clause in the bull in which the Pope claimed the right to excommunicate the French king and free his subjects from their oath of obedience. For the first time since the prohibition of 1673, the lawyers insisted upon the right to issue remonstrances. Controversy flourished in the discontented state of society, in a capital uneasily aware that another minority was soon to begin. There was talk of a general council, even of schism. D'Aguesseau denounced the 'idol of Roman grandeur' and saluted Noailles as 'the man of the nation'. It was heady stuff and in a society which lacked a forum for overtly political debate, material for the politically minded. *Parlement* could now see itself as the bulwark against arbitrary government.

Ailing, exasperated, Louis betrayed the strain. D'Aguesseau had been urged by his wife to face imprisonment rather than give in to Louis; Louis reminded him that they were not far from the Bastille, and shouted that if *parlement* resisted he would 'make them crawl on their bellies'. Louis, who had shown such dexterity in using Gallican sentiment to gain his political ends, but had then turned ultramontane to show himself a good Catholic, was trapped between the two most powerful forces in the world of ecclesiastical politics. Perhaps he understood that Jansenism was stirring up the underground opposition that he had so long needlessly feared. Associating itself with the idea of a national church, *parlement* threatened king and pope alike. Not surprisingly Louis wavered. In July, he projected a national council which should obtain the submission of Noailles and the clergy. He was a dying man, the extraordinarily tough physique was breaking up at last. The political stability of the reign (expressed by his own controlled, masterful personality) had been based, if not on the reconciliation of opposites, at least on a balance between particular interests, with the entrenched corporate bodies that represented them, and the crown, which had to take a wider view of its responsibilities to the people. Was this regime now breaking up, together with the man, so self-controlled and masterful, who had so long embodied it? The answer was to lie in the experience of the regency: necessitated by the third successive royal minority, it turned out to be different from the previous two and from what might have been expected by the more radical *parlementaires* or the more critical of courtiers and clerics.

Further Reading

Seventeenth century France, like England in the same period, may prove daunting to the student when he is confronted by the volume of material and variety of interpretation. In this bibliography I mention only a handful of books and articles which may prove most useful – and accessible. A longer bibliography will be found in my book, *Seventeenth Century France* (2nd edn, London, 1981). Another, skilfully succinct, introduction to French history in this period, is R. Briggs, *Early Modern France, 1560–1715* (Oxford, 1977). The two relevant chapters in the *New Cambridge Modern History* are J. Lough, 'France under Louis XIV' (vol. 5), and J. Meuvret, 'The condition of France, 1688–1715' (vol. 6). Useful collections of documents include: O. and P. Ranum, *The Century of Louis XIV* (London, 1972), and R.C. Mettam, *Government and Society in Louis XIV's France* (London, 1977), which is invaluable for Colbert. C.W. Cole, *Colbert and a Century of French Mercantilism* (2 vols, London, 1965), is still the best full study of the great minister. J.H. Shennan, *Government and Society in France, 1461–1661* (London, 1969), though mainly concerned with an earlier period, has a helpful introduction.

Mazarin still awaits his biographer, though there is no lack of writing about the Fronde, and his early life at least is well covered by G. Dethan, *The Young Mazarin* (London, 1977). For government during the whole period of the cardinals see R.J. Bonney, *Political Change under Richelieu and Mazarin, 1624–61* (Oxford, 1978). The same author's article, 'The French Civil War, 1649–53', in *European Studies Review*, 8 (1978), provides some correctives to A.L. Moore's *The Revolt of the Judges* (Princeton, 1971), which, with E. Kossman, *The Fronde* (Leyden, 1954), provides the best account of the Fronde. But see also R.J. Knecht's Historical Association pamphlet, *The Fronde* (1975).

There are a number of lives of Louis XIV, most unbalanced by excessive emphasis on the court. Ragnhild Hatton's bibliographical essay in the *Journal of Modern History*, 45 (1973), offers a valuable survey of 'recent gains in historical knowledge'. J.B. Wolf's *Louis XIV* (London, 1968) is solid and authoritative. P. Goubert, *Louis XIV and Twenty Million Frenchmen* (London, 1970), offers a more balanced picture of the reign while Ragnhild Hatton's *Louis XIV and his World* (London, 1972) is a stimulating essay within a brief compass. The same writer has edited two valuable volumes of essays, *Louis XIV and Absolutism* (London, 1976) and *Louis XIV and Europe* (London, 1976), which touch on most aspects of the period. The student would be unwise to proceed far in the study of Louis XIV's foreign policy, for example, without consulting the latter. An insight into Louis XIV's character and values can be gained from his *Mémoires for the Instruction of the Dauphin*, ed. P. Sonnino (New York, 1970). For the years 1680–1715 see R. Hatton and J.S. Bromley (eds), *William III and Louis XIV* (Liverpool, 1966), *Essays by and for M.A. Thomson* (1968), and G.N. Clark, 'The character of the Nine Years War', in *Cambridge Historical Journal*, 11 (1954). For absolutism, see also the notes after chapter 5. In the context of Louis XIV, however, David Parker's

The Making of French Absolutism (London, 1983) should be mentioned. There are some illuminating articles in J.C. Rule (ed.), *Louis XIV and the Craft of Kingship* (1974). Other articles in R.F. Kierstead, *State and Society in Seventeenth Century France* (New York, 1975), like Leon Bernard's on 'French society and popular uprisings', illuminate some forms of resistance to the regime. R. Mousnier, *Peasant Uprisings in Seventeenth Century France, Russia and China* (London, 1971), contains a study of the Breton revolt of 1675. For a more general view of society, see P. Goubert, *Ancien Régime, 1600–1750* (trans. A. Cox, London, 1973). For his work and that of Ladurie and Braudel, see also the bibliographical note after chapter 1. While some of the finest French historical writing has been devoted to regional studies, a characteristic of the best of them, like Ladurie's on Languedoc and Goubert's on the Beauvaisis, is the way they throw light on the history of the country as a whole. Two other good examples of the genre are G. Roupnel, *La Ville et la campagne au 17e siècle* (1922), about Dijon; and P. Deyon, *Amiens, capitale provinciale* (1967).

For cultural aspects of the reign, D. Maland, *Culture and Society in 17th Century France* (London, 1970), is valuable; J. Lough's *Introduction to 17th Century France* (1954) uses texts aptly to illustrate the social and literary life of the period; there are also sound political summaries. J. Klaits, *Printed Propaganda under Louis XIV* (Princeton, 1976), is an important contribution to an understanding of the later years of Louis XIV's reign, as, in a more wide-ranging way, is L. Rothkrug, *Opposition to Louis XIV* (Princeton, 1965).

For religious questions see also chapter 3. Mention should be made here, however, of the outstanding book on the revocation, J. Orcibal, *Louis XIV et les Protestants* (1951), and, for its consequences, G.H. Dodge, *The Political Theory of the Huguenots of the Dispersion* (1947), and W.C. Scoville, *The Persecution of the Huguenots and French Economic Development, 1680–1720* (1960). For the Jansenists, a good, concise survey is that of L. Cognet, *Le Jansenisme* (1961). A good introduction to Fénelon is through his *Selected Letters*, ed. J. McEwen (1964), which has helpful introductory essays. *Louis XIV's View of the Papacy* by P. Sonnino (Berkeley, 1966) is a sound introduction to the Gallican question.

8

LOUIS XV

The Regency

Louis XIV died on 1 September 1715, leaving a child of 5 to succeed; it was the age at which he had come to the throne seventy-two years before: ironic coincidence, some might have thought, even ominous. Previous royal minorities, those of Charles IX and Louis XIII, his own, had been blighted by civil war. It is possible to speak of a consensus in the political nation till 1700, if not beyond. By 1715, at least on the surface, this had gone; in its stead were the murmurs and intrigues of discontented parties. There was a powerful, general desire among influential courtiers for relaxation of the strict surveillance of manners: the *dévôts* were isolated, on the defensive. Politically, the main thrust came from those who wanted a shift in the balance of power, with more weight in council and with executive posts going to the king's traditional advisers, who had been deliberately excluded in favour of the professional administrators, close-knit groups, several belonging to the dynasties established by Colbert and Le Tellier. Orléans was known to be sympathetic to such views. But his position was threatened from several quarters. Men such as Torcy, Colbert's nephew and Louis XIV's foreign minister, had unrivalled experience. The leading luminaries of 'the old court', men like Harcourt and Villeroi, would not readily accept any abrupt break with their king's regime. The dukes of Maine and Toulouse, legitimized by the king's controversial edict of 1714, expected their special position to be respected by the new regime: the former had been appointed by the king's will to be guardian of the young Louis. Many favoured the king of Spain, though he was debarred by the terms of the peace of Utrecht, for the succession to the French throne, in the event of Louis XV's dying young. That ensured that the succession question would not merely be a domestic question but a vital concern of diplomats. Altogether the situation was both complicated and hazardous. But there was to be no civil war. That in itself says much about what had occurred during Louis XIV's reign: the balance did indeed tilt, but only slightly. It also says something about Louis XIV's nephew Philip of Orléans. Some of the difficulties that he faced at the outset were of his own making and reflected justifiable mistrust of his character. The relatively sound position that he bequeathed to the king eight years later was equally a tribute to his resourcefulness and realism.

At Louis XIV's death Orléans bid skilfully for the support of *parlement* as the price for his release from the constrictions of Louis XIV's intended council of regency. Louis had stipulated that decisions were to be taken by vote of the majority, without which Orléans was not to act. At the crucial meeting of *parlement*, peers and princes of the blood, on the day after Louis XIV's death, soldiers ringed the Palais de Justice to prevent a counter-stroke by the duc de Maine. Inside he claimed office by right of birth in accord with laws and precedents. He had already promised to carefully chosen notables posts in the councils which were to be the instruments of aristocratic participation in government. Villars was to be president of the war council, Noailles of the finance council; the latter's brother, the archbishop of Paris, was also secured for the cause: a key figure, given the Jansenist temper of the capital. *Parlement* leaders like Joly de Fleury were already apprised of Orléans's intention of ruling 'assisted chiefly by your counsel and wise remonstrances'. Even without the cordon of troops round the Palais it is unlikely that *parlement* would have denied him the title of regent, freedom to appoint to high offices, to nominate the members of the regency council and to keep the household troops under his direct command, which altogether effectively annulled the dead king's provisions. So from the outset his power rested on the approval and co-operation of the magistrates and the participation of the aristocracy in the system of government that came to be known as the *polysynodie*. It was a bloodless coup, in political terms a reaction rather than a revolution.

Forty-one years old in 1715, his purple face witnessing to the heavy drinking that was already undermining his strength, a myopic squint lending an air of genial cunning, Philip, duke of Orléans was the son of Louis XIV's younger brother. Like his father, who had performed notably well at the battle of Cassel, then been denied further command, and who had adopted an effeminate dandyism perhaps in conscious parody of the royal style, Philip found that prowess as a soldier did not endear him to the royal family. As a young man, in Flanders, in titular command in Italy and Spain in 1706–7, he had shown the courage and understanding of tactics that might have made him a great soldier. In other ways too he was almost embarrassingly talented. Skilfully taught by Abbé Dubois, who founded his own brilliant career on the relationship of the schoolroom, he enjoyed philosophical questions and could hold his own in arguments about theology with Fénelon. He was a discriminating collector of paintings and patron of poets, notably Fontenelle. He loved music and composed at least two operas. He was a particularly keen amateur chemist and fitted up a laboratory for the Dutchman Wilhelm Homburg; there they made the experiments that aroused gossip at the time of the royal deaths in 1712. He provided further ammunition to his enemies by his avowed scepticism, his preference for Paris, with its informal ways and uninhibited demimondaines, to the ceremonious life of Versailles. When he emerged as a possible regent, a provocative style matured into a serious prospectus for an alternative system of government as Saint-Simon and his friends rallied round the man they hoped would restore to the princes of the blood and the *ducs et pairs* their rightful place in government. Up to a point he did not disappoint them. He made shrewd, pacifying concessions to lawyers and magnates, without surrendering his own freedom to act decisively. He lived long enough to see the monarchy through perilous times, not long enough to make significant reforms. Indeed it may be doubted whether he could have done so: he relished the exercise of political authority, yet lacked both stamina and principle.

He was tragically flawed; and his tragedy was inevitably his country's. Like his great-grandfather Henry IV, he pursued women, in a greedy, inconstant way that contrasted with his lasting, serious friendship with men. He seemed always to be afflicted by a sense of aimlessness. He was not wholly a bad man; rather one who had the misfortune, in Saint-Simon's phrase, 'to be born bored'. The regency has come to be identified with lax morals and frivolous manners. As in the political field, so in the cultural, there was an underlying continuity, with more serious purpose than is usually allowed. But there was a sharp break when the old king died: his presence had ensured decorum, his sincere piety had set the tone. With the regent came release: frustrated libertines could now say and do what they wanted, knowing the regent to be one of themselves. The delicate, flippant art of fashionable painters like Watteau and Lancret portrays the regime at its most attractive: for the rococo artist, prettiness is all. The ostentatious dissipation of the duchess of Berry, Orléans's unstable daughter, and her circle, was typical of its less salubrious aspect. Another representative figure was Orléans's friend, the poet Fontenelle. When he died, aged 100, in 1757, the fastidious *litterateur* had lived long enough to see the publication of the first volumes of the *Encyclopédie*. By then the gap between official, clerical attitudes to religion and prevalent modes of belief and behaviour had widened to such an extent that it is possible to identify two distinct upper-class cultures: scepticism and materialism had so permeated the fashionable world that monarchy was actually being weakened by association with the Church which had previously provided its most important sanction. Fontenelle, the skilful popularizer of scientific ideas, had played his part in the process.

Louis XIV had never done more than suspend *parlement*'s right of remonstrance. Taxation of the privileged classes was presented as exceptional and temporary. None the less, royal power had advanced to positions from which it would not willingly retreat. When the regent restored latent powers to *parlement* he was giving away less than some *parlementaires* may have hoped. In 1717 *parlement* refused to register a financial edict and secured from the government a detailed account of national income and expenditure which was rendered to a group of commissioners nominated by them. In 1718 successive remonstrances against financial policy forced the government to have recourse to a *lit de justice*: monarchy's claim to complete legislative power was reaffirmed, the right of remonstrance was curtailed and, to enforce the lesson, three judges were arrested. In 1720, after *parlement* had refused to register a financial edict, the regent ordered the whole body to be exiled to Pontoise. At the same time *parlement* was forced, under threat of further exile and the creation of new courts, to swallow *Unigenitus*.

The main innovation of the regency, in appearance replacing Louis XIV's councils, was the *polysynodie*: a pretentious name for what was in fact a device to give a few notables a share in the making of policy, and to some more of the nobles the illusion that, by sitting alongside experts and veterans of government, they were also so sharing. Meanwhile essential continuity was maintained, in unofficial ways, through firm central direction and through informal reference to ministers. There were some enforced resignations: notably, as a gesture of intent, the experienced, devout Pontchartrain, epitome of the old order, was ordered to leave the council. Membership of the council was largely dictated by political expediency. Representatives of the old court, like Harcourt, sat with necessary grandees like Bourbon: Louis XIV would never have tolerated such a man, dull grandson of the great Condé. Around the central regency council there were seven satellite councils, each headed by grandees: in some cases, like Noailles and Villeroy, presiding respectively over the councils for finance and commerce, they were chosen simply because Orléans wanted to neutralize them. The councils had no authority to issue decrees; it was their sole responsibility to prepare material for the regency council. It met on different days to discuss the matters which had formerly been the province of the several special councils of Louis XIV, so it was, in effect, that council on its allotted day. Patronage was all important, as Orléans proceeded warily towards his goal: the transfer of sovereignty to Louis XV. Political equilibrium was the aim, but Orléans guarded against loss of efficiency and of the trained, knowledgeable men who could ensure it. In two critical areas he kept control. Torcy, Colbert's nephew and Louis's experienced foreign minister, who lost his ministerial post, was put on the foreign affairs council in 1716. Orléans needed his expertise, and the bulging files accumulated from his control of the postal service, but Dubois was the main architect of his foreign policy. In matters of finance the regent gave his support from the start to Law and his ambitious schemes. In September 1718 the councils for war and finance were suppressed and secretaries of state took over. The finance council remained, with a team of professional administrators under d'Argenson, but they did not challenge or alter the arrangements made between Law and the regent. Another to survive was the navy council, where Toulouse was effective and good work was done. But the system never represented the realities of government under Orléans. For that reason it is misleading to talk of its failure for it served the purpose for which Orléans had established it. By neutralizing opposition and spreading responsibility at the time when cohesion was more important than anything else it contributed to the success of his rule.

Without some such system it is hard to see how Orléans and Dubois could have avoided serious opposition over foreign policy. 'In appearance much like a ferret . . . outspoken in contempt for loyalty, promises, honour, truth . . . a toady, a trimmer': with more in this vein Saint-Simon depicted Dubois, the clerical parvenu who served Orléans's interests, and his own, so faithfully. Whatever may be thought of Saint-Simon's partisan description (and he was never one to sacrifice artistic effect for the dull truth), and given that Dubois was happier in the role of politician than that of priest, it is not clear that any other policy would have better served France's interests. Orléans and Dubois sought security. The equilibrium in Europe remained precarious so long as the ambitions of Spanish king, Austrian Emperor and Jacobite pretender were unsatisfied. Philip V of Spain did not accept that his renunciation of the French throne in favour of Orléans was valid. If Louis XV were to die young, or without an heir, then the Orléans supremacy and, Orléans would argue, the stability of France, would be jeopardized. Philip V's throne was still claimed by the emperor Charles VI who had fought so hard to win it; he possessed Naples, however, and Philip was bent on recovering it for Spain. England's king, George I, had to face the Jacobite challenge. His chief minister, Stanhope, saw the advantages of an entente with France. After so many years of conflict, only Philip V, or more positively his queen Elizabeth Farnese and minister Alberoni, was willing to go to war. Like Talleyrand, after 1815. Orléans, with an apparently weak hand, was able to exploit the general desire for settlement. His object was to weaken the aggressive potential of the Grand Alliance, which had done such damage in the last war, by associating with its principal members, even at the cost of a breach with Spain and of allowing England advantages in the commercial and colonial spheres where, as critics of his policy have urged, France should have been making her own claims. But in these years France was in no position to ask a high price for her alliance. Alberoni's impetuosity might have forced England and France together even if Dubois and Stanhope had not already come to an agreement. The failure of the Jacobite challenge of 1715 showed that there was no future for France in supporting that bankrupt cause. Orléans needed to ensure adherence to the terms of Utrecht, among which was Philip V's renunciation of the French crown. Equally France required respite from war which could be secured by a system of collective security such as the Triple and Quadruple Alliances provided: the latter (1718) added Austria to the alliance of France, England and Holland. The minor operations against Spain of 1718–19 brought the success that might have been expected from the weight of the alliance and the power of the British navy. With Alberoni gone, the way was clear for Dubois to negotiate for the alliance with Spain which was formalized by the treaty of Madrid, foundation of the later 'family compact'. It was cemented by the projected double marriage, one half of which, the marriage of his third daughter to Philip's elder son, was accomplished by Orléans's death.

John Law

In the last two years of Louis XIV's reign, the *contrôleur-général*, Desmarets, had pursued an orthodox deflationary policy: with the reduction of demand had gone a dip in commercial activity. Money was hoarded; bankruptcies, debts and unemployment mounted; troops went unpaid and roamed about, seizing what they could. Noailles's finance council had initiated some reforms and economies. They adopted the usual, relatively easy expedient of 'making the financiers disgorge'. A committee of *parlementaires* was set up to scrutinize accounts, exact repayments and cancel contracts. The reduction of royal debts by such arbitrary means was no remedy for the ills of the system. Despite individual casualities, the old financial system and its most skilful operators, with their farms and syndicates, remained intact. But the war had demonstrated the power of credit and the value of state banks. As the regent was sufficiently perceptive and unconventional to realize, radical reform was now required. In John Law he found the man to implement it. Son of an Edinburgh goldsmith and banker, Law had already had the sort of colourful career to qualify him for a place in the select company of adventurers, like Alberoni and Ripperda in Spain, for whom a sovereign's friendship was a passport to power, but a temporary one, renewable only on condition of success. He had been imprisoned in England for fighting a duel. It was as a gambler that he had attracted the attention of the regent. He had a fine presence, a genial manner, a clear mind; unspoiled by success, he was to prove philosophical in misfortune. He liked analysing and solving problems and he wrote well enough to demonstrate the validity of his schemes. He could be called a visionary but his schemes were founded on knowledge of financial affairs. There were awkward gaps and time-lags in his reasoning which meant unprecedented risks. But the times were hard, and orthodox policies and time-honoured expedients appeared to be inadequate. Because the regent had had to defer to the aristocratic interest for the sake of political stability, one line of reform, fair and proportionate taxation, was debarred. He therefore decided on a new strategy.

Law held that the circulation of money was more important in the enrichment of a country than the mere acquisition of capital. To stimulate the productive process paper money had to be printed to a value in excess of the wealth to back it, but to a value which reflected the amount which would be created by this process: the reasoning and method is not far from that of Maynard Keynes, stipulating the preconditions of recovery from the recession in the 1930s, though Keynes's emphasis, in an industrial society, was more on full employment. Law had less reason than Keynes to rely on the generation of economic activity through the manipulation of the money supply, for he was planning for a society in which, unlike England or Holland, which provided him with so much of his data, the mercantile values were overlaid by the structure and mentality of absolutism, erected above a society of orders and corporations, tenacious of rights. To implement his schemes Law required greater state intervention; but that was what had been so powerfully resisted during Louis XIV's reign; now, during the regency, when the full authority of the crown was in abeyance, the current flowed even more strongly against it.

A bare resumé of the facts conveys the drama of Law's rise to the management of his financial empire, and of his sudden fall. In May 1716 he founded his *Banque Générale*. In April 1717 the payment of taxes by bank notes was authorized. At the same time Law was engaged in founding the Mississippi Company to exploit Louisiana. In October 1718, the company's financial base was strengthened by his acquisition of the expanding tobacco tax farm. In December 1718 he took over the Senegal Company, making the first of the acquisitions which led by the following June to control of all the state companies for overseas commerce. In July 1719 he was granted the sole right to coin money. In August he bought out those tax farmers who remained and took over their fiscal responsibilities. He was then able to make the daring leap to full responsibility for the national debt, buying out the *rentes* and offering to their holder the same rate of interest as on his company shares – 4 per cent. In October he was charged with raising the direct taxes. In January 1720 he was made *contrôleur-général*. In February his bank and company were united. So he had achieved, in less than four years, the ultimate monopoly: maritime and colonial trade, together with a bank of issue empowered to raise taxes, to coin and to print money. To maintain and exploit this mighty castle of credit he made regular issues of company shares: they were increasingly expensive but eagerly sought. At the same time he increased the amount of paper money in circulation. Business boomed, prices soared, speculation became the rage. The inflationary process acquired its own momentum; shares of 500 *livres* face value were sold for 18,000. As the gap between the circulating paper and the metals backing widened, the question of public confidence became all important. At this point the opposition of treasurers, tax farmers and bankers whose monopolies were threatened by the audacious interloper became significant; it was easy for them to point out that the commercial companies could not show profits or prospects remarkable enough to justify the weight of credit mounted on them. Selling developed and everything fell apart.

In May 1720 Law decreed a drastic devaluation, which only shook confidence further. Dismissed from the office of *contrôleur-général*, he none the less remained influential. He tried to restrict the circulation of paper money, but he could not save his system. The regent was staunch in the face of threats to burn down the Palais Royal: he was too far committed for it to be politic to repudiate the system entirely. But he beat a tactical retreat while Law slipped out of Paris, Orléans maintained his firm front towards *parlement*. However, through decrees of the regency council, he took palliative measures, culminating in the withdrawal of paper money from circulation. Many had lost; a few were ruined. A few others made money, by luck, selling at the right time or by exploiting in some way the booming business conditions created by the system and Law's insistence on low interest rates. Nor was all lost in the subsequent slump. Law's reorganization of companies under the supervision of the Compagnie des Indes, reconstituted in 1722–3, undoubtedly contributed to the important revival of overseas trade in the next decades. It is possible to regard Law as a charlatan. But the weight of evidence supports a more generous verdict: though perhaps fatally careless about detail, he was a man of rare perception, convinced that his diagnosis and plans were right, caring more about implementing them than about his own fame. The financial record of the *ancien régime*, between Law's downfall and that of the monarchy, speaks for him. Law pointed the way towards an enlightened regime in which the abolition of financial privilege should work to enhance the power of the state, and its ability to mobilize credit. The manner in which Law failed and the immediate consequences of failure, so unnerving politically to the regent and his successors, together go a long way to explaining why France never achieved such a regime and therefore never enjoyed the advantage of an efficient mechanism of state banking.

Fleury

Orléans died, in December 1723, of a stroke, in the arms of his mistress. The tone of society over which he presided had certainly been relaxed but his trusteeship had been firm. In the narrow political sense he had set a standard of responsibility. It was to be maintained by Cardinal Fleury who brought to the management of affairs as much shrewdness and firmness as the regent had shown and, as befitted a venerable prelate, a more cautiously traditional stance in domestic affairs. Immediately, however, Orléans was succeeded as regent by the duc de Bourbon, the next prince of the blood: he was at least sensible enough to attempt to strengthen his position threatened by the growing independence of the young king and his inclination towards his old tutor, André-Hercule de Fleury, bishop of Fréjus (1652–1743). Believing that the need to strengthen the succession in the direct line outweighed all other considerations, he negotiated the marriage of Louis to Maria Leszczynska, daughter of Stanislaus, ex-king of Poland (1725). It was done hastily, and without regard for the feelings of the Spanish court, who assumed that Louis, as had already been arranged, would eventually marry the 5-year-old infanta. When Bourbon tried to secure the removal of Fleury from the royal council, he was abruptly dismissed and ordered to reside upon his estate of Chantilly. And so in June 1726, with the trusting support of a diffident but affectionate king, and with the deceptive ease which characterizes much of his political career, Fleury came to a position which gave him greater power than had been exercised by any minister since Mazarin. In his strong *dévôt* ideology, far-thinking and realistic diplomacy, in the ruthlessness with which he dealt with opposition, he more closely resembles Richelieu. A century on, authority was more firmly established and there was less need for drastic measures. Fleury's self-effacing and amiable manner was well suited to the tasks of maintaining harmony among conflicting interests and getting the most out of able ministers, without sacrificing any essential elements of royal authority.

The Fleury years, which ended effectively in 1741 and war, only two years before his death, coincided with the most prosperous years of the eighteenth century. There was a healthy growth in economic activity, nature was relatively benign, and until 1739 there were no serious famines. The population began to grow, revenues were buoyant. To this last happy condition Fleury contributed by a wisely cautious approach to international relations: with only a modest increase in the fiscal demands of the state, during the only two years of a war whose scope and scale were prudently limited, the economy was given a chance to grow in something approximating to the 'natural' conditions favoured by the physiocrats and their predecessors in that liberal school of thought. Inasmuch as he was responsible for economic policy, his was a conservative regime. It began with the fixing of the value of the coinage; less sound in principle was the return at the same time to the old system of collecting indirect taxes by means of the *fermiers-généraux* who had been suppressed by Law. More directly important than Fleury in the management of financial affairs was the *contrôleur-général* Orry who held the office from 1730 to 1745.

Colbertist, by inclination cautious and reluctant to innovate, he was content to work on the basis of existing institutions. Thus in 1739 he put the *corvée* to regular use for the building and upkeep of roads. Even the peasant who built them might benefit in the long term, though less than traders, from the fine system of roads which eventually covered the country. To meet the exigencies of wartime Orry twice reintroduced the *dixième*. But in the years of peace he managed to keep expenditure slightly below revenue without raising extra taxes. In the light of subsequent events it was to seem a notable achievement. Meanwhile criticism of a tendency to regimentation in economic affairs was lulled by the evidence of improving trade. It could be seen in the imposing and elegant streets and squares of Bordeaux, Nantes, Aix and a number of smaller cities where merchants and magistrates displayed their wealth and taste.

In domestic affairs, for which he could assume direct responsibility, Fleury was capable of acting in a briskly autocratic manner, in a way that showed perhaps his age and his *dévôt* pedigree. He suppressed the Entresol club, where the supposedly subversive literary and political conversations of well-born *habitués*, d'Argenson among them, gave him cause for concern. Possibly he was over-sensitive about the wide-ranging discussions of advanced opinion; it is also arguable that the monarchy would have been stronger in its last years if censorship had been more rigorous. But then again there might have been less need for censorship subsequently if government had not taken, in these years, such an intransigent line about Jansenism. The courts had eventually to accept his ban on interference in any matter relative to the recognition of the bull *Unigenitus*. But *parlement* had appeared throughout the dispute to be more moderate and restrained than the crown; by contrast, Fleury had acted in an arbitrary fashion, with scant respect for legal forms, at the very time when the secular trend in political thinking divested monarchy of its traditional sanction of divine ordination. *Parlement* was left defensive and sore. Monarchy had tried out the authoritarian line, to which it was to return at the end of the reign, with more directly fateful consequences; meanwhile a valuable fund of loyalty had been needlessly squandered. For the moment, however, the damage was contained because the crown was solvent and financial issues did not arise to strengthen *parlement*'s hand and further embitter relationships. Also Fleury, frail though apparently immortal, primarily interested in the delicate issues of the Polish succession, became more circumspect and amenable. It is on his handling of that question especially that his reputation for statecraft principally depends.

Just as in ecclesiastical matters Fleury was the product of the conformist thinking of Versailles during Louis XIV's last years, so in diplomacy there are echoes of those years of defeat, expressed in profound scepticism about what could be achieved by military force alone. At the start of his ministry, European peace seemed to him to be doubly endangered: first by bellicose moves by Spain and Britain, reflecting respectively the ambitions of an old, decayed imperial power stirring under more energetic leadership, and thrusting merchant capitalism; second by the Austro-Spanish axis formed by the first treaty of Vienna in 1725, after the Spanish had reacted furiously to the news of Louis's hurried marriage to Maria Leszczynska.

For British statesmen the favourable treaty of Utrecht could either be regarded as a mandate for the uncompromising assertion of British interests, or as the basis for a balanced state system in which Britain's authority should be used as arbiter, if need be, to preserve harmony. It was only gradually that Fleury, who leaned at first upon the British alliance, decided that Walpole was trying to have the best of both worlds and wanted influence without commitment. Fleury acted as broker in the complicated negotiations which were concluded by the first treaty of Vienna in 1731: the danger of war between Britain and Austria was then averted, though none of the fundamental issues was resolved. He had by then been disenchanted and begun to judge Britain's policy correctly in its insular context, after Walpole refused to become involved in action to expel the Austrian invaders of Parma in 1730. 'Peace-keeping', Walpole's avowed aim, could look like cynical isolationism on the French side of the Channel. So France and Britain drifted back into their old positions of rivalry. It is likely that colonial ambitions would have had the same effect in any case. Colonies and commerce were not, however, the main concerns of the war party with whom Fleury had to contend at Versailles. It consisted in the main of soldiers and courtiers less concerned than British 'hawks' with material benefits: a contrast that can be seen most strongly in the decisive conflict that was to be fought over colonies and foreign trade. All the more reason for Fleury, advised by the financier Paris-Duverney that another war would be fatal to France's chance of financial recovery, to try first to avoid, then to limit the war that proved to be unavoidable.

In 1733 King Augustus II of Saxony and Poland died, leaving Augustus III as heir in his Saxon lands and, if the electoral magnates should so decide, king of Poland. They did not, but chose instead Stanislaus, who hoped that France would sustain him more successfully than had Sweden during his earlier adventure.[1] Inevitably an opposition formed, backed by both Russia and Austria, and chose Augustus III as king; more powerful than the voice of the electors was the Russian army which chased the luckless Stanislaus out of the country. Fleury could not ignore such an insult to Stanislaus's royal son-in-law. He allowed Chauvelin, officially keeper of the seals but effectively minister in charge of foreign affairs under Fleury, to organize a coalition with Spain and Sardinia, while keeping open his own line to Walpole to ensure British neutrality. Chauvelin wanted war on a grand scale and for the traditional objectives. For the elder statesman the lesson of the great war was that to negotiate was better than to fight; among those who

[1] See pp. 543–5 for these events in their Polish context.

had been young men then there was a yearning for *revanche*: not for the last time in French history it swamped more sober counsels. Fleury's skill was exercised thereafter in limiting the scope of the war. In particular he saw to it that the French did not alarm the British by operating in the Low Countries. Nor did he venture upon a campaign in Poland. The French armies did just enough in the Rhineland (they occupied Lorraine and captured Phillipsburg) and in the Milanese where the veteran Villars fought his last campaign, to provide him with cards to play at the negotiating table.

There emerged a settlement characteristic of the best and worst of the old diplomacy. Honour had to be satisfied, the balance of interests preserved; subjects were of no account. When the masters of European chess had finished moving their pieces about the board, in 1736, France emerged with the prospect of Lorraine. Though granted for life to Stanislaus, his French chancellor proceeded to run it so that when it was eventually absorbed into France, at Stanislaus's death in 1766, it was already virtually a French province. The Emperor was compensated for its loss by the transference of Francis of Lorraine, soon to become his son-in-law, to Tuscany, and France's recognition of the Pragmatic Sanction; the Emperor also gained Parma, though Naples and Sicily were abandoned to Don Carlos. Fleury had used his two advantages, Walpole's determination not to become involved in a war over a distant country and the Emperor's need to secure his daughter's succession to the family lands, to the best possible advantage. More important than the incorporation of a valuable province, where the elegant architecture of the capital, Nancy, was to provide a fitting memorial to the civilized essay in diplomacy, was the avoidance of a larger war, possibly against the Anglo-Dutch-imperial alliance which had already proved too formidable. He could now afford to secure the dismissal of Chauvelin. He could also send his ambassador to negotiate the peace of Belgrade between the Turks and Austrians (1739).

Drift and Disaster

Another fruit of Fleury's diplomacy was the treaty of the Escorial with Spain: the first of the family compacts which were part of the diplomatic pattern of the next forty years. France then had an obligation as well as an interest when Britain went to war with Spain in 1739 over trading rights in South America on the pretext of the alleged injury to the ear of Captain Jenkins. When in 1740 Frederick the Great invaded Silesia and opened up a new, initially unrelated area of conflict, the pressure on the ageing minister became harder to resist. It did not deter the comte de Belle-Isle and his friends that France had so recently guaranteed the rights of the Austrian queen. Frivolous and opportunistic, they appear to have been more aware of France's traditions than of her present needs. Louis XV was persuaded, against Fleury's advice, to embark upon a war which could only be justified on the narrowest traditional grounds and on hope of an early victory. It lasted seven years more, brought setbacks, the rapid retreat from Bohemia (1742), the defeat at Dettingen (1743), but also some resounding victories: notably at Fontenoy (1745), Roucoux (1746) and Laffeldt (1747). The victor, Marshal Saxe, joined the select company of France's greatest soldiers, and retired to write his memoirs, embodying his considered thoughts about the practice of war to which he brought such distinction. France made no significant gains, however, at the peace of Aix-le-Chapelle (1748) for none of the victories had been decisive and most of the military action had indeed been irrelevant to the important issues. Large debts, not yet crippling but large enough to justify Machault's renewal of the *dixième* in 1749, underline the point that the war was as wasteful as it was irrelevant.

At Aix, France recovered Louisbourg in Canada, but its earlier loss was a warning of worse to come. The effect of British sea power was felt in the way, by 1748, French overseas trade was brought virtually to a standstill. There was sense in the current argument that, just as France had been successful in Flanders, she could bring pressure on Britain through military action against Hanover. It was essentially Pitt's strategy, defined by him as winning Canada 'on the banks of the Elbe'. But Pitt was to be successful largely through the instrument of a strong navy. And so the French entered the next war, in 1756, in the worst of both worlds. Their navy was not strong enough to outmatch Britain's; they were heavily and unnecessarily committed to Austria. How had that come about?

Inasmuch as France's intervention enabled Prussia to keep Silesia, it contributed to the weakening of Austria. At the same time, however, it strengthened the hand of Austrian ministers: Haugwitz, who planned for the renewal of imperial authority and the enlargement of her armies, and Kaunitz whose main diplomatic aim, successfully encompassed in 1756, was to draw France in again, but this time on the side of Austria. He seized the initiative and achieved a great coup, the central feature of the diplomatic revolution, in the shape of a treaty with France. News of the defensive agreement signed between Great Britain and Prussia, the convention of Westminster (January 1756), provoked the French to what Britain had feared when they joined Frederick's camp. The first treaty of Versailles was simply a defensive alliance with Austria to preserve the peace of Europe. At that stage French ministers still hoped that they could concentrate on an overseas war and provide the necessary support to Dupleix in India and Montcalm in Canada. Along the Ohio river, as in India, hostilities had continued sporadically since 1748: the colonists had their own scores to settle; their chiefs had their own designs. By 1755 there were regular troops fighting on both sides in Canada. In 1756 their war was subsumed into the main action of another world war.

As so often it was what seemed to be, and not what was, that precipitated the next action. Frederick was not the man to wait to be hit. He invaded

Saxony to gain the advantage in the war against Austria. France's defensive alliance was thus converted to a new offensive alliance and the country was committed to help Austria to fight to recover Silesia. The inconsistency needs no stress. France, in the person of Louis XV, conducting his own foreign policy with the advice of Conti and Broglie, had let itself be used as the instrument of Austrian strategy. France had to fight on two continental fronts to check the growth of the power which they had helped to rise. It was Louis's misfortune that Frederick was as tough as he was unscrupulous; and so the war was prolonged. Misfortune was compounded by the emergence of William Pitt as war minister, a man of masterful personality uniquely well endowed with the vision and ability to exploit to the full Britain's advantages: her commercial and financial strength and her navy. France had a disastrous experience in the Seven Years War. After a hopeful start, when they secured the capitulation of Cumberland at Klosterseven (September 1757), weakness in command was exposed at the battles of Rossbach in November 1757 and Minden in 1759: both were serious defeats, the former ended in a humiliating, long-remembered rout. Napoleon was to call it the single most important event in the collapse of the French monarchy. The navy started well by worsting the unfortunate Admiral Byng and subsequently taking Minorca, but its operational scope was limited by the British policy of blockade and then in 1759 the two main fleets were defeated, that of Conflans by Hawke at Quiberon Bay and that of La Gallissonière by Boscawen off Lagos. Choiseul's invasion plans were thus foiled and colonial possessions, particularly those in the West Indies, were left vulnerable to Pitt's well-mounted expeditions. Meanwhile Prussia's epic defence enabled her to survive against all expectation and by securing Hanover, a potential source of embarrassment to Pitt, at the same time to upset another of France's strategic calculations, namely that British forces would be used to defend the electorate.

The duc de Choiseul came to power in 1758: a nobleman from Lorraine and a soldier who had seen action in Flanders. He inherited the storm and had to endure its worst effects, although he was supported by the favour of Mme de Pompadour. He brought professional skill and shrewd judgement to what could only be a salvage operation. After Wolfe's brilliant attack on Quebec and Amherst's expedition to Montreal, Canada was irretrievably lost. The audacity of Clive, his victory at Plassey and subsequent consolidation of British rule in Bengal, meant the disappointment of French hopes of a more extensive and profitable empire there. As one West Indian island after another fell to Pitt's amphibious operations, Choiseul brought off a useful diplomatic coup when Spain, having safely received her annual treasure fleet, declared war against England (October 1761). It was more important to the French that Pitt resigned, having failed to gain his way and secure the Spanish fleet by a pre-emptive strike against Spain. Ministers, taking their cue from the young King George III, who had acceded in 1760, and more concerned with economies than with conquests, went to the negotiating table in a mood of what seemed to Pitt to be irresponsible moderation. At the peace of Paris in 1763, France ceded a lot: Tobago, Grenada, St Vincent, Dominica, some stations in West Africa, above all Canada. But she received back rich Martinique and Guadeloupe, solace to the merchants, especially those in the rapidly expanding sugar trade. Choiseul had saved something from the wreck and he looked for opportunities to do more. The frustrating question for the French, after their defeats at sea and in the colonies was: how could they set their still formidable army against the British? How to get to grips? Significantly, within two months of making peace, Choiseul was again considering plans for invasion and working on the construction of a naval force. Now more than ever, after defeats and losses so keenly felt, honour was at stake. The revolt of the American colonies was to provide the opportunity for *revanche*.

In 1780, the alliance with Austria was strengthened by the marriage between Archduchess Marie Antoinette and the young dauphin: the basis of peace in western Europe was thus laid. There would now be no question of war in the Netherlands, and the Rhineland and France would be left free to concentrate all their resources against Britain. In the same year, however, when Choiseul was preparing to come to the aid of the Spanish over the Falkland Islands, he was dismissed, and it was Vergennes who in 1778, with the young King Louis XVI but four years on his throne, who made the fateful decision to go to war on behalf of the American colonists. Even without French assistance the colonies might have won their independence but in the crucial years 1770–81, culminating in the surrender at Yorktown, temporary French naval supremacy in American waters played a significant part. It is debatable, however, whether the French gained anything from the discomfiture of their old enemy for the British held Canada. Admiral Rodney's victory at the Île des Saintes in 1782 restored to the British command of the seas and reduced French bargaining power in the peace parleys. The cession of Tobago and Senegal at the treaty of Versailles in 1783 was not worth the cost to France's ailing finances. The germs of colonial liberalism were carried home into a system which, in its manifold expression of privileges and constraints upon human rights, was all too susceptible to such infection; and ministers faced a burden of debt which was, within six years, to prove insurmountable without recourse to radical measures: the consequent meeting of the estates-general in 1789 was to be the prelude to revolution.

Then, with a vengeance all the more terrible for its being so long delayed, the crown was to pay the penalty, not only for wrong decisions, such as that to go to war in 1778, but for the shortcomings of royal diplomacy, characterized by the personal initiatives of kings who did not know enough, or see clearly enough, to create a coherent policy out of the discordant advice that they received. The arbitrariness of policy was an unhappy departure, as its critics saw it, from the tradition of responsible authority, working through recognized departments, in a spirit of legality, mindful of precedent and principle.

The Indifferent King

Before the end of the regency, Louis XIV's system of government had been re-established. Between then and the Revolution there was little change; and that was in emphasis rather than formal structure. The only significant addition to the five councils of Louis XIV, foreign affairs, war, finance, 'dispatches' or home affairs, and religion, was that of commerce: nor was that entirely new for it had been established in 1700 and was only given new form in 1730. The councils were less important than in Louis XIV's time because even when, after the death of Fleury in 1743, Louis XV did undertake to be his own *premier ministre*, like his great-grandfather, individual ministers were more independent than Louis XIV had allowed them to be. That is not to say that they were necessarily effective. No minister, in the years of Louis XV's personal rule, achieved as much as had Colbert or Louvois. Conflict and confusion characterize policy in the three last decades of his reign. The mounting deficits were only sustainable because of growth in the economy and that appeared to owe less to government policies than to a general expansion of demand, production and trade. It was not entirely Louis XV's fault. While Louis XIV had maintained his authority he had not used it for fundamental reforms; nor had he abolished the institutions and offices which he deprived of power; and so alongside cherished traditions there were shells, ready for a new generation to inhabit and utilize when circumstances were favourable. *Parlements*, estates, financial officers and corporations were ready to obstruct, as well as to serve; or to serve on their own terms. They could do so because government, king and ministers did not present a united front and because decisions were made which were to prove costly, not only in the financial sense but, equally significant, though harder to measure, in the erosion of authority. That is why Louis XV is generally reckoned to have failed, not simply as a man, where judgement must necessarily be to some extent subjective, but as a sovereign. There the way in which he failed to measure up to the needs of the system allows objective appraisal, and there historians, like his contemporaries, differ only in emphasis, according to their particular concern or viewpoint. Louis XV was king at a time when absolute power, wielded half-heartedly and capriciously, was a formula for disaster greater than if such power had not existed at all. If it was his misfortune, it was also that of the French monarchy and all who served it, that he should have reigned, and reigned so long.

Yet this prince, who retained all his life, along with traits of the spoilt child, something of an instinct for rule, roused hopes at the outset and affection throughout; more than he seemed able to respond to. Early in his reign people thought well of him, as they heard reports of his courage and good nature: then he was still '*le bien aimé*' and there were fervent prayers for him when he nearly died of smallpox in 1745; there was still sympathy as well as shock when in 1757 he survived the attempt of Damien to assassinate him. As early as 1749, however, Bishop Douglas reported great opposition to a proposal to build a new square in Paris, with the king's statue in the centre. Criticism centred then, however, on Mme de Pompadour, whose star was in the ascendant and who was held responsible for the peace of Aix, with its concessions, so incomprehensible to those who had been fed news of great victories. Another Englishman, Thicknesse, who noted his 'handsome goodliness' and addiction to the predictable slaughter 'that the French call hunting', referred also to his notorious pursuit of women: 'nor has any man been more indulged in that way'. He was as greedy in that respect and more inconstant than Louis XIV. Louis XIV, with middle age and Mme de Maintenon, became devotedly uxorious. Louis XV, as he wearied of Mme de Pompadour, indulged himself in a specially established house of young girls before settling to a more or less steady relationship with the amoral though amiable Mme du Barry, illegitimate daughter of a cook, and wife, after many affairs, of a notorious rogue. But these are not the most important differences between the two kings. Whereas Louis insisted upon decorum and upon a clear line between public business and private relationships, Louis XV allowed his weakness to affect the tone of court and administration. Mme de Pompadour, who for about ten years after 1745 came as near to being a wife to him as any woman could to such a self-centred man, was the source of vital patronage, not only in the arts: she could make and unmake ministers and influence policies. She was intelligent, and not without some sense of duty to the state. But she represented an extra political interest, and so was the cause of further confusion in already tangled lines of authority.

Only fools were honest, loyal or chaste in the court of Louis XV: that is the message of memoirs and letters, not only those of social lightweights but of powerful ministers, men like d'Argenson, and Choiseul, protégé of Mme de Pompadour, who knew the workings of government and had experienced both favour and sudden disgrace. Choiseul served Louis for twelve years and in the disappointed aftermath recalled only his faults: 'He was jealous of authority and weakly submissive to ministers ... his vanity is inconceivable but he cannot give it scope for he is rightly aware of his incapacity ... his character resembles wax on which the most diverse objects leave their trace.' D'Argenson's judgement may reflect his rancour after being abruptly dismissed from the foreign secretaryship. Louis disliked working with ministers 'as the finances are so bad, and their fear of him creates his fear of them. So they shirk decisions leaving everything to him, and he fears to make mistakes.' Perhaps most telling, because it comes in the middle of a sympathetic portrait of a well-intentioned man, is that of the comte de Cheverney, a diplomatic official: 'he spoke of affairs as if someone else was on the throne'. In all descriptions there comes across the laziness and indifference to business which led to more being done behind the scenes or in the minister's bureau. 'In council,' wrote the cardinal de Tencin, 'only a very small amount of state business is discussed; after the rapid reading of a memorandum our opinion is asked on the spot, without any time for undisturbed reflection and summing up. Moreover, the king appears to show no interest and the profound silence he maintains is shattering.'

Louis was not, however, inactive. He travelled, in his younger days to the eastern frontier, to fortresses or field manoeuvres, later round his palaces. He sought ways of escape from routines that bored him but he could not but be effected by the oppressive climate of the court, so claustrophobic and isolated from honest opinion or even undoctored news from the provinces and towns of the greater France. He concerned himself with the lobbying for power which his own irresolution served to encourage. He had the weak man's love of gossip and intrigue and the pursuit of secret lines of policy. The tragedy is that his secret correspondence reveals a man who had ideas of his own. He worked behind the backs of every foreign minister until Choiseul, hiding much even from him; he studied reports from his agents in other capitals. He had his small circle of confidants but his ministers were kept in the dark and left to guess. After Fleury's departure he relied much on Marshal Noailles, veteran of the War of the Spanish Succession and president of the council of finance under the regency, a man of integrity and ability: it was he who was responsible for the choice of Marshal Saxe to command in Flanders in 1743. For a few years Noailles was first minister in all but name. It was Louis's misfortune that he did not find another such. He seems to have needed an authoritative, fatherly figure, for he lacked confidence in his own judgement. Conducting his *sécret du roi*, the private dealings which often crossed official lines of policy, Louis had the reassuring sense of being in charge in a private world in which his judgement could not be tested before experts. He did not, however, have the satisfaction of success. The Seven Years War began with France being outmanoeuvred by Austria in crucial diplomatic exchanges; after a deceptively bright start there ensued a crushing sequence of defeats at the hands of both the main enemies, by sea and by land. The pursuit of a Polish throne for a French prince was a cherished aim of his private diplomacy; before he died, Poland's partition, excluding France altogether, revealed its barrenness.

Louis XV's reign ended with a show of determination as Maupeou and Terray carried out their onslaught on *parlement* in pursuit of more revenue, for which there was an ever pressing need. Louis supported them, agreeably surprised perhaps at the effect of ministerial co-operation and concerted moves, backed by his authority. It was a beginning – but it came late, after years of drift when projects of reform had failed because the king had not sustained the minister concerned. It is hard to imagine Louis XIV abandoning Colbert as Louis XV did Machault over the question of the taxation of the clergy in 1749. Because they found it difficult to serve the king and were unsure of his support, ministers sought to build their own empires. D'Argenson wrote of the royal council as consisting of the heads of factions, each thinking of his own concerns, one of finance, another of the navy, another of the army, and each achieving his ends according to his greater or less facility in the art of persuasion. He had the satisfaction, between 1743 and 1747 of pursuing a complicated personal policy, but also of being rendered powerless before his dismissal by the interference of the king. In this situation corporate interests could obstruct policy and individuals could create pressure groups for their own ends. Thus the Church mounted its successful campaign to avoid any tax other than the *don gratuit*; and thus the Jesuits were assaulted and isolated by a skilfully orchestrated campaign, until the point was reached when the king, as it seemed to him, had no option but to acquiesce in their expulsion (1764). Louis really seems to have had the worst of both worlds. The odium of arbitrary measures of ministers bent on forcing through fiscal measures and dealing with obstruction by that still effective weapon, the royal will, as expressed through *lits de justice* or sentences of exile or imprisonment, was accompanied by the contempt of those sufficiently close to him to see the way in which he caved in to organized interests or changed his policy to suit a whim or prejudice, not always his own.

Parlement, Jansenism and Sedition

Among the inner group of the most powerful ministers, the most important was still the *contrôleur-général*. His wide-ranging powers over all areas of the economy were the legacy of Colbert. Since the regime's authority depended on sound finance, his role was always central and sometimes critically important. Experience and continuity were especially important in this field. None of his successors, however, enjoyed anything like the length of tenure of Orry, Fleury's protégé (1730–45). Louis XV was served by some notable *contrôleurs-généraux*, Machault, Bertin and Terray among them: their ability and reforming initiatives only serve to highlight the magnitude of the problems that faced the monarchy. A firm, far-sighted policy was required; it was exactly what was lacking. On the contrary the impression was one of incoherence, a hardening of privileged positions, and the steady movement of nobility back into government. This in turn reflects the consolidation of the noble class, with the distinction between *robe* and *épée* fading into relative insignificance. While the upper tiers of wealth and rank were forming a single plutocratic élite, at the other end of the scale the caste was remarkably open and accessible to aspiring bourgeois. During the eighteenth century at least 6500 bourgeois acquired nobility through office, and a much larger number thereafter came to enjoy noble status by inheritance from the newly ennobled. By mid-century all *intendants*, most bishops and most holders of the major offices were noble; so were all members of the sovereign courts. The nobility possessed between a third and a quarter of the land; they dominated social and cultural life. One aspect of the closing of ranks was the near monopoly of commissions in the army. Another was the 'feudal reaction', which remains a useful way of describing the tendency of seigneurs to extract more from their feudal dues, so long as it is understood that the feudalism in question was that of a new and potent grouping, using the language of the old order but imbued with the values of lawyers and business men.[1]

Politically most significant of all was the development of the idea, expressed cogently by Montesquieu, of a distinctive public service performed by nobilities of various kinds as intermediary bodies which prevented monarchs from becoming despots. 'The nobility,' wrote Montesquieu, 'enters in some way into the essence of monarchy, whose fundamental maxim is: no monarch, no nobility; no nobility, no monarch.' If behind this formula there lay the ideal of a natural harmony of interest, the political reality was ironically different. Louis XV's reign was marred by recurring conflicts between his ministers and *parlements*. The fiscal demands resulting from the exceptional cost of war were the main reason for an increasing emphasis on the role of *parlements* as guardians of what was proper, and so they came to exercise a negative power, enabling them to obstruct policy, but not otherwise to influence, let alone dictate, it. The wealthy grandees of *parlement*, hereditary representatives of long-established legal dynasties, were still imbued with a sense of responsibility for the maintenance of order in the realm. Resisting the periodic attempts of the crown to extend its powers, *parlement* tended to adopt a style that had a wider appeal. The philosophy was conservative, the rhetoric was radical, in effect, if not in intention: for example in the use of the word 'nation' signifying an interest higher than that of any institution or individual. *Parlementaires* could be demagogues and all the more effective in that role because of their reputation for prescience and probity. The circulation of their remonstrances strengthened their hold on Parisians; the struggle was carried to the country, as it was reported in gazettes, and as their example was copied by other *parlements*.

In this period too the estates played a more prominent part, notably the 3 most active of the 5 that remained: Brittany, Languedoc and Burgundy. The inhabitants of the *pays d'état* were more lightly taxed and they had

[1] Like most specific areas in which historians have looked for causes of revolution this has been the subject of widely differing interpretations. For convenient summary of the state of controversy, see W. Doyle, 'Was there an aristocratic reaction in pre-revolutionary France?', *Past and Present*, 57 (1972). See also pp. 32–3 and 330.

more control over administration. They were, therefore, envied and influential in promoting the spirit of hostility to centralized, authoritarian government which became more articulate in eighteenth-century France. That was but one aspect of the alienation of public opinion to the point at which the exercise of legitimate power was regarded with suspicion, with the consequence that when government did behave in an arbitrary way, the privileged body or individual under attack was sure of general sympathy. By 1774 'despotism' had become a term of common recourse. France was not even then on the eve of revolution; nor was royal authority wholly ineffective. But it was seriously compromised by the inconsistency of the king's actions and appointments, as well as by the more obvious failures. It may seem then that Louis XVI inherited a form of government, absolute in theory, but hedged about with the constraints upon his freedom of action normally associated with a monarchy limited by representative institutions. Of course he made matters worse by the egregious blunder of entering the War of American Independence; the balance in the fiscal battle was then tilted against the indebted crown, as it was to prove, with calamitous effect.

Another kind of war, no less unnecessary, was that waged by Louis XV against Jansenism.[1] Its cost cannot be reckoned so exactly but it created bitterness and nurtured political opposition in a period of relative prosperity, when financial needs were less pressing and might not, therefore, in themselves have been the cause of constitutional conflict. The regent had successfully reaffirmed the crown's claim to complete legislative powers and at the same time dealt, it might have seemed conclusively, with Jansenism as a problem of government. The break between Gallican and ultramontane was papered over by *parlement*'s reluctant acceptance of *Unigenitus*. Jansenism did not die, however. Fleury saw it as an ecclesiastical matter in which the Church must be supported by the state. In 1730 he issued a declaration demanding that *Unigenitus* 'being a law of the church . . . should be regarded too as a law of our kingdom'. *Parlement* was overawed neither by a *lit de justice*, at which judges were forbidden to discuss legislation enforcing the bull, nor by attempts to divide *parlement* by persuading the normally co-operative *grand chambre* to comply. The decree of the royal council affirming the Church's right to enforce its spiritual censures without reference to a secular power only stiffened the lawyers' determination to stand firm upon the traditional Gallican position. In 1731 a decree of *parlement* asserted that the secular power alone had the power of coercion and that clerics were subordinate to temporal law. Fleury curtailed, temporarily he assured them, the magistrates' right to freedom of speech on such questions of authority. Excitement was then generated by the case of the young deacon Paris, who had lately died and was lamented by his fellow Jansenists who believed him to be a saint. With miracles allegedly being performed and convulsionaries dancing around his tomb,

[1] For Jansenism in the wider religious context, see also pp. 101–5.

the government was compelled to act: in January 1732 the churchyard was closed and *parlement*, perhaps needlessly, was forbidden to debate any matter relating to the bull. When magistrates declared themselves ready for a judicial strike, Fleury arrested and exiled their leaders. Most of the rest then resigned. Government forbade legal strikes and called another *lit de justice*; then, the magistrates still resisting, 139 of them were exiled. Since government was dealing with some wealthy men, influential in finance as well as in law, a compromise was clearly required: the crown suspended the declaration forced through by the *lit*. Subsequently the unimaginative determination of the archbishop of Paris, Christophe de Beaumont, to enforce *Unigenitus* by refusing the Sacrament to those who could not produce a *billet de confession*, proving that they had confessed to an orthodox priest, ensured that the pot was kept boiling. But the chief ingredient in later Jansenism, was the militancy of the lower clergy, radical in their demand for better treatment for themselves and their parishioners who could easily be roused to morbid enthusiasm by the extreme rhetoric adopted by Jansenists to express their own quest for spiritual perfection. They craved miracles, signs and saviours not of this world. In this world they heard, however, of authority, apparently 'fanatical' and censorious and blind to their needs. They heard too the anti-clerical phrases used by those they came to see as their spokesmen. Through the remonstrances of rich *parlementaires*, and the sermons of poor *curés*, the *sansculottes* of the future were trained to reject authority. The diarist Barbier, well acquainted with the people of Paris, summed it up: the dispute would destroy the spirit of submission which was 'the offspring of ignorance but necessary to the well-being of a great state'.

On the Jansenist issue, and until the 1750s, the language and conduct of *parlements* remained on the whole moderate: they were content to remain on the defensive, standing for a well-established Gallicanism, the position of 1682, and the rule of law. Between the period when the notion of divine right apparently satisfied the need of thinking men to find some theoretical justification for absolute monarchy and the emergence of the idea of the nation as embodying the natural and inherent rights of its citizens, the sanction of law was especially important. Monarchy, to be legitimate, must be exercised with restraint and respect for the fundamental laws: they epitomize cherished traditions and represent the moral norms. By that standard Fleury appeared intemperate, his successors unwisely rigid. Was it that they underestimated *parlement*'s force of conviction or that they thought it right to challenge it on the grounds of a higher authority? But what credibility did that higher authority have, when the intellectual *avant-garde* was eroding the idea of a supernatural sanction? At the very time when monarchy needed all the support it could gain from association with the rules and with rationality, it chose to attack the body which, for all its limitations, could best represent law and absorb the assaults of the *philosophes*.

The *Philosophes*

Enough has been said to show why the *philosophes* began to look to other countries and sovereigns to implement their enlightened reforms.[1] It was not that they necessarily opposed the idea of absolute sovereignty but that they lived under a government which was neither effectively absolute nor, by their standards, enlightened. The regent's relaxation of censorship, which had made possible publication of Montesquieu's *Lettres persanes* in 1721, had proved to be a false dawn; but that entertaining satire upon contemporary institutions and attitudes, through the transparently fictitious account of an ingenuous outsider, set the tone for the critical onslaught that was to be the main work of the *philosophes*. They were a party only in the sense of sharing certain assumptions: notably that human reason was the best guide in the search for a society which offered fewer obstacles to the pursuit of happiness which was man's proper aspiration. They became aware of being a party in the critical mid-century decades when they experienced enough persecution to alienate them and create a sense of solidarity and mission, but not enough to silence them. In 1748, *parlement* ordered the burning of Toussaint's *Les Moeurs*, a mildly deistical tract. Diderot was imprisoned briefly at Vincennes, in 1749. His *Encyclopédie* was banned in 1751: the start of a prolonged saga of obstruction which delayed but did not prevent the completion of the great work, in thirty-five volumes, by 1786. Voltaire, banned from France by the king, found a congenial retreat on the Swiss border; the next twenty-four years, till his death in 1778, were to see his reputation grow to the point at which he could be described as the most famous man in Europe. How effective then were the efforts of government to censor and check subversive writing? Evidently they did not prevent those who wished to obtain a banned book from one of the numerous *colporteurs* who, with the publishers prepared to risk printing an illicit book, were in the front line of this war of ideas. Was it a serious war at all? The crown struck, but as it were apologetically; it condemned, and yet connived. Chancellor d'Aguesseau allowed Montesquieu's *L'Esprit des lois* to be printed in Paris – so long as the name of a foreign town appeared on the title-page. Even disapproval cannot be assumed. Occupying from 1750 to 1763 the key post of director of the *Librairie*, without whose sanction books could not officially be published, Malesherbes saw to it that those he was supposed to be censoring came to no harm. But could they do much good?

[1] For the *philosophes*, in the context of the European Enlightenment, see also pp. 153–63.

Neither stimulated nor disciplined by the prospect of power, the *philosophes* exhibited the typical vices of a permanent opposition. They dealt blandly in abstractions, concentrated on relatively safe areas where abuses were obvious or where science was irrefutable, and vented their frustration in largely destructive criticism. It is instructive to compare the energy and passion that went into the attack on the Jesuits with the paucity of serious thinking about questions of education, law or, most damning, relief of poverty, the condition of that large number of Frenchmen whom Voltaire habitually referred to as *canaille*. It is sobering to reflect that the expulsion of the Jesuits, which appeared to be the greatest triumph of *l'esprit philosophique*, was due primarily to traditional *parlementaire* Gallicanism, reinforced by Jansenism and marshalled by a determined minister. In their comfortable cultural milieu individual *philosophes* were revered; politically they appeared to be irrelevant. Inevitably they looked outside, to apparently more malleable societies, more responsive rulers: Voltaire to Frederick II of Prussia, Diderot to Catherine II. When Jean-Jacques Rousseau, author of the *Contrat social* (1762), sought objective criteria by which to make political judgements, he referred to an idealized Sparta or Rome. Montesquieu dwelt upon England, where the rule of law was to be observed, a standing reproach to the arbitrary government of France; he misrepresented to some extent the English constitution when he drew particular attention to 'the separation of powers'. The work of a profound, subtle and original mind, 'the best system of political knowledge that, perhaps, has yet been communicated to the world', in Hume's opinion, *L'Esprit* was remarkable mainly for its critical insights, for example into the nature of law or the characteristics of a republic, rather than for sustained enquiry.

The *Encyclopédie* was inspired by the idea of knowledge as a social function: it was assembled, in the words of Diderot's own article, entitled 'Encyclopédie', 'so that our children, better instructed than we, may at the same time become more virtuous and happy.' It was the work of men who did not envisage for themselves a political role or expect to achieve their goals by political means. The physiocrats, the small but articulate band of economic theorists who from the late 1750s advocated the removal of what they believed to be the artificial obstacles blocking the 'natural' economic order of a free market for the produce of the land, addressed themselves intelligently to the actual problems of society but they ignored, for the most part, the question of political implementation. In the writing of Quesnay and Mirabeau, however, a common programme can be discerned. When Turgot became *contrôleur-général* in 1774, they saw one of their number put theory into practice with a series of measures more radical than anything seen before. By contrast, the *philosophes*, confronted by the fundamental question of political authority, could only agree upon certain general principles. Montesquieu, whose special concern was the sanctity of human law and established custom in government, favoured greater authority for the nobility. Voltaire wished rulers to use their authority to aid their subjects by freeing them from superstition and the abuse of archaic laws. When occasion arose, as it did in the action of the demonstrably biased magistrates of Toulouse who were responsible for the death after torture of Jean Calas, in 1762, he was able to treat a peculiar case and an archaic law as symptoms of a more general wrong and appeal to the 'enlightened' audience with his resounding warcry: '*écrasez l'infame*'. By then the audience was growing: already the *Encyclopédie* had gone some way, in its editor's words, 'to change the common way of thinking'. It was Diderot who responded to the critical conflict between Maupeou and the *parlements* in 1771, with his celebrated judgement:

> Each century has its characteristic spirit. The spirit of ours seems to be that of liberty. The first attack, against superstition, has been violent, beyond measure. Once men have dared in some way to launch an assault upon the barrier of religion, the most formidable of barriers, as it is the most respected, there is no stopping them.

More significant than the rhetoric is the fact that on the Maupeou issue Diderot and Voltaire, the two men who had done more than any to combat 'superstition', were diametrically opposed, Voltaire approving, Diderot condemning the chancellor's policy.

There is no doubt that the assault upon 'despotism' would have been more effective if, at that juncture, the *philosophes* had presented a united front. In the event the accession of Louis XVI did more for *parlement* than all the pamphlets of their protagonists. Meanwhile, however, the war of words had begun to affect the regime in a way analogous to the effect of earlier controversies over Jansenism on the Church. Montesquieu's definition of despotism had become widely accepted: wholly bad, corrupt by its very nature, destructive by principle, maintained by violence, bloodshed and the promotion of ignorance. He did not specifically accuse Louis XV of being despotic. But his account of Richelieu and Louis XIV leaves the reader of *L'Esprit* in no doubt about what he feared. And his warning was clear: servitude, he said, begins with sleep. Many, it seemed, in 1771, were awake. Montesquieu's works became an armoury where *parlementaires*, fighting for their rights, could find the weapons they wanted. His doctrine of intermediary powers took on a new significance. By then, of course, the word 'despotism' had become a cliché, signifying any kind of authority which its user might find objectionable. By then too, the language and ideas of Rousseau were appearing in the political pamphlets. In at least one quarter *philosophes* could point to progress. A commission was at work upon the dissolution of the smaller monasteries and the reallocation of their revenues. There was talk, even among the bishops, of the need for toleration.

Is it possible to strike a balance? The *philosophes* continued to move in different directions and to speak with discordant voices. After the publication of Holbach's *Système de la nature*, they fell into two distinct camps: those who accepted and those who rejected his dogmatic atheism. Voltaire, who thought that Holbach had committed an act of intellectual tyranny, was among the latter. Not surprisingly, their challenges were uncoordinated; their record, whether measured in political or social terms, was modest. It was the *salons*, to a lesser extent the learned societies, which were chiefly affected. But they were unlikely to become cells of political radicalism, like the clubs of revolutionary France which were made possible by the novel political opportunity of 1789. Jacobins and Cordeliers were recruited from among the frustrated young journalists and lawyers on the edge of the professional élites, who had picked up what has been called 'gutter Rousseau-ism', those elements in the paradoxical philosopher's work that fitted in with their sour view of a society that denied them scope for their talents. Essentially that was a social rather than an intellectual phenomenon, having little to do with the aspirations and values of the *philosophes*. Meanwhile the ordinary educated Frenchmen continued to pursue traditional interests: 60 cent cent of all titles published in provincial France in the 1780s were religious. Even in the intellectual world the case for orthodoxy was stoutly maintained, as by the pugnacious Fréron. The vigour of counter-attack does show, however, that the *philosophes* had done some damage. By persistently emphasizing the ability of man to manage his own affairs without divine intervention, and aided by the public quarrels within the Church, they had undermined confidence both in the Church and in the state which supported it. By using in print all the resources of a language that in its logic and clarity was so well-suited to public debate, they had introduced to the nation ideas that challenged the inequalities and anomalies of the regime. Partisans for *parlement* talked of *nation* and called themselves *patriots* and *citoyens*: old concerns but a new language, potentially that of revolution. The *philosophes* had played their part in discrediting the regime, so that when the crisis came there was a fatal failure of confidence in its validity among those who should have been its committed supporters. Only when it had disintegrated and *citoyens* had to make a fresh start and design new institutions, did it turn out that they took for granted the axioms and standards of the Enlightenment: reason, humanity, utility. By its inadequacies royal government had provoked, out of a number of talented writers, the crusade of the *philosophes*; by its fall it endowed them with a retrospective glory. It had not been destroyed by external assault. It had simply broken down through inherent weaknesses, leading to bankruptcy.

Financial Manoeuvres

Government, seen to be arbitrary in the matter of Jansenism, could only command respect if it passed the most important practical test, that of solvency; mostly it did not. Therefore, it had to have recourse to further arbitrary actions. Yet the financial legacy was less unfavourable than might have been expected after the huge deficits of Louis XIV's last decade and the failure of Law's schemes. The ruin then of many investors engendered mistrust and discredited the idea of the state bank which was what France so badly needed; but the general debacle did enable government to carry out a drastic repudiation of debts and reduction of interest rates. It could also be seen retrospectively that Louis XIV's government had made a decisive breakthrough with the *dixième* of 1710. *Parlement* had then ceded, in effect, the principle that the privileged classes should pay tax. It was, therefore, reduced to two lines of opposition: first, to any attempt to alter the existing system for raising taxes and loans, second, to the levying of further taxes in peacetime. The first was easier after the fall of Law and the triumph then of the old financial regime. But the second rested on the dubious assumption that the financial provision was adequate for government expenditure. Periodically in peacetime, invariably in wartime, it proved not to be. Then *contrôleurs-généraux* found themselves hamstrung by the rigidity of the system. To make occasional scapegoats of exceptionally greedy or peccant financiers was no substitute for the capacity of rulers of some smaller states, like Prussia, to shape the system to meet the needs of the state. Ministers, whom *parlements* naturally saw as unscrupulous predators, were reduced to expedients more or less radical according to the temperament of the minister and to the degree of emergency. It is this haphazard way of proceeding, by ministers sometimes frustrated, sometimes taking the easy way out, knowing that they could not rely on the king to back them if they chose, like Bertin in 1763, to challenge *parlement*, that creates the impression of years of wasted opportunity; all the more because all the evidence points to France's growing prosperity in these years.

Between 1730 and 1770 national income rose faster than that of England. The long run of good harvests during those years was broken only in 1739–41, the years, as it happens which saw the fateful departure from the pacific foreign policy of Fleury. Low wheat prices during these forty years show that production was rising to match the growth of population. Indeed the evidence suggests that food production in some areas may have doubled. Agricultural rents certainly doubled, reflecting the keen search for land, with younger sons looking for holdings sufficient to support their families. The benefits were unevenly distributed and most peasants remained poor; some were still indigent and beggars, but there were no serious famines.[1] The ambition of *intendants*, the pressure of local men of substance, the administrative and strategic needs of government, were responsible for the supplying of men to work on the hated *corvée* which was giving France the best roads in Europe. Canal making was important; though the vaunted

[1] Olwen Hufton's study of *The Poor of Eighteenth Century France* (1974) provides a sombre corrective to any idea that the general improvement in economic conditions did much to improve the lot of the majority of the population. See also pp. 46–52 above.

'Canal of the Two Seas' was of little commercial value, more modest undertakings, like that which joined the Oise and Somme (1734), helped to reduce costs and delays. Tolls remained a formidable barrier to trade, the target of the physiocrats who placed their trust in the free market. Away from the trunk roads or negotiable waterways, villages were linked, for the most part, by simple tracks and limited to local markets. That is one reason why it is hard to gauge the precise effects of increased purchase power, together with improved facilities for the conveyance of goods, upon the overall level of demand. It is likely that the poorer classes, the majority, simply ate more. For the minority of *laboureurs*, on the other hand, those who had substantial holdings, good harvests, resulting in lower grain prices, were a mixed blessing. But such men had the capital to divert to other forms of production. It was of course to the small but disproportionately influential class of large landowners that prosperity, translated into higher rents, brought the greatest benefits; the effect was to be seen in greater spending on those luxuries for which French craftsmen were already justly famous, fine porcelain, fabrics, glass, clocks, jewellery, and so on. But the contribution of the increasing number of middling people, the small officials and professional men, the better-off craftsmen and shopkeepers, should not be ignored. They benefited generally from the rise in economic activity. Spending normally about a fifth of their income on bread and flour, they found themselves with a larger margin for expenditure on all those goods in the area which cannot be classified strictly as either necessary or luxury, whose production sustained the economy of towns, large and small: knives, locks, buttons, hats, soap, paper, glass, pewter and metalware of all descriptions, and they required specialist skills and services which were not to be found in the villages.

With 60 per cent of all national production accounted for by agriculture, the sequence of good harvests was clearly a major factor. Similarly when, with bad harvests in 1770–1, the sequence broke, the fundamental limitations of the agrarian economy were exposed, as the country encountered the subsistence crisis which, rather than any long-term plan, evoked the drastic measures of *contrôleur-général* Terray. Meanwhile there were other factors at work outside agriculture. In this early phase of development, before anything so dramatic as to justify the phrase 'industrial revolution', there was greater regional specialization in manufactures and a notable expansion in the textile industries, in particular in linen manufacture. The woollen industry of Languedoc was capturing the Mediterranean and Spanish markets from the Dutch, assisted by the friendly relationship between the French and Spanish governments which was one of the enduring benefits of foreign policy. In Normandy the cotton industry grew apace, doubling between 1732 and 1766, before an even greater advance in the next twenty years. A strong school of thought, represented notably by Raynal, opposed the whole colonial system, but on moral as well as on material grounds. It did not prevent the growth of the colonies, with a prime market in the West Indies, giving valuable stimulus to exports. The French captured the lucrative northern European market in sugar and pioneered the coffee trade. The leading city in the re-export trade, which grew overall eightfold in their century, was Bordeaux, handling a quarter of all the country's export trade, and re-exporting most of the coffee and sugar that came in.

The question that faced successive ministers is easier for us to frame than it was for them to resolve: how to ensure that the state gained a proportionate share of the wealth that was being created, so as to meet its expenses and reduce dependence on borrowing. It was in part an administrative question, in part political. Accountancy and the servicing of debts was in the hands of officials whose main concern was to preserve the importance and profitability of offices which represented a large capital investment and security for their families. By comparison with the British and the Dutch it was not the size of the French debt that was remarkable, at least until after 1778 and the American war, but the rate of interest that had to be paid: at 6 per cent nearly double that of its rivals. Because there was no efficient state system, ministers were dependent on private credit and on financiers operating within a restricted market in which they occupied a privileged position, with access to ministers at the highest level. Acting as individuals or as members of a consortium, they were able to produce the money but at rates which reflected not only economic conditions, but also current views of the soundness, or otherwise, of the regime. This was the background to the recurring drama of conflict between government and *parlement* which is the central political theme of the reign. The interaction of religious and financial issues showed that it was, in reality, a matter of authority. The crown had to show that it was in control. As we have seen it did not always choose wisely the ground or the weapons. By adherence to foreign policies leading to wars it incurred financial obligations which reduced its bargaining power; failures in those wars, particularly after 1756, further weakened its hold on public opinion and therefore, as shown by Louis XV's pusillanimous conduct in the 1760s, the nerve to assume the full powers of autocracy.

In 1749 Machault d'Arnouville won a limited victory, over the *vingtième*, a new tax, required to meet the cumulative deficit incurred in the War of the Austrian Succession: 5 per cent on all incomes, whether derived from property, office or commerce, it was designed to be levied on all classes of society. It was forced through by means of a *lit de justice*, but its value was reduced when the clergy, after a loud and well-orchestrated campaign, supported by the queen and the dauphin, secured their exemption. The war minister, d'Argenson, helped to undermine his colleagues' standing when he joined the abolition lobby: it pinpoints a crucial weakness. There was an outcry against the inquisitorial methods of the assessors, reminiscent of the opposition to the excise bill in Walpole's England: it was, declared the Toulouse *parlement*, 'not unlike a census of slaves'. The provincial estates, too, flexed their political muscles and enjoyed a chance to orate on real issues, securing out of the general clamour a relatively light treatment for their already privileged provinces, the *pays d'états*. In 1753 *parlement* fought on familiar ground when framing the *Grandes Remonstrances* in answer to the crown's attempt to move the Jansenist dispute to the *grand conseil*, in order to bring it nearer ministerial control. They were emboldened to fight back when, in 1756, Machault persuaded the king to issue a number of edicts, designed to limit the power of *parlements* to resist the crown. They prohibited recourse by the judiciary to closing the courts (the judicial strike) and to repeated remonstrances. Two of the five *chambres des enquêtes* were suppressed so that the balance of power was shifted to the *grand chambre*. The result was an unprecedented union between all five *chambres*, half the *grand chambre* and the provincial *parlements*.

The onset of the Seven Years War in 1756 left the crown little room to manoeuvre. *Parlement* accepted a second and third *vingtième* on the understanding that they would be temporary. (Of course they weren't, though the third *vingtième* was cancelled because of opposition in *parlement* in 1763: Bertin, then *contrôleur-général*, who wanted to retain the tax to reduce the high level of borrowing, resigned.) The crown effectively withdrew its edicts; two *chambres* were indeed suppressed but their personnel were transferred to other courts. Machault, who had managed to antagonize all important interests, clergy, provincial estates, *parlements* and financiers, was transferred to the navy, a department better suited to his authoritarian temperament, though a gruelling assignment, as it was to turn out.

The Coup Maupeou

Indirectly it was the needs of the navy which led to the boldest challenge to the regime and thence to the sternest response by the crown. The government wanted to make the Bretons pay for the new military roads, designed to link their ports. The naval operations of the Seven Years War had emphasized the strategic importance of Brittany. The province was no longer a backwater in military terms, but it remained for the most part poor and scarcely able, without substantial levies on the rich, to provide the funds for the government's projects. The autocratic governor, d'Aiguillon, clashed with the province's *parlement*, the most aristocratic in the country, and in particular its *procureur-général*, La Chalotais. The struggle could not be contained within Brittany for the principles at stake were fundamental ones, affecting the authority of the crown. When the king created a new judicial court at Rennes, other *parlements* declared their support for the original *parlement*; when La Chalotais was found to be pressing his case at court he was arrested. In March 1766 Louis held his notorious *séance de la flagellation*, a *lit de justice* so called because of the scathing terms in which he expressed his rejection of *parlement*'s claims as unacceptable novelties. He was a different man from the demoralized king who had abandoned Bertin and his *vingtième* in 1763. His own definition of absolute power was comprehensive and unequivocal:

> It is to me alone that the legislative power belongs, without dependence and without sharing; it is by my authority alone that the officers of my courts proceed, not to the making of the law, but to its registration, its publication, its execution. . . . The entire public order emanates from me, as the rights and interests of the nation . . . are necessarily one with mine and rest only in my hands.

He spoke in traditional terms but the climate had so changed that he now sounded like the despot against whom Montesquieu, now much read and respected, warned, when he wrote of *parlement*'s limiting role. No good government, he felt, could be extreme: 'one can not speak of these monstrous governments without shuddering.'

When the 'Coup Maupeou' of 1771 showed how flimsy was the defence against such government, the argument was not ended; on the contrary it was taken up and extended to the dangerous point at which compromise began to seem like weakness. On the one hand writers like Le Mercier advocated 'legal despotism' under a monarch controlled by the law, not man-made but that of nature. On the other hand, following such parts of the richly ambiguous Rousseau as suited them, there were now writers to put forward the idea that *parlement* embodied the will of the nation: and if *parlement* could not act effectively, then it must be replaced or joined by a representative body which could. They found a ready response. There had been a number of confrontations with the courts of Besançon, Grenoble and Toulouse; those of Pau and Rennes had been dissolved and remodelled. Such attacks on rightful property, as their offices were regarded, inspired the defensive doctrine of classes, the idea that the separate courts were only classes of a single indivisible *parlement*. At the same time the courts began to make much use of the vocabulary of rights, with emotive terms such as *nation* and *citoyen*. When in 1771, the cry for an estates-general was first heard, it fell on friendly ears throughout France.

Maupeou was an experienced lawyer who had distinguished himself upholding the king's interests before *parlement*. When he became chancellor, however, in 1768, it does not seem that he intended to force a showdown, let along abolish *parlement*. He was a dry, unsentimental little man, the 'Seville Orange' to his detractors, essentially pragmatic in his approach. He was, however, determined to overthrow Choiseul and to this end he provoked *parlement* in order to be able to accuse Choiseul of encouraging its defiance. Possibly Louis XV was influenced against Choiseul by his new mistress, Mme du Barry, who wanted to promote d'Aiguillon. He was undoubtedly concerned about the prospect of Choiseul dragging France into war; and he was resolved – for once the word can be used of him – to teach *parlement* a lesson. In December 1770 Choiseul was curtly dismissed. But the *parlement* persisted in the judicial strike with which it had replied to Maupeou's first attack. Early in 1771 Louis sanctioned Maupeou's brutal coup. The magistrates were banished to country towns, their venal offices were abolished and a new network of lower jurisdictions was established which should be easier to access than those they replaced. The offices in the new courts were to be by appointment, not for sale; judicial fees were abolished. When the provincial *parlements* protested, they too were remodelled. It is not hard to see why historians have been impressed by the achievement, and correspondingly critical of Louis XVI's restoration of *parlement*; nor why there was a storm of protest at this unprecedented act of tyranny from the legal establishment and its eloquent friends. Voltaire, however, applauded the chancellor for his courage and looked forward to the implementation of his promised reforms, in particular a new code of law. There is less inconsistency in his view than may appear. He could suspect *parlement* when it espoused the cause of Jansenists against clerical tyranny, or attacked the Jesuits. But he had no illusions about its character, reactionary and concerned essentially with its own corporate interests. Nor was he alone among the *philosophes*: Condorcet declared that '*Parlement* was less advanced towards reason than it was two centuries ago.' It is a reminder that *l'esprit philosophique* was fundamentally opposed to *l'esprit juridique*, something that had been obscured during the conflict over Jansenism, which had created a common front, united by anticlericalism. Standing firm in the centre of the storm, Maupeou was undoubtedly brave, but he was no radical. His code never materialized and his free justice had to be paid for by higher taxes. He had acted as he did because he was convinced that it was essentially to clear the field for his colleague Terray, who was wrestling with the consequences of the most serious economic crisis of the reign.

The *abbé* Terray, *contrôleur-général* since 1769, was perhaps underestimated, certainly widely misunderstood. For example, it was rumoured that he was in league with sinister profiteers in an alleged *pacte du famine* (and criticism of Mme du Barry in this context touched the king himself). In fact he reimposed controls, regulated the grain trade and built up stocks of grain through purchases in the less afflicted provinces in order to provide practical relief for the starving after the first of a sequence of crop failures which affected altogether a third of the country. In this respect of course he was offending the main precept of the physiocrats, which was fast becoming the conventional wisdom: that local shortages of grain were due to regulations hampering the free passage of grain from one province to another. Such theorists are never happy to allow for natural phenomena. Complacency had been encouraged too by the series of good seasons which were largely responsible for what Pierre Goubert writes of as the 'unprecedented blaze of prosperity which nourished the kingdom between 1763 and 1770'. They had come to an end with a vengeance and Terray was better placed than any previous *contrôleur-général* to know the full extent of the shortages and suffering. Goubert calls him 'the veritable creator of French statistics': he obtained uniquely thorough reports, from all provinces, of production, population and price movements. Grain prices rose in 1770 higher than at any time in Louis XV's reign; higher too than in any subsequent year till 1789. It was an unhappy coincidence that the crown had just, in 1769, given its sanction to the enclosure of common lands: in increasing numbers peasants lost the rights to graze animals or gather firewood which might just make the difference between survival and ruin. But rents continued to rise and there was increasing speculation in land values. The gap between the richest and poorest widened ominously. At the same time industrial workers in town and countryside suffered from the decline in manufactures, mainly textiles, which inevitably accompanied a rise in grain prices; with unemployed men faced with dearer bread, reports of bread riots fill the *intendant*'s reports. Trading was affected at all levels: there were 2500 business failures in 1769–70 and several prominent financiers were ruined. Terray was faced by a crisis of confidence, with private bankruptcies weakening the credit of the government, dependent as it was on private finance. He pre-empted events by declaring a partial bankruptcy while protecting the credit of the royal treasurers. He turned misfortune to good account by abolishing many financial offices and tightening up the accounting process. The great tax farmers had thereafter to yield more in funds and take less in payment. He nationalized, as it were, the royal treasury, and so placed crown spending directly under the control of his department. He had no difficulty in securing approval of increased taxes from the remodelled *parlements*. The figures show what might have been achieved if France had not entered the American war. In 1763 the government's deficit was 50 million *livres*; it had been reduced to 40 million by 1774; in 1786 it reached 112 million.

Louis XV died of smallpox in 1774. It is significant that, when Louis XVI restored the old *parlement*, it was at first disposed to co-operate: the magistrates had realized their essential weakness and were prepared to give a new regime the benefit of the doubt. That it was in a position to make a confident beginning (too confident, critics might say of Turgot's doctrinaire measures) was to some extent the result of the reforms of Maupeou and Terray. Those reforms may have been forced on them, but by their courage and intelligence they had elevated the authority of the crown to the point at which it had more to gain than to fear from reasonable change. It may be that their critics are right and that Maupeou and Terray did not have the vision to travel further along the road of reform. But it seems on balance a misfortune for France that they did not have longer to try: a misfortune compounded by the accession of a king who undoubtedly cared more for his subjects than his grandfather had done, but understood even less about their government.

Further Reading

Inevitably the Revolution casts its shadow over the history of France in the reign of Louis XV, as can be seen from the assumptions behind such contentious questions as the extent of 'the feudal reaction' and the role of the Enlightenment in preparing for the Revolution, as, indeed, from the title of a recent pamphlet by J.H. Shennan, *France Before the Revolution* (London, 1983). The emphasis on the Revolution does, however, concentrate the mind on the events of the preceding years. This is the effect of a stimulating and forceful book by William Doyle, *Origins of the French Revolution* (Oxford, 1981): despite its title, it is essential reading for Louis XV. The picture of his reign has been transformed during the past twenty-five years and the process of reassessment is still continuing. The reader will do well to consult the first chapter of M.S. Anderson's stimulating *Historians and 18th Century Europe* (Oxford, 1979), for an objective summary of views, past and present. The student now has plenty of material to work on: it includes some particularly forceful and appealing works, like those of Ford, McManners and Hufton, listed below, each of wider interest than their titles suggest.

In A. Cobban, *History of Modern France*, vol. 1 (Harmondsworth, 1969), the reader will find a useful introduction, which he may supplement with the same author's chapter in the *New Cambridge Modern History*, vol. 7, 'The decline of divine right monarchy', and in essays like '*Parlements* of France in the 18th century', in his *Aspects of the French Revolution* (1968), in which he develops themes that are cursorily treated in his *History*. In the collection *France, Government and Society*, ed. J.M. Wallace-Hadrill and J. McManners (1957), J.S. Bromley's 'The decline of absolute monarchy' is still valuable. J.H. Shennan provides a constitutional account of the reign in the later sections of his *Parlement of Paris* (1968). His *Philippe duc d'Orléans* (London, 1979) offers a reliable account of the regency as well as of its central figure. Though his main thesis, that there was a merging of the interests of the aristocracies of 'robe' and 'sword', has been disputed, F.L. Ford's *Robe and Sword* (Cambridge, Mass., 1953) is invaluable and a model of writing which wears its learning lightly. The vital work of the *intendants* is studied in V.R. Gruder, *Royal Provincial Intendants: a Governing Elite in 18th Century France* (Ithaca, 1968). An article by Peter Burley in *History Today*, 34 (January 1984), 'The *ancien régime* in debt', explains the financial situation at the end of Louis XV's reign.

Louis XV does not tempt the biographer. The best account, though emphasizing affairs of court and diplomacy in the traditional way, is still that of G.P. Gooch, *Louis XV* (London, 1976). J.H. Shennan's essay, 'Louis XV, public and private worlds', in *The Courts of Europe*, ed. A.G. Dickens (London, 1978), deserves mention. The opinions of Englishmen and Frenchmen respectively may be studied in C. Maxwell, *The English Traveller in France* (1932), and J. Lough, *An Introduction to 18th Century France* (1960), with its useful summaries of the political story and the social scene. Social history may be approached through C.B.A. Behrens,

Ancien Régime (London, 1967). Sombre but compelling in its weight of evidence is Olwen Hufton's *The Poor of Eighteenth Century France* (Oxford, 1974). Besides other local studies mentioned in the previous chapter, works which relate to this period particularly include the same author's *Bayeux in the Late Eighteenth Century* (Oxford, 1967); J. Kaplow, *The Names of Kings: Parisian Labouring Poor in the 18th Century* (The Hague, 1972); T.J.A. Le Goff, *Vannes and its Region: A Study of Town and Country in Eighteenth Century France* (Oxford, 1980); and R. Forester, *The House of Saulx – Tavanes, Versailles and Burgundy, 1700–1830* (Baltimore, 1972).

The history of ideas (for which, see also chapter 4) may be approached through P. Hazard, *The European Mind* (trans. 1953), and J. Brumfitt, *The French Enlightenment* (London, 1972). T. Bestermann's *Voltaire* (1969), A.M. Wilson's *Diderot* (Oxford, 1972) and R. Shackleton's *Montesquieu* (Oxford, 1961) are each written with the authority of long study. A fine study of Voltaire is by H.T. Mason, *Voltaire* (London, 1981). D.D. Bien has written a powerful account of *The Calas Affair* (London, 1979). Concerning religious life, J. McManners has written memorably and with rare humour in his study of Angers, *French Ecclesiastical Society under the Ancien Régime* (Manchester, 1969). The religious counter-attack against the Enlightenment is the theme of R.R. Palmer's *Catholics and Unbelievers in 18th Century France* (1939). Another important topic is dealt with in D. van Kley, *The Jansenists and the Expulsion of the Jesuits from France (1757–65)* (New York, 1975).

9

SPAIN AND PORTUGAL

War and Revolts

Newly king, 16 years old, Philip IV (1621–65) had addressed his *cortes* concerning Spain's mission 'to aid the rebel Hollanders again and to defend everywhere our sacred faith and the authority of the Holy See'. It was the manifesto of a Christian imperialism, sincere, chivalrous and less impracticable than it may appear in the light of subsequent experience. It appeared menacing enough to Protestants when Spinola occupied the Lower Palatinate and again when he captured Breda (1625). Until the entry of Gustavus Adolphus into the war in 1631, there was no power in Germany to stand up to the victorious Habsburgs. Olivares's plan to establish a base on the Baltic received a setback when Wallenstein failed to secure Stralsund in 1628 but it still appeared to be feasible, linked as it was to the Emperor's plan to recover the secularized bishoprics of northern Germany. Philip IV had not exaggerated unduly when he claimed in 1624 that the Spanish had 300,000 men under arms, in field armies, garrisons and the navy which boasted some 50 new galleons. Had Cardinal Richelieu not come to power in that year the Spanish hawks, who had ousted Lerma in 1619 on the war issue and who had seized on the Bohemian revolt of the year before as a golden chance to promote Spain's *reputación* and to recover the separated provinces of the Netherlands, might have been proved right. It was not only Olivares's decision to enter the Mantuan succession contest (1628–31), but Richelieu's intelligent exploitation of the issues that made it such a fateful turning point in the war. It could be argued that Spain's purpose was still primarily defensive, though in the context of positions and claims that were to Richelieu unacceptable. For him there was no doubt about the aggressive nature of Habsburg manoeuvres. Along with the sturdy resistance of the Dutch, it was his implacable hostility to the house of Habsburg and his readiness to associate with Lutheran Sweden in the interest of French security that checked defeated Spain. By 1640, the year of the Catalan and Portuguese revolts, the crisis of the Spanish state became plain for all to see. The art of government had long been the art of improvisation. The troops had been paid no more regularly in the sixteenth century than in the seventeenth. They continued to fight well when they were well led. The administration remained steady; indeed the king, taking more on himself, displayed a new seriousness of purpose; it showed itself in an unyielding attachment to his rights, a mixed blessing for his subjects. So there was no sudden collapse in this war of attrition; but the monarchy's resources, human and material, were expended at a rate which could not be sustained indefinitely.

There was a drastic reduction in the level of silver coming in from America in the 1640s: it can be measured in the drop in remittances to the army in Flanders: an average of 4 million crowns between 1635 and 1641; 1.5 million in 1643. It was not, however, the decisive factor. Not the least remarkable feature of the Spanish war effort is the crown's ability to find the wherewithal for each year's campaign from its own resources. Paradoxically, the general European recession may have helped since there was no shortage yet of hungry recruits. Condé's victory at Rocroy (1643) was a staggering blow to the prestige which was so important in the maintenance of recruitment and discipline; yet the Spanish forces were able to regroup the next year. In Flanders, where the garrisons held on stoutly; in Catalonia, where the French invaders were soon hated more than the Castilians for their arrogance and exactions; even in Italy, the natural focus of Mazarin's ambition, despite the promising opening there provided by the Neapolitan revolt in 1647, decisive victory eluded the French. Success at Lens (1648) did give Mazarin a useful counter in the final stages of negotiation. By then, however, his adopted country, enmeshed in commitments and debts, needed peace as badly as Spain: the Fronde underlined the failure to make such a peace along with the other settlements of 1648. It was due as much to Spanish obstinacy as to French ambition that peace had to wait for another eleven years.

Philip IV and his ministers, notably Haro, 'the diffident *valido*', Olivares's less ambitious and less autocratic successor, were encouraged by a revival of Spanish fortunes. In 1652 Barcelona capitulated to the king's illegitimate son, Don John, and Caracena succeeded, where the mighty Spinola had failed, in capturing Casale. The recovery of Dunkirk, nest of privateers and Spain's most advanced base until Turenne captured it in 1658, suggested that Spain would be able to consolidate its position in Flanders under the energetic direction of the young Austrian archduke Leopold William. The successes were, however, in large measure due to the way in which the French government was incapacitated by the Fronde, in which at different times both Turenne and Condé fought for the Spanish. The spectacle of Spanish soldiers pitching their tents on French soil, as in the 1590s, only hardened the French resolve to fight for complete security: given the Spanish weakness that would take them beyond existing frontiers. Meanwhile the blood-letting went on: between 1638 and 1643 alone Spain lost 30,000 soldiers and sailors, many of them on the Peninsula. The losses were the more serious because of the steady erosion of the resources of Italy. The revolt of the Neapolitans under Masaniello in 1647, taking their cue from the Sicilians of Palermo, stirred up by Mazarin's agents, was caused essentially by twenty years of mounting exactions: after Castile and Milan, Naples contributed more soldiers and taxes in proportion to the population than any part of the Empire. The revolt was repressed. But in 1655 plague, which had already visited Genoa and Milan, brought frightful mortality to Naples's crowded tenements. By then few Italians were fighting in the *tercios*; in their desperation the authorities were recruiting Irishmen, ever the last resort of needy governments.

Like his contemporaries Richelieu and Strafford, the count-duke of Olivares (1587–1645), Philip IV's *privado* or chief minister from 1622, made himself loathed by his ruthless efforts to keep the state afloat. He had bullied bankers, sanctioned debased currency and issued more government bonds. He had introduced reforming decrees: the reduction of offices, restrictions on dress and jewellery and the closing of grammar schools. But results were trivial: the court and bureaucracy defied retrenchment, while Philip IV, despite good intentions and conscientious efforts to read state papers, showed a discouraging lack of moral or political stamina. In administration Olivares had achieved more efficient operation through small *juntas*, staffed by men devoted and responsible to him. At the top, the *junta de ejecución* made policy under his direction. He had the courage to attack the Church and the nobles: cathedral chapters and abbeys were made to pay unprecedented sums and hidalgos were made to serve in the army at their own expense. Prodigiously active and inventive, devoted to Castile, Olivares had represented the hopes of the *arbitristas*, the academic authors of schemes for the restoration of Spain's industries, for fairer taxes and a reduction in the swollen mass of office holders and rentiers living comfortably off government bonds. He understood moreover the need to correct the imbalance between Castile and Aragon, so gravely weighted against Castile as the American trade fell away and other provinces paid relatively little in taxation: Aragon sheltered behind its constitution, Valencia was impoverished by the expulsion of the Moriscoes. He cared much for uniformity but deserted fields and despairing tax farmers spoke more loudly than any theory. It is typical of his grandiose style, however, that he conceived a plan

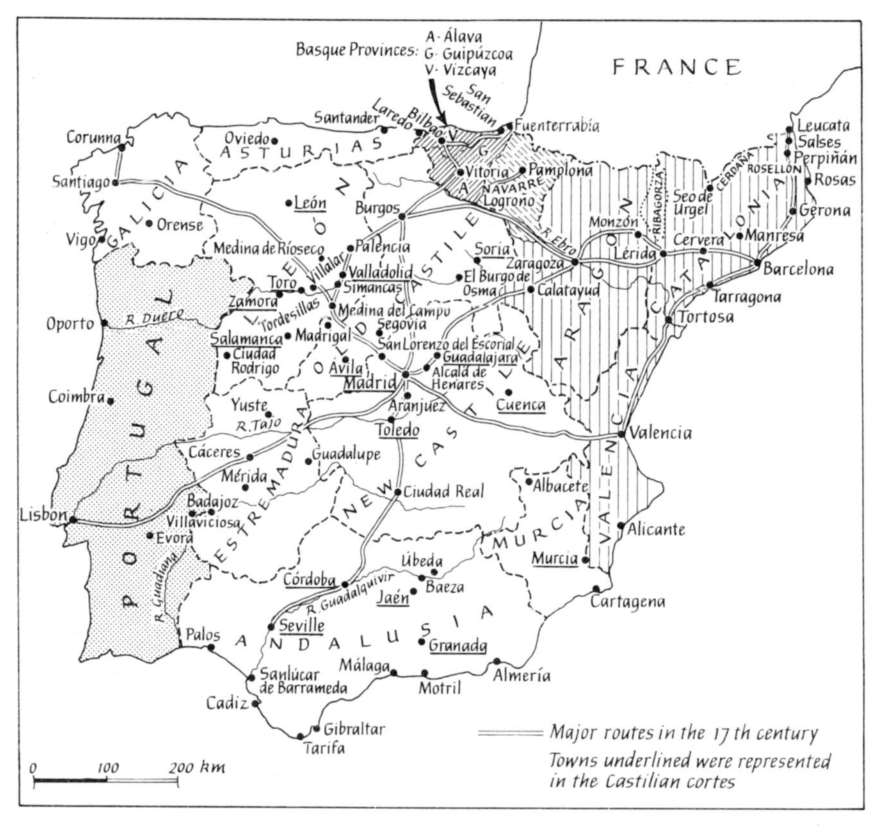

Map 9.1 *Habsburg Spain*

to answer several needs at once. His Union of Arms, projected in 1624, was an attempt to equalize contributions from the different provinces of the empire, according to their size and wealth, and to create a larger army to relieve the pressure upon Castile and to prepare the ground for the full political and economic union, '*un rey, una ley, una moneda*', envisaged in his famous memorandum. As in France, England and in the lands of the Austrian Habsburgs, the most sensitive areas were those on the periphery: provinces that did not wish to pay for the doubtful privilege of royal government. Today, when the unitary state is under challenge from lively separatist movements, Breton, Scottish, Basque, it is easier than it was to appreciate the passions aroused by the first steps towards central direction in the state; in this case the lack of enthusiasm shown in Catalonia for Olivares's 'sole cure for all the ills that can arise, namely that as loyal vassals we all unite'. The policy failed, for lack of administrative machinery and military force to overcome the reluctance of the provinces to behave like vassals or to subscribe to an ideal of unity which simply meant to them Castilianization – and higher taxes. From 1635, as the war with France brought new burdens, the monarchy's relations with Catalonia and Portugal deteriorated. The Catalans would not provide, or pay for, troops for their own defence against the French. The Catalans had indeed lost much Mediterranean trade; but Barcelona was still the richest city in Spain and, to a Castilian, the Catalans appeared more concerned with protecting their privileges than with assisting the monarchy at its time of need. Olivares regarded the province as 'entirely separate from the rest of the monarchy and useless for service'. But it conveys something of the primitive state of administration, and the handicaps under which a seventeenth-century statesman laboured, that Olivares estimated the population of this province at 1 million while it was in fact around 400,000.

In 1638 the French invaded Guipúzcoa; but Catalonia sent no troops. In 1639 Olivares deliberately mounted a major campaign and pressed the Catalans for money and troops in order to involve them in the war. By the time Olivares realized that he had misjudged the situation, a series of clashes had developed into a general revolt. The *Diputació*, posing as defender of Catalan laws, made contact with the French. Demagogues found mass support among the lesser peasantry and casual labourers. In June, the viceroy Santa Coloma was murdered on a Barcelona beach as he tried to escape the mob. Olivares, though unwilling to conciliate, was unable to conquer. In January 1641 the marquis de los Vélez, a royal commander, was defeated outside the walls of Barcelona. The better-off Catalans soon regretted their separatist enthusiasm as the revolt acquired a radical character; but the province proved hard to reconquer. In January 1643 Olivares resigned, a defeated man. In 1644 Philip IV guaranteed the Catalan constitution. The French showed that they cared more for Catalonia's strategic use than for its constitution or economy, but the outbreak of the Fronde weakened their war effort. In 1651–2 Philip took advantage of Catalan divisions to mount a more energetic campaign: in October 1652 Barcelona surrendered to Don Juan. Thereafter, operations were confined to the frontier as both sides sought counters for peace negotiations. In the peace of the Pyrenees (1654) Spain lost Roussillon and Cerdagne to France. The Catalans had lost far more than two provinces. Ironically, French requisitions, billeting, war damage and the disruption of trade had reduced the province to a near-Castilian condition. To cap all, the great plague of 1650–4 decimated the population, claiming 36,000 victims in Barcelona alone.

Since the union of the crowns in 1580, Portugal had been a valuable strategic and economic asset to Spain. With Portugal, Spain had acquired a navy and a colonial empire: Brazil, and stations in the East Indies and West Africa. To some extent, the two commercial empires were complementary. Portugal, whose empire was a commercial one without extensive settlements, needed Spanish American bullion for exchange purposes; Spain needed the pepper, spices, silks and other eastern goods which her own empire did not provide. The conditions on which Portugal was incorporated in the Spanish empire were not extreme, but based on Philip II's governing principle of devolution: the Portuguese were left to administer their own empire, the country was to be garrisoned only by Portuguese forces; the *cortes* was not to be convoked outside Portugal and the king would not legislate for Portugal in a foreign assembly; the council of Portugal would be drawn from men of Portuguese birth. Unhappily for the Portuguese, with Spain's protection they acquired her enemies. In the 1590s the Dutch began to attack the Portuguese monopoly in the Far East: a process which was to end in its destruction. Because the Spanish were fully occupied in defending their own empire Portuguese interests in Asia and Brazil were neglected. Spain's involvement in the Thirty Years War was a disaster for Portugal. Her overseas interests were crucially affected by decisions in which she had no say, decisions moreover which seemed to be taken with regard exclusively to Castilian ambition and pride.

Portugal was not immune from the difficulties that beset Castile. With steady emigration, and numerous casualties amongst the sailors engaged upon the oceanic voyages, men whose skill and hardihood had long been a marvel of Christendom, besides the ravages of epidemics, culminating in the plague of 1599, the population could not grow; in 1640 it was 1.2 million. There were too few peasants to maintain the cities' food supplies with any margin of safety, but the non-productive members of society grew in numbers. The Church flourished, as in Spain, while commerce was largely taken over by the *conversos*, nominal Christians of Jewish extraction. Persecuted by the Inquisition, often fined, sometimes driven to emigrate, these crypto-Jews yet performed a useful trading service. But they undoubtedly roused Portuguese resentments. The government in Madrid exploited their weak position, offering, then withdrawing, concessions for cash. Disgruntled Portuguese suspected collusion. Some envisaged a Jewish plot, directed from the Sephardic Jewish colony in Amsterdam whose members had emigrated there from Lisbon in the 1590s, involving too the Madrid community, which was protected against popular resentment, for his overriding financial reasons, by Olivares. It was a short step from there to the notion that Castilians were subscribing to an unholy alliance of international capitalism to take over the Portuguese empire.

It was against this unpropitious background that Olivares sought to exact a higher contribution to the imperial war effort: Portugal might not be interested in Mantua or Artois, but they could be expected to pay for their own defence. In 1634 a royal governor, in the person of Princess Margaret of Savoy, arrived in Portugal with instructions to exact a fixed annual levy of 500,000 *cruzadas* for that purpose. Madrid showed belated concern by mounting an armada for the recovery of Brazil – but had difficulty in persuading the Portuguese to contribute to its cost. Much was at stake for Brazilian sugar alone was worth 4 million *cruzadas* a year to Portugal. The

Dutch had first attacked the sugar ships, and then established themselves in Pernambuco in north-east Brazil. Its restoration became a prime Spanish condition for any peace with the Dutch. The expedition that finally sailed from Lisbon in September 1638 was a dismal failure because of the incapacity of the commander, the conde de Torre. At the same time that the Portuguese were bewailing their losses in Brazil, the Spanish were reasserting their monopoly in their own parts of America, where the Portuguese had been operating profitably since the union. The revolt of Portugal was born of the fiscal troubles of Spain and the contraction of her American trade; the revolt made both much more serious.

Tax riots in Évora and other Portuguese towns in 1637 had petered out because the upper classes gave no lead. By 1640, however, grandees and merchants had grounds for revolt. They hoped that the Dutch would moderate their attacks on the empire if Portugal severed its link with Spain. They produced a claimant in Don John, duke of Braganza, a weak man but with a valid dynastic claim. The Jesuits, strong in Portugal and Brazil, supported the revolt out of antipathy to the Dominicans, their rivals in theology and in missionary tactics. When the duke was proclaimed King John IV on 1 December 1640 there was little Portuguese opposition; and little that the Spanish could do about it. When the Catalan revolt had been overcome and Philip IV tried to recover his position in Portugal, the Portuguese had acquired confidence and allies. The Spanish were defeated at Elves in 1659, at Ameixial in 1663 and, decisively, at Villaviciosa in 1665. In 1657 the insurgents had gained indirectly from Cromwell's Elizabethan-style sally into the war, leading to the Redcoats' capture of Dunkirk: Spanish troops were diverted to meet the Anglo-French challenge. After 1661 the Portuguese had the benefit of the English alliance, cemented by the marriage of Charles II to Catherine of Braganza and the cession to England of Bombay and Tangier. They had proved their ability to look after their own interests by fighting back against the Dutch, who had tried to exploit their difficulties and had occupied Luanda. In 1648 the Portuguese captured Luanda; in 1654 they recaptured Recife and drove the Dutch out of Brazil. Their independence was a fact long before the death of Philip IV in 1665. He had held rigidly, fatalistically, to the dynastic view. His widow, the regent Mariana, was compelled to be more realistic. The frontier province had been cruelly afflicted by Portuguese raids and by the billeting of their own soldiers. Population was down, tax returns were negligible. On 13 February 1668 Spain recognized the country's independence. Portugal was free thereafter to pursue the course mapped out by the pioneers of commercial imperialism. In the seventeenth century its economy depended largely upon entrepôt trade in tobacco and sugar and the export of salt; in the eighteenth, while the staples were not abandoned, it came to be based more upon slaves, gold, leather and wine. Revolving round the busy port of Lisbon, Portuguese trade was influenced jointly by Anglo-Dutch capitalism and by the colonial economies out of which was emerging the new nation of Brazil: a source of much needed gold for Europe and prosperity in the short term for the mother country. Portugal, peasant-style conservative and uniformly Catholic, shielded from innovation by the vigilance of the Inquisition, could not have sustained, even at a relatively modest level, an independent role in international relations without its empire and the participation of its dominant landed class in a profitable foreign trade.

Bad Government

The Thirty Years War was a testing ground for economic structures which might have survived reasonably intact the strains of small, short wars but were exposed in their inherent fragility by the forty-five years of total war which began when the council decided to attack the Dutch and Spain was 'drawn into the policy of violence, prestige and energy from which there was to be no honourable retreat'. Alcalá Zamora writes with something of that wistful pride that characterizes the century in which 'enormous reserves of energy were expended in the most continuous and disproportionate effort ever made by a people'. They were required because the rules of orthodox finance were flouted from the outset. The war was fought on a combination of unlimited deficit – financing and extra-economic revenue. For an analogy one may turn to Britain in 1939–45, with her empire, experience and resources; consider the effect of that war on those resources and then consider what it would have been if the war had been prolonged much longer. Of an annual Spanish budget of up to 15 million ducats, about half had to be earmarked for payment of interest on royal debts. Between 1615 and 1625 revenue increased 25 per cent against an increase of 250 per cent in expenditure. Unsound finance became more damaging as Europe entered what was to prove a long recession in economic activity. Spain was the worst hit of any country and, within Spain, Castile experienced the steepest decline in national productivity and income, the sharpest fall in population (except for areas of Germany directly affected by war) and the most damaging fluctuations of currency values. There is no lack of statistics to give an impression of scientific validity to any interpretation of Spain's decline in economic terms, but they should be treated with caution. It is in any case difficult, as the decline gathers momentum, to distinguish cause from effect. It becomes apparent too that analysis which is too mechanistic fails to account for certain unique features of Spain's tragedy. At the beginning of the century, when it was feared, as at the end when it was patronized, if not pitied, Spain had the fascination for other westerners of a country that was distinctive in attitudes and manners, as well as in institutions. To avoid superficiality it is necessary to go back to certain fundamental traits and to longstanding weaknesses which belong to the sixteenth as much as to the seventeenth century, although it was then that they were exposed.

Politically Spain had never advanced far beyond the situation created by the union of crowns, of Ferdinand of Aragon and Isabella of Castile, in 1478. With separate crowns, constitutions, *cortes* and laws it was in no sense an organic union but a loose federation, analogues to that of England and Scotland between 1603 and 1707. It is recorded that when the humanist Nebrija presented Isabella with his Spanish grammar, and she asked him what it was for, he replied: 'language is the perfect instrument of empire'. Isabella's vision of such an empire, a political, religious and cultural union of the Peninsular kingdoms, with command of North Africa, had never been fulfilled. Instead Spain had been diverted by the Italian ambitions of Ferdinand, the Burgundian commitments, and imperial mission of Charles V towards goals that were to prove – as the leaders of the Comuneros, whose rebellion he had faced at the outset of his reign, had foretold – both elusive and irrelevant to the country's needs; towards a future which the poet Garcilaso de la Vega (killed in France in 1535) caustically prophesied, after speaking of the waste of war – 'the curse upon this our time':

> The nation's thanks? A place in history?
> One day they'll write a book, and then we'll see.

From the outset the union was dominated by Castile, the larger state and the one in which royal government was most advanced. In Aragon, a corporative state *par excellence* in which the ruler could only govern effectively by coming to terms with powerful estates, orders and towns, there were four distinct units: Aragon, Valencia, Catalonia and Majorca. When Spain became, by marriage and inheritance, part of a larger chain, including the Netherlands and other parts of the Burgundian inheritance (notably Franche-Comté, whose loss in 1678 was to be the bitterest of blows to an already humiliated monarchy), then with the accession of Charles V, the Austrian family lands and the dignity of Holy Roman Emperor – so poor in endowments but rich in responsibilities – it was in effect Castile that bore the brunt of the religious wars and of the duel with Valois France. At the same time Castile prospered mightily from her monopoly of the American treasure and trade which made possible the crusading imperialism directed by Philip II, which would otherwise have been completely beyond the country's resources.

Philip II's reign had closed in an atmosphere of frustration and reappraisal. He had failed in three important aims: the subjugation of the Netherlands, the conquest of England and the exclusion of Henry IV from the French throne. The golden years of colonial trade were giving way to a time of contraction and a new balance less favourable to the mother country. After the turn of the century less silver was entering Spain. Between 1591 and 1600 the peak of 83 million ducats was reached; the figure for the years 1611–20 was 65 million; for 1621–30, 61 million; for 1631–40, 40 million; for 1641–50, 31 million. Meanwhile fewer manufactured goods were being exported. American trade was passing into foreign hands. The great plague of 1599 and succeeding years killed about a million people: the high mortality was partly caused by overcrowding in towns which itself resulted from the drift from the land as sheep farming replaced arable, and hungry men looked for jobs or alms. Madrid, the rapidly growing centre of bureaucratic government, and Seville, less parasitic and unproductive than the capital, but grossly enlarged around the money-spinning activities that stemmed from the American trade, were exceptional in their prosperity, products of a far from prosperous economy. The plague caused a temporary shortage of labour which gave a further twist to the inflationary spiral at a time when Dutch, English and French merchants were taking advantage of peacetime conditions to enlarge their operations.

1609, the year of the twelve-year truce with the Netherlands, was also the year of the expulsion of the Moriscoes, about 275,000, mostly field labourers. The expulsion conforms to a pattern of Spanish life of that time, along with the retreat from humanism, the hardening of attitudes towards everything foreign and the almost obsessive concern with orthodoxy. It mainly affected Valencia and its overall effects are hard to evaluate, but the loss of hard-working and skilful farmers and craftsmen could only be damaging. Castilian industries, already hampered by the restrictions imposed by the guilds, by shortage of capital and by a cost inflation more severe than that experienced by foreign competitors, never recovered from the setbacks of these years. Whether the Spanish economy would have suffered some form of collapse in any case is open to argument. Certainly the decision to go to war again was made at a time when only stringent measures of reform could have saved the economy. Government was too weak, social pressures too strong, for such reforms to succeed under any but the most favourable conditions. As it was a general recession and an all-consuming war made both political and economic reforms virtually impossible. That in sum was the tragedy of Spain, and of Olivares, who stands out among Spanish ministers of the seventeenth century as the man who had the clearest vision of Spain's imperial role and policy for her future development. At the same time, with his cavalier reluctance to cut his coat according to his cloth, he fairly represents a society in which Church and aristocracy held all the important keys to status and influence.

If Spain was not precisely that 'republic of the bewitched' described by Cellorigo in 1600, 'living outside the natural order of things', yet it was certainly a society in which, in the words of a minister of 1641, 'each in his own sphere and station desires honour and estimation above everything else'. The Spaniard, though given to self-analysis, has often proved unwilling to accept the logic of new situations. It is significant that Spanish intellectual life in the seventeenth century was largely untouched by the new mathematics and the scientific thinking of the time, whether empirical or rational. Everything militated against the sort of economic growth being achieved in Holland and England, where there was a more open culture and greater mobility between classes; where the middle classes had incentives to invest in trade and manufactures. Even in France, where feudal attitudes also died hard, there was a greater dynamism in the economy. One should be chary about elevating economic growth as the supreme good and should not too readily dismiss, because it was out of the cultural mainstream, the values of a society that could produce the masterpieces of the late Spanish baroque. Along with the melancholy of the age of *desengaño* or disenchantment, so movingly portrayed for example in El Greco's sombre painting, *The Burial of the Count of Órgaz*, with its grave attendant grandees, there surely survived too some of the passion and energy of the Castilian that finds expression in song and dance – and in the heavily accentuated language that made *fuero* out of the sober Latin *forum*! And yet the isolationism and sterility of much of Spanish life in the seventeenth century provides an unhappy picture. It is sobering, too, to reflect upon those *fueros* which arose from the clamour of the market place, the intense bargainings of earlier centuries, the 'crystallised deposit' as they are called by J.B. Trend, 'of the thought and feelings, the private lives and public institutions, the agriculture, industry and commerce' of an earlier Spain. The *fueros* of the privileged classes and of the peripheral provinces, were honoured and intact. But in most Castilian towns, economic decline had rendered them worthless. Here again is the yawning gap between idea and reality which characterizes Spain in this period.

Philip IV (1621–65) may be called the king that Spain deserved. There was in Spanish political life a certain naivety, a waiting upon miracles, a soul-searching that stopped short of the more awkward questions; in all an inward-looking posture inhibiting adaptation. In Philip we see in particular the stubbornness of an essentially irresolute, egotistic man whose actions and attitudes undermined the dynasty in which he professed such pride; furtive womanizer of Madrid theatres and brothels, and morbid penitent of mornings after; happier in the company of courtiers and artists than of ministers who brought sobering reports and expected steady application to work. Despite the heavy blank look of the great Velázquez portraits, Philip was neither fool nor weakling. The correspondence of his latter, remorseful years, with the abbess Sor María, reveals a soul profoundly troubled though incurably self-indulgent. 'Woe to the land whose king is a child', a Catalan had written in 1626 on the occasion of his first and last visit to that province. It was Spain's misfortune that this king never quite grew up. When he wrote to Sor María, in 1645, that he was grateful for her intercession with God on his behalf, since 'before everything must come the salvation of my soul . . . and after it the good and tranquillity of this monarchy', there is no reason to doubt his sincerity. But he never found the humility or courage to rise to the idea that he was king of a people as well as head of a dynasty. He provides rich material for the student of the complexities of human nature; a lesson too in the dangers of this style of monarchy, at the halfway stage between the feudal and the bureaucratic. With the excessive responsibilities of a Charles V and a Philip II, and an inadequate apparatus of government, he lacked the unswerving devotion to duty, the zeal and inner toughness of those kings of the 'golden age'. He fathered at least twenty illegitimate children, but left as his sole legitimate heir a malformed and backward child of 4. No wonder that pious Spaniards, like their discredited king, saw in their misfortunes the anger of God.

In 1653 the Venetian ambassador declared that Spain was the most poorly governed country in the world. Yet the structure was imposing enough. A series of viceroys represented the king in each dependent province such as Navarre, Sicily, Peru. In Madrid, a number of councils attended the king. It was through councils for each province that the king was, in Olivares's somewhat optimistic phrase, 'considered to be present in each one'. These councils received reports from the viceroy concerned, advised the king and then sent instructions back to the province. Above the territorial councils there were others with responsibility for the entire empire: finance, war and the Inquisition were thus dealt with, while the council of state considered questions of high policy. Castile possessed a formidable apparatus of government. A network of officials acted under the instructions of the council of Castile. In each important town *corregidores* enjoyed powers comparable to those of the French *intendant*. They supervised municipal councils and other local institutions; acted as military governors, as judges and fiscal agents. In Castile moreover the nobility had no representative institutions. The *cortes* consisted of but 36 representatives of 18 towns. Their readiness to vote taxes was limited only by the inability of many communities to pay what was required.

This was not an absolute monarchy, weak only because misdirected. Respectful of their subjects' rights, the Habsburg kings were also beset by checks and controls. As the seventeenth century proceeded the nobility increased their grip upon government at all levels until it had the appearance of a regime administered by the nobility for the nobility. Spain was not just Castile. Outside Castile, the king ruled by contract, or in conformity with local customs which left him little room to manoeuvre. In Navarre, the ordinary people did not pay taxes to the king; nor could they be conscripted. When Olivares tried to collect a salt tax and to raise troops in Vizcaya, one of the three Basque provinces in which the king ruled as constitutional monarch, the people rebelled. In Aragon, the king ruled only on condition that he observed the *fueros* from which, to quote a Catalan statement, 'the prince can no more exempt himself than he can exempt himself from a contract'. In effect the king could secure no grant from the Catalan *cortes* until its grievances had been met. He could touch no law without its consent. Only a minute proportion of any subsidy voted by the Catalans went to the crown. The income from royal lands in Catalonia was less than half that of the council of its capital Barcelona. Barcelona, after the great Castilian plagues probably the most prosperous city of Spain, was virtually an independent republic.

Castile was the major part of Spain. It was the rapid deterioration within Castile that led Castilians to demand help from the other provinces. It is unlikely that its decline would have been arrested even if that help had been forthcoming. For the appearance of untrammelled royal power within Castile was misleading. Under Lerma's extravagant administration, the nobility, kept at some distance by Philip II, had moved back into government. Olivares attempted to curb the grandees, like Richelieu, but without his success. In the last twenty years of Philip IV's reign they gained control. In Charles II's reign all important posts at court, in the councils, viceroyalties, embassies and armed forces were filled by the grandees; the lesser posts were infiltrated, if not monopolized by the middling nobles, *caballeros*; these men also became *corregidores*, judges and deputies to *cortes*. Under these circumstances it is conceivable that the crown could have retained its grip on the basis of a Prussian-style co-operation with the nobles, had not the administration at the same time been at every level corrupted by the sale of offices. Local pressures, some not far removed from gangsterism, often abetted by the needy state, had delivered most of the larger towns into the hands of local nobles who owned municipal offices and could pass them on to their children.

The nobles of Spain were essentially town-dwellers. There were 'noble cities', Madrid, Seville, Toledo among them, where office-holders had to go through the business of *probanza*, showing purity of blood from Jewish or Morisco traits, and proof that they abstained from manual labour, were not '*viles y mecánicos*'. The towns moreover enjoyed jurisdiction over large surrounding areas. This Spanish version of the lord–vassal relationship meant that large areas were virtually immune from royal control. The greater part of the Spanish countryside was administered in any case by the church or nobility, enjoying *señoríos* which provided a wide range of feudal dues and monopolies. Besides rights of mill, oven, wine press and slaughter house, with road and ferry tolls, there were sometimes tithe and pasture rights and even the right to take the *alcabala*, the 10 per cent sales tax. The last illustrates vividly the weakness of the crown in relation to its privileged subjects, its inability therefore to enforce government or to protect those who most needed it. Many places had commuted their dues for a fixed annual sum. The community or their *señor* might once have secured the right in return for an annual payment which inflation had rendered of little value to the crown.

In sum the nobility had gained more in local power than they had lost in political influence. For most Spaniards the *pueblo* and its surrounding *país* was more important than the province, let alone Spain, that abstract term of Madrid officialdom. And for most Spaniards the *señor* was more important than the king. The king might of course own the land and it was generally held preferable to be under a royal than a private *señorío*. A grandee's agent was the power that dominated the lives of very many Spaniards; he would maintain upon the backs of his peasants and townsfolk an almost royal court, a local centre of government from which *corregidores* would deal out justice and administer affairs as if the king hardly existed. The hordes of servants, officials and pensioners kept by the wealthier nobles ensured a strong position in the management of towns – all the stronger as the towns decayed. It was a far cry from the medieval ideal of the Spanish people, *Del rey abajo ninguno* – King and commons with no lords between! It is hard to conceive a system less conducive to the well-being of the monarchy or to that of the mass of the people. In simple but not wholly misleading terms, Spain may be described as a land of grandees, hidalgos and priests – and of those who served their interests, in relatively secure and respected capacities, as lawyers, doctors, teachers, or as beasts of burden. That it was not also an entirely wretched, joyless and uncreative society says more for the resilience of human nature and for certain specifically Spanish qualities than for any merits in this regime of exploitation.

Broadly speaking, the European states that advanced in 'the age of absolutism' did so either by subduing the nobles or by coming to some mutually beneficial arrangement with them. Poland is an extreme case of a country in which the nobility remained dominant, socially and politically. Spain was another. Here there were extremes of wealth and poverty that find no parallel until we reach the Poland of the Sapiehas and Radziwills, and the Hungary of the Esterhazys. The nobility had acquired status from its traditional military function, and a special lustre from the heroic, elevating experience of the *reconquista*. The *fuero de hidalguía* assured the nobles of exemption from personal taxes and the normal processes of law. The crown persisted in its belief that aristocracy provided the natural, most loyal and useful talent at its disposal. It is an illustration of the way in which incessant war fostered demands and attitudes remote from economic realities; the same phenomenon can be studied at Versailles in the heyday of Louvois and French militarism. The role of education was also crucial. The Jesuits worked by preference through the upper classes. Their new Colegio Imperial was founded in the reign of Philip IV for the elder sons of the higher nobility 'because they are the principal part of the state and for good or for evil they lead the rest; moreover they subsequently control the government and administration of the kingdom'. In the universities the nobility now monopolized the *colegios mayores*, foundations originally intended for poor but clever students.

Traditional attitudes apart, wealth was the basis of the social divisions of Spain. There were pressures on government to reinforce class distinctions: decrees prohibited the use of silk by artisans and their wives and limited the possession of coaches. But there were tensions within the aristocratic class as the *nobleza de sangre* sought to establish their position in the face of massive hidalgo encroachment by purchase or by military or civil service. Castilian hidalgos numbered about 650,000 in 1600, about 1 in 10 of the population. Such men, 'eating black bread under the genealogical tree', would have little land, perhaps none at all. They might beg, do menial work secretly, serve on each other's tables, struggle to maintain a façade. Such a life of pride and patches was the butt of satirists, the despair of the *arbitristas*. And yet the coat of arms, the sword, the documents that proved *limpieza de sangre* came to mean all the more as Spain's economic decline continued. Among the more enterprising of hidalgos there was always the effort to rise to *caballero*, or hidalgo of middle rank. Such a man would live in a town house, drawing his income mainly from his estates and annuities from investments; he might have a *regimiento*, a seat in a town council; he might look forward to the chance of becoming a procurator in the *cortes*. The more ambitious among them aimed to become *caballeros de hábito* and *comendadores*, the latter members of the military orders, without function but held in great honour and supported by a useful income in the shape of an *encomienda*. Again, money might buy entry into the coveted ranks of the *títulos*. Counts and marquises were, however, held at their distance by the *grandes*, members of the *grandeza*: these, as defined by Charles V, consisted of a mere twenty-five families.

Olivares used preferment to attract and reward, seeking to create a more flexible aristocracy of service. In 1640 the crown made 10 new *grandes*, each being responsible for a military contingent. The older families were affronted by Olivares's methods, but after his death they tightened their grip over the state. The enlargement of the aristocracy seems to have been in inverse proportion to the fortunes of the monarchy. In thirty-five years Charles II sanctioned the creation of as many titles as in the previous two centuries: 12 viscounts, 80 counts and 236 marquises. Domingo Grillo, Italian banker to the crown, who bought a marquisate in 1682, was promoted to *grande* only eight years later, for 300,000 *pesos*. For *grandes* and *títulos* there was relative security. Many were encumbered with debts, incurred through the payment of dowries, unremunerated service to the crown or the cost of the obligatory palace and retinue in Madrid, but they could usually rely on the crown to provide for them by *encomienda* (a grant of lordship in the New World) or *mercedes* (monetary grants) which were costing the treasury 3 million *ducats* a year by the end of Philip IV's reign. The *mayorazgo*, or entail, protected their estates from alienation. But for lesser nobles life could be an anxious business. Over the social battleground roamed the lawyers, whose profitable business it was to investigate claims to nobility. The crown had an interest in curtailing numbers because of the cost of tax exemptions. It also made efforts to secure something concrete in return for noble rights: for example *grandes* were pressed to send men from their estates to the army; they were also employed as governors and ambassadors for scant remuneration. Behind all lay the monarchy's lack of money. Hence stemmed the alienation of *señoríos* which was transforming the political balance, and the sale of even the highest offices to nobles which weakened the independence of the crown and its willingness to reform. *Grandes* tended to divide into factions; then they could be overcome. When they combined together, as they did to destroy Valenzuela, they were invincible. Their protected economic position was damaging in less obvious ways. Notably it reinforced the prevailing bias against agricultural labour: the large landowners, who were in the best position to improve farming and estate management, failed to do so. If one contrasts the neglected fields and deserted villages of Castile with the ostentatious spending of the great families (not much of it however on the arts or civilized living), it is hard to resist the conclusion that the aristocratic way of life blighted Spanish society.

A Religious Nation

During the Peninsular War the duke of Wellington observed, 'the real power in Spain is in the clergy. They kept the people right against France.' As an Irishman he would understand that power. For two centuries would-be reformers had criticized it, pointing, for example, to the contrast between the opulence of the Church and the poverty of the countryside. At first sight the facts are startling. There were, in 1700, at least 150,000 secular and regular clergy; men in minor orders and nuns brought the total figure to 200,000. An eighteenth-century estimate of the number of religious houses was 3000. In 1797 a census showed that there were 53,000 monks (including novices and lay brothers) and 24,000 nuns. In Castile the Church possessed one-seventh of the *señoríos* in extent of land, a quarter if assessed by income: that was land given in perpetuity and inalienable. The Church reflected the prejudices of a society which lacked the taste or talent for country life *à l'anglais* – and priests, like nobles, thronged the cities. Some decayed towns preserved a religious establishment which appeared to be impervious to economic decline. In Burgos, with a population of 8000 in 1700, there were 14 parish churches and 42 religious houses. Of the situation in Valladolid in 1683, a minister reported that 'the most important part of the inhabitants consists of the ecclesiastical chapters and other clergy, infinite in number'. There were 53 religious houses and 17 parishes – so that it seemed that 'this city is made up principally of consumers only'. The cathedral at Toledo was, after St Peter's, the richest in Europe: here there were 60 canons, 20 of them called *extravagantes* because they were only required to attend on certain occasions. The cathedral at Saragossa employed 349 priests, while that of Seville was equipped to say 100,000 masses a year. The concentration of priests in certain privileged communities gave rise to most of the complaints about frivolous or scandalous behaviour. At the same time, the lack of educated clergy in sufficient numbers to minister to the villages helped to preserve the grosser superstitions, so that peasants continued to live in a world inhabited by witches, sorcerers and devils. The children of Valencia wore little fists of ivory or glass to protect them from the evil eye. Some clergy, perhaps sensibly, took a complaisant view of pagan tradition. Others may have connived at tricks to impress the devout. The Spaniard was inclined in any case to be literal-minded: congregations would extend their arms to receive a blessing which otherwise would not touch the heart. Here was a people in love with religion. It was for the people, not for an aesthetic élite, that artists designed the vast *pièces montées* of the high baroque – one thinks of the *Transparante* of Toledo (1732), that astonishing altarpiece of Nicolás Tomé, perhaps the most daringly theatrical of such compositions – with their dynamic use of sculpture, stucco and paint, their bold montage of saints, martyrs and angels all conveying religious exaltation in the most sensuous fashion. The simple people who listened devoutly to the homely teaching of the Franciscans and Capucins in the primary schools were animated by the same spirit as the fashionable theatre-goers who knelt before the viaticum. The most successful playwright of his time was the devout Pedro Calderón de la Barca (1600–81) whose mystery plays, full of rich symbolism, combining sermons with biblical plots, offer a significant contrast to the French favourites, Molière, anathema to many Christians, and Racine, whose themes and language were often more stoic than Christian. Bartolomé Murillo devoted himself for years to the painting of huge pictures of the Immaculate Conception. Spanish priests and lay brotherhoods worked together to organize the Church's feasts in an idiom which was traditional, popular, Christian and pagan, the celebrations of a distinctive culture in which Christian zeal and pride of community were almost indistinguishable. Indeed, words like devotion inadequately convey the sentiment of that seventeenth-century Sevillean *caballero* who challenged to single combat any who should doubt the Immaculate Conception (which was not proclaimed a dogma until 1870).

There was thus nothing remote about the religion which inspired the holy-day festivals which still flourish in modern Spain, with their tabernacles and carnival giants, chanting children and hooded penitents like those whom Madame d'Aulnay observed whipping themselves so that onlookers were splashed by their blood. Catholicism was not merely a creed and a liturgy but a way of life, offering something to everyone in a society which had not as yet experienced the separation of two cultures, that of the educated élite and that of the simple masses, which was occurring in western societies as they came under the influence of scientific rationalism. It is a paradox that, in this most aristocratic of countries, where there were such extremes of riches and poverty, there was still a whole culture. Part of the answer lies in the Church's continuing dominance over Spanish lives and minds. The records of the Inquisition, the universal and still popular judge over all aspects of faith and morality, show that there was some anti-clericalism. Cases of sacrilege were common. Sexual morality was lax. It was acceptable that priests should have concubines; brothels catered for the laymen and perhaps preserved their marriages. Priests were often surprisingly liberal, to judge from manuals of confession, for example about abortion. But the friar who boasted in 1655 that 'atheism has never been known in Spain and is not congenial to Spanish minds' was not entirely wrong. Outside the fringe, the vagabonds and gypsies, Spaniards might deviate and sin; they did not knowingly defect from the faith.

How adequately did the church respond to this devotion? As a conservative force in society, notably through the Inquisition, it prevented the spread of new learning, harried the potentially useful citizens of Jewry and contributed to Spain's isolation. The second half of the seventeenth century saw a series of *autos-da-fé* directed against Portuguese *conversos* in Spain. It was one aspect of an impoverished society, a diversion for the poor, a lucrative process for the state through fines and confiscations. The Index of Prohibited Books contained most of the authors whose work was creating in the rest of Europe the culture of the Enlightenment, Descartes, Grotius, Bayle among them; in the eighteenth century Montesquieu and Voltaire. The decay of the universities, which were essentially secular institutions, was however due to other causes besides the predominance of the Church: they had become training grounds for the royal bureaucracy, and the aristocracy deserted them for their own colleges.

Too much land and capital were immobilised under the 'dead hand' of the Church: approximately a fifth of the total, compared to the nobility's three-fifths. Lack of investment capital was certainly one factor in Spain's economic malaise; it is also to be weighed alongside the craze for *hidalguía* and the contempt for 'vile' labour. The crown expressed concern about the large numbers of men trying to enter the priesthood; an edict of 1689 put a temporary stop to ordination because 'in many villages it is hard to find a young unmarried man who is not in orders'. It is common for weak administrations to attack symptoms because they are unwilling or unable to identify the cause. Yet the Church was faithful to its mission in aiding the poor. Bishops and monasteries provided food for unemployed and beggars in thousands. An eighteenth-century archbishop of Granada provided daily bread for 2000 men and 3400 women. Some of the highest dignitaries had humble origins. One eighteenth-century archbishop was the son of a charcoal-burner. A bishop was usually, however, drawn from the modest hidalgo class, educated by way of a scholarship at one of the *colegios mayores*; he was expected to reside in his see and to give away all his surplus income in charity. The conscientious Spanish bishops indeed compare favourably with those of Catholic France or Protestant England. What the moralist would praise the economist might, however, deplore: indiscriminate alms provided a cushion for the idle. The Church which responded so closely to the aspirations of Spanish society and reflected so plainly its shortcomings could not escape entirely the censure of that society's critics.

One of the best known of those was himself a priest, Fray Benito Feyjóo (1676–1764), a Benedictine monk and professor of theology, who set himself the formidable task of interpreting modern learning to his blinkered fellow countrymen. The gist of his argument was that Spain was blessed with the finest theologians and enjoyed religious unity, but it had lost touch with science. He adopted the empirical method of Francis Bacon to attack what he held to be false religion: obscurantist theology, exaggerated devotion to the saints and concern with the externals of faith. In the encyclopedic range of information, in his zeal as correspondent and educator, he might be called the Bayle of Spain. But it is significant that he did not criticize the achievements of Spain's former intellectual leaders. He remained devoted to his faith and attacked ignorance and its effects in the spirit of a true Christian and Spaniard. 'Thanks to the immortal Feyjóo,' wrote one admirer, 'spirits no longer trouble our houses, witches have fled our towns, the evil eye does not plague the tender child and an eclipse does not dismay us.'

The Spanish Enlightenment came late and in peculiarly Spanish form. Its targets were broadly the size and excessive privileges of 'the useless classes'; more specifically such obstacles to progress as the system of entail and the wealth and influence of the religious orders. The Church lacked a statesman of the stature of Cisneros, the great sixteenth-century archbishop of Toledo, humanist and founder of universities, to reform, to educate, above all to purge the religious orders. It is hard to believe that Cisneros would have tolerated the neglect of the peasants: it has been reckoned that there were, in 1700, 2000 villages without priests. The eclipse of humanism and the lack of reforming initiatives were part of the price Spain paid for the triumph of the Counter-Reformation. Perhaps it would have been better for Church and society if there had been more heretics. As it was, the Church suffered from lack of competition and objective criticism; it operated in a society of closed minds and devoted much care to keeping them closed. It is in its complete lack of the pragmatic spirit that was abroad in western Europe from around the beginning of the seventeenth century that the Church most accurately reflected the parent society.

Spain and the New World

Defeats, revolts, commercial failures and an all-pervading conservatism, at once timid and arrogant, with irrational and panicky measures of government, could be called symptoms of withdrawal in a society that had lost some of its essential supports. The flood of treasure from the new world had profoundly affected the mind as well as the economy of Spain. Like twentieth-century oil it provided what was, in a sense, an unearned income which made men undervalue the essential business of production: so Spaniards stood back from plough and forge and held out their hands for their daily bread. American silver had sustained imperial designs and an extravagant court. In the seventeenth century, however, the relationship between Spain and America was transformed. After imports of bullion had reached their climax in the last decade of the sixteenth century, and after a plateau had been held for two further decades, there was a period of contraction until the mid-century years, when the decline of Atlantic trade became part of the general crisis of the Spanish state. That decline has two aspects: within, colonial trade and the colonial economies; without, the blows from hostile forces.

Castile's monopoly of American trade had survived because of the financial assets of the Seville merchants and those of foreign capitalists, and because of the common interest that merchants, shippers, officials of the *Casa de Contratación* and Andalusian magnates had in keeping outsiders out. For typically conservative bureaucrats, clinging to a system that had once worked well, it seemed that there was no viable alternative: the Catalans were occupied with the recovery of their share of Mediterranean trade, while Aragon was severely affected by the mid-century recession. Supremacy within Castile was passing meanwhile from Seville to Cadiz. In the first half of the century Seville still had 60 per cent of the trade but her population was drastically reduced by recurring plague; more serious was the difficulty of access to Seville as the Guadalquivir became silted up: as ships became larger navigation became more hazardous. Cadiz by contrast was one of the few places (Bilbao was another) to show vigorous growth; it was favoured by foreign shipowners, who by 1665 were handling most of the trade, because of its good facilities and favourable dues. In 1670, France's consul wrote to Colbert that 'the trade in this port of Cadiz is the greatest and most flourishing in Europe'. It was all the more remarkable because trade overall was shrinking.

Ruled always by short-term financial needs, Spanish methods were self-defeating. Convoy and harbour defence was financed by the *avería*; this tax became so heavy in the war years that merchants, finding themselves at a disadvantage compared to foreigners, tried to avoid payment. Tax evasion meant weaker defence measures and slimmer armadas. Government pressure culminated in the periodic confiscation of private bullion; fraud and contraband destroyed what should have been a relationship of mutual advantage between government and merchants. Excessive customs rates encouraged smuggling, while the extension of colonial taxation brought only diminishing returns from that source. The Indies were exploited by the sale of offices and *encomiendas* (grants of Indians who paid tribute in labour or cash) to meet the domestic demand for place and pension.

Through this decadent version of absentee landownership thousands of Indians toiled for Spanish gentlemen who had never set eyes upon Mexico or Peru. Altogether it appears to be a prime example of killing the goose that lays the golden eggs. But it may be that a more responsible, less embattled government could still have done little to check the trend. For the decline of Spanish American trade reflects not only changing conditions in America itself as the colonies adapted their life and trade to meet their own problems, but also foreign competition which was robbing the Spaniards of much of the profit of their own colonial trade.

In the sixteenth century, the once numerous Mexican people had almost ceased to exist in the course of one of the worst of human calamities. They had lost their land and water supplies to settlers and succumbed to imported diseases such as smallpox and measles, and to alcohol. The Indian population of central Mexico, which may have been as high as 20 million in 1519, had fallen by 1670 to a million and a half. Landowners became increasingly reluctant to put money into mining, which became more expensive as the best seams were worked out. Other factors included the psychological shock to all concerned of the disaster of Matanzas, when the Dutch captured the entire treasure fleet (1628); the revolt of Portugal in 1640, bringing with it the worst phase of *vellón* inflation and the most damaging fiscal measures; and the inevitable decline in ships and seamanship, as it became more difficult to maintain the ships and to recruit crews. The Dutch presence in Brazil was more of a threat than privateers in the Caribbean; hurricanes were more serious than either.

In the face of such problems the resilience of the Spanish was impressive. The convoy system worked well. With the exception of Jamaica (to England in 1653) no important territories were lost during the seventeenth century. In the face of renewed buccaneering in the 1680s, the Spanish refurbished their Pacific defences. The crisis occurred, not because the colonies were collapsing but because they were developing. The Mexican economy was being reorientated, from mining to farming, based upon the haciendas – great landed estates which produced wheat or maize, cattle or sugar, and achieved a self-suffiency characteristic of the whole colonial economy. Mexico was retaining more revenue for its own purposes. In Peru the transition was less dramatic and more rapid: there was no demographic disaster comparable to that of the Mexican Indians. The native population was much smaller in the first place and, after Inca rule, more inured to exploitation. As in Mexico, Peru's white population increased in relation to the Indian: by 1650 it was 70,000 against 1.4 million. Earlier than Mexico, Peru ceased to become an important market for Spanish goods. As early as 1590 the viceroy was reporting of Peru that it was virtually self-sufficient in foodstuffs and the coarser textiles, and the Philippines trade was supplying it with finer textiles. Potosi, 'the mountain of silver' high in the Andes, voracious consumer of the unfortunate Indian miners, with 160,000 inhabitants by 1650, continued to produce profitably after that time, but a growing quantity of its silver found its way back into the Peruvian economy. Only 20 per cent (36 million *pesos*) of the income of the Peruvian treasury between 1651 and 1739 was remitted to Spain. Thus, developing their own profitable ways of farming, building their own ships and weaving their own textiles, trading outside the restricted markets prescribed by mercantilist theory, the Spanish colonies came of age, shaking off a submission to the mother country that had lasted for barely a century.

Silent Looms and Neglected Fields

Even without the falling off of American trade, the Spanish economy would have experienced a recession during the seventeenth century. Many peasants left the land in despair and sought a living in overcrowded cities; less food was produced and the country became dependent on imported grain. Neither impoverished peasants nor town workers, spending their wages largely on food, had money to spend on manufactured goods. The rich tended to buy goods from abroad. The prejudice against manual work and commercial operations was damaging. As in France, capital was diverted from relatively insecure manufacturing enterprises to office, property and government bonds. Sales of office had soared in the early 1600s and the trend continued, despite several efforts to check it: from viceroyalties and councillorships to postmasterships and bailiwicks, all was for sale. Government, taken up with military and fiscal concerns, ill-informed and naive in economic matters, was slow to adjust to changing economic conditions. Outside Cadiz and Madrid there were no substantial money markets. The limited amount of trade at other centres did not create enough business to attract financiers. Heavy purchase taxes and internal customs barriers discouraged production and hampered distribution. As early as 1616 Gondomar pointed out that it was cheaper for consumers from Galicia in the north-west or Valencia in the east to obtain their cloth from London, than from Segovia in the centre of the country. Spaniards also preferred lightweight English cloth to the native product. It was the textile industry which endured the worst effects of recession. Cuenca, a one-industry town, had lost two-thirds of its population by 1700; neither Avila nor Cordova had many looms working by then. The once great trading city of Burgos, one of the main motors of the economy, was in full decay. Granada, the biggest industrial city in Spain, with a population of 100,000, a fifth of them silk-workers or in ancillary trades, was so badly affected by 1700 that it took another fifty years to restore old levels of production. The story in Valencia, where French competition was the bogy, was similar. It was the earlier vitality of such places that had suggested good prospects in the early sixteenth century for native entrepreneurs who might have imposed their values on society and earned from government some of the support they needed; their slump reveals how strong were the forces of adversity. Toledo, like some other Spanish cities, gives the modern visitor the sensation that life stopped at some point in the seventeenth century. It is explained by the successive collapse of the three industries which had once made it the boom town of Spain's golden age. The number of cloth looms in operation had fallen by three-quarters by 1660; then the silk looms began to close down; meanwhile the forges, which had made the name of Toledo mean fine steel for swordsmen all over the continent, ceased production. From 50,000 in 1600 the population of the city had dropped by 1690 to 22,000.

For the metal industries, as for ship-building, war at least should have provided constant demand. But Spanish businesses were unable even to meet domestic requirements. In the 1550s, 300 ironworks were producing 3300 tons of iron and steel goods a year; a report of 1634 noted a drop to under 1000 tons. The country was exporting iron ore, but importing iron manufactures. In Charles II's reign, Spain was importing most of its arms equipment from England and France. Difficulties in obtaining good timber and other essential commodities (with the Baltic, North Sea and English Channel dominated after 1640 by the Dutch and English), the recession in the Indies trade, shortage of skilled labour, rising costs, and technical shortcomings which made even Spanish owners prefer foreign ships reduced the shipyards of Bilbao, Guipúzcoa and Barcelona to relative inactivity. Spain's floating castles, fifty years behind the lighter and more manoeuvrable Dutch and English vessels, offer another image of this suddenly isolated country, living under the all-too-potent spell of its glorious past.

It is wrong, however, even of Castile, to think of complete collapse. Alongside the plight of some industries must be placed the survival of others providing adequately for local demand: leather, gloves, soap, for example. Outside Castile, Barcelona prospered until the Catalan revolt, and was thereafter quick to recover: the population was 32,000 in 1600, 50,000 in 1700. Bilbao was sustained by wool exports. One observer at the turn of the century wrote: 'There is so much building that the city is nearly twice as big as it used to be.' Patchy though it is, the evidence points to a modest revival in the economy in the last two decades of the century. There were trends at work, largely unaffected by government policy. It was helpful that the Spanish were not engaged after 1678 in a major war. Most of the fighting in the War of the Spanish Succession (1702–14) was confined to Aragon. There was a lower tax requirement, and the sheer inefficiency of the regime may have allowed a breathing space here and there. So it is legitimate to speak of a modest revival in Charles II's reign, before the accession of the Bourbon dynasty to whose more vigorous and enlightened policies such revival has traditionally been ascribed. But the picture remains a sombre one, and a lesson in the fragility of industrial enterprise when demand fails and investment is insufficient; when political and social factors are unfavourable; when demoralization passes the point when short-term remedies can work. There was no lack of analysis. Cellorigo had written a particularly perceptive study of the problem in 1600, when he placed the greatest stress on the shortage of labour (after the 15 per cent loss by plague) and the consequent upswing of wages at the end of the century which put the country temporarily but fatally out of line with her competitors. As the century proceeded, ministers were bombarded with advice. Prohibition of imports was a favourite remedy of the *arbitristas* but measures such as the great *Pragmática* of 1623 to prohibit the import of textile, leather and other goods for the home market failed under the pressure of vested interests. The decline in manufactures would have been even more serious had it not been for the export of raw materials. In 1600, Spanish wool was regarded as superior to its nearest rival, the English, and was more acceptable in continental markets: that was the chief justification for the monopoly of the Mesta, the sheep-owners' guild, which otherwise had such unhappy effects on the balance of Spanish farming and the health of rural communities. That export was sustained. The country also exported wine, olive oil and iron ore. Shipping losses, together with the need to import not only manufactured goods but also staple commodities, were responsible for the continuing deficit on foreign trade, despite bullion imports which held up remarkably well in the later years of the century.

Throughout the seventeenth century Spain was importing wheat, and so we come back to that aspect of Castilian life which most vividly displayed to natives and foreign observers alike the distress of Spain. Only in the valleys and irrigated plains was nature kind to the cultivator. In the lower parts of Aragon and in the Basque lands, smallholders, relatively unburdened by the dues that oppressed the Castilian and Valencian peasants, made a steady living. The expulsion of the Moriscoes from Valencia, in 1609, affected the production of the basic crops of the region, wheat, rice and sugar – and sugar was hit by Brazilian and Caribbean competition. In Galicia, land of small enclosures, there was sufficient rainfall, though the soil was mostly too acidic. But it was on the high lands of Castile, where alternating droughts and spells of torrential rain made farming at best a cruel and hazardous occupation, that there was most evidence of distress, in waste fields and reduced and deserted villages. Again, there were favoured situations: the irrigated, garden-like lands round Valladolid; the remote villages of the sierras of Old Castile, where timber supplemented the pastoral economy; the fertile *vega* of Granada with its varied crops; the wine districts round Jerez. Some even of the bare, treeless districts of the centre and south, which so appalled travellers, were more productive than they may have seemed. It was easy to mistake the tawny stubbles that stretch into the distance for waste. Villages were sometimes far apart, but many labourers lived in the towns and travelled out to the fields. The ploughs were primitive and only scratched the soil; but the use of deeper ploughs, urged by some reformers, would have damaged the soil irreparably. It was the thin soil, starved of manure, that determined the level of cultivation, together with the low rainfall: less than 20 inches a year in central Spain, and that usually heavy, for short periods, causing flooding and soil erosion. There were other important factors. Much of Andalusia and Estramadura, arid regions to the south and west of New Castile, was the land of the latifundia, peopled largely by overseers and landless labourers, given over to huge fields of wheat, barley and fallows, or olive monoculture, bull ranches or, increasingly, scrub pastures grazed by sheep in great flocks that crossed Spain from summer to winter pasture, protected by the Mesta. Here the white buildings of the *cortijo*, with its great gate and tower, not so much a farm as a garrison, with small permanent staff and barns for the itinerant *jornaleros*, hired seasonally from the towns, dominated the landscape and the economy. Twenty per cent of all Spaniards (more than in all Aragon) lived in these two provinces. Central Spain, the two Castiles and León had nearer 30 per cent. It is significant that when the population started to rise again in the 1670s from its mid-century nadir, of about 6 million, the increase was confined almost entirely to the peripheral regions.

The latifundia were but one aspect of the problem. Climate and soil were most important. In provinces like Avila, with its stony soil, conditions were as difficult as anywhere in Europe. There was exploitation everywhere of a defenceless class, verbal leases constantly renewed, high rents, *servicios* and *millones*, tithe, feudal dues and interest to pay on private and communal debts. After paying his tributes to *señor*, priest and king, the peasant was left with about 50 per cent of his meagre product to feed his family and buy stock and seed. It is not surprising that he did not improve his land, or that he fell easy prey to disease; or that he would try to direct his children into one of the escape routes, a ship to America, the acquisition of a little Latin leading to professional qualifications or a place in a nobleman's house or in a monastery; or that he would give up the struggle and wander off to fight, beg or scrounge. So the flight from the land, at least in the short term, actually enhanced the traditional structure that was itself responsible for so many of the obstacles to efficient production. At the same time, it contributed to the national mood of *desengaño*, the disenchantment and cynicism that enveloped the country and paralysed the efforts of those who tried to alleviate or to reform. Until the later years of the eighteenth century, no serious effort was made to effect agrarian reforms. The repartition of estates was in itself no answer. There was little heart in the land, or in the cultivator, and the system told against him at every level. Agrarian misery points to the moral decadence of the Spanish upper classes content to draw their income from oppressed and hungry peasants whom they rarely if ever saw; also to the limitations of a monarchy which had surrendered so many of its rights and powers to the nobility, and which had to accept what a minister's memorandum of 1669 described as 'a state of prostration unprecedented in our history'.

Charles II: a Modest Recovery

Charles II, 'the sufferer', lived till 1700. If Philip IV was among the worst of kings, Charles was surely the most unfortunate. In 1665 the economy of Spain had apparently declined beyond the point at which it could recover without constructive action by the state. That in turn was possible only if the privileged classes could be persuaded, or compelled, to co-operate responsibly. It was a situation in which the king had to inspire respect for his will and judgement. Instead, Charles II, whose mother Mariana of Austria was his father's niece, might have been designed by a geneticist to illustrate the hazards of inbreeding. He would have been an object of sport or pity in the poorest Spanish village. With the jutting Habsburg jaw so pronounced in him that he could neither chew nor speak clearly; with the effects of childhood rickets, with recurring internal disorders of every sort, rashes and epileptic seizures, he was so self-conscious that except in profile and in a darkened room, he would not be seen on state occasions. Gloomily he endured the ceremonial motions of the dullest court in Europe. The papal nuncio described him at the age of 25 as having 'a melancholic and faintly surprised look' and found him 'indolent, seeming to be stupified'. His subjects thought him bewitched because he had no child by his two wives, Marie Louise of Orléans and Mariana of Neuberg. His ministers used him as a cypher. He governed in name only, while a succession of chief ministers exercised what authority they could muster. They achieved more than might have been expected of them.

While foreign diplomats anticipated his death with schemes for the partition of his territories, for example the secret treaty between Louis XIV and the Emperor Leopold in 1668, Spanish armies failed in successive wars to make but a token effort to defend them; Luxembourg, Franche-Comté and large parts of the Netherlands were lost to the French. At home there was progressive devolution of power to the grandees and the provinces. Castile, whose western lands had suffered cruelly from the Portuguese wars, now underwent further harrowing experiences: between 1677 and 1687 the countryside suffered from plagues of locusts, prolonged droughts and great floods. Andalusia and the regions round Seville were worst affected. In 1684 the city authorities reported to the government on their distress after nearly a year of absolute drought which had 'left the fields barren and devoid of crops'. With peasants flocking to the towns and malnutrition weakening resistance, disease was rampant. Severe outbreaks of plague between 1676 and 1685 brought losses amounting to a quarter of a million people, checking the recovery in population which had begun after the previous great outbreak of mid-century. Quarantine measures did more to disrupt trade than to prevent contagion. Labour shortage affected all productive activities. The revenue from taxes diminished. The reckless debasements of Philip IV's reign had driven gold and silver out of circulation. In the first fifteen years of Charles II's reign, while prices elsewhere in Europe were stable or declining, the government was unable to control inflation. The deflationary measures eventually enacted in 1680 were shattering in their immediate effects. Even the normally buoyant wool trade of Segovia succumbed; local trade and production were almost completely paralysed. With some parts of Castile falling back on barter, with towns and villages protesting that they were unable to meet even the main part of their tax quotas, with lamentable reports flowing in from all parts, the government was compelled in 1686 to carry out a partial revaluation.

There ensued a period of relative price stability. From 1680 there seems to have been a new spirit abroad. There were tentative beginnings of reform, a growing awareness, at ministerial level at least, of the need to copy the methods of other countries. It was not so much an 'enlightenment' as a time of readjustment to more modest circumstances. The loss of family lands had been painful to dynastic pride, but it stimulated a long-overdue study of the country's interests; resources were fewer – but so were commitments. At home, so many Castilians of all classes had had first-hand experience of the effects of economic decline that there was discernible, behind the flurry of proposals, a greater readiness to accept change.

Mariana, regent for ten years, had preserved the *junta* set up by her husband Philip IV to prevent her choosing a *valido*. The *junta* was, however, so divided that it could do little to prevent the rise of Nithard, an Austrian Jesuit who became inquisitor-general, exercised a complete control over the queen mother and was for a time her chief minister. He never secured a sufficiently broad base of support to impose his authority effectively. Don John, the illegitimate son of Philip IV and Maria Calderón, took the leadership of an aristocratic faction which overthrew Nithard in 1669, but failed to follow up his success. For a few years, Mariana governed with junta advice before succumbing to the bold personality of Fernando Valenzuela. His prominence is a comment on the weakness of the junta and the state of the country. In origin an obscure army officer, he made a business of patronage, dealing in titles, pensions, contracts and directing theatrical presentations. He became *valido* of the queen mother, then of the king, who came of age in 1675, when he was 14, but remained under his mother's sway. In September 1676, already laden with titles, Valenzuela became *primer ministro* – the first to be so designated – and the junta was abolished. He achieved little, being more concerned with people than with policy; but he did provoke something like unity among the grandees, who saw the degeneracy of monarchy as both opportunity and justification for a stronger assertion of their political rights. They formed a solid block behind Don John.

Somewhat chastened by his earlier failure, Don John had more to offer than might at first appear. Handsome, with a large following among the people, but hitherto uncertain about his proper role, he now showed sound political instinct. He enjoyed the backing of Church and army leaders, and he was the first Castilian politician of note to take seriously the claims of the eastern provinces. With his base in Aragon he had already made some contribution to the welfare of that province. The army with which he marched on Madrid in the coup of January 1677 was largely composed of Aragonese hidalgos. He obtained the disgrace of Valenzuela, who was sent to prison in the Philippines, while Charles was left to consider the meaning of this coup: no Spanish king since the Middle Ages had had a minister imposed upon him in this way. Could Don John be the strong man, *el caudillo* that the country needed? Engulfed in problems beyond his control, he could only improvise. The Dutch War, in which Spain fought against France from the outset, ended in 1678 with the loss of Franche-Comté, the army demoralized and the clergy resenting higher taxes. Don John died in September 1679 leaving the way for government on a more stable basis than the efforts of a single man.

The 1680s are the years of Medinaceli and Oropesa, neither of them negligible figures. The former, a leading grandee who had been president of the Council of the Indies, worked modestly and without illusions to save crown and country from the worst effects of harvest failure, famine and depopulation. His orthodox monetary solution to inflation, a revaluation, was overdue; in the circumstances it could be said that it was too extreme. Commodity prices fell by 50 per cent, farmers were caught between adverse growing conditions and lower prices for their products. Demand fell and commerce was depressed. The partial devaluation of 1686, together with some good harvests, then restored stability. For the first time for a hundred years, the country stood on a reasonably sound financial base. This, together with the slight recovery in population level, probably did more to promote the modest revival of manufactures and business of the last years of the century (for example some stocking factories were established in Valencia and Madrid, and began to export to England) than the *junta de comercio* which the government set up in 1683. That institution, reconstituted in 1705, was however to have a useful future under the Bourbons.

When Oropesa became first minister there was no important break; he had been the man promoted by Medinaceli to succeed him, though the latter may not have expected to be replaced so soon. Oropesa promoted some sound financial measures: influenced by French ideas, he set up a new office to take charge of fiscal affairs, the Superintendencia de Hacienda, under the marquis de los Vélez. He cut court expenditure, reduced office holding, whittled away at pensions and *mercedes*; what could not be abolished was taxed. A major assault was launched upon the *juros*, pensions paid in respect of an advance of capital, now negotiable pieces of property and a charge on the revenue, by 1667, of 9 million ducats a year. Arbitrary annulments and restrictions upon interest rates brought temporary hardship for holders and the disruption of some commercial houses. But the measures did end speculation in *juros*, reduced the burden on the state and prepared the way for their final liquidation in 1727. With measures to reduce the weight of the *millones*, the consumption taxes which fell most heavily on the poor, the lowering of tax quotas for impoverished communities, and negotiations with Rome for a higher tax contribution from the clergy, the reform programme was courageous and characterized by wise fiscal and social priorities. Oropesa also campaigned against excessive ordinations in the Church and set up a *junta* to investigate the Inquisition. At least enough was done to dispel the characteristic mid-century sense of helplessness in the face of events and to keep alive hopes of more substantial reforms. This was as well for Oropesa fell in 1691, and the rest of the reign was given over to the problem of the succession, to puny efforts to defend Flanders, Catalonia and Italy in the war of 1689–97 and to experiments in government which owed more to the ambitions of certain magnates and of Queen Mariana than to any philosophic reappraisal of the merits of devolution over centralized government.

The history of Spain in the 1690s is the history of factions, trying to secure for themselves the most favourable ground from which to bargain with whatever regime should follow, French or Austrian. Government was virtually in abeyance. The English ambassador Stanhope reported in 1694 that the country was 'in a most miserable condition; no head to govern, and every man in office does what he pleases without fear of being called to account'. In 1699 another bout of famine brought Spain close to social revolution. After violent bread riots in Madrid, Charles II was lifted off his sickbed to appear before the mob and promise them aid. He was soon to make a more important gesture of kingliness. Since the fall of Oropesa, Queen Mariana had been filling the council of state with her own clients, Spanish and German. The sister of Emperor Leopold, she was designed by the Austrians to be the agent of union between Austrian and Spanish crowns, or at least a favourable partition of lands. She played her part with gusto, but with little sense of the Spanish mind. When she handed out high offices to some magnates she merely offended others. Her experiment in devolution, allotting four parts of the kingdom to four governors, encouraged feuding between faction, and reduced the central administration to farce. While the diplomats of Austria, France and the maritime powers devised schemes of partition (the treaties of 1698 and 1699), Charles was beset by doctors and priests, purged and exorcised. Diplomats lobbied at court for their respective interests. The queen had overplayed her hand and aroused a stout reaction in favour of a French claimant and – much more important than the man – reversion of the Empire, whole and undivided. In October 1700, guided by Portocarrero, cardinal archbishop of Toledo, the king signed a will leaving all his dominions to Philip of Anjou, grandson of Louis XIV. After his death in November, while ministers were trying to raise money to pay for his funeral, Louis XIV accepted the will on his grandson's behalf. War ensued in 1701, and for twelve years Spain was the scene of fighting between French and Anglo-Austrian armies. During this war, with the new king and some of the upper class making common cause, with ordinary Castilians contributing to what came increasingly to look like a war of liberation, a sound basis was laid for the work of the Bourbon dynasty.

Bourbon Spain: Alberoni and Ripperda

Philip V (1700–46) was fortunate in the military aid he received from France to stiffen the erratic native troops, and no less in a cadre of experienced French officials, entrusted by Louis with the onerous task of raising funds for the war, who regarded government as a challenge to be met by proven French methods, rigorously applied. With devoted aid from his young wife, Marie Louise of Savoy, only 13 when she came to Spain but purposeful and steady beyond her years, and with the spirited and intelligent, if somewhat egotistic guidance of the princess of Orsini (her title coming from her Italian husband), whom Louis had chosen to be the queen's principal lady-in-waiting, Philip, ever willing to be led by women, displayed courage and aptitude enough to win support. The loyalty he evoked owed something to traditional hostility to Protestant England, whose navy and troops were partners in a war which was ostensibly about the rights of the archduke Charles to the throne of Spain but was primarily, Castilians believed, about commerce and that particularly in America. The archduke's stiff manner did not commend his cause while, by making his base in Aragon, he began at a disadvantage. As the war proceeded it took on something of the character of a civil war as the antipathy of Castile and Aragon emerged as one of the main issues. Indeed for Catalonia, it was a second twelve-year war, ending in 1714, as the first had in 1652, with the siege and capture of Barcelona and the loss of further privileges. There were dramatic changes of fortune and twice at least Philip seemed to be close to losing his throne. In 1706 and 1710 he was forced to evacuate Madrid. But Castile was vast and Madrid was not London, or even Paris, in relation to the rest of the country. For the British and the Dutch Spain was inevitably less important than Flanders. Even the Emperor never gave it such priority that he committed to it his best troops or most successful general, Eugène. After the Tories came to power in the election of 1710, the English were already looking for a way out of the war and the initial pledge to fight for the archduke's claim. When in 1711 Joseph died and Charles became Emperor in his place, it no longer made diplomatic sense to soldier on for a union of crowns that would have created as great an imbalance as the union of

France and Spain. Louis, by contrast, cared intensely about the outcome in Spain, all the more after his defeats in Flanders and Italy. Berwick's victory at Almanza in 1707 had heartened the old king at a dark hour. In 1710 he sent Vendôme, one of his best generals, to bolster up the Bourbon forces after imperialist victories in the summer: he it was who was responsible for another dramatic turn in the fortunes of the war by defeating Stanhope and Starhemberg at Brihuega and Villaviciosa in December. The victories were decisive, but in retrospect it may be concluded that this was a war which the allies could never have won. It is clear that many of the *grandes* were careful not to commit themselves to either side so long as the issue remained uncertain. But hidalgos and peasants, with less at stake, were more easily roused by the call to defend the homeland. The Church, following the lead of Portocarrero, was solid for the Bourbons. Napoleon was not to be the first alien to discover the fervour of Castilian feeling for their land, and the power of the priesthood to incite resistance.

After the war, the disloyalty of the Aragonese provided Philip with the chance of cancelling the traditional *fueros*. By the terms of the *nueva planta*, in 1707, Catalonia, Aragon and Valencia had already lost their old constitutions, their own viceroys and *cortes*. They had been given a tax system based on ability to pay, and an *intendente*, French in character, to enforce it. With some useful guidelines from the Medinaceli–Oropesa years Philip also had two exceptional administrators at his disposal. Under the much disliked, relentless Jean Orry, the royal household and councils were reorganized on the French pattern. More flexible and statesmanlike than Orry, the lawyer–diplomat Amelot was primarily responsible for the suppression of provincial privileges. He and Orry helped to win the war and laid the foundation for a better-governed country. The peace of Utrecht, which confirmed the Bourbon kinship, could have been the start of a further period of constructive reform. Spain was shorn of the rest of the Netherlands, the Milanese and Tuscan *presidios*, Naples and Sardinia, Gibraltar and Minorca, and therefore had smaller commitments and expenses and correspondingly less need for taxes. But it was the loss of credit that weighed most with her sovereign, and with his new queen, who brought with her claims in Italy which provided, fatally for the peace of Europe and for hopes of radical reform within Spain, the opportunity to recover that credit.

Philip married Elizabeth Farnese in 1715, a year after the death of his first wife. Vivid, talented, intrepid, she had energy enough for the two of them: he loved her slavishly and would not let her out of his sight, or even make his confession without her. Her first action as queen was to send home the princess of Orsini who had been led by Alberoni, Parma's minister in Madrid at the time of Marie Louise's death, to support the Parma marriage as the means through which she could perpetuate her own influence over the unhappy king. Thenceforward, Elizabeth ruled Spain, in the name of her enfeebled husband, at first in partnership with Alberoni. The son of a

Parmesan hairdresser, his name has suffered from treatment so summary or patronizing as to approach caricature: he is paraded as a diplomatic gigolo, the Italian of low birth and high ambition who first made a queen, then encouraged her in a course of foreign adventure which brought inevitable Spanish defeat. It is to do him less than justice.

Elizabeth remained at heart a princess of Parma and therefore opposed to the Habsburgs. She was concerned above all for the future of the duchies of Parma and Piacenza, which lacked a male heir and would therefore revert to the imperial power, already strengthened by the acquisition of Milan. Elizabeth was determined to secure from the great powers, by diplomacy or force, acceptance of the right of her elder son, Charles, to succeed to the duchies. She also dreamed of a larger Italian principality, including Milan and Tuscany. Her ambition accorded well with her subjects' concern for *reputación*. What was right for Parma could also appear to be right for Spain. From a traditional standpoint, it was intolerable that the Habsburgs should be allowed to dominate Italy. Nor was Alberoni's diplomacy entirely unrealistic. He knew that Britain valued her postwar commercial treaties with Spain. Was not even Stanhope at one stage prepared to barter Gibraltar for the sake of peace with Spain? It was understandable too that Alberoni should rely on the normal hostility between France and Austria. He may also have sensed a reluctance among the western powers to go to war. And so he hoped to be able to deal with Austria in isolation: a *casus belli* was offered by Charles VI's negotiations with Savoy for Sicily, which Alberoni declared to be a breach of the peace settlement. Unfortunately for him, in Stanhope he encountered a seasoned soldier–diplomat, no lover of Spain, where he had fought fruitless campaigns in a hostile countryside; now a minister, enjoying the favour of his Hanoverian king, he valued the new stability of Europe and his country's new alliance with France. Alberoni's policy was therefore reduced to a tissue of expedients: intrigues against the regent in France, threats of support for the Jacobites against England, a lure to Savoy in the form of Milan. Nothing if not resourceful, he approached the Hungarian nationalist, Rakoczy, and urged the Swedes and Russians to make common cause against Hanover. He tried to force the pace and sent the Spanish fleet to attack Sardinia. Charles VI then turned to the western powers; and the Triple Alliance of Britain, France and Holland became the Quadruple Alliance of 1718. At Cap Passaro the British attacked the Spanish fleet before it could concentrate, and destroyed it. Dubois exposed Alberoni's intrigue against Orléans and persuaded the regent to endorse an attack on his fellow Bourbon. While the Spanish were failing to follow up early successes in Sicily, the French army invaded Spain and was successful enough to persuade Philip that he must rid himself of Alberoni (December 1719).

Cardinal Alberoni (he received his hat in 1717) had played the diplomatic game skilfully, if without finesse: he was no Mazarin. Adventurer is not an unfair description. But his domestic enterprises show an interest in the well-being of his adopted country, a furious energy and an imagination that recall the early career of another Italian, Napoleon Buonaparte. In search of greater flexibility, he reduced the councils to mere honorific status and established a system of government by the sovereign's personal advisers that was to become the eighteenth-century norm. Tax reforms included constructive measures in Valencia, where a single customs duty and salt tax replaced damaging sales taxes. A sharp axe fell on pensions, *mercedes* and *juros*. Into the chaos of Spanish coinage, with its *reales* and *piastres* of varying origin and value, he introduced a new piece of 2 *reales*, to be current throughout the Empire. He reformed the tariff system so as to place foreign goods at a disadvantage while, amongst other Colbertist measures, he attracted foreign craftsmen with the bait of exemption from food taxes. Using Spanish timber, ropes and pitch, and Cuban copper, he set about the construction of a modern fleet. He experimented with the Indies trade, sending single ships instead of mounting expensive convoys. His naval college at Cadiz and new shipyard in Barcelona witnessed to his intelligent understanding of Spain's role in the world. It is all the more unfortunate that his Italian project should have diverted Spanish resources from more fruitful undertakings. Yet the pursuit of economic autarky and the diplomatic chauvinism were but two sides of the same coin. Alberoni had retreated into the smaller world of Italian politics when Trevisoni painted the fine portrait that is now to be seen at Badminton. The strong, confident features – and corpulence – may recall Cardinal Wolsey, as do the audacity of his diplomacy, and the plans and accomplishments that survived his fall.

Jan Ripperda was a Dutchman from Gröningen, brought up as a Catholic but later converted to Protestantism; colonel and friend of Prince Eugène in the War of the Spanish Succession, he was a deputy to the estates-general of the United Provinces before becoming envoy to Spain in 1715. His bold, picaresque career throws further light on the odd contradiction at the heart of Spanish society in this period: the absolute monarchy, designed for the autocratic exercise of power by the sovereign becomes a vehicle for the foreigner and adventurer. Drawing upon his knowledge of Dutch commerce and administration he presented the sovereigns with plausible designs and was regarded by Alberoni as a useful lieutenant. On Alberoni's dismissal he was made director of the new state manufactures; he planned expansion of the cloth industry, a larger trade with the Indies. Illusions of grandeur led him to devise a novel foreign policy. If Elizabeth could not win Parma against the Habsburgs she might do so by co-operating with them: the idea took shape in the treaty of Vienna (1725). Elizabeth had been steeled for the *volte-face* by the clumsily insulting action of the French ministers who decided to marry the young Louis XV to Maria Leszczynska of Poland, despite his formal engagement to the young infanta. In return for commercial concessions in the Spanish empire for his new Ostend Company,

Charles VI offered his two marriageable daughters to the sons of Elizabeth, and support for the recovery of Gibraltar and Minorca. Ripperda boasted prematurely. Nor did he allow for the grudging attitude of Charles, most narrowly dynastic of sovereigns, and still unreconciled to the idea of the Parma succession. When his ambassador asked for Ripperda's dismissal, the latter was rash enough to inform the British ambassador, not only of the secret terms of Vienna, but also of the bribes he had received from the Emperor.

Ripperda was dismissed in May 1727 and set off for Africa, where he helped to organize Moorish resistance to Spanish expeditions, became a Muslim, indeed founded a new Islamic sect, and was asked by some Sicilian refugees in Tunis to become their king. When he died, in a Moorish prison, he was planning to travel to Rome to ask the Pope's forgiveness. Meanwhile his work resulted in a war between Spain and England (1727–8): neither the Spanish siege of Gibraltar, nor the English blockade of the treasure fleet in Porto Bello were pursued with energy. Out of the turmoil certain salient features emerge. Walpole and Fleury wanted peace above all. The Emperor was increasingly concerned with his Pragmatic Sanction to safeguard the rights of his daughter Maria Theresa to succeed to the family lands: under the circumstances Spain had sufficient nuisance value to secure concessions. With England and France committed after the treaty of Seville (November 1729) to the succession of Charles to Parma, and the Emperor determined not to let the duchy go, war became imminent when its duke died (1731). A second treaty of Vienna brought temporary respite: England recognized the Pragmatic Sanction, the Emperor suspended the Ostend Company; Charles received Parma and the reversion to Tuscany when its duke should die. In 1732 the British fleet escorted him to Italy. In that year too Oran, lost to the Moors in 1708, was reconquered by a Spanish expedition. In 1733 the treaty of the Escorial, or family compact, was signed between France and Spain. Spain therefore became involved in the War of the Polish Succession which acquired a second front when the French occupied Milan and Charles marched south to occupy Naples. The result of further campaigns and prolonged diplomacy was in one respect disappointing for Spain since Cardinal Fleury abandoned the 'perpetual' alliance of the Escorial for the greater prize of Lorraine, whose duke had to be accommodated in Tuscany. Charles was, however, promoted. In return for ceding the duchies of Parma and Piacenza, which were joined to imperial Milan, he was recognized as king of Naples and Sicily (1737).

Elizabeth may by then have thought her game worth the candle. But she nursed ambitions for her other sons. Louis had already been provided for by the archbishopric of Toledo. For Philip she looked for an Italian principality. The opportunity came when Britain, rather than seek a peaceful settlement of the conflicts over trade in America, chose to make an issue of the notorious affray in which Captain Jenkins lost an ear and gave his name to the war that followed (1739). A second war began with the death of the Emperor and Frederick of Prussia's attack on Silesia (1740). All was bound together in what became known as the War of the Austrian Succession but was in reality several distinct conflicts related only by the alliances which each country made to further its particular ends, and by the decision of France, undoing Fleury's cautious diplomacy, and dishonouring her commitment to the Sanction, to go to war with Austria. Elizabeth and her husband, rousing himself from squalid torpor like some old, sick hound at the prospect of the hunt, sent all the troops they could muster to Italy. The situation presented Sardinia and its foreign minister d'Ormea, with an excellent opportunity to exploit its position, lying as it did between France and Austrian Milan. At the treaty of Worms, England's foreign minister Carteret bid high for its alliance (September 1743) but that only provoked France to renew the family compact and to pledge herself to secure an Italian principality for Philip and to recover Gibraltar and Minorca for Spain. Genoa also came over to the Bourbon camp. Since, however, Frederick extricated himself from the war as soon as he had gained Silesia (1745) and the Austrians were able to concentrate upon defending their Italian possessions, the elaborate diplomatic plans of d'Argenson, envisaging no less than a complete reconstruction of the Italian states, came to nothing. While Marshal Saxe was winning notable victories in Flanders, the Italian war, pursued through the vicissitudes of six campaigns, ended in the complete failure of the Bourbon armies. At least, however, Austria's concern with recovering Flanders, and building up diplomatic support for another war for Silesia, meant that they were prepared to let Parma go; and so at the peace of Aix-la-Chapelle, in 1748, Philip was confirmed in his rights in the duchies. Nor was that position disturbed in the war of 1761–3, which began when Charles III (as the former king of Naples became when he became king of Spain in 1759), concerned about the growing strength of Britain overseas as a result of her victories in the Seven Years War, renewed the family compact. By then, Spanish priorities had changed, and there was becoming apparent that shift of emphasis to the country's commercial concerns which had long been the care of her best ministers but had been concealed by the preoccupation with dynastic interests.

Philip's successor, Ferdinand VI (1746–59), was pacific by temperament and content to leave foreign affairs to his minister José de Carvajal. Up to his death in 1754 Carvajal followed the intelligent and moderate course which his sovereign approved, preserving Spanish neutrality between the poles of Austria and France, aiming for a position of influence from which to help preserve the balance. To secure this position a commercial treaty was made with England (1750). Meanwhile steps were taken to revive industry. That so much had been done already without inspiration from the crown speaks for the ability of successive ministers. Until the accession of Charles III progress depended on the application and judgement of such men; outstanding among them was José Patino. Born in Milan of a Spanish family, he made his reputation as *intendente* of Estramadura, that province of three million sheep, only half a million people. As president of the *casa de contratación*, he did wonders to bring the fleet up to operational standard. After temporary eclipse, until after the fall of Ripperda, Patino was again given responsibility commensurate with his ambition: for a time he had charge of finance as well as of the navy. The great fleet which sailed from Alicante and conquered Oran (1732) was Patino's creation. He managed to secure increased taxes from the once-more prosperous Indies trade. He was unable to achieve comprehensive reforms, but he saw to it that money was available to support Elizabeth's diplomacy. Another constructive reformer was the marquis of Ensenada, who earned promotion through naval administration and a title for his work with the fleet that helped to conquer Naples. Minister of finance after 1743, he was a great projector, infected with the optimistic spirit of the times. His new road over the Guadarrama, linking the two Castiles, was the first major project in this vital but neglected sphere.

No significant body of reform could, however, be carried out without firmer direction from above. The Spanish Enlightenment was being thoroughly prepared through the writings of men like Fray Feyjóo, who exposed Spanish backwardness in his essays and preached the criterion of social utility in a society still obsessed with honour and display, and in the work of reformers like Ensenada, who had already done the detailed planning for a single tax to replace the manifold imposts when he fell from power in 1754. It reveals much about Spanish government that his decree of 1749 to put this tax into effect had not been carried out mainly because the officials did not understand it. It is not surprising that the reigns of the first two Bourbon kings should have seen only piecemeal and limited reforms. In the vital areas of agriculture, commerce, education above all, there needed to be a strong directing hand. That was to be the role of Charles III. It is only in his reign that we can speak of enlightened government, with its characteristic flavour of anticlericalism, its faith in the criterion of reason, and pragmatic measures designed to promote the prosperity of the people.

Charles III and the *Luces*

Charles III (1759–88) is justly regarded by Spaniards as the greatest of their monarchs: superior to Philip II, comparable only to Isabella the Catholic. Part of his appeal, then and now, lies in simple manners and homely, traditional values. Devoted to religion, hunting and his wife, chaste after her death in 1761 and more zealous than ever in government business, Charles was far removed in character and style from his greatest contemporaries; but not in his aims and achievements. No picture of the age of enlightened absolutism is complete without an account of his reign, of which a modern authority, Raymond Carr, has written that 'there is no practical reform of the nineteenth century, no reforming attitude of mind, that cannot be traced back to one of the servants of Charles III'. He picked and backed intelligent, bold ministers: Squillace, Aranda, Campomanes, Flóridablanca were all open-minded men in touch with the ideas of the *philosophes*, committed to practical reforms, especially in the economic sphere. The impulse towards reform, in this most conservative of societies, came from the king himself. 'I devote all my attention to improving the welfare of my subjects, since I wish to save my soul and to go to heaven': in a man of less obvious sincerity the words would have sounded sanctimonious; in Charles, Spanish-style utilitarian, they were a text for action. Goya's famous picture of Charles, with gun and dog, against a verdant landscape, with long face and shrewd grin, as of a farmer appraising his crops, portrays the king who brought monarchy back to the people. He could not perform miracles, but he could persuade them that progress was possible.

Charles started with no obvious advantages. His inheritance was not reassuring: his father Philip V had suffered from bouts of insanity, his half-brother Ferdinand VI had ended his days a melancholy recluse. But he came to Spain with a solid record of reforms in Naples, where he had been king since 1734. He had gone there determined, in the words of his minister Tanucci, 'to sweep away feudalism'. To some extent he had succeeded. He had also established industries where there had been none before, built palaces, and an immense poor house as well; patronized archaeology and the arts, and shown the courage to stand up to vested interests, as he did to the clergy over his unpopular decision to admit Jews into the kingdom. He owed his throne in Naples to the fierce determination of his mother, Elizabeth Farnese; the lesson of her successful diplomacy was that boldness, allied to shrewd judgement, can produce great results. There was, however, nothing of the gambler about him. Even his more controversial actions in the field of foreign policy, conditioned as they were by natural feelings of resentment towards the British, in particular because of their continued occupation of Gibraltar, were based on rational assessment of risk and potential. He went to war twice against Britain: he entered the Seven Years War in 1761 and the American war in 1779. In the epic siege of Gibraltar (1781–2) the British garrison held out against the odds. In the ensuing negotiations, leading to the peace of Versailles (1783), although the French and Spanish held strong cards and British opinion was divided about the value of Gibraltar, the Spanish had to be content with the cession of Minorca, along with that of Florida. Gibraltar remained a strategic asset to Britain but an obstacle to friendly relations between that country and Spain – which may have been the intention of the French foreign minister Vergennes when he refused to back the Spanish claim. Perhaps Charles should have been prepared for it since the French had also failed to support the Spanish when, in 1770, they occupied Port Egmont in the Falkland Islands. They subsequently had to withdraw when the British threatened to fight over it. Louis XV, seeing the British characteristically stiff on the question of sovereignty and concerned about the prospect of war over so small a matter, dismissed his foreign minister Choiseul and wrote to Charles III: 'my minister would have war, but I would not'. Such failures and rebuffs may be held to outweigh the gains of Versailles. More serious was the cost of the wars to Spain's fragile economy. Yet it was to this area that some of Charles's most strenuous reforms were directed.

It was an important characteristic of Charles that he could learn from mistakes and that he remained sensitive to realities. The decree of July 1765 proclaimed free trade in grain and abolished price controls. Prohibiting all monopolies, companies and guilds in the grain trade, together with 'illicit dealings or ill-gained profits', it offended powerful local interests. The government was unlucky in that the succeeding harvest was poor: its effects were exacerbated by hoarding and the indolence of local authorities charged with supply. There were widespread riots in 1766. The most serious were those of Madrid in March, and they, unlike the rest, were undoubtedly political and manipulated by certain grandees and churchmen who saw their privileges threatened and fomented opposition in the taverns and the churches to bring out 'the monstrous crowd of the lower classes' who congregated in the squares of the capital. Agitators were provided with a cause by the zeal of the king and his unpopular Italian minister Squillace for cleaning up and lighting the notoriously dirty capital, and their attempt to rouse Spaniards to a sense of their isolation and backwardness by reviving former decrees forbidding the long capes and wide-brimmed hats beloved by the bravos (and convenient for the lawless since the hat's brim enabled the wearer to conceal his face). Typically the mob who sacked Squillace's house also destroyed the new street lamps. He was forced into exile and Charles had to revoke his edicts. He proceeded to work more cautiously to reassert his authority and promote reforms. The aristocracy may have been reassured by the promotion of the count of Aranda, but the clergy were not, since his chief function as president of the supreme council of Castile was the preservation of royal rights against those of the Church. With the Jesuits earmarked for special treatment, since they made little attempt to conceal their interest in preserving the old clerical regime, the pattern of the reign was being established.

In 1767 the Jesuits were expelled from Spain, and Monino, who was responsible for the administration of the order, was rewarded with the title conde de Flóridablanca. He was to become chief minister in place of Grimaldi in 1776. A fellow minister was Pedro Rodríguez, conde de Campomanes, attorney-general, a man in the best tradition of the *arbitristas*, tireless author of reports on subjects for reform. They were very different men from the haughty, patrician Aranda, but the three had in common a devotion to monarchy and to the cause of reform, together with the broader European view and the willingness to experiment which give this period a quality, new to Spain, of radical enterprise. 'It is an old habit in Spain,' wrote Campomanes, 'to condemn everything that is new, however good and suitable it may be.' Upon that habit the king and his ministers waged persistent and subtle war.

Conservative bodies fought back. The power of the Inquisition is illustrated by the fate of Olaveide, a talented administrator from Peru who was put in charge of the Sierra Morena project of resettlement of empty lands, largely by German immigrants. With its symmetrical arable plots along the bandit-infested roads, its industrious Lutheran farmers and severe classical buildings, not least its ban on the religious orders, it was a provocative showpiece of the new order. And Olaveide, with his 'pornographic pictures' in the style of Boucher and Fragonard, was an irresistible target for the guardians of the old Spain. After prolonged, meticulous trial by the Inquisition on the charge of being a formal heretic, his judges, having produced among other damning documents his correspondence with Voltaire, Olaveide was convicted and condemned to live for eight years in a convent, from which he later escaped. Perhaps the king's favour preserved him from the flames; but the king was too wise, or too good a Spaniard, to attempt any drastic action against the Inquisition.

There is little intellectual distinction or originality about the Spanish *Luces* (Enlightenment) and its disciples. Even if there had been, the obscurantism nurtured by the universities would have deprived them of a significant audience. The spirit of acceptance was stronger than that of enquiry. 'You will search in vain in Spanish history,' wrote Rousseau, Charles's French biographer, 'for a savant like Galileo, Newton, Lagrange or Lavoisier.' Charles might issue an edict like that of 1762 praising 'literature as one of the chief adornments of a state', but books were little read. In this climate it is not surprising that the emphasis of the reformers was utilitarian; it is rather more noteworthy how much they achieved than how much was left untouched. A brief selection of the enterprises and innovations of the reign bears this out.

Utility rather than blood was the criterion of social value; utility rather than tradition the principle behind legislation. As in so much else Charles set the tone. 'Appointments,' he wrote, must only be filled by the best informed, the most balanced, and the liveliest.' In 1771 he created a new order that opened nobility to the *gollilas*, the bourgeoisie. The changing emphasis at the centre was matched by action at the local level to abolish hereditary offices, even to introduce elections for certain posts. The best solvent for old attitudes was the force of new ideas, given the seal of respectability by official sponsorship of the arts and sciences. Charles founded an astronomical observatory and an immense hospital. He completed the botanical garden in Madrid and commissioned the building of the Prado, which was originally designed to be a natural history museum. He finished the building of the royal palace in Madrid and was the first Spanish king to live there. The cost of such works could be justified in the stimulus to all the building and decorative crafts; they were showpieces in a wider programme of patronage, protection and subsidy. Royal factories were created for the manufacture of clocks and porcelain. Some of the restrictive practices of the guilds were ended. New roads were built. Under the direction of Flóridablanca and his corps of engineers, a road system was begun, radiating from Madrid, symbolizing the new energy of central government. The first national bank of Spain was founded, while in the provinces a number of economic societies were founded to spread technical knowledge; significantly they were sometimes called 'patriotic' societies. There were even enlightened churchmen, like the bishop of Siguenza, for whom workshops and model farms were a sounder way of dealing with poverty than the indiscriminate alms-giving for which the Church was much blamed by enlightened followers of the new gospel of progress.

Of course the most general source of poverty was the backwardness of agriculture. Campomanes was able to bring about some curtailment of the powers of the Mesta. Ambitious irrigation works were carried out, model farms and colonies were established. Some common land was parcelled out and enclosed and some private land that was uncultivated was redistributed. The simple proposition behind agrarian reform was that surplus land should be allocated to surplus labour. It proved to be more complicated than that. Possibly Charles's greatest contribution, as in other branches of production, was to counter the traditional Spanish prejudice against work, by his own example, for he would go off to work sometimes in one of his own factories, as much as by edicts like that which declared that the trades of tanner, blacksmith, tailor and shoemaker did not degrade the person practising them, or his family! It was not so much attitudes as institutions that provided the main obstruction to the reformer. While government became more effective through the *corregidores* Charles could do nothing in the face of the *fueros* of the Basque provinces and of Navarre, exempt still from Spanish conscription, taxation and customs duties: the national customs frontier ran along the river Ebro. More serious was the sheer size throughout Spain of the local administrative body and its inertia, with the extra factor of unresolved differences between Castilian and local codes of law, making the little republics of the municipalities the last and weakest link in the chain of authority.

Ironically it was in the area where Charles's reforms had their greatest impact that they also had their most disastrous consequences. Reform in the American colonies appeared to be necessary since weak government meant inadequate revenue for defence, and weak defence meant that foreign competitors would gain ground. The last thing that the creoles of New Spain wanted was more honest, efficient government; they were excluded, as untrustworthy, from the new system under colonal *intendantes*. Even where Charles's reforms brought local prosperity, as in the viceroyalty of Buenos Aires, they only increased the spirit of independence. To the great Spanish civil servant Gálvez, reform meant 'an enforcement of a more rigid adherence to the paramount interests of the mother country'. To the creoles, not surprisingly, it meant subjection. They wanted free trade and the fruits of office; they would soon be fighting for their independence.

Further Reading

Many students of Spain will continue, rightly, to approach seventeenth-century Spain through one of two books. J.H. Elliot's *Imperial Spain 1469–1716* (London, 1970) is thin on the second half of the period, specially good, as might be expected from the author of *The Revolt of the Catalans* (Cambridge, 1963), on the middle years of the century. The second volume of J. Lynch's *Spain under the Habsburgs*, entitled *Spain and America, 1598–1700* (Oxford, 1969) is specially strong, as the title suggests, on the colonial relationship. A mine of information about climate, landscape, rhythms of trade and the condition of the people is F. Braudel's *Mediterranean and the Mediterranean World in the Age of Philip II*, vols 1, 2 (English edns, London, 1972, 1973): though the period treated is earlier certain structural characteristics persist. At the other end of the period, Raymond Carr's volume in *The Oxford History of Modern Europe – Spain, 1808–1939* (Oxford, 1966) – has a valuable section, the first eighty pages, summarizing the character of eighteenth-century Spain and the achievements of the Enlightenment. Among textbooks of the period, P. Chaunu's *La Civilisation de l'Europe classique* (Paris, 1966) is specially rich in statistics and insights.

The much debated question of the decline of Spain may be approached through articles like Elliot's 'The decline of Spain', *Past and Present*, 20 (1961), and H. Kamen, 'The decline of Spain: an historical myth?', *Past and Present*, 81 (1978). (See also books on the general crisis cited after chapter 5.) Still important is E.J. Hamilton, 'The decline of Spain', *Economic History Review*, 8 (1938), a distillation of the arguments in his major works: the most authoritative is *War and Prices in Spain, 1651–1800* (1947). Similarly R.A. Stradling's 'Seventeenth century Spain: decline or survival?', *European Studies Review*, 9 (1979), offers an introduction to themes and arguments to be found in his longer study, *Europe and the Decline of Spain* (London, 1981). His work, along with that of J.I. Israel, *The Dutch Republic and the Hispanic World, 1606–61* (Oxford, 1982), is considered in a review article by J.H. Elliot, 'A question of reputation? Spanish foreign policy in the seventeenth century', *Journal of Modern History*, 55 (1983). In his own recent work, *Richelieu and Olivares* (Cambridge, 1984), Elliot sets out to answer the question: how far was the decline of Spain due to extrinsic causes, notably the restoration of French power after a period of civil war? For the *arbitristas*, contemporary analysts of crisis, Elliot offers an interesting study, 'Self-perception and decline in early seventeenth century Spain', *Past and Present*, 74 (1977). For an assessment of the period to which various categories of decline have to be related, see A.W. Lovett, 'The Golden Age of Spain: new work on an old theme', *Historical Journal*, 24 (1981). The six works that he reviews, looking at different parts of Habsburg Spain, each present distinctive pictures and no one conclusion entirely supports another. As in other fields, the law appears to be: 'the more is known, the less safe it is to generalize'. For one of the distinctive regions see J.G. Casey, *The Spanish Kingdom of Valencia in the Seventeenth Century* (Cambridge, 1979). For a master's *tour d'horizon*, see P. Vilar, *Brief History of Spain* (Oxford, 1967) or his article, 'The age of Don Quixote', translated and reprinted in P. Earle (ed.), *Essays in Economic History, 1500–1800* (Oxford, 1974). H. Kamen has just written a new, balanced account of the country, *Spain 1469–1716: a society of conflict* (London, 1983), which includes the main arguments of his bold revisionist study, *Spain in the Later Seventeenth Century* (Harlow, 1980). He claims to be trying 'to establish a general context for further work in early modern Spain'. He does so with an impressive if one-sided range of evidence but his theme is not entirely original: the gist of the argument can be found in Juan Regla's chapter in the *New Cambridge Modern History*, vol. 5 (Cambridge, 1961).

Eighteenth-century Spain has not recently received the same intensive treatment as preceding centuries, though a useful narrative account is that of W.N. Hargreaves-Mawdsley, *Eighteenth Century Spain* (London, 1979). Richard Herr's *The Eighteenth Century Revolution in Spain* (1958) is therefore invaluable and, with J. Sarrailh, *L'Espagne éclairée de la second moitié du XVIIIe siècle* (1955), it still commands the field. There are useful chapters in the *New Cambridge Modern History*, vols 7, 8, by J.O. Lindsay and J. Lynch respectively. An important Spanish work awaits a translator: G. Anes, *El Antiguo Régimen: los Borbones* (1976). L. Rodríguez, 'The Spanish riots of 1766', *Past and Present*, 54 (1973), illuminates a crucial episode in the reign of Charles III whose robust character is well analysed in an essay by Nicholas Henderson in *History Today*, 18 (10–11) (1968).

10

GERMAN EMPIRE, AUSTRIAN STATE

The Holy Roman Empire

The political history of early modern Germany is that of a federation of territorial princes and free towns. Changing constantly with the accidents of marriage, inheritance and acquisition by fair means or foul, their number fluctuated around 300. The reckoning at any time depended upon what was held to belong to the German Empire, itself a part of a larger entity, or rather myth – for that is what the Holy Roman Empire had become by the seventeenth century. The medieval emperors' claim of universal sovereignty was hollow long before the Reformation destroyed the underlying ideal of Christian unity. Ferdinand II (1619–37) called for the support of German princes while concerting with Spain a Counter-Reformation strategy in which the princes saw more of dynastic ambition than Catholic zeal; he put the traditional idea of empire to the test when he claimed the right to adjudicate over the succession to the Italian duchy of Mantua (1627) against the claim of the French-supported duc de Nevers. At the diet of Regensburg, in 1630, the princes ruled that he had no such right. They still cherished the idea that they belonged to what they called, in more parochial terms, the Holy Roman Empire of the German nation.

The ambition of Ferdinand and of the kings of France and Sweden had turned what began as a German civil war, when the Elector Palatine defied the Emperor by accepting the crown of Bohemia, into a wider European war, subsuming other conflicts, notably that in the Netherlands between

Spain and the Dutch. Thirty years of war left a mass of claims to be resolved. The prime objective of the diplomats of Westphalia was to ensure a lasting security and protection of the rights of German princes against future aggressors from without and within. The best that they could do was to work for a balance of interests, as for example by the partition of Pomerania between Sweden and Brandenburg. The need to restore order and to facilitate negotiations led them to a more precise definition of boundaries and sovereignty. They laid down that the rulers' powers were not those of complete sovereignty but territorial supremacy. They excluded from negotiation the Burgundian circle, one of the ten groupings created by the Emperor Maximilian I (1477–1519). (These groupings, *Kreis*, were administrating 'circles' within the Empire.) Maximilian's object had been the creation of a mechanism of central control and taxation; he had been thwarted by the constitutional party among the princes, led by Berthold of Mainz, which wanted to create a federation which could provide effectively for the defence of the Reich without infringing upon the rights of individual princes. The conflict of interest was to persist, but the Germany that emerged from the crucial decade of reforms in the 1490s was nearer to Berthold's than to Maximilian's ideal. It was a two-tiered federal system. Above the territorial assemblies within the German states were imperial assemblies at national level to which the heads of the states belonged and where they could discuss and direct German affairs. The *Reichstag*, *Reichskammergericht* and *Reichshofrat*, the imperial assembly, supreme law court and court of appeal respectively, in which the Emperor sat only as *primum inter pares*, gave dignity and meaning to the Reich, to that which pertained to the German princes in common, as distinct from that which was *Kaiserlich*, signifying the Emperor's own powers of direction and administration.

Each German state had the right to control its own domestic affairs and was in effect free to negotiate with foreign powers. Princes, ecclesiastical and secular, counts and representatives of the imperial cities, enjoyed the right of representation to the *Reichstag* which dealt with matters of interest to the Empire as a whole and met under the presidency of the Emperor. His office was nominally elective but had become virtually hereditary in the Austrian branch of the Habsburgs. The Emperor was understood to have certain 'reserved rights' which allowed him to veto measures submitted by the *Reichstag*, to make promotions in rank and bestow fiefs, titles of nobility and university degrees. The first of the three *curiae* in the *Reichstag* was the college of electors, the eight who carried out the imperial election. Second was the college of princes, counts and barons (including the ecclesiastical princes), and third the college of the imperial free cities. There were sixty-five ecclesiastical states; they were usually small but they included the three electors of Mainz, Trier and Cologne, Mainz having special influence through the archbishop-elector's hereditary office of arch-chancellor of the

Empire, which gave him the status of 'second only to the Emperor' and the opportunity to influence policy in the *Reichskammergericht*. The forty-five dynastic principalities, with 80 per cent of the land and population, contained several states large enough to pursue independent policies, as Bavaria had done during the Thirty Years War, and possessing the potential for further growth which, along with the likelihood of diplomatic involvement with foreign powers, posed the greatest threat to the federal system. The sixty dynastic counties and lordships, having altogether but 3 per cent of the land, might appear to have poor prospects for survival alongside such giants as Saxony or Brandenburg. But the well-documented experience of Lippe, in Westphalia, shows not only the powerful sense of a separate identity under a well-established line of rulers but also a will and capacity to survive in complete independence which appears to have been typical of the minuscule states of Germany. Vulnerable, as it proved, to economic rather than to political pressures, were the sixty imperial free cities and towns. Status did not necessarily correspond to size or importance. Leipzig had only *Land* status under its prince, while some imperial towns were little more than villages, with under a thousand inhabitants. Outside the political structure, as defined by membership or right to representation in the *Reichstag*, were the imperial knights, over a thousand of them. By the fifteenth century they had formed cantons within their own regions in the Rhineland, Swabia and Franconia. They enjoyed in legal terms the same independence as the highest princes, having no overlord but the Emperor himself. But their cantons were never joined to the federal institutions of the German Empire and they had neither seat nor vote in the imperial assemblies. Altogether possessing but 2 per cent of the land, each of them claimed rights of landlordship and justice that amounted to virtually independent sovereignty. Most significantly they claimed *Landherrschaft*, allegiance only to the Emperor in his capacity as president of the *Reichstag*.

It was only the Emperor who gave the semblance of unity to this federation, for the Emperor could only act effectively in concert with the princes or through his courts. There lay the strength and weakness of an Empire which was bound together by the feudal ties of allegiance and strengthened by the sentiment of nationality; which existed in some respects in the world of medieval universalism, in others in that of the modern nation, without belonging wholly to either. The traditional loyalties were commonly subordinated to material interests, particularly in the actions of the larger states. Religious schism created new frontiers and new criteria for policy. The nation had no clear frontiers. The elector of Brandenburg ruled East Prussia, which was outside the Empire and still a fief, in 1648, of the king of Poland. Not only did mainly Slav Bohemia belong to the Empire, but its Habsburg sovereign, in his capacity as king, was also a member of the college of electors. The king of Spain kept a toe-hold through his representative in the Burgundian circle. Within the intricate patchwork there was further fragmentation and fracturing beyond the capacity of any historical atlas to convey. First, feudal jurisdiction and lordships overlapped in ways that could be understood only by the local lawyers. Second, inheritances and partitions meant a constant shifting even of such lines as could be drawn. Third, and most important, there lacked any clear idea of state, or sovereignty, for Germany as a whole. It is easier, then, to say what the German Empire was not than what it was. It fits into no traditional category, such as those which Aristotle bequeathed to successive generations of political theorists, which led the Great Elector's adviser Pufendorf to dismiss it as 'a monstrosity'. Yet it is becoming increasingly plain, through the investigation of particular states in this period and their dealings with the imperial authorities, that the German Empire was still a working political reality. It is essential therefore to ask the right questions. How did the Germans view the Empire? How did it work?

The educated German's conception of the Empire and the state within which he lived cannot be described exclusively in political terms. It was a product of social and economic conditions which were as different from those of France, Spain or the Netherlands as they were from those of Russia or even Poland. It was influenced too by the predominance of universities within the Empire, a unique feature, as well as by intellectual trends in those universities which therefore affected society as a whole: in particular the development of native doctrines of natural law and cameralism and, within the Lutheran confession, the phenomenon of Pietism.

The population started to recover at once from the losses sustained during the Thirty Years War, as high as 50 per cent in the Palatinate and Württemberg, 30 per cent in Bavaria, and around that figure in Germany as a whole. It had returned to the prewar level, around 15 million, by 1700. Trade and industry were not so easily restored. The gradual shift of the axis of the European economy from central Europe to the Atlantic seaboard, with the decline in activity in the Mediterranean area, and latterly the growing influence of colonial possessions, would have had adverse effects even if there had been no great war; because of it the decline was, however, more general and severe: markets were disrupted, capital was dispersed; trading expertise went to waste. Apart from the irreversible decline of the cities of south Germany, the exports of grain and textiles from the Baltic ports were never to return to prewar levels; in Rhineland commerce there was no significant growth till the second quarter of the eighteenth century. Everywhere the individual capitalist lost standing. The men who had made cities like Nuremberg, Augsburg and Frankfurt am Main so prosperous and splendid were replaced by the princes: ubiquitous and paramount in states large and small, they became prime agents in economic affairs. Whereas there was little, if any, growth in the old trading cities, new building beautified the state capitals, providing for the officials, courtiers, their households, and the tradesmen who provided for their needs. Cities

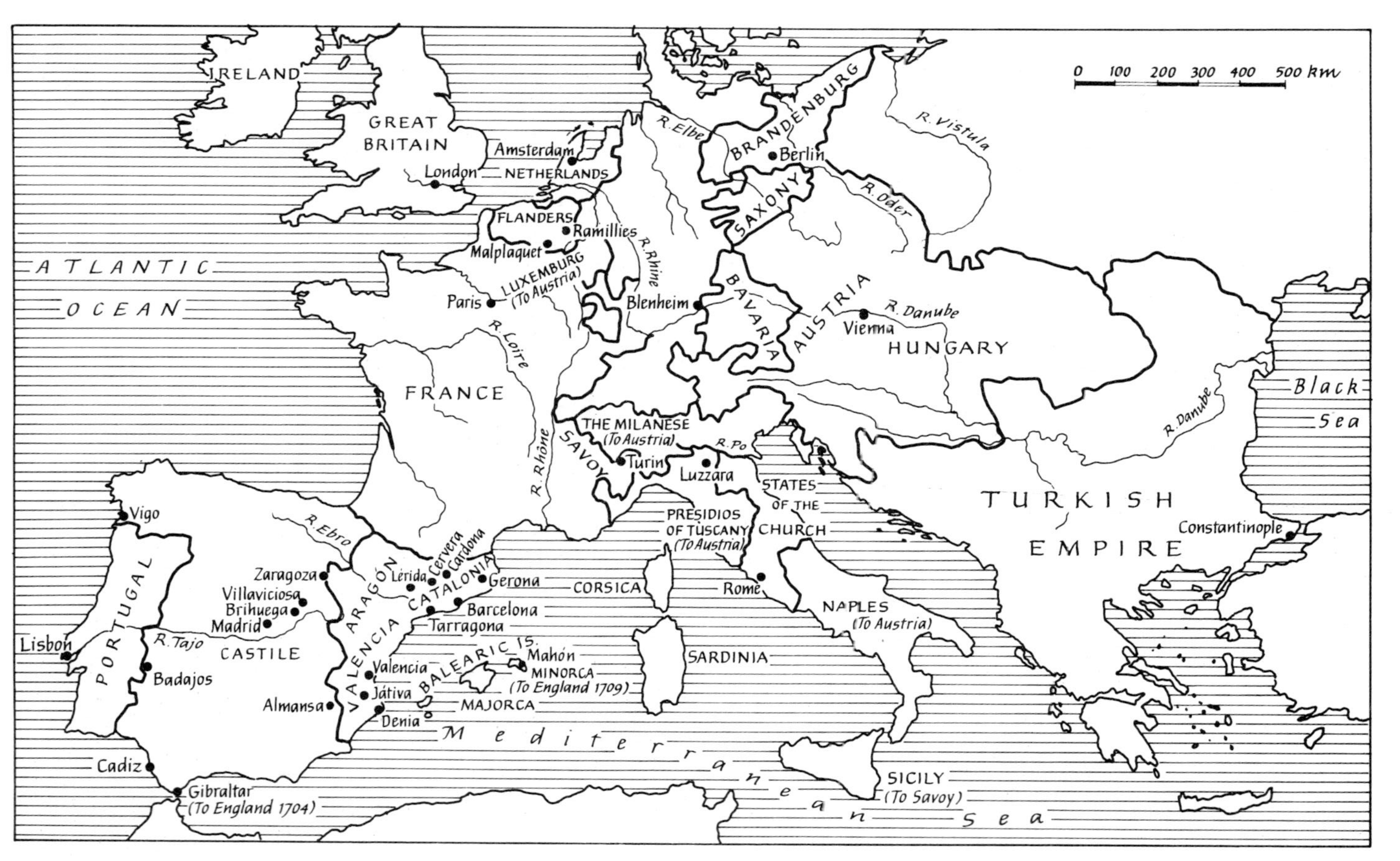

Map 10.1 *Europe at the time of the War of the Spanish Succession*

like Dresden, Stuttgart and Hanover were the showplaces of the Germany of the princes. At Weimar and Munich a third of the inhabitants depended directly on the prince for their livelihood. In such places the patterns of demand and spending established by princely patronage meant that most of the rest were in some measure dependent. There could be no vital entrepreneurial class because producers and traders were managers within a bureaucratic structure rather than entirely free agents. Numerous customs barriers inhibited the development of trade between states that were already dominated by cautious, parochial officialdom. The Elbe was a great natural waterway but because of the many toll points it was cheaper to carry goods by land. The guilds were both numerous and powerful. After the liberal Reich law of 1731 relating to their powers and functions, there was some growth in the number of manufacturing enterprises outside the guild organization. From the middle of the century there was more pronounced economic progress, and an increasingly important part was played by private enterprise. By the 1790s over 1000 concerns in Germany employed more than 10 workers. Large units were becoming more common, particularly in textiles. But there were still significant differences between Germany and the developing economies of the west: there were fewer entrepreneurs; there was a larger role for nobles, particularly in mining enterprises; the attitude and energy of the prince were still of overriding importance.

In no other country were universities so important as in Germany. By 1800 there were nearly 50; in France at the time there were 22, in England 2. Between 1600 and 1800 there were 24 new foundations. Not all were as vigorous as Göttingen, founded in 1737, thereafter leading the way in research and teaching, not only in mathematics and natural sciences, but in the humanities as well; or Halle, where all the important Prussian civil servants of the eighteenth century were trained. In general the universities dominated intellectual life. Catholics recognized the superiority of the best Protestant universities which led individual students to travel north in search of a better training and eventually compelled the authorities to set their own houses in order. The authority might well be the prince. German rulers valued universities, and their teachers were respected and influential because they served the state by providing the officials required for tasks of government that were no less complicated where the state was small; indeed might be more so since there was less scope for specialization. And so far from being ivory towers German universities were firmly integrated into the local community and its government. Teachers moved in and out of government posts, while the majority of their students became servants of government in one way or another: in Lutheran countries, that did not just include lawyers and administrators but also teachers and clergy, since education and religion were under the control of the state; the minister might well be in charge of the local school; if he were not he would still be the government's agent in publicizing decrees. It is likely too that he would lose no chance of instilling respect for duly constituted authority. It is the subservience of church to state that has led historians to emphasize the importance of Lutheranism in the evolution of a distinctive German attitude to authority. In the eighteenth century moreover it was given a new flavour through the pervasive influence of Pietism.[1]

Essentially a devotional movement, Pietism was imbued with an active reforming spirit: it found expression in orphanages and workhouses; it practised the morality of the good neighbour to such good effect that it came to enjoy a commanding position in the Lutheran establishment. Their individualism brought Pietists into conflict with orthodox Lutherans but in one vital respect they remained faithful to the tenets of the founder: they believed with Luther that religion should not be mixed with politics. Only by spiritual means should they try to establish God's kingdom on earth. Stressing the supreme values of prayer and work they impressed upon the faithful the corresponding values of duty and obedience. Even those who did not enter their own somewhat intense world were affected by their values. Of most Protestant intellectuals, it can be said that they were influenced by Pietism in their youth. But the earnest religious spirit which affected life at all levels was not confined to the Protestant confessions. Anticlericalism tended to be an issue in the Catholic states because of the prominent role of the Church, religious orders in particular, as landowners and educators. But there was nothing comparable anywhere in Germany to the revolt of western intellectuals against traditional dogma. To be a philosopher, in Germany, was not to be a sceptic: rather the reverse. Amid all his speculations, Leibnitz, who more than any other influenced the way thoughtful Germans felt about life, held to the idea of a personal God existing apart from, not subject to, the limitations of the materialist universe. Devotion, not indifference, impelled him to search for grounds for Christian reunion. His disciple Wolff, the central figure of the *Aufklärung*, whom even Frederick the Great respected, believed that reason and revelation could be reconciled. The Pietists secured his expulsion from Halle on the charge of doctrinal unorthodoxy. The rational philosopher and the emotional revivalists shared none the less essential Christian beliefs. In Halle there evolved, out of the fusion of Pietism and Wolffism a new scientific theology which was both orthodox in such doctrines as the Trinity and progressive in the spirit of the *Aufklärung* which had no truck with philosophical materialism.

It is not hard to see the appeal of religion in the Germany of Schütz, Buxtehude and Johann Sebastian Bach, of the baroque style in building and ornament, so majestic in the larger edifices but appealing and homely in the parish churches. But the wealth of sacred writing, music, building and painting is not enough to account for the apparent immunity of German intellectuals from the contagion of secular rationalism – and that in a period

[1] See also pp. 107–9.

when the French appeared to be influential in every aspect of culture. One has to look to other features of the German tradition to account for the uncompromisingly Christian character of the *Aufklärung*. First is the general acceptance after 1648 of the principle *cuius regio, eius religio*, with mostly open frontiers for those who wished to migrate to another state where the prince was of their religious persuasion: following the lead of Brandenburg, princes tended to be more relaxed about the danger from religious minorities. At the same time the ruler's authority in ecclesiastical matters was enhanced and there was less need or scope for conflict of the kind which did so much in western Europe to foster doubt about authority, spiritual as well as secular. Second, it is no accident, given the prevailing intellectual climate, the responsibility of each Protestant ruler for religion in his state and the double authority of the sovereign in the Catholic prince-bishoprics, that a high proportion of German rulers were pious and conscientious and that some actively promoted reforms. In most dioceses attempts were made to improve the training of priests, with it the quality of services; also to reduce the wealth and privilege of the regular orders. Programmes of reform were facilitated by the association of so many academics with the Church and with government. Johann von Hontheim (1701–90), better known as Febronius, leader of the campaign to restrict the powers of the papacy and to reform the Church – the German equivalent of Gallicanism but with less of law and more of piety about it – was both a professor at Trier University and a suffragan bishop. It can be added that the religious spirit of the time was an aspect of the general conservatism in which the role of the lawyers and the nature of the law they taught was crucial.

The advocates of natural law in the eighteenth century, following the lead of Grotius and Pufendorf, argued in a secular context. They argued that a system of law could be constructed logically from rational axioms so that it was reason, rather than custom or faith that enabled man to decide what was right. In the hands of men like Christian Tomasius (1655–1728) and Christian Wolff (1679–1754) natural law endorsed absolutism. They might be accused of rationalizing the existing situation: it is a common trait of political philosophy in all periods. But Wolff, who owed his great influence less to his originality than to his gift for making difficult ideas both plain and palatable, found no difficulty in presenting the case in strictly logical form. He argued that natural law was identical with reason; every action of the state in accordance with reason was therefore lawful. The ruler was absolute. Echoing Tomasius, Wolff declared that 'he who exercises the civil power has the right to establish everything that appears to him to serve the public good'. He and his followers accepted that the state had its origin in a contract and that there were certain civil rights: they advocated religious toleration and humane justice. But they did not affirm the need for any constitutional safeguards. Security against arbitrary actions on the part of the ruler was to be assured by the rule of law. Wolff lived in a world apart from that of Locke or of Montesquieu. For him there could be no separation of powers. His sovereign, as delineated in *Rational Thoughts on the Social History of Mankind*, was legislature, executive, judicature all in one: he was also to be a positive force in the land, benevolent in every sphere touched by modern 'welfare' provision: as it were Luther's 'godly prince' in eighteenth-century dress, serving his people's needs, material and cultural as well as spiritual. Such a prince was the ideal of the cameralists, who treated government as a science. In the universities and the bureaucracies they served the principles of natural law, and cameralism gained widespread acceptance, in Catholic no less than in Protestant states.

The emperor Joseph II exemplified the cameralist ideal, absolute, responsible, and active in pursuit of reform. By his time, however, there was a vigorous reaction against the rationality and practicality of the natural law school, with its emphasis upon regimentation. The generation of Goethe, Schiller, Fichte valued above all feeling and spontaneity. The *Weltanschauung* of the literary revival appeared to be favourable to political liberalism. But unlike writers of 'romantic' persuasion elsewhere in Europe the Germans of the *Stürm und Drang* did not effect a significant change in the way in which their countrymen regarded political authority. The political regime tended to muffle dissent or divert it into harmless channels: few intellectuals were in any way independent. The scholarly Herder, whose ideal *Volk*-state would have had a republican form of constitution (indeed no rulers since 'their existence is regarded as a denial of the rule of law'), had little impact until later writers explored his dense, difficult works, then only to use the more conservative elements in them. It is not surprising that Herder eschewed controversy: he was *Generalsuperintendant* of the clergy of Weimar. Even Kant, who was opposed to cameralism and advocated the separation of powers, with the participation in politics of a large part of the population, the man who might seem most likely to have stirred up a radical political movement, would not allow the right of revolution. In his most influential work, *Was ist Aufklärung?*, Kant distinguishes between the public and private use of one's reason: future generations of German idealists, faced by a sharper challenge to their integrity than Kant, loyal subject of the king of Prussia, could have envisaged, were to find his distinction helpful. Kant advanced the significant paradox, with Frederick the Great in mind, that 'the ruler with a well disciplined and numerous army could provide more liberty than a republic'; moreover, in words which offer another text for modern German history, 'a high degree of civil freedom seems advantageous to a people's *intellectual* freedom, yet it also sets up insuperable barriers to it. Conversely, a lesser degree of civil freedom gives intellectual freedom enough room to expand to its fullest extent.'

That was Kant's experience, and with him we return to the essential feature of German political thought, perhaps too the most important point to grasp about German history. The peculiar structure and development of the Empire, in particular its territorial fragmentation, created a distinctive notion of *libertas*. Because the prince combined the role of executive within his own state with that of representative within the Reich, and because the theorists were involved so closely in government within the intimate, parochial establishment of their state, there was no stimulus to the development of ideas of constitutional liberty. The German associated political liberty with the authority of the state. He was loyal to his city, county or principality. Brunswick, Württemberg, Bamberg, each meant more to its inhabitant than Germany. His own state was 'fatherland', 'abroad' was another state. Between the Saxon and Bavarian lay differences at least as great as those which separated the Italians of Naples from those of Milan. For a lead in time of crisis, for support in dealings where right and law were involved, the princes had recourse to their Emperor who was still, in the vital feudal sense, the overlord of his vassals. He alone bestowed titles; it was by virtue of this charter that a free city maintained its independence; bishops owed homage to the Emperor for the lands that they ruled. All that did not mean that all the Emperor's subjects were necessarily amenable or that they could be relied upon to sacrifice their own interests even in a crisis: 'The *Reichsarmee*, never more than a fraction of its nominal strength, mobilised late and demobilised early' (Blanning). There was in general, however, an inclination to loyalty. One can see it in the agonized reluctance of the Lutheran Elector John George of Saxony to oppose Ferdinand II in the 1620s, until he was driven to it by the Emperor's unconstitutional acts. The level of co-operation was likely to be in inverse ratio to the political activity of the Emperor at the time. Quiescence was expected of him, except of course in times of danger, like a Turkish invasion: then he was expected to lead.

Where common policy or action was sought within a region the circle provided the forum for princes to associate, to arbitrate, to coerce the recalcitrant. At the imperial level there were too many territories for common interest to operate. That is why the *Reichstag*, permanently seated at Ratisbon after 1663, was normally occupied with minor disputes; also why the imperial authorities failed repeatedly to take effective action in the face of external threats, as over Louis XIV's annexation of Strasbourg in 1681, or the Russian invasion of Mecklenburg in 1716. The circle, however, comprising territories which were likely to be economically interdependent and to have similar laws and customs, provided a valuable intermediate level of federal government. It was specially important where, as in Westphalia, there was no state large enough to act effectively on its own. Co-operation within the circle, over such matters as coinage for example, but also over potentially disruptive quarrels over property and other rights, suggests that there was a wider recognition of common German interests. The experience of the Thirty Years War had taught princes the unwisdom of contending over religion and of allowing succession disputes to go unresolved. The

Catholic majority in the *Reichstag* was restrained in the use of its strength, however rigorous the policy of individual princes might be within a state. It was better to be reconciled to differences than to let in the Swede or the Frenchman, quick to exploit the grievances of a minority, like Charles XII those of the Silesian Lutherans, or Louis XIV those of the Catholics of Strasbourg. Arbitration was to be preferred to aggression in this world of delicately balanced interests: for that the *Reichskammergericht* still served. Its mechanism for arbitration, for instance, protected the counties of Isenburg and Solms from annexation by the ruler of Hesse-Darmstadt. Its authority restrained ambitious rulers, like the duke of Württemberg, from pursuing territorial claims. The record of peacekeeping between 1648 and the dissolution in 1806 contrasts favourably with that of the period before or after. Subsequent critics were to complain of cumbrous procedure and delays. In 1772, 61,000 cases awaited trial. Evidently there was also a continuing demand for the justice that the court alone could provide. It was more than a court of law. It functioned also as the chief federal executive, in matters of police, debts, bankruptcies and tax claims.

Even in the Empire's old age there was more life and utility in its institutions than was to be allowed by historians of the next century, their judgement affected by what had happened by the time they came to investigate its odd, by then archaic, forms. By then German political thought had travelled far along a nationalist path: of its time, but characteristically German. In place of the mathematical, rational principles on which classical political theory rested, idealists of the romantic counter-revolution offered the 'organic' ideal of a group-mind, or *Gemeingeist*; for the supposed ailment of political disunity, they proposed the remedy of a powerful state. The old loose federal system was discredited. Yet, in the century and a half after Westphalia, it had provided practical solutions to many of the problems of German society. There is material for satire: the princes who aped Versailles, one even going so far as to build a wing of his palace for his mistress – in title only, for he was a virtuous man; or the eighteenth-century Elector Palatine who had thirty regiments, a quarter of whose members were officers, and a grand admiral to command his several barges on the Rhine. Undoubtedly the political atomization, together with the stability of the state system, encouraged rulers to maintain an establishment beyond their means to support, unless by harsh taxes. In Leiningen, for 70,000 subjects there were 50 councillors and 72 other officials. But it can be argued that it was no bad thing that in these smaller political units there were a disproportionately high number who could experience some responsibility. It was a positive advantage that bourgeois officials were brought into daily contact with nobles: each class could learn from the other. Social tension was reduced by the sheer volume of patronage available to the prince so that German states did not suffer from the existence of a disaffected class of literate outsiders, unemployed lawyers, frustrated writers such as played an important part in fomenting agitation in contemporary France. That would have been thought good by Germans, children of the Thirty Years War, and their children, for whom the all important fact was the general peace. It rested on the authority of the princes but also on their ability to co-operate at both levels, the circles and the Reich. It did not necessarily mean a supine attitude towards authority. The Estates survived and proved effective in a number of states. In 1728 the Estates of Mecklenburg-Schwerin persuaded the Emperor to depose their unpopular duke. The long struggle of the Estates of Württemberg with their duke Karl-Eugen (1737–93) left them in a strong position. A ruler with despotic tendencies was liable to find himself relatively powerless because, without the co-operation of the Estates, he was unable to raise sufficient money. In states where an autocratic ruler had apparently little to fear from either constitutional bodies or the advance of liberal ideas, the impressive feature is commonly the sensitivity and benevolence of government. Mainz is only the best documented of states (tiny Lippe is another) where, so far from crumbling, the traditional establishment showed a mature ability to contain and to utilize the new potentially disruptive ideas. Arbitrary though some rulers undoubtedly were, the most prominent characteristic of the time is respect for the law.

It is clearly illustrated by the case of King Frederick William I of Prussia (1713–40) and the matter of the succession to the duchies of Berg and Jülich, long claimed by the Hohenzollerns and desirable as a means of rounding off their Rhineland territories; since 1614 they had possessed Cleves and Mark which had gone with the other duchies before the division enacted at the treaty of Xanten in that year. The king's dynastic claim was a strong one but it required ratification by the Emperor. In 1728 an agreement was reached with Charles VI by which the succession of Berg was guaranteed to Prussia while Jülich was to go to the river claimant of the Pfalz-Sulzbach family: in return Prussia guaranteed the Pragmatic Sanction and the rights of the Emperor's daughter. Such patience and respect for the legal process was, however, ill-rewarded by the Emperor who repudiated the claims when he made his treaty with France and the maritime powers in 1738. Frederick II's first action on coming to the throne was to renege on his father's treaty. The Habsburgs were made to pay dear for the way they had slighted the Hohenzollerns. After the invasion of Silesia the Empire was never the same again. Allegiance to the Emperor had to rest on a firmer basis than the merely juridical; nor was administrative convenience enough to hold back indefinitely the advance of individual states. The federal military system had helped to keep Louis XIV at bay and to defeat the Turks. When the Turkish threat receded it was necessary to find a new role and a policy as unifying as the external challenges had been. This the Empire did not find. So for all its usefulness in particular ways, its days were numbered.

1740 was the fateful year when the accession of Maria Theresa to the family lands and the provisions of the Salic law, which did not allow a woman to become Emperor, necessitated the choice of a non-Habsburg Emperor. It was also the year when Frederick II of Prussia, by his invasion of Silesia, precipitated the series of wars which lasted till 1763, leaving the central issue of supremacy between Austria and Prussia unresolved and the constitution fatally weakened. Even so it is more surprising to see Maria Theresa's son Joseph II spurn the Empire in his efforts to create a more coherent block of family lands, than it is to see his mother, more conservative and in tune with current German opinion, seek to restrain her son, so lacking in a sense of history. Joseph was a child of the *Aufklärung*, with its cardinal principle that reforms were best achieved through the agency of a single, absolute political authority. He was also heir to the Austrian cameral tradition of emphasis on self-sufficiency and planning from the centre. His view was not moderated by respect for old forms nor apparently by fear of what might replace them. The view from Vienna was no longer naturally an imperial view. After 1772 non-German-speakers were in the majority in the Habsburg lands. Not surprisingly it could seem to Austrian officials that the institutions of the Empire were moribund, the idea behind them obsolete, at best irrelevant. Joseph, partitioner of Poland, did more even than Frederick the Great to weaken the structure and morale of the Empire. When he tried to turn the Bavarian succession crisis to his advantage in 1784 he was checked by a league of German princes, led ironically by Frederick, who appears to have seen, in the Emperor's rejection of the federal Empire, a chance to increase his own influence within it by championing its integrity. But it was evident that it was the Prussian army, not the German constitution, which prevented Austria from becoming the super-power of southern Germany by the acquisition of the Bavarian lands.

When in 1806 Napoleon declared that he no longer recognized the German Empire and Francis II resigned the title, only the most conservative could have felt more than a sense of the inevitable. Successive emperors had sought to balance the interests of the house of Austria: Catholicism, the imperial authority, the *Hausmacht*. Only at certain favourable times did they plainly coincide, as in 1683. Not till the accession of Joseph II did the *Hausmacht* emerge in brutal clarity as the dominant motive. The contradictions may not have been so clear before. But they can be seen in earlier reigns, notably in that of Ferdinand II, the Emperor of the Thirty Years War, who acted as if he trusted that what was good for Austria was also good for Germany and Rome.

The Illustrious House

The Thirty Years War, which had begun in 1618, in Prague, with an act of defiance to Ferdinand II, had been prolonged by his insistence not only upon enforcing conformity to Rome in conquered Bohemia, but also upon extending the principle to those German ecclesiastical lands which had been secularized since 1555. In the process the war had spread, drawing in other countries and conflicts – in France and the Netherlands, north Italy, Scandinavia and Poland. It was never thereafter merely a German war; religious issues that affected every western country could not be so confined. Nor was it exclusively, some would say even primarily, a religious war. At the outset, however, Germany was at the storm's centre; within Germany, religious differences provided motives and pretexts for war. Ferdinand II, impatient and masterful, staked the future of the Empire upon his cherished design. To his conception of empire, authoritarian and Catholic, he subordinated the German liberties that meant more to princes like John George of Saxony than any difference of creed. Arbitrarily, he transferred the Palatine electorate to Catholic Bavaria and gave imperial titles to his general Wallenstein. True, he was confronted by the radical force of Calvinism. German interests, furthermore, had been interlocked with those of Spain, France, Denmark and the United Provinces long before the fateful edict of restitution in 1629. When the Elector Palatine accepted the crown of Bohemia he had activated long-prepared alliances. It is, however, not unfair to see Ferdinand II as the prime actor in the prolonged mêlée; nor would he have shrunk from the title. He was singleminded to the point of obsession.

A century and a half later (he became Emperor and co-regent in 1765, sole ruler in 1780) Joseph II governed no less ruthlessly but in the rational spirit of a new absolutism and a new morality. For Rome and Austria, Ferdinand overrode the German constitution; for 'reason' Joseph risked revolution within his family lands. Both men, in their different ways and circumstances, sought uniformity and conformity, Ferdinand through priests, Joseph through teachers of German. Both were arrogant, but sincere, exponents of the Habsburg interests. Whatever the rationale of government the interests of the family came before all. The rulers of the intervening period were less extreme, apparently less remarkable guardians of the tradition. The pressure of events counted for more than the logic of faith or reason, but they were not for all that, notably less successful. Ferdinand III (1637–57), Leopold I (1657–1705), Joseph I (1705–11), Charles VI (1711–40) and Maria Theresa (1740–80) all had in common the Habsburg instinct for clinging on to lands and rights, and sufficient sense and determination to preside over a century and a half of reappraisal and change without loss of dignity or control. There were crises, failures, defeats and retreats. But after 1648, 1683 and 1740, the Habsburgs demonstrated their capacity for recovery and for exploiting a situation which appeared to be unfavourable. Austria both survived and evolved. It was no mean achievement.

To Ferdinand III, who had been the co-victor, with his Spanish cousin, at the battle of Nördlingen (1634), the latter stages of the war brought bitter disappointment. The Habsburg armies were badly led; morale was low; Bohemia and Moravia were never free of enemy troops. God seemed to have deserted the house of Austria. Before the disastrous battle of Jankau (1645) the statue of St Wenceslas was found shattered in the local church. The peasantry inclined to sedition and heresy; crowds of them flocked to outdoor Lutheran services staged by the Swedes. The war ended where it had begun, in Prague, with Jesuits, students and burghers grimly defending their walls against the Swedish general Königsmarck. In the treaties, important territories were ceded to France. In return for recognition of his unlimited authority in the family lands Ferdinand had to concede measures of 'satisfaction' to the Protestant states of the north: Sweden, Brandenburg, Mecklenburg and Brunswick. That meant the immediate secularization of many church foundations and the lasting security of Protestantism in north Germany. After intense bargaining, the German states, with whom the Emperor now dealt as with fellow sovereigns, agreed upon a compromise between Catholic and Protestant which was essentially political. The year 1624 was chosen as the criterion for judging local disputes between churches over property and rights of worship: after the suppression of the Bohemian revolt, but before the greatest victories of the Catholic party. Rome was still to have individual successes, like the conversion of the elector Augustus of Saxony. But a convert ruler could no longer enforce his creed upon his subjects: Saxons stayed Lutheran. The new settlement did not end all frictions: Lutherans continued to harass Calvinists, Catholics exploited every missionary opportunity. But with rulers, for the most part, concerned more to attract new subjects than to drive out dissenters, rival confessions learned to coexist. To the Pope the peace was a disaster and he called down anathemas on those responsible. The Empire had failed to fulfil the hopes of Counter-Reformation Rome. Central Europe had represented Rome's last chance of exercising political influence. The Pope's hegemony was now reduced to the confines of Italy and his chagrin is understandable. The Germany of Leibnitz, protagonist of Christian reunion, was far removed in spirit from the ideal of a Catholic Germany; a disappointing outcome for those who had seen the edict of restitution as the beginning of the end for German Protestants. But all was not lost for the Church or for the Habsburgs. No longer defensive in the face of militant Catholicism, the princes of Germany were less suspicious about the implications of Habsburg patronage. Ferdinand II had to fight hard and negotiate skilfully for the election of his son Ferdinand III; the election of Leopold I was also to be an expensive and uncertain business; but there was to be no question about his successor.

More intelligent and flexible than his father, Ferdinand III was able to build on his father's achievement. As many individual conversions show, his necessarily cautious and undogmatic policy towards his fellow princes did not weaken the Catholic cause in Germany while in the family lands the church's grip was continually strengthened. It was in the reign of this still underestimated ruler that the pattern of confessional absolutism was established: church and autocracy, twin hierarchies, partners as it seemed in a system of mutually beneficial support. It was to be the basis of the victorious years of Leopold I; it was to sustain Maria Theresa. Protestantism was at first widespread through the family lands. But the spirit of the Counter-Reformation permeated the political and administrative structure; all posts in government went to Catholics; universities were solid for the faith; the religious orders, revived and ardent, sent missionary teams to combat heresy and ignorance in the remotest regions. As in the personalities of successive emperors, religious zeal and political authority worked together. Ferdinand III enjoyed untrammelled sovereignty over the family lands and Bohemia and used it to achieve the desired conformity. His unrelenting rigour might have been expected to repel rather than to attract the unaligned princes of Germany. But Ferdinand and his successors, relying on the co-operation of the favoured upper classes and the subjection of the towns, enjoyed further advantages. Imperial government represented the only possible embodiment of order in central Europe. In the face of external challenges, whether from Turks or from Frenchmen, the Habsburgs were the natural leaders of a German resistance.

In the course of his long reign, Leopold I (1657–1705) sustained this part in a way that belies his reputedly modest abilities and invites reappraisal. Ferdinand III's younger son, he had been intended for the Church and the plurality of bishoprics which enabled great princes to play their part in the family business without financial embarrassment. When his elder brother died in 1654 he was summoned from Spain and theology to undergo the laborious, costly business of election to the several crowns. He wore them with dignity and brought to court and government a strong sense of duty and a readiness to listen to older men, notably his civilized, perceptive uncle, Leopold William, who had learned political realism in the hard school as governor of the Netherlands for the Spanish. He was far from passive, but he trusted subordinates, perhaps to the point of being deliberately blind to their faults; he was therefore himself trusted, respected and loyally served. It is instructive to compare him with the cousin with whose destiny his was so closely bound. Two centuries of dynastic rivalry had conditioned Leopold and Louis XIV each to regard the other with a mistrust which their respective policies did nothing to allay. They were rivals for strategic advantage in the Rhineland and north Italy, for influence in Germany, and for the greatest prize, the Spanish succession. Leopold could never have played the Frenchman's part of assured principal in a brilliant court. The heavy ecclesiastical style of the Hofburg which, by contrast with Versailles, is an integral part of the city, better suited his sensitive, cautious, self-effacing character. The formalities of court, each in its way influenced by

Spanish notions of etiquette, that enabled Louis to dominate and glitter, protected and sustained the artistic, introverted emperor. Both men could be petty. Leopold's pride sometimes made him seem ungracious, as in his grudging response to John Sobieski after the relief of Vienna. Louis XIV was more susceptible to flattery; his self-esteem was potentially more dangerous since it inspired an aggressive foreign policy. Both men were strong, showing stoicism in the face of family bereavements: Leopold, between 1668 and 1673, lost two sons and his beloved first wife Margaretha, the Spanish princess whom he had first known as a child from Velázquez's wonderful painting; then, in 1676, his second wife Claudia, following the death of two infant daughters. He was faithful in marriage and rewarded by a contented third marriage, to the admirable Eleonora of Pfalz-Neuburg, mother of 10 children of whom 5 survived. He was religious in a way that showed his sense of the smallness of men, even of kings, before God; he was an artist, a lover of books and music, indeed a prolific and competent composer; in all there was a versatility and sensibility, with further points of contrast with Louis, not all to the latter's advantage.

With his long face and the jutting lower lip and jaw of the Habsburgs, habitually sombre expression on formal occasions, and pedantic manner, Leopold invited sneers. His ample private correspondence reveals, however, another, lighter side and a well-stocked, curious mind. Slowness was sometimes deliberate though he became increasingly irresolute with age. An exasperated French ambassador described him as 'a clock always waiting to be wound up'. A papal envoy wished that 'the emperor would trust less in God so that he might take a more practical view of his business'. The Emperor, it might be thought, allowed the Jesuits too much power. By 1700 there were 1300 of them, influential through their six universities and their schools, as well as through careful attention in the architecture of their churches and the sermons preached in them, to the emotional needs of their congregations. There were by then fifteen Jesuits at court but Leopold's two most intimate clerical advisers were Capucins, Sinelli and d'Avianto. They were licensed to criticize and to advise on political and military as well as spiritual matters. More generally it might be objected that Leopold's devotion to religious observances, with what seemed to the less ardent an unending succession of Masses and litanies, was beyond what was required of a secular ruler. But there was statecraft too. Regular pilgrimages to his favourite shrine of the Virgin at Mariazell, visits and regular gifts to the monasteries and for the relief of the poor of the capital were means through which he could play, and be seen to play, a role with which his subjects could identify. His manuscript book of private prayers and his close attention to confession and preacher speak of an unaffected piety. Like Louis XIV he insisted on conformity and did not shrink from using force. But while Louis can be censored for inconsistency and opportunism, as he was by Pope Innocent XI, Leopold's partner in the Holy League, there was a compelling logic in the Emperor's actions against heresy. It was that of a faith which supplied the unifying ideal to appeal to the aristocrats of Hungary and Bohemia, and to bind together, in the ordinary routines of government or the special demands of a crusade, people of divergent cultures and races. The religious principle gave to Leopold's rule the quality of Christian stewardship: the master who was also servant. It guided his descendants, not least Maria Theresa, and gave to the regime claims and rights more powerful than those of administrative convenience and family interest. Solid and caring, it represented a return to the sanity of the central tradition of the Counter-Reformation, back from the esoteric interests of Rudolph II, patron of alchemists, or the vaulting political ambitions of Ferdinand II.

It could also be said of Leopold, whose reign saw the conquest of Hungary and the defeat of France, that he was a lucky ruler, not least in his opponents' mistakes. The failures of French diplomacy over Poland, Louis's aggression in the Netherlands and the Rhineland, his obvious manoeuvres to win over the German Catholic princes, combined with his refusal to lend aid to the Emperor against the Turks, all helped to create the impression that Leopold was the more acceptable patron of German interests. The victories of Austrian arms, the successive 'miracles of the House of Austria' which Leopold received so calmly, were won by talented generalship, of Montecuccoli, Charles of Lorraine and Eugène of Savoy, certainly not by competent administration. There lay the central weakness, stemming directly from Leopold's irrational and fatalistic nature and only mitigated by the efforts of his soldiers and diplomats in ways that stored up trouble for his successors. Leopold regarded the poverty and mismanagement of the public purse less as a challenge than as a further argument for caution. While Louis XIV was supporting Colbert in drastic and unpopular reforms Leopold allowed Sinzendorf to remain in charge of the treasury from 1656 to 1680 initiating virtually nothing in the field of manufactures and directing most of his efforts to negotiating with financiers the farming of state revenues and to securing a share of the proceeds for himself. Leopold received ample, constructive memoranda from the cameralists, men like the tireless, talented friar Rojas y Spinola and his protégés Becher and Hörnigk, who urged the need for tighter central control and positive government, particularly in the economic sphere. But it was not in him to act with the ruthless singlemindedness of the Great Elector. Austria was no Brandenburg: Hungary was less malleable than Prussia; the problems were not dissimilar, notably the feudal spirit of the magnates, but the scale was far larger. Unique in the breadth of his responsibilities in many lands, Leopold undoubtedly failed at times where action was called for by a stubborn reluctance to act that bordered at times on the perverse. Yet it is arguable that this homely, decent sovereign served the interests of his subjects better by his realism and caution than did the grander, bolder Louis XIV those of France.

An Uncertain Rule

The Habsburg Empire has invited caricature throughout its history. That it survived and grew larger, against the odds, until the final collapse of 1918, suggests that there was more at work than the famous good fortune of the house. Habsburg strength had been created by an inspired sequence of dynastic marriages. It was maintained by expert diplomacy, usually directed in some way towards exploiting differences, not only those between foreign powers but among the diverse races of their own lands. Every force they encountered – Protestantism, Ottoman and French imperialism, and ultimately German nationalism – was blocked or exploited for Habsburg ends until, in the end, the dynasty succumbed to the combination of Slav nationalism and democracy. The peoples evolved; possessions were won and lost; the Habsburgs remained, the obstinate survivors, most august of dynasties. The diversity of the subject races enabled the rulers to play off one interest against another; a backward economy meant that towns and the urban middle class were relatively unimportant. The greatest interest was that of the landowners, who wanted above all to maintain the status quo.

Essentially a dynasty of landowners, the Habsburgs concentrated, after 1648, upon developing their family lands. That does not mean that they ceased to take seriously their role as Holy Roman Emperors. Within Germany the Habsburg ruler was still fortified by the respect accorded to the man who was duke in Austria, king in Bohemia and Hungary, but Emperor only by virtue of presiding over the Holy Roman Empire. In the long term it was an advantage that Vienna was no longer able to rely on Spanish support. The Habsburgs could enrol allies among the German states if they appeared, as now, one among the German princes, pursuing a common interest, respected, but no longer as suzerain to vassal. The defence of Vienna against the Turks cast the Emperor in the role of defender of Germany against barbarism. Louis tried, without success, to outbid Leopold for the allegiance of the Catholic states by revoking the edict of Nantes (1685). Although the federal institutions of the Empire continued to provide modestly effective means of government, large questions were decided for the most part by Saxony, Bavaria, Brandenburg or bodies, such as the elector of Mainz's League of the Rhine, in which small states gained weight through co-operation. In this situation no emperor could afford merely to think imperially. There were times of course when there was no clash between Habsburg and 'imperial' interests, as during the Turkish invasions. But after the recovery of Hungary, the acquisition of Belgium and north Italy, the family interests were so vast that practical questions of government became crucial. Germans were now in a minority in the Habsburg Empire. Milan came to Leopold's successor to seem more important than Strasbourg. It was still possible, however, to turn imperial authority to advantage. Duke Ernst of Hanover, who was being cultivated by French diplomacy, was quickly won back by the offer of an electorate (1692). The promotion of the elector of Brandenburg to status of king in Prussia (in 1700; Prussia was conveniently outside the Empire) brought an even more valuable ally to the imperial camp. The Habsburgs were slow to relinquish their traditional position in Germany. Even after the eventual dissolution of the Empire, Metternich was able to secure for Austria the presidency of the new Confederation of Princes (1814). But inevitably the centre of gravity was shifting from the *Reichsidee* to the *Staatsidee*, from the institutions which embodied the idea of empire to those that solely served the state. There was a long-standing struggle between the Austrian court chancery (*Hofkanzlei*) and the imperial chancery (*Reichskanzlei*), which also worked in Vienna but was still in letter and spirit an organ of the Holy Roman Empire. In the early 1700s Schönborn, who as imperial vice-chancellor and nominee of the elector-archbishop of Mainz, the chancellor of the Empire, was the guardian of the old tradition, was steadily edged out of the inner councils of state by the Austrian court chancellor, Sinzendorf, and his nominees.

In 1564, when the emperor Ferdinand I died, his provinces had been shared out among his three sons. The view of lands as private property was to persist into the eighteenth century; it was the master principle of the Habsburg dynasty. But the partition was even then looked upon as a trifle eccentric at a time when rulers, following English and Spanish examples, were trying to concentrate powers in a central authority. It was not until the middle of the seventeenth century that the Habsburgs set about constructing the semblance of a unified state, nor until a century later that significant progress was made, with reforms in the army and administration, towards raising revenues and maintaining troops on a scale commensurate with resources. Reforms were only achieved under the impact of external stimuli, such as the defeats in the Thirty Years War, the challenges of France and Turkey and, after 1744, the loss of Silesia and the rivalry of Prussia. Each of the three main components of the monarchy was itself a collection of smaller parts. The river Enns divided the Austrian lands into two: Upper Austria with its capital at Linz, Lower Austria with the capital Vienna. The main *Länder* of Inner Austria were again separate in character and had their own capitals: Styria, Carinthia and Carniola were most important, their capitals being respectively Graz, Klagenfurt and Laibach. The family also owned the Tyrol and lands in south-west Germany, such as Freiburg; these were controlled from Innsbrück. Not until 1665 were all these lands united under one ruler. The traditional separatism was reflected in his different titles. The Emperor was a duke in Austria, a count in the

Tyrol. It was the same in Bohemia, where geography and history divided the ancient kingdom into three – Bohemia, round Prague; Moravia, round Olmutz; and Silesia, round Breslau; here the Emperor was king of Bohemia but only margrave in Moravia.

With its well-defined historical frontiers, mainly rivers or mountains, but sharply differing patterns of settlement and forms of culture, Hungary presented the oddest anomalies. The lands to which the crown of St Stephen had once laid claim – Croatia, Slavonia and Dalmatia – were for most of Leopold's reign in Turkish hands. Transylvania had achieved the status of an independent principality – and was even represented at Westphalia. Barely a third of the kingdom, in the west and north, was controlled by the Habsburgs. Altogether there were six distinct races under Habsburg rule: Germans, Czechs, Slovaks, Magyars, Croats and Serbs, even before the peace of Rastadt added Italians and Belgians. While arguably this made it less difficult to identify with ruler and state than the theorists of nationalism in the nineteenth century were to claim, it meant as much of a problem of government as, for example, the difference between Castilian and Catalan, or Irish and Anglo-Saxon in the seventeenth century, involving, beside the diverse customs of close-knit societies, the practical problem of language.

The years after the end of the Thirty Years War were a time of economic recession throughout the continent. Least severe in the north and west of Europe, the recession was especially severe in lands remote from the sea – central France, central and southern Germany. In the Habsburg lands, opportunities for economic growth were specially limited. The dominance of nobility and clergy, the development of large, self-sufficient estates (especially in Bohemia after 1621) and the decline of towns were related aspects of a landlocked society. The population of Bohemia had declined during the war by nearly 50 per cent; Upper and Lower Austria suffered little less. There had been as many as 100,000 emigrants from Austria after the repression of the risings of 1627–8. In some south German villages as many as half of those baptized were of Austrian origin. More than 40,000 Protestants were expelled from Upper Austria alone. One significant career further afield suggests the cost to the state of enforced religious conformity: Georg von Derfflinger, who emigrated from the village of Linz, became a field marshal in Brandenburg and carried out the reorganization of the Great Elector's army. Everywhere, shortage of labour made landowners restrict the movement of their serfs and demand more labour services from them. It was a rigidly immobile society.

With its long, open, eastern frontier, Hungary suffered chronically from the plague, while Turkish exploitation of the Magyars and periodic wars against the Austrians did not encourage settled cultivation of the fertile plains. The Habsburgs were feeble in dealing with external pressures and vested interests at home because they were chronically poor. There was iron in Austria, salt in the Tyrol, mercury in Istria, and a little gold and silver in Slovakia. But mining enterprises were feeble by comparison with those of Sweden or England. Everywhere, oppressive taxation helped to depress demand. The wealthy tended, as in Poland, to buy their wares from Italy or France. Merchants were defensive-minded, dominated by restrictive guilds who were more concerned with preserving their share than with creating more wealth. Communications were everywhere poor and customs barriers between provinces made them worse. The Church was resolute in defence of its privileged status and landed wealth. Land was bequeathed inalienably by pious laymen; the 'dowries' of wealthy novices swelled monastic revenues. The ambitious reconstruction of abbeys has left superb memorials of the high baroque, as at Benedictine Melk, cathedral and palace in one grand building. Church wealth was lightly taxed, land and capital were immobilized; the Church's influence over education and the broader issues of state policy was sustained by a material wealth out of proportion to its needs.

Since the fifteenth century, the majority of Czechs had been heretics or schismatics of one sort or another. In two decades after the battle of the White Mountain the Roman faith was everywhere restored in Bohemia and Moravia; only in a few mining communities and near the Saxon and Silesian borders did some underground Protestantism survive. In Silesia, freedom of worship was allowed since the elector of Saxony had secured that concession for its inhabitants in 1648. The breaking of Protestant resistance elsewhere, the development of a new agrarian economy, and the suppression of liberties in town councils and universities, were related to the extension of royal power. The nobles, secure in their economic and social position, were prepared to tolerate the presence of royal officials. Some of the greatest were of foreign origin, descendants of the *soldatesca* of the Thirty Years War who had moved in at the time of the massive transference of land, around 50 per cent of the total, which followed suppression of the revolt. They were unlikely to make common cause with the mass of the people. The nobility, old and new, predominant in the diet, as elsewhere in the Empire, controlled the purse strings and, even where they were supervised by royal officials, continued to run the administration, law courts and police. The *Landesoffizier* in Bohemia, like his counterparts in Austria and Hungary, was still a local magnate; among other duties he presided over the diet. The aristocracy nodded towards Vienna but continued to put its interests before those of the state.

In Vienna the Emperor dealt with affairs sometimes through royal officials, more often in conjunction with magnates or bishops, their agents and lawyers who provided local justice and government. At the centre he had ministers, specialists and councils. In form and spirit government was an extension of the royal household. Policy was nominally made in consultation with the privy council (*Geheimer Rat*), a small group of court officials and councillors under the major-domo (*Obersthofmeister*), the best-paid if not most important of officials under Leopold. The administrative body was the court chancery, which dealt with the foreign policy of the monarchy as a whole, and domestic matters in the Austrian lands. There was a separate chancery for Bohemia. The *Hofkriegsrat* conducted military affairs and dispensed most of the money that the *Hofkammer* could raise. It was responsible for the standing army, some sixty regiments by 1690, in positions from the Rhine to the Save, and for the garrison of the long frontier zone, where even the villagers lived under martial law. The *Hofkammer* or court chamber was the central treasury; it decided the budget and had general oversight of commerce, manufacture and mines. Here there might have been scope for growth since there were always some commoners among its members, aware of contemporary trends concerned to extend the powers of the state and to develop the crown's neglected industrial resources. From 1656 to 1680 the treasurer was Sinzendorf. He was Colbert's contemporary but he saw his work very differently; he initiated virtually nothing in the field of manufactures and trade. Most of his efforts were directed towards negotiating with financiers the farming of state revenues and to securing a share of the proceeds for himself. No support was given to promising enterprises like de Luca's Eastern Company (1665), which sought to develop Balkan trade with Turkey, bypassing the Venetians. In this single contrast can be seen much of the difference in economy and government between Bourbon and Habsburg monarchies.

Since each province was a *Ständestaat*, or state in which the ruler had to share power with the Estates, it follows that there was no unified political machinery. The monarchy transacted its business with the separate Estates through four chancelleries: Austrian, Bohemian, Hungarian and Transylvanian. (The Netherlands and Lombardy were attached after 1714 to the Austrian.) The Estates provided a *contributio* or war tax, levied mainly on the peasants. Pressure could be exercised – particularly in Bohemia – but Estates took a provincial view and paid reluctantly. There were able men to serve the dynasty, but they were not usually Austrians. The chancellor from 1667 to 1683, Johann Hocher, was the son of a professor from Freiburg. His successor, Theodor Strattmann, was a Rhinelander. Bartenstein, Charles VI's chief adviser, came from Strasbourg. Successive presidents of the *Hofkriegsrat* were soldiers or organizers of note: Lobkowitz, Annibale Gonzaga, Montecuccoli, the margrave of Baden – none was either Austrian or German.

The Hungarian Problem

It is impossible to isolate a single main reason why the Habsburg rulers could only proceed tentatively towards reducing their lands to obedience when other monarchies were taking large and decisive steps. The separatism of provinces, the supremacy of great landowners, the dominance of a church that fully accorded with the pious ideology of the rulers, and the lack of resources in a backward economy, comprise interrelated parts of the total problem. The same interaction of cause and effect can be seen in the story of the Empire's wars and diplomacy. The relative weakness of the army forced the government to make concessions; these in turn prevented the reforms which would have enabled it to make more of its resources. One legacy of the Thirty Years War was a standing army; but the government was chronically insolvent. Leopold's election as Emperor in 1658 was financed with Spanish money. In 1704 the duke of Marlborough had to offer his own fortune as security before the Viennese bankers would advance money to pay the wages of Prince Eugène's troops. Charles VI could muster at most 100,000 troops from his 25 million subjects, though he could draw on some of the best fighting races in Europe, whereas Frederick William I of Prussia could raise 80,000 out of 2.5 million. The foreign policy of the state was not, however, tailored to match its meagre resources. Resistance to France, pursuit of the Spanish succession and the reconquest of Hungary from the Turks were concurrent concerns. The winning back of Turkish Hungary was part and parcel of the assertion of Habsburg authority and ideals over the part of Hungary that had remained unconquered but had also preserved an unruly independence.

The reconquest of Hungary was to provide the monarchy with the chance of bringing a people whom suffering and occupation had done little to prepare for submission under direct German-style government. The process was to be neither continuous nor straightforward. In this chequered, restless, suffering land, where self-help was the necessary rule, the Habsburgs were used to compromise: they granted and withdrew their concessions according to the needs of the time. The extensive plains were potentially rich cattle and corn country, but banditry was endemic and the Hungarians of the frontier lands between Turkish and imperial zones suffered almost as badly from raids and looting as those who lived in the much larger 'occupied' lands. Their leaders did not scruple to take advantage, however, of the respective needs of Turks and Austrians. They in turn were divided: mainly between those who looked to Vienna for salvation and those who preferred their quasi-independent status to that of a province of the Empire. As elsewhere in eastern Europe, the nobility enjoyed privileges which set them apart from the mass of the people. In Hungary, moreover, they had a caste sense and a political tradition which made them peculiarly hard to deal with. The closest analogy is to be found in the attitudes of the Polish magnates and gentry during this period. The 30,000 noble families were the Hungarian 'nation'; they alone had the political rights which had been enjoyed by the free and equal community of mounted warriors who had first settled around the middle Danube in the tenth century. Serfs, the 'sandalled' poor nobles and the inhabitants of the royal free boroughs, mostly German colonists, were excluded from these rights. The small class of magnates (about 200 of the leading nobles) sat in the Upper House of the bicameral diet, along with state officers and bishops. In the Lower House sat the representatives of the nobles with a handful of town deputies. To secure a modest degree of co-operation the Habsburgs negotiated with the magnates, on whom they relied to organize the defence of the ever shifting frontier. Some of them were remarkably rich. According to a recent calculation 37 per cent of Hungarian villages were in the hands of 13 families. They could afford to be independent, but no one of them could rise above his fellows without either accepting the patronage at the disposal of the Habsburg ruler or – the desperate but not unattractive alternative – taking the path of rebellion. A number of great Hungarians built palaces in Vienna and adopted an Austrian outlook, but they remained outside the Austrian establishment, speaking Magyar and set apart by their strange dress and manners. At times of crisis such men would be likely to rally to the crown. In 1683, for example, Archbishop Szelepcsény found money and valuables worth nearly half a million florins to pay the troops. As in Bohemia the Jesuits played their part, bringing a number of leading nobles back to Rome. The crucial factor throughout was religion. In the cult of Mary, in the heroic style of the fashionable baroque, in the lives of ascetic friars and hermits, and in the lavish material resources of the Church, freely given to the leading families who subscribed to the militant faith of Counter-Reformation Catholicism, there was the appeal of a common ideology strong enough to overcome prejudice against German language and officialdom. The pattern of mutual support can be studied in the career of Pál Esterházy, an astute politician, loyal to Leopold but on his own terms, builder among other palaces of Eisenstadt where, a century later, Joseph Haydn would live and compose under the wing of the Esterházy of his day. Pál was elected Palatine at the turbulent diet of 1681, and he held the post till his death in 1713. He built churches, led his tenants on pilgrimage and saw no less than six of his sons enter the Church.

Alliance on such terms as bound the Esterházys to the Habsburgs was only of limited value to the regime because of a system of local autonomy, unique to Hungary, and the unruly haven of neighbouring Transylvania, which would have created problems even without the special conditions of the frontier, marauding Turks and local banditry. The nobles elected deputies to their county diet, which passed local laws and elected officers. Magyar in blood, language, clothes and customs, it was they who ran the counties, often clung to their Calvinism or Lutheranism, defended their liberties and maintained the Magyar ideal, a powerful fusion of history and legend, faith and magic. Neither terror nor missionary enterprise availed: they were too tough and entrenched in their ways to be suppressed. Hungary could be described as a colony; it was never a province. Even after the treaty of Szatmár, following the suppression of the second great Hungarian revolt (1711), the native constitution survived. The crown

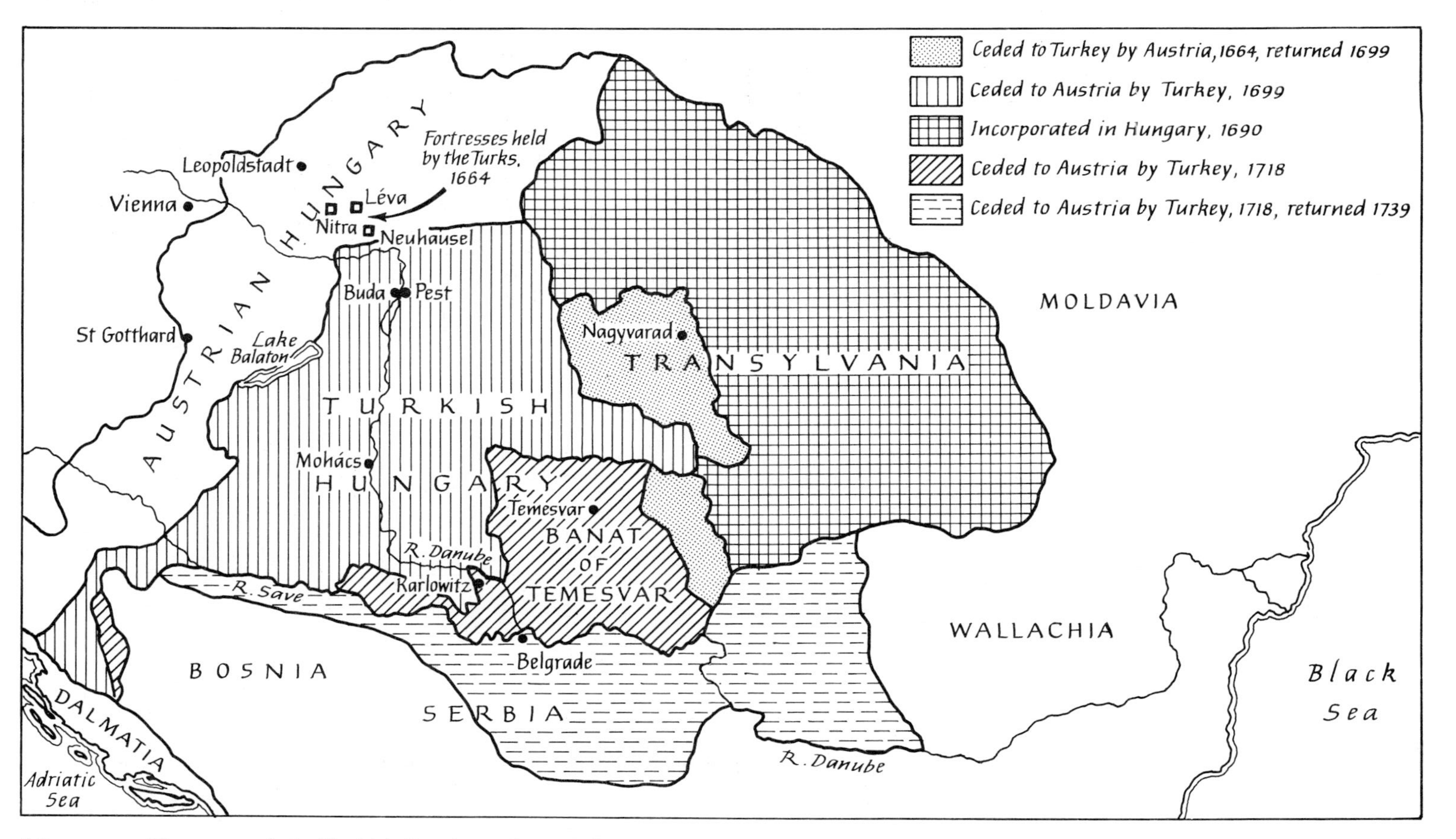

Map 10.2 *Hungary and the Turkish frontiers, 1600–1718*

became hereditary but the diet, usually well attended, could still dispute the royal will and present its own grievances. The Palatine, chosen by the diet from four royal nominees, executed such policy as could be agreed upon between sovereign and estates. His deputy presided over the king's court of appeal. The Habsburgs had to work through the institutions of Hungary and, as Joseph II was to find to his cost, they would not be incorporated in the detested German system without a fight.

Turkish Challenges, Austrian Triumphs

Leopold succeeded, at 16, to a crisis which reminded men of the opening of the Thirty Years War. Charles X of Sweden had attacked Poland and captured Warsaw, and George Rakoczy II of Transylvania, who also had an eye on the Polish crown, joined forces with him (April 1657). Fortunately for the Habsburgs, Charles had to return to defend his country against the Danes. The Turks also objected to the actions of Rakoczy. The new Grand Vizier, Mehmed Köprülü, determined to crush the Transylvanians. For four years that fierce people, inspired by radical Calvinist ministers, spiritual brothers of the sectaries and visionaries of Cromwellian England, fought against the successive onslaughts of a Turkish army, reformed and inspired by the ambitious Mehmed Köprülü. Rakoczy defeated one invasion at Lippa (May 1658). But the Austrians were slow to help. The Turks ranged freely, seizing vital fortresses and ravaging the countryside. In May 1660 Rakoczy died of wounds. His successor, Janos Kemény, was defeated and killed at Segesvár in January 1662.

The fall of Transylvania removed the Carpathian buffer between the royal part of Hungary and the Turks, now elated and hungry for conquests. The Austrian effort had been reduced by their operations against Denmark and acute shortage of money. It had been particularly expensive to secure the Emperor's election in August 1658 against the influence of Mazarin, though the German electors, suitably rewarded, had finally shown their traditional preference for the Habsburgs. Now Leopold had reason to appeal for something more tangible than moral support. In April 1663 the Turks began their drive up the Danube. The heroic defence of the fortress of Neuhausel saved Vienna for the year. Meanwhile Spain, the Pope and several German states sent men and money; Louis XIV allowed 6000 'volunteers' to join the imperial army. Bohemia raised the exceptional sum of 2 million *guilders*. In August 1664 Montecuccoli, with his army of the nations, stood on the river Raab, defending the capital 50 miles away. There, near the monastery of St Gotthard, he defeated the Turks as they tried to force a crossing. The Austrians promptly made a peace at Vasvar which seemed to the resentful Magyars a weak postscript to a great victory. The Turks were to evacuate Transylvania but the country was to remain under the Sultan's suzerainty. Leopold gave some monetary compensation to the Turks and, unaccountably, the Turks were allowed to keep three key fortresses in Slovakia. The Hungarians felt more exposed than ever to the Turkish menace.

Why had the Emperor not followed up his victory? His forces were still meagre and perhaps insufficient for a campaign to expel the Turks from Hungary. He was beginning to think of the Spanish succession. In 1665 Philip IV of Spain died; in May 1667 Louis XIV went to war to secure part of Spanish Flanders. Leopold did not, however, join the Triple Alliance powers opposed to Louis. At this stage it was his policy, encouraged by Lobkowitz, to work with Louis rather than against him. In January 1668 he made the secret partition treaty which would have united Austria with Spain and Milan (though not the Netherlands, Franche-Comté or Naples). His concern with such prizes might have caused him to lose Hungary.

Stung by Leopold's apparently callous rejection of their cause, Hungarian conspirators turned to the Turks. The conspirators, led by Ferenc Wesselényi, Ferenc Nádasdy, chief justice of Hungary, and Peter Zrinyi, had little reason, beyond their oaths of allegiance, to be loyal to the Austrians. They seem to have wanted an independent Hungary, free to elect its own king in return for tribute to the sultan. They were unofficially encouraged by Louis XIV's ambassador, Gremonville, since it suited Louis that the Austrians should be distracted from western affairs while the French completed their plans for the invasion of Holland. The death of Wesselényi in April 1667 removed the only leader who was capable of giving unity and purpose to the disaffected magnates. Louis would not commit himself and the Turks were preoccupied with the siege of Candia. Zrinyi betrayed the plot to Vienna, confessed his own part and then resumed his intrigues. Ferenc Frangepan led a force against Zagreb and was easily repelled. There was no further military action and the movement collapsed. Patriotic motives were lost in the medley of personal designs. The Hungarians let themselves be seen as faithless, incompetent bunglers. Nothing in the history of their ruptured country had given them the political experience to enable them to work together in a common cause. They therefore exhibited the worst features of a feudal aristocracy. Zrinyi, Nádasdy and Frangepan were tried by an Austrian court and beheaded. It may be noted that the Hungarian leaders were all Catholic; but in the reprisals that followed it was the Protestant communities that suffered worst. The country was occupied by Austrian troops. In the words of the imperial vice-chancellor: 'The Magyars have rebelled and thereby have lost all their privileges.' Hungary was now to be placed, like Bohemia before it, under the direct rule of Austria, represented by the new archbishop of Esztergom, Gyrgy Szelepcsényi, the king's lieutenant, and Leopold Kollonich, another bishop, president of the Hungarian Chamber. In 1673 a *Gubernium* was set up, under Johann Ampringen, titular Grand Master of the Teutonic Knights. Conditions favoured the autocratic solution.

Germans despised Magyars, Catholics appreciated the chance of suppressing the Protestant communities which had managed thus far to preserve their rights, and the soldiers had a free hand to establish reliable bases in what was effectively occupied country. Superficially, Hungary lay prostrate; and for ten years, with Turkey battling against Poland and Russia in the Ukraine, Leopold was unusually free to attend to the problems of the Netherlands and Germany. One result of Louis XIV's attack on Holland was that it wrecked the understanding fostered by the Francophil Lobkowitz between the Emperor and Louis and made Leopold adopt the now feasible alternative role of leader of the German states. Militarily, at first, despite the stubborn Dutch resistance and a skilful performance by Montecuccoli on the Upper Rhine, the French still held the upper hand, but a new balance was evolving.

Leopold's lands paid highly for his new militancy. Bohemia was the worst affected. These were the years of darkness, *temno* as the Czechs called it. Crushed between the demands of landowners for ever greater services and the exactions of the royal tax collectors, distressed further by the famine of 1679 and the plague which reached Hungary from the Balkans in 1678, and Bohemia two years later, the peasants voiced their grievances to the Emperor. He was almost as powerless within the stresses of his system of government as the peasants themselves. When he forbade appeals to the king and revoked the serfs' remaining privileges he was merely following the line of the landowners who were the real rulers of the country. The bitter, futile peasant revolt of 1680 was easily suppressed as the peasants were armed mainly with scythes and clubs. The *Robotni patent*, issued by the crown to define the extent of labour services, fixed the normal maximum at three days a week and contained a plea for humane treatment, but it was soon widely ignored. The dominant families of Bohemia, like the Liechtensteins, with sway over 19,000 peasant families in 1690, had every reason to be loyal to the Habsburgs. Not for them the financial embarrassments of the ruling house, on whose behalf they exercised government, to whom they might lend money on their own terms. Work on royal buildings was to be suspended during the war of 1701–14, but their palaces rose, in their splendour and profusion witnessing to the realities of power.

The Bohemians had been suppressed after 1620 because there was no political support of any importance and no hostile power on the border. The Hungarians posed tougher problems which, as the second crisis of Leopold's reign showed, had not been solved. Exiled lords of the 'patriot' party made common cause with the Transylvanians who formed robber bands in north-west Hungary. Since Leopold had supported Calvinist Holland against him, Louis XIV felt justified in supporting the Emperor's rivals. The main project of his anti-Habsburg diplomacy was an alliance between John Sobieski of Poland and Prince Apafi of Transylvania. In Imre Thököly, the rebel cause found a leader of talent; he was a young man, ambitious, wealthy, well-educated. In 1678, with some Polish troops and French officers to lead and advise, Thököly made war on the Austrians in northern Hungary. Ranging west as far as the borders of Silesia and Moravia, he had overrun most of northern and western Hungary by 1680. The Turks, thwarted in the Ukraine, saw a promising new opening. The new Pope, Innocent XI, clear-sighted enough to see the wider significance of the Habsburgs' frontier problem, persuaded Leopold that he must negotiate with the Hungarians to save Europe from the Turks. At a meeting of the Hungarian Estates in May 1681, he restored their traditional liberties: regular meetings of the Estates, the right to elect a Palatine, the independence of the Chamber, the right of Hungarians to fill high offices; even the restoration to Protestants of the liberties of 1608. The extent of the concessions, reversing as they did the trend of Habsburg policy for sixty years, shows how seriously the Emperor took the threat of Turkey. Events swiftly showed that he was right.

Thököly went to the new Grand Vizier, Kara Mustapha, and offered him allegiance and soldiers. The sultan declared him king of the whole of Hungary and Croatia, as vassal of the sultan. In the summer of 1682 an immense Turkish army moved across the plain into upper Hungary. Fortresses fell, and Leopold tried to buy time with a truce: he ceded to Thököly all Hungary east of the Hron. While Louis XIV's lawyers asserted his right to 'dependencies' of recently acquired lands on his eastern frontier and his troops moved in to effect the *réunions*, the Pope's nuncios were busy constructing an alliance to defend Christendom. On the same March day in 1683 that John Sobieski pledged his support, the Turks began their historic march from Adrianople. Apafi joined the host in Hungary; Thököly provided a diversion in Slovakia, but was halted at Pressburg. The imperialists fell back to the west, leaving Hungary to the invaders. From July, the Austrian capital was ringed by the Turkish army, Leopold had prudently retired up the Danube, maintaining the government at Passau while the brave and skilful Starhemberg directed the defence of the city. His first action was to order the suburbs to be burnt down so as to deprive the Turks of their cover. The siege was a savage affair; Christian captives were massacred outside the walls, Turks decapitated or flayed alive by the imperialists. Dysentery was as great a threat to defenders and attackers in the August heat as the mines and bombards of the Turks and the fierce forays launched by Starhemberg to delay the progress of the siege. Each day of early September, with desperate fighting around the outer walls beyond the Hofburg, brought nearer the final assault and collapse of the garrison. Had the Turks possessed sufficient heavy guns, had Kara Mustapha been prepared to accept the loss of life and destruction that an assault would have entailed and had he even taken proper precautions against a relieving force, Vienna must have fallen. The imperial army, with Poles, Saxons and Bavarians, 70,000 in all, commanded by Sobieski and guided by Duke

Charles of Lorraine, relieved Count Starhemberg and his garrison in the nick of time. The Turks had already breached the walls and mined some bastions. On 12 September the imperial and Polish army completed their march through the Vienna woods, descended 'like a stream of black pitch' from the heights of Kahlenberg and swept the Turks before them.

It was the second great deliverance of the reign. This time, unlike the sequel to St Gotthard in 1664, the victory was to be followed up. The allied strength was greater than in 1665, the leadership more resolute. The Turks were in disorder and looked for scapegoats; the Grand Vizier was strangled in Belgrade in December 1683; the sultan Mehmed IV was deposed by mutinous troops and imprisoned in November 1687. The Ottoman troops had been needlessly exposed to a defeat which altered the balance of power in the east; and, as Louis would soon understand, not only in the east. The battles of Flanders were later to be won on the fields of Hungary. The revival of Austrian military power, the patronage of the Pope and the attraction of the imperial alliance for Germans, Dutch and English, together created an entirely new situation. The initiative had passed to the enemies of Louis XIV. From Versailles it looked as if Leopold and his successor Joseph I were engaged in a gigantic bid for power: the old fear of encirclement was revived.

For the Empire the truce of Ratisbon (1684) secured the necessary peace in the west. The formation of the Pope's Holy League brought concerted pressure to bear upon the demoralized Turks. While the Venetians laboured to revive their former greatness in the Aegean, and the Poles campaigned in Moldavia, the imperial troops recovered Turkish Hungary. Neither Venice nor Poland had the strength to benefit as their rulers hoped from the Turkish retreat. The Habsburgs benefited vastly. In 1687 Archduke Joseph was crowned king in Hungary. The crown was declared hereditary in the male line with a formula which reserved, though vaguely, powers to disregard constitutional rights. In those heady days, before war aims were complicated by the clash of French and Austrian interests in the Rhineland and Spain, Habsburg ambitions swelled with every victory. Thököly was driven out of Slovakia; Apafi was made to accept Habsburg troops; Budapest fell in September 1686 and the Turks were defeated again at Nagyharsany. Imperial troops pushed on into Bosnia. In September 1688 they captured Belgrade. Bulgarian Catholics raised their heads. George Brancovitch, Serbian patriot and writer, and his brother, an Orthodox bishop in Transylvania, were stirring up the Serbs. Cantacuzene, prince of Wallachia, recognized Leopold's suzerainty. The lands beyond the Carpathians, around the Danube as it turned east below Belgrade, and around the Save and Una rivers, beckoned to the eager generals. They won glorious victories against the faltering Turks, at Zalankhamen in August 1691 and, after years of stalemate as the armies manoeuvred among the tributary rivers of the Danube and their surrounding marshlands, at Zenta on the river

Tisza (September 1697); there Eugène's victory prepared the way for the Karlowitz peace (1699). After the resumption of war in 1716, further victories at Peterwardein and Belgrade preceded the treaty of Passarowitz, in July 1718, which took Habsburg rule even further than had Carlowitz. To Hungary was added the Banat, Little Wallachia and the most fertile part of Serbia, with Belgrade.

Though it would be wrong to talk of anticlimax, the prospects of 1688 were never fully realized. From that date the Habsburgs devoted an increasingly large part of their strength to the western fronts. With so much at stake in the Rhineland, Spain and Italy, the Emperor committed his forces to a widening theatre of war. Louis had tried to settle his Rhineland frontiers while Leopold had been carving at the Turkish dominions. The ruler of Lorraine, Duke Charles V, was Leopold's brother-in-law and general of his army in Hungary. Elector William of the threatened Palatine was Leopold's father-in-law. Cologne, where Louis wanted to impose a client of his own, was a Wittelsbach interest; Leopold was intent on binding the Bavarian Wittelsbachs to his cause. Victor Amadeus of Savoy represented a crucial alliance in any struggle for power in northern Italy. So family ties and strategic interests compelled the Emperor to look away from Danube and Drava to Rhine and Po. He was well served by his allies: William's dedicated struggle in the face of disappointments, Marlborough's cool mastery and his fruitful partnership with Eugène helped to overcome the difficulties inherent in an alliance of divergent interests and aims, with several fronts to maintain. Before Leopold died, his troops under Eugène had taken part in the battle of Blenheim (1704), a resounding prelude to years of victory in the west, as significant for the Habsburgs as those of the eastern marches.

Blenheim altered in one day the military and political balance of Europe. Leopold's son Joseph (1705–11) inherited victory and experienced little else. He died suddenly of smallpox, leaving questions about what he could have achieved which historians might have pursued with more interest if he had been a more interesting man. As it is there appears to be little in his character or contribution to suggest that he would have ruled more flexibly than his brother or taken advantage of peace to promote radical reforms in government. That is not to say that there were no solid achievements. Administrative disorder continued to exasperate the generals but there was one useful innovation, that of the *Konferenz*, a small standing cabinet to act as the supreme advisory body. Dependence on individual financiers, like 'the court Jew' Samuel Oppenheimer, whose death in 1703 was followed by the collapse of the whole structure of credit which he had sustained, left the regime embarrassingly short of ready money: the foundation of the Vienna city bank on the model of the bank of Amsterdam, made possible wider investment and went some way towards solving the problem of raising credit. A conventional man, more worldly than his father or brother but devoted to hunting with a fervour remarkable even by

Habsburg standards, Joseph made predictable decisions in matters of foreign policy where decisions could not fail to be significant: chief among them was to take advantage of Eugène's victory at Turin in 1706 to press for more lands in Italy: in the short term this strained the alliance though the British and Dutch were prepared to pay the price, Milan, for Austrian co-operation. It also antagonized the Pope, who was already reluctant to recognize Charles as king of Spain. In the long run such opportunism was to have its legacy in Spanish moves after the war to recover ground in Italy, the cause of further wars. The second revolt of the Hungarians, under Rakoczy, which diverted Austrian forces for eight years, was eventually repressed in 1711, the peace of Szatmár). Only in Spain was there failure, and there Charles's claim to be king became less important when he became Emperor. In sum these were triumphant years. Three years after Joseph's death the peace of Rastadt (1714) brought all that he could have desired: Flanders became Austrian, so did Milan. But because there was no gain in efficient authority, acquisitions only exposed the essential deficiencies of the state.

Charles VI and the *Hochbaroch*

A ten-year reign in Spain was the worst possible training for the Emperor Charles VI. With Spanish advisers and Spanish manners he brought back in 1711 a lasting resentment at having lost the crown he assumed to be his by right. His manner was cold and haughty but he was neither idle nor insensitive: he hunted strenuously throughout the year and rode in the elegant school which he founded in Vienna for the practice of the formal Spanish style of horsemanship and which can still be seen there; he led the court orchestra and composed an opera. Above all he kept the religious festivals with a regularity and fervour which discomfited courtiers and Catholic ambassadors. Like his father he venerated the cult of Mary. Outward forms meant much and he insisted upon the 'Spanish reverence', the deep genuflection that any man must make before speaking to him. Austrian court ceremony was becoming more elaborate just at the time when it was being relaxed elsewhere; the contrast with the economical, workaday household of Frederick William I of Prussia is specially significant. The Emperor was enveloped in solemn rituals which made it more difficult to think or to act as objectively as the problems of his Empire required. At the end of the reign defeats at the hands of the Turks were followed by the treaty of Belgrade (1739) in which the Austrians gave up many of their conquests, including Belgrade itself. They were paying the price of failures, in domestic policy, to reduce privilege, to economize (notably at court, where there were over 2000 paid officials and some 30,000 hangers-on, with or without titular posts), to reform the army, to integrate the provinces and, not least, to stimulate learning, science, and the free intellectual climate in which ideas about reform could flourish. Charles lived on the capital and credit of the years of military success against Louis XIV and the Turks, and he added little. Politically the high point of his reign was the imperial diet's acceptance of the Pragmatic Sanction. As became immediately apparent in 1740, such diplomatic exercises were worth little against the material weakness of the regime. The great powers measured Austria's strength by her record in war and internal government – and acted accordingly.

Charles VI shared some crucial Austrian views, anti-Semitism among them. He fostered the values of the *Hochbaroch*, the union of spirit between an aristocratic society and a privileged church that is to be seen embodied in resplendent baroque interiors where craftsmen collaborated in paint and stucco to impart a fulsome vision of the divine order. The style is theatrical and exuberant, with daring innovations of line in place of the sober conservatism of Italian baroque. The eye is led past the attendant court of angels and apostles to the crowning glory of the heavens and a sublime, mysterious God. From the worshipper awe, veneration and absolute submission are required. In church and in school the Church taught acceptance: of doctrine and tradition, of the degrees of society, of wealth and of poverty. Abraham à Sancta Clara, a Viennese monk from the Barefoot Friars of St Augustine and Leopold's court preacher, used to dwell on the blessings of that poverty which gave the poor man the opportunity to reach heaven through suffering, the rich man through his giving. The rebuilding of monasteries such as Melk, dramatic on its steep cliff above the Danube, with their lavish apartments, library, theatre, museum and princely lodgings for the abbot (even, as at St Florian, imperial apartments), indicates that some abbots took a more worldly view of their responsibilities.

Inevitably some critics have stressed the obscurantism and the lack of that concern for the material interests of the people that they would expect from a high clerical culture. Others have seen the new Vienna of architects like Fischer von Erlach and Lucas von Hildebrandt, the palaces and churches springing up from the debris of 1683 around the enlarged and modernized Hofburg, as the apotheosis of the Austrian spirit, at its most forceful and joyous. As elsewhere in Germany, artistic achievement and political sterility are different aspects of one culture: to admire the one it is not necessary to ignore the other. In the Hofbibliothek in Vienna Fischer von Erlach's design lays out precisely for scholar and sightseer the pretensions of his patron. The library celebrates the pre-eminence of Charles VI as conqueror and patron of the arts. The twin pillars of the central hall, like those of the Karlskirche, represent the pillars of Hercules and thus the claim to the Spanish inheritance. There was nothing original about the exploitation of art as an instrument of propaganda: in their different ways the Escorial and Versailles aimed at the same effect – the exaltation of the ruler – as, in the twentieth century, do the creations of Socialist Realism or Fascism. To set the majestic and subtle splendours of the Hofbibliothek against the People's Palace or Rome railway station is instructive: two centuries only, but politically, socially and aesthetically worlds apart. In the *Hochbaroch*, the collaboration of German, Italian and French artists created a style that was international, expressing the values of an élite with wealth to spare and a yearning to spend it ostentatiously – and yet it was essentially Austrian (or more broadly south German). European civilization would be immeasurably the poorer without the baroque, the baroque the poorer without the patronage of the aristocracy, following the example of the court. One thinks of Erlach's Karlskirche, of Hildebrandt's Kinsky palace in Vienna and his exquisite summer palace, the Belvedere, commissioned by Prince Eugène. Rewarding employment was provided for skilled craftsmen, masons, glaziers, plasterers, carpenters and painters. The province of Vorarlberg in particular was a nursery of builders and craftsmen who travelled all over the Habsburg lands and south Germany. On the other hand, Vienna drained the provinces of wealth and vitality. Great nobles visited their country estates only to hunt. Their new palaces were provided by the labour of peasants, who were exploited, sometimes brutally, with more concern for immediate returns than for long-term improvement. Neglected agriculture was to be one of the main concerns of the reforming Emperor Joseph II.

Charles VI, more artist than accountant, leaned towards an aristocratic form of government. There was a gradual wilting of local independence, but more from the apathy of the estates than any central initiatives. He merely tinkered with the institutions. New chancelleries were added for the Belgian and Italian possessions. The privy council had grown so large that policy discussions and decisions took place in the smaller 'privy conference'. The real head of the administrative machine was Bartenstein, a former Protestant from Strasbourg, the only commoner among Charles's advisers. Maria Theresa, looking back on this period in her *Testament*, was to describe Bartenstein as 'a great statesman'; she leaned heavily on his advice in her early years. Efficient though he was, he made little attempt to work for uniformity: the Emperor gave no radical impulse or lead. Prince Eugène did what he could to strengthen the army; he was in touch with developments in other countries and painfully aware of the deficiencies. Shortage of money was ever the problem. The Habsburgs understood that poor subjects made a poor country. There was no lack of analysis or experiment: there were state textile and porcelain factories, companies founded to trade abroad. Little came of these efforts, though the state bank, *Wiener Stadtbank*, continued to prove useful. There was a chronic shortage of capital and little spontaneous investment; no business expertise among the administrators; in short, no social foundation for economic advance. The Oriental Company, based on Fiume, went into liquidation because of shortage of capital; the East India Company of Ostend was sacrificed, after it had made a hopeful start, to satisfy British commercial interests and to secure British acceptance of the Pragmatic Sanction. Charles did not lack good advice. One of his councillors in the *Hofkammer*, Christian von Schierendorff, worked hard to promote the ideas of the seventeenth-century mercantilists. He proposed that burghers and peasants should be better represented in the diets so as to gain more equal assessment of taxation; that lords should be made to grant leases to their peasants and to commute labour services; that Protestants should be tolerated. Charles was not, however, the man to direct a revolution, to challenge feudal tradition, the myopic defensive regulations of the guilds, the attitudes of a church which was still so imbued with Counter-Reformation attitudes that it made conformity its priority in evangelism and education alike.

Charles VI's constant concern, and his particular contribution to the interests of the dynasty, was gaining the assent of other powers to the Pragmatic Sanction. It grew from a private Habsburg agreement to a public article of the constitution and the sacred cow of Habsburg diplomacy. The monarchy was to pass whole to Charles's eldest son, or daughter if he had no more sons, instead of to the daughters of Joseph, his elder brother. In 1716 Charles's son died. In 1717 Maria Theresa was born: she became sole heiress. His efforts to persuade the other powers to accept the Sanction inhibited his diplomacy. Within the Empire, he had to make concessions to the diets in order to win their loyalty to his daughter. The succession question both hampered the internal development of the state and involved him in sacrifices and commitments abroad which helped to expose Austrian weakness. It did not cause, but it did complicate, the problems of the dynasty. Nor did the marriage of Maria Theresa to Francis, duke of Lorraine, help her cause, since it was regarded by the war party in France as a provocative move to check the French policy of gradually absorbing his duchy. The hawks of Versailles had reason to be optimistic about French prospects in case of war against the traditional enemy. By 1740, following the treaties of Vienna (1738) and Belgrade (1739), the Habsburgs had lost Naples, Sicily, Lorraine and much of southern Hungary. The army, demoralized by defeats, defended loosely bound provinces, controlled by an administration which, by French or Prussian standards, was rudimentary. Large debts loomed over an insufficient income. But there were, on paper, a number of pledges from the great powers that they would not exploit such weakness by depriving a princess of her inheritance.

Maria Theresa and the Silesian Wars

Maria Theresa was 23 years old when her father died. She had been married to Francis of Lorraine for four years. Within two months of her accession, in December 1740, Prussian troops marched into Silesia. Frederick II had demanded the surrender of the province, in return for 2 million *thalers* and his vote for Francis in the forthcoming imperial election. She had resisted the majority of her councillors, who had advised negotiation, and returned a proud answer: 'Never, never will the Queen renounce an inch of all her hereditary lands, though she perish with all that remains to her. Rather the Turks in front of Vienna, rather cession of the Netherlands to France, rather any concession to Bavaria and Saxony than renunciation of Silesia.' After fourteen years of fighting, she had to accept the loss of most of that desirable province: it was part of the price for years of neglect. And so she began her reign with a gamble, but it was an intelligent one; by personal example she showed the way, not only in queenly gestures but through sensible measures as well. She saved her crown; she also left it stronger.

Maria Theresa was less disposed than her son Joseph to press matters to their logical conclusion. Her instinctive conservatism was that of many of her subjects: she was an Austrian of her age, a devout Catholic who ruled unquestioningly under God when many of her contemporaries were rejecting that notion of authority and finding secular reasons for more unscrupulous behaviour. As tenacious of her rights as she was respectful of those of others, she used to the full the advantages that nature conferred. She inherited the good looks of her mother, Elizabeth of Brunswick: with her large blue eyes, fair hair and full figure went an appealing gaiety. She was immensely strong, managed with little sleep, rode and danced whenever she could, and bore 16 children in 20 years. Her husband, like her ministers, knew that her determined look was not misleading; she normally had her way. Standing out against extremes, she none the less accepted necessary reforms, chose intelligent ministers and backed them against often formidable opposition. It is hard to imagine any person better suited to rule the Habsburg possessions at this critical juncture, nor any who would have been more successful. That is not to devalue the work of her reforming ministers, Bartenstein, Haugwitz and Kaunitz. One has only to think of her son-in-law, Louis XVI, and his failure to support ministers against court interests, to appreciate the value of her strong, instinctive understanding of the right and the good.

It is tempting to take a sentimental view of Maria Theresa; it is a natural reaction, however, to the brutal cynicism of Frederick the Great. One should recall, however, her decidedly unsentimental relations with her children; they were regarded with affection but used as pawns in the dynastic game. She loved her husband, the amiable, business-like Francis of Lorraine, and was grieved by his failures in war. But she managed him as she did the rest of her family. *Casa nostra* was her ruling passion, as it was that of all the successful Habsburg rulers. But again one can see something more. She fought two dynastic wars which cost her subjects dear. She believed that her cause should be theirs, but she came in her later years to understand that their cause must be hers.

At the battle of Mollwitz (April 1741), a weak Austrian force under Neipperg, who had already failed badly in the Turkish campaigns, was defeated by the superior Prussian infantry. France, Spain and Bavaria, who had been waiting to see how Austria would fare, then joined in the war; the two larger powers undertaking to support the claim of Elector Charles of Bavaria to the imperial title, and to keep any lands that were won from Austria in the process. The British offered Austria support, as a guarantor of the Pragmatic Sanction, on condition that part of Silesia was abandoned to Frederick. It was British policy, a mixture of honour and self-interest, to divide the allies and to concentrate upon France. Maria Theresa had cause to doubt Frederick's reliability: after he had made an agreement (the secret Convention of Klein-Schnellendorf, October 1741) he came back into the field to obtain more. In July 1742 he was granted nearly all Silesia, after British mediation. Meanwhile the Austrians had recovered. The turning point had been Maria Theresa's appeal to the Hungarian 'nation'.

In September 1741 the Hungarian diet had been summoned to her castle at Buda. There she had placed herself under their protection and the nobles had responded by declaring the *insurrectio*, the old formula by which they pledged themselves to fight: 'Life and blood for our king'. The price, hammered out with the diet in the following month, included the registration, as a fundamental law, of the right of the nobility not to pay taxes. They offered a military contribution of 100,000 men. There was a chivalric element in the Magyar response to their injured queen. She deserved their loyalty, for she had the nerve to break down the barriers of mistrust which her predecessors had helped to build. On 12 February 1742, Charles of Bavaria was elected Emperor by unanimous vote. Two days later he lost his own capital. Khevenhüller, the best Austrian general, had staged a diversionary invasion of Bavaria; the French invaders of Bohemia were trapped in Prague; by the end of the year they had all retreated from the country. In 1743 there was a second Austrian invasion of Bavaria; again Charles was bundled out. In June, the Pragmatic Army of British and Germans defeated the French at Dettingen.

The war developed into a world struggle. In the end peace was negotiated over the heads of the Austrians. One undisputed fact was the military superiority of Prussia, at least when fighting against Austrians alone. Frederick entered the war at his convenience: he occupied Bohemia in 1744, accepted the peace of Dresden and the status quo in December 1745; he held the initiative throughout, compelling the Austrians to limit their other operations, on the Rhineland and in Italy. Maria Theresa could congratulate herself on having secured the imperial crown for Francis, who was elected in 1745 after the death of Charles Albert. But losses rankled: Silesia to Prussia, some Italian estates to Savoy (the price of its alliance), and Parma and Piacenza to Spain; the high-handed conduct of Britain and its failure to defend the Netherlands suggested that Maria Theresa might look elsewhere for an ally. 'Why am I excluded from negotiations which concern my own affairs?' she asked the British envoy during the peace negotiations at

Aix-la-Chapelle (1748). 'My enemies will give me better conditions than my friends'. On Kaunitz's return from Aix he wrote a memorandum in which was foreshadowed the diplomatic revolution: its decisive move was alliance between Austria and France; behind it lay Kaunitz's perception that Prussia had replaced France as a far more dangerous hereditary enemy to the Habsburgs.

The consequence of the 'revolution' was another instalment of war. It is sometimes regarded by British historians as a brilliant but cynical exercise in power diplomacy. Judged by results it may also appear to be futile. For Austria, the terms of the peace of Paris (1763), after a ding-dong struggle in which Frederick, against reason and nature, survived the combined assaults of Austria, France and Russia, were a repetition of Aix. The loss of Silesia was no easier to accept after a war in which the Austrians had won several battles: Kunersdorf in 1759 had been such a complete victory that the Austrians believed they had won the war, and against any ruler but Frederick it would have been so. The reasoning behind the reversal of alliances, the new alignment with France and Russia was sound enough. Maria Theresa was entirely in sympathy with the Bohemian nobleman Kaunitz, at 47 a young man by Austrian official standards, whom she promoted in 1748, above all who disagreed with him, to be *Staatskanzler*, a title held after him only by Metternich. There is room for criticism, however, about the way in which the reversal of alliances was followed up. It is reasonably certain that Maria Theresa intended at some point to attack Prussia. Her alliance was plainly not a defensive one. The attachment of Russia to the Franco-Austrian alliance, and subsequently Sweden, gave it great potential. Then, as later when Joseph urged some aggressive action (such as the occupation of Zips in 1769), she had misgivings about the morality or wisdom of tactics to which her own sprawling empire was also so vulnerable. In this case, however, she regarded the hostilities as an inevitable consequence of Frederick's original sin. The rape of Silesia had to be followed by measures to recover honour and lands. It is therefore surprising that war preparations were so leisurely, that the Austrians allowed themselves to be caught out by Frederick's sudden attack upon the Saxons in August 1756. It is all the more surprising in that the years between the wars had been used to promote those military and administrative reforms which were the main achievement of Maria Theresa's reign.

Haugwitz and the Great Reform

> The Empire, like the House of Austria, is without a Supreme Head, the finances of Austria are in a state of confusion, the armies decayed, her provinces sucked dry by war, plague, famine and by the terrible burden of taxation they have had to bear up to the present.

It was in these terms that Frederick assessed his opponent in 1740. The queen, in her own *Testament* (1749), was to confirm his diagnosis: she had begun, 'without money, without credit, without an army, without any experience or knowledge of my own and finally without any kind of advice'. It was not only that ministers treated her as an amateur and a female one at that. It was also that they still thought in terms of the *Ständestaat*, a mentality conditioned by centuries of struggle between sovereigns and their estates. The ruler had rarely been in a position to impose terms upon a province without compromise, while the magnates' duty and interest had been to protect their province and their class. Now the loss of Silesia, a province which paid a quarter of all direct taxes levied in Austria and Bohemia, was comparable to the revolt of Bohemia in 1618: not a mortal blow but warning of worse to come unless effective action were taken.

Such action could not be expected from Sinzendorf, head of the Austrian chancellery, aged 70 in 1740; from Starhemberg, who had been head of the treasury for thirty-seven years, and was now 77; nor from *Landmarschall* Harrach, aged 71, or his relatively youthful brother Joseph, president of the War Council, aged 63. The Bohemian chancellor, Kinsky, had been responsible for the feeble defence arrangements which Frederick had so easily brushed aside, and was the most obstinate opponent of all plans to make war more effectively. Kinsky epitomizes the separatist spirit of which Maria Theresa wrote:

> Owing to the division between the provinces, none of the Ministers was really trying to rescue me and the state from this terrible embarrassment. At first, all proposals of a sort to inflict the smallest hardship on any province were immediately rejected by the officials in charge of that province, and everyone cared only for his own interest.

By the end of the war, however, all the veterans were dead or retired – except for Joseph von Harrach, entrenched in his office until 1762.

Maria Theresa later described how, on the cession of Siberia, 'my state of mind suddenly changed, and I directed my whole attention to internal problems and to devising how the German Hereditary Lands could still be preserved'. She had fortunately several devoted servants for whom the scourge of Frederick was also a salutory challenge. There was Bartenstein, who 'lighted the true candle', guided her in her early years, and to whom, again in her words, she 'owed the preservation of the monarchy'; Ignaz Koch, secretary of the cabinet from 1741, and Sylva Tarouca, comptroller of her household from 1744 to 1771, both essentially palace men, kept her supplied with information; and to be well-informed was half the battle; only perhaps in Poland was it more difficult than in the Habsburg lands. Above all loomed Friedrich Wilhelm, Count Haugwitz (1700–65), uncouth but intelligent and masterful. When Maria Theresa and her husband (who appears to have been a model of loyalty and discretion) supported Haugwitz and his plans against the opposition of the rest of the special council called to discuss them, in 1748, they were initiating the process of reform in the only way that could ensure its success – by uncompromising assertion of the queen's sovereign rights. The action was as significant, and as brave in its way, as her more dramatic appearance of 1741 before the diet of Hungary.

The son of a general in the Saxon army, Haugwitz had become a Catholic as a young man, entered the Austrian service and become one of the leading administrators of Silesia. After the loss of that province, a rankling experience, he came to Vienna to work for its recovery. He was made responsible for the rump of the province, where special conditions allowed him to act as virtual dictator. Student of the *Aufklärung*, admirer of Frederick the Great and prodigiously hard-working, he sought to convince his mistress that the methods which worked in Silesia, where, after 1744, taxes were assessed and collected directly by the state, could be applied to the rest of her dominions. It was a simple matter of nerve: the powers were there. In 1747 he was sent as commissioner to Carniola and Carinthia, which had fallen into arrears with payments, and promptly empowered state bailiffs to take charge of all fiscal and administrative affairs. When the estates of Carniola complained about their taxes they were peremptorily informed that 'the crown expressly commands them to grant these sums voluntarily'. In the same year, Maria Theresa accepted the estimate of her military advisers that she needed an army of 108,000 men (excluding the military frontier levies, the Hungarian, Netherlands and Milanese forces), involving an upkeep of 14 million *thalers*. To raise the money, Haugwitz proposed that the provinces be required to extend the land tax to the previously exempt demesne lands of the nobles, in return for relief of expenditure arising from the supply of troops billeted on them and alleviation of interest rates upon their debts. To the estates of Bohemia and Moravia at least it seemed to be a fair exchange of rights and obligations: they had an interest in being properly defended, and they accepted it readily. There was greater resistance from the Austrian estates because it was the assertion of a radically new policy which, when fully implemented, meant the end of self-government. The estates were left the right of voting the money once every ten years for the ensuing decade and were to see to its collection monthly; thereafter the money was at the disposal of the state.

In each province a *Representatio* was set up (on the Carinthian model), equal in status to the Estates and independent of them. Not only did the Estates thus lose most of their administration and judicial functions; at a lower level the *Kreis* (circle) offices, formerly local agencies of the Estates of Bohemia, were transferred to the use of the *Representatio*. The *Hofkammer* was deprived of its supervision of Austria and Bohemia, its reduced revenues being applied to servicing the national debt and to court and official expenditure. Finally in 1749 the Bohemian and Austrian court chancelleries were abolished and were replaced by two Prussian-style bodies: the *Directorium* for administration and finance (under Haugwitz) and the *Oberste Justizstelle*, combining the functions of the ministry of justice and supreme court of appeal. Measures enacted by both courts applied to the whole of the two provinces. Thus the German, Austrian and Bohemian provinces were brought under central control in all business above that of manor and borough. The forms and titles of the governing bodies were to be changed. But the crucial step had been taken in the development of the unitary state, whose parts received, and acted upon, the orders of a sole authority in Vienna – the same for all.

Superficial unanimity covered but scarcely affected provincial variations. The Netherlands, Italy and Hungary were not affected. Maria Theresa would not venture far into the Magyar nettle-patch. She tried to neutralize the local sympathies of the great magnates by drawing them to court. She did not summon the diet for the last fifteen years of the reign. Power lay with the gentry in their county organizations – the *comitati*. As Britain found with Ireland, to ignore the problem did nothing to solve it. Haugwitz's reconstruction had been inadequate because the object of the reformers had been short-term – the provision of an efficient army. Kaunitz went further to check the particularism of the Estates. It was agreed by his critics that he went too far in the concentration of authority: by comparison with the Prussian administration there were excessive delays. The endemic fault was the lack of a trained corps of officials; too many were amateurs and attuned to local powers and interests. As Maria Theresa complained: 'It is always the fault of those provincial officials who do not do their duty.' It is this inefficiency that explains the increasing concern of the queen and ministers with social reforms, above all with education.

Allowing for exceptions and shortcomings, there was more unified government for ordinary men, as the reformed offices of the circles took on public health, weights and measures, the regulation of markets, roads and other such matters. It is in the operations of local government that we can see most clearly the pragmatic spirit in which the reformers worked. Maria Theresa did not believe that it was possible to abolish villeinage. Humanity and reason demanded, however, that the peasant should be fit to work productively. Circle officers were instructed therefore to see that the peasants were *steuerfahig* – fit to pay their dues. Conversion of peasant to demesne land was prohibited. Though labour services were notoriously hard to regulate, some effort was made to correct abuses of *Robot*. The remote province of Slavonia, never properly surveyed or administered before, was the scene of a pilot scheme; there, the government laid down the proper size of a peasant's holding and with it the rents due, in cash, kind and services.

The loss of Silesia emphasized the need to stimulate economic growth in the remaining provinces. In 1746 a supervisory body was set up with the resounding title: *Universalkommerzdirektorium*. The results were neither 'universal' nor spectacular but some provincial organizations were effective. In Bohemia, Count Hatzfeld laid the foundations for a more prosperous economy with measures to stimulate the linen, woollen, cotton and glass-refining industries. Maria Theresa would have been shortsighted indeed if she had neglected the economic factor in her calculations. It would have been natural for her to pay lip service to the fashionable nostrums of the time or she might have been expected to concern herself mainly with taxation matters. It is impressive to see how clearly she grasped the complex interaction of economic, social and political problems, how assiduously, with the instinct of a good housekeeper, she scrutinized the small print. Cameral records contain many examples of comments and requests in her own handwriting. Of course, economic policy was a patchwork: short-term considerations weighed strongly. Maria Theresa's reforms served the overriding purpose of her government, the punishment of Prussia: Silesian workers must be drawn to Bohemia, trade diverted from the Elbe. The Austrians had hitherto had low general tariffs, fiscal rather than political in purpose. Now the Bohemian lands were made into a customs union and protected by a tariff of 30 per cent, which was extended to Hungary in 1755, Austria in 1756. It is also possible, however, to see an overall philosophy at work, and a constant evolution, from mercantilist to physiocratic notions. It was a mark of the more realistic, perhaps more pacific policies of Maria Theresa's later years that trading policies became more liberal: in 1775 the general level of tariffs was lowered while those between Germany and the Austrian and Bohemian provinces were abolished. Meanwhile the enlargement of the Adriatic port of Trieste and the search for new export routes and outlets in Russia and Turkey indicated the reorientation of the Habsburg economy from Germany.

The main object of the reforms was to find more money for the army from the vast resources of lands which could have been the basis of an enduring European power: it was to implement the policy advocated by Hörnigk in his pamphlet of 1684, *Oesterreich über Alles*, and kept in the minds of educated Austrians through no less than sixteen editions of the work. The fact that Frederick survived his ordeal of war on two, sometimes three, fronts and emerged from the Seven Years War still in possession of Silesia should not in itself obscure the solid achievement of the army reformers or discredit Kaunitz and his diplomacy. *Feldzugmeister* Daun, the chief planner of the new army, proved to be less inspiring in the field than he was as a trainer of troops; a textbook soldier, cautious to a fault, he let himself be outpaced by Frederick on several occasions; yet he won victories, notably those at Kolin (1757) and Kunersdorf (1759) which would have put paid to any opponent less resilient than Frederick: his genius was Austria's misfortune. Moreover the French performed lamentably, a factor that Kaunitz could not have anticipated when he negotiated the French alliance.

Finally the abrupt Russian withdrawal after the death of the Empress Elizabeth in 1762 saved Frederick when he seemed to be on his knees. All in all the Austrians reaped a poor reward for the sensible remodelling of their army.

The war council was reorganized: a new infantry manual was introduced; small arms, artillery, engineers were all brought up to Prussian standards; training schools for young officers served the double purpose of imparting professionalism and attaching the nobles to the regime. If there is some truth in the old gibe that Austria always acted too late, it cannot be said in this context that it did too little. Thorough and wholehearted, the effort is impressive, bearing the mark of the queen, *mater castrorum*, as she was termed on a commemorative medal. For a time the recovery of Silesia and the humiliation of Frederick took priority in her mind over all domestic reforms. This usually magnanimous woman never forgave Frederick: she 'always detested his false character', as she admitted in her *Testament*. She lost popularity with taxpayers and – which was perhaps more significant for the future – with the other German states, as her image changed from romantic victim of Prussian aggression to vindictive dynast, allied to alien powers to crush the gallant Frederick. Yet under all the stresses Maria Theresa never lost sight of the economic and human factors; intelligent measures were adopted to minimize the social cost. Austria did not suffer as badly from the war as either Prussia or France. The war only temporarily deflected the queen and her advisers from pursuing their grander objectives, from promoting royal authority and the well-being of her people: for Maria Theresa that meant their spiritual as well as working condition.

Kaunitz and Joseph

Prince Wenzel Anton von Kaunitz (1711–94), Maria Theresa's chancellor from 1753, negotiated the treaty of 1756 with France which was the centrepiece of the 'diplomatic revolution' and was, from that time, one of the leading statesmen in Europe. But he came to think that his diplomatic efforts had been wasted by incompetent direction of the war and by the failure to exploit the Empire's resources to the full. He was unfairly critical of Haugwitz's reconstruction of government and replaced Haugwitz's *Representationen* by ten *Gubernia*, and his *Directorium* by a united chancellery (1765), the old *Hofkammer* in new form. Of greater value was his innovation of a central council of state (1761), with eight senior ministers, under his presidency. This body brought to the making of policy a degree of unanimity which had hitherto been lacking and made possible a concerted policy of reform. So great was Kaunitz's influence in government after the death of Maria Theresa's husband Francis of Lorraine and the entry of their son Joseph into government as co-regent in 1765, that the next fifteen years of rule can be envisaged as a triangle, with the queen at the apex, still emphatically in charge. Kaunitz advised but did not dictate. Yet he enjoyed an ascendancy which is the more remarkable as he was a world apart from her in character and ideas. Vain but shrewd, he was indeed oddly composed of virtues and eccentricities. He hated fresh air, fretted about his health and would not hear of death: if a colleague died he had to be told that he was 'no longer available'. His foibles would have been absurd if he had not been so impressive intellectually. 'I was born', he wrote, 'with the spirit of order.'

Sceptical and anticlerical, Kaunitz affected to despise the homely values of the Austrian *Hausfrau* which the queen personified. Yet nothing could shake her faith in his judgement. She knew that he could be relied on to perceive the true interests of the state and to put them before those of his class. 'I cannot advocate putting the nobles and the Estates back in their high places', he wrote (in 1763): 'I am myself a Bohemian noble and a landed proprietor, but my duty to Your Majesty comes first.' He referred to the dangers of noble power in Hungary, Transylvania and Belgium and concluded that the reintroduction of rule through the nobility would 'at a blow, cut off all improvements and hopes, and deal a most sensible blow to your supreme power'. With that ability to use people to the best advantage, which characterizes the skilful manager, Maria Theresa could see that his talents complemented her own. He was specially useful as the one minister whom the opinionated Joseph could respect. Kaunitz outlived Joseph. In a letter to the latter's successor Leopold II, by way of warning for the future, Kaunitz assessed Joseph, in a way that suggests his own moderation and practical wisdom: 'Harshness, exaggerated severity, over-hasty decisions, despotic behaviour, obsession with innovations ... ambitious projects which advertised hazardous aims or which gave cause for alarm, aroused everywhere antipathy and distrust.'

The legislation of the short reign of Joseph II (1780–90) was to break new ground. But for the most part he simply took further, in some cases to extremes, the measures of earlier years when Maria Theresa was trying to initiate practical reforms, while guarding essential principles against her son's impetuosity. He was given the special job of presiding over the *Hofkriegsrat* after the death of Daun in 1766. He was required to sign, after her, all royal documents, but he was allowed relatively little executive freedom and inevitably he resented his subordinate status. His mother's mind remained clear, her will and energy unimpaired. Unsentimental, utilitarian, contemptuous of history and its ubiquitous presence in institutions and customs, Joseph believed in radical action to create the unitary, secular state. No other ruler of his time went so far in the pursuit of equality. Nobility and clergy were allowed no prior claims upon his state. His views, combined as they were with fervent admiration of Frederick II and a foreign policy which matched that of the old master in ruthless opportunism, were anathema to Maria Theresa. War had been a disillusioning experience for her. She had good cause to believe in the sanctity of treaties and to respect the rights of other sovereigns, even elected kings of Poland; but over the question of the Polish partition (1772), through which Austria gained Galicia and 2.5 million inhabitants, she was overruled. She bewailed the morality of the act and prophesied that people would see 'what is the outcome of this violation of every accepted standard of sanctity and justice', but she could perceive that it would be dangerous to stand by and let Prussia and Austria take all. Her correspondence with Kaunitz on the question of Turkey reveals her typically sensible approach: honour precluded 'the acquisition of Bosnia and Serbia, and the only provinces which would bring us advantage'. And so the Empire would have to be content with Moldavia and Wallachia, 'unsalubrious, devastated countries, exposed to the Turks and Russians, with no fortresses, lands on which we should have to spend many millions of money'. Presciently she warned: 'Our monarchy can do without enrichment of this kind which would end by ruining it altogether.'

Maria Theresa was no lover of *Realpolitik*. But she believed in furthering the interests of her dynasty, in the traditional way, through the marriage market. Her own strength and fecundity gave her ample opportunity. Joseph was married first to Isabella of Parma (1761). He loved her and was heartbroken by her early death in 1763, but let himself be persuaded to marry, again for solely dynastic reasons, Josepha of Bavaria: she in turn died of smallpox (1765). Maria Theresa took an unsentimental view of marriage. Of her daughters, Caroline was given to Ferdinand IV of Naples, after the death of her elder sister Josepha, the intended bride. Maria Christina was the instrument of a useful marriage alliance with Prince Albert of Saxony; Maria Amalia had to be content with the duke of Parma. The youngest daughter, by contrast, was provided with the brilliant – though, it was to transpire, ill-fated – match with Louis XV's grandson, the dauphin of France and future Louis XVI. To Leopold, who was to prove an enlightened ruler of Tuscany, was allotted Maria Luisa of Spain; to Ferdinand, Maria Beatrice, heiress to Modena; the youngest son, Maximilian Francis, entered the Church in order to prepare for his responsibilities as prince bishop and elector of Cologne.

Maria did not relinquish her hold over her children when they were married; indeed they were pursued with advice about how to behave. Nor was Joseph exempt. Heir to the largest of eighteenth-century empires, a man who knew little happiness in his domestic life, whose conception of what was right and necessary differed so radically from his mother's, Joseph was painfully frustrated by these further years of tutelage: the cumulative effect can be seen in the self-destructive haste of the decade when he was at last his own master. Before he died (in 1790) he was bitterly conscious of failure and the widespread rejection of his measures of rationalization and centralization: Belgium and Hungary were in open revolt and he was having to retreat and compromise. He had assaulted traditional institutions, Estates, guilds and the Church, and he had shaken the confidence of the privileged at all levels: nobles, abbots, guild masters and provincial officials. A flood of edicts had sought to give effect to his views on what was required to bring about and improve the health and well-being of his people. In all this activity the attention to detail is remarkable: women brought up in state institutions were forbidden to wear corsets; dwellers by the Danube were forbidden to bathe or wash in its, doubtless, dirty waters; Viennese were advised not to eat gingerbread; peasants were enjoined to mix vinegar with spring water. Such examples convey the obsessive side of this ruler who could not leave well alone: the Emperor's opinion became the subject's law. But running through all can be seen Joseph's concern for the human resources upon whose health depended the grander objectives: the creation of a self-sufficient economy, of a single administrative system and Austrian hegemony in Europe. All his work was characterized by faith in the power of laws to shape society, by the urge to systematize and control, by disdain for the voices of the past and reluctance to listen to those of the present (unless they happened to agree with him): marks of the political ideologue in all ages. But he was less dangerous than some later examples of the species, for his ideology was that of the Enlightenment, with its emphasis upon the dignity of the individual. He did not subscribe to a mystical view of the state as a higher good, in whose name so many have been crushed. He did not consider that the principles of the Enlightenment were incompatible with the interests of the state; on the contrary he held that the state was best served by reforms which had a rational basis, were therefore right in themselves and relevant to the country's needs. Undoubtedly he paid too little attention to the prejudices and fears of those he sought to help: the tenant of the dispossessed abbey, or the craftsman suddenly deprived of the protection of his guild and exposed to the blast of competition. It can be argued however that those of his reforms which survived his death and his successor Leopold's brief reign of reaction and reappraisal (1790–2) contributed in the long term to the survival of the Habsburg Empire till 1918.

With little grasp of the way ordinary people thought and felt, this most original of monarchs sometimes found means to reach their hearts: as when he opened the royal gardens to the citizens of Vienna. This reputedly unlovable, egotistical sovereign was also capable of acts of imaginative sympathy which it would be churlish to attribute solely to his desire to stand well in the eyes of enlightened opinion. The uncompromising statist who wanted the Church to be wholly subject to the secular authority was also a sincere Christian after his fashion; his emphasis on the importance of pure devotion, uncluttered by material aids, was that of some of the most thoughtful of his subjects, who saw too much of the Church's wealth being spent on paint and plaster rather than on schools and hospitals. His redistribution of parish boundaries offended vested interests and showed scant respect for history but it was intended to ensure that no parishioner should be more than walking distance from his church and that the priest, paid from the central state fund, should be fairly treated. Of the vast sums extracted from the churches and from the amalgamation of lay brotherhoods, much was devoted to the building of orphanages, hospitals and medical academies. New homes for unmarried mothers, the blind, deaf mute and lunatic, may be compared with what was provided – or rather not provided – for such people in George III's England. Joseph instructed his commissioners to see what could be done to make blind or crippled children self-supporting and to check that 'dishonouring punishments of unfortunate girls' had been abolished; doctors were reminded that they were bound 'by the highest laws and by their oath to come to the aid of the truly poor at all times'. Such humane consideration is no less representative of Joseph than the harsh cynicism of the partitioner of Poland or the vanity that led him to take command of the ill-fated expedition against the Turks in 1788. This extraordinary man cannot be reduced to simple dimensions.

Conservative Reform

Joseph's full achievement and significance lie outside the scope of this work. As one observer, Baron Risbeck, wrote: 'As soon as Joseph stands alone at the helm, a revolution will take place here that will render the present inhabitants a phenomenon to the next generation.' Joseph belongs properly to the age of revolution, just as plainly as his mother, scornful of the precepts of the Enlightenment, epitomizes the values of the *ancien régime*. It was his misfortune to antagonize many of those who should have been the dynasty's natural supporters – on their own terms. Realistic about the need to survive, Maria Theresa was prepared to accept those terms. For all that, her record as social reformer does not compare unfavourably with that of the 'revolutionary emperor'. Her deep unquestioning faith was accompanied by a sensible view of the value of religion as a force in society. 'What could exist', she asked, 'without a dominant religion? Tolerance and indifference are exactly the surest ways of destroying the established order. What else is there to control bad instincts?' It was in accord with the feelings of the mass of her subjects who loved their painted churches, the amiable discipline, the consoling rites and evocative images of south German Catholicism. Nor was she immune, unfortunately, from their prejudices. It was one of her quirks that she would only speak to Jews behind a screen. It was left to Joseph to relieve the disabilities of Jews and Protestants. But as a rule she deserves to be judged by her actions rather than by her manners. As a child she had learned, from the history of the investiture contest, that the Emperor was right to stand up to the Pope and his claim of *plena potestas* over all sovereigns. She improved taxation on Church lands, limited the jurisdiction of Church courts and forbade the publication of papal bulls of which she disapproved. The Church carried surplus fat while the state was lean: so she discouraged further donations to the clergy and castigated idle monks. In 1745 she secured the abolition of twenty-four Church holidays on the ground that it was in the interest of the Church that Catholics should be made to work as hard as their Protestant rivals.

Before Maria Theresa's death Protestants were allowed to take degrees at Vienna University. During the last twenty years of her reign censorship was relaxed and the privileged position of the Church further pared in ways that showed that she was convinced by its critics. They argued that the Church's excessive landholdings contributed to the sluggishness of the economy and that its virtual monopoly in education was an obstacle to the progress of ideas. The Church was under fire from within and without. Jansenism had been spreading for some time from sources in the Austrian Netherlands and northern Italy, through interested laymen, or members of religious orders, notably Dominicans who had studied there: Jansenists were hostile to the Jesuits and critical of ultramontane papalism, baroque forms of devotion in churches and scholastic methods in universities, with their heavy emphasis on classical learning and logical exercises. In Maria Theresa's reign several Jansenists secured key positions in Austria: so an attitude became a movement, with political and social implications far beyond the theology from which it stemmed. The central figure, one of the most important in Austrian history, was Gerhard van Swieten, a Belgian and protégé of Kaunitz, who had come to Vienna as the queen's doctor in 1754. He used his position of trust to forward the careers of like-minded men. So it was that Karl Martini became professor of law at Vienna in 1754, Simon Stock director of theological studies in Austria and Ignaz Müller a confessor to the queen. '*Die Grössen*', as they were called, became a formidable force because they had clear objectives, worked together and enjoyed the protection of Kaunitz. If Austrians were to move beyond the intellectual confines of Poland or Spain, and if schools and universities were to provide the trained administrators who, as the example of Prussia showed so forcefully, were the necessary precondition of a sound and prosperous state, education and the press had to be liberated from a conservative clerical establishment: that is what was being achieved before Joseph took control. After a long struggle with the Jesuits they gained control of the censorship commission: and so works as potentially subversive of received constitutional ideas as Montesquieu's *L'Esprit des lois* became available. A ministry of education was founded, with an explicit brief to secularize the universities. Directors of faculties were appointed to reform curricula. In medicine, van Swieten's special concern, where students had been going abroad for proper facilities, the reforms were to give Vienna a lasting pre-eminence. In law and political science the emphasis was vocational; modern languages, mathematics and accountancy were given priority. In 1770 a separate institute was set up for the training of merchants. Even in the theological faculty the curriculum, drawn up by Abbot Rautenstrauch, was shaped to enable students 'to learn only that which is useful for the cure of souls and consequently for the good of the state'. The same principles applied to grammar schools where the addition of subjects like geography, history, mathematics and, of course, German, destroyed the predominance of Latin; and to the foundation of a teachers' training college which was intended by Johann Felbiger, who was brought from Silesia to set it up, to be the means through which the masses could receive the benefits of the new learning.

It was probably the vocational bent of the reformers that appealed to the queen, together with their emphasis on loyalty to the ruler and service to the state. There was a practical motive in the great creations in which the queen took a personal interest: the State Archive, the Military Academy, the Oriental Academy, which developed from a school for interpreters into a cadre for diplomats, and the Theresianum, an academy for the sons of nobles. Always too there was the smouldering sense of loss, resentment at Prussian progress, and the realization that if Prussia were to be overcome, it must first be copied. She was prepared therefore to ordain change, ruthlessly, over the heads of legal bodies, if the public good required it. She was deaf to the appeals of outraged papal officials when they asked her to defend the Church against the measures she had sanctioned. She would not change her view of doctrine or her liking for proper ceremony. But she required funds and the monasteries, providing for a dwindling band of inmates, had them in abundance. In 1769 measures which had been tested in the Habsburg duchy of Milan were extended to the hereditary lands. Under the aegis of a special department in the court chancery, directed by Franz von Heinke, a former pupil of the rationalist Christian Wolff, Church land was frozen by a law forbidding the acquisition of new land by religious bodies; they were then required to submit estimates of income and expenditure and of numbers; no one was allowed to take his religious vow before the age of 24 and a novice's dowry was severely limited. Empirical in approach, mild in effect, these measures might not have been judged sufficient to alarm the Pope in the decade which saw him sanction the dissolution of the Jesuits (1773) – which Maria Theresa was most reluctant to implement. But he clearly saw, behind the moderation of the old queen, the anticlericalism of her minister; behind the new emphasis upon the rights of the state in ecclesiastical matters, the threat of schism and the establishment of an independent state church. Joseph seemed to be moving in that direction when he ordered the dissolution of all religious houses 'which served no useful purposes'; upon this odd criterion numbers were reduced from 65,000 to 27,000.

Maria Theresa can be seen as taking the steps necessary for the health of the monarchy, or as letting herself be swept along with a tide which was to endanger its very foundations. Evidence to support the former view is provided by her record on the crucial issue of serfdom, where the status quo in the form of the traditional alliance of sovereign and her nobility, was challenged by those who pressed the claims of humanity, or the fiscal needs of the state. In both Bohemia and Hungary the issue was forced by the actions of the peasants themselves. After 1763, Bohemian lands ravaged by war and epidemics suffered from successive harvest failures. With the fall in population went an increase in the landowners' demand for *Robot*. By its drastic action against particular noblemen who abused their rights the state did enough to suggest sympathy towards the peasants. There had already been a number of local revolts when, in January 1775 a more concerted movement began, under the leadership of a secret society directed by a free peasant, Antonin Nyvlt. Armed bands roamed the countryside, threatening stewards and bailiffs, pillaging manor houses, even churches. Inevitably the risings were suppressed for the peasants were no match for regular soldiers, and Nyvlt was killed. But all was not lost for the peasants. In August a government edict was read out, by soldiers in the villages so that the people should know their rights, limiting *Robot* to three days a week. On a number of royal estates the crown introduced a more radical scheme, devised by Franz von Raab: *Robot* was changed into a cash payment and domain land was cut up into leaseholds for a free peasantry. In Hungary Maria Theresa lost patience with the obstructive *szlachta*, after years of negotiations over the issue of labour and services. When the peasants brought matters to a head by passive resistance, simply refusing to work, she intervened and forced reform of the laws by decree (1767). This was action in the best paternalist tradition, but far short of what reformers wanted and what Joseph later sought to achieve through his great land survey. It showed, however, in Maria Theresa a thoughtful concern for the well-being of the people, with a strong sense of what was possible, but a willingness to act against privileged groups when the higher interest of the state appeared to require it. By 1780 the state was appreciably stronger than in 1740, its claims better understood, more readily accepted. The rights of privileged sections of the community had been successfully challenged. The power of local estates had been curtailed and the Church had been shown that it enjoyed no special immunity. There had been a significant shift in the balance of power.

Further Reading

Recent work on the Holy Roman Empire has led to a more generous view of its role and importance. For the workings of imperial institutions, Roger Wimes, 'The imperial circles, princely diplomacy and imperial reform 1681–1714', *Journal of Modern History*, 39 (1967), should be consulted. Court life in the German states, with examples drawn from Würtemburg, is described in A. Fauchier-Magnan, *The Small German Courts in the Eighteenth Century* (1947, trans. 1958). For background, G. Barraclough, *Origins of Modern Germany* (Oxford, 1946), and F.L. Carsten, *Princes and Parliaments in Germany* (Oxford, 1959), are invaluable. In *The*

Development of the German Mind, vol. 2 (1962), F. Hertz does not confine himself to cultural history. An important theme is conveyed by the title of G. Parry's article, 'Enlightened government and its critics in eighteenth century Germany', *Historical Journal*, 6 (1963).

The effects of the Thirty Years War should not be neglected. Henry Kamen, 'Consequences of the Thirty Years War', *Past and Present*, 6 (1963), gives a balanced picture. They are the starting point for E. Sagarra's *Social History of Germany 1648–1914* (London, 1977).

Besides such general histories as those of W.H. Bruford, *Germany in the Eighteenth Century*, (Cambridge, 1953), R. Flenley, *Modern German History* (revised 1969), and H. Holborn, *A History of Modern Germany*, vol. 2: 1648–1840 (London, 1964), several area studies have demonstrated the utility of imperial institutions and validity of the federal structure. Notable studies, the former narrower, the latter wider in implication than the title suggests, are: G. Benecke, *Society and Politics in Germany, 1500–1750* (1974) (about Lippe); and T.C.W. Blanning, *Reform and Revolution in Mainz, 1743–1803* (Cambridge, 1974). See also G.L. Soliday's study of one of the most important of the 'Free Cities', *A Community in Conflict, Frankfurt Society in the Seventeenth and Eighteenth Centuries* (Hanover, New England, 1980); and, for a city which ceased in 1681 to be part of the Empire: Franklyn Ford, *Strasbourg in Transition, 1648–1789* (Cambridge, Mass., 1958).

Habsburg history has been enriched recently by the work of R.J.W. Evans. *The Habsburg Monarchy* (Oxford, 1982) draws extensively on the archives to show the character and workings of confessional absolutism. Belated justice is done to one of its more formidable exponents in J.P. Spielman's *Leopold I of Austria* (London, 1977). The crisis of his reign is well described in J.W. Stoye's *The Siege of Vienna* (1964). In *The Austrian Achievement 1700–1800* (London, 1973), E. Wangermann provides a helpful synopsis of a period which is otherwise liable to be presented either with distorting emphasis on individual rulers or with a dulling concentration on administration. J.W. Stoye's article, 'Charles VI, The Early Years', *Transactions of the Royal Historical Society*, 5th series, 12 (1962), brings to life, against the odds, a sovereign who has still received no satisfactory biography. By contrast, and deservedly, Maria Theresa's reputation is higher than ever, even though there is still scope for a new life which could utilize the work of Austrian scholars like F. Walter on the government of her lands, revealing Maria Theresa and her ministers as innovators, and Joseph, by contrast, often as follower. Meanwhile, C.A. Macartney's short *Maria Theresa* (1969) and his commentaries in the documentary collection, *The Habsburg and Hohenzollern Dynasties of the Seventeenth and Eighteenth Centuries* (London, 1970), are as judicious as would be expected from the author of a major work, *The Habsburg Empire, 1790–1918* (1968): its early chapters put the eighteenth-century achievement in perspective. Another authority on later Habsburg history, Edward Crankshaw, has written an informative and sympathetic life, *Maria Theresa* (1969). The emphasis in G.P. Gooch's *Maria Theresa and Other Studies* (1951) is on court and family diplomacy; but then they did loom large in the queen's life.

Strictly speaking the reign of Joseph II falls outside the limits of this book, belonging to the revolutionary decade. My brief sketch is intended to indicate the extent of his influence during the years of joint rule, besides his unique contribution. Chronological constraints apart, the title of S.K. Padower's lively biography,

Revolutionary Emperor (2nd edn, 1967), suggests the difficulty of placing him: of the *ancien régime*, yet reaching out beyond it. The effect of books like E. Wangermann's *From Joseph II to the Jacobin Trials* (Oxford, 1959), T.C.W. Blanning's admirable introduction, *multum in parvo, Joseph II and Enlightened Despotism* (Harlow, 1970), with its documentary supplement, has been to rescue him from myth and caricature (and his own propaganda). They replace the picture of a daring, single-handed innovator, modelling the lives of his subjects, with that of a well-intentioned, industrious ruler, generally pursuing his mother's aims, limited, like her, by the social and economic structure of his lands, thwarted at the end by the problems they presented. If anything, Joseph's stature is enhanced by the kind of realistic assessment offered by P.P. Bernard, *Joseph II* (New York, 1968). His views reflect his earlier study of Joseph as exponent of *Realpolitik, Joseph II and Bavaria: Two Attempts at German Unification* (1965). For the effect of 'Josephism' in one area, see W.W. Davies, *Joseph II: An Imperial Reformer for the Austrian Netherlands* (New York, 1974).

For Hungary, C.A. Macartney provides short introductory histories in *Maria Theresa* (1969) and *The Habsburg and Hohenzollern Dynasties of the Seventeenth and Eighteenth Centuries* (London, 1970). There are works by H. Maczali, *Hungary in the Eighteenth Century* (Cambridge, 1910), B. Kirali, *Hungary in the Later Eighteenth Century* (1969), and, incorporating results of recent research, E. Palmeniji (ed.), *A History of Hungary* (London, 1975). For Bohemia, see R.J. Kerner, *Bohemia in the Eighteenth Century* (1932), and for a view of Austrian rule of northern Italy, see D. Limoli, 'Pietro Verri: a Lombard reformer under enlightened despotism and the French Revolution', in *Journal of Central European Affairs*, 18 (1958). For economic aspects, see W. Wright, *Serf, Seigneur and Sovereign: Agrarian Reform in Eighteenth-century Bohemia* (Minneapolis, 1967). There are also useful articles by H. Freudenberger: 'Industrialisation in Bohemia and Moravia in the eighteenth century', *Journal of Central European Affairs* 19 (January 1960), and 'The woollen goods industry of the Habsburg monarchy in the eighteenth century', *Journal of Economic History*, 20 (1960). See also, A. Klima, 'Industrial development in Bohemia, 1648–1789', *Past and Present*, 11 (1957); also, R. Betts, *Essays in Czech History* (London, 1969).

Military history can be studied through N. Henderson, *Prince Eugène of Savoy* (1964). There is also an article, 'Prince Eugène of Savoy and Central Europe', in *American Historical Review*, 57 (1951). Lavender Cassels describes the vicissitudes of campaigns in the east in *The Struggle for the Ottoman Empire, 1717–40* (London, 1966). See also C. Duffy, *The Wild Goose and the Eagle: a Life of Marshall von Brown, 1705–57* (1964); and G.E. Rothenburg, *The Austrian Military Border in Croatia*, 1522–1747 (Urbana, Ill., 1960).

A distinctive Austrian culture is described in A. Kann, *A Study in Austrian Intellectual History from Late Baroque to Romanticism* (1960). For late eighteenth-century Vienna, see M. Brion, *Daily Life in the Vienna of Mozart and Schubert* (trans. 1961). An essential aspect of south German culture is the subject of N. Powell, *From Baroque to Rococo* (1959).

II

THE RISE OF PRUSSIA

The Hohenzollern Tradition

The foundation of the Prussian army state has been called the most remarkable accomplishment in German political history. The state whose foundations were laid down by the Great Elector survived until 1945. Exactly 200 years after the accession of Frederick the Great in 1740, as German troops marched through Paris, men had cause indeed to brood upon the way in which the rest of Germany had been grafted on to the Prussian state; upon the character of that state; upon the succession of policies and accidents that had finally fused the traditions of the Prussian army with an exclusive nationalism and 'state socialism' into a Nazi state that yet remained in some respects the Prussian state of earlier times. The army was destroyed at Stalingrad and in Normandy; the state was dismembered at Potsdam in 1945. Königsberg, capital of Prussia, is today the Russian town of Kaliningrad. There is special interest in the beginnings and causes of such a dire fulfilment; equally, there is scope for distortion and myth. The failures of liberalism in the nineteenth century were not solely due to the success of Prussian autocracy or the strength of military tradition. The French Revolution did as much as Frederick the Great to shape the Germany of Bismarck. But no revolution had destroyed Prussia's *ancien régime*: the army reformed by Scharnhorst after Jena preserved the traditions of the earlier Hohenzollern rulers.

They were remarkable men. Ability was manifest in the persistence and flexibility of the margrave Frederick William, the 'Great Elector', his acquisitiveness tempered by caution. King Frederick William I toiled devotedly to implement his heroic though limited vision of the state. Few men have been better equipped in mind and temperament for the direction of an autocratic regime than Frederick II. Part of his claim to greatness lies, however, in his epic response to the challenge of a war, brought on by his own act of aggression, and the cause of appalling suffering and loss to his country. 'The world does not rest more securely on the shoulders of Atlas than does Prussia on such an army,' declared Frederick after his victory at Hohenfriedburg in 1745. But it is questionable whether the existence of such an army, his chief inheritance from his father, its great size out of all proportion to the resources of the country, was conducive to wise statesmanship or the well-being of the people. In Prussia, the state existed as much for the army as the army for the state. The tendency can also be observed in Louis XIV's France and in Peter the Great's Russia; but nowhere else was the logic of militarism so extreme in application, so little checked by tradition or alternative policies. In scale and character, in the combination of centralized administration and military methods, the work of the Hohenzollerns was indeed unique. The Thirty Years War had stirred venturesome, power-hungry princes throughout Germany; only in Brandenburg did an enduring power structure emerge.

If an objective and well-informed observer of German affairs had been asked in 1648 which of the German states, Austria apart, would play the greatest part in the ensuing years, it is likely that he would have selected Bavaria or Saxony; they were larger and richer, their rulers esteemed among their fellow princes. Bavarian government, under the electors Maximilian and Ferdinand Maria, was absolute and pretentious. Bavaria had acquired the Upper Palatinate and her ruler electoral rank during the Thirty Years War. Her lands had been cruelly ravaged and an intolerant Catholic policy militated against a rapid recovery of population. But that was roughly in line with the instincts of a people accustomed to a paternalist state and priesthood. If the wealth of the Church inhibited economic development, as in Austria, it also provided a useful counterweight to the power of crown and nobles. Bavarian autocracy demanded less in taxes than the Prussian, and spent less of what was collected on the army. The peasantry had more land and were less oppressed by feudal dues and labour services. As in Saxony, it had been the policy of previous rulers to encourage peasant smallholders in order to curtail the power of the nobles. During the Thirty Years War John George of Saxony had been the only important rival to Maximilian for the leadership of the princes in the confused situation arising from religious and dynastic rivalries and territorial ambition. John George was a fairly ineffective conservative. The Saxon estates were relatively strong; Saxon absolutism was muted and easy-going. By material standards, Saxony or Bavaria were better places for the mass of the people to live than

Brandenburg. In part that was a matter of soil and resources. It also, however, reflects the character and aims of the rulers. For Frederick William, and for his successors in the tradition that he established, the demands of the state were paramount. In the stringent conditions imposed by infertile and thinly populated lands, faced by the new challenges of postwar Germany, the Hohenzollerns worked for survival and strength by exploiting their few assets and forcing their scanty population to serve their dynastic interests, with a single-mindedness and lack of sentiment that sets them apart from their chief rivals.

Besides the quality of the ruler and his distinctive response to the political and economic challenges, the rise of Brandenburg may also be seen as the product of new conditions in Europe after 1648. That year was a landmark in the decline of the Empire as a political and moral authority in Germany. The retreat was not sudden, nor was reappraisal complete, as will be seen; for the Habsburgs, like the vassal princes of the Empire, continued to wish to have the best of all possible worlds. But, after the failure of the policy of restitution of Church lands during the German wars, as later after the victorious wars against the Turks and the recovery of Hungary, there was a perceptible change in Habsburg objectives. Imperial authority was still valuable for diplomatic purposes; but it was effective precisely because it was seldom used to justify political interference in the affairs of the German states. The failure of Ferdinand II and Wallenstein's grand conception of a military empire reaching to the shores of the Baltic had left a vacuum for the northern powers to exploit. For political and commercial reasons, the struggle for mastery of the Baltic sea and shores affected not only Sweden, Denmark and Poland but directly or indirectly every European power. To draw the maximum advantage from this struggle was to be one of Frederick William's prime aims. His success, though limited by the requirements of his French patrons and the paucity of his own resources, laid down the lines for the future development of the state. No less crucial were the methods of taxation which he adopted to provide the military strength to achieve his diplomatic objectives. There was a general rise in the scale of armaments in Europe as France's example was followed by the other great powers. In the coalition wars that followed France's invasion of Holland in 1672 – that grand blunder – Louis XIV and his enemies were bidding for alliances and troops with lavish subsidies. Several German princes, like John George of Hanover, accepted doles and levied taxes on their subjects to provide a bigger army and then used that army as a lever to bargain for further subsidies.

The competitive arms drive was not confined to Brandenburg but it was there most skilfully integrated with the business of state building. In furthering that business, the elector enjoyed hidden advantages in what otherwise seemed to be the greatest of his misfortunes. After a century of relative decline in economic activity, reflected in the impoverishment of

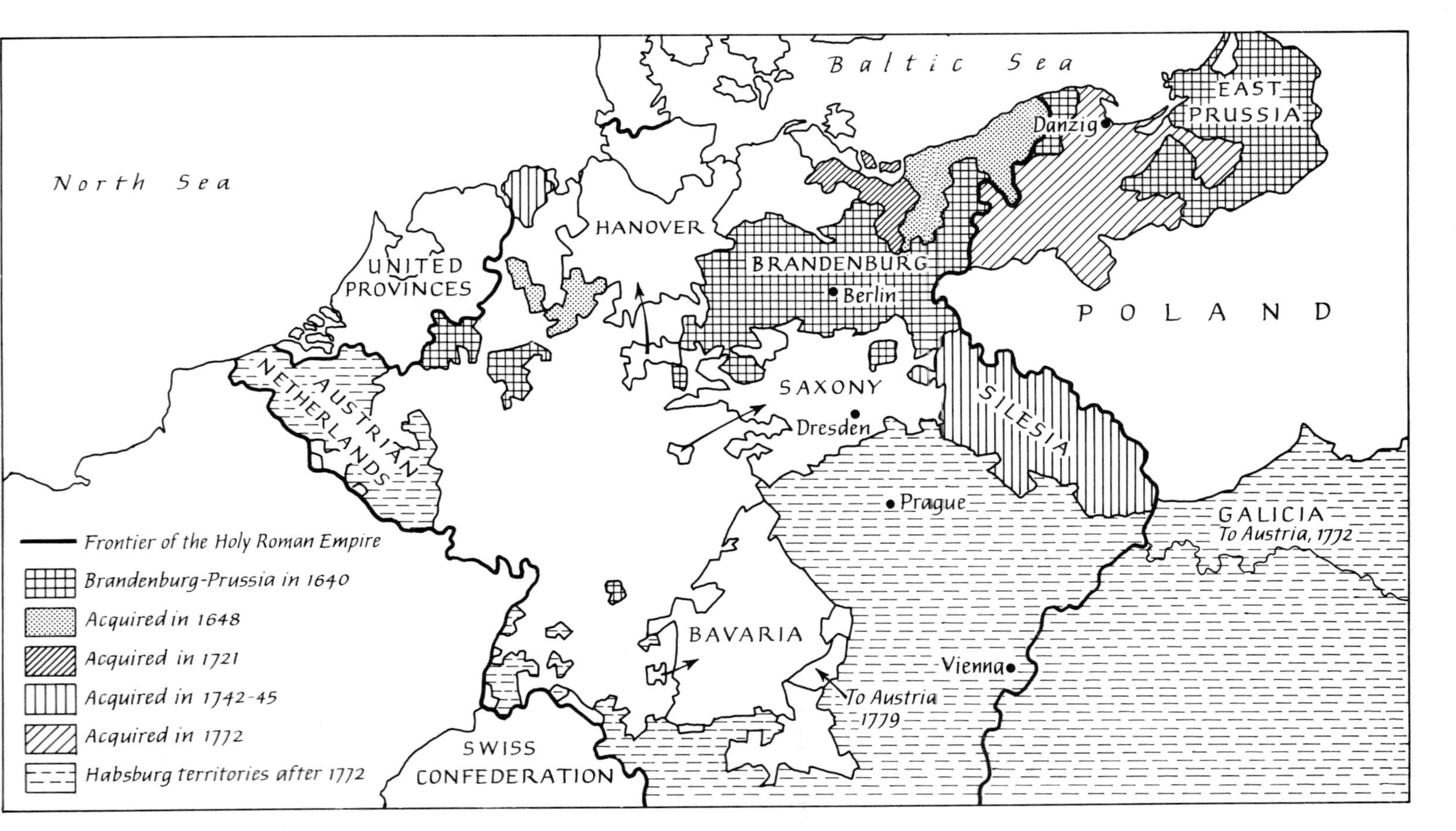

Map 11.1 *The growth of Brandenburg–Prussia, 1648–1772*

many German towns, the Thirty Years War had brought new dimensions of human suffering and economic damage. Demographically, Germany had suffered the greatest calamity since the Black Death of the fourteenth century, although the pattern of loss was less even, and the economy more resilient than in that all-devouring plague. Few areas of Germany had suffered more than Brandenburg, and few could so ill afford to suffer such loss at all. Yet by skilful management, and by good luck, Frederick William wrested political advantage from his impoverished lands. For as the wealth and security of landowners and merchants had declined so too had their will and means to resist the advance of government through the constitutional bodies which still provided, in theory and recent usage, the means to check a ruler's attempts to enlarge his powers or raise new taxes. Frederick William, knowing what he wanted, impatient of tradition and prepared to do a deal with his most powerful subjects, built a fortress base from which to govern on his own terms. It was how he conceived his duty to a dynasty which might be parvenu by Habsburg or Wittelsbach standards but lacked neither resources nor tradition.

Since the day in 1417 in the market place at Constance when the Emperor had invested Frederick I of Brandenburg with the dignity of elector in return for his oath of allegiance, the house of Hohenzollern had held its place among the greater princes of Germany. Frederick 'Irontooth' (1440–70) had acquired the New Mark from the Teutonic Knights and curbed the power of the towns. In 1511 Albert, a Hohenzollern cousin, was elected to the Grandmastership of the Teutonic Order; after the Reformation, in 1525, its lands were converted into a hereditary duchy for himself and his heirs, though held by him as vassal of the king of Poland. After the death, in 1618, of the childless Albert Frederick of Prussia, his duchy was united to the electoral house. The legacy of the Teutonic Knights, colonizers by virtue of cross and sword, business-like with their professional officials and financial expertise, can be recognized in the subsequent evolution of Hohenzollern government. As elsewhere, the study and dissemination of Roman law helped to foster theories about sovereignty: the University of Frankfurt an der Oder became a noted centre for such studies. The Reformation might also have been expected, as in England and Sweden, to take the ruler some way along the road to absolute monarchy, since he acquired control over the Church and further economic resources from Church lands. As in England, however, the gains of the ruler were offset by the relatively greater gains of some of his leading subjects.

The combination of princely extravagance, rising prices, and the grant or sale of lands created a new constitutional situation, in which successive margraves retained goodwill at the expense of crucial concessions. In 1540, in return for a money grant, Joachim II undertook to decide nothing that affected the country's well-being, and to make no move in foreign policy, without the consent of the Estates. In 1549, the Estates took over the collection and administration of tolls and taxes. In 1610, according to the principle of *Indigenat*, all offices and benefices were reserved for Brandenburg noblemen. The first Brandenburg forces mobilized in the Thirty Years War were officered entirely by native noblemen, nominated jointly by margrave and Estates: all soldiers had to take their oath to both, and every military move required the consent of the Estates. In Prussia, the duke had to contend with the implications of Polish overlordship. After 1566, for example, the Estates were empowered, if ever a duke infringed their privileges, to ask the king of Poland to maintain them. Any alliance needed the consent of the Estates and of the king. Prussian noblemen always looked enviously at the liberties of their Polish counterparts who could attend a diet where each representative enjoyed the right of veto. A more remarkable man than George William (1619–40), elector during most of the German war, might have found it hard to pursue an effective policy under such constraints. No wonder that he trailed hopefully in the wake of the Emperor, and suffered accordingly from the collapse of Habsburg plans to recover Church lands and imperial authority in Germany. Not until the Habsburgs abandoned that policy and France began to assert herself more effectively in German affairs was there any solid ground for a more independent diplomacy.

The Great Elector

Frederick William (1640–88) was styled, in the preamble to the treaty of Wehlau (1657), margrave of Brandenburg, head chamberlain of the Holy Roman Empire, and electoral prince of Magdeburg, Prussia, Jülich, Cleves, Münster, Stettin, Pomerania, the Cassubians and Vandals; also duke of Crosna and Carnovia in Silesia, burgrave of Nuremberg; prince of Halberstadt and Minden; count of Mark and Ravensberg and lord in Ravenstein. The miscellany of titles summarizes a history of acquisitions and inheritances; it also reminds us that sovereignty was exercised in each part by virtue of his title in that part. There were several embryos but there was nothing of an organic state. When the titles are transposed into places on the map, the practical problems of government become evident. From Rhine and Meuse to Niemen, the Hohenzollern lands were spread out across the German plain. East Prussia, which remained fief of Poland till 1657, was separated from Brandenburg by the bulk of Polish West Prussia (containing Danzig and the mouth of the Vistula); also by Eastern Pomerania, the poorer half of the duchy which was claimed by the Hohenzollerns after Duke Bogislav's death in 1637, on the basis of an old agreement, but was divided with Sweden in 1648 to provide that country with 'satisfaction' for her war effort. Magdeburg, the reversion to which was also ceded in 1648, was adjacent to Brandenburg. Minden, Ravensberg and Osnabrück were 200 kilometres to the west. Mark and Cleves (the latter on the Rhine), acquired with Ravensberg by the treaty of Xanten (1614) which settled one of the most tangled succession questions of the century, complete the tally of states under direct rule. In 1648 the population of all these lands was about 700,000. Lacking in natural frontiers and open to invasion, particularly from Sweden, Brandenburg had suffered most severely from the war. Berlin had 6000 inhabitants compared with 14,000 in 1618, Frankfurt an der Oder 2000 instead of 12,000.

It was a small inheritance, much spoiled, poor in assets and prospects. Brandenburg was for the most part a featureless country of sandy soil and scattered woodlands of birch and fir, similar to the Breckland of East Anglia. The population density – about 13 to the square kilometre against Saxony's 55 or Bavaria's 45 – tells its own tale. The figures reflect the war losses, higher than 50 per cent in east Brandenburg (as in Pomerania) compared to 10 per cent in most of Saxony. Whole districts had been so ravaged that they had reverted to waste; small towns had lost their function as market centres. The war had accentuated the trend of the previous hundred years, a period in which landowners developed large estates. They provided their own services, breweries, tanneries and transport, thus curtailing the role of all but the larger towns as markets, suppliers of craftsmen and specialized industries, and employed direct labour from their peasants rather than receiving rents in the western style. There were obstacles in the way of enlarging the demesne farms at the expense of peasants' holdings, since the German peasant, unlike the Polish, had legal rights and could not be arbitrarily evicted. Enclosure was therefore piecemeal and gradual. Mainly because of their financial interest the princes of Prussia, Pomerania and Brandenburg did not oppose their nobles' efforts to have the law amended to facilitate enclosure. War also swept clear large tracts; peasant refugees returned to find they could not prove title or recover rights. Unpromising land was put to the best use, and north-east Germany joined Poland as grain producer for the Mediterranean countries. The social and political effects were momentous. The *Junker*, dispenser of justice, patron of schoolmaster and minister, indeed master of every aspect of the peasant's life, enjoyed a growing influence in the estates; townsmen were also represented there but their economic base was crumbling at the same time as that of the *Junkers* was being reinforced. The Hohenzollerns did not, like the early Stuarts, feel themselves irreconcilably opposed to their most powerful subjects; they accepted the *Junker* supremacy and worked with it for their own ends. They based government and army upon alliance with the dynamic capitalist class. Whereas in western Europe that class was largely composed of townsfolk and merchants, in north-east Germany it was the landowners, aiming beyond self-sufficiency for an increasing margin of profit.

Samuel Pufendorf (1632–94), a Saxon, and professor of international law at Heidelberg, was for a time Frederick William I's privy councillor and historiographer. In his pamphlet, *De statu imperii Germanici* (1667), which became a textbook in Swedish and German universities, he offers an interpretation of the Thirty Years War, and of the role of Brandenburg, which put the 'Great Elector' and his policy in the best possible light. The war, in this view, was largely caused by religious dissensions exploited by Austria, a 'foreign power'; Brandenburg suffered especially because of the failure of George William (1619–40) to identify himself clearly with the German patriotic party. His successor exploited this over-simplified view of events to justify his own tortuous and brutal policies. Posing as a 'good German', he made and broke alliances without scruple. This champion of 'German liberties' browbeat the Estates in each of his provinces, and secured the co-operation of the *Junkers* at the expense of an overburdened peasantry. It can be argued that strong government was preferable to the occupation of the country by foreign armies; within his own terms of reference Frederick William did well. Inevitably his achievements cast a backward shadow over the reign of his unfortunate father. George William had followed the path of appeasement; latterly he had become a mere spectator of events. When he died he was a refugee in Prussia and most of Brandenburg was occupied by the Swedes. To Cleves and Mark he clung 'as to an eel's tail'.

George William's reign had illustrated the vulnerable position of any ruler who did not arm himself for survival in the competitive world of the military powers, old and new. Frederick William's boyhood had provided some painful lessons in the ways of that world: once, he had had to hide in the forest of Letzlingen to escape invading troops. Watching the abortive though ambitious efforts of his father's minister, Schwarzenberg, to strengthen the electoral government he resolved that he would be his own first minister: Schwarzenberg's death in 1641 enabled him to take over almost at once. He admired the Swedish king Gustavus Adolphus for demonstrating what a small country could do once the ruler had gained control over his subjects, but he also determined to oust the Swedes from their German footholds. Even more important for the Grand Elector was the example of Holland. The United Provinces, in the later stages of the great war against Spain, may be compared to Israel in the fifties and sixties of the twentieth century. The siege mentality did not inhibit, but actively fostered the creative, inventive spirit of a community in which scientists, soldiers, administrators and artists felt themselves engaged co-productively in a heroic enterprise: among the Dutch militant Calvinism went hand in hand with open-minded exploitation of economic assets. Frederick William was 15 when he was sent to Holland for safety and education. He spent four years there, at Leyden University, and in the entourage of the *stadholder* Frederick Henry. In long letters to his father, describing Frederick Henry's campaigns, and illustrating them with sketches, he evinced the beginnings of his life-long interest in war. From his mother Elizabeth Charlotte of the

Palatinate, and from his great-grandfather, William the Silent, he had inherited the ideals of the foremost Calvinist families. As a boy, he adopted for his motto the words of the Psalmist: 'Cause me to know the way wherein I should walk for I lift my soul up to thee.' Under Dutch influence, his devout Calvinism broadened into a rule of life. Under the exigencies of political struggle his outlook coarsened. The tender, intelligent Louise Henrietta, the daughter of Frederick Henry, whom he married in 1646, played her part in restraining his imperious instincts. After her death in 1667, a second marriage brought a stiff broom, and a governessy manner, to bear on the household in the shape of Dorothea, widow of the duke of Brunswick. Throughout, his severely purposeful life was grounded essentially on the powerful Calvinist conceptions of an omnipotent God, the receipt by the elect of His special grace, and the need to justify election by austere and dutiful conduct. His rising fortunes were to be a clear token that he was earning God's approval.

To this prince it may have been clear in 1640 that the idea of a German empire in which the princes sought to act together in defence of the constitution under Habsburg patronage had no future. That had been the reasoning behind the peace of Prague in 1635, at which John George of Saxony, followed by George William, had made his peace with the Emperor. But the continued military presence of Sweden and France, the swift military decline of the Habsburgs in the later stages of the war, suggested that safety lay in an independent diplomacy emancipated from the imperial tradition. The army, if it can be called such, consisted of some 2000 demoralized men, dispersed in garrisons. Schwarzenberg had understood the need to break the power of the estates, but was evidently powerless to do it. Military and economic deficiencies and constitutional traditions were knotted together in a bundle of weakness. The Hohenzollern lands would forever be at risk unless the elector could recruit and maintain a disciplined army. The war showed that a ruler's problems were only beginning when he succeeded in recruiting a sufficiently large army to carry out his immediate objectives: Austrian, Bavarian, Swedish armies had each degenerated to the point at which their master's aims were foiled, their authority compromised. Regular pay and supplies depended on regular taxes which, given so small a population, must be at an unprecedented level. The estates must therefore be persuaded if the elector were to have adequate force behind him. Add the fact that taxes, even if granted, depended upon the condition of farming and trade, both severely affected by war, and it becomes clear that, for Frederick William, the stakes were high, the options few. Despite early setbacks, notably in Cleves, where he failed to secure from the Estates the requisite supplies to pursue his forays into Berg, held by his Catholic rival of Palatinate–Neuberg, it is his skill and resource in operating within a limited range of options that commands admiration. In the negotiations that led to the peace of Westphalia, and at the famous recess of the Brandenburg Estates in 1653, he gained room to manoeuvre for subsequent more ambitious operations.

A recess was a meeting of a comparatively small number of representatives rather than a full diet. The diet of Brandenburg, convoked the year before, had been so obstructive that the elector resorted to calling the smaller body. At the time, the agreement between elector and representatives had the appearance of a compromise, even something of a surrender on the part of the elector. He confirmed the principle of *Indigenat*, though it flatly contradicted his absolutist principles and the centralizing policies of his regime. He made an easy promise to consult the Estates about alliances and other foreign policy matters, knowing that the Estates had already given up trying to influence foreign policy. He confirmed the lord's rights of jurisdiction and police and provided penalties against a subject's appealing against his lord's decision without sufficient cause. He reaffirmed the condition of serfdom where it already existed: the onus of proving that he was free was to rest on the peasant. On him too, rested the burden of the unofficial social compact by which the nobility yielded control of the purse, and with it political control and responsibility, in return for the consolidation of an oppressive landowning regime. For this, the elector gained consent to a tax of 530,000 *thalers* spread over six years: after five years of having to rely on forced levies to maintain his tiny peacetime army, he had now established a principle and precedent. The timing was significant. In France, the Fronde had just collapsed. In England, Cromwell was groping towards a new-style autocracy. In Russia, the paternalist tsar was emerging strongly from the revolts that had threatened his authority. The elector's achievement, like his grant, might appear comparatively modest. It was the beginning, not the end, of his constitutional tussles. But it enabled him to wrest more advantage from the northern war than appeared likely when Charles X of Sweden first overran Poland and then led his army into Prussia, forcing the elector to parley. The treaty of Königsberg (January 1656) gave him the bishopric of Ermland – but he had to accept the suzerainty of Sweden, in place of that of Poland, in Prussia.

When all credit has been given to the elector for skill and good timing, there remains the element of luck. It was apparent in Mazarin's generous patronage at Westphalia. It was also fortunate that the Poles rallied unexpectedly in the face of the Swedish onslaught: with the forces that rendered more evenly balanced the alliance of Brandenburg became once more worth paying for. And so the elector won from the Swedes renunciation of sovereignty over Prussia, and accepted it without reference to Poland (November 1656). As a result, when Denmark attacked Sweden he was left to face the outraged Poles alone. He might have regretted his unscrupulous conduct if the Habsburgs had not intervened. The Emperor Ferdinand III had just died, and his son Leopold needed Brandenburg's vote in the imperial election. His agent, Lisola, therefore mediated between Poland and

Brandenburg. At the subsequent treaty of Wehlau in 1657 Frederick William gained the full sovereignty in Prussia which so greatly enhanced his status among his fellow princes.

Meanwhile Frederick William had used successive emergencies as argument or pretext for raising taxes and conscripting troops. When Louis XIV invaded Holland in 1672, the Elector had a standing army of 20,000. He joined the coalition formed to aid the Dutch; received a sharp lesson in 1672 when only a swift retreat saved his troops from being cut off by Turenne; kept out of trouble in 1673; but rejoined the coalition in 1674. A Brandenburg contingent fought at Seneffe, Condé's bloody victory of August 1674. But it was a smaller battle that brought the elector his first success. In June 1675, at Fehrbellin, with Marshal Derfflinger, he directed his troops in a famous and fruitful victory over the Swedes, swept on into Swedish Pomerania and captured Stettin. By the end of the Franco-Dutch war, Frederick William was in possession of Stralsund and Stettin; in the winter of 1678–9 he repulsed a Swedish army sent to recover the province. But the subsequent peace negotiations brought bitter disappointment. Demonstrating the value of their alliance, the French were able to insist upon the return of Western Pomerania to their client Sweden. Realist as ever, he turned his back upon the Habsburgs who had so let him down and accepted French subsidies. Only when Louis's seizure of Strasbourg and other 'reunions' threatened further aggression against Germany, did Frederick William prepare for the last of his diplomatic somersaults. The Emperor's brilliant success at Vienna against the Turks in 1683 and Louis XIV's assault upon the Huguenots, provided political and moral arguments. So the 'Great Elector', as he was called after Fehrbellin, welcomed Huguenot immigrants and returned to the Imperial–Dutch alliance. In all his tortuous dealings, it is likely that it was there that his true sympathies lay, overlaid as they had been by tactical considerations. His choice of password for the Guard at Potsdam issued on the day before his death, on 9 May 1688, may have been significant: 'Amsterdam and London.'

The Great Elector had not begun with a set plan of making himself absolute but was prompted, in successive emergencies, by the paramount need to build up his army to adopt unconstitutional methods. He was forced often to take the short-term political and tactical view. Were his measures to assist a backward economy narrowly fiscal in purpose? Would he have regarded the nearly fourfold increase in the annual revenue of the state as a sufficient measure of the achievement of his reign? He was certainly aware of the importance of accurate information about his subjects. He ordered the publication of annual *Populationslisten* for Berlin and Brandenburg. His 'mercantilism' was plainly imitative but there is evidence of an adventurous spirit in some of his enterprises: he built a small fleet of ships under the supervision of his Dutch director-general of the navy, Benjamin Raule; he bought a trading post in the West Indies and founded Great

Fredericksburg on the coast of west Africa. Though his squadron fought in a modestly successful encounter with the Spanish in 1681, none of these enterprises prospered. A better use for the meagre capital available was the great Oder–Spree canal linking the Oder and Elbe and diverting Silesian traffic away from Swedish Stettin.

He was alive to the importance of internal colonization. Drawn by financial incentives and the prospect of religious tolerance, Lutherans came from the Palatinate, Calvinists from Saxony. Over 20,000 Huguenots settled after 1685, many of them in Berlin, making a vital contribution to the economy. In customary fashion the elector was swift to exploit a situation. An electoral edict stated, in detail, the rights and benefits that he proposed to give the French expatriates. They were to have free transport, passport facilities, building materials for repairing ruined houses and money to set up businesses. In short, they were treated as favoured citizens. The edict of Potsdam demonstrates the meticulous Hohenzollern paternalism at its most astute. More commonplace were his measures to promote manufactures. State companies were set up, for the production of textiles, glassware, iron, copper, paper and other basic goods which otherwise would have to be imported. Such conventional attempts at economic planning could not make Brandenburg self-sufficient, and the country relied heavily on the export of primary products to pay for imported manufactures. But the elector's enterprises ensured scope for the skill of immigrants and at least the basis for future growth. His policy of stimulating productive enterprise was practicable because of the network of revenue and recruiting officers, and balanced by the artificial separation of town and country for the purpose of collecting the excise. Industry was prohibited in villages, and townsmen were discouraged from buying land. Again, the decisive reforms took place in Brandenburg, under the elector's eye, and under the stimulus of war. The *Generalkriegskommissariat* came into being during the first Northern War in 1655, with responsibility for all financial matters concerned with the army – as most were. During the Dutch War, a *Feldkriegskasse* was instituted, a central treasury to which the provincial chests had to account. The commissars, whose credit depended entirely upon their success in exacting taxes, were responsible to their ruler alone, scornful of local rights, and the élite of the new military state. Their duties extended beyond the collection of taxes into the field of general economic management.

The excise upon towns, a copy of the Dutch tax, was a logical step towards broadening the basis of the elector's revenues which till then had been derived from his own land, rents, and the *contributio* – whatever the Estates offered or the elector took. It has to be confined to the towns, because the nobles would not renounce their privilege of exemption from taxation. It was calmly received: rates were not crippling and the tax did establish, in theory, a common interest between ruler and burgomasters in a prosperous urban economy. The preamble of the elector's order establishing the excise in Brandenburg (1667) spoke of 'the poor and needy condition of our towns' and of the need 'to save them from final ruin' and to distribute the public burdens more fairly. It was fair in that it bore on all inhabitants, 'each contributing much or little according to whether his consumption is large or small'. It would have been fairer still if the nobility had not so successfully upheld their privilege of exemption from taxation that towns under noble jusisdiction became exempt. There was more at stake in this than fiscal privilege. The nobles realized that the excise could grow to the point at which the elector would no longer be dependent on the Estates. Although it was at first entrusted to town officials, it was soon taken over by the elector's men, responsible to him alone. All goods brought into a town were checked and listed at the gates. For all transactions, an excise receipt had to be shown. Powers of search and confiscation led to bullying; low payment meant that officials were susceptible to bribes. With the spread of the excise came the inevitable inflation of office. In tiny Halberstadt, most modest of the elector's principalities, there were some seventy officials. However, the development of the excise brought the elector valuable dividends. It contributed to the dramatic alteration, within a virtually static north European economy, in the balance between the income of the public and private sectors of society. The towns may have gained in security, but their citizens had to pay an unremitting, inescapable levy. At the same time they lost all but the vestiges of self-government. No politically mature middle class could develop under these circumstances. Already the eighteenth-century pattern was taking shape: that of docile burghers, an all pervading bureaucracy, a privileged and complacent *Junker*-dom. Here were subjects who would do what they were told.

During the Northern War, the elector recruited troops and seized taxes without waiting for the estates to make their grants. At one point, in 1659, more than 100,000 *thalers* a month were being collected in Brandenburg, twelve times the prewar levy. The Estates of Cleves–Mark, which had been in such a strong position at the start of the reign, because of remoteness from Berlin, were offered a settlement in 1660, to be accepted on pain of military execution. In effect they were required to trade the grant of regular subsidies (about the same per head of population as those of Brandenburg) for confirmation of their rights: to free assembly and to the limitation of offices to natives of the duchies. That was as far as Hohenzollern power was to go in these pastoral lands, where the inhabitants lived in modest prosperity, unaware of the mineral wealth beneath their soil which was to make it the industrial heart of modern Germany. The elector did not impose the excise there, unwilling apparently to support his *Oberkommissar* against the officials of the estates.

The experience of Cleves–Mark provides a valuable insight into the elector's thinking. He could only envisage local government as being carried on by landowners, and of the authority of the state as being upheld by an alliance of landowners and princes. The mild landowners of the west, content with tax exemption, were a different breed from the corn-farming, serf-owning eastern *Junkers*. The elector could not transplant the *Junker* and the social structure of the east; and so, with typical realism, he left well alone. By contrast, Prussian society provided some of the essential preconditions for his strategy; it was on Prussia therefore that he concentrated his attack in the second half of the reign. There, the pro-Polish party among the nobles had the support of Königsberg merchants who resented the elector's tolls because they damaged the city's trade. With its 40,000 inhabitants, Königsberg was easily the largest city in the elector's domains. With its busy export trade in rye, hemp, flax, tallow and malt, and no less than eighty-two craft guilds (according to a list of 1671), it was the one place with anything comparable to the civic pride and independence of the trading cities of the west. The elector had good reason to suspect the burghers of leaning towards Poland. Like the *Junkers*, they wished to be left in peace, to enjoy the privileges of a frontier province without the burdens; they recognized no obligation to the Emperor, no need to support the territorial ambitions of the house of Hohenzollern. Fortunately for Frederick William, who could not sustain his army without Prussian taxes, the Prussians were divided. In Königsberg, as in western cities like Bordeaux and Amsterdam, the merchant princes feared the levelling tendencies of the less affluent tradesmen. The estates were separate, each having its own system of assessing and paying taxes. When in 1661 the urban commons, led by the lawyer Hieronymus Roth, declared that the transfer of sovereignty to Prussia was invalid without their consent and sent a deputation to King John Casimir to ask for his support, the aldermen of Königsberg repudiated their action. The city was unable therefore to resist the elector's army; Roth was abducted and imprisoned, and resistance was crushed.

Such brusquely efficient use of his army, maintained on a war footing by the elector, underlines the importance of his deal with the estates of Brandenburg ten years before. In their turn, and in return for concessions (1663), the Prussian estates recognized Frederick William's sovereignty and granted taxes. With triennial diets and formal control of taxation in their hands, Prussian 'liberties', in the narrow upper-class sense of the word, seemed to be intact. But there was no doubt who was master. In 1670 Christian von Kalckstein, the leader of the pro-Polish party, who continued to agitate against the extension of Hohenzollern government, was abducted from Warsaw by the Brandenburg envoy, and was tortured and executed, in defiance of international law and noble privilege. The billeting of soldiers upon the townspeople was enough to bring Königsberg to heel after renewed resistance to tax demands in 1674. The *Junkers*, who resented having to pay the land tax, repeatedly urged the elector to impose the excise which he had recently introduced into Brandenburg. Empirical as always, concerned more with political than with economic advantage, Frederick

William refused to change a system which offered such scope to divide and conquer. While the estates drifted further apart, the officials of the new *Generalkriegskommissariat* began to take over the work of natives. In the course of time the *Junkers* fell into line with those of Brandenburg and accepted service in the expanding state organization. As elsewhere we see the pressure behind the expansion of bureaucracy and army: both offered an honourable alternative way of life to landless younger sons of landowners in a virtually static economy. They were taken out of a world of private lordships and loyalties into one of overriding obligation to the ruler. Meanwhile, at home, the head of the family was left undisturbed in the oversight of his estates. He might be appointed *Landrat* by the elector but he had previously been elected by his fellow *Junkers*. Since Frederick William had gained the political assets of a standing army under his sole direction, a regular income in the shape of the excise beyond the control of the estates, and a civil service to collect and spend it, he could afford to leave the peasantry to be managed by their natural masters.

The Power of the Sword

The reign of Frederick William's son, Frederick I (1688–1713), falls into two halves. In 1698, the fall of Eberhard von Danckelmann, a career official in the mould of the Great Elector, and his replacement by Kolbe von Wartenberg, ended a phase of prudent government. There ensued a change of policy and tone. Frederick lacked his father's ability and dedication to business. He was easily flattered and led. Wartenberg played on his vanity and taste for ceremony, to further his own ambition and provide for his family and friends. His policy was plausible: Frederick had inherited a strong bargaining position which he should use to win the title that would set him above all German princes. Only the Emperor could confer a crown. In 1700 he designated Frederick king in Prussia in return for renewing his father's treaty of alliance. It is much more a measure of the Great Elector's achievement than of the skill of Frederick's diplomacy that the alliance was held by the Emperor to be so valuable. It was a limited concession, since Prussia lay outside imperial territory. But its symbolic importance was great, as Prince Eugène realized when he said that the Emperor's ministers should be hung 'for their perfidious advice'. The coronation at Königsberg in the following year, staged with unprecedented pomp, raised the elector's prestige throughout his lands. The royal title was held only in respect of the former duchy of Prussia; but official institutions and armies throughout the Hohenzollern lands were now called royal. 'The redoubtable Prussian foot' of Churchill's phrase played a useful part in Marlborough's victory at Blenheim and in subsequent campaigns. After the overwhelming success of the allied armies in the War of the Spanish Succession, Frederick might claim to have chosen the right side – with a just reward. When his successor later gained Stettin and most of Western Pomerania in 1720, it was because France was too weak to support her old ally Sweden.

If Frederick had used his strength and enhanced status with more moderation his reputation would have rested securely upon a distinctive achievement. As it is his reign is usually seen as a diversion, at best a soft interlude between the iron, purposeful reigns of the two state-builders, his father and his son. 'Great in small matters, small in great' was to be Frederick II's verdict on his grandfather. Pretentious, histrionic, Frederick I is apparently the odd man out among the early Hohenzollerns though he might have been recognized by contemporaries of the Kaiser William II. Each man suffered from a physical disability: the Kaiser from a withered arm, Frederick from a spinal deformity that gave him a hunchback stoop. The power of his state serves only to emphasize the shortcomings of the man. Like the Kaiser, his descendant, indeed like Frederick II in 1740, Frederick I craved the glory but did not count the cost. Prussia was called on for an effort out of proportion to the resources of the minor power which, in relation to France, the Empire, Holland, it still was. It is possible that Frederick's commitment to the Grand Alliance lost Prussia the chance of intervening effectively in the great Northern War. It is certain that Frederick's ambition and extravagance nearly ruined his country. He left debts, mortgages, alienated rents and revenues. Along with the 600 horses in the royal stables, the bodyguard in crimson satin, the army of cooks, the *castrati* and all the hangers-on so contemptuously dismissed by his economical son, and the essential artificiality of the imported baroque style, should be weighed some positive contributions to the growth of a native culture. The palace of the Charlottenburg, named after his Hanoverian wife Sophia Charlotte, though it typified the obsession of so many German princes with the style and values of Louis XIV, is a beautiful building in its own right. Frederick founded the University of Halle in 1692, and academies of art and science. His wife, more discerning than he, patronized Leibnitz and Christian Wolff. All was *à la mode*, but there were positively good elements in the rational and tolerant ideas of Leibnitz. There was also a moral earnestness and commitment to social reform in the teaching of the king's Pietist protégés Spener and Francke, which was to inform the character of a university-trained middle class of officials, pastors and teachers; and there was fruitful ground for the raising of a native German culture more gracious, more sensitive in outlook and pursuits than that of the *Junkers*.

King Frederick William I (1713–40) perfected the military regime which was to survive till the battle of Jena in 1806 and the surrender of Prussia to Napoleon. 'It cannot be done with the pen if it is not supported by the power of the sword': Frederick William's words were the unofficial motto of the Hohenzollerns. As a young man, Frederick William served with Marlborough in Flanders. His conduct at Malplaquet earned the praise of Prince Eugène. Afterwards he conducted himself and his kingdom upon strict military principles. He was impressed, like his grandfather, by the sober, frugal ways of the Dutch, and disgusted by the waste and frivolity of his father's court, irrelevant as it seemed to be to the interests of the state. He saw that Prussia was being used as a pawn, her soldiers fighting other men's battles. The paramount objective, he held, must be independence; that was conditional upon possession of a large army and the resources to pay for it. Making no distinction therefore between fiddlers and pastry cooks, equerries and valets, he began his reign by dismantling his father's court, cutting staff and salaries to the bare minimum. His father had maintained 25 châteaux, he managed with 5. He was soon able to boast that he was no 'king for hire', unlike some of his fellow princes, but could fight 'at his own expense'. Under the Berliner Schloss, which housed the leading bureaucrats, he built a strongroom to house the treasure minted out of his father's gold and silver objects.

It was all the more urgent to work for independence because of the poor condition of the province of Prussia, afflicted in the early years of the century by plague and cattle disease. But it was not mere political or financial calculation that dictated his policy. From his Huguenot tutor Frederick William learned the stern Calvinist doctrine of predestination. It was not until he was 20 that he believed he was saved: the underlying anxiety remained to torment him, only to be assuaged by unremitting toil. He lived ever under God's judgements, acutely conscious of the penalties of failure. He gloried in the gospel of work, and looked for the outward signs that it was being well performed. Like a zealous *Hausfrau* he swept and scrubbed, peered into corners and hunted restlessly for irregularities. He was a sincere but obsessive moralist. 'Harlotry,' he would bellow, 'is the most terrible sin.' His faith in himself and the state he served so devotedly appeared to armour him against criticism. If his subjects did not like their medicine, that was proof that it was doing them good: he had no need of their love. There was surely a paranoid side to his brutal temper. He was tormented by the fear that round the corner, out of earshot, officials, servants, his wife and children, were mocking him. Physical ailments came with middle age: gout, migraine, piles, perhaps the porphyria (supposed to have been George III's malady) which brought mental deterioration along with such physical symptoms as stomach cramps; towards the end dropsy made him grotesquely fat and unwieldy. His normal peppery manner did not mean that he expected always to be taken literally, as for example when he threatened to have all his medical officials branded if they failed to check the plague in Prussia; he did have the corpse of one corrupt official displayed for several weeks outside the administrative building in Königsberg. He went to alarming extremes in his treatment of his elder son, the crown prince. He was driven into a frenzy by what he deemed Frederick's 'self-willed evil disposition'. He could not abide 'an effeminate chap who has no manly leanings, who to his shame can neither ride nor shoot, and at the same time is personally unclean, wears his hair long and curled like a fool.' The king himself was constantly washing and changing his shirt; men of his time were not usually so fastidious. He persecuted Frederick as if he saw, in the man whom he expected to continue his own good work, the embodiment of the traits he most despised. Frederick was musical, and enjoyed reading and writing. Might he not turn into another Frederick I, a waster of inheritances, more interested in the delights of court than in the labours of rule? Frederick William accordingly beat and mocked the unfortunate prince. In 1630 he compelled him to watch his friend von Katte being executed for his part in a plot to remove Frederick back to England; he even contemplated having him shot as a deserter from his beloved army. Frederick conformed, resentfully, even later with wry appreciation of his father's outlook, but at a cost to his own personality. He trained himself methodically and intensively for kingship. When the opportunity came he departed from his father's advice in one respect. In 1722 the latter wrote: 'I beseech my dear successor in God's name not to start any unjust wars and not to be an aggressor, for God has forbidden unjust wars and one day you will have to account for every man who has fallen in such a war.' Frederick invaded Silesia. After that initial coup, blunder or stroke of genius as it might be, Frederick was to spend his life in defending and restoring his inheritance. In his rational, fastidious way he was to prove as good a Hohenzollern, as zealous a manager, as devoted a servant of the state as ever his father had been. Frederick the Great was as much a legacy of the 'Drill-sergeant of Potsdam' as was the country he ruled.

Frederick William hated 'bad vassals', those who were reluctant to serve or inclined to argue, and any who did not belong to his narrow world, like Jews, artists and actors. He distrusted foreigners, and refused, for example, to let noblemen attend universities outside Prussia. The combination of his dynastic chauvinism and his naive interpretation of the foreign scene made him a laughing-stock among other princes. He despised intellectuals and artists, and was often scornful of the civilian officials of the state machine which he drove so relentlessly. He respected noblemen, if they were prepared to serve the dynasty, soldiers, hard-working craftsmen and peasants. His Table of Ranks of 1713 established a new order of precedence in accord with his idea of the superiority of the military to the civil branch: at the summit, a field marshal took precedence over the lord chamberlain and so on down the line. He liked to supervise and to regulate down to the smallest details. His code of conduct for the General Directory left little to chance: if they met after 1400 hours, 'we order our Marshal that he shall bring them food and drink and in such manner that half may eat while the others work'. If any minister or councillor came more than an hour late without leave, '100 ducats shall be deducted from his pay'. He had neither the temper nor the talent for political management. Not for him the subtleties of negotiation, for getting the best from men by appealing to ideals or satisfying needs. How different was his approach to that of a Walpole or a Fleury; but then so was his situation. Delegation required a sufficiency of educated men, used to certain rules and conventions, understanding and accepting the ruler's objectives; but Prussia's system, like the country, was raw. Rustic nobles, traditional functionaries, were fighting a rearguard action to preserve their own way of doing things.

In his bluff, direct style of government, with his insistence upon obedience and concern for what brought results and was practical, as in his contempt for polite conventions and his penchant for shock tactics, the king recalls the tsar Peter whom he so greatly admired. Like Peter, Frederick William spent much of his time travelling about his dominions, inspecting his officials, checking tax and rent rolls. He liked to visit cottages, workshops and customs stations, to see for himself what his subjects were doing. The arrival of the bulky king could be an alarming experience. In Potsdam, where he was most often to be found if not on tour, he once belaboured the postmaster with his stick when he found him asleep and neglecting his early morning customers. In nights spent with a few cronies discussing state affairs and army gossip over pipes and beer, he managed to combine business and pleasure: Peter would have felt at home at these 'tobacco parliaments'. As in Russia the army was the prime object, and the ultimate guarantor, of government. Frederick William started the practice which was to become a convention among European sovereigns, of wearing an officer's coat throughout the day. He personally wrote the Infantry Regulations (1715) which were to be influential in European armies for the rest of the century. The showpiece of his army was the celebrated regiment of giant grenadiers. They were recruited from all over Europe; his envoys were encouraged to recruit exceptionally tall men, even to kidnap them. Naively he would defend such unscrupulous practice by reference to his Bible, where in the First Book of Samuel, it was written, 'When Saul saw any strong and valiant man he took him unto himself'. His giants were not toy soldiers. Their exercises and tactics became the model for the whole army, which by 1740 was the fourth in size, though Prussia was but thirteenth in order in population, among European states. Its 80,000 men were equipped and drilled to the highest standard, and regularly paid. The king worked on the formula of the Great Elector: an officer corps drawn almost exclusively from the nobility supplied and trained their own men. It was a new-style feudalism in the service of the state, answering to both the military and political requirements of the ruler. In the development of this reign we see also the impress of a sovereign who expected subordination from all. As the military tradition was consolidated, there was a levelling process within the officer corps. From cadet to colonel there were no distinctive badges of rank: all, rich and poor, belonged to the same caste and had to accept the same discipline. They were expected to live in the image of their godly, self-denying king. Every commander sent him regular reports upon all aspect of the officers' lives. It was the ideal of Gustavus Adolphus: 'a godly army is an efficient army'.

Everywhere in Europe, younger sons, bred on the estate, receiving an education which qualified them to follow their fathers but deprived of the benefits of the estate, finding doors shut upon them as soon as they had reached their maturity, had been a prime cause of unrest in society. In Britain there were openings in politics, trade, an expanding navy and colonies. In Prussia, with its relatively limited economic opportunities, the army and bureaucracy expanded to provide honourable careers. Frederick William's achievement was to use the aristocratic principle in this most aristocratic of ages in such a way as to neutralize its more dangerous characteristics: its caste pride, contempt for political authority, separatism, its insistence upon privilege – all were subordinated to the overriding loyalty.

The Prussian army had to live and train on native soil. That posed problems of supply and discipline which affected the life of the community as well as the running of the state. There were scarcely enough peasants to meet farming needs; inevitably there were many foreigners among the rank and file. It was difficult for commanders to pay for them; ferocious discipline could not prevent, sometimes caused, widespread desertion. The solution lay in the development of an informal militia system. Officers recruited their own serfs, saving money for mercenaries and letting the serfs work on the land for much of the year. In 1733, Frederick William established the canton system and made the part-time army an official institution. In one respect it was the completion of the state of which a minister was later to write that it was 'not a country with an army but an army with a country which served as headquarters and food magazine'. At the same time, it was a realistic concession to the needs of the land: every peasant could be a soldier, but many soldiers could still be peasants. Prussia was divided into regimental cantons, subdivided further into company and squadron cantons (the latter for cavalry). The captain registered serf boys at the age of 10 and kept track of their progress. They were sent for military training for two years, thereafter released for farm work for most of each year. In early summer, between sowing and harvest, they went on manoeuvres. Even foreigners were given extended periods of leave to work as labourers. At the officer level, the army played a vital part in knitting the country together. The ordinary soldier played his part in the machine without disrupting the economy. The army thus consumed the minimum of labour while providing a steady market for goods. It played a crucial role in a protectionist economy and a centralized administration.

Frederick William's measures to protect and stimulate the economy also show his paternalism in a favourable light. His assumptions were traditional, his actions intelligent. He introduced a system of short leases in the hereditary lands and gave the lessee, the crown bailiff, as well as the customary feudal rights and dues, further powers which enabled him to improve the estate. By this means the king encouraged the growth, alongside the *Junkers*, of a new rural middle class, and ensured a regular and expanding cash revenue from his demesne. Through his commissaries, with their wide police powers, the government increased its control of industry and trade. Under their supervision the excise played the main part in regulating the flow of trade to the advantage of home production. 'Mercantilist' measures of protection included the prohibition of imports of Polish grain (1732) and of the export of raw wool (1718); and of imports of foreign cloth and cotton. Prussia played the main part in securing an agreed measure of the imperial diet (a rare event) to curtail the excessive powers of journeymen, one of the worst faults of the German guild system, which remained stronger than in England or France, and a serious barrier to the advance of capitalism. In Prussia, however, a new industrial code (1732–5) brought the guilds under strict state supervision so that they became instruments of the government's industrial policy. In this field as well, old forms were adapted to serve the impersonal police state. It may seem that there was more efficiency, less freedom. Certainly the emphasis shifted, so far as the protection of an individual's rights were concerned, from the corporation or guild to the state. That does not seem to have deterred immigrants. Frederick William maintained the tolerant and welcoming attitudes of his predecessors. A large group, Protestants evicted by an intolerant bishop in 1632, came from Salzburg. Prussian agents were always on the look-out for promising citizens. Many seem, however, to have come without persuasion, attracted by empty lands or manufacturing jobs. By immigration and natural increase, the population of Brandenburg trebled in the course of the eighteenth century. It was the fastest rate of increase anywhere in Europe.

Besides his cherished army, Frederick William left his son a system of government which was the logical expression of his own reluctance to delegate and of his ideal of a bureaucracy disciplined like an army. 'One must serve the king with life and limb, with goods and chattels, with honour and conscience and surrender everything except salvation. The latter is reserved for God. But everything else must be mine.' All the more galling to the soldier king was the discord that existed between the two administrative bodies, the Great Elector's war commissariat, reorganized on Swedish collegiate lines in 1712, and his general finance directory, which controlled the royal lands by means of provincial chambers. Each of these bodies had gained ground from the antiquated relics of the estates; each in the process became infected by the possessiveness and jealousies characteristic of established officialdom. There was also a genuine conflict of interests: excise officials of the war commissariat wanted cheap food and fair prices for manufactures, while domain officials, mainly concerned with protecting rents and dues, worked for fair prices for farm products. Frederick William's solution, in 1723, was to merge the two bodies in a general directory, with six ministers as vice-presidents and some councillors. Each minister had a special responsibility for a particular area, together with special brief for a department; it might be post office, mint or army supplies, land utilization or boundaries. The king was to be president: 'I have command over my army, and should I not have command over a thousand damned pen-pushers?' In practice he rarely attended, preferring to govern by commands and minutes from his desk. But his portrait was hung over his empty chair in case ministers should need any reminder of his authority. It was unlikely. By example and exertions he instilled into those who served him the idea that work was good, service its own reward.

'Under Frederick I,' wrote Frederick II, 'Berlin was the Athens of the north; under Frederick William she became the Sparta.' But this was still a Sparta in the eighteenth-century manner: one of Frederick William's last notable actions was the appointment of Samuel von Cocceji to be minister of justice (1738) with a brief to compile a common body of law, with uniform procedures. Uniformity and rationality were prime aims of the 'enlightened' autocrats, though Frederick William was hardly 'enlightened' in the way that Christian Wolff would have understood the word. Wolff was expelled from Halle University and from Prussia (1723) because the Pietists argued that his ideas could be used to justify desertion from the army. Pietism dominated higher education, inculcating values of self-discipline, frugality and modesty that accorded well with the principles of the king, and the development of a sound bureaucracy. The king did not approve of higher education except as a vocational training, erected upon the broad base of elementary literacy which he envisaged when he ordered (1717) that there should be instruction in the three Rs and scripture for all up to the age of 12. To improve the standards of central government, he founded two chairs in cameralism or government studies, incorporating economics, administration and law. A significant contrast comes to mind. Much of the future course of two peoples was being determined, in the one case, by the methodical, vocational Prussian approach, and, in the other, by the complacently amateurish attitudes of young English gentlemen studying classical literature at Oxford and Cambridge, or preparing for public life by inspecting classical ruins on the 'grand tour'.

Frederick the Great

On an early summer's day in 1785, the year before Frederick II's death, Friedrich von der Marwitz watched his king returning to Berlin from an inspection of his lands:

> The whole Rondell and the Wilhelmstrasse were crammed with people; all the windows full, all heads bare, everywhere the deepest silence and on faces expressions of reverence and trust. The king quite alone in the

front, greeted people by continually taking off his hat.... The crowds stood still, bare-headed and silent, all eyes on the spot whence he had gone, and it took some time before a person collected himself and went quietly on his way.... Yet nothing had happened – an old man of seventy-three, shabbily dressed, covered in dust, had returned from his day's work. But everybody knew that this old man was toiling for him, that he had devoted his entire life to that labour and that he had not missed a single day's work in forty-five years.

Frederick II's state had expanded from 119,000 to 185,000 square kilometres. The population, despite heavy losses in war, had risen from 2.2 to 5.8 million. He had obtained Silesia by conquest, East Friesland by inheritance and West Prussia by negotiation from a position of irresistible strength. Berlin had grown, from 98,000 in 1740, to 150,000 by 1786, reflecting the growth of bureaucracy and the crafts and services required in a sophisticated capital city. He had directed indomitably and resourcefully, a war of survival; his state had grown larger and stronger and, potentially, richer; he had become the object of a cult. The young Goethe, considering the 'lawful misuses' of the imperial constitution and the 'lawless misuses' of the French, looked north where 'shone Frederick, the Pole Star, around whom Germany, Europe, even the world seemed to turn'. Among European statesmen he comes second only to Napoleon in the attention, and literature, he has subsequently attracted. However they might differ in emphasis upon aspects of his achievement, historians are agreed that his influence was immense and not confined to Prussia. Now, as then, his virtuosity on the battlefield commands attention. With the inventive spirit and the flair for the dramatic which never deserted him, he had perfected new tactics, notably the attack in oblique order, and kept his enemies guessing: opponents like Daun were criticized for being cautious – but they had reason to be so. In his first successful attack on Silesia (1740) and its subsequent defence, he acquired a moral superiority: by his brilliant victories of Rossbach over the French, in November 1757, and Leuthen over the Austrians, in the following month, he had enhanced it. Rossbach, Napoleon called 'a masterpiece of war'; at Leuthen he defied the accepted rules by attacking an enemy twice his strength. But the title 'Great' was truly earned after the catastrophe of Kunersdorf (August 1759) when his strategy was successfully countered by the Austrians and Russians. He wrote then 'of an army of 48,000 I have less than 3000 men left. All flee and I am no longer master of my men. Berlin must look to its own safety. This is a terrible event and I shall not survive it.' It was not the least of the miracles of the house of Brandenburg that he did survive it.

Kunersdorf and the desperate actions that followed showed that the outcome could have been tragically different for the state and the king who had put all at risk. Within five months of his accession in May 1740, he was writing to Voltaire that the death of the emperor Charles VI had 'destroyed all my peaceful thoughts'. In fact it had enabled him to put into action a long pondered project: one that had been considered by the Great Elector and was supported by several of the young king's advisers.

There was much to be said, if the author of *Anti-Machiavel* could set aside moral considerations, for taking the chance afforded by Austrian weakness to capitalize on his predecessor's gains and create a wider, richer basis for the Prussian state. There was an old claim to Silesia which Frederick's lawyers dressed up for public consumption. Frederick took it lightly though generations of Prussian schoolboys were thereafter to learn it by heart. Frederick William I had felt constrained to swallow his humiliation in 1738, when the emperor Charles VI repudiated Prussia's far stronger claim to the Rhenish provinces of Jülich and Berg. Now Frederick was not sorry to take the chance of avenging himself on the Habsburgs.

In December he invaded Silesia and so launched the sequence of wars, 1740–2, 1744–5, 1756–63, in which he fought to retain the province against Maria Theresa's resolute efforts to recover it: first in alliance with France, latterly in the Seven Years War, with Britain, but against France, Russia, Sweden and Saxony as well as Austria. Frederick incurred humiliation in his first action, at Mollwitz (1741), when he was escorted from the field, only to learn later that his infantry had held steady and won the day. The experience only sharpened his self-confessed craving to 'make a name for myself' and the interest in military science of which he became such an original and effective practitioner. But boldness was always thereafter tempered by prudence.

After the peace of Breslau (1745) which he hailed as the great and happy end of an event which 'brings one of Germany's most flourishing provinces into the possession of my house', he recognized the need 'to call a halt'. Unfortunately he could not do so. He underestimated the character of Maria Theresa, her resolve to recover a valuable part of her inheritance, and her ability to carry out, at the same time, reforms in army and administration which enabled the Austrians to fight on equal terms. He was virtually isolated by the diplomacy of Kaunitz and he was confronted, in the diplomatic manoeuvres of 1755–6, by the intransigence of the tsarina Elizabeth and her ministers. He was fortunate in the support of Britain and the strategic vision of Pitt, who appreciated the need to provide Frederick with large subsidies and a second army to contain and defeat the French. However, he tasted defeat and his country came near to ruin in bitterly fought campaigns. The old blue coat which he habitually wore, torn by bullet holes and roughly darned, witnessed to a style of royal generalship which Europe had not seen since the death of Charles XII. Frequently depressed, culpably careless on occasion in his preparations for battle, he exhibited a fatalistic kind of courage, balanced by the resilience which enabled him to rise repeatedly to the expectations of his devoted aides, foremost among them his younger brother, Henry, who was himself a capable soldier.

Somehow after Kunersdorf fresh levies were raised to fight for the new campaign. The victories of Liegnitz, Torgau and Burkersdorf show Frederick at his perceptive, tireless best. Yet he was close to despair again by the end of 1761. By then he had exhausted all possible expedients: he had debased the coinage, melted down silver and economized on the salaries of his much tried officials. With Prussia occupied by the Russian army and Silesia by the Austrians it looked as if he would have to concede peace on his enemy's terms.

Whether or not Frederick deserved fortune it came in spectacular fashion. The death of Tsarina Elizabeth and the accession of Tsar Peter III brought an immediate reversal of Russian policy: in May 1762 Russia withdrew from the war. During the next eighteen months successive treaties brought peace with Sweden, Austria and France. The Empire was brought into the general pacification with the conclusion, at Regensburg, of treaties of neutrality between Prussia and the electorates of Bavaria, the Palatinate and Cologne, and the duchy of Württemberg. Frederick was now set to adopt his new role, that of good imperialist. The next time Prussian forces were mobilized, in 1778, for the Potato War against Austria (so called because the manoeuvres of both armies were influenced more by the needs of the commissariat than by the desire to meet and fight the enemy), it was for the constitutional rights of Bavaria. It was an irony that he could well savour, for his own state was by then apparently secure. Frederick had done more than merely survive. The ceaseless strain of the Seven Years War had confirmed the soundness of the fiscal administration. During the war the army had been the essence of the state, with the king constantly in camp. No longer, as in the first war, could Frederick's axiom hold good: that 'the burgher should not be aware that the soldier is at war'. Between 1756 and 1763 the king was constantly on the move, usually within his lands, preoccupied with strategy and supply, marches and entrenchments. In all that time he made but one visit to Potsdam. Officials were used by Frederick primarily to expedite deliveries for the army. Not only was Frederick commander-in-chief; he was in effect war minister, for there was no other. The shared experience under arms, the loyalty of officials and their proven ability to rise to emergencies and provide the necessary means to carry on the war generated a further cohesion. It is that especially which distinguishes the second, creative period of peacetime government, that of 1763–86, from the first, the interlude, as it had proved, between wars.

The effect of war was devastating. As Frederick himself wrote in 1763:

> It is necessary to imagine whole countries ravaged, towns ruined completely, others half burnt, 13,000 houses of which not even the vestiges remain, lands not sown, inhabitants destitute of food, farmers lacking

> 60,000 horses for labour and in the provinces a decrease of 500,000 people, which is considerable in a population of 4,500,000 souls.

The king had no reason to exaggerate the extent of a disaster for which he might be called to account: we need not doubt the figures or their significance in the record of Frederick's reign as a whole. But war took up only 13 out of 46 years. Frederick, the manager of state business, was as accomplished as Frederick the soldier. He gave to the manifold, exacting tasks of Hohenzollern government the vigilance, method and self-fulfilling zeal that he had come to admire in his father, together with the luminous intelligence that gives to humdrum routines an air of distinction: the king's keen glance, his incisive, often caustic tones, bring the records to life.

His own voluminous writings, in particular those on political and philosophical subjects, reveal the facility that enabled him to hold his own with the *philosophes* and command their respect, even when they came to be disillusioned with views so much at odds with their own. He can be criticized for his excessively rational and mechanistic vision of society. But he never became the prisoner of theory. Like the self-appointed leaders of the Enlightenment who welcomed, on hearing of his first liberal acts, so fortunate a combination of intellectual and autocrat, subsequent generations have been attracted, or repelled or simply puzzled in ways that reflect the extremes and contradictions within his personality. They may warm to the talent of the patron who could design, with his architect Knobelsdorff, such an elegant rococo masterpiece as his palace of Sans-Souci, and of the flautist who also composed for his favourite instrument. They may then encounter the cruel, often crude wit, the callous militarism or the shallow, pretentious side: the egocentric young king's craving for fame at any price, the embattled veteran's vicious propaganda, the misanthropy of 'Old Fritz' who liked best to walk alone with his whippets. Among women he cared only for his eldest sister Augusta. He was childless; indeed his marriage with Christina Elizabeth of Brunswick was probably never consummated.

To some extent Frederick was the victim of his own publicity for it has obscured some of his better traits, notably his devotion to duty. He exemplified the cardinal principle of his political philosophy, that the state should have the first claim on the life of the king, as of his subjects. In 1741 he delivered a strict order to his minister Podewils, in case he should be captured: 'my orders in my absence are not to be followed and the state is not to do anything unworthy to obtain my release'. It was repeated during the Seven Years War when, several times, his cause apparently lost, he contemplated suicide. In war he never shrank from danger. 'Dogs, would ye live for ever?' he bellowed, as he rallied his faltering infantrymen at Kunersdorf. But in the ordinary dealings of life, starting with his frightening relationship with his father, he became an advanced student in the art of self-preservation: he had learned not only to conceal and to deceive, but also to separate the private world of a cultivated gentleman from the métier of a prince, and its disciplined labours.

He was bruised by the experience. A wretched note is sounded in some of his letters: he was 'heartily tired of life' or 'a poor God-forsaken man'. In camp, in 1759, De Catt recorded some conversations with the king 'whose intellect never slept'. 'You see me very busy reading and writing. I need the diversion from the gloomy thoughts that agitate me.' At such times he would enter into a second, no less real world. 'Some get drunk, I relax by versifying.' The intellectual and the artist came also, however, to find fulfilment in war and government, in a kingship which was the expression of a personality so self-conscious and self-sufficient, at the same time so gifted, that it is profitless to pursue the broader questions: was he 'enlightened' or was he a 'good German'? Like any other creative artist, Frederick deserves to be judged by his achievements.

The inheritance which Frederick fought so hard to extend was, at the outset, a favourable one. The collapse of Swedish power, the anarchic conditions in Poland under her Saxon kings, and the weakening grip of the Habsburgs over their outlying lands, make it easy to understand why the young king, like Louis XIV when he came to his inheritance, was keen to build on strength. The strength was not merely founded on his rivals' disarray. Specially significant was the dual character of Prussian rule. Like his neighbours Hanover and Brunswick, which also spent heavily on their armies, Frederick was bound by the laws of the Empire; but as ruler also of lands outside the Empire, he was able to circumvent the rulings of the imperial court and so to override the privileges of provinces, and of bodies and individuals within them, who should otherwise have been protected against arbitrary measures. So far from being committed in any dogmatic way to the principles of centralization, Frederick understood the need to respect local authorities and customs. He actually restored a semblance of power to the local estates by working through their nominated officials, the *Landrats*. In this, as in other ways, he reinforced the already high standing of the nobility. Personal preference apart, his policy was a reflection not of weakness but of confidence in his own ability to keep a grip on government. Nor would he have gone so far as his great-grandfather, who contemplated the subdivision of his lands among his heirs; but he always referred to 'my states'. Such particularism was less damaging to the Hohenzollerns than it was to the Habsburgs who had to contend with racial and linguistic differences as well. In the Prussian lands there was always more scope for positive action by the state. Like his father, Frederick gave priority to developing the economies of East Prussia, Silesia (after 1745) and, after the partition of Poland in 1772, West Prussia. The acquisition of that neglected province, whose recolonization and restoration was to be the chief object of Frederick's government in the last years of his life, completed the process which had begun with the Great Elector's acquisition of Eastern Pomerania, in

1648, by which the state came to be concentrated on the Baltic, its rivers and ports.

Servant of the State

The political essays of Frederick's bold youth and seasoned old age, *Anti-Machiavel* (1740) and *Essai sur les formes de gouvernement* (1777), both defined the monarch's role in idealistic terms. He was to be the first servant of the state. It is possible, for Frederick was of a more philosophical cast of mind than his father and readier to think in abstract terms, to distinguish between the outlook of the two men: the Calvinist Frederick William, concerned in traditional fashion with the dynasty; Frederick essentially secular and rational, thinking of the state. That state was not, however, conceived of in a mystical way but rather as the sum of the material interests of its subjects, making by virtue of their trust and dependence its own transcendent claims. In effect the function of the king remained much the same after 1740 as before. The emphasis was on duties rather than on rights; on utility rather than on ceremony. The tone was set at the outset when Frederick refused a solemn coronation. Even when he could live in his favourite Sans-Souci, the king's style was simple. Diplomatic visitors, accustomed to the pomp of thrones and lackeys, found a solitary, shabby person, his coat invariably dusty about the shoulders from his favourite snuff. Like his father he was reluctant to delegate in matters which he could deal with himself and he did not bother to conceal his contempt for slower men, even if they were his ministers. 'He does everything for himself ... ministers are mere drudges of limited importance.' The French ambassador's words of 1740 proved prescient in some respects. Frederick's way of running the state was that of a soldier, in peace as in war, direct, peremptory, unequivocal: as for officers, so for civilian officials, he preferred men of noble birth. Government was by personal decree. He was no more sentimental about introducing foreigners into government than he was about using mercenaries in the army. In 1765, needing to raise more money from the excise, he called in French customs officials and entrusted them with the management of the *régie*, a general form of the indirect taxes. By the end of the reign the *régie* was producing a sizeable surplus but at the cost of such antagonism from taxpayers and rival officials that Frederick had already felt compelled to reduce its powers. He may have seen it as a means of preventing the bureaucracy from controlling the whole fiscal system. With sons following fathers, the official body was acquiring traditions and interests of its own which, if allowed to develop unchecked, would have represented a check on that freedom of action which above all he sought to retain.

Perhaps inevitably, in a man who guided his state through such critical passages, in a commander whose army was controlled on the principle that a soldier had to be more afraid of his officer than of the enemy, the tone of government could be harsh, the judgements terrible. An extreme case was that of the Jesuit father Faulhaber. A recaptured deserter declared that he had told him at confession that while desertion was a great sin, it was one that could be forgiven. Frederick had Faulhaber hanged, without any kind of trial, and upon a gallows which had had the body of a deserter rotting on it for weeks. The highest official might suffer along with the humblest. In 1778 Johann von Justi, since 1765 director of state mines, was imprisoned because certain foundries had not reached their targets and because of alleged deficits. Such cases reveal the harsh face of a government in which all depended in the last resort on the will and temper of the king. But more typical of the reign as a whole was the concern for fairness and efficiency which made so many 'proud to work for the king of Prussia'. The much used phrase suggests the appeal of the king's service to men from all over Germany who found the service worthwhile because there was creative work to be done, and cash available for it. Such a man was Friedrich von Heinitz, a Saxon of international repute as a mining engineer who was appointed in 1776 to run the mines department and was successful in persuading Frederick to invest heavily in Prussia's mines and foundries, in particular coke furnaces and steam power, and therefore in its industrial future. Heinitz could draw inspiration from the king as a model of industry: 'there is nobody,' he wrote, 'with his abstemiousness, his single-mindedness, his ability to occupy himself fruitfully'. But the vital fact was that the minister was left a free hand to work and plan for the future. It is a feature insufficiently recognized by those who have concentrated on the centralization of the regime as it is reflected in institutions like the General Directory.

Frederick was no innovator in the forms of government. To his father's General Directory he was content to add new departments for specific purposes: mines, excise, for example. The hallmarks of his method of government were a lapidary style and a concise and relevant marshalling of the facts. Mirabeau described it thus:

> The king rose at 5.00 a.m. and worked for two or three hours, not with his ministers but with his secretaries. Ministers have authority and opinions and exert influence upon the purposes even of enlightened princes, while they direct those of ordinary sovereigns. The secretaries of the king of Prussia were but scribes.

The sprawling bureaucracy was thus goaded and checked. The speed with which documents were circulated and business completed was unsurpassed in Europe. But as the physical bounds of the state were enlarged, the role of the state expanded proportionately. Inevitably more and more came to depend on Frederick's directing intelligence. He never faltered. His legacy was a supremely well-ordered state. Yet it can be argued that Frederick attempted too much. Therefore, argues W.L. Dorn, 'harmonious co-ordination of the central administration was notoriously lacking'. And there were limits to what one man could do to energize the separate departments of government. A bedside box, opened after his death by one of his ministers contained a bundle of edicts with a label: 'none of these carried out to my knowledge'. Frederick could not ensure total obedience in his lifetime. After his death, what then? Too much depended on him. 'If ever a foolish prince ascends this throne,' wrote Mirabeau, 'we shall see the formidable giant suddenly collapse, and Prussia will go the way of Sweden.' Frederick was succeeded by a prince, Frederick William II, who, if not foolish, was quite incapable of managing personally what had become a large and complex business. Power therefore reverted to local officials who went by custom and the book. The state was thus conditioned for the catastrophe of Jena and the temporary incorporation of Prussia within the Napoleonic order.

Where, in all this concern for results, and absorption in the drudgery of administration, was there room for the concerns of the *philosophes*, in particular for education and the assertion of human rights? In February 1763, before the signing of the peace treaty, Frederick committed himself to an intensive drive for primary education. No pains were spared to ensure that it was provided: there were detailed regulations about the hours of teaching, syllabuses and books. The impetus was maintained. In West Prussia, between 1772 and 1775, 750 schools were built. In this case education was clearly allotted a role in the political process of assimilation. In general the extent of primary education continued to depend on the whim of landowners and bailiffs who tended to fear that schooling would spoil the ploughboy. The king might take a more enlightened view, looking as he did for ways of making his subjects think more independently. But it becomes plain, not least through his shabby treatment of universities, that his overriding purpose was to provide for the training of officials. It was the inspiration behind the Higher Education Commission of 1770 which led to the introduction of a state examination system. Frederick had to his credit the abolition of torture throughout his lands. Far more than the relatively modest advance of education it is the reform of the law that is the glory of his reign. This extensive work of rationalization and humanity had been initiated by his father when he appointed Samuel von Cocceji (1679–1755) to head a commission of reform; it had been carried a long way before Cocceji's death, and effectively completed by Carl Schwarz by 1784, but it was not published as a comprehensive code until after the king's death in 1791.

The preface to a new edition (1970) of the *Allgemeine Landrecht* describes it as easily the greatest codification of German law. Its editor, Schwarz, summarized, among other principles: precaution against one class or estate impairing the rights of others, regard for civil liberty, and the rights and possessions of subjects, and complete religious and intellectual freedom.

Cocceji claimed for the Prussian law which he was establishing that it was based on commonsense and the constitution. Since, however, it incorporated the right of petition to the king, and since the king was able to dismiss judges, the law, *certum et universale* as Cocceji might call it, remained in effect what the king willed, and he never hesitated to intervene when he thought there was incompetence or a miscarriage of justice. The case of the miller Arnold shows to what lengths he would go and how unsatisfactory the result might be, even by his own criterion, protection of the rights of the subject. Arnold claimed, against the judgement of the Neumark Chamber, that the *Landrat* had diverted water by digging a carp pond so that he had been unable to pay his rent – and so been dispossessed. After exhaustive enquiry his plea was upheld by Frederick who also sentenced six councillors of the provincial chamber to nine months imprisonment. For justice Frederick had perpetuated a heavy injustice.

Frederick justified the freedom of the press with the resounding words: 'Gazettes, if they are to be interesting, must not be molested.' Yet, after the relative freedom of the first decade, he restored the traditional controls. The right of individuals to speak their minds could not be allowed to impair the interests of the state. A glimpse into Frederick's mind is afforded by his refutation of an anonymous essay, probably the work of Holbach, critical of despots and strong for the principle that man is made for the truth. 'Man is made for error', declared the king, explaining that in political and religious matters, lies might be an essential part of good government. It is not surprising that Frederick seemed to some to be guilty of applying double standards. Lessing, the great German writer who, in the end, repudiated Prussia and its king, wrote in 1769 to a friend who had enthused about Prussian freedom:

> This freedom may be summarised as solely that of saying as many *sottises* against religion as one likes.... Just let somebody try to write as freely about things in Berlin as Sonnefels writes in Vienna.... Let one man stand up in Berlin for the rights of the subject and against exploitation and despotism, as now happens even in France and Denmark, and you will soon find out which country is to this day the most slavish in Europe.

Frederick did little to court German writers and artists. Indeed he did not conceal his low opinion of them and his preference for the French. He relished Voltaire's remark: 'Germany was for soldiers and horses.' It is fair to say that he typified the dominance of French culture in Germany whose states and cities were generally too small to sustain a wealthy class of patrons outside the courts. Balthasar Neumann, the most gifted German architect of the time, had to submit his drawings for the *Residenz* of the prince bishop of Würzburg to Parisian architects before they could be approved. Frederick was proud to think of himself as 'a member of the Republic of Letters' and wished to foster cultural values. But he seemed to have envisaged them as belonging to a world apart from the body politic and irrelevant to its needs: it was an aristocratic and cosmopolitan world. He never mastered the German language, indeed wrote habitually in French. Among French writers it is significant that he most admired Racine: he once told d'Alembert that he would rather have written *Athalie* than won the Seven Years War. He would argue, with the authority of one who used it with rare facility, that the elegance, clarity and economy of classical French made it the best possible vehicle for the expression of ideas. The Prussian Academy was dominated by Frenchmen: its first permanent president was Malpertius, its first prizewinner, d'Alembert. His court painter was Antoine Pesne, his favourite painters were Watteau and Boucher. Frederick was in a uniquely strong position to challenge this cultural colonization. The great art historian Winckelmann was recommended to him as librarian and asked for a salary of 2,000 *thalers*. 'For a German 1000 *thalers* is enough', the king decreed. Frederick was a patriot who loved and toiled for his country but despised its civilization. The paradox is more apparent than real for his country was not Germany but Brandenburg–Prussia. It had a genuine popular culture, based on Lutheranism, strengthened by Pietism. Frederick was moved when he heard the soldiers sing Luther's hymn, *Ein Feste Burg*, as evening fell on the corpse-strewn battlefield of Leuthen; but for Lutheranism, its rites and doctrines, he had no more use, or indeed instinctive sympathy, than for the idea of a greater Germany.

Prussia was a militarist state: that was true no less of peacetime, when the army was maintained at full strength, than of the thirteen years when the country was actually at war. The requirements of the army affected society at many points. Before the Seven Years War, the army numbered about 150,000: 3 out of 4 were natives, 4 out of 5 were combatant troops. At the end of the war, despite the high annual rate of casualties, there were over 200,000 men under arms, about 4 for every 100 of the population. During the war the army was indeed 'the essence of the state': the state was governed from army headquarters, for that is where the king would normally be. It was a strategic advantage that the king was able to fight on interior lines, with his armies based normally on his own lands; but the burden on resources and administration was correspondingly heavy. It is all the more remarkable that Archenholtz, who served in the army in the Seven Years War and subsequently wrote about it, could claim: 'the Prussian army was never without pay, bread or forage, very rarely without vegetables, even more rarely without meat'. The militia system ensured that a high proportion of the king's male subjects would have experience of military service, with its emphasis upon drill and its stern discipline. Despite, or perhaps because of that discipline, the desertion rate was about the highest in Europe, thousands every year taking the risk of being recaptured and so having to run the gauntlet which might lead to their being flogged to death. Frederick felt it necessary to decree officers should acquaint themselves with the rougher country round their garrisons so that they could hunt deserters more efficiently. In battle the Prussian soldier was steady. It was an important factor in Frederick the Great's victories, and recuperative powers after defeat, and it was partly due to the high morale of the officer class, superior to that of the Austrians or French. By 1756 almost all officers were native-born and noble. They could be relied upon to serve loyally as members of a close-knit caste, whose standing in society depended largely on their commissions and who could readily identify both with the sovereign who was their commander and with their fellow soldiers; and so they were ready to share the privations of camp and campaign, and to brave shot and steel in the thick of the fighting. They were shareholders in an enterprise of territorial expansion which could be to their immediate advantage.

Economic considerations had influenced his decision to invade Silesia. Whatever the predominant motive the consequences are beyond any doubt. The acquisition of 40,000 square miles of Silesia, confirmed by the peace of Hubertusburg (1763), was a big stride towards the consolidation of an independent state, with its centre of gravity east of the Elbe, straddling Germany from east to west. It would still suit Frederick at times to be a good German and constitutionalist, especially when the emperor Joseph's efforts to gain Bavaria, an issue similar, in the blend of right and *Realpolitik*, to that of Silesia, enabled him to enter the lists, to check the Emperor and so to win the approval of the German states. It was a role that Frederick probably enjoyed, as a student of international law and political theory. In his *Political Testament* of 1768 he considered the question of 'whether, and under what circumstances, the welfare of the state demands the breach of a treaty', and concluded: 'The sovereign is judge of what the welfare of the state requires.' In the case of Silesia, Frederick may have had doubts about his judgement during the worst passages of the Seven Years War. But by 1750 it was producing 45 per cent of total exports. With its metallurgical industries and coal mining, old established linen industry and new glass manufacturers, it contributed to Prussia's overall self-sufficiency and her increasing trade surplus. It fitted into Frederick's conception of orderly economic policy. He used the state's economic resources recklessly; but he took care to replenish them. In 1741 he added to the General Directory a fifth department with responsibility for the Hohenzollern lands as a whole, charged with planning for trade, manufactures and agriculture.

Frederick showed no inclination towards the economic policies of the Enlightenment. Trade fairs, like that of Frankfurt an der Oder, were harmed by transit taxes on exhibits: there were import and export restrictions. But Frederick saw more risk than advantage in exposing Prussia's infant industries to competition from outside. By 1773 there were 264 new factories of various kinds, including sugar refining, tobacco and silk. The royal porcelain works in Berlin, exploiting the Meissen techniques which the Prussians discovered when they occupied Saxony, succeeded beyond expectation. But some enterprises failed, and more would have done without protection. Fiscal considerations were also important. In fifteen years after 1763, largely because of the *régie*, the customs yield was doubled. For Frederick, the most pragmatic of rulers, the growth of the state and the health of the economy were inseparable. He was not interested in surpluses for their own sake, but in planned enterprise to produce higher revenues. Always, however, there was the quality of imagination which sets him apart from other rulers. In his *Essai* he wrote that the ruler should

> imagine himself in the situation of a peasant or industrial worker and ask himself: If I had been born into the social class where one's hands are one's sole asset, what would I expect of my sovereign? Whatever his common-sense tells him ought to be done, that he must do if he is to fulfil his duty.

Charles XI of Sweden had seen the value, in a period of sluggish economic growth, of recovering the crown lands, to secure revenue and to provide a solid foundation for royal authority. The efficient management of the demesne lands, among other sources of revenue, had been one of the chief concerns of King Frederick William I and the aspect of his work that Frederick came most to value. It is also that which explains the apparent lack of principle which the *philosophes* came to deplore when they perceived him to be maintaining the rights of the *Junker* and, in particular, serfdom.

As in Russia the keys to the situation were that it was not land that was short, but labourers, not material resources but cash. The Seven Years War, in which Prussia lost 10 per cent of its population overall, but a much higher proportion in those lands directly affected by fighting and occupation, further distorted the balance of supply and demand. On royal lands it was Frederick's policy to commute labour services into payment in kind. He continued his father's policy of offering short term leases which reflected market value. *Junkers* were not allowed to exact more than four days service a week and physical punishment was forbidden. Further he could not go. The sympathies of the *Landrat*, on whom the crown relied for local administration and justice, were those of his province and class. The lord himself retained rights of jurisdiction as part and parcel of his landownership: *Gerichtsherrschaft* went with *Grundherrschaft*. In this far from ideal world Frederick may well have served his peasants better by his caution than he would have done by taking the course of the Emperor Joseph. To *philosophe* critics who dealt with more tractable kingdoms of the imagination, Frederick had his answer. In his *Essai* he wrote: 'Whoever should suddenly desire to overthrow this abominable administration [serfdom], would entirely overthrow the mode of managing estates, and must be obliged, in part, to indemnify the nobility for the losses of their revenue.' Even on the most strictly managed private estates the peasant enjoyed some bargaining power: he was a valuable asset and he had to be adequately fed and housed. Taxes and dues, at around 30 per cent, were less burdensome than those endured by his contemporaries in France and Spain. All depended on sound farming practices and expanding production. A land survey was undertaken to establish the extent of the lands and the scope and need for improvement. The impressive result can be seen in land reclamation and technical innovation: winter stall-feeding of cattle and the cultivation of fodder crops, like sainfoin and clover, which were in line with the advanced practices of British and Netherlandish farmers. Demesne revenue had notably increased by 1786 while the improvements on private estates as well justified the policy of agricultural protectionism. There were no serious famines even in the worst years of cattle plague or bad harvest; only in Silesia, where events in the Austrian lands affected opinion, was there any significant conflict between landowners and serfs during the later stages of the reign. To sustain their privileges the *Junkers* needed the authority of the state and also its patronage to provide the opportunities for suitable employment. So it was that Frederick looked to that class for his officers and rationalized necessity by writing about their superior fitness for such service, as men of honour and natural aptitude for command. Upon this basis of mutual advantage rested the stability which contrasts so strikingly with the situation in neighbouring Habsburg and Romanov lands, to take the two extremes of liberal experiment and repressive autocracy; it was the most beneficial aspect of Frederick's idiosyncratic but essentially practical regime. It was perhaps what Bismarck perceived when he wrote that Frederick had 'two gifts which advanced each other, strategic ability and a sober understanding of the interests of his subjects'.

Further Reading

It is not surprising, in a Germany that has so much else of interest, that the historian should still concentrate on the rise of Prussia. A bibliography published at the centenary of his death listed about 2700 books and articles relating to Frederick II alone. What will the figure be at the bicentenary? It is all the more important that the history of Brandenburg–Prussia should be approached through the Holy Roman Empire of which it was a part (see the bibliography following chapter 10) and against the background of an earlier Germany. A good introduction which places the Prussian achievement in that wider perspective is that of G. Barraclough, *Origins of Modern Germany* (Oxford, 1973), specially valuable because of the author's strength in medieval history. So, for the same reason, are F.L. Carsten's *Princes and Parliaments in Germany from the Fifteenth to Eighteenth Centuries* (1959) and his *Origins of Prussia* (London, 1982). More than any other historian, Carsten, a Prussian-in-exile, has made his country's history intelligible to the English reader. His other work includes an article on 'The Great Elector', *English Historical Review*, 75 (1950), and one on King Frederick William I, 'Prussian despotism at its height',

History, 40 (February 1956). Of the former, there is also a biography: *The Great Elector*, by F. Schevill (1957).

Hohenzollern government may be studied through H. Rosenburg, *Bureaucracy, Aristocracy and Autocracy: the Prussian Experience, 1640–1815* (1966); H.C. Johnson, *Frederick the Great and his Officials* (New Haven, 1975); and through two articles by Walter Dorn: 'The Prussian bureaucracy in the eighteenth century', *Political Science Quarterly*, 46 (1931) and 47 (1932). Justice is done to the achievements of the 'sergeant king' in R.A. Dorwart, *The Administrative Reforms of Frederick William I of Prussia* (Cambridge, Mass., 1953). There are some useful documents in C.A. Macartney (ed.), *The Habsburg and Hohenzollern Dynasties in the Seventeenth and Eighteenth Centuries* (London, 1970). Two articles explore the character of the *Junkers* who played such a prominent part in that government: F. Carsten, 'The origin of the *Junkers*', *English Historical Review*, 62 (1947), and H. Rosenburg, 'The rise of the *Junkers* in Brandenburg–Prussia, 1410–1653', *American Historical Review*, 49 (1943–4, two articles). Two books which deal with the army in Prussian history are also inevitably in some respects studies of the *Junkers* who provided the officers: Gordon Craig, *The Politics of the Prussian Army 1640–1945* (1955) (earlier chapters), and Karl Demeter, *The German Officer Corps in Society and State, 1650–1945* (1965).

In his interesting study of the historiography of Frederick the Great in *Historians and Eighteenth Century Europe* (1979), M.S. Anderson says that 'there is no great historical figure of whom the judgements of posterity have fluctuated more violently': he was reviled by the romantics as a cold, life-denying rationalist; revered by nationalists as a good German; subjected again to more hostile scrutiny in the aftermath of the twentieth century wars. There was a Frederick the Great for each age, as historians pondered the affairs of Europe in which Prussia or a Prussian Germany played so large a part. Sentiment counted for more than the records. Recently, however, scholarly analysis has concentrated on the nature of Prussian government under Frederick, as in the solidly informative *Frederick the Great*, by Walter Hubatsch (London, 1981). The student may find it helpful, however, to approach the king through D.B. Horn's dry but balanced account; his *Frederick the Great and the Rise of Prussia* (1954) benefits from the author's understanding of eighteen-century diplomacy. He will find a fair verdict on Frederick's stewardship in Gerhard Ritter's life (translated by Paret, 1968). Paret has edited a useful compilation of extracts from different writers, and he discusses the contradictions within Frederick's personality and rule in his *Frederick the Great: a Historical Profile* (Berkeley, 1968). Conflicting views are also assessed in G.P. Gooch's urbane study, *Frederick the Great* (1947).

The military side of the reign is authoritatively dealt with in C. Duffy, *The Army of Frederick the Great* (Newton Abbot, 1974) (see also books after ch. 6). Economic aspects are dealt with in W.O. Henderson, *Studies in the Economic Policy of Frederick the Great* (London, 1963); reform of the law, in Herman Weil, *Frederick the Great and Samuel von Cocceji* (1961); political philosophy, in F. Meinecke, *Machiavellism* (New Haven, 1957) and H. Brunschwig, *Enlightenment and Romanticism in Eighteenth Century Prussia* (Chicago, 1977); and last but not least should be mentioned a stimulating examination of a still controversial topic: E.J. Feuchtwanger, *Prussia, Myth and Reality: the Role of Prussia in German History* (London, 1974).

12

HOLLAND

Born to be Free

In 1648 at Münster the United Provinces made peace with Spain. Apart from a truce from 1609 to 1621, war had been waged continuously since 1572, when the Sea Beggars captured Brill. The country had been literally made by war. The Union, first established at Utrecht in 1579, had been a makeshift. Holland, Zeeland, Utrecht, Gelderland, Overijssel, Friesland and Groningen, each separatist in outlook, led but not overawed by Holland, the largest and richest of the provinces, had joined to defend their rights; they were then more aware of their common interest in fighting Spain than of their different customs and cherished liberties. The lines of demarcation between north and south corresponded to no division of culture, religion or language. The southern provinces had made their own union because they could see no future in resistance. The patterns of fighting imposed by the rivers Rhine and Maas made an artificial frontier along strategic lines of defence. For material and sentimental reasons William the Silent had fought for a union of all the provinces. Towards the end of the great war, when it was plain, after the revolts of Catalonia and Portugal in 1640, that the Spanish could not recover the north, some Dutchmen still dreamed of conquering the south: their hopes prolonged the war. But by then the United Provinces, originally the poorer northern half of the seventeen provinces of old Burgundy, had become a nation and, in relation to its size, probably the richest nation in Europe. From any standpoint it is an extraordinary development. There was a dualism in what

Map 12.1 *The Dutch Republic in the second half of the seventeenth century*

had formerly been one culture. In learning and art Holland now led: there was rich soil for all the growths of civilized life. But the cost was high. One view is forcibly expressed by Professor Geyl, for whom the split of north and south represents 'a disaster brought upon the Netherlands by foreign domination'. Dutch, and latterly Belgian, pride has tended to obscure the damage done by the disruption of a once coherent Netherlands culture by the accidents of war. Like the severance of East and West Germany after 1945, equally the product of war, the division created new interests and fostered new ideologies which have made balanced judgement of the cultural and moral issues specially difficult. There is less room for doubt about the political and economic consequences.

The military success of the United Provinces is not surprising, given that they had the will to survive the fierce initial onslaughts in both phases of the war. The extensive commitments of Spain in the Thirty Years War, especially after the War of the Mantuan Succession (1630) and the entry of France (1635), ensured a progressive weakening of Spain's forces in the Netherlands. There were moreover chronic disabilities: there was never enough money to pay the troops and this imposed a defensive strategy on the Spanish commanders. The fact that the Dutch commander Frederick Henry also adopted a cautious strategy meant that the war developed into a stalemate, relieved only occasionally by great events, like the capture of Breda by Spinola in 1625 and its recapture by Frederick Henry in 1637. All the time, the condition of the Dutch was improving. It is the positive aspect of the Dutch achievement that is impressive, the courage and enterprise with which they exploited their assets. Behind the dour defence a small people, about two million, lacking a centralized administration and divided in religion, became a great power.

Utrecht again was the scene, in 1713, of a great congress, in which the diplomats of Europe met to settle the frontier after three long wars in which the Dutch had stood up to, sometimes defeated, the armies of France. It was the fourth congress of its sort to be held on Dutch soil, Breda (1668), Nijmegen (1678) and Rijswijk (1697) being the others. The Dutch had fought with various allies; since 1689 with England and the Empire. They had provided the core of the opposition on what was for France the main battlefront – the southern Netherlands. Great-power status could not thereafter be maintained by the United Provinces. It had always been a *tour de force*. The seventeenth century was Holland's golden age; and during it the Dutch showed, at least until 1648, that war could benefit a country's economy; and after 1648 that economic strength could provide a small country with the resources to hold its own against what in political and military terms might seem to be overwhelming odds. Dutchmen were stirred not only to make money and to defend their gains, but to realize in the quality of their lives the opportunities afforded by successful resistance.

The Dutch were probably the best-fed people in Europe; they certainly took most care of their urban poor. Calvinist faith was influential, as ministers expounded the austere doctrines that gave their congregations a sense of being a chosen people. Godliness and the new patriotism marched together. Besides painting, which had more extensive roots, Dutch literature enjoyed a minor renaissance in the hands of men like Marnix, translator of the Bible, and Van Mander, author of the popular Scriptural songs. The new University of Leyden was the centre of a vigorous Dutch intellectual life, besides being an outpost of Protestantism in Europe. Daniel Heinsius, the poet, expressed the mood succinctly: 'Wherever you, Spain, are not, there is my fatherland.' He was born at Ghent, but he wrote as a northerner when he said: 'We were born to be free.' As Antwerp, occupied by the Spanish and blockaded by the Dutch, declined, Amsterdam became the financial capital of the world. Immigrant southerners brought their capital and skills to the cities of the north. Dutchmen traded profitably in the East Indies, Africa and India. But this nation of seamen and merchants – Louis XIV's despised 'cheese merchants' – was also the nation of Rembrandt and Vermeer, Huygens, Leeuwenhoek and Spinoza. Over against the Spain of Olivares and the France of Louis XIV it offered, besides commercial rivalry, an alternative way of life. The civilization and the trading empire were inseparable. The sturdy, stubborn character, the success against military odds, the resourceful engineering, the adaptability, all stemmed from the way in which they mastered their native element.

Traders of the World

The inhabitants of Holland and Zeeland, the flat reclaimed lands threaded by waterways, dotted with expanses of lake, under the wide skies that their painters have made so familiar, lived at sea level. Water was everywhere. The sea was their historic enemy – the persistent challenge and the potential ally. It was easier to travel by boat than by road and natural to fish for a living. In *buizen* built specially for the conditions of the North Sea, decked with holds for salt and barrels, the Dutch fishermen pursued the herring shoals, operating mainly from ports at the mouth of the Maas, under the regulation of the College of the Fishery. A modern estimate of the value of this industry is that 'equivalent to the total export value of Britain's famous cloth industry'; this moreover leaves out of account the valuable cod and whale fishing. Salted herring and cod provided security against famine in winter months and a valuable export to other countries. To acquire salt of sufficient quality the Dutch went to the Bay of Biscay and to Setubal in Portugal. To build their ships they imported timber from Norway and the Baltic. Sandbanks in the Zuider Zee and the narrow channel of the Vlie meant that the larger ships had to be discharged from lighters. The development of the *fluyt* was therefore specially significant. First made in Hoorn at the turn of the century, flat-bottomed and of shallow draught, economical to build and to run (a ship of 200 tons could be manned by a crew of 10 men), with a large hold, the *fluyt* gave the Dutch a crucial trading advantage. Throughout the seventeenth century the Dutch were able to offer freight rates a third to a half lower than their English competitors.

By 1670 Dutch-owned shipping was larger in tonnage than that of all the European merchant fleets together and held a dominant position in the Baltic grain, timber and metals traffic. Dutchmen traded between Mediterranean ports; they carried tobacco, sugar and dyestuffs across the Atlantic; pepper, cinnamon and nutmeg from the Far East. Their factories were to be found all over the world: at Archangel on the White Sea, at Accra on the Guinea Coast, at Batavia in the Indonesian archipelago, at New Amsterdam in North America, at Pernambuco in Brazil and Nagasaki in Japan. They penetrated into the hinterland of Asia and to the furthest islands of Indonesia. The range and audacity had been anticipated by the Portuguese. Now operating from a sounder base, with greater resources, the Dutch took over from the Portuguese as predatory heirs of the first colonial empire. The Dutch East India Company (founded in 1602) and the West India Company (1621) were backed by large and well-spread investment; they were states within the state, authorized to make war and peace with the native powers, to maintain naval and military forces and to govern in the regions with which they were concerned.

After 1620, and the renewal of the Spanish war, the Dutch pressed their attack against Portuguese and Spanish possessions. There were some isolated triumphs. Piet Heyn's capture of the Mexican silver fleet in its Cuban harbour (1628) gratified his shareholders but aroused hopes which were not subsequently fulfilled, since the Spanish held on to most of their possessions. The Portuguese suffered worse. Brazil, the Gold Coast, Angola and Cape Verde were partly or wholly conquered and an inroad made upon their lucrative trade in gold, ivory, slaves and sugar. By the treaty of Münster (1648) Philip IV recognized the right of the Dutch to conquer and hold all the Portuguese colonial lands claimed by the Dutch India companies. The West India Company had a disappointing record in the second half of the century. But the East India Company forged ahead. Jan Maetsuycker, governor-general in Batavia from 1653 to 1678, was the greatest among colonial administrators of this period. Something of his spirit may be gauged from his answer to the Portuguese envoy who came to demand the cession of Negumbo in 1644 when Maetsuycker was governor of Ceylon and after the Portuguese had just made a truce with the Dutch: 'We are not servants to the Prince nor States but to the Company, from whom we have received no such order; nor when we shall receive such order will we surrender it but by force.' In fact the governor had already received orders from the company to grab as much Portuguese territory as possible before the truce took effect. Such were the pressures that were building up behind the protagonists of profitable war. The states-general cherished peace in theory; many merchants, particularly those operating in Europe, wanted it in fact, understanding the dangers of their country's diplomatic isolation. As Rijkloff van Goens told the governors of his company (1655): 'There is nobody who wishes us well in all the Indies, yea we are deadly hated by all nations ... so that in my opinion, sooner or later, war will be the arbiter.' The directors were under no illusions; but they continued to endorse a 'forward' policy. In 1652, van Riebeck founded Dutch South Africa when he took possession of its southern tip in order to protect communications with the east. In May 1656, Colombo fell after a long siege and Ceylon was almost entirely controlled by the Dutch. From there they set up trading stations on the coasts of south India. With a depot in Canton, outposts in Siam, and a monopoly in dealings with the haughty Japanese, the trading octopus could grip with many tentacles the sources of the riches of the east. Eastern trade was never so important however as the Mediterranean; both were dwarfed by the 'mother' or Baltic trade.

Danzig, Riga, Stockholm and Copenhagen were the key places in the framework of the Dutch economy. War between Denmark and Sweden, as in 1645 or 1658, brought the Dutch fleet into the Baltic; it was in their interest to hold the balance. The Dutch were, moreover, as Defoe pointed out in the next century, 'the Middle Persons in Trade, the Factors and Brokers of Europe'. Their industries depended largely upon imported materials: they refined sugar, milled oil, prepared tobacco, finished cloth and made guns from imported raw materials. Their goods were in sufficient demand to attract the buyers and silver of other less fortunate or less well-organized countries. Spanish silver fleets often sailed direct to Holland to pay for the goods which Spain required. Colbert noted the success of the Dutch in a world economy of static demand and planned to imitate – and to crush – the trader state.

In Holland there was little land available for purchase and it was correspondingly expensive. More than in other countries, therefore, those who made money sought opportunities for investment in commerce, or in municipal loans. The Exchange Bank of Amsterdam (founded in 1609, characteristically with municipal backing) had 2698 depositors by 1701. Even in the crisis of 1672, when French troops threatened the city and the de Witt regime was overthrown, the bank survived. A low interest rate attracted foreign borrowers and made England, with its expanding economy but relatively high interest rates, a profitable field for Dutch investment. Charles II's England never knew less than 6 per cent. Under de Witt interest fell as low as 4 per cent. Richelieu sent subsidies to his allies by way of Amsterdam; the Emperor Ferdinand II borrowed there on the security of his silver mines. Dutch capital helped to found the Bank of England in 1694, in imitation of the Dutch bank. Marine insurance was another flourishing 'invisible export': in the naval wars of the 1660s and 1670s even enemy shipping was insured at Amsterdam. The city also benefited from the growth of speculation in shares and commodities. Commodity price lists were circulated throughout Europe; in 1686 there were 550 quotations. A flourishing trade in arms made no distinction between allies, neutrals and enemies. Immigrants from the south contributed to the growth of such services, and to some of the manufacturing industries which supplied ballast to this well-diversified economy. Diamond cutting, still today a speciality of Amsterdam, originated in Antwerp. The spectacular growth of Leyden as a textile centre provides another example of this beneficial movement. Calvinist refugees came from Hondschoote in Flanders, negotiating as a body with the city authorities. In the period between the siege and relief of Leyden (1574) and the turn of that century, the cloth production of this ancient but depressed textile town was doubled. Labour was cheap, and there was some exploitation of immigrants. As in the early stages of Britain's industrial revolution, the price of expansion was paid by sweated labour; conditions of work and housing were grim. But Leyden became the prime producer of the new lighter cloth that was making life more agreeable for the affluent and fashion-conscious. Production and population were at their peak when the French attacked Holland in 1672 and began the series of wars which was to be the undoing of Dutch industry; by then, Leyden was second only to Lyons among the industrial cities of Europe.

In economic matters the Dutch were the schoolmasters of Europe, like the Scots of the eighteenth century. So great was the immigration into other countries that, between 1669 and 1750, a series of decrees were aimed by the states-general against the emigration of skilled workers. They were apparently abortive. The opportunities abroad became more tempting as the growth of the Dutch economy slowed down: a trend to which the loss of so much skilled labour must have contributed. Cornelius Vermuyden drained the English Fens for the Duke of Bedford. Other Dutchmen drained the Pontine marshes for the Pope. The van Robais family from Middelburg became the biggest textile manufacturers in Abbeville. Van Geer settled in Sweden and acquired a supremacy in the mining of copper and iron that was as profitable to himself as it was to the Swedish kings. Peter the Great learnt about ship-building in the yards of Zaandam, and English landowners studied from Dutch experts the latest methods of crop husbandry. Dutch merchants controlled the wine trade of the river Loire and ran the mint of Poland. Dutch merchants purchased cloth cheaply in Silesia, had it processed in Holland and sold it back, more expensively, as a Dutch product. For England the second half of the seventeenth century was what Cunningham called a period of 'conscious imitation of the Dutch'. When William III prepared his expedition against James II in Ireland in 1689 he could not find an English contractor to undertake the food supply: the Amsterdamer Jean Pereira took it on.

An Open Society

The traffic of men and ideas was not all one way. The Holland which received at different times the young Charles II, Clarendon, the disgraced minister, and Shaftesbury, his defeated opponent, which such independent spirits as Descartes, Spinoza, Locke and Bayle found so congenial for life and thought, was the most open society of its time. The thousand or so Sephardic Jews, refugees from the Inquisition in Spain and Portugal, made a disproportionate impact in finance and scholarship. Another and greater dispersion, that of the Huguenots in the 1680s (about 50,000 came altogether), proved as great a benefit to the economic and intellectual life of their new land as it was a loss to France: Huguenots introduced the manufacture of brocades and velvets, and stimulated the production of books and pamphlets in those significant years of scientific discovery and of a reappraisal of traditional religious and political views. Pierre Bayle, the encyclopedist, was a Huguenot émigré who established his base in Holland where, with his friend and former colleague at the college of Sedan, Pierre Jurieu, he was given a chair at the Illustre school at Rotterdam. He used it for an assault upon accepted beliefs which was comprehensive and sharp enough to entitle him to be considered one of the fathers of the Enlightenment.

A more central figure however in the Dutch culture of the time was Baruch Spinoza (1632–77). He was the descendant of immigrants; a grinder and polisher of lenses; a Jew who was actually expelled from the Amsterdam synagogue for his heretical views; a philosopher whose writings fell under the official ban and who dared, in 1670, to write a book, *Tractatus Theologico-Politicus*, which considered the Bible as the work of men; a rationalist and deist who was widely but wrongly held to be an 'atheist'; and he received money from de Witt and other regents and was left unmolested by the civil authorities. He recognized his debt to a freedom of thought which could be found nowhere else in Europe at that time, and which made Amsterdam 'great and admired by the whole world', a city where 'men of every race and sect live in the greatest harmony'. There he was just another craftsman in a cosmopolitan city of craftsmen and traders where Baptists, Mennonites, Lutherans, Sephardic and Ashkenazi Jews lived alongside the predominant Calvinist and Catholic communities.

Amsterdam was a city of 200,000 souls by 1700: about a tenth of the size of the whole country. It was not Holland, any more than Holland was the United Provinces. The character of the other provinces, except for Zeeland, was mainly agricultural and modestly seigneurial; in Gelderland there was a strong noble class, German in character; in Friesland and Groningen the small freeholder was still important. But Holland provided more than half the total revenue and was responsible to an even greater degree for the country's economic and military strength – and for the vigour of her culture.

Among the eighteen towns of the province which enjoyed the traditional right of sending delegates to the states of Holland, ranging from decayed places like Purmerend to affluent Dordrecht, Rotterdam, Delft and Leyden, Amsterdam was acknowledged queen. As a masterpiece of town planning with carefully regulated development along the concentric canals, it can still be studied; for it has been miraculously preserved from nineteenth-century industrial development, and twentieth-century bombs. In the seventeenth century it was a boom town. It is characteristic of that period, as well as being specially Dutch in its disciplined neatness. The riches garnered from all parts of the world went to build a city in which individual ambition and taste was subdued to the needs of the whole. As in other Dutch towns shortage of timber and building stone necessitated the use of brick. Moreover, since many wanted to live on canals, they had to accept a narrow frontage. From this derive the tall narrow façades surmounted by the gevels which lend variety to the formal scene. Early in the seventeenth century the city council adopted plans for building along three new concentric canals, along which would be town houses for merchants, while the lower-middle class and artisans lived more humbly along the radial canals. The council had powers of compulsory purchase; the land was divided into plots averaging 26 by 180 feet (of the latter, half had to be garden). Certain industrial purposes were debarred. The brick, even the piling foundations had to be approved. The owners had to pay for the cobbled streets and stone walls of the canals. The council achieved symmetry and paid nothing. The *huisvrouw* gained a house which needed relatively little domestic help, with abundant water for scrubbing the tiled floors. She has been immortalized by Pieter de Hooch and Jan Vermeer and the other painters whose work epitomized the sedate values of this bourgeois culture. Outside, the streets were so clean, we are told, that foreigners refrained from spitting on them. There was of course another Amsterdam. The Joordan in the west was developed by speculators to provide cheap tenements for immigrant workers. But one last thing should be noted about this city. The finest and most ostentatious building in Amsterdam was not a private palace but the new town hall of Jacob van Campen who, in Constantiÿn Huygens' words, 'From our stricken and disfigured face, the Gothic squint and squalor did erase.' Standing on the Dam, a royal palace since 1808, it has nowadays lost its *raison d'être* and is even anomalous in the heart of the city which so stoutly opposed the Orange dynasty. But its decorations can still be examined. Their symbolism is clear. On the pediment, sea gods and creatures from every continent gather to pay homage to the figure of Amsterdam. The style is related to contemporary French baroque, but its ethos is altogether different from that of the Palais Royal or later Versailles. It is the tribute of an oligarchy of business men to the ideal of civic patriotism.

'Wonder is No Wonder'

The qualities of Dutch painting can best be appreciated in Dutch cities and under Dutch skies. It is so much part of Dutch society, and that society has left such solid memorials of its golden age, that one walks from a picture gallery (for example the Mauritshuis at the Hague, the classical building, *circa* 1640, designed for John Maurits, governor of Brazil) straight out into the urban landscape that the artist depicted. This was far from being an art of the court, or of a social élite. Travellers noted that fine paintings were to be found in taverns and in the houses of ordinary people. John Evelyn held that men bought paintings as a form of investment in a country in which land was scarce, an explanation that may appeal to the twentieth century but was hardly adequate for its time: nowhere was there such scope for commercial and financial investment as in Holland. Beyond doubt, the Dutch liked paintings as they liked tulips. Introduced from the east, tulips were cultivated with fierce rivalry and at one time 'tulipomania' produced a speculative boom all of its own. When they could not buy oil paintings the Dutch bought prints. The painters had successfully adopted their style to the public taste when the patronage of the Church was abruptly stopped. They were very numerous, and regarded themselves as craftsmen, belonging, with glass-painters and bookbinders, to the guild of St Lucas. They attended carefully to the requirements of the man of middling income, and they specialized in the more successful genres: winter scenes, flower pieces, views of town and country. 'Still-life' and 'landscape' are Dutch terms, Dutch inventions. Portraits were usually of head and shoulders only, to suit the domestic setting. Groups, however, sometimes commissioned portraits, like Hals's *Militia Men of Haarlem* or Rembrandt's celebrated *Night Watch*. Since the supply evidently exceeded the demand, artists competed for perfection of technique. Realism was the keynote, though it was not always taken to its ultimate lengths. For example, flower pieces often contain the flowers of different seasons; landscapes were composed in studios. But precise drawing, a scientific approach to the problems of texture and tone, a technique based in general upon minute study of what could be seen, on the assumption that the client would look for what he normally saw in a room, a harbour or whatever took his fancy, all characterize an art in which painters worked for their clients in the harmonious spirit that could only come from agreed values.

In the two central decades (1640–60) the roll of artists then painting some of their best works is impressive indeed. It includes Rembrandt, most intellectual of portrait painters, whose insights into character are equalled only by his mastery of the medium; Frans Hals, master of colour, who is said to have used twenty-seven different kinds of black; Jacob van Ruisdael, whose landscapes, like those of his uncle Salomon van Ruisdael and the more naturalistic Meindert Hobbema, have fixed in the minds of countless admirers the precise features of this flat country; Paulus Potter, who was the foremost in the new genre of animal painting; Jan Steen, supremely successful as a painter of children: Jan Vermeer, who could make of the apparently commonplace – a kitchen maid pouring milk out of a jug, or a street scene – something that is completely satisfying and moving in its evocation of the simple dramas of every day; Pieter de Hooch, more animated than Vermeer, a genius in the effect of light upon colour. The list is far from complete, even for the greater artists. Some will look for the names of Van der Velde, marine artist, or Gerard Ter Borch, whose *Helena van der Schalke as a Child* recalls Velázquez in its restraint and dignity. Even to compose such a list is to be made aware of the impossibility of conveying the nature of genius by the recital of names; while at the same time hinting at one aspect of the wealth of this society.

Besides paintings, the Dutch produced other goods in which usefulness and beauty are pleasingly compatible. After Chinese porcelain had been introduced into the country it was only a matter of time before Dutch potters found means of making their own. The decline of the Delft breweries made buildings available just when demand for 'china' was making its manufacture – and export – a profitable enterprise. Delft which had long filled the Dutchman's belly now filled his wife's cabinet. The exquisite engraved glass made, notably, by the *Muidenkring*, a circle of aesthetes, provides an example of high skill and sensibility applied to a specialized craft. More popular in demand and inspiration were the painted tiles beloved of the Dutch. Purely practical objects found notably elegant expression in the form of the maps and charts of the house of Blaeu (the great world atlas of Jan Blaeu was produced in eleven volumes in 1662). Maps, like paintings and prints, were hung on walls. The navigator's need subserved the taste of the connoisseur.

Holland lacked a universal genius like Leonardo da Vinci, artist, inventor, scientist in one. None the less, as in that earlier southern renaissance, the artistic life of the Dutch should be seen as a part of a whole society's pursuit of knowledge and understanding. The scientific spirit pervades the pursuit of technical perfection by such men as Hals, Vermeer and Hoogstraten – 'the passion for finding things out' which Kenneth Clark ascribes to Leonardo, and which is the hallmark of this society. In seventeenth-century Europe, artists, craftsmen, men of business, scientists, were not specialists belonging to distinct cultures: they understood one another, lived in the same world, discussed problems of common interest in untechnical language. The scientist was just another seeker after knowledge. The new mathematics, the new techniques of observation, facilitated the search. Like the artist, the scientist recorded and investigated, without prejudice or constraint, in a liberated and secular spirit. The importance of accurate time keeping in a business community needs little emphasis. Appropriately it was Christiaan Huygens, greatest of Dutch scientists, whose pendulum clock set new standards of precision, and whose invention of the balance spring made possible the development of the pocket watch. Minute observation was important to artist, soldier or doctor. Huygens' telescope, through which he observed the rings of Saturn, and Leeuwenhoek's microscope, through which he first saw protozoa in rainwater and bacteria in the human mouth, with their multiple utility and promise for the future, symbolize the creative character of the Dutch. As formerly they had found means of mastering their elemental enemy, the water, now, with their growing material resources, they sought to improve the conditions of life. The same combination of high endeavour and commonsense that marked their conduct of finance and business, exploration and war, land reclamation and town planning, can be seen in the intense cultural life of a society whose motto could have been that of Huygens: 'The world is my country, to promote science is my religion.'

Universities in the seventeenth century were somewhat in decline, whether because of religious strife, war (as in Germany), economic decline (as in Italy and Spain), or because outworn curricula and methods of study and teaching were inappropriate to modern needs. Few men achieved eminence as university professors; most of the great work in all fields was done outside academic circles. A few of the better universities showed signs of intellectual vitality and openness to change. But it is evident that the widespread growth of new institutions, academies and learned societies was catering for a demand for learning and the facilities for research which older institutions were not supplying. Leyden University offers an interesting exception. It was the first of the new universities of Holland and it remained the greatest. Its foundation (1575) was endowed fittingly out of the lands of a dissolved abbey, soon after the siege and relief of a city which had made its name a byword for patriotic resistance. It was governed jointly by two curators, chosen by the states of Holland, and the four burgomasters of the city, and by the *rector magnificus*. It was relatively free from traditional patterns of learning and from the requirements of church authority. No tests of religious orthodoxy were required. Students came from many countries. The English were specially well represented. The great French classical scholar Scaliger was enticed to take a chair; Galileo was asked, but refused. The governors sought talent where they could; though there was no shortage of it in Holland. The growth of the city as an industrial centre may have contributed to the vitality of the university. The parallel rise of the publishing concern of the Elseviers certainly did. The French emigré Lodewijk Elsevier was a strong Calvinist; he had come to Leyden in 1580, established himself as the greatest of the many Leyden printers, and specialized in works of theology, classics and oriental languages. The firm's Amsterdam branch was later to print works of Grotius, Descartes, Milton and Hobbes. As the century proceeded, more books were produced in Dutch and French. But it was the use of Latin that enabled a Dutch printer to find a world-wide market for his books among the educated classes. The Elseviers were only the most prominent among the printers of Holland whose work was so prolific that it has been suggested that more books were published in Holland in this century than in all the rest of Europe together.

At Leyden can be studied that interaction of the world of learning and of practical affairs that is so marked a feature of Dutch life. For the mathematician Simon Stevin, whose motto was 'wonder is no wonder', who produced treatises on bookkeeping by double entry, navigation and decimal coinage, Prince Maurice had founded a school of engineering. Leyden's anatomical theatre was the only place, apart from Padua, where the human body was publicly dissected for teaching purposes. Holland's eastern empire lent purpose to the study of oriental languages and provided specimens for the botanical garden. When an observatory was built in 1632 for the mathematician Willibrod Snellius it was made open to the public. Students queued in the early morning to attend the lectures of Hermann Boerhaave (1669–1738), the outstanding medical teacher of his time. He wrote a textbook, *Institutiones medicae*, that was used everywhere; he held audiences spellbound while lecturing in Latin, and did not shrink from putting his theories to the test. It was as a clinical teacher, working in the local hospital, that he had most influence upon the development of medicine. Pupils of Boerhaave pioneered the medical schools at Edinburgh. Few men have made a greater contribution to the alleviation of physical suffering.

Regents and *Predikants*

The modern traveller is likely to be surprised at the concentration of towns in Holland. Dordrecht and Rotterdam, Delft and the Hague, Leyden and Utrecht are but a day's walk apart from each other. Inevitably the towns dominated; there was little space for the development of the large estates and dependent peasants of other lands. Land was largely owned by burghers: the nobility was weak in numbers, a closed caste, enjoying little political power. Within the towns, as in the other provinces, affairs were managed by small, interrelated groups who provided councillors for the states and together constituted an exclusive aristocracy of office. The revolt had enabled the 'regents' (the urban magnates who monopolized posts on the council) to secure power. By the end of the seventeenth century they had so consolidated this power that it was difficult for an outsider to enter the circle: they could grow rich in safety.

Although their strength derived in the first place from trade, and the furtherance of trade remained the main factor in deciding policy, they were tending to withdraw from business to concentrate upon finance and investment so as to provide a stable base, and the leisure, for politics. One family history is typical of many. Christiaan van Eeghen founded the family business when, in 1662, he moved from Flanders (having become a convert to the Mennonite creed) to settle in the north as a linen manufacturer. His son Jacob, with an expanding business in Amsterdam, became a dealer in a wide range of commodities with interests in western Europe, the Baltic and Mediterranean; he also ventured into finance, bill and foreign-loan transactions, even into land speculation in New York. His son William (1700–47) presided over a period of consolidation symptomatic of the trend of the Dutch economy. By his time the transition from industrialist to financier is complete: the creative period is over.

The education of well-off Dutchmen was designed to produce literate lawyers and administrators. As Temple, England's ambassador for much of Charles II's reign, an admirer and shrewd observer of the country, wrote: 'The chief end of their breeding is to make them fit for the service of their country in the magistracy of their towns, their provinces, and their State.' There was loss and gain. The loss was to the out-going spirit which had made the empire that they now so soberly, and complacently, administered. The inertia that settled upon the country – and which is reflected in Dutch painting with its sudden loss of inspiration (the painters were ever faithful recorders of their society) had several causes. One was a prevailing fear, after the coup which overturned the de Witts and showed the regents the brute power of the mob, of the forces of disorder that lay beneath the placid surface. Economic stagnation only made the problem worse, as unemployment grew, traditional markets were lost, and demand wilted. Ironically the Dutch were to suffer, in the eighteenth century, though in far less acute form, something comparable to the economic decline, with some of the accompanying social problems of seventeenth-century Spain. There was an admirable dignity about the élite of public servants so tenderly described by Pieter Geyl: 'level headed and lucid, not amiable but bold and steady, such were the burgher regents at their best'. More sophisticated than the middle class, they none the less, for the most part, shared (though grander ways with a distinctive dress came in during the 'periwig period') the old values: sobriety, frugality and balanced ledgers. But superficial appearances could not conceal the loss of wholeness when defensive and class-conscious attitudes came to permeate what had been perhaps the best-integrated society in Europe – and the regents came to fear the freedom that had formerly been the hallmark of that society.

One element that could not be reconciled to the compromises of the bourgeois republic was that of the militant Calvinists. The dispute between moderates who followed the liberal teaching of Arminius and the hard-liners who lived by literal acceptance of Calvinist dogma (notably, in theology, predestination, and in church government, the clear separation of church from state) had been resolved at the synod of Dordrecht (1619). Ministers or *predikants*, who preached holy war against the enemies of God and were therefore the natural allies of the house of Orange and the anti-

Spanish party, had been allowed victory on points of doctrine. Maurice of Nassau had acted decisively and Oldenbarneveldt had been burnt: a rare sacrifice to the cause of religious orthodoxy. The regents retained, however, effective control of church government. *Predikants* were paid by the state, public office was restricted to those who accepted the rulings of Dordrecht, and Holland became, in Huizinga's words, 'a people cast in a Calvinist mould'. Practice was, however, more important than official doctrine. That there were no prosecutions, such as that of Galileo in Italy, was not because there were no guardians of traditional views. When Voetius thundered against the new cosmography he had a receptive audience. But there were no effective sanctions. The loose structure of the republic favoured intellectual freedom. Moreover the Calvinism of official and intellectual circles was mostly moderate. The *predikants* were deterred from burning witches (unlike their brethren in Germany), from banning the picturesque ceremonies of the people or persecuting Roman priests. The burgomasters of Amsterdam rejected a plea by the consistory to close the town theatre. Puritanism was held in check. Had it not been so, the inventive and artistic genius of the Dutch would have been denied free play. The Remonstrants, as the liberals were called, were only a small group but they were influential. Hugo Grotius, one of their leaders, spent most of his life abroad after escaping from Loeuvenstein castle. But others remained, to build their own church in Amsterdam, and to defend the spirit of toleration: 'In essentials unity, in doubtful matters liberty, in all things charity.' Meanwhile militant Calvinism remained a potent popular force at the service of Orange dynasticism.

The Disunited Provinces

It was usual for Dutchmen to say that the federal republic was the sure guardian of their religion and society. The extraordinary success of the 'disunited provinces', as Temple called them, when compared to their size in territory and population, appears to confirm the conventional view. Yet there were strains inherent in the condition of the state: the divided interests of the provinces caused delays in vital decisions; and the prestige, the wealth and claims, of the house of Orange were scarcely compatible with the entrenched power of the city oligarchs. During the Spanish war, when war and economic growth apparently occurred together, it was easier to see the benefits than the dangers of division. Thereafter, as the interests of Orangists and the regents became more sharply defined, the balance of opposites led to more serious conflicts. It was then possible for Downing, the English ambassador, to write (1664) of the advantages enjoyed by the British government over that of the Dutch, 'such a shattered and divided thing'. The slowing down of economic expansion in the second half of the century and the relentless toll of the French wars upon the country's resources later contributed to disillusion. The Dutch came near to revolution in 1650; but the history of other crises suggests that even if William II had succeeded in his coup of that year and taken Amsterdam by force, some compromise would have emerged. The regent class was always divided between those who enjoyed and those who wanted office. Moreover the regents lived in constant fear of the middle and lower classes, the best-educated tradesmen and artisans in Europe: sceptical of the pretensions of the oligarchs, and more vulnerable than they to the mischances of war and trade they were always a volatile element. The regent class, the Amsterdam regents in particular, held on to their supremacy in government and economy by dint of concession (as to the *predikants*) and compromise, as between the interests of the maritime provinces and the rest. In war their position was precarious indeed. Dutchmen were realistic enough to appreciate the danger – and futility – of extreme attitudes in politics. The history of Holland, between the ascendancy of the de Witts (1650–1772) and the French Revolution, was one of periodic violence within, and a gradual retreat from influence in external affairs. But there was no revolution: the Dutch were able to change their rulers without overturning the political and social order.

Sovereignty lay with the seven provinces separately; in each, the states ruled, and in the states, the representatives of the towns (though nowhere else so preponderant as in Holland where, of 19 delegations, 18 represented towns and 1 the nobility). Action could not be taken without a unanimous vote; it was therefore common for issues to be referred back to the town corporations. Only in Friesland did the peasant farmers, grouped in self-governing associations, have a voice. The towns were largely immune from interference with their affairs; they also exercised some control over the provincial states and therefore, indirectly, over the Republic itself. The states-general of the Republic dealt with the affairs of the state: diplomatic and military measures and taxes. Its members were ambassadors, closely tied by their instructions; when they could not agree, they had to refer back to their province. The system could only have worked in a small country. As it was there were serious delays. On the eve of the French invasion, in 1672, Gelderland and Overijssel wasted precious time by withholding consent to new recruiting measures. The Netherlanders had fought to preserve their provincial rights against the foreigners – and they would not readily forgo them. The treaty of Münster (1648) provided Ter Borch with the subject of a famous painting: he depicts the Dutch delegates standing, hands raised, to swear the oath of ratification. Each province had sent its own delegation to Münster. Negotiations were carried on against a background of public debate. The Utrecht ambassador refused to sign the treaty and the Zeeland man boycotted the ceremony of ratification. The Dutch nation came of age officially in the eyes of the world – by a breach of the rules. If the occasion was an impressive exercise in the testing of public opinion such as would have been possible nowhere else in Europe at that time, it was not precisely the display of national unity depicted by the painter.

Policy-making came to revolve round two officials and their respective parties. The chief legal officer of the states of Holland, the stipendiary councillor, representing the province which paid more than half the taxes, was able, by various forms of influence, to secure support for his proposals. The *stadholder*'s power was based more upon patronage. He was originally the duke of Burgundy's lieutenant in each province. Since the revolt, the prince of Orange had usually been *stadholder* in Holland, Zeeland, Utrecht, Overijssel and Gelderland, while the Nassau cousins held the post in Friesland and Groningen. The posts of captain-general and admiral-general, with overall command of the armed forces, had usually been conferred upon the prince of Orange by the states-general. Without the title of the king, the prince fulfilled some of the duties, and possessed the means to support the dignity, of a monarch. The family estates in the Netherlands, Germany and France were large enough to have placed the Orange family well up in the league of German princes. Their name would ever speak of the heroic war leadership of William I and his sons, Maurice and Frederick Henry. William III was the grandson of Charles I of England and great-grandson of Henry IV of France. He himself was to become king of England in 1689. Round the core of the Orange party, officials, tenants on the family estates and officers in the army and navy, clustered all who opposed the ruling clique of Holland. At all times this was a formidable interest. At times of crisis the party showed that it had the will and organization to seize the commanding heights. At such times, as in 1653, when the English were winning the war at sea, and in 1672, as the French advanced on Amsterdam, Orangist feeling became a hysterical clamour.

The essential differences between Orange men and the regents of Amsterdam can be simply stated. The regents preferred peace, in the interests of expanding trade and lower taxes. They regarded military (preferably naval) operations as a last resort if Dutch commercial interests were threatened. They were seldom entirely free agents. In the English wars the force of popular opinion drove the Dutch government into a reluctant show of chauvinism. In 1672 the French invasion left no alternative but to resist. The Orange party had to consider the security of their estates and the interest of their relatives. They would have liked to support the Stuarts in the civil war. They clung to the dream of a united Netherlands. They saw themselves as the natural defenders of the country against aggression, French as well as Spanish. War was their métier; about bills and debts they were notoriously indifferent. The regents, by contrast, believed it to be their duty and interest to protect the liberties of town and province, their legacy from the middle ages, and to resist all attempts at imposing a central autocratic authority. Three times in the seventeenth century, in 1618 (the

Oldenbarneveldt affair), 1650 and 1672, these differences came to a head. In 1747, true to tradition, the Dutch again responded to a French invasion by calling on William IV to be *stadholder* of all seven provinces. Not until 1815 was the logical conclusion reached in the establishment of William I as king.

The resumption of war with Spain in 1621 had been the inevitable result of Spanish aggression in the Rhineland; but Maurice and Frederick Henry were not unhappy to accept the challenge. Between 1625 and his death in 1647, Frederick Henry, less intransigent in domestic policies than his brother, raised the reputation of his house to new heights. He preserved constitutional forms, but married his son into the Stuart royal house. William II succeeded Frederick Henry and tried to capitalize on his achievements. Brashly he planned to renew the war against Spain in return for French support, first for intervention in the English civil war on behalf of the Stuarts, second for a *coup d'état* against the regents of Holland. He knew that they would oppose him, for with a debt of 140,000,000 *guilders* already, they wanted to reduce the size of the army. He could rely upon the support of the army, many Calvinist ministers, and all who had reason to resent Holland's supremacy over other provinces. What little unity the Orange party possessed would, however, have been shattered if his supporters had known his ultimate aims.

In 1650, after the states-general, in deadlock over army reductions, tried to call the tune, the commanders of companies maintained by Holland were told that they would not receive their pay. With powers similar to those given to his uncle Maurice in 1618, William was authorized by the states-general to suppress the disorder that was spreading through the country. With a cavalcade of officers he travelled round Holland but could not persuade the towns to obey his orders. In July he imprisoned six Holland regents in Loeuvenstein castle and marched towards Amsterdam. The town closed its gates but negotiated. In return for the freeing of the prisoners, the city dismissed some of its regents and promised not to obstruct William's policy. Amsterdam had shown little spirit. But it was one thing to overawe the city, another to persuade the Hollanders, over a long period, to pay the price of his ambitions. It is possible that his policies would have united the whole republic against him. He certainly failed to secure the approval of the states-general for war against Spain. Yet the monarchical principle, centralizing, autocratic, militaristic, which he represented, was soon everywhere in the ascendant. If William had learnt to be more of a Dutchman than a Frenchman and shown something of the tact of his family, Dutch history could have been very different. Or there could have been a revolution. The question remains unresolved for on 6 November 1650 William died of smallpox. Without him, his party disintegrated.

In January 1651 the so-called 'Grand Assembly' met at the Hague, after the states of Holland had by-passed the states-general (and the Orangists) and invited provinces to send new delegates to a special meeting. Undoubtedly the examples of Parisian *frondeurs* and English republicans were noted. The upshot was, however, neither radical nor positively republican: after a series of negative decisions (for example no new captain-general, admiral-general or *stadholder* was elected for 5 out of the 7 provinces) the provinces emerged with greater powers: war could not be declared, nor peace made, without the consent of all the provinces. Like contemporary Poles and Germans, the Dutch showed themselves to be separatists above all. But what was lacking in those countries existed in the United Provinces: one province, capable of influencing and dominating the rest, and a sophisticated leadership, capable of the diplomatic and administrative exercises required to make the provinces work together. Holland assumed, and because of its wealth the rest could not deny, the right to lead.

Johan de Witt

From 1653 to 1672, when he was lynched, the pensionary Johan de Witt (son of one of the regents imprisoned by William II) was the most important figure in the republic. When William II died, the regents caused a medal to be struck bearing the text: 'The last hour of the prince is the beginning of freedom.' A few months later, Princess Mary bore the son who was to be the future William III, *stadholder* – and king of England. The child inherited the quarrel, now embittered by the events of 1650. Like de Witt he was to prove serious and dedicated to the interests of his country. De Witt was only 27 in 1653; there could eventually have been a fruitful partnership between the two men. But plots and propaganda kept alive the spirit of rivalry. Between de Witt's 'system of true liberty', as his adherents called it, and Orange dynasticism, no compromise appeared possible. It was essential to de Witt's purpose to keep William out of the *stadholder*-ships. In all but Friesland and Groningen the office was left vacant.

De Witt was a scholar who translated Corneille's *Horace* into Dutch, a mathematician who pioneered life insurance on a practical basis, a fine representative of the generation who were brought up for a career in the public service. He showed skill in handling the complicated machinery of Dutch politics. He made his reputation by his energetic direction of the war effort in the critical months of the first English war; he enhanced it by the dexterous financial policies which reduced the republic's heavy war debts. The de Witt who protected Dutch interests in the Baltic against the ambitious operations of Sweden's Charles X, and who forged with England and Sweden the Triple Alliance (January 1668) to check the aggression of Louis XIV, was a European statesman of the first rank. Perhaps he had his share of 'the narrow class egoism' with which Geyl has charged the leaders of Holland in this period. He was as determined to preserve the supremacy of his party within Holland, and of Holland within the republic, as the Dutch as a whole were to preserve their advantage against their unfortunate brethren of the south. In his world there was little room for sentiment about unity. As he said, the United Provinces were not *respublica* but *respublicae*. But he lived simply and eschewed display. His salary was small and he was incorruptible. Temple noted that he was usually seen in the streets alone and on foot, 'like the commonest burgher of the town'. His regime also made a consciously rational appeal to the literate classes. The brothers de la Court and the philosopher Spinoza were among those who lent their pens. There was an air of sophistication very different from the more homely regime of Jacob Cats, Holland's favourite poet, convenor of the Grand Assembly and de Witt's predecessor as pensionary.

De Witt could be sure that most of the regents would support a regime which guaranteed their hold upon office. His problem was to broaden his support. His attitude towards dissenting sects was latitudinarian, less from conviction about the positive value of freedom than from fear of upsetting the economy. Extreme nationalism or insistence upon religious orthodoxy were luxuries which a trading nation could not afford. More than half the country dwellers were still Catholic. Then there were small sects representing various degrees of liberalism. On both flanks therefore of the well-organized body of orthodox Calvinists, who comprised about a third of the population, were dissenters who were natural supporters of the de Witts and their policy. Inevitably they lacked political organization. At times of emergency there was little to mobilize against the popular appeal of the house of Orange. The lower-middle classes, *predikants* (largely recruited from this class), shopkeepers and small tradesmen were not impressed by the rule of an enlightened oligarchy. Social animosities were heightened by the failure of the government to solve the economic problems whose effects were felt most keenly by the poorer classes. The trade wars against England (1652–4, 1664–7, 1672–4) contributed to those problems. Ironically, the government which should have been most single-minded in pursuing peace and trading advantage was first weakened by the depression of trade which affected all countries in the 1650s and 1660s, and then overthrown by war. There is much to admire in the dexterity of de Witt's statesmanship in these years. Most of the problems were not of his making. The partisanship of the trade wars was the bitter fruit of the buccaneering years, when the Dutch looted and grabbed the Portuguese empire. He inherited an exposed and isolated position – analogous to that of the British Empire at the close of the Victorian era – rich, tainted with arrogance. In retrospect it seems that the most the Dutch could do, given Colbert's aggressive trade policies on the one hand, and the stirring of British rivalry on the other, was to maintain the defensive. This would have required a restraint which was hardly to be expected from a country so new, and hitherto so successful. De Witt, the epitome of intelligent conservatism, sought to maintain Dutch power in a hostile world. His motto might well have been that of William the Silent: *je maintiendrai.*

The three Anglo-Dutch wars of the seventeenth century make sorry reading. Greed and shortsightedness characterize the attitudes of both sides. 'What we want,' said the English admiral, Lord Albemarle, 'is more of the trade the Dutch now have.' To Shaftesbury, Holland was 'through interest and inclination the eternal enemy'. The perhaps unconscious arrogance which so infuriated Englishmen and Frenchmen can be seen in the inscription of the medal struck by the states to commemorate the Triple Alliance in 1668: 'After having reconciled kings, preserved the freedom of the seas, brought about a glorious peace by force of arms, and established order in Europe....' They had reason for pride. It is in Britain, in the National Maritime Museum at Greenwich, that de Ruyter is described as the greatest seaman of his age; van Tromp was not far behind in contemporary estimation. Dutch merchants and politicians, working closely with the naval strategists, thought that they could find cheap means of obtaining commercial superiority. Naval fighting was of course relatively inexpensive; part of the cost was paid by the sailors who died in those startlingly bloody actions: 10,000 were killed or wounded in the Four Days Battle in June 1666. Even in an age that was ultra-sensitive about matters of precedence, the question of the flag seems to be a trivial one: the English claimed the right of salute in 'British seas'; at the treaty of Breda, in 1667, the Dutch succeeded in limiting the 'British seas' to the English Channel. Along with the touchiness and opportunism, however, rival principles can be seen. The English, obsessed by 'mercantilist' ideas, held that there was a sum total of world trade and that their share must be won from their rivals' share: they further believed in their right to dominion in British seas. The Dutch argued, in the spirit of Grotius, father of international law, for the freedom of the seas. Their argument seemed hypocritical to the English. As Downing pointed out, in 1664, 'It is *mare liberum* in the British seas but *mare clausum* on the coast of Africa and in the East-Indies.' Where the East India Company operated there was indeed no question that the Dutch were shameless monopolists. Nearer home, they had kept the mouth of the Scheldt closed to foreign shipping since the treaty of Münster – to spite Antwerp. The Dutch attitude seemed to be the more reprehensible because it was generally held that they were capable of operating more cheaply and efficiently – and would therefore win in open competition. The wars were perhaps inevitable; they were also inconclusive. They ended when it was realized on both sides that there was a greater threat to both of them, in the shape of France. In 1672 Shaftesbury was prepared to speak to the theme '*delenda est Carthago*', urging war; by 1674 he was more concerned about the growing prestige of Catholic and absolutist government. Some Englishmen were anxious to make common cause with the enemies of France; others were content to see France and the United Provinces exhaust their resources in a war of unprecedented fury.

The Baltic corn trade fell off badly during the *stadholder*-less period: bad harvests in the Vistula area, recurrent wars, a fall in the demand for corn in western and southern Europe were contributory causes. De Witt's intervention in the Baltic question illustrates the vigour of his foreign policy when Dutch commercial power could be used to full effect. The Swedes had emerged from the peace of Westphalia in a strong position: the Dutch now supported the Danes in order to maintain the balance. Having resolved the question of dues to be paid to the Danes for the use of the Sound (350,000 *guilders* a year), and secured a guarantee from Sweden that Dutch trade would not be interrupted, de Witt was able to stay neutral in the first Northern War. When, however, in 1658, Charles X attacked Copenhagen with a view to dethroning the Danish king, de Witt sent the Dutch fleet to the Sound; it defeated the Swedes and relieved Copenhagen. After busy diplomacy, a joint decision by England, France and the Republic, at the concert of the Hague (May 1659), that peace should be imposed on the combatants, and the use of the Dutch fleet to that end, the peace of Copenhagen was signed (1660). The episode showed that the Dutch could not defend their commercial interest without adopting the stance and methods of a great power. De Witt showed, by his patience and ultimate firmness, and by acting with France and England, that power could be exercised in a responsible way. He hoped to go further and make a defensive alliance between the three countries. With England, negotiations broke down over the question of freedom of the seas; but with France he concluded an agreement (1662) which proved its usefulness in the second Anglo-Dutch war, when the French sent troops to help the Dutch beat back the invasion of the bishop of Münster.

After two years of war in which, if anything, the Dutch had the better of the naval fighting, in June 1667, de Witt authorized the daring and successful raid on the Medway and then negotiated the moderate peace of Breda: Cape Coast castle in Africa and New York were ceded to England, Surinam was gained in return. But it was with reluctance that he signed the Triple Alliance, between England, Holland and Sweden, in the following year. He had tried to come to acceptable terms with Louis XIV over the southern Netherlands, which Louis had invaded in the previous year. De Witt was driven to make the alliance by pressure from the states of Holland who were angered by Colbert's tariff policy, rather than by Charles II's apparent concern about the growth of French power. In appearance a check to French aggression, it was to prove to be the undoing of Holland, and of de Witt. Within two years, the French and English kings were making the treaty of Dover (1670). For the French king the treaty and the subsequent war – which was intended to crush the Dutch as a military and commercial rival – were a fateful departure from the policy of the cardinals: he jeopardized his country's strong diplomatic position in Germany and northern Europe. Even allowing for the foreceful reasoning of Colbert and the cruder arguments of the military advisers, Louis seems to have been activated by doctrinaire reasons: their Calvinist austerity and business values, the separatism of provinces and town, the stress upon freedom in economy and society set the Dutch apart in the Europe of centralized administrations and regulated economies. De Witt himself embodied the traits which Louis most distrusted and – being young and complacent – despised. During his period of office the Dutch had grown if anything further apart from the movement of ideas and the development of institutions elsewhere. Dutch cartoonists depicted the sun of Louis being eclipsed by a round Dutch cheese moon. Louis went to war to teach republicans a lesson and to put merchants in their place.

William III

De Witt had striven to accommodate the house of Orange. From the policy of exclusion he had moved towards the more constructive policy of initiating the young prince of Orange into state business. Since it was de Witt's intention that William should be a good republican, it was essential to resist the movement in other provinces to restore the prince to his ancestors' offices. He feared that the restoration of William would open avenues of influence to the English. During the second English war the Orange household was purged of notorious intriguers and the states of Holland abolished the *stadholder*-ship of their province altogether by the Eternal Edict (1667). De Witt did not wholly fail. William III was bitter about the regents: 'the promoters of Liberty and Privileges are not anything but promoters of their own liberty and prestige'; but he did learn some of the lessons that the Grand Pensionary tried to instil. By comparison with Frederick Henry, for example, his view of the national interest was less narrowly dynastic. Meanwhile de Witt could not prevent William moving into a position of political as well as military authority. In 1670 he entered the council of state. In February 1672 the states-general appointed William captain-general, albeit for one campaign. When the campaign opened with the French attack in May, the weaknesses of the army were at once exposed. It is tempting but misleading to compare de Witt's regime with that of de la Gardie in Sweden. In both countries, antimilitarism and economies had sapped the morale of the army. But it was the trade wars that had compelled de Witt to put expenditure on the navy before that of the army. Moreover, in Holland, the Dutch commanders were handicapped by the fact that each province now had authority over the battalions paid for from their contributions. The young captain-general had no option but to order his forces, outnumbered by 3 to 1, to retreat behind the 'water line', the flooded zone between the Zuider Zee and the river Lek. By the end of June 1672 Louis's troops controlled Utrecht and Gelderland. The nobility of Overijssel submitted to the bishop of Münster; everywhere in the eastern provinces the Catholic clergy took over their old churches; it seemed as if the Union were breaking up.

Defeatism infected army and politicians. De Witt invoked the heroic past and talked of turning Amsterdam into a great redoubt. Louis XIV made excessive demands, the Orange party beat the national drum and instigated popular disturbances against the regime. Towards the end of June de Witt was attacked in the streets and wounded. On 3 July the states of Holland proclaimed William *stadholder*. Negotiations were broken off. Anger and suspicion continued to stalk the streets, feeding on bad news. Early in August, de Witt, recuperating from his wounds, resigned his office. In the eyes of the extreme Orangists this was not sufficient expiation. On 20 August, with his brother Cornelius, he was caught by a hysterical mob at the Hague, dragged into the main square and murdered; their corpses were hung upside down, then cut up for souvenirs. William appeared to condone the murder while *predikants* praised a godly deed. About one-third of the regents of Holland were compelled to resign. They were replaced by men of similar background but Orange sympathies, expected to co-operate with the regime. With the fears and furies engendered by the invasion, and the chronic existence in every city of a layer of unemployed and poor, the violence is not surprising. Clarendon might have met a similar fate had he not chosen exile – in Holland – after the disaster of the Medway. The comparison prompts the further reflection: that it would have been admirable indeed if the civilized de Witt had been allowed to live and to use his leisure to write his history of events. He had not, however, like Clarendon in England, witnessed a revolution, either in 1650 or in 1672. William had been appointed in legal form. He had assumed powers appropriate to an emergency; but he had produced no revolutionary programme. He made no basic changes in the form of government: the regents continued to monopolize office as before. There was a gradual evolution towards a new and, for military and diplomatic purposes, more workable version of the old order: the regents governed the republic, but now in the interest of the Orange family. Only in the eastern provinces reconquered from the French did he achieve anything approaching sovereignty as it was understood in France; in 1673–4 Utrecht, Groningen and Overijssel were asked to agree to a 'government regulation' giving him control of all the chief appointments in town and province. In Holland and Zeeland, however, the office of *stadholder* became hereditary. But in those provinces, and in the face of the states-general that they dominated, William always had to struggle to show that what was good for Europe was good for Holland. By being so extreme in his terms when the Dutch were apparently on their knees and by his aggressions of the 1680s, Louis XIV provided William with the arguments which he needed.

Between 1672 and 1714, the United Provinces were the heart of successive coalitions against France and, until his death after a fall from his horse in March 1702, William was, with Louis XIV and Leopold, one of the leading statesmen of Europe in a period of almost continuous war. The Dutch bore the burdens, financial and military, of twenty-seven years of war with a resilience which gives some idea of the resources of the nation; but in trade and manufactures a ceiling had been reached. The small size of the land and the population began to tell; the military effort was disproportionate. William may have had reason to be impatient with the reluctance of the regents of Amsterdam to back his master plan for thwarting the king of France; but they had reason to be concerned about the steady attrition of Dutch wealth.

William was only 21 in 1672. He was slight in build, with a stoop and a weak chest; pale, fastidious in appetite; reserved in manner, especially with women. He proved himself nevertheless a brave, patient, and ultimately accomplished statesman. Above all, in adversity and triumph, he remained a student of men and affairs. From the loneliness of youth, with a grand tradition and an uncertain future, to the rude coming of age in conflict with the greatest military power the world had yet seen; in the success of his gambler's throw for the crucial prize of the English throne; in his efforts to conjure supplies and troops out of his adopted country; in the bleak reverses of the Nine Years War; in the final diplomatic manoeuvres round the moribund empire of Spain, in all he displayed a pliability and grasp of essentials which enabled him to win where more brilliant men might have lost. He derived strength from the puritan zeal of the orthodox Calvinists, who identified the struggle against France with their own campaign against laxity of faith and morals in the congregations. Louis XIV's treatment of the Huguenots only confirmed the attractively simple view that the French were the enemies of God. Throughout, William kept his eyes fixed on his supreme aim – the defeat of France. In his hands, the Orange party gave moral leadership to a cause which united the provinces. His character is far from simple. Along with the vital ability to take long-term views and the dogged persistence that recall William the Silent, there went a certain daring. As a soldier, unlike Frederick Henry, he always looked for the decisive combat in the field. He was matched successively by Condé and Luxembourg: he was defeated bloodily at Seneffe (1674), more seriously at Cassel (1677) and again at Steenkerke (1692) and Neerwinden (1693). In all the campaigns of the Nine Years War the capture of Namur was his only important success. Yet, in all disappointments, he never lost his moral authority over the army and politicians. He used, without seeking to break, the institutions which embodied the liberties and pride of the people. By his moderation he persuaded the regents of Amsterdam that the security of Europe was compatible with the interests of trade and Protestantism. He retained solid support in the face of rising taxation (direct and indirect taxes were more fairly levied than the French, more onerous than the English);

the reasonable complaints of those who grew impatient at the long duration of the wars (fifteen years during William's rule) and who suspected after 1689 that Dutch interests were being subordinated to British.

After his death in 1702, there ensued a second *stadholder*-less period; after 1689, with William concentrating his attention upon his role as king of England, Anthony Heinsius, who became Grand Pensionary in that year, assumed tactical direction under William of Dutch policy. The objectives remained essentially unchanged. William fought primarily to prevent the Spanish Netherlands coming under French control. It was easier to persuade taxpayers that there was a sound economic purpose behind the war, because French occupation of the southern provinces interfered seriously with Dutch trade. By the terms of the peace of Utrecht (1713) the 'barrier' forts were recognized; the southern provinces were transferred, needless to say without their inhabitants being consulted, to Austria. But one fundamental war aim was not achieved. For all their expenditure of money and men – 8000 died at Malplaquet alone – the Dutch, deserted and bullied by the English who, from 1710, had pursued their own negotiations with France, were unable to preserve their commercial predominance in the Spanish empire. The trade was debarred to the French; but it was the British who gained, with Gibraltar and Minorca, potential mastery of the Mediterranean, and, with the *asiento*, entry into the valuable South American trade.

The Periwig Period

Some Dutch historians quarrel with the generally accepted view that the eighteenth century was one of decline for the Republic. About some aspects there can be no doubt. Art historians accept that the genius of Dutch painting died with the seventeenth century. No one would place the flower painter, Jan van Huysum (1682–1749), among the supreme artists of the golden age. High prices were paid for the work of Adrien van der Werff (1659–1722), but he was painting at a time when there was relatively little competition. It may be significant that one of the most important artists of the periwig period was Daniel Marot (1663–1752): he was a Huguenot immigrant, and worked as architect and designer on such large commissions as the palace of Het Loo for William III, and the Trevesaal, the states-general's reception hall for foreign ambassadors; but the style, though attractive, was entirely French. Or, if military success be the touchstone, again there is no doubt: the Dutch effort in the War of the Austrian Succession was insignificant compared to that of earlier wars; and when the Dutch joined Britain's enemies in the American war (1780), in Charles Wilson's words, they were 'hopelessly beaten, their commerce reduced to nothing, the Bank of Amsterdam ruined, and Dutch capital lured away by French propaganda from the safest investments in Europe'. It is true that the picture of Dutch decline was painted in unnecessarily sombre colours by the 'patriots' of the revolutionary period and romantics of the nineteenth century. It is possible to sympathize with the words of B.M. Vlekke who writes: 'We admire Erasmus who, in a turbulent period, described the conversation of friends in a beautiful garden as the height of civilised entertainment; yet we are disgusted with his 18th century followers who put his theory into practice.' Tranquil lives were lived by those who could afford them, but economic stagnation meant unemployment and poverty for large numbers of the population. There is ample evidence to show that the Dutch did not benefit much in trade and finance from the neutralist policy of their rulers: there were weaknesses and failures in precisely those areas of the economy where they had once been so strong.

The population grew at a slower rate than that of the rest of Europe. In 1700 it was 1.85 million; in 1790, 2.08 million. Amsterdam, which, like London, might have been expected to show growth, had the same number of houses in 1795 as in 1740. In less favoured places, decline was widespread. Boswell wrote in 1764 of finding 'their principal towns sadly decayed'. Evidently the process was most severe in the small sea towns of north Holland, Zeeland and in some of the formerly important inland towns, like Leiden and Delft.

Greater competition, protectionist measures by other countries, and a change in eating habits help to account for the decline of the herring, cod and whale fisheries which affected towns like Enkhuisen and Zierikzee, now so attractive to modern tourists in their preserved but lifeless state. Just as the benefits of intensive fishing had brought opportunities for employment in ancillary crafts such as coopering and rope-making, so now its decline caused a shrinkage of demand which made its effects felt throughout the economy. The Dutch share of the Baltic timber trade fell from 65 per cent in 1730 to 32 per cent in 1780. Sawmills closed and sailors looked to other markets. The Society of the Free British Fisheries, founded in 1750, for example, found most of its skippers in Holland or Denmark. In the American war, the Dutch were able to find only half the sailors they required to man their ships.

The technical superiority enjoyed by the Dutch in their golden age was now lost, not merely in map-making and navigation, but in the vital business of ship-building. Of the possible causes – shortage of capital, lack of skilled craftsmen, sheer conservatism – the last seems to be most important, for it is characteristic of the whole society. There are signs too of some loss of morale in the great trading companies: though still profitably in business they were losing ground to the British. In 1643, there were 85 Dutch Indiamen in Asian seas; in 1743, 48 of about the same size. The Dutch had nothing to show that compared with the spectacular advance of British interests in India in the age of Clive and Hastings. One sea trade flourished in this period: Dutch smugglers traded profitably with Britain in tobacco and brandy, and high duties in Holland encouraged smuggling into the country at all levels. Advocates of lower duties argued that the Dutch were losing valuable entrepôt trade; in the trade in sugar between Bordeaux and the Baltic in 1750, it was Hamburg, and not, as formerly, Amsterdam, that handled most of the business.

In 1740, an exceedingly cold winter was followed by a wet summer. The poorer classes suffered badly. The setback was temporary, but the fact that some Dutch historians have dated the decline of the United Provinces from this year indicates the central importance of farming, which still employed more than all other occupations together. The overall picture is one of stability: cattle plague was a recurring threat, as in other western countries (the English destroyed infected cattle and were relatively immune). In the plague of 1744–5, 75 per cent of the cattle died in some provinces. Butter and cheese continued to be valuable exports. In Holland the distinctive market-garden business developed, while in Friesland they concentrated upon potatoes. In marked contrast to Britain, farmers were slow to innovate. To make this comparison is to be reminded of the importance in Britain of the large landowner and his capital. In Holland heavy provincial taxes, a serious effect of the French wars, and the paucity of great estates militated against land improvement. However, in the second half of the eighteenth century there was a general improvement of prices which, together with more intensive grain farming and the cultivation of reclaimed land, brought modest prosperity.

Manufactures were less fortunate. In 1775 the cloth production of Leyden was under a third of what it had been a hundred years before. Shipbuilding presents a gloomy picture too. There were several hundred ships on the stocks at Zaandam, when the young Tsar Peter visited the place; in 1770 he would have found about thirty. There were pockets of prosperity, notably diamond cutting, paper-making, and gin and brandy distilling; but a relatively small domestic market and a chronic dependence on other countries for raw materials together worked against the Dutchman and emphasized how exceptional and precarious had been the prosperity of the seventeenth century. Dutch exports fell as other countries developed their own trades and industries: the English, for example, no longer required them to 'finish' their linen and woollen goods. Moreover, English and French tariffs were followed by similar tariffs by the other countries. Russia and Prussia and even, on a smaller scale, Denmark, whose rulers sought to develop the resources and powers of the state by meticulous protection, provide examples of what the great trading republic was up against. It did not comfort the Dutch that so many skilled Dutchmen were working in Germany and Russia. This diminishes the force of the argument, popular among industrialists at the time, that high wages and costs made Dutch manufactures less competitive. Diagnoses and remedies were plentiful: the Dutch were fully conscious of their reduced state. It is misleading to see the Dutch experience in the light of what happened in Britain, where the industrial revolution, gathering momentum in the eighteenth century, was exceptional: there a swelling population brought cheap labour, commercial success made capital available, science contributed to an advancing technology and raw materials abounded, notably iron and coal. Within his own limited field of opportunity, however, the Dutchman was no longer the force he had been. 'We are no longer innate inventors,' wrote a contributor to a Dutch journal in 1775. 'Nowadays we only make copies.' There is nothing, however, surprising about the development of a nation of traders into a nation of *rentiers*. (There was a similar tendency, though largely concealed by the wealth of empire, in late Victorian England.) The social prestige of the merchant had always been higher than that of the industrialist. Where in other countries the successful manufacturer or merchant might purchase land, the Dutchman in similar circumstances refined his techniques of buying and selling.

The financial sector prospered without greater effort than was required by decisions about the most profitable use of ample funds. The shrinking volume of domestic demand discouraged the investment in manufactures which alone could stimulate demand. Inevitably the merchant bankers, investing in foreign funds and enterprises, were accused of financing the country's rivals. Inevitably it became a political issue. The regents were drawn almost exclusively from the financial establishment whose wealth and power were thus self-perpetuating. After the death of William III in 1702 there had been no *stadholder*. The decentralized structure of the provinces, which had served the country well in the seventeenth century, now proved dangerously obsolete as foreign competition became more effective. No change was made in the financial arrangements. Provincial rivalries even prevented the construction of roads and canals. Holland had pioneered some of the most important advances of the Enlightenment. In the eighteenth century she was able to benefit relatively little from them. As in 1672 the frustration of the lesser burghers and professional men, and the anger of hungry workers, trapped now between static wages and rising prices, gave a sharper edge to controversy. As in 1672 the aggrieved saw their oppressors as the regents and their hopes of redress in the house of Orange; as then they took to the streets in the shock and panic of a French invasion. In 1747 William IV, of the Friesian line of the family, was elected *stadholder*. He was expected to break the power of the regents and to revise their financial policies. The meetings of the *Doelisten*, who took their name from their original meeting place in Amsterdam, demanded an end to the sale of offices, the restoration of guild regulations and the election of militia officers from the citizenry.

The movement spread through the larger cities, taking a radical form in Leyden, where unemployed workers supported the establishment of a rival town government. But it did not succeed, for neither William IV, nor his successor William V, a minor when he became *stadholder* in 1751, was interested in fundamental reform. Once their own supporters had been placed in key position the Orange princes maintained a system as exclusive and corrupt as it had ever been. Until the 'patriotic' movement which first brought about Dutch intervention (1781) on the side of France and the American colonies, then used defeat in the war as the pretext for launching a programme of American-style constitutional reform (1782), the dynasty was secure in power. There ensued five years of humiliating exile till the counter-coup of 1787, led by the king of Prussia, William's brother-in-law, re-established him in authority. The 'patriots' bided their time till the French Revolution brought them a second chance to bring about what they saw as the salvation of their country.

Further Reading

The best general survey is by a great Dutch historian, P. Geyl, *The Netherlands in the 17th century*, 2 vols (1961, 1963). His perspective is that of the seventeen provinces of the Burgundian state, so tragically separated and demarcated, north from south, by a line made by war. Thereafter the history of the southern provinces is overshadowed by that of their masters, Spain until 1714, Austria thereafter. H. Pirenne, *Histoire de Belgique* (begun in 1906, completed in 1929), is still the fullest history: vols 4 and 5 are relevant to this period. Even Pirenne, a Walloon, teaching history in French to Flemish students at Ghent, the only public university in the Dutch-speaking part of the country, was not exempt from the charge of bias: objectivity is hard to achieve amid the linguistic and cultural diversity of the southern state as Geyl explains in his essay, 'The national state and the writers of Netherlandish history', in *Debates with Historians* (1955). Even allowing for the difficulty, there is a remarkable paucity of good writing in English about 'the cockpit of Europe' which had been the scene, before the debilitating war between Spain and the northern provinces, of so much fruitful activity in manufacturing and the arts.

By contrast the successful Dutch state has received ample treatment. Good surveys include K.D.H. Haley, *The Dutch in the 17th Century* (London, 1972), C.H. Wilson, *The Dutch Republic and Civilisation in the Seventeenth Century* (1968), and P. Zumther, *Daily Life in Rembrandt's Holland* (1962). All are illustrated, which is important in the treatment of a state whose art expressed so much of its character. Sir William Temple, *Observations upon the United Provinces of the Netherlands*, ed. G.N. Clark (rev. edn, Oxford, 1972), goes a long way to explaining the favourable impression made by this state upon foreigners and gives a clear picture of its constitution. A work by M. Bowen, *The Netherlands Displayed* (1926), describes individual provinces. J. de Vries, *The Dutch Rural Economy, 1500–1700* (New Haven, 1974), V. Barbour, *Capitalism in Amsterdam in the Seventeenth Century* (Baltimore, 1950) and 'Dutch and English merchant shipping in the seventeenth century', in E.M. Carus-Wilson (ed.), *Essays in Economic History* (1954), C. Wilson, *Profit and Power: A Study of the Dutch Wars* (1957), and G.N. Clark, 'The Dutch alliance and the war against French trade, 1689–97', *Cambridge Historical Journal*,

(1954), are all valuable. For the Dutch overseas, see particularly C.R. Boxer, *The Dutch Seaborne Empire* (London, 1977), and *The Dutch in Brazil, 1624–1654* (Oxford, 1957). For one great Dutch sailor, see P. Blok, *The Life of Admiral de Ruyter* (London, 1976).

Though there is no adequate biography of de Witt, the gap is partly filled by the translation of another of P. Geyl's works, *Orange and Stuart* (1969), covering the years 1641–72. Stephen Baxter, *William III* (1966), appears sounder to the English reader than to the Dutch: they claim that he distorts the position of William's opponents in order to establish the greatness of his subject. The religious questions which were so important politically within the United Provinces may be studied in D. Nobbs, *Theocracy and Toleration* (Cambridge, 1938). The importance of immigration from the south is explained in P. Dibon, 'Le Refuge Wallon, précurseur du réfuge Huguenot', *XVII siècle* (1957). The following books may be chosen from many to represent the many-sided cultural achievement: D.W. Davies, *The World of the Elseviers* (The Hague, 1954); E. Labrousse, *Pierre Bayle* (The Hague, 1963); A.E. Bell. *Christian Huygens and the Development of Science in the Seventeenth Century* (1947); G.A. Lindeboom, *Hermann Boerhaave* (1968); G.L. Burke, *The Making of Dutch Towns* (1956); J. Rosenburg, S. Slive and E.H. ter Kuile, *Dutch Art and Architecture, 1600–1800* (Harmondsworth, 1972). The list could be twice as long. It suggests the richness and versatility of seventeenth-century Dutch culture. By contrast, reflecting relative decline, there is a paucity of writing about the eighteenth century. In chapter 10 of Boxer, *The Dutch Seaborne Empire* (cited above), the reasons for decline are succinctly stated. See also Alice Carter, 'Dutch foreign investment, 1738–1800', *Economica*, 15 (1953), and her *Neutrality or Commitments: The Evolution of Dutch Foreign Policy 1667–1795* (London, 1975); C. Wilson, *Anglo-Dutch Commerce and Finance in the Eighteenth Century* (1941); also his 'Decline of the Netherlands', *Economic History and the Historian* (1969).

13

SCANDINAVIA

The Baltic Sea

The Baltic Sea is nearly a thousand miles long from furthest east to west. But for three narrow outlets to the North Sea, the Great and Little Belts and the Sound, it would be a lake; tides are small, the water is only slightly salt and therefore freezes easily. But several of the longest rivers in Europe flow into the sea: the Oder, Vistula and Dvina. Teeming with fish, endowed with excellent harbours, the sea played a dominant part in the lives of the states on or near its shores. The commodities produced in the Baltic states were important to the other states of Europe. The trade routes from the north and east of Europe to the west pass through the Baltic. The economies of the western powers came to depend increasingly upon those commodities because of the disruption and shortages directly or indirectly caused by war. Thus the Baltic was both the centre of a struggle for power among the local states and the concern of more distant powers: Holland, England, France, Spain and the Empire. The series of wars, small in scale by western standards, but intensive in relation to the size of the northern powers, which culminated in the Great Northern War should therefore be seen as it was by contemporaries, not as mere scrapping on the margins of Europe but as a vital part of the struggle of the larger states for lands, fortresses and markets. Like Gustavus Adolphus in the Thirty Years War, Charles XII was to become a crucially significant figure.

Europe's ship-building depended on the timber and tar of the northern forests. The great plains of Prussia and Poland provided surplus grain for

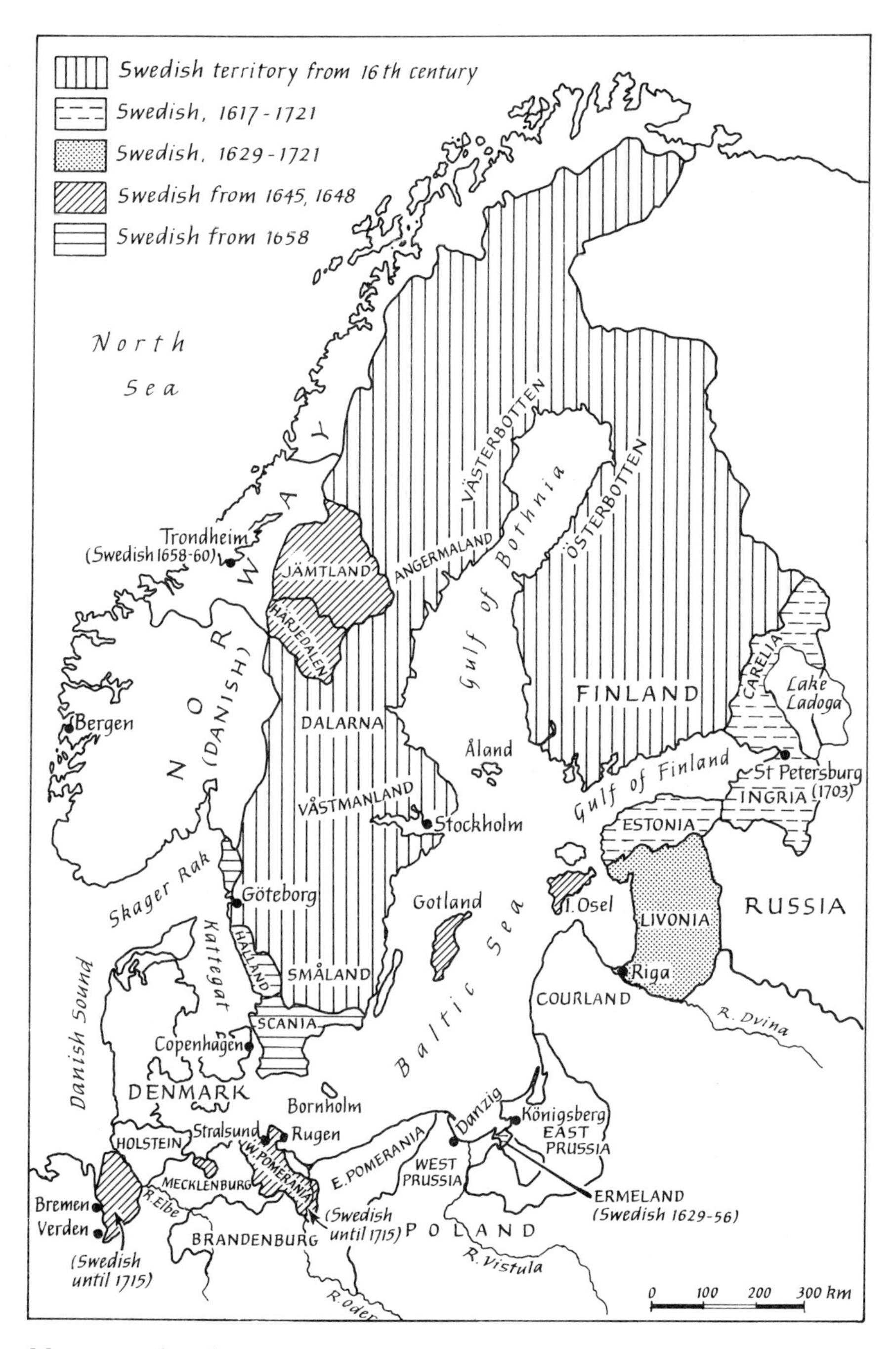

Map 13.1 *Scandinavia, 1600–1721*

the more densely populated countries of southern Europe. The growth of armaments stimulated production of iron ore and copper: Sweden's rich copper mines helped to finance her own war effort during the Thirty Years War. In exchange, the Baltic provided markets for the textiles of Britain and the Netherlands, the wines of France, and the tea, sugar and tobacco flowing into Europe from the east. The Hanse towns had once controlled the region's trade; but although there remained some flourishing trading companies, the Hanse declined. At the start of the seventeenth century, the Dutch dominated Baltic trade in a way that contributed to the economic strength and political influence of their republic. Even without the Dutch example the northern states were bound to fight for control of the Sound, bordered on both shores by Danish lands, for the rivers and harbours, and for the dues that could be levied on waterborne traffic. The struggle became more intense as the states faced mounting bills out of revenue which still came mainly, in the traditional way, from the land. With small and often primitive communities scattered over large areas, it was easier to collect dues in kind than in coin. Complicated dealings with merchants who advanced money in return for goods, or the farming out of estates in return for a share of the proceeds, were no substitute for a reliable flow of money. The Danes tried to raise their Sound dues and were to be frustrated by military defeats. The realistic reaction to that failure was to sell crown lands, to raise indirect taxes and to impose a land tax: the latter proved politically feasible because of the constitutional victory of the crown over the aristocracy. In Sweden the problem was more intractable, despite the remarkable success of her armies in the German war; some of the strains which led to the revolutionary situation of 1650 came from a victorious war and the acquisition of an empire beyond native capacity to sustain.

The warring dynasties of Europe appreciated the importance of securing allies in the north. The rise of both Sweden and Brandenburg owed much to the patronage of France. The Habsburgs sought to establish themselves on the Baltic shore during the Thirty Years War; it was also their steady concern to defend the interests of Catholic Poland. The maritime wars of England, Holland and France, between the first English Navigation Act in 1652 and the peace of Nystad in 1721 (which in this context can be treated as an extension of the peace of Utrecht), resulted in part from those countries' concern about the Baltic and their urgent need for naval supplies. It was in the interests of all to keep the Baltic open. Three times a year, a great Dutch fleet sailed for Danzig, Königsberg, Riga and Reval, laden mainly with Dutch fish and cloth, French and Portuguese salt, French and German wine, returning with Prussian corn and Norwegian timber, Silesian linens and Swedish iron. The trader republic watched keenly every shift in Baltic affairs; in this, as in other ways, teaching its rivals lessons in the use of sea power. The English in particular were concerned because they had become dependent on the Dutch for materials for ship-building. Colbert was not the first Frenchman to look grudgingly at the profits made by Dutch merchants from shipping French goods. The security of Holland depended on her maintaining a balance of power in the Baltic. This balance was threatened first by Sweden, then by Russia.

Denmark: a Study in Absolutism

Sweden established a foothold in Germany and her superiority over Denmark in a series of wars which brought her the provinces of Scania and Halland and, with them, control of the Sound. Yet of all the Baltic states at the beginning of the seventeenth century it was Denmark which seemed to be in the strongest position. The German-speaking Christian IV (1588–1648) was father-in-law of James I of England. His German estate of Holstein gave him a private income and a seat on the imperial diet; his Sound dues provided revenue and a measure of bargaining power. It is arguable however that they were a mixed blessing, since they entailed expenditure on defence, embroiled Denmark with the maritime powers, caused delays in shipping, and in the end cost Denmark the eastern part of her kingdom. The position adopted by Christian in his pamphlet, *Mare clausum* (1638), claiming supremacy over the Baltic, was an unrealistic one. The chain of islands, leading to the eastern shore of the Baltic (Bornholm was the most important) lay athwart Swedish communications: they were both an asset and a standing provocation. In short, Denmark's position was an exposed one. The Bohemian revolt and its aftermath encouraged Christian to gamble: his Lutheranism was a sufficient pretext; and he was ambitious to play a larger role. Ruler of a bare million subjects, Christian sought to strengthen his authority over the nobles, to expand from his base in Germany, and to recover what he regarded as Danish lands from the Swedes. He failed in all three objectives. Far from asserting the ancient hegemony of Denmark which had been broken with the ending of the union of Kalmar in 1523 by the Swedish Vasas (a union under Danish kings dating from 1396), he lost by precipitate moves, not only the chance of expanding trade in the distant lands around the Gulf of Finland, but also the security of his homelands. The Swedes shed no tears over the defeat of Christian and the Lutheran cause at Lutter (1626). For nearly a century after that, the Swedes were a force to be reckoned with in Europe, while the Danes failed to recover their lost advantages. Yet the history of the country does not lack distinction. Its relative failure in the power stakes can be seen in perspective in the eighteenth century, when Sweden, like Holland, settled back into a role in keeping with its resources.

We may speculate what might have been if the Danes had won Lutter or the Swedes lost Breitenfeld (1631). But there there were sound reasons for each event. Sweden's victory was prepared for by an efficient exercise of royal authority, and won by inspired training and generalship in the field.

Christian's ill-disciplined and archaic force reflected a contrasting weakness in government and the attitudes of a nobility who resisted all measures of reform. The monarchy was elective. The Oldenburgs secured their succession at each election by granting a 'capitulation', therein accepting a system of government in which king and council, the *Raad*, shared power with the nobility. The Assembly of Estates was irrelevant; the peasant estate no longer met; the clergy were dependent on the nobles; the towns were controlled by family cliques and would take no initiative. The nobles everywhere extended their privileges. As estates grew, peasants slid into serfdom. The crown was able to tax on its own estates but not on others: this is one reason for the importance attached to the Sound dues. The *Raad* was dominated by nobles. They had refused to attack Sweden in 1611 on the grounds that that country was too poor to sustain an invading army. They had reason to suspect Christian's policy of expansion, which they rightly saw to be part of his larger design of strengthening his own authority. Christian failed, where Gustavus succeeded, in establishing a basis of common purpose and effort from which to launch an ambitious policy. When he died, in the year of Westphalia (1648), trading companies, new roads and harbours, fine buildings in Copenhagen and the new city of Christiana (Oslo) witnessed to his energy and foresight; but the Swedes had secured, in a brief and inglorious war, free sailing through the Sound (1645).

Christian's second son and successor, Frederick III, was accepted by the nobles of the Assembly only in return for the surrender of his father's rights – and more. Frederick was not even allowed to leave the country without their leave. Frederick was a man of some learning, but naive in political judgement, insensitive in his attitudes. Leonora Christine, wife of his first, subsequently disgraced, chief minister, Ulfeld, was imprisoned on trivial grounds for twenty-two years in the Blue Tower of Copenhagen castle. The organist at Elsinore, the great composer Buxtehude, left Denmark in 1668 to spend the rest of his life at Lübeck. The Denmark of the *Kongelow* (king's law) was not a lively cultural scene. A successful war offered the best chance of restoring Frederick's authority. In 1657 he attacked Sweden. With Charles X occupied in Poland, the Russians poised to invade Swedish Ingria and Brandenburg eager to help, the time seemed propitious. Not for the first or last time, however, a Swedish king upset the odds by daring and skill. In a campaign that Danes would wish to forget, Charles X expelled them from Holstein and overran Jutland. After a garrison of gentleman soldiers had made a poor show of resistance, he captured the fortress of Fredriksodde (October 1657). In the unusually harsh winter that followed, Charles wrote a chapter in military history when he crossed the ice of the Little and Great Belts to the island of Sjaelland, threatened Copenhagen, and dictated terms of peace. The treaty of Roskilde (1658) was harshly punitive. Scania, Halland and Blekinge, with the island of Bornholm, were ceded to the

Swedes, as well as Trondheim and Bohuslan in Norway. Denmark was to renounce all anti-Swedish alliances and to prevent hostile warships from entering the Sound. The latter condition stung the Danes and caused delay. Charles, more soldier than diplomat, tried to execute a *coup de grâce*. He attacked again (July 1658) and captured the fortress of Kronburg overlooking the Sound. But Copenhagen was defended stoutly; and the Dutch, till then cautiously neutral, now sent their fleet. Copenhagen was relieved. In May 1659 a concert of powers, England, France and the United Provinces joined to impose a peace. When Charles X died, in February 1660, the main obstacle was removed. The Danes recovered Trondheim and Bornholm; moreover they cherished hopes of recovering their other lost provinces. As Alsace and Lorraine were to beckon the French in 1871, so Scania and Halland, for strategic, economic and sentimental reasons, enticed the Danes to a war of revenge. Meanwhile, with a second minority in Sweden offering respite, they embarked on overdue reforms.

Events in Denmark exemplify on the small scale what was happening all over Europe at this time, when princes built anew from the wreckage of foreign and civil war. They were able to benefit from the economic and social difficulties that made subjects look for direction and regulation, as well as from the apparent decadence of a society of orders which no longer provided a secure framework or a guarantee of liberties. The smaller the country the more efficiently could the prince grasp his opportunities. As so often happens, as even in Poland, after the first partition, a drastic surgery, however bitterly resisted, provided the shock that prepared the patient for a more organic cure, and to some extent dictated the conditions and methods of treatment.

The failures of the Danish army had exposed the selfish pretensions of the nobles. King and burghers had made common cause in the defence of Copenhagen. In 1660, a meeting of the states displayed a new mood, patriotic and purposeful. The nobles were demoralized; the more capable of them, like Hannibal Sehested, sided with the king, but the majority fought to preserve their immunity from taxation and their control of the great offices. The burghers, led by Hans Nansen, mayor of Copenhagen, and the clergy, led by Hans Svane, bishop of Sjaelland, petitioned for a declaration of hereditary monarchy. The *Raad* refused to discuss it; but Frederick presented his cause to the people. The nobles gave way to the mounting hostility and in October 1660 the estates recognized the principle of hereditary monarchy. It was a complete surrender of rights, a textbook example for students of Hobbes. In January 1661 the king, working with a small group of advisers, was declared 'absolute sovereign lord'. The *Kongelow* (drafted and preserved until after Frederick's death in secret) defined the rights of the crown in terms as absolute as any that Louis XIV would have employed. Its author Peter Schumacker, a burgher's son, ennobled with the name of Griffenfeldt, had visited Paris and studied the French system of government. Monarchy it was said owed its origin to a surrender of the supreme authority to the king by the estates. The only limitations on his power were that he should maintain the unity of the realm and the status of the Protestant religion. The king was 'supreme head here on earth, elevated above all human laws', and he recognizes 'no other judge, either in secular or spiritual matters, than God almighty'.

The question of sovereignty thus resolved in fact and theory, the way was open to reforms. Sehested, now chief minister, directed changes in the administration: the Swedish system of colleges was introduced and local government was brought under central control. The national debt was reduced by the drastic expedient of alienating royal property to the major creditors; but a new land tax increased the revenue. The evolution in Denmark was from rents to taxes – unlike Charles XI's Sweden, where the opposite course was adopted. The accession of Frederick's son, Christian V (1670–99), did not interrupt the process. He was neither clever nor modest, but his athletic prowess and bluff manners impressed his personality on the people. He identified himself with the patriotic group who wanted war against Sweden. More important at first was his chief minister, Schumacker. He concentrated authority in his own hands and used it to further absolutism in the approved French style. Work proceeded on a new code of law (completed in 1683); trade was protected and subsidized by orthodox mercantilist measures. Copenhagen was enlarged: there were 60,000 inhabitants by the end of the century. Danish scientists acquired a distinction in this period that recalled the famous Tycho Brahe. Roemer published in Paris, where he had been elected member of the French Académie des Sciences, his calculation of the speed of light. He developed and invented scientific instruments, including a thermometer with a Fahrenheit scale, and at the end of his life, as burgomaster of Copenhagen, introduced the first regular system of street lighting. Stensen, who studied medicine at Leyden, proved that the heart was a muscle, while his work on fossils makes him one of the founders of geology; he later abandoned science for religion and became a bishop.

While the old aristocracy was undermined, a new privileged class, largely composed of Holsteiners or other Germans, promoted for service to the regime, moved into the dominant position: the titles of count (*greves*) and baron (*frihere*) hitherto unknown in Denmark, and a new order of merit, the *Dannebrog*, were introduced. Griffenfeldt was one of the first *greves*. He was also a member of the revived medieval Order of the Elephant. There was no large-scale transfer of land to the peasants. The crown still possessed a quarter of the land, nobles or burghers most of the rest. Farms grew larger as landowners switched from cattle to corn. German methods brought higher yields but the peasantry suffered in income and status: it was to be the trend throughout northern Europe.

War between France and Holland (1672–8) jeopardized Griffenfeldt's constructive policies.[1] In 1674 Denmark joined the coalition against France, along with the Emperor and Brandenburg; this entailed war against Sweden. In 1676 the war party secured Griffenfeldt's dismissal on grounds of treason and he was subsequently imprisoned for life. His caution and pacifism were justified by events. The Scanian war (1674–9) brought reverses for Sweden but no corresponding benefits for Denmark. In 1676 the young King Charles XI crushed the Danes at Lund. On the other hand, their admiral, Juel, won control of the sea, with the support of the Dutch. When Louis XIV imposed the treaty of Fontainebleau (1679), Scania remained Swedish. Charles XII's defeat at Pultava in 1709 tempted Frederick, despite an earlier reverse in 1701, to try again. At least in 1720, by the peace of Fredriksberg, the Danes gained the Schleswig lands of the duke of Holstein-Gottorp. The equilibrium which ensued after the Great Northern War was to be that of two relatively minor powers, neither of whom could hope to aspire to supremacy in this region, let alone make an impact upon Germany and the west. The farsighted proposals of Gyllenstierna, author of the secret articles of Lund (1679), were based upon a realistic view. The open treaty only confirmed the terms of Fontainebleau. But the private clauses – not revealed until 1870 – provided for the close co-operation of the two countries for their mutual advantage. In the face of the growth of Prussia and Russia, with greater resources than Swedes or Danes could ever command, such a partnership offered the only secure base for the future. Meanwhile traditional hostility counted for more than material interest. Denmark had still some harsh lessons to learn. Charles XII had to live out his triumphs and disasters; the Great Northern War had to be fought out to the bitter end.

Sweden: Domestic Crisis and Foreign War

When Gustavus Adolphus died on the battlefield of Lützen, in November 1632, he was at the height of his powers. The Thirty Years War was a cruel testing ground of armies and generals: perhaps it was as well for his reputation that he did not live to experience his successor's struggle to maintain the position that he had secured for his country. That there would be such a struggle was almost certain, for idealism and impulse had carried him far beyond the bounds of traditional Swedish policy, to the Rhine and as far as the Habsburg lands in search of the decisive combat.

The scale of his initial triumphs in 1631 had overborne the sober calculations upon which he based his first campaign in Germany. His death came as a relief to his French paymasters. It can be argued that he had been unwise to adopt an aggressive role in the first place, that Sweden's interests would have been better served if he had taken the role of jealous house dog,

[1] The ensuing passage should be read in conjunction with pp. 512–19, for a fuller account.

rather than predatory wolf. It may be fairer to see the 'crusade' of Gustavus as an intelligent variation upon a consistent theme. Like Charles X, Charles XI and Charles XII after him, Gustavus had begun his reign in 1611 ringed with enemies. To each king in turn, attack seemed not just the best but the only means of defence. From 1611 to 1721 the Swedes were engaged in a restless search for security. It is that which gives a degree of unity to a period which, if viewed in terms of domestic politics, appears to be one of near-revolutionary upheaval. The sharpest change, that of Charles XI's reign, from a degree of constitutionalism to a military autocracy, was again dictated by the need to adapt to postwar circumstances: shortage of revenue, social tensions, above all the pretensions of an aristocracy reinforced by new men, successful soldiers and courtiers, some of them German, who sought to drive harder bargains, whether with the government or with peasants on their estates. Circumstances changed, but the problem of security remained constant. After 1648, the ambition of the Habsburgs to secure a footing on the southern Baltic could be discounted, even though they continued to support the Polish kings, enemies of Sweden since 1592; then the Swedes under Charles Vasa, who became Charles IX, overturned Sigismund, the ruling Vasa, Catholic convert and elected king of Poland. The more successful the Hohenzollerns of Brandenburg were in fastening their rule upon their scattered lands, the more determined they became to master the Baltic rivers and ports. Denmark sought to recover her grip on the Baltic Sound.

The Swedes emerged from the Thirty Years War with a large indemnity for the army and with bases and lands in north Germany: Western Pomerania, a further tract between Elbe and Weser, Bremen, Verden and Wismar providing security against Denmark; ports in Mecklenberg and an alliance (amounting to a protectorate) with the duke of Holstein-Gottorp, who looked covetously at Denmark's German lands. The war brought lasting benefits, notably in the development of the iron industry; copper had become a vital export – but the mines were nearly worked out. The government had used all possible means to further trade. Dutch ships were discriminated against; Swedish ships were allowed free through the Sound – a concession wrung from the Danes by the treaty of 1645. Stockholm benefited especially from the channelling of exports through its port, and the city had grown to 50,000 by 1670. Riga's advantages were not exploited in the same way: the conservatism of the burghers and the government's concern for Stockholm's monopoly account for that failure. The value of the Russian and Polish export trades still ensured that the Swedes would stoutly defend their Ingrian and Estonian ports. There was no lack of planning. The *kommerscollegium*, under the guidance of Eric Oxenstierna from 1652–6, had a role similar to that of the French *conseil de commerce* and other government bodies set up during this period to encourage and direct commerce and manufactures. It ran the Swedish African Company, started in 1649 with a fort in Guinea, and maintained New Sweden on the banks of the river Delaware. That little settlement was abandoned in 1655, however, while neither the African venture, nor attempts to develop an overland trade through Russia to Asia brought much return. The Dutch supplied much of the capital for these ventures. They had such a large stake in the Baltic that they would go to great lengths to preserve the balance of power in the region. It was to be Dutch intervention that stiffened the resistance of the Danes in the latter part of the war of 1655–60 and checked Swedish demands. In that war, Charles X gained the vital provinces on the Sound but not the political and economic mastery of the Baltic for which he hoped. Sweden lacked the maritime resources of the Dutch republic.

Gustavus Adolphus and his chancellor Oxenstierna had launched their German campaign largely upon the expectation of German dues and river and harbour tolls. These had proved lucrative but were not sufficient to make the army, as was hoped, self-supporting. An empire of around 2.5 million inhabitants, of whom a bare million were Swedes, became, after 1648, victim of the process to which it had given such momentum: the growth of armies. Sweden could not afford to maintain a force sufficient to defend her provinces but she could not afford not to try. The alternatives eventually became clearer: either reliance on foreign subsidies or better use of economic resources. The first meant undesirable commitments, the second exploitation and regulation. Both entailed the risk of war. Meanwhile the situation was complicated by domestic disorders which victories in war concealed but could not cure. After 1632 Oxenstierna had to deal with the usual difficulties that accompany a minority, and with diminished royal authority. He derived strength, however, from the reforms and the personal prestige of Gustavus.

The Swedish administration, with its five specialized 'colleges', the head of each sitting in the *Riksrad* (council), was the most efficient in Europe. The chancellor's success testifies also to his political skill. The strength of his system lay in the co-operation of a group of relatives and dependants who turned the *Riksrad*, guardian of the 'balanced constitution', into the instrument of a close-knit oligarchy. Beyond them ranged the soldiers and officials, whose appetite for land had grown with their sense of Sweden's new place in the world, and the established nobles who did not mean to be left behind by the *nouveaux riches*. They were impressed by what they saw of German methods of exploiting the land and suppressing the rights of peasants. Whether for immediate revenue or for political influence, it was inevitable that Oxenstierna should sell or give away crown land. He did so apparently without qualms, at least so long as Queen Christina remained a minor. Besides his authority as the queen's first minister, he also enjoyed the wealth and status of a great landowner; and he accepted the values of his class. He believed, no doubt, that rural society was best left to the care of private landowners. He may have been convinced by his own argument that the money that came from new indirect taxes would make up for the loss of traditional dues. The process by which Swedish peasants were being brought into the framework of the manor not only reduced their status to that of dependents, subject to labour services and restricted in their movements, but also diverted money from the state to the landowner; for whereas the free peasant paid half-taxes, the manorial peasant paid none. More than revenues were put at risk by this great transfer of property. Burghers and clergy had their own reasons to be resentful: the former because of increased competition for office, the latter because of abuses of lay patronage and loss of tithe. Responsible citizens feared that the crown was abdicating its social responsibilities, and was courting disaster by allowing such a concentration of fiscal privilege and political influence in the hands of what amounted to a new aristocracy. Queen Christina's minority ended in 1644; under her own rule these fears were intensified. She seemed to delight in giving away lands as the fancy took her – to an unemployed colonel or to a court physician. Returning commanders were lavishly rewarded. The annexation of Verden, for example, was less valuable than it should have been because so much of the land was given to its governor, Hans Königsmarck, a German officer who had made his fortune in the Swedish service. Bremen came off best in a long struggle to maintain its status as an imperial free city with a place in the *Reichstag*. For fear of alienating German opinion, the Swedes refrained from bringing military pressure to bear on the city. In Pomerania, the ducal land of dispossessed Bogislas was frittered away among Swedish officials, local nobles and burghers. Here the Swedes, even Charles XI, were never able to enforce absolute government but had to respect and share power with the estates. Weaknesses were compounded by Christina's feckless generosity. In her 10 years the number of counts and barons was multiplied by 6. There was little system about either ennoblements or endowments. Indeed, when she made a grant of land it was often with the proviso that it did not already belong to someone else. The state's revenue fell by 40 per cent. If the process had continued, the crown would have become bankrupt and as weak as that of Poland.

When, in 1650, matters came to a head much, therefore, was at stake: the survival of the independent peasantry, and their constitutional role in the *Riksdag* (assembly); the balance that was provided by a healthy middle class with prospects of advancement and service; the survival of the authority of the crown in the face of the dominant interests in the *Riksdag*, who claimed at first to be consulted, and aspired ultimately to a monopoly of legislation and taxation. The clergy asked whether she was to be 'crowned queen of the Swedish lands or queen of tolls and excises'; the compilers of the Protestation asked: 'What have we gained beyond the seas, if we lose our liberty at home?' They were challenging the system of government, but they were attacking the privileged magnates, not the crown itself. This was the advantage which Christina grasped. She had one paramount objective. Uncertain of her own future she intended to secure the throne for her cousin

Charles – son of Gustavus's half-sister Catherine and John Casimir of the Palatinate. To do so she had to overcome the resistance of the *Riksrad* which contained no less than four Oxenstiernas and secure the approval of the *Riksdag*.

When the *Riksdag* met in July 1650 the people were suffering from the effects of the previous year's harvest, the worst in the century. The news from abroad conveyed that it was, in an English observer's phrase, 'a time of shakings'. In London, Paris, Amsterdam and Naples authority was flouted. Jakob de la Gardie was convinced that 'they want to do as they have been doing in England and make us all as like as pig's trotters'. Manifestos and sermons denounced the oppressions of the landlord. The three lower estates showed unprecedented unity and spirit. The lower clergy and burghers upheld the grievances of the peasants, demanded *reduktion*, that is recovery by the crown of alienated land, and drew up a Protestation whose language echoes some of the claims of the English parliament and French *parlement*. Its authors' demands were for equality of all estates before the law: for offices to be open to all according to merit, and payable by fixed salary; for private prisons and torture to be banned. They appealed to 'fundamental law'. They claimed, in contradiction of the ordinance of 1617, that a majority within the estates was decisive. The nobles realized that they were confronted, not only with the risk of a peasant *Jacquerie* (Oxenstierna confessed to being afraid to visit his country houses), but with an articulate and coherent opposition, led by such men as the lawyer–politicians, Nils Nilsson and Nils Skunk. The queen received popular deputations with sugared words. She encouraged the commoners to attack the nobility. The situation may have appealed to the gambler in her – and she won. By the end of August the nobility were asking for her protection. She gave it, in return for the acceptance of Charles as hereditary prince. She forced the lower estates to give up the *reduktion*. Each class was given a concession, and their unity collapsed. The clergy won a grant of privileges, the peasants an ordinance limiting labour services; the leading burghers some civic posts. It was a triumph of will and personality in the finest Vasa manner. Yet even while she was proving her ability as a ruler she was considering the possibility of abdication. She was already on the way to becoming a Catholic. She may have feared that so long as there was no direct heir to the throne the nobles would be restless; and she was determined not to marry. Her uneasiness is reflected in her increasingly capricious behaviour in the last few years of her reign. At the Abdication Diet of 1654 the estate of peasants begged her to stay. But there was also widespread relief, not only among the nobles. She went to Italy, joined the Roman Church and settled in Rome. Her action won a temporary éclat, but the world soon forgot her.

Charles X was well fitted to rule. He had studied at Uppsala University and travelled widely. He learnt soldiering under Torstensson and he ended the German war as commander-in-chief of the Swedish army. At the age of 32, he appeared to be at the height of his powers. Quiet, firm, modest if not moderate, he worked for essential reforms in a spirit of compromise. At the same time he took a soldier's view of Sweden's problems. He invaded Poland because he believed that John Sigismund's country was on the verge of a collapse, even disintegration, from which Russia and Brandenburg would benefit, unless Sweden acted to forestall them. To further Sweden's imperial interests, he was ready to postpone urgent fiscal reforms. The Russians, acting in concert with the insurgent Cossacks under Hetman Chmielnicki, were fighting to secure White Russia, Severia and that part of the Ukraine which lay to the east of the Dnieper, large areas nominally ruled over by Poland and eventually won by the peace of Andrussovo (1667). Charles foresaw that the Russians would not rest until they had established themselves in Swedish Estonia and Livonia. Charles first angled for a Polish alliance, on terms which the Poles, who had never acknowledged the Vasa dynasty in Sweden, proudly rejected. He then attacked.

Two Swedish armies, starting in the spring of 1655 from Riga and Stettin, stormed deep into Polish territory. Charles occupied Warsaw and Cracow, and John Sigismund found temporary refuge in Silesia. The elector of Brandenburg, unwilling to commit himself, made an agreement with the Swedes by which they gained privileged access to the ports of Memel. The Polish general in Lithuania accepted Swedish suzerainty. Local surrenders like this seemed to bear out the theory that Poland was on the point of dissolution. The Swedes seemed once again to be masters of the Baltic lands. But fortunes could change quickly in these wars. Behind imperial dreams lay an encumbered estate: much royal land alienated, the inhabitants by no means united, it was vulnerable to its neighbours. Charles showed a lack of imagination in failing to appeal to the peasants of Poland against their masters. The brutalities of his troops pointed the argument the other way. Noisily patriotic as ever, the Poles found a rare degree of unity in resistance to the Nordic invader: they proved themselves as hard to conquer as they were hard to govern. Charles lost the alliance of Brandenburg when the elector made a deal with the Poles: in return for military support he was granted full sovereignty over Prussia. For this advantage the elector had to thank the Emperor, who was roused by the Swedish invasion to look to the safety of outlying Hungary and Silesia. Charles X, dangerously over-extended, sought allies outside the accepted range: not only the Cossack insurgent Chmielnicki, but also George Rakoczy of Transylvania and the Tartar Khan of the Crimea. Only Rakoczy moved, and it was perhaps lucky for Charles that news of Danish aggression forced him to break off the campaign. He left Rakoczy in the lurch and hurried home to direct the brilliant operations that were to bring destruction to the Danes. In Poland he had failed, though without discredit. In Denmark he succeeded all too well. Having secured what Sweden could be forgiven for seeing as their natural frontier, and the island of Bornholm to complete control of the Sound (by the peace of Roskilde in March 1658), Charles made further demands, invaded again to secure them, and provoked a spirited resistance which won the support of all the Baltic powers, including Russia. England, France and Holland tried to restore peace; he made it possible by dying.

Charles can be praised for anticipating the threat of Russia and for going halfway to meet it. He was Vasa enough to believe attack to be the best form of defence. Like Gustavus he believed that war should pay for itself. He reminded potential enemies that the spirit of Gustavus was still alive. But his aggressions also served to concentrate the enmity of the Baltic powers on Sweden. In the long term this was to have serious consequences, though it seems likely that it would have happened in any case. Even his marriage with the daughter of the duke of Holstein-Gottorp, on the face of it a sensible defensive move, was seen by the Danes as a provocative intrusion into their sphere of influence. Had he lived longer, he might have anticipated some of the work of his successor. As it was, he began the process of the redemption of crown lands, established the first Swedish bank, and endowed his University of Uppsala with a new constitution. The inevitable difficulties of the third regency of the century did not tarnish the image of a strong king.

King 'Greycoat'

In 1660 Charles XI was only 4 years old. Charles X had tried by deathbed arrangements to ensure that the council of regency, under the queen mother Hedwig Eleonora, should be controlled by supporters of the dynasty. Within months the estates, under the influence of the nobles, had declared his will invalid; his nominees had been forced to resign, and new officials appointed who could be relied upon to uphold the rights of the aristocracy. The record of this new government was not disgraceful. Peace treaties at Oliva (1660) and Kardis (1661) put an end to the wars with Poland and Russia respectively. The programme of *reduktion* was of course abandoned. But the treasurer, Gustav Bonde, made some sensible economies and the chancellor, Magnus de la Gardie, was intelligent enough to realize the importance of keeping the peace. Trade was encouraged, the navy strengthened. The foundation of the University of Lund (1668) would help towards the cultural assimilation of the Scanian provinces. But the government had no answer to the chronic problem of how to maintain the armed forces in sufficient strength and preparedness without imposing an impossible strain on the economy. Resolute leadership was lacking, for the amiable, extravagant de la Gardie did not see far beyond the interests of his class: he lacked energy and persistence and devoted more time to designing castles on his numerous estates than to the conduct of affairs. The principle of his foreign policy was to receive the greatest possible aid from France. French subsidies offered a comfortable way of postponing those reforms which, though they alone could restore Sweden to independence, would cost the great landed families their monopoly of social and political privilege. In the end, however, the regents found themselves in a position where they could neither remain safely neutral nor benefit from war. They had tried to maintain great power pretensions on the cheap. The offers of mediation, the lavish embassies, failed to impress. Lionne and Pomponne, Louis's foreign ministers and Sweden's bank managers, were sceptical: their client represented a sizeable investment in cash and goodwill, and had to be supported, but they expected little return.

When Louis XIV, having invaded Holland, demanded satisfaction, Sweden lurched into a war for which she was ill-prepared. The elector of Brandenburg had sided with the Dutch. In 1674, a Swedish army launched an invasion from Pomerania. The commander had no option because he had run out of supplies: Swedish policy was truly bankrupt. The only significant military action occurred at Fehrbellin in July 1675: it was little more than a skirmish, but the Swedes were beaten by the Brandenburgers. Promptly, Denmark joined in war, imprisoned the duke of Holstein-Gottorp, and made a compact with the elector. He was fighting for Pomerania, Christian V for the Scanian provinces. The Swedes could only protect themselves by retaining command of the seas. In a series of battles their inexperienced navy was defeated by the Danes and Dutch. Sweden's outlying provinces were therefore at the mercy of her enemies. In these grim circumstances, Charles XI rose to his responsibilities, made his name by his bravery, and laid the foundations for a successful reign by winning the confidence of his people.

Charles had come of age in 1672, but at first remained in the background, patronized and snubbed. To de la Gardie and his sophisticated circle, he was a dull, plain, awkward adolescent. Little could be expected of a youth who was word-blind, painfully shy, quick-tempered but slow in conversation. Until the outbreak of war he lacked a role. When, in the autumn of 1675, he left the capital to lead his army, he cut himself off from the influence of the grandees, and found ardent supporters among the young officers of the army. Under the guidance of Johan Gyllenstierna, de la Gardie's relentless rival, he began to take decisions without consulting the council. From the pettiest routines to the exhilaration of the battle, he loved soldiering. His answer to most tactical problems was to attack as furiously as possible. When he led his men to victory against the odds at the bloody battle of Lund (1676), he did more than save the Scanian provinces. He took the first step to becoming a military dictator.

The experience of these early months of war provided the basis, indeed the inspiration, of his subsequent reign. Young bloods contrasted his style of heroic leadership with the complacent rule of the oligarchs. Older and wiser men, like Gyllenstierna, saw their chance in the moulding of a party of king's men at a moment when the men of the regency lay under the cloud of a commission of enquiry, appointed in 1675, to determine responsibility for military failures. By the treaties of St Germain, and Fontainebleau (1679), Sweden suffered virtually no loss of territory. Meanwhile the king had seized the constitutional initiative. De la Gardie's rearguard action was abruptly ended when the king relieved him of his office, 'kicking him upstairs', and into political insignificance, with appointment as High Steward.

The wealthiest Swedish subject of the century, the greatest patron of the arts and learning, was of course a prime target for the new royalists, army officers, lesser nobles and officials, men whose expectations had been roused by the reforms of Charles X and since disappointed. War had provided Charles with the opportunity to gain their allegiance and assert his authority. He now proved that he could extend it. He had a simple, firm grasp of the needs of his people in a hostile world. He proceeded to conduct a retreat to positions of strength with such skill that he deserves to be known, not only as the most absolute of Swedish kings, but also among the wisest. The example of France at the zenith of her power and influence, the nearer model of Denmark, the proven failures of aristocratic constitutionalism, and the instinct of the Swedes to follow a soldier, all favoured the king's efforts. As elsewhere, Lutheran clergy were ready instruments of royal government; in this period they seem to have been much influenced by current Oxford ideas of divine right. None the less the Swedish constitution was apparently full of life. The events of 1650 had shown that the *Riksdag* could act effectively when several of the estates combined, and the *Riksrad* appeared, at least till the war, to have consolidated its position as the guardian of the constitution against extremes, whether royal or popular. Appearances were misleading, however. It was to the crown that officials looked for promotion, the clergy for moral government, the mass of the people for security and prosperity. Under war conditions the *Riksrad* was exposed as irrelevant; they were now to be shown that they were the servants, not the masters, of the state.

In 1680 Charles secured from the *Riksdag* favourable answers to a series of loaded questions. The experience of centuries of constitutional government was thrown away like old clothes. The king was declared responsible to God alone. The *Riksrad* was not an estate of the realm as its members claimed; nor was the king required to consult it. He was not bound by the Form of Government; he could alter it as he wished. Two years before, the *Riksdag* had presented the crown with a programme of domestic reforms. Now they abandoned every lever they possessed, except for the right to grant and withhold taxes – which they had never used; on the contrary the *reduktion* was approved as a means of reducing the dependence of the crown on taxes. In 1683 Charles was granted power of legislation for the recovery of crown lands. There ensued that series of confiscations which ranks as one of the toughest things done by any government in this period. All lands in the conquered provinces, and 80 per cent of all alienated lands, were reclaimed. The economic power of the aristocracy was broken, the crown's finances restored, and the peasantry saved from subjection to the nobility. In 1693, after granting the king the power to levy extraordinary taxes, the *Riksdag* declared him to be 'an absolute sovereign king, responsible to no one on earth, but with the power and might at his command to rule and govern the realm as a Christian monarchy'.

Their trust was surprising but appeared to be justified. Gyllenstierna's plan for an entente between Denmark and Sweden foundered soon after his death in 1680 because of tensions over the position of Holstein-Gottorp which both countries regarded as a legitimate sphere of influence. As they negotiated for allies, the Swedes with the Dutch in 1681, and the Danes with the French in 1682, relations continued to be uneasy. Though Denmark for a time occupied part of the disputed duchy (she returned it by the treaty of Altona in 1689), the subject continued to be a sensitive one. But Charles XI showed more restraint than other Vasa kings: bent on reorganization, he husbanded his army and his money. His foreign policy has been compared to the reaction of a hedgehog that curls up into a prickly ball of defence against all comers. In his domestic policy too, a few powerful instincts, stubbornly followed, were apparently at the root of his actions.

Charles seemed to accept his limitations; he respected older men like Gyllenstierna and von Ascheburg, but he was no cypher. He would accept criticism from experts, but he expected to be kept informed. No foreign dispatch could be opened except in his presence. The royal quartermaster checked lists and bills with meticulous care. He made journeys to all parts of his kingdom, inspecting property and checking on the work of administrators. The Table of Ranks, published in 1680, had accomplished one of the aims of his supporters, promotion by merit. The growth of an adequately paid civil service, dependent on the king, was one legacy of the reign; indeed local administration and the collection of taxes were incomparably efficient. As elsewhere in Europe, the expanding state, military and bureaucratic machines provided the scope and prospects which a virtually static economy seemed to deny. From the king himself – King 'Greycoat', in his shabby clothes, always happy to escape from formal occasions to his papers, to review his troops, or, as ever bent on saving money, to eat simple meals at his mother's house – down to the raw scion of a country family who had scrambled on to the bottom rung of the official ladder, there was a common zeal to serve the state. His harsh, narrow, plodding but devoted spirit gripped the political community. As with Prussia, the size of the country was an important factor. Not so large as to be incoherent – not suffering from undue pressure of people upon resources, nor therefore from the social upheavals which, as in France, followed from such pressure – and yet not so small as to be negligible in war and diplomacy, Sweden was recognizably a nation. Among contemporary rulers, only perhaps Brandenburg's Great Elector can be compared to Charles XI for vigilant, accurate management. The man of whom it was said that he rose at 4 in the morning after his wedding night to inspect the troops, cannot be accused of letting sentiment interfere with duty. There was, however, a gentle side to him: he adored his Danish wife, Ulrica, and was heartbroken when she died in 1693. He looked after the interests of his friends. His colleagues in the great *reduktion* were rewarded by grants of leases on favourable terms; but when some of them took advantage of their position to feather their nests illegally, Charles duly punished them. He ruled without fear or favour.

Naval weakness had marred Sweden's war efforts in the past. Charles XI enlarged the navy until it possessed an efficient fleet of forty ships. The new naval station of Karlskröna, in south-east Blekinge, was to grow into one of the finest naval bases in Europe. The army was closest to Charles's heart. The perennial problem of maintaining it in peacetime at home without crippling expense was met by the principle of settling the native conscript army on the land. By the *indelningsverk*, lands or rents were assinged by the crown for the maintenance of troops. According to their rank they became farmers, smallholders or labourers. Effectively they were paid in kind. The system brought order to the crown's finances. In all these measures, the wholeness of Charles's policy can be seen. The land released by the *reduktion* made possible the new arrangements for the army. The autocratic powers assumed by the king made possible the *reduktion*.

All had been possible because Charles had shown himself capable of responding to the emergencies of war and to the aspirations of the mass of his subjects. The reversal of previous trends, the realistic, though according to mercantilist notions eccentric, retreat from the cash economy, from emphasis upon a greater mobility of capital, resources and troops to an acceptance of a more static, defensive role, adds up to something original and important. The *reduktion* was the central process in a revolution in the power of the state as far-reaching as that which occurred at the time of the Reformation. There was a price to pay. The reign of Charles XII, an absolute monarch who was also a soldier of genius and ambition, was to reveal the dangers inherent in his predecessor's victory over constitutionalism. The reaction of the eighteenth century was to show the vitality of the aristocratic tradition. Charles XI's reign represents a clean break in the continuity of Swedish constitutionalism; what was restored in the 'limited' monarchy that followed the death of Charles XII was essentially government by a faction of the aristocracy through powerful committees. The *Riksdag* was restored: it was largely dominated by officials, and divided, as was the administration, along party lines. The *Riksrad*, which had been the guardian of the country's liberties and laws since the Middle Ages, an estate of the realm, controller and mediator, the body to whom sovereignty reverted between reigns, was relegated to honourable insignificance. The absolute monarchy of Charles XI was not destined to last. Meanwhile the old balance of the constitution which had been destroyed in its making was never to be recovered.

Charles XII and the Great Northern War

Charles XI died of stomach cancer in April 1697. He was only 41, but he had lived longer than any other Vasa king. While his body was still lying there, the old castle at Stockholm was burnt down. It was probably an accident – but some Swedes, victims of arbitrary power and the *reduktion*, rejoiced at the fire that marked their deliverance. Others felt that it was the end of an age. Charles XII succeeded. Not quite 15, he was moulded already by a thorough education in the principles of government. In manner and habits he was like his father whom, perhaps, he came more consciously to imitate after his mother's death when he was only 11. He was cleverer than his father, with a talent for languages and mathematics. In 1703, when he lost the key, he was able to use from memory the complicated cypher devised for his military correspondence. He was rash in the face of physical danger, but cool in political calculation. He was apparently well schooled for management at a dangerous moment in his country's history, apart from one important defect. He was too young to have acquired the sympathetic and intuitive understanding that might come from normal family life. Now, suddenly thrust into a position of authority, faced with the need to make quick decisions, surrounded by advisers who had their own reasons for promoting the absolutist cause, and soon to lead his troops, he assumed at once the hardness and directness that impressed all who dealt with him. It was a superficial manliness with which went a dangerous naivety of judgement. His heroic will to succeed took the world by storm. In 1706 the *Dictionnaire historique*, published in Paris, devoted its longest entry to the new lion of the north: 30 columns to Louis XIV's 22. But there was a corresponding capacity for self-destruction. His imagination was starved. His idealism was a mixture of traditional Vasa patriotism, a fervent Lutheran piety and the impatient promptings of an adolescent. Sweden's enemies were preparing a hostile union; the country's domestic condition was stronger than at any time for fifty years. The war was not of his making – but he would strike first.

The national debt had been reduced to a manageable sum, 11 million *thalers*, and there was a small reserve. The army was in good shape, even though the logic of Charles XI's reforms was that it should be used mainly for home defence. The bureaucratic machinery was functioning smoothly. Its efficiency was to be proved during the long absences of the king, when taxes were regularly paid and the royal authority maintained as if he had been living in Stockholm. The official class had not yet acquired that habit of independence that was to characterize the 'Age of Liberty'. All was not harmonious. The vindictive spirit of the *reduktion* and the ruin of some great fortunes had made for bitterness; something of the tradition of noble service which had helped make Sweden great had been lost. In Sweden proper, the royal revolution had been in an exact sense a popular revolution: lesser nobles, peasant farmers and clergy approved. The policy of Swedification had, moreover, been markedly successful in Scania. In Livonia, on the other hand, it had provoked patriotic resistance; there Patkul looked to foreign allies to aid him against the oppressive state. The untried king lost no time in challenging the doubters and those who hoped that he might halt the *reduktion*. His first constitutional act was to obtain from the *Riksdag* an assurance of his absolute power. He crowned himself – and took no coronation oath. The superstitious marked that the crown 'slipped off his head'. But when a clergyman, Boethius, already well known for his opposition to absolutist rule, spoke and wrote against conferring unlimited authority upon a boy, he was arrested and condemned to death; though the sentence was commuted to life imprisonment. The whole country seemingly depended on the judgement of one man. More than he may have realized, he was the tool and accomplice of the absolutist party, led by men like Wallenstedt and Piper. They believed it necessary to make the new order plain to all. They soon found that the king had a mind of his own. No wonder that he was sometimes moody, as he struggled with his problems: for instance, whether to make a dynastic marriage, or to settle the Holstein question. Even within the absolutist party there were divisions enough to convince him that he must decide for himself.

When Frederick IV succeeded to the throne of Denmark in 1699, conflict could not long be postponed. Once again, Holstein-Gottorp was the cause. When Charles XI died, Danish troops had pulled down the duke's fortifications. Charles XII helped the duke to restore them, gave him his sister in marriage, and made him commander-in-chief of Swedish troops in Germany. In the new year Charles was preparing for battle and not against Denmark alone. The Livonian Patkul persuaded Augustus of Saxony and Poland to fight on his behalf. He could not persuade the Elector Frederick of Prussia to enter his league: Frederick was concentrating upon the imperial alliance and securing the title of king. But Tsar Peter undertook to invade Ingria and Karelia. Charles did not hesitate. He believed that Peter would not move until he had finished with his Turkish war. An Anglo-Dutch fleet entered the Baltic (on behalf of the duke of Holstein) as guarantors of the treaty of Altona. Charles therefore felt secure at sea and led his army to Zeeland, threatened Copenhagen and extracted terms from King Frederick (August 1700). When he heard that the Russians were invading Ingria he shipped his army across. He marched to relieve Narva and there routed the large but ill-trained Russian army (20 November 1700). Fought in a snow storm which blew into the faces of the Russians, decided by the superior discipline of the Swedes and the generalship of

Rehnsköld, Narva did for Charles XII's reputation what Lund had done for Charles X. He had led his troops, gloried in the danger, and received a bullet in his cravat. The spoils included over 100 Russian cannon. The Swedish army suffered more from sickness in their encampments in the ensuing winter than from casualties in battle. That disagreeable experience led Charles thereafter 'to get some air', to move the battle zone away from the Swedish lands, to keep his armies on the move and his enemies guessing, above all to ensure that the brunt of war, destruction, famine, disease fell not on Swedes but on Courlanders, Saxons or Poles. It had been the principle of Gustavus. Charles XII's disciplinary measures also recall the master. Soldiers were taught by their chaplains to respect the God of battles; prayers and hymns sustained them. Seeped in Lutheran theology, the king was devoutly fatalist in battle, hardy in his ways. He wore no wig, dressed plainly, ate frugally, slept on straw or on a couch of fir twigs. There was art as well as instinct in his style of leadership. Like other successful generals, he understood that it was important for his men to know him. His distinctive features, long head, big nose and jutting lower lip were easily recognized. He often talked to the ordinary soldiers, visited outposts and sentries; on the battlefield he was ubiquitous. He became known for his pungent remarks. 'Hungry dogs bite best,' he said before Kliszów, when urged to let his men rest.

In the same month as Narva, Charles II of Spain died, leaving a French prince to inherit – and to fight for – the Spanish empire. The interested parties made their dispositions for war, and courted the alliance of Sweden. The Northern War was soon to become a part of the larger struggle, the king of Sweden a key figure in all diplomatic calculations. His actions in 1701–2 showed that Narva was not a fluke, and put a premium on the Swedish alliance. In July 1701 he crossed the river Dvina and defeated a Russian-Saxon army. Then could have been the time to stop, to secure Livonia, even to invade Russia. For sound military reasons, he decided to deal with Augustus first. He was outraged by Augustus's unprincipled aggression and swayed by promises of support from the Sapiehas, the leading family in Lithuania. He was sceptical from the start about the lasting value of such support, but believed that he could defeat Augustus. At Clissow, on the anniversary of the Dvina crossing, he was proved right. It was a more notable feat of arms than Narva: a silent march through woodlands, a surprise attack to the front followed by a switch to the flank, hand-to-hand combat against stubborn Saxon troops, were all conducted by the king with a veteran's skill. The duke of Holstein-Gottorp was killed; on the other side, Patkul escaped, disguised, in a peasant's cart.

The victory made it possible to plan the deposition of Augustus and the installation of the native king Stanislaus Leszczynski, who would be Sweden's ally. The Swedes would assist Poland to recover lands lost to Russia; in return they would benefit in the Baltic; Charles might become duke of Courland. Clissow promised much but decided nothing. It was one thing to defeat an army, another to destroy the combined armies of Russia and Saxony, another again to hold down the vast spaces of Poland. Poland had no natural centre, and government was only possible if the new king commanded widespread patriotic support. In the end, a military solution was found: the enemy armies were split, the Polish-Russian part confined in the east, the Saxon in the west of the country. Daring in conception, masterly in execution, the operation enhanced Charles XII's high reputation as soldier and statesman. But the cost was high. The Swedish soldiers terrorized and antagonized ordinary Poles. The size of the country, the divisions among the leading families, the failure of Stanislaus to win general support, meant that a solution could only come from the army. Charles felt that he had been drawn into a web from which he had to slash his way; unfortunately the strands stretched towards Russia. While he was involved in Poland, the Russians were conquering Livonia and reforming their army.

The Russian venture has been criticized as a reckless gamble, yet it followed logically from Charles's Polish entanglement, just as his original decision to invade Poland had stemmed from the need to break out of the hostile ring. Always he sought the radical, final solution. It can be argued that he should have adopted a defensive strategy from the first. But Narva had shown that aggression could pay and Kliszów appeared to confirm the lesson. Behind his actions was the reasonable fear of the political and economic power that an integrated Polish-Saxon state might possess. Beyond that power was Russia: a permanent threat to Sweden's Baltic interests. He may have divined that ultimately there was to be no denying Russia's place on the northern Baltic shore. Meanwhile he could do his best to put off the evil hour. Peter was opposed and loathed by many of his subjects. The chance that he might be overthrown was one of the factors in Charles's reasoning. Charles believed in God, his cause, his judgement – and his troops. His was a nature for large decisions. He had learnt to live without women and without comforts and schooled his body and mind for a life of self-sufficiency. His laborious life left little room for philosophy. He relished power. And yet there was little in his make-up of the illusions that overcome great conquerors, the paranoia, or even the sense of infallibility. Some of the criticism from chancery officials came from the natural split between military and civilian advisers at a time when the government of the country was in two places: the executive in camp with the king, the administration in Sweden trying to cope with his requirements. The king liked, as councillors said, to 'tighten the bow'. The stream of young recruits, like the 13-year-old Maximilian of Württemberg, who came to learn war as volunteers with the Swedish army, testify to his reputation. Well-informed opinion in Europe held the Swedish king to be the first man of his time. The sale of medallions and prints contributed to the growth of a cult; but its hero did not cease to be a rational person.

In April 1704 Charles defeated the Saxons again at Pultusk. In October, he captured Thorn and with it control of the basin of the Vistula. While Augustus went to Russia for aid on stringent terms, Charles built up his party among the Polish nobles. In July 1704 their confederation, well supplied with Swedish money, had secured the election of Stanislaus Leszczynski. The object of Charles's next campaigns was to eliminate the forces of Augustus. He was successful enough to be able to crown Stanislaus (September 1705); but the Polish nobleman was but king of a faction. In 1706 Charles took the war into Saxony. In February, his general Rehnsköld defeated the main Saxon army in a two-hour battle worthy of his king; but the Russian army made its escape and Charles was therefore frustrated in his strategic purpose – of luring the Russians into Saxony to support their ally, of then annihilating them. Charles pursued them to Pinsk, but then fell back to Saxony. In September, at Altranstädt, near Leipzig, he imposed humiliating terms on Augustus. The unhappy man renounced the throne, gave up his alliance with Peter, and surrendered Patkul, who was subsequently broken on the wheel.

Poltava: the Decisive Battle

Charles XII was courted by the western powers. The duke of Marlborough himself went to Altranstadt to try to persuade the king to join the Grand Alliance. He found Charles determined to finish with Russia, and much less concerned about war in the west. Charles's main interest was that the war should continue, France and the Emperor remaining evenly balanced. He extracted from the Emperor, in August 1707, an agreement guaranteeing the rights of Silesian Protestants. It was in character that he should have been concerned about them. Sweden was guarantor of the peace of Westphalia; Charles never wavered in his evangelical faith. He then marched towards Russia with the finest army that Sweden had put into the field since 1631: more than 40,000 strong. His main objective was to relieve the pressure on his Baltic provinces, and to stop Peter supporting Stanislaus. He hoped to bring the main Russian army to battle. His army, smart in new uniforms of blue and yellow, well-provisioned and armed with the best flintlock muskets and pistols, was in high spirits.

Peter had tried to postpone the contest. He had offered to surrender all his Baltic conquests except for St Petersburg and the river Neva. He had offered troops to the western allies if they would mediate on his behalf. Before Prince Eugène and Prince Rakoczy, imperial commander and leader of the Hungarian revolt respectively, he dangled the prospect of the Polish throne. These moves Charles interpreted as signs of weakness. He knew that Peter was harassed by the prospect of a Cossack rebellion, and that his religious policies had caused widespread discontent among the Old Believers. To the Swedes at Charles's headquarters, the Russian army was a laughing stock. On any reading of the evidence, Peter was vulnerable. Charles resolved to strike at the heart of his empire. He was urged to concentrate first upon recovering the Baltic provinces. Instead he pointed his army towards Moscow: if he could win the decisive battle, the Russians would evacuate the Baltic provinces.

Peter's conquest of Estonia and Livonia had given him confidence and a sense of direction. His new capital was rising above the Neva marshes. He had begun necessary reforms of the army. Charles's plans were magnificent, but they took little account of the possibility of failure at any point. The central thrust was supported by his general Lewenhaupt, marching from the north with reinforcements and supplies. A quarter of Charles's force was left in Saxony to co-operate with Stanislaus in a policing action before following the main force. The summer of 1708 saw Charles making his way across the great northern plain to cross the Dnieper. At Holovain, on 30 June, he won a fierce battle: a brilliant cavalry charge led by Rehnsköld decided the day. The Russians were mauled but they were not destroyed. When Lewenhaupt fell behind schedule and failed to join him (August), Charles moved south-east to outflank Russian troops covering Smolensk. It was an important error. The Russians closed in on Lewenhaupt; at Lesnaya he was defeated, with the loss of half his troops and most of his supplies. When at last he caught up with Charles XII, at Severia, the main condition for success was missing. Swedish strategy was thereafter dictated by the need to find food. All the way the Russians had laid a carpet of 'scorched earth'. So Charles moved into the Ukraine. Mazeppa, chief of the Dnieper Cossacks, from whom much had been hoped, was a disappointment. He resented having his hand forced by the Swedes and he brought only a small following. The winter of 1708–9 was everywhere the most severe in living memory. In the Ukraine it took heavy toll even of the hardened Swedes. Charles's force was reduced to about 22,000. He managed to enlist some southern Cossacks; marvellous horsemen, they were yet no substitute for the Turkish troops that he would have liked, or for the reinforcements expected from Poland, which never arrived. In May 1709 Charles laid siege to the fortress of Poltava, in order to lure Peter to battle. He faced an army very different from that which he had beaten at Narva; he had been wounded in the foot and had to watch the battle from a litter. A night attack went astray; on the day, a part of the Swedish infantry was held up by the Russian redoubts; the cavalry could give little support; the rest of the infantry were gradually overwhelmed. The Swedes lost nearly 10,000 killed or captured. The king went to Turkey to raise help. Lewenhaupt was left to extricate the demoralized force, but surrendered when the Russians came up.

It was not until November 1714 that Charles XII returned to his native land. Up to that time he was in Turkey, presiding over his tiny court, trying to order the increasingly desperate affairs of Sweden by courier, playing chess and planning economic reforms for his embattled country. The Russians controlled Poland again. The Danes invaded Scania, but were driven out by Stenbock in 1710. With the plague sealing off the Austrian frontier he could not return. Instead, he tried to spur on the Swedish council to raise fresh armies to renew the offensive in Poland. Not surprisingly they took a more pessimistic view. The Swedish commander Stenbock was unable thereafter to move far from the coast. He could not exploit his victory over the Saxons at Gadebusch (December 1712). He attempted an invasion of Jutland but was trapped and forced to surrender by a superior army of Danes, Russians and Saxons, in the Holstein fortress of Tonning (May 1713). Meanwhile Charles XII had been acting as adviser to the Turkish army. In 1710, acting on his plans, the Turks had surrounded the Russians at Standerci on the river Pruth. They had allowed Peter to buy his way out of a critical position by the surrender of Azov, and the return of Livonia and Estonia to Sweden; the latter he had no intention of doing. Thereafter the frustrated Charles was nothing but an embarrassment to his hosts.

In June 1713 the peace of Adrianople was signed by Russia and Turkey; in the same year, the peace of Utrecht marked the beginning of the end of the western war. The Turks tried at one stage (February 1713) to evict Charles: at the 'tumult of Bendar' he was literally smoked out of his house at the end of a day in which he had been besieged by 10,000 Turks. By then he had lost credit with the western powers. Eventually he was allowed to make his way back through imperial lands. Austria and England were becoming uneasy about the expansion of Russia, and the threat to their interests in the Balkans and Baltic respectively; but Charles failed to make good use of this change in the diplomatic climate. It is at this point that the man's limitations become plain. The unwillingness to accept defeat, the rejection of offers of British mediation, have their admirable side. He was as brave as ever. But he went on living in the belief (virtually true until 1709) that 'the war paid for the war'. Since then, two large armies had been lost, the Swedes had been afflicted by the plague. George I of England, as elector of Hanover, signed, with the king of Prussia (whom Charles could have wooed as an ally), an agreement to maintain their respective positions in Germany. Sweden was no longer a German power. Charles's own position was less secure than it had been. It was only the firmness of his chancellor Arvid Horn that had prevented the estates from placing Charles's younger sister, Ulrica, at the head of the government. Charles had for some time been reported to be either dead or mad. News of his return, however, evoked pathetic joy. He placed his hopes in a renewed military effort, on divisions among his enemies and a general war-weariness which might be expected to result in concessions. Unfortunately for him, Peter the Great was equally determined to see the Baltic business through to the end.

In 1715 Sweden found herself at war with Prussia, Hanover, Saxony, Poland and Denmark. Charles was unable to prevent the surrender of

Stralsund (December 1715). Thence he came to Sweden to raise money and troops. He was assisted by his new minister, Baron von Goertz, officially in the service of Holstein-Gottorp, a fervent admirer of Charles and a resourceful diplomat. Charles put into effect the reforms upon which he had brooded in Turkey. The economy was mobilized under an 'exchequer of contributions'. Government was conducted by six 'expeditions', each under its departmental head or *ombudsman*, the chancery being limited to the conduct of diplomatic business. The economic management was ruthless and skilful. In particular the iron industry was mobilized: iron masters were forced to sell to the state, which exploited its monopoly and the scarcity of iron in Europe to push up prices. Taxes on the rich (a luxuries tax in 1716, a capital levy in 1718) alienated the privileged classes and brought nearer the time of aristocratic reaction. Charles's brother-in-law, Frederick of Hesse, found supporters for his claim to the succession from among such people. It is this connection that links his name with the theory that Charles was murdered in 1718 by one of his own side – for which there is otherwise no conclusive evidence.

Behind a diplomacy so hectic and complex that it is hard to see what was screen and what was sincere, Charles made his preparations for further campaigns. Undoubtedly the object of war was peace. But it would have been peace only on his terms. As he observed to one of his generals a few days before his death: 'We once fought a thirty years war, and we might yet fight a forty years war.' From rumours that the tsar was dying (the death of his heir Alexis suggested that there might be another succession struggle) he derived hope for the future. Meanwhile he resolved to teach the Danes a lesson. He launched an invasion of Norway which showed that he had lost nothing of his grasp of military science. He was taking part in the siege of the fortress of Fredriksten when he was shot, at suspiciously close range. Frederick of Hesse's wife, Charles's younger sister Ulrica, was promptly proclaimed queen. Whoever fired the bullet could claim to have struck a blow for the Swedish people. Charles had fought a brilliant, epic rearguard. In the long perspectives of history it is hard to see that he could have prevented the decline of Sweden into a second-class power. By the treaty of Nystad in 1721, Livonia, Estonia, Ingria and Karelia were ceded to Russia. Sweden's former German possessions had already been lost to Prussia. Of her footholds in the Empire there remained only Wismar, Stralsund and the Greifswald district of Pomerania. In one reign Sweden had lost nearly a third of her adult male population.

The *Frihestiden*

The death of Charles XII was another landmark in Sweden's continuing constitutional debate. It was followed predictably by a reaction against royal absolutism. His long absence and his failure to produce a direct heir to the throne ensured that opposition groups were well prepared for the emergency. In 1719 Baron Görtz, Charles's 'grand vizier', was tried and executed. The *Riksdag* elected Ulrika in preference to Charles Frederick of Holstein-Gottorp, who bowed out with the famous comment that the Swedes had been in too much of a hurry to move the clock from XII to I. She was soon induced to abdicate in favour of her husband, Frederick of Hesse-Cassel. As was expected by his adherents, he accepted a constitution which reduced his power to the point at which he was little more than president of the council (*Riksrad*). The restrained baroque grandeur of Tessin's new royal palace in Stockholm was far removed from the realities of power. It had been designated for Charles XII. His successors could only select *Riksrad* members from a list drawn up by the *Riksdag*. Later, the device of the facsimile royal signature made it possible to bypass royal opposition to majority decisions of the *Riksrad*. The *Riksrad* no longer consisted of the heads of the colleges. Only the president of chancery preserved the former link. With the growth of parties in the *Riksdag*, the principle was slowly established that councillors should change according to the standing of parties in the *Riksdag*. Inevitably, the *Riksrad* declined in authority as important decisions came from the most influential of the committees of the *Riksdag*, the *Sekrata Utskottet*.

The *Riksdag* as a whole tried to guard against the concentration of power in any body while, within the *Riksdag*, divisions between the four estates and within the order of nobility itself acted as a further check upon any revival of a strong executive. Both the clergy (the bishops and about fifty elected clergy) and the burghers, usually town worthies with trading interests, were normally anti-aristocratic in bias. The fourth estate, representative of the free, landowning peasants, were suspect to all the other estates because of their preference for a strong monarchy to maintain them against the exactions of landowners and officials at a time when, as the country saying went, 'Everyone who wears a wig thinks himself a king.' In the *Sekrata Utskottet* there were fifty nobles, equal to the combined strength of the clergy and burghers, while the peasants were only called upon issues of special gravity. The most important estate was therefore that of the nobility. The head of every noble family, some thousand in number, enjoyed the right of sitting in the *Riksdag*. They worked together to uphold their economic privileges and their grasp of high offices. But they were a far from coherent body. The largest group was that of the lesser nobles who relied on government service for a livelihood rather than on land. Older and richer families were in a better position to make money out of new trading or mining enterprises, but they did not enjoy political power proportional to their wealth. There was thus a conflict of interest: out of it developed the party struggle which gives the *Frihestiden* – the 'Age of Liberty' – its special character, and which accounts for (though it also conceals) the fact that the real rulers of Sweden in this period were the officials. Superficially, it was a time of aristocratic constitutionalism; essentially it was a bureaucratic regime, refined and tested under Vasa absolutism but subject now to the less stringent and regular pressure of the prevailing party in the *Riksdag*. Like the army, the official class was dominated by the nobility. Moreover this nobility was not an exclusive caste but was constantly reinforced by new creations: there were 725 between 1719 and 1792. Just as it was accepted that a nobleman might also be an official or take part in trade and industry, so influence and talent in many fields were rewarded by ennoblement: the names of Linnaeus and Swedenborg, for example, figure among new creations.

While appointments to new offices provided the bread-and-butter issues of politics, the differences of the parties were polarized by the ever sensitive question of the succession to the throne. The claim of the Holstein-Gottorps was derived from the marriage of Frederick of that house to Charles XII's elder sister Sophia. His son had been disappointed but his nephew Adolphus Frederick succeeded, mainly by Russian influence, in 1751. Uncertainties about the succession provided opportunities for leverage within the *Riksdag*. They were important also because they represented alternative approaches to foreign policy. The Holsteiners favoured a détente with Russia as the best means of recovering the Baltic provinces. They were weakened by the death in 1727 of Tsarina Catherine and the temporary withdrawal of Russian support for the Holstein claim. Count Arvid Horn's Hessian party banked rather on the Hanover alliance, involving Britain and France; but as the Franco-British alliance disintegrated in the 1730s Horn found that conciliation was not enough. For nearly twenty years, as president of chancery, he strove, in the manner of a Walpole or a Fleury, to preserve a degree of unanimity in the *Riksdag* and peace abroad. He was helped by a strong pacifist sentiment after the ordeal of the Great Northern War, by association with the Anglo-French entente and by the sympathetic support of some of the great Francophil parties. Eventually a younger generation of 'patriots' emerged as an effective opposition. Calling themselves 'Hats' (signifying the finery of a soldier's headgear), they ousted the 'Caps' (or 'Nightcaps' – sleepy old men). Their election campaign for the *Riksdag* of 1738 shows how much Swedish politicians had acquired of the skills of party organization. The campaign recalls the early years of party in Charles II's England, with meetings in coffee houses, wearing of emblems, political entertaining, pamphleteering – and the shameless acceptance of foreign money. Throughout the period, Russians, French and British spent money on Swedish politicians. Against the relatively liberal policies of the Hats, the Caps urged aggressive mercantilist measures to exploit the strength of Sweden's industries (notably iron, technologically the most advanced in Europe). They demanded strong action to recover the Baltic provinces. The militancy of the Hats found scope in the diplomatic imbroglio of the years between the invasion of Silesia and the peace of Paris

(1740–63) and support among those who had forgotten or never known the privations of earlier generations.

In 1741, under pressure from the chauvinists, the Swedes went to war with Russia. But party rivalries had affected officers in the army; the farmer–soldiers of the *indelningsverk*, moreover, were now reluctant warriors. The Russians overran Finland and took advantage of their success by imposing their candidate (Adolphus Frederick) as heir to the throne (peace of Abo, 1743). Peter of Holstein-Gottorp, Peter the Great's grandson and grand-nephew of Charles XII, had been the choice of the *Riksdag*, but he had already been earmarked by Tsarina Elizabeth for her heir. He had duly embraced the Orthodox faith a few days before the Swedish deputation arrived in Moscow to offer him the throne.

In the Seven Years War worse was to come when the Swedes joined the war against Frederick of Prussia in order to recover Pomerania. Once again, constitutional and foreign issues interacted. Queen Louisa Ulrica, Frederick the Great's sister, had made a determined attempt to build up a court party. After bitter fighting over appointments and policy, culminating in an abortive coup in the summer of 1756, she was forced to concede entire control to the estates. She had to listen to a lecture upon her constitutional position by the spokesman for the clergy, the king was threatened with the loss of his throne, eight of their supporters were executed – and the *Riksdag* struck a medal to celebrate their victory. The war against Frederick that ensued brought no advantage, however, to the Hats or to Sweden. On the face of it, there was an ironic but promising reversal of the role of Sweden in Charles XII's time: then ringed with enemies, now member of the alliance which closed in upon Frederick. But the Swedish army was not the force of Charles XII's day; there was little popular support for the war; Frederick did not collapse. In 1762, freed at last from Russian pressure, Frederick directed his army against the Swedes and they were glad to accept peace on the basis of the status quo. The prestige of the Caps suffered accordingly. A younger generation of Hats came to the fore, in a coalition supported by peasants, burghers and clergy. The Caps relied upon Russian money to preserve the peace and the Swedish economy.

It was to make the country more independent, to prevent development of another Polish situation, rather than to defend the privileges of the nobility, that Gustavus III, Adolphus's son, king from 1771, carried out his bloodless coup in August 1774 (the year of the first partition of Poland). He was strongly influenced by French ideas and wished to try out the 'legal despotism' that was recommended by the physiocrats. On 21 August he surrounded the *Riksdag* with soldiers. Its members voted a new constitution. He proceeded to implement the reforms which entitle him to a place among the 'enlightened' sovereigns of his day. In appearance his coup, about a century after Charles XI's assumption of absolute power, seems to be another of those dramatic Swedish revolutions. His reign was an important one in the history of the Enlightenment. Like Charles XI he represents a European fashion. There was a break – but it should not be exaggerated. There was much in the Sweden of the *Frihestiden* that the *philosophe* could approve. It had been shown that changes of party and policy could be brought about peacefully. There was corruption – but the press was free. Useful experience was gained and spread about many of the political and articulate people – themselves a large proportion of this small country. With its rising population, Sweden had remained modestly prosperous. The *Frihestiden* represents in some aspects a return to the central tradition of Swedish public life: the nobility had become once more the guardians of the people's liberties. The moderate way in which that trust had been exercised helped to prepare the people for the extension of political responsibility in the nineteenth century. Sweden may have been a minor power but it was an important school of political experience.

Struensee: Experiment in Enlightenment

In the eighteenth century Denmark's experience was in some ways similar to that of Sweden. In both countries there was protectionist fostering of industry and trade until, about the middle of the century, the principles of economic freedom began to gain ground; the cult of rationalism flourished here as elsewhere. Politically, however, there was a sharp divergence. For the Swedes, this was *Frihestiden*, the Age of Liberty, but the Danes accepted with docility the autocratic rule of the house of Oldenburg, and benefited materially from the absence of party strife. The dynasty's good record was maintained by Frederick IV (1699–1730) and to a lesser degree by Christian VI (1730–46). Frederick cared keenly about the well-being of the depressed peasants. Latterly he came, under Pietist influence, to concern himself more particularly with their souls. Just before his death a 'Sabbath Ordinance' laid down heavy penalties for non-attendance at church and for the indulgence in worldly pleasures on a Sunday. His son too was an ardent Pietist. The court was a sombre place, since the king disapproved of dancing and cards, but as ceremonious as ever. The playwright Holberg, the Molière of Denmark, turned his attention to writing a history of his country, since the Copenhagen theatre, burned down in the great fire of 1728, was not rebuilt. In one ordinance Christian provided for the setting up of primary schools for the peasantry on the model of those on royal estates. Less enlightened, and more to the taste of the landowners, was the decree of 1733 – the hated *stavnsband* according to which peasants were tied to their estates from the age of 14 to 36, or until their service with the militia had expired. Landowners were understandably concerned about the scarcity of labour. Even so the *stavnsband* well illustrates the power of the landlord interest in the Europe of the Enlightenment, even under a benevolent ruler.

Frederick V (1746–66) was dissolute but had the sense to leave affairs to competent ministers, notable among whom was Bernstorff, foreign minister from 1751 to 1770. Bernstorff lived to see his great design fulfilled by his nephew: Schleswig and Holstein were finally secured, with the help of Russia, in 1773. The erratic, perhaps schizophrenic, personality of Frederick's son Christian VII (1766–1808) disturbed the tranquillity of Oldenburg paternalism and led to a brief, eccentric episode, the dictatorship of Dr Struensee, which provides an object lesson in what absolute monarchy, in a small and well-drilled state, could achieve when it was directed by a man of imagination and the will to change society.

Johan Frederick Struensee, a Holsteiner who made influential friends among his patients, was a student of Rousseau and other prophets of social reform. After treating the young king he obtained a hold which has aroused speculation: it is possible that he used some drug, like concentrated cocoa bean, to control the king's wayward temper. When he cured the crown prince by 'a double inoculation' he won the affection of Christian's neglected queen, George III's daughter, Caroline Matilda. She became Struensee's mistress and the willing accomplice in his plans. They secured the dismissal of Bernstorff in 1770. With the king confined under a well-briefed keeper, Struensee was able to dictate changes in the teeth of the majority of the political and clerical establishment. He worked at a pace which suggests the adventurer who knows that his time is short. His reforms reveal some startlingly liberal traits but he is not a completely isolated figure. The trend in Denmark had been towards rational, humane government. The atmosphere was more conducive to the exchange of ideas than in the German states where similar political systems seemed to impose a greater degree of conformity. In 1755 Frederick V's subjects had been invited, on the initiative of Bishop Erik Pontoppidan of Bergan, to submit proposals for economic improvements which were later published at the crown's expense. But no one was prepared for the pace, and radical character, of Struensee's reforms. He celebrated Bernstorff's fall by announcing the complete freedom of the press – and received the compliments of Voltaire. Hampered by the council, he abolished it. With a commission of enquiry into their grievances he bid for the support of the peasants.

In July 1771 he assumed the powers of a dictator. The architects of the new monarchy in 1660 had hardly envisaged such a turn – an unbalanced king and an omnipotent favourite. Over a thousand laws were promulgated in under two years. The official class was purged and bullied; their salaries were cut while Struensee lavished money on court entertainments. His measures to bring about a new climate of morality have left their mark on Denmark to this day: illegitimate children were given equal status with legitimate, free love was no longer a crime, a chapel was converted into a clinic for the treatment of venereal diseases, brothels were relieved of police supervision; and the gardens of Rosenbourg were opened to the public for music and dancing, seven days in the week. Struensee's economic policy again bore the marks of the doctrinaire and the exhibitionist: an attempt to fix a maximum wage level brought predictable hostility. His regime ended, as it had begun, with scenes reminiscent of comic opera. In January 1772 conspirators, approved by the dowager queen, led by the captain of the guard and armed with the king's warrant, seized the dictator. He was tried, condemned and executed before an approving crowd. The barbarity of the execution makes an ironic end to the life of this wayward son of the Enlightenment, and the fate of the 'queen of tears', a tragic postscript: she was divorced and died soon afterwards in exile.

Further Reading

The two best general introductions are French: P. Jeannin, *L'Europe du nord-ouest et du nord aux XVIIe et XVIIIe siècles* (1969), and C. Nordmann, *Grandeur et liberté de la Suède 1660–1792* (1971). Jill Lisk, *The Struggle for Supremacy in the Baltic 1600–1725* (London, 1968), is therefore particularly useful. Denmark is not well served by general histories in English and there seems to be here an opportunity for some historian to establish a bridgehead, if not the kind of ascendancy which Michael Roberts has long enjoyed in the Swedish field. An attractive introduction is, however, provided by Stewart Oakley, *A History of Denmark* (London, 1972). Specially useful for an understanding of Danish history in the crucial period in which absolutism was pioneered is E.L. Petersen, *The Crisis of the Danish Nobility, 1580–1660* (1967). Otherwise, there is L. Krabbe, *Histoire de Danemark* (Copenhagen, 1950); also K. Larsen, *A History of Norway* (New York, 1948).

The best outline history of Sweden is Ingvar Andersson, *A History of Sweden* (1956). E.F. Hecksher, *Economic History of Sweden* (Cambridge, Mass., 1954), is an abbreviated translation of a famous book by the author of a standard work on mercantilism. Nils Ahnlund, *Gustav Adolf the Great* (Princeton, 1940), is described by M. Roberts as 'a classic discussion by a supreme authority'. The latter words might well be applied to Roberts, author of a two-volume life, *Gustav Adolf: A History of Sweden* (1953, 1958). Most valuable for the student of this period is his *Essays in Swedish History* (1967), containing a long essay on Charles XI and one on Queen Christina's crisis; also his *Sweden as Great Power, 1611–97* (1968), which consists largely of documents; and *Sweden's Age of Greatness, 1632–1718* (London, 1973), edited by Roberts, which fills further gaps with essays on Charles X, by Stellan Dahlgren, and on Magnus de la Gardie, by Göran Rystad. 'The experience of empire: Sweden as a great power' is the title of another of the essays, by Sven Lundkvist. Sweden's pre-eminence came to an abrupt end in the reign of Charles XII, the subject of many biographies, starting with Voltaire's, all eclipsed by the splendid life, *Charles XII* (London, 1974), by Ragnhild Hatton, which makes full use of the author's extensive knowledge of the diplomatic history of northern Europe. Eighteenth-century Sweden is less well served, but there is B.J. Hoyde, *The Scandinavian Countries, The Rise of the Middle Classes* (2 vols, Boston, 1944). There is an analytical account of the Age of Liberty in Sven Ulric Palme, 'The bureaucratic type of parliament: the Swedish Estates during the Age of Liberty, 1719–1772', in *Liber Memorialis Georges de Legarde* (1968). See also the essays by M. Roberts, one in A. Goodwin (ed.), *The European Nobility in the Eighteenth Century* (1953), and another, in *Essays* (cited above), on the Hats and Caps.

14

POLAND

The Royal Republic

When John Casimir was elected to the Polish throne, following his brother Wladislaw IV, in November 1648, one month after the end of the Thirty Years War, he became ruler of the kingdom of Poland and the grand duchy of Lithuania: some 350,000 square miles inhabited by some 7 million people, less than half of whom were Poles. East of the Bug and San rivers were Lithuanians, White Russians and Ukrainians, though many of the nobles in these eastern regions were Polish. The Jews, perhaps 5 per cent, were to be found mainly in the east and in the towns. There were also Germans, recent immigrants from the war zones. These were lands of peasants and gentry, of extensive grain lands, forests, marshes and steppes. Even townspeople were often farmers as well, while the *szlachta*, or gentry, were remarkably numerous, about 1 in 20 of the population. 'Noble' status extended often to freeholders, living remote and simple lives in their single-storey wooden houses, modest in estate but not in the pride derived from former colonizing times when knights had claimed equality with their lords. Certain great magnates with vast estates towered above the mass of the *szlachta* but all were equal in law and constitutional rights. There were no peers, no Polish titles; though some were called 'Prince', it was an honorific title only. A crucial problem of government was the discrepancy between the social and political status of the gentry, with incomes often little above those of their peasants. They tended to seek the protection of the great families; this made even more dangerous the power that they could exercise through their voting rights in the diet.

It is tempting to view Polish history as a long prelude to the eventual tragedy of the partitions (1772, 1793, 1795). In 1772 the essential deficiencies were the same as they had been in 1648. The country lacked an educated body of diplomats, legal and financial experts; a sufficient body of regular soldiers and adequate revenues to support them; a secure and prosperous community of merchants and manufacturers. But it need not be assumed that the political and economic weaknesses of the country were therefore beyond hope of remedy in 1648. The examples of Brandenburg and Russia show how states could evolve in similarly unpromising circumstances. Personalities and circumstances play an important part in the decline of Poland. It was Poland's misfortune that rival states produced rulers of the calibre of Frederick William I of Brandenburg, Peter I of Russia and above all a succession of able Vasa kings of Sweden. Yet John Casimir and John Sobieski were men of ability and spirit. The latter inspired the alliance and led the army which delivered Vienna from the Turks in 1683. Physical obstacles were less formidable than those which Alexis and Peter encountered in Russia. It was mainly the eccentricities of the system of government that defeated attempts to build a modern state and even to repair the old one.

Poland had suffered relatively lightly in the Thirty Years War. After the treaty of Stummdorf (1635) which ended the war against Sweden, she had been neutral, but at a price. When Livonia and the administration of the West Prussian customs were ceded to Sweden, Poland lost much of her Baltic trade. The aggrandizement of Brandenburg, which received Eastern Pomerania in 1648, further threatened her interests. John Casimir also inherited a war against the Chmielnicki Cossacks: rebellions were in fashion in 1648. Wladislaw IV's efforts to mediate in the European conflict had met with snubs; Poland was not even represented at the final negotiations. The unwieldy body of Poland–Lithuania, second only to Russia among Christian states in its extent, displayed some alarming symptoms, but there was no reason to diagnose a fatal outcome. It had been one of the great powers of Europe in the early sixteenth century, still expanding at that time in such a way that contemporaries compared the European movement eastward and northward to the colonizing of the Indies; the conquistadores in East Prussia, Livonia and the Ukraine were Polish and Lithuanian lords, with their client gentry, seeking new lands and sources of income. The state, however, neither directed nor controlled the exercise. Since there was practically no gold or silver to be mined, farming, with increasingly profitable exports of corn, timber, skins and salt, became the mainstay of the economy. Landowners turned cash rents into labour dues wherever possible. With ample land, cheap labour and rising corn prices, they set up a dominant position at the expense not only of the peasantry, who were

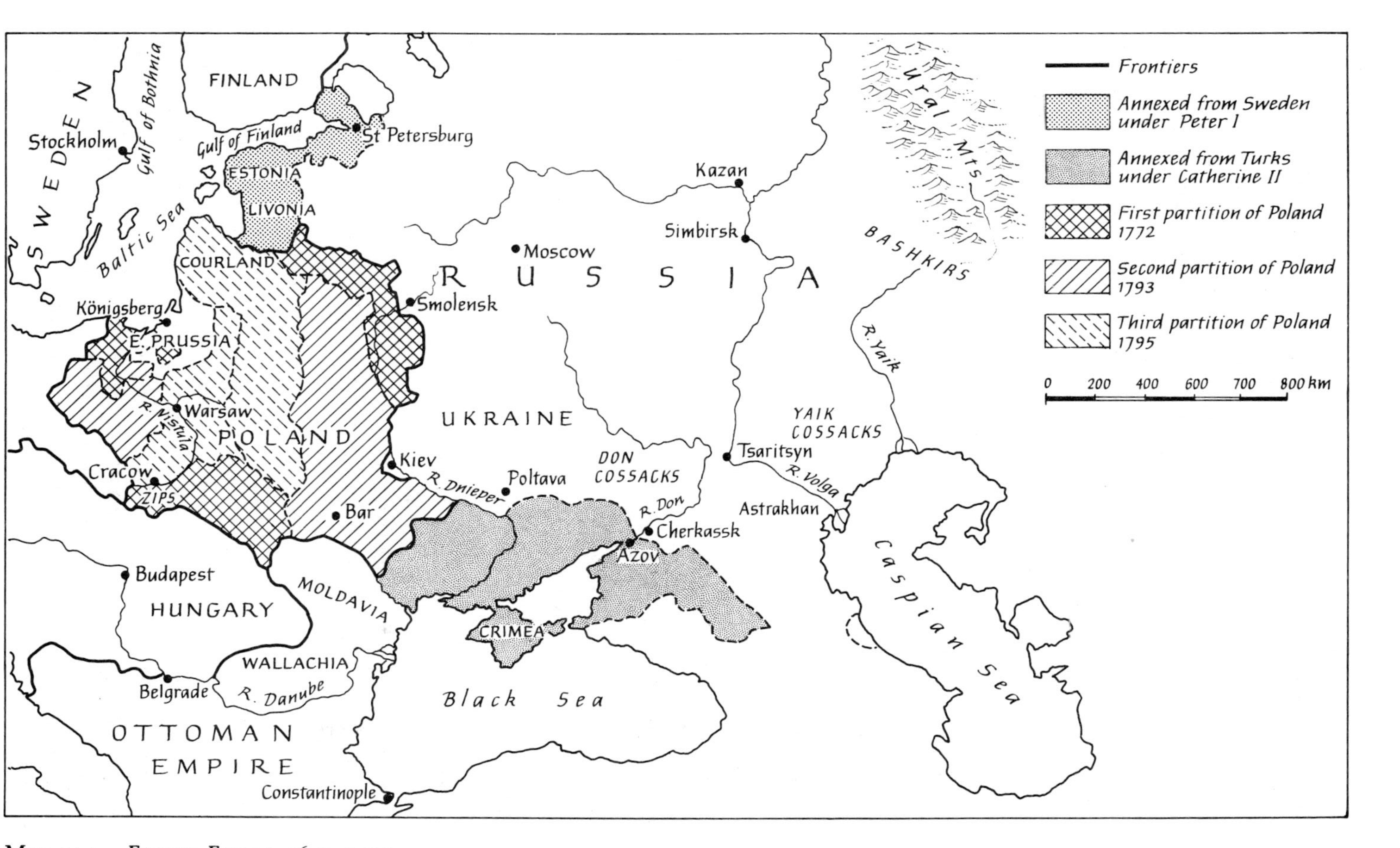

Map 14.1 *Eastern Europe, 1640–1795*

reduced to servile status, but of the inland towns, since they traded through their own agents and used the rivers, which were largely customs-free, to take their produce to the ports. These advantages were reflected in their monopoly of political power in a diet which represented the *szlachta* exclusively and an elective monarchy which gave the diet unique opportunities to exact concessions.

Even after 1667, when a large area beyond the Dnieper, 68,000 square miles, was surrendered to Russia, Polish lands stretched from that river nearly to the Oder, and from within a hundred miles of the Sea of Azov to the Baltic. But there were no true frontiers. There was a strong emotional feeling of nationality, at least in the kingdom of Poland proper, but little political coherence. 'Sarmatism', an early flowering of Slav nationalism, flourished in the eighteenth century among the gentry, but it was based on pride in the very institutions and customs that made the Poles so weak. If the state had a *raison d'être* it was that Polish kings afforded some protection to landowners in their far-flung domains without asking much in return. The very conditions of wartime emergency and economic contraction which enabled the Great Elector, secure in his hereditary status, to drive such hard bargains with his *Junkers* enabled the landowners of Poland to consolidate their position. For 55 out of the 70 years after 1648 the Poles were engaged in war. With such large numbers of that particular class of gentry which was supposed to nurture the bravest men, it might be expected that the state could have produced a large army. In the eighteenth century, however, the army at the disposal of the king was barely a quarter of that maintained by Prussia: the military revolution passed Poland by.

There were religious minorities, Orthodox in the Ukraine, Uniates (product of the union of 1596 between Catholics and Orthodox Christians, obeying the Pope and Catholic doctrines while following their traditional rites), and pockets of Lutherans, mainly of German origin. The state was Catholic, however, having been recovered for Rome largely by the missionary efforts of the Jesuits towards the end of the sixteenth century. It was a boast of the Poles that they had had no religious war. Government was simply never strong enough to enforce conformity.

In the 1640s the Orthodox revival radiating from the monasteries and brotherhoods of Kiev, Lvov and Wilno was a strong attraction to the peasantry in the eastern districts, who associated Rome with Polish-speaking landowners, and an important factor in the great Cossack revolt. In the eighteenth century the 'great powers' were able to exploit the grievances of the relatively small numbers of 'dissidents', Protestant and Orthodox. The vitality of the Roman Church, displayed in missionary work, education and architecture, which affected Polish life so profoundly in the first half of the seventeenth century, declined thereafter with that of the state. The Jesuit fathers maintained their monopoly in education but they gave the impression of caring more about religious orthodoxy than about free learning. They helped to undermine the idea of responsible citizenship which was essential if the free institutions of the *szlachta* were to be useful to the state. The system needed the collaboration of the educated classes. What could then be achieved was briefly shown in the years of reform that followed the first partition (1772). Education and attitudes were crucial. The urgent need was for teaching to fit young Poles for the altered circumstances of the nation. Pointing to the work of Frederick the Great in Prussia, the reform-minded Staszic was to ask: 'Why cannot we have our boys learning trades also?' The Jesuit *ratio studiorum* was designed rather for the needs of a literate élite. But the decline of schools and universities was part of a general demoralization for which methods of education were not primarily responsible.

The Polish constitution rested on a contract made between king-elect and the people, represented by the *seym* or diet, defining the mutual obligations of both parties. The *pacta conventa* was first formally enacted in 1573 on the election of Henry of Valois. It remained a special institution of public law to the end of the commonwealth (*Rechtspolita*). But it was only binding for the lifetime of the sovereign; at each new election the clauses were redrafted. Those of 1573 set out principles that were repeated in every subsequent bargain: the monarchy was to be elective forever and the king might take no step to influence the choice of a successor. The king could move only within carefully defined limits; if he exceeded these limits his subjects had the right to withdraw allegiance. The *seym* and the senate represented the rights of the subjects; two parts – the king being the third – of the General Crown Diet which legislated for the whole *Rechtspolita*. The *seym* was an assemblage of gentry, about 180 in number, and contained no representatives of towns or clergy. Furthermore its members were deputies, sent by the gentry of their district. The senate was not representative in this way: there bishops, *voivodes* (governors) and other officials were members by virtue of their office. The king could summon this diet; in theory it could not meet without him. For legislation there had to be concurrence between the three estates: deputies, senators and king. In voting, all must be unanimous. By a refinement of this principle the *liberum veto* evolved: a single adverse vote was sufficient not only to defeat a proposed measure but to invalidate all previous legislation of the diet.

In the local *diets* (about seventy) which sent representatives to the *seym*, there was a steady accretion of duties and powers. These bodies, which all the gentry had the right to attend, voted special taxes, maintained local troops and appointed their commanders. They voted by majority, inevitably, since many thousands might assemble for an election to the *seym*. The constitution of 1717 reformed the *diets* and limited their powers to the military sphere; but they had a free hand in financial matters until 1768. In the former year the size of the army was hopefully fixed at 24,000. Attempts to recruit an army to supplement the small core of regulars failed entirely. The *starostas* (sheriffs) found it inconvenient to apply even selective conscription, and the Cossack guard raised to defend the Dnieper frontier was of little use. Poland, which should, upon contemporary calculations, have produced an army of at least 60,000, could rarely mobilize a third of that number. For the size of the army depended on taxes; but such wealth as could be tapped was concentrated in the hands of the larger landowners, and they controlled local *diets*, whose delegates in the *seym* spoke mainly for provincial interests; they referred back demands for taxes to the provinces which had deliberately refused to empower them to accept such taxes. The crown was unable therefore to build up a new tax system to replace the dues and rents which had fallen into the hands of the landowners. The country came increasingly to look like a federation of aristocratic estates; while Poles talked of *aurea libertas* and unique constitution which preserved both liberty and order, diplomats grew more sceptical about the chances of survival in the world of absolute monarchies.

In the absence of an effective royal bureaucracy the gentry supplies most of what government there was. The tribunals which steadily took over the exercise of law from the traditional royal judicature were appointed by, and consisted of, gentry. The *starosta* also freed himself from the king's influence and could be relied upon to serve the interests of the dominant class. A distinctive product of the idea that the gentry were the natural guardians of liberty was the confederation: this was a union of leading members of society formed for specific ends. Confederations were formed during every interregnum when the power which had belonged to the king reverted to society. They were also formed during his lifetime to further the interests of a party or bring pressure in some local or national issue. Headed by marshals, bound by oath, they were all the more effective because so many of the lesser gentry, in worsening economic circumstances, were content to accept the status of client to a magnate in return for security. Inevitably they became, therefore, an instrument in promoting political ambitions. The great families of this 'noblemen's commonwealth', Czartoryskis, Potockis and their like, fought for influence; one or other party of them manipulated the state during the Saxon period. A Czartoryski setting out for his estate with 400 horses and 14 camels; or to a fashionable spa, with 100 wagons; the Branickis, in their palace at Bialystock, with its stables for 200 horses, and only 170 books – such men dominated the Poland of the Saxon kings. They displayed a perverse pride in the un-western character of their country, but they went to French architects and Italian dressmakers.

The Great Cossack Revolt

John Casimir, formerly a Jesuit and a cardinal, was the second son of Sigismund III, and he succeeded his brother Wladislaw IV. Father and sons in succession occupied the throne from 1587 to 1668. Yet no progress was made during this time towards establishing hereditary monarchy. John's accession coincided with the rising of the Cossacks under the *hetman* (leader) Chmielnicki. When the *seym* was meeting to choose their king, Chmielnicki was operating within 150 miles of Warsaw. It was the beginning of two decades of war, conspiracies, confederations and invasions in a tangle monstrously hard to describe and interpret. The Cossack lands came, east and west, under Russian and Polish influence: 'rule' would be an inapt description. An earlier rising under Pavluk had been suppressed by Wladislaw, who had taken the chance to extend Polish power: he settled Poles in Cossack lands and planned to turn the Cossack horse into a unit of his own army. But there was no controlling the magnates who were the real power in the land. Enterprising men like Jerome Wisniowiecki carved out vast estates: he had a miniature principality on the left bank of the Dnieper with his own capital at Lubny, far into the Ukraine, his own officials and soldiers, and the forced labour of many thousands of peasants. His courage and style suggest the vitality that went to waste because the crown lacked the moral authority and physical resources to control it. As in the case of Wallenstein, the imperialist entrepreneur of the German war, Wisniowiecki was exploiting not the strength of his state but its weakness: in the king's name he fought, colonized, and made enemies for the king among those who wanted to preserve the freedom of the steppes.

Chmielnicki, a Cossack by birth, latterly a Polish officer, had seen service with the French: he revolted apparently on the score of personal grievances but seems to have dreamed of making an independent Ukrainian state. Within months there was a vast *Jacquerie*, spreading beyond its centre in the Ukraine. Peasants believed that they were to be released from serf overseers, recruiting officers, tax collectors, the Jews, and the Jesuits whose missionaries had worked so tirelessly to overturn Orthodoxy in the Ukraine. Chmielnicki was aided in varying degrees by the Tartars of the Crimea and George Rakoczy, the Calvinist prince of Transylvania; he tried to marry his son to the daughter of the prince of Moldavia. Tsar Alexis was tied at first by the revolts which threatened his own administration and caused him to impose a more rigorous serfdom. In 1649, despite the brave resistance of Wisniowiecki at Zbaraz, Chmielnicki extracted terms from the Poles under which he ruled part of the Ukraine in virtual independence. He had Polish advisers, but Polish troops were withdrawn; Jews and Jesuits were expelled, the Uniate church dissolved. In 1651 he was defeated by John Casimir at the three-day battle of Berestczko. The king could win a battle against odds but could not impose a political solution: it was to be the normal pattern, with bravery in plenty but no unity; patriotic Catholic sentiment but no way of canalizing it; no claim to loyalty to override the claims of province and family interest; no sanctions effective against rebels.

In 1654 the tsar, by the treaty of Peryslavl, agreed to the incorporation of the Cossacks into the Russian state. Thereafter the settlement of the Ukraine was bound up with the wider war which began when Charles X, fearing the consequences of Russia's success in Poland, launched his own attack (1655). Though individual Cossack gangs and their leaders might do well for themselves, the Ukraine did not benefit from Russian intervention. It is doubtful whether it was to the advantage of Russia to take on so great an extension of responsibility, though it could be argued that the anarchy of the southern marches left no third way between advance and retreat. At least the Russians could unfurl the banner of Orthodoxy. In however crude a form, moreover, the Tsar had the political authority and military strength to meet the challenge – as the revolt of Stenka Razin in 1667 and its ruthless suppression were to show. The ensuing period for Ukrainian historians is 'the ruin'. For a period it was a time of troubles but not without hope. The latter years of John Casimir were to show signs of a will to survive, together with a revulsion from foreigners that was at least the negative precondition of recovery.

In 1654 the Russians took Smolensk; in 1655 Wilno, capital of Lithuania. The Radziwill princes, pre-eminent in that province, fearing Russians more than Swedes, recognized Charles as their feudal superior. The Palatine Opalinski led a party of magnates that favoured the Great Elector, while Frederick William needed little encouragement to throw off his allegiance to Poland as vassal in East Prussia. It suited him rather to accept the suzerainty of Sweden: by the treaty of Königsberg, in January 1656, East Prussia became a fief of the Swedish crown and the Swedes gained privileged access to the Prussian ports of Memel and Pillau. But in the longer term Frederick William looked forward to seeing the Swedes pay the penalty for upsetting the always delicate balance of northern power. His judgement was sounder than Charles X's, for Charles, pursuing the dream of *dominium maris Baltici*, penetrated deeply into Poland. The Habsburgs were uneasy at the presence of a Swedish force in Cracow, within striking distance of Silesia and its Protestant communities. The Dutch, in 1656, sent their fleet to prevent Danzig from falling to the Swedes, which encouraged the Danes to attack Sweden; that was to change the course of the war, even though it provided Charles with an opportunity for his most spectacular campaign and the Danes with their most humiliating experience.

In July 1656 Prussians and Swedes (fighting together for the last time) won a famous victory outside Warsaw. Offering partition to the victors, Charles X spun a web of alliances to consolidate his position: Tartars, Cossacks, the Carpathian princes. Of these only George Rakoczy of Transylvania, with some Cossack support, moved effectively. When he reached Warsaw, however, Charles was hurrying back to Pomerania to fight the Danes. The Polish revival had taken heart from the sacrificial defence led by Prior Kordecki of the monastery of Czestochowa with its precious medieval painting of the Black Madonna (December 1655), but it had hitherto been confined to local patriotic movements; it now bore fruit. Rakoczy had to retreat. His force disintegrated and he only reached home after paying a huge indemnity. The Poles were able to make a separate peace with Prussia, to whom they ceded sovereignty in East Prussia (at Wehlau in 1657). The year 1660 saw the death of Charles X and the peace of Oliva: the Poles ceded Livonia formally, a meaningless sacrifice since that province had been in Swedish hands since the time of Gustavus; nothing else. The Russian war dragged on until the peace of Andrussovo (1667) which confirmed Polish losses in White Russia and the Ukraine, and gave Russia Smolensk and Kiev. Altogether those lands amounted to about a fifth of the whole kingdom, but they were frontier lands, sparsely populated: they had not been truly governed and they could not be defended.

The war had shown how vulnerable Poland was to foreign invasion. Its open plains offered no natural obstacles; its troops were inadequate in numbers, weapons and training. Safety might lie temporarily in the divisions of its rivals, but those rivals could sink their differences in the pursuit of easy spoils. The always fragile economy had suffered severely. The birth rate fell sharply in the 1650s, as it was to do again in the 1670s, the period of the Turkish wars. Extravagant issues of copper and debased silver coins brought price inflation while lagging wages reduced the level of demand, and with it the activity of manufacturers. Conditions that were experienced to some extent throughout Europe (and which affected adversely demand for Poland's surplus grain) were most acute in Poland, notably in those regions around the Vistula basin where the Swedes made war, lived off the land and burnt what they could not use. The peasants suffered worst but with them too the smaller landowners. The magnates guarded their position by exacting more labour services from the reduced population, and gentry joined their households as courtiers and clients. In this way war conditions produced a greater imbalance in society, making more difficult, but also more urgent, those radical changes in the constitution which alone, in the long run, could save the state.

John Sobieski

In 1652, a deputy Sicinski used the *liberum veto* to secure the dissolution of the *seym*. His action was a portent of the increasing power of the magnates, exercised through the formation of factions among deputies, financed or encouraged often by foreign envoys; and of their ability to check the executive at will. Of the 58 biennial sessions after 1652, 48 were destroyed in this way. The king being childless, there was talk of revising the constitution to avoid the disruption that might ensue upon his death. A constructive scheme, drafted by the chancellors of Poland and Lithuania (1658–61), proposed to alter the voting system so that a two-thirds majority on a secret ballot could bind the majority. At the same time the crown was to accept a limited right to veto bills passed in this way. *Seyms*, moreover, were to meet annually for six weeks. For lack of support from either court or nobles, this scheme foundered. The merit of the scheme was that it contained the positive good in the 'royal republic', its balance between sovereign and representatives, but corrected its negative trend. The simpler plan of the queen, Louise Marie, for nominating a successor during her husband's lifetime, pointed to hereditary monarchy and to absolutism: it would have stood little chance even if the court candidate had not been a Frenchman, the duc d'Enghien. Resistance was led by the Grand Marshal Lubomirski, acting, as he undoubtedly believed, in the spirit of the Polish constitution. He led an open revolt in 1664 which only ended two years later with a compromise by which the tired king renounced all schemes of reform. After his wife's death John Casimir abdicated and retired to live at the abbey of Nevers in France in 1668.

There ensued the sort of election that he had worked to avoid. In 1669 against lavishly promoted foreign candidates a native nobleman, Jerome Wisniowiecki's son, Michael, was elected. He could boast of descent from the Jagellon kings and he married the emperor Leopold's sister. But he was as feeble as his father had been tough. It was his misfortune moreover to be faced by a new threat to his southern frontier when the sultan Mehmed IV invaded on behalf of the Cossack leader Doroshenko. Two-thirds of Poland's southern frontier lay alongside the Turkish dependencies of Moldavia and Transylvania and the Tartar principalities of Yedisan and the Crimea; it was a stretch as long as that which the Habsburgs had to defend. In 1672 the Turks gained Podolia and what was left of the Ukraine. They were operating with extended lines of communication and they experienced difficulties analogous with those of Poland, in controlling their own tributaries Wallachia and Moldavia, but their success was assured by the notorious weakness of the Polish fortresses on the southern frontier and the complete failure on the part of the *seym* to provide for defence. In 1672 the *seym* broke down in bitter recriminations; with a confederation of Habsburg partisans defying another which represented French interests, civil war seemed near. Faction politics bedevilled defence in a way that illustrates the handicaps that hindered the Polish statesmen. Men from Lithuania or from western Poland could not take seriously what happened in Podolia; not only was it too remote, but there was also the danger that, by over-reacting, the Polish king might invite further assaults from the northern powers. Fortunately for the Poles, their chief commander, John Sobieski, combined a shrewd understanding of Polish affairs with a flair for the sort of generalship that won battles in these primitive wars.

John's handling of cavalry was to be proved on the heights of Kahlenberg on a September day in 1683 in one of the decisive battles of history. His victory of Chocim ten years earlier was less spectacular but it was timely. Michael died on the eve of the battle. In 1674 Sobieski was elected king in his place with significant French support. The yearning for a native leader, which had brought only disappointment in Michael, now promoted a soldier-statesman of high calibre. To satisfy his supporters and fulfil his ambition he had to divert patriotic sentiment from self-indulgent posturing to the service of the state. Throughout Europe absolutist principles were gaining ground at the expense of aristocratic constitutionalism. In 1680 the Swedish *Riksdag* surrendered its remaining rights to a king who recognized no check upon his sovereign authority. In less spectacular fashion the elector of Brandenburg was overcoming the resistance of his various estates. Was Poland alone to persist in its eccentric course, its patriots wallowing in talk of *aurea libertas* and of the glorious sixteenth century, that age of expansion that had culminated in the union with Lithuania and the victories of Stephen Bathory against the Turks?

There were broadly two lines of policy open to John. He could appeal to the *szlachta*, whose interest appears to have lain in curbing the pretensions of the magnates; many of the gentry depended on the favour of some great family, but there was a robust tradition of equality written into the constitution. Or he could make a trial of strength with the more recalcitrant of the magnates. John was one of them and he could play their game. His early military experience had been acquired while fighting for the Swedes against the king. His subsequent political advancement owed much to his wealth as the heir to three huge estates but much also to the patronage of the French queen, whose lady-in-waiting, Marie Casimir, he loved and eventually married. The disgrace of Lubomirski, Grand Marshal, enabled Sobieski to succeed him in the highest military office. From the outset, and inextricably, he was therefore leader of a faction; without it he would not have risen; having so risen he was beset by enemies. Against them he could parade his reputation as a soldier for Christ. As a boy, growing up at the family seat of Zolkiew, he could gaze upon the relics of his grandfather, *hetman* Zolkiewski: his bloodstained cloak and the sword of honour sent him by the Pope. He became professionally earnest, single-minded and altruistic about his mission to fight the infidel. He abandoned the French alliance because French diplomats appeared to be half-hearted about that aspect of Polish policy; he thought that they let him down in the negotiations of 1676 which led to the cession of much of Podolia. He believed that he could unite the nation by adopting the Habsburg cause in the crisis of 1682–3; but there may have been more instinct than calculation in a decision which brought together the strands of his own career and of his reading of Polish history in such a satisfying logic – and with such spectacular success that he may justly be called Europe's last crusader. The sequel to the relief of Vienna, with his own arrogance in dealings with Leopold, the latter's ingratitude and suspicion, the persistent attempts to conquer Moldavia while *seyms* refused supplies and factions undermined his standing at home, exposed the precariousness of his position. His outstanding service to the Habsburgs brought disappointing political dividends. But it is hard to say that he was wrong, taking a narrowly Polish or the wider European view, to offer the Polish army to the Emperor. There were sound military reasons too for the decision to go on hammering the Turk after the relief of Vienna. His campaign in Moldavia ended in stalemate but contributed indirectly to Austrian successes in Hungary.

One motive in Sobieski's forward policy in the east was to find a principality for his son James. As prince of Moldavia he would be in a stronger position to bargain for the Polish crown than as merely son of Sobieski. John treated him as heir-apparent and secured his marriage to Elizabeth of Neuburg, the niece of the Emperor. However, opposition within the family spoilt the king's plans. As his health declined, his wife began to work for the election of one of her younger sons, fearing the loss of her position if James should succeed. In 1692 she signed a private agreement with Louis XIV. Meanwhile in Lithuania the all powerful Sapieha family, controlling army and treasury, planned for the succession for themselves, agitated against John's scheme, and threatened the secession of Lithuania. John's campaigns were represented by his rivals as the pursuit of dynastic ambition. They appeared to cost more than the country could afford, certainly more than the *seym* was prepared to produce. The army went unpaid and John had to act firmly to prevent their forming a confederation to secure their wages. Since John made no convincing attempt to appeal for support beyond the court circle to the mass of the *szlachta*, it is impossible to say what their reaction would have been. In 1689, after attacks on him by senators, some of them demanded a 'horseback *seym*' (in which all the gentry could have taken part). *Mutatis mutandis* it is possible to imagine what a Swedish Vasa could have made of such an opportunity. As it is we are left with a poignant mixture of complacency and cynicism in the tract of Stanislas Lubomirski, *De vanitate consoliorum* (1699), in which the author argues the case for 'golden freedom' and asserts that all state institutions become corrupted in the course of time so that no change is worth making.

The Saxon Kings

John Sobieski died in 1696. Augustus II of Saxony was crowned king of Poland in Cracow in September 1697. For the next half-century Poland was to be tied to Saxony by a personal union, which was the outcome of more than a year's manoeuvring during the longest interregnum of Poland's history. The Russians had promoted the Saxon candidature to counter the election of the French prince of Conti, who had actually been declared king by his supporters when Augustus arrived to claim the throne. With the Polish army behind him, besides his own Saxon troops, Augustus was able to complete a bloodless coup. The union promised certain benefits. The manufacturing skills of hard-working Saxons, combined with the raw materials of Poland, could bring dividends in Baltic trade. Augustus's territorial designs also had some logic behind them. Austrian Silesia and the Prussian Oder lands, both formerly Polish, divided Poland from Saxony. The example of Brandenburg suggests what might have been achieved by some degree of integration. But Brandenburg's success was the product of efficient administration and of a military power beyond anything that a Polish king could muster. The union with Saxony also brought mutual resentments which cancelled out the additional resources. The events of the Great Northern War exposed the weakness of Poland, the shortcomings of the new king, and the dubious value of the Saxon alliance.

Augustus's early measures for a renewal of war against the Turks were spoiled by the open revolt of the Lithuanian nobles. He none the less entered the alliance against Sweden which was being canvassed by the Livonian leader, Patkul. Like the rulers of Denmark and Russia, he underestimated the quality of his opponent. The Poles besieged Riga in February 1700. After their failure to capture it, Augustus would have liked to retire from the war. Unhappily for Poland, Charles XII decided to follow up his victory over the Russians at Narva (November 1700) by throwing his whole strength against the union in order to depose Augustus and check what he regarded as a serious threat to Sweden's interests. The Sapieha family of Lithuania, and Cardinal Radziejowski, archbishop of Gnesen and primate of Poland, declared for Charles. He could also count on France. The *seym* voted Augustus an increase in army and revenues; the Cossacks revolted once more, however, and he had to detach valuable forces to suppress them. Charles XII's army was victorious, though he could only control the regions in its immediate vicinity. He declared that he had no quarrel with the people, only with their ruler, but his soldiers brought destruction and terror. In some areas *szlachta* and townsfolk fought together for their liberty but, as ever, the war effort was paralysed by the dissensions of the magnates: in July 1704 one of their number, Stanislaus Leszczynski, was elected king by a gathering of *szlachta* to the accompaniment of salvoes of Swedish guns.

For Sweden, Stanislaus was to prove useful at first, but soon an embarrassing liability. Augustus had meanwhile to endure an invasion of Saxony. In February 1706 his commander, Schulenberg, was defeated at Fraustadt on der Oder by the Swedish general Rehnsköld. In September Charles set up his standard at Altranstädt, as defender of the Protestants and liberator of Germany. But when, in the following year, he marched towards Russia, he set in motion the train of events that was to lead to the battle of Poltava, the destruction of his army and the irrevocable decline of his country. Augustus recovered his throne after years of damaging civil war, in which the Russians had established a commanding influence. The pattern of the next fifty years was already determined. Augustus tried to use Russian backing for his own ends: to strengthen sovereignty, to make it hereditary and to build a territorial bridge between Saxony and Poland. The Russians rebuffed plans of partition but they were interested only in maintaining a weak Poland which would be unable to challenge them in their newly conquered Baltic lands. Like the Prussians, they championed any group among the magnates which was prepared to accept their money and to disrupt the *seym* whenever there was any chance of reform. They backed the *szlachta* confederacy of 1715 which was formed to expel the Saxons. The treaty of Warsaw (November 1716) between Augustus and the confederates, and the meeting of the *seym* that was called to ratify its provisions served only to narrow the ground on which Augustus could manoeuvre. The Saxon army and officials were to leave the country; all the king's decisions were to be subject to the approval of the majority of senators. The formation of confederacies was, however, banned. There was also a positive gain for monarchy in the shape of a fixed standing army, supported by permanent taxes, although these turned out to be inadequate even for so small a force: at 24,000 a bare third of the size of the Prussian army. The power of the *hetman* was curbed and special courts were set up for cases of persons prosecuted for dealings with enemies of king or state. The finances were brought under budgetary discipline for the first time and the treasurer was to account to each *seym*. The army was to make its own arrangements for the collection of the poll tax, which typically fell on the peasantry and was assessed on an out-of-date basis: a reflection upon administrative standards and a check to hopes of future development.

The package was incomplete; but it did represent a start of sorts to the process of setting up the French-style absolutism which he, like other German princes, believed to be the ideal form of government. There was even talk among the authors of the Warsaw treaty of abolition of the *liberum veto* and the institution of majority voting. At the next *seym*, in 1718, there were proposals from the court for a larger army and measures to stimulate the economy, cancel private customs duties and reform the coinage; others to limit the power of the Church, increase tax upon its estates and reduce the scope of its courts. All was in the spirit of the time, pointing to some of the critical weaknesses of the state. It was Poland's tragedy that they were not put into effect. What a Sobieski might have achieved, given a sufficient following among the *szlachta*, a Saxon king, dependent upon Russian goodwill, could not.

In the Polish setting, there is an ironic sound about Augustus's title 'the Strong'. Boastful even in remorse, he is said to have confessed on his deathbed: 'my whole life was one continual sin'. He possessed neither the stamina nor the subtlety, nor even the interest in Polish affairs, to achieve his objects: the *szlachta* were right of course to assume that he did not want a hereditary monarchy for the sake of his Polish subjects. At a time when *aurea libertas* wore a tarnished look after so many years of war, there was still little appeal in the alternative of German government, bureaucratic and militarist in character, even if it were not taken to Prussian extremes by the more easy-going Saxons. Neither Russian tsar nor Polish *hetman* was prepared to accept it. Augustus was also constricted when it came to initiatives in foreign policy. He asked the *seym* of 1719 to ratify his treaty of Vienna providing for the evacuation by the Russians of Mecklenberg and Poland, which he envisaged as the basis for a new alliance of Austria, Sweden, Poland and Saxony. The deputies, fearing the renewal of war with Russia, rejected the treaty. The direct consequence was the Potsdam agreement of Russia and Prussia (1720) to impede another Saxon succession and protect Polish institutions. So the *seym* continued to meet, and to disperse, in futile fashion: 23 out of 28 held under the Saxon kings were deliberately wrecked. Some deputies continued to receive foreign money. The Czartoryskis, known as the 'Family', who supported Stanislaus Poniatowski, commanded the allegiance usually of the greater number of the *szlachta* and held at least to some constructive and reforming ideas, were matched by the Potockis, less well educated and public-spirited than their rivals, adherents of Stanislaus Leszczynski; enthusiasts for confederacy when it suited their book, the Potockis were ready to adopt any means to keep their grip on the grand offices of state: for many years one brother was Grand *Hetman*, another primate. Each faction believed that what was good for them was good for Poland. The *seym* was their battleground; the veto was their weapon; the result was stalemate. Until the first stirrings of a genuine reform movement in the 1760s, under the impending threat of partition, nothing material was done to put Poland's house in order.

The Great Northern War which had such fatal political effects also wrought havoc upon the country's already backward, always precarious economy. Between 1700 and 1721 the population of Poland fell by at least a million, to six million. Between 1700 and 1716, the exactions of Russian, Swedish and Saxon armies amounted to considerably more than the total revenue of the state during this period. Danzig, the one city never to fall to a foreign army, 'contributed' several hundred thousand *thalers*. In the one year of 1706 the Swedes gutted 140 villages on the estates of one of Augustus's followers. In 1716 the Saxon army ravaged the estates of the confederates. Nowhere in Europe were military operations conducted with such contempt for civilian rights. The continent's last great outbreak of bubonic plague, together with local famines, compounded the miseries of war as communities dissolved into refugee bands. The survey of crown properties carried out in 1710–15 reported widespread desolation. In some districts 90 per cent of the farms were abandoned. Shortage of labour led to a tightening of the bonds of serfdom as landowners sought to keep their estates going. A drastic fall in medium-sized peasant holdings witnessed to the deterioration in the life and productivity of the peasant. It became harder for the peasant to prove his rights to land or to recover an estate lost in war; and so landless labourers became more numerous, an anomaly in this vast and underpopulated country.

The trend towards self-sufficient demesne farming further damaged the towns. For besides the direct damage of war, with its forced levies and interruption of trading routes and facilities, there was the more insidious process by which the landowners simply bypassed the towns; they provided their own services, felled and sold their own timber, and brewed ale; they even maintained their own workshops, manned by serfs in their own corner of the town, importing direct whatever goods they required from abroad. The same process can be studied in Prussia; but there it was government policy, for fiscal reasons, to protect the urban middle class and to foster trade. In Poland, the towns simply decayed as price control upon manufactured goods further benefited the *szlachta*, whose self-sufficiency in essential goods and services was already so harmful to a country suffering above all from lack of demand. Besides Warsaw, which enjoyed a somewhat artificial prosperity, supplying the needs of the court and aristocracy, only Danzig, Wilno, Cracow, Lvov, Thorn and Lublin remained considerable towns, with 10,000 inhabitants or more. Most towns had but a thousand or less. Ruined houses and deserted streets spoke of the plight of the surviving artisans who could make a modest living only by farming outside the walls. The Jews, preserving their strict social and moral discipline and inured to slights and setbacks, became the Polish 'middle class': traders, craftsmen, agents and farmers of estates, and protected by the nobility whose estates and business concerns they managed so efficiently.

So Poland continued to exhibit features of an underdeveloped economy at a time when Europe was enjoying a modest period of growth. There was a chronic shortage of capital both for farming and for manufactures. Merchants, usually mere agents, were unable to accumulate reserves for investment. Demand was depressed by a cash famine at a time when Europe as a whole was benefiting from easier monetary conditions. Frederick the Great, armed with dies from captured Saxon mints and a network of agents, sucked in good coin and issued debased, making a profit equal to the value of all the British subsidies in the Seven Years War. But, even before that masterpiece of economic warfare, there was always a surplus of copper coins; silver ones were debased; and only gold kept its value. Banking was in its infancy and in the hands of a few foreigners. In sum, it is not surprising that neighbouring rulers should think that they could make better use of some parts of Poland than could the Poles themselves. The *Rechspolita* was in precarious shape – and yet the crown of Poland was accounted a prize worth contesting.

Another aspect of Poland's isolation is revealed by the hardening of religious orthodoxy at a time when the government might have been expected to encourage immigration from relatively populous Germany. Was it mere perversity that made the Poles march so confidently out of step with contemporary movements of thought? Polish orthodoxy had its positive side. As in Spain on Europe's other flank, reasons are to be found in

Poland's earlier history: Spain's *reconquista* is matched by Poland's conversion from Lutheranism by the Jesuits; crusade against the Turks was a way of life for eastern Poles, a still lively tradition throughout the *Rechspolita*. For the illiterate peasant and educated gentleman alike, Roman Catholicism was an essential feature of a national identity which distinguished the Slav Pole from Russian barbarian or German tradesman. Under the influence of their Jesuit schoolmasters the *szlachta* found the common ground for action against Lutherans and Orthodox Christians that they could not achieve in the political sphere. The ever-adaptable Jesuits tended to suit their methods to the communities they served. At the same time in their pursuit of what seemed good for Rome and their order, they might lose sight of the wider needs of their people. The very success of conversion and teaching upon the principles of the *ratio studiorum* now limited their understanding of Poland's political and material crisis. The Renaissance-style classical curriculum did little to prepare young upper-class Poles for a realistic approach to contemporary problems of government and society but encouraged them to believe unquestioningly in their race and class and to despise what was different. Loosely worded articles in the Warsaw treaty encouraged Catholic militants to gnaw at the remaining Protestant rights. In 1733 it was decreed that non-Catholics should be excluded from civil offices. Augustus III was the first Polish sovereign not required by his accession oath to keep the peace between the Christian denominations. How little his predecessor, Augustus, had been able to do so is revealed for example by the tumult of Thorn. In Thorn barely half the people were German Lutherans but they dominated the city through the craft guilds. In July 1724 after provocation by a Jesuit seminarist, a Lutheran mob desecrated the Jesuit chapel. The king, who could have dealt with the matter himself, referred it to the chancellor's jurisdiction. The exclusively Catholic court decreed death for the twelve chief rioters, besides the mayor and his deputy for not checking the riot. The victims of this severity appealed to Protestant powers of the west. Several protested, but effective action was prevented by the lack of support from Russia and Prussia, and by Augustus's evident powerlessness. On this occasion, as often later, the Russians turned a deaf ear to the pleas of minorities because they wished to preserve the goodwill of the border magnates. Continual Catholic pressure was, however, building up a situation in which oppressed minorities afforded plausible pretexts for direct intervention.

The War of the Polish Succession has to be set in a wider context than that of Polish politics and the ambitions of the Wettin dynasty if the interest of the western powers is to be understood. First the French were anxious to check the rising influence of the Emperor in Germany, where all members of the German diet, except for Bavaria, Saxony and the Palatinate, had accepted the Pragmatic Sanction in 1732. Cardinal Fleury, 80 years old but still alert and far-sighted, would have preferred to maintain an entente with Austria; but the Austrians had made the treaty with Russia in 1726 which did so much to determine the future of those countries in the Balkans and made possible common action over Poland; the British cold-shouldered Fleury and renewed their alliance with Austria (Vienna 1731). Fleury was pushed towards war by the traditionalist war party at the French court, led by Chauvelin. The French were directly involved because of the marriage of Louis XV to Maria Leszczynska, daughter of ex-King Stanislaus. Superficially the establishment of an outpost of French power in the north, together with the prestige that would accrue to Louis XV if his father-in-law regained his throne, looked attractive. France prudently insured against the prospect of a Saxon succession to Poland by means of a treaty with Augustus II in 1732. But Augustus had also come to terms with Frederick William of Prussia by which that country, together with Austria and Russia, would receive portions of Poland in return for guaranteeing the hereditary succession of the Saxon dynasty in Poland. When Augustus died, in February 1733, the Russians and Austrians preferred the bird in the hand, in the shape of a dependent Poland, to whatever might be in the bush; and so Courland was earmarked for Tsarina Anna's favourite, Bühren, the new elector of Saxony was put forward for the throne and Prussia was left with nothing. Frederick William naturally, therefore, let Stanislaus go through Prussia on his hasty journey to Poland and the throne to which the *seym* duly elected him (September). Feodor Potocki had meanwhile used his position as primate to persuade the *seym* to pass a resolution excluding foreign candidates from election. But when 30,000 Russian troops marched into Poland, Stanislaus, the 'Autumn King', had to flee to Danzig; impressed by Russian bayonets, the deputies in Warsaw thereupon elected Augustus III king in his place. It is fair to add that the Lithuanian party amongst the electors preferred him; they were closest to Russia.

It looked as if the contest of kings would lead to a major war along the lines of that of the Spanish Succession, as Fleury wove a web of treaties: with Spain (the 'family compact' of 1733), Savoy and Bavaria; while Turkey and Sweden hovered on the fringe, ready to settle old scores against Russia. But Fleury was wisely moderate. He carefully avoided provoking Britain, so that Walpole was able to maintain neutrality and to turn a deaf ear to Austrian requests. The expedition that Fleury eventually dispatched to help Stanislaus at Danzig was small enough to allay British fears about the Baltic and therefore of no use to Stanislaus, who had to surrender Danzig in July 1734. While French troops seized Lorraine, Fleury did not pursue his advantage; in Italy the French effort was half-hearted. There was no attempt to link up with the Bavarians, or to invade the Habsburg lands; and no encouragement was offered to Turkey. The Emperor, therefore, was allowed to extricate himself, and preliminaries of peace were signed at Vienna in October 1735 (the final settlement was delayed until November 1738 while Fleury negotiated to extract the maximum benefit for his country). As an exercise in dynastic diplomacy and limited war, the episode may be regarded as a cynical, more or less futile performance, or as a civilized, even though laborious, way of settling complex disputes with the minimum of bloodshed. In the light of what was to follow from the more direct approach of Frederick the Great (his invasion of Silesia in 1740), there is much to be said for the latter interpretation. From a Polish standpoint, however, the outcome was unsatisfactory. Stanislaus was compensated for his disappointment by the duchy of Lorraine, which proved to be a manageable theatre for his modest but agreeable talents.

And so the Poles were left with another Saxon king. Augustus III was stolid and unenterprising, a pious Catholic though he had only been converted as a young man on his father's orders. He spoke no Polish and, apart from his enforced stay during the Seven Years War, he spent but two years in all in Poland. He was content apparently to leave Polish affairs to his Saxon minister, von Brühl. Between the Czartoryskis and the Potockis, between Russia and Prussia, von Brühl sought to make the royal authority more effective, to persuade the aristocracy to render some service in return for their privileges. They, however, continued to provide material for that crushing verdict of a Polish historian who wrote of the Saxon period that Polish history 'turns out to be that of a handful of families'. The embroilment of the great powers in the War of the Austrian Succession and the Seven Years War afforded some respite, and even some limited opportunities for constructive bargaining. Once again opportunities were wasted. In the *seym* of 1744, the Czartoryskis proposed measures of rearmament: the Russians approved, hoping for support against Prussia; the king promised Josef Potocki command of the new army. But the Potockis were not to be enticed: they were bribed by Prussian agents and the *seym* broke up in angry recriminations. In 1748, the cause was different, the outcome similar. The Czartoryskis wanted the king to bestow office regardless of family or party. If their proposals had been implemented Poland would have had at least the beginnings of aristocracy of service upon the formula that had served Prussia so well. Not unnaturally the Potockis saw the ambitions of the 'Family' behind this apparently altruistic policy. A bitter conflict developed over the composition of the *Trybunal* and for a time judicial administration was at a standstill before a compromise was patched up. Von Brühl became disillusioned with the Czartoryskis and tried to build up his own party which only accentuated the Family's mistrust of the Saxon dynasty. Foreign troops were on Polish soil in one area or another throughout the Seven Years War – but no patriotic movement could make headway against the jealousies of magnates when all they seemed to have in common was dislike of the foreign king. Poland was on the edge of civil war in 1763 when Augustus III suddenly died.

Polish Enlightenment

It was the hope of the Czartoryskis that by co-operating with the Russians to secure the election of Stanislaus Poniatowski they would be able to bring about the reforms which a significant number of Poles were now talking about. Their protégé, Stanislaus Konarski, a Piarist priest, had long been active in the reform of the Piarist schools. He introduced a new curriculum in which stress was laid upon critical thinking and clear expression; training for citizenship was grounded upon the teaching of science and modern languages. The Jesuit schools were compelled to follow suit. In 1761–2 Konarski produced, in three impressive volumes, *On the Effective Conduct of Debates*, the case for a government responsible to a two-chamber parliament abiding by the decisions of the majority. His reforms had to wait till after the first partition (1772) had induced a spirit of urgency. It is notable, however, that after 1762 no single *seym* was disrupted.

Stanislaus was elected with Russian support in September 1764. It soon became clear that he was well fitted to play the part of enlightened sovereign. He was a discerning patron and collector of works of art. He began the amassing of materials for a 'modern museum' which included, besides jewels, engravings and relics of the past, contemporary fabrics and china. His work as patron can be criticized for its dependence on the work of foreign artists who included Fragonard. The king also provided stimulus for native arts and crafts; his new porcelain factory outside Warsaw was soon producing pieces comparable to those of Dresden or Berlin. His court, so enterprising, so optimistic, has been called the 'last Renaissance court in Europe'. The title has an ironic ring in view of the impending destruction of the Polish state.

The crucial area of change was constitutional: the reforms that were to follow the first partition unfortunately only served to convince Tsarina Catherine that it would be dangerous to allow an independent Poland to survive. It can be argued that reforms were too late – though hardly too little. Poland died with a flourish and with style. Out of the French and Italian manner that Stanislaus preferred to the Saxon rococo of his predecessor's reign there was evolving, during this period, a distinctive Polish classicism to be seen at its most splendid in the Lazienski palace or Gucewitz's remodelled cathedral at Wilno. In these years, the cities were beautified by architects like Fontana and Merlini, and the countryside graced by those pillared, Palladian manor houses that became the fashion among the gentry.

Stanislaus had been acceptable politically and personally to the new Tsarina Catherine; he had been her lover and she intended him to be her puppet. His independence and reforming zeal were therefore unwelcome. She was not, however, necessarily unprincipled in her defence of the claims of the dissident Polish members of the Greek Orthodox Church. An ardent pupil of the Enlightenment in the early years of her reign she may have been genuinely shocked by the chauvinist attitudes of the Catholic clergy and gentry; she also understood the political value of her patronage of a persecuted minority. Stanislaus found himself occupying uncomfortable middle ground between Repnin, the Russian ambassador, whose brief was to secure complete equality for the dissidents, and the dominant Catholic party among the gentry, grouped around defence of their traditional faith. Inevitably they opposed constitutional reform when it was advocated by a king and politicians whom they suspected of selling the pass to Russia. And so they approved the confirmation of the *liberum veto* in the *seym* of 1766; once again a foreign power and Polish traditionalists combined to weaken the constitution and the state. Now, however, Russia tried to push her advantage beyond what most of her Polish allies could accept.

Radziwill and his party of Lithuanian magnates did indeed support the Guarantee of 1768 by which Catherine secured toleration for Orthodox Poles and 'guaranteed' the constitution. But a more typical reaction was that of the confederates of Bar (in Podolia) who proclaimed the right of Poles to manage their own affairs. At the eleventh hour, Catholic, patriotic Poland asserted itself. It was bravely done – but in the wider political context it looks naive. The Polish gentry had chosen the wrong time and they had acted for the wrong reasons. When France incited Turkey to go to war against Russia, Poland became so entangled in the eastern question that nothing but Russian military defeat could save her. In the event, the Russians occupied Moldavia and Wallachia; Austria and Prussia moved together to protect their interests against Russian aggrandizement. At least that was how the emperor Joseph II defended the Austrian occupation of Zips, the small but rich province south of Cracow (1769).

Joseph's rash action upset the balance of power and set in motion the process of partition. The benefits to Prussia of such a partition were sufficient to outweigh Frederick's mature caution. He therefore offered Catherine Austro-Prussian mediation to end the Turkish war in return for the cession of that part of Poland which separated Brandenburg from Prussia. In 1771 the Russians managed to conquer the Crimea, but they were so exhausted that they were glad to accept the Prussian offer and make peace with Turkey, handing back Moldavia and Wallachia but keeping the Crimea. Hence came the first partition treaty of 1772. A look at the map suggests that Austria was the principal beneficiary, receiving 11.8 per cent of the entire Polish state, an area with 2,130,000 inhabitants, nearly 20 per cent of her total population; it was mostly good agricultural land, with rich salt mines to compensate for the earlier loss of Silesia. Prussia received less, but joined Pomerania to East Prussia by means of Polish or West Prussia. Prussia thus made a further stride towards a compact, defensible state. Besides, Danzig was cut off from the rest of Poland and Frederick could now control Vistula commerce as he pleased. The Russians, who gained sparsely populated tracts beyond the Dvina and Dnieper rivers, had been manoeuvred into a false position which Catherine's later aggression did little to redeem. The second and third partitions of 1793 and 1795 gave her the lion's share of what remained of Poland. But it might have been better for Russia to have kept the real advantages of control over a nominally independent Polish state, together with a balance of power that kept her rivals in check. Poland was an indigestible meal, as the history of the next two centuries was to show. Russia moreover was suffering not from lack of resources but means of effective government: the state was already too large.

Maria Theresa realized the danger of Joseph's partition policy to her state, held together as it was, not by common race or language but by loyalty to the dynasty alone; she called it 'a blot on my whole reign'. Arrogant and greedy, the partitioners represent autocratic diplomacy at its worst; such contempt for the rights of a sovereign was also dangerous at a time when the rights of people were becoming a dynamic force in politics. It is revealing that all three aggressors invoked the principle of the balance of power in justification; yet their action destroyed that very balance which was the soundest achievement of the old diplomacy, and which even Frederick the Great's invasion of Silesia had not entirely overthrown. Vergennes, French foreign minister, noted soon after the first partition:

> For two centuries the great powers have concentrated their entire attention, often to the point of exhausting all their resources, on preventing any one of them from becoming preponderant. Now a new combination has replaced the general balance; three powers have set up one of their own. It is based on the equality of their usurpations and thus the balance of power is made to tip heavily in their favour.

For Poland, partition did not at once appear to be a disaster: two decades of constitutional reform and economic progress showed that a slimmer Poland could thrive. But the very success of Stanislaus's experiment in enlightened constitutionalism prepared the way for the final acts of butchery. Except for twenty years of independence (between 1919 and 1939) Poland's fate was to be a puppet, Napoleonic, tsarist, Soviet; its frontiers and constitution decided by others; its people left with little but their faith to console them.

Further Reading

For English readers the situation has recently improved with the publication of two large works. The first of two volumes of Norman Davies's *God's Playground. A History of Poland* (Oxford, 1982) takes the story up to 1795. Ten out of the thirteen articles collected in J.K. Fedorowitz (ed. and trans.), *Republic of Nobles: Studies in Polish History to 1864* (Cambridge, 1982), relate to the early modern period, and so this book is specially valuable. Three chapters in the *New Cambridge Modern*

History, by H. Jablonowski in vol. 5 and by L.R. Lewitter in vols. 7 and 8, provide reliable narrative. Lewitter's on the partitions also touches on the neglected subject of the Polish Enlightenment. The sections of J. Stoye's textbook, *Europe Unfolding, 1648–88* (London, 1969), which deal with Poland are authoritative because of the author's special knowledge of northern and eastern Europe. In this context may also be mentioned the same author's *Siege of Vienna* (1964). A useful biography by O. Laskowski is *Sobieski, King of Poland* (1944). A.B. Boswell, who contributed the chapter on Poland in the collection of essays, *European Nobility in the 18th Century* (1953), ed. A. Goodwin, also wrote a general study, *Poland and the Poles* (1919). The partitions are also dealt with in H.H. Kaplan, *The First Partition of Poland* (1962), and in L.R. Lewitter's two essays in *History Today*, 8 (December 1958) and 9 (January 1959). Another article of specific interest is that of W.F. Reddaway, 'Great Britain and Poland (1672–1772)', *Cambridge Historical Journal*, 4 (1934).

15

RUSSIA

The Service State

The Slav Russians emerged as a recognizable people in the ninth century from a welter of tribal movements, Scythian, Sarmatian, Hunnish and Bulgar. They were thinly spread but occupied the greater part of 'European' Russia within an area flanked by Novgorod, Pskov and Polotsk in the north, Smolensk and Rostov in the centre, Kiev and Chernigov in the south. Ever since, Russia has been both in and beyond Europe and its civilization. Until the seventeenth century the whole land of Russia was in constant flux. Its princes were adventurers and empire builders in near empty lands. At the beginning of that century Russia stretched to the Caspian sea, the Ural mountains and the Arctic ocean. Swedish and Polish lands barred her from the Baltic. Novgorod, recovered from the Swedes in 1617, Smolensk (1657) and Kiev (1667), both acquired from Poland, subsequently extended the frontier to the west. In 1648 Oknotz was founded on the Pacific shore. Siberia had already been penetrated by a few fur traders and colonists. With its nomad tribesmen and its handful of forts, Siberia, Russia's backyard, was as yet of little economic importance. The historic role of Russia, according to Klyuchevsky, had been to act as guardian of the eastern gate of Europe 'which it defended against the attacks of the nomad plunderers of Asia'. In the process 'it saved European civilization from the onslaught of the Tartars' but so 'fell behind the rest of Europe'. The process can be studied in the events of 1632–4 when an invasion of southern Russia by the Crimean Tartars contributed to the failure of Russian attempts to seize Smolensk from Poland. It should be added, however, that during the two expansionist reigns of Ivan III (1462–1505) and Ivan IV (1533–84) it was not so much the drive across the steppes to the Ukraine and Black Sea as the effort to secure a footing on the Baltic shore that strained the resources of Muscovy. The Baltic had to be reached and colonized if Russia were not to retreat upon herself and lose fruitful contacts with the west. In the sixteenth century Russia was not, in the opinion of Western diplomats, a European power. It was still fashionable to despise the Russians in the next century. Descartes, for example, wrote in 1648 that a small piece of the Palatinate was worth more than all the empire of the Tartars or the Muscovites. Yet by then the process had already begun which was to bring Russia into the front rank among states.

In that process the harsh imperatives of geography were at least as important as the impact of race invasions. Immense spaces unbroken by natural obstacles, together with a climate of extremes, gave an elemental character to the people's fight for survival. The great Russian plain which stretches from the Arctic circle to the Carpathian mountains, from the Baltic and the rocky hills of Livonia to the north–south line of the Urals, is not entirely featureless: it is a series of low plateaux. It has a rainfall of less than 20 inches a year. The relatively short growing seasons, between 120 and 150 days, with periodic dry springs and summers, meant recurring harvest failures: 34 either partial or complete were recorded in the eighteenth century. It is the lack of an east–west mountain range to draw the rainfall from the sea winds, to interrupt the advance of Arctic conditions, that creates the notorious Russian winter. The climate becomes indeed more extreme as one goes south-eastwards into the continent, so that Siberia has colder winters, as well as hotter summers, than St Petersburg. The average temperature in January at Tsaritsyn (Volgograd) is −10°C. It is not surprising that the celebration of spring plays such a large part in Russian literature. Within the plain, there are great expanses of steppes, virtually treeless. Northwards stretch the forest lands, scrub and tundra, the latter virtually impossible to cultivate. Moscow, a natural political centre, lies in the one district where a west European might feel at home, with its deciduous trees, oak, elm and beech. Russian rivers start from low watersheds: from the gentle Valday hills in the province of Novgorod flow the Western Dvina to the Baltic, the Volga to the Caspian and the Dnieper to the Black Sea. It was easy to travel from one river's headwaters to another's. The rivers are slow-moving and sinuous, broad natural waterways flanked and fed by extensive marshes, often providing defence, and always the main arteries of colonization and trade.

Klyuchevsky believed that the Russian landscape moulded the Russian people. The open lands and boundless horizons of the steppes created the frontier peasant knight, later harboured the outcasts of Muscovite society, the resourceful Cossacks, horsemen, soldiers, brigands. More than half

Russia's population lived in the forest lands: theirs was the stubborn conservatism of a people who lived by lumbering, cultivating patches of land cleared by fire for a few years, then moving on, always circumscribed by the immensity of the forests. The great rivers were by contrast, a gentler influence; there voyagers and traders could meet in a comradeship of mutual interests. One should be wary, however, of a sentimental view of the life of the Volga boatmen, human draught animals. By 1815 it was reckoned that 7000 of them died on the job every year. Rivers were so important because roads were mere tracks. In rainy seasons long stretches became impassable seas of mud. There were no metalled roads till the nineteenth century. Everywhere, the Russian was but loosely tied to the land, having few possessions, ever ready to move on. The times of political disorder such as the Time of Troubles (1598–1613), external pressures such as those of the Tartar invasions or Livonian Wars of the sixteenth century, and the relentless battering of authority, whether it was the landowner exacting his labour dues or the state seeking to bind subjects within the framework of service, all combined to induce a frontier mentality.

Countries like France and Spain were made up of smaller communities, provinces and districts, tenacious of their customs, rooted in places where generations had forged their tools, sweated to clear wood and scrub and to till the soil, and cherished their beasts and crops; each region was as distinctive in character as in landscape; and so we find everywhere particularism, and material and psychological barriers, against those who sought to usurp local rights, to enforce the decrees of a royal government which belonged to an alien world. Russia, with its monotonous tracts of uniform vegetation, possessed an open character which is hard for the westerner to grasp. The survival of the peasant lay in passive endurance or in flight. When plague and famine also assailed the people, the survivors were pressed all the harder by taxation, labour services and recruitment for the army. There was thus a steady emigration to the remoter lands of the south and east, where the soil was more easily worked, officialdom less oppressive. As in nineteenth-century America the role of space is important: the open frontier prevented economic, political and religious tensions from becoming too acute. The boundless, bare, fringe lands militated against the typical western process of concentration.

At the end of Ivan IV's reign, around Moscow, more than three-quarters of the cultivable land was lying waste. Everywhere deserted villages were commonplace. Shortage of labour was the crucial problem of the Russian government. Until the abolition of serfdom, a landowner's wealth was reckoned not in acres but in 'souls' – the number of peasants he possessed. All Russia had around 14 million inhabitants at the start of the seventeenth century, scattered over 3 million square kilometres; the density of 4 to the square kilometre may be compared with France's 40. The validity of the state depended upon its ability to create conditions in which peasants would stay put and cultivate the soil. The defence of the state required troops and taxes to pay for them; yet if nobles were to serve the state satisfactorily they must be ensured an adequate work-force. These apparently conflicting requirements could only be reconciled by coercion. Serfdom, the tying of peasants to the land with the enforcement of labour services, was a logical development.

The role of the state was perforce negative. Until Peter the Great came to change the style with his radical, unsentimental philosophy and violent methods, the manner in which the tsar lived and worked was priestly and paternalist. But the tsar's officials had always been essentially a military police. Russia was hierarchic but it had never been feudal, for it was never dominated by the knightly class or affected by concepts such as fealty; the status of vassal was unknown. Nor was it, like Germany, a corporate society; there were no provincial estates, municipal corporations, university colleges, even craft guilds. There was no strong class of burghers. The foremost among the merchants, *gosti*, were state functionaries rather than private businessmen. They came under the direct authority of the tsar and ran, on his behalf, the customs and certain monopolies. Apart from the state and the *gosti*, no one had much capital to invest in trade. Russia was not in any sense a capitalist society. It can, however, be described accurately as a society of service since the social hierarchy was arranged in such a way as to provide the ruler with what he needed to control and to defend his lands. Duties, as conceived by the tsar-proprietor, provided the criteria – not rights. The *knyazhata* or princes of the royal blood, decimated by Ivan IV, the remainder of them bitter, potential rebels, had long lost their right of counsel, and were insignificant compared with the magnates of west European states. Boyars, next in order, were themselves graded according to the length of time their families had served the tsar. Some had been deported, as many as 10,000 had been killed by the *oprichniki*, Ivan IV's civil and military agents, through whom he had sought to break the power of the old landowners and create a new class, privileged but dependent for their status upon the tsar. Under weaker tsars, the idea of the *oprichnina* foundered. But their activities had served to shatter what existed of that bond between lord and peasant; the vital element in that sense of community that characterized rural areas in other parts of Europe was thus absent. What survived were two categories of privileged state servants. The *votchinniki*, or medium-sized landowners, were granted lands on condition that they performed specified services; below them ranged another layer of service, the *dvoryane*, petty gentry, sometimes peasants who had distinguished themselves in war. In principle, 'the activities and obligations of all subjects, from greatest lord to meanest serf, were determined by the state in pursuit of its own interests and policies' (Blum). In practice, the efforts of successive tsars to create a stable framework had so far been ineffective, and would remain so until the authority of the tsar was raised securely above those bodies in society which sought to control him or to escape from him. Meanwhile Russians could say 'The Tsar is a long way up and God is a long way up.'

The First Romanovs

The death in 1598 of Theodore I, last of the Ruriks, was followed by a period of social calamities, notably the great famine of 1601–3, and succession disputes leading to foreign invasions. It was during the Time of Troubles (1598–1613) that the crisis was reached in the political conflicts which had to be resolved if Russia were not to disintegrate. The status of the tsar as hereditary proprietor of the state was at stake. The strength of the autocratic tradition of 'Holy Russia', Byzantine in origin and style, was in danger of being wasted. Baron von Herberstein, imperial ambassador at the court of Muscovy, had written of Tsar Vasily III (1505–53):

> He has unlimited control over the lives and property of his subjects. Not one of his councillors has sufficient authority to dare to oppose him, or even to differ from him on any subject. They openly confess that the will of the prince is the will of God.

After Ivan IV had 'applied his red-hot iron to Russia' (Mousnier), and Theodore had died without issue, anarchy reigned. A true tsar had to be a born tsar. Invasions and revolts showed how feeble were the sanctions when the legitimacy of the ruler was in doubt. The humiliation of the Polish occupation of Moscow and the election of King Sigismund to be tsar (1610) stirred up a patriotic counter-movement in the provinces against the Roman Catholic foreigner and the boyar-dominated government of Moscow. The intruders were expelled, and a *Zemskii Sobor* (national assembly) elected Michael Romanov, aged 16, as tsar (1613).

Three centuries later, Nicholas II, last of the Romanovs, was to abdicate and die at the hands of revolutionaries. During two of those centuries Russia was to be one of the prime military powers of Europe. Towards the end, her social structure and economy were being transformed: absolutism and bourgeois liberalism were coming awkwardly to terms. Yet it does not seem that the government of the last of the Romanovs had found an answer to the perpetual dilemma of Russian history. Throughout, the genius of Russians was grounded in their awareness of belonging to a distinctive culture. At the same time, they were drawn inexorably by diplomacy and trade to imitate the methods and institutions and to use the weapons of the 'advanced' powers of the west. Tsar Alexis (1645–76) seems to have recognized the ambivalence, and tried to build up the monarchy. He encountered violent prejudices but survived two critical challenges, the urban riots of 1648 and the revolt of Stenka Razin. Peter the Great (1689–1725), differing from his predecessor more in outlook and methods than in essential aims, resolved some of the practical problems but created new tensions by his violent efforts to make Russia strong and self-sufficient. He was the most effective of the tsars, a giant in will and vision as in physique; yet beside Russia's immeasurable conservatism he is a dwarf. His immediate successors faced a reaction and only survived because of the divisions of their opponents. During the eighteenth century the state had to moderate its demands upon the nobles; while no longer bound to serve the state they maintained, and even strengthened, their hold upon the serfs. The effects of this reaction were to be felt in Russian society until the Revolution of 1917.

Tsar Michael (1613–45) ruled as an elected tsar, with the assembly, the *Zemskii Sobor*. His father, patriarch and prime mover in the coup that brought him to power, played the main part in securing the support of the boyars. As their power declined in face of the competition of the *dvoryanstvo* who, by 1678, were estimated to own more than half of the taxable land in the country, the tsar's authority grew correspondingly. There was a modest growth of manufactures, some recovery of agriculture, and a significant influx of Germans from their war-torn homelands. The support of the *dvoryanstvo* enabled Michael and his successor Alexis to resist pressures from the *Zemskii Sobor*; indeed, Alexis gave up summoning that body at all. Encased in a profuse and ceremonious court, but a thoughtful man and no cypher, Alexis bought security at the price of concessions to his more privileged subjects. It was a conservative alliance of the sort that was being forged, under very different circumstances, in the Great Elector's Prussia. Ruler and gentry were bound together in revulsion from the anarchy of the Time of Troubles and in defence of the status quo. The contrast between the benevolent purposes of the ruler (and the best of his advisers), and the cruel demands of a struggle to survive, is strikingly shown by the events of 1648.

Extra taxes, levied to make up arrears, together with the blatant privilege of officials, were common grievances. In Moscow there was particular resentment at the exemption allowed to important households. Merchants disliked the favours granted to foreigners; the *streltsy* demanded regular pay. The mob which surrounded the tsar as he emerged from church, rampaged about the city, setting fire to the houses of prominent citizens and eventually besieging the tsar in the Kremlin, was reinforced by malcontents from the provinces. Alexis did not manage to reassert his authority or to placate the mob before two of his officials had been handed over, to be lynched in Red Square, and the hated Morozov, his most influential minister, sent into temporary exile. As to the young Louis XIV, soon to undergo similar humiliations in Paris, it was a shaking lesson in politics: it appeared that there must be a more detached, effective royal authority, resting on a strong, loyal army. Subsequent riots in Pskov and Novgorod, where grain exports to Sweden at a time of scarcity after a poor harvest were the main cause, highlighted a further danger. Robustly independent, with a tradition of autonomy, tied by commerce to the cities of the Baltic, those cities invited outside interference. It took a punitive expedition and a three-month siege to suppress Pskov. In Novgorod, Archbishop Nikon played an important part in the quietening of the rioters, by delivering sentence of excommunication, but not before he had been nearly beaten to death in his cathedral. It emphasized the value to the tsar of the authority of the Church, and of a specially vigorous cleric.

It was ostensibly in response to demands for reform emanating from the *Zemskii Sobor*, which was summoned in the aftermath of the Moscow riots, that Alexis's government produced the great code of 1649, the *Ulozhenie*. Hastily compiled from many different sources, in 967 articles, the *Ulozhenie* brought uniformity and publicity to existing law. Its weaknesses, notably the absence of any definition of legal ideas, reflect ignorance of Roman Law, except for some Byzantine maxims, and of the lack of a class of lawyers, trained in the Roman tradition. It paid lip service to the needs of every class of subject while it reaffirmed more emphatically and comprehensively the rights of the state. Its authors sought to freeze Russian society in its existing shape. The Church was not allowed to increase its estates, or townsmen to leave their towns, or countrymen to compete in town trade; no one outside the ranks of the *dvoryane* was to be allowed to enter the class. While the state's fiscal rights were thus protected, the boyars were confirmed in their hereditary rights. Little attempt was made to define precisely the legal relationship of lord and peasant. Its provisions to protect the rights of landowners and tax collectors and its vagueness about what little protection in law the serfs still enjoyed, made the *Ulozhenie* a landowner's charter. Peasants were regarded as legally attached to the estate on which they resided: this applied to 'all who shall be born after the census – because their fathers are written in the census book'. Thus serfdom became hereditary.

Underlying the legislation is the idea of the peasant as a chattel. A law of 1625 had ordered anyone who killed a serf belonging to another master to give the latter 'one of the best of his own peasants, with his family'. Though the state protected its fiscal interests by forbidding the removal of serfs from land held by one type of tenure to another, they could otherwise be transferred without restriction. The time-limit upon the recovery of the runaway serf was removed, a regulation designed to discourage the landowner from employing a fugitive, as well as to frighten the serf into staying put. The master himself was not exempt from social discipline: he was expected to treat his peasants well, not to provoke them to fight, not to make them work on a Sunday. For serious offences the master might be given the knout. Besides the earnest paternalism and the typically Russian sense of belonging to a community of mutual obligation can be seen the practical need of the state to exact as much as possible from the peasant in taxes and services.

In the half-century after 1648 serfdom became almost universal. In 1500 the more or less independent peasants were in the majority of cultivators; by 1700 they formed 7 per cent. In a sluggish economy, threatened by anarchy, it made sense for the government to buy the co-operation of the privileged classes for social concessions which were, at least in the short term, relatively cheap. Continuous peasant revolts and the bitterness aroused by Russian serfdom suggest that the true cost was higher. The *mir* or village community, which could have been a stabilizing influence, lost its authority. In such matters as the allotment of land or the proportions of tax and labour dues, the orders of the landowner's steward counted for more than the judgement of the village elders. Trapped by their own laws and attitudes, governments reacted to peasants' demands by giving landowners ever greater powers. In practice they took the law into their own hands. Measures to secure the labour of the serf drove the more desperate ones to the lawless fringe. In 1664–5 the records of one county on the edge of the steppe reveal 2994 runaway peasants. Sometimes whole villages moved. The danger was compounded by the existence of a vast frontier region, by the cultural and spiritual diversity of the land, and the scope for intervention of outside powers. The ruler was haunted by the fear that the unwieldy state would disintegrate; his greater subjects knew that their castles of privileges were built on shifting sands. And so tyranny was legalized, violence remained endemic. The majority of the Russian people, in Pares's vivid phrase, was 'driven underground'. In a society clamped in place by many kinds of bondage, the language of government was characteristically that of the bully: the response of the governed, one of servile obedience. Perhaps some upper-class consciences were sensitive to the stresses of a society living under duress but it was not till the nineteenth century that a sense of guilt and revulsion became prominent in the outlook of westernized gentry and intellectuals and a theme of Russian literature in its golden age.

The Cossack Challenge

The rising of the Ukrainian Cossacks against Polish overlordship (1648) and the subsequent struggle to maintain the rights they had won by the peace of Zborow (1649) tempted the Russians to intervene in an area which they had formerly been content to leave as a refuge for outcasts from their own society and a conveniently independent no-man's-land between Turkey, Poland and Russia.[1] When the Poles fought back and the Cossacks faced

[1] For a fuller account of the Russo-Polish war and its affects on the Ukraine and Poland, see pp. 506–7.

defeat, their leader, Bogdan Chmielnicki, turned to Moscow. Hitherto Ordyn-Nashchokin, the tsar's foreign minister, had been primarily concerned with reaching the Baltic; now he had to weigh the risks of intervention against the danger of Russia's southern flank from a Polish Ukraine. In 1643 a *Zemskii Sobor* had urged the tsar to take the Cossacks 'under his mighty sovereign hand'. In January 1654, a Cossack council approved Chmielnicki's proposal for union with Moscow. The subsequent agreement was not an alliance, still less was it direct Russian annexation. The tsar took the Cossacks under his protection and into his service; his envoys were asked to swear to uphold Cossack rights, but they would not commit their sovereign to anything beyond the act of grace. The words of the Moscow boyars witness to the potential strength of the Russian monarchy. 'Never has it been demanded that sovereigns should take an oath to their subjects, and as to the fact that the kings of Poland used to swear an oath to their subjects it is improper to quote this as an example, since these kings are heretics and are not autocrats.'

In the war that ensued the Cossacks, weakened by faction rivalries, failed to benefit from their attempts to play off Poles against Russians. When Yuri Chmielnicki (Bogdan's son) sought Russian protection again in 1659 he had to accept harsher conditions: the election of a *hetman* required the tsar's consent; *hetmans* lost their diplomatic rights; Russian *voivodes* were imposed on the chief Cossack townships; the Cossack army could be employed by the tsar without restrictions. By the peace of Andrussovo (1667) between Russia and Poland, all the Ukraine east of the Dnieper and Kiev, with some land west of the river, became Russian; Poland retained only the western Ukraine. Thus the war in which the Cossacks had fought for autonomy under the protection of one or other of the great powers ended with their being divided between them. For Poland the peace was a milestone on the road to her decline; the country's faults of structure, her inability to defend her frontiers were cruelly exposed. By contrast Russia's advance meant a lifting of horizons. In 1645 Alexis had notified his accession only to neighbouring Poland and Sweden, to England, Holland and Denmark; in 1673 Moscow was promoting the idea of a European coalition to meet the Turkish danger. In 1686 the peace of Andrussovo was accepted by the Poles as the basis of a permanent treaty because they wished to secure Russia's adherence to the Holy League against the Turks. In the following year the first of Prince Golitsyn's Crimean campaigns heralded the beginning of her great crusade against the Turks in Europe, a process of attrition which was to last until the twentieth century.

The Polish war had brought Russia into the orbit of the western powers. At the same time, with the Ukraine, Russia had acquired a new dimension to her chronic social problems. How dangerous was shown by the revolt of Stenka Razin. Razin, the 'little Stephen' of Russian mythology, was an outlaw who established himself in a fortified settlement on the river Don and used it as a base for raids and robbery in the surrounding countryside. By 1670, he was installed in Astrakhan and preying on the trade routes of the Caspian Sea. When the Russians tried to bring him to heel, he appealed for popular support and evoked a response which shook the state. Up the Volga to Novgorod, westwards to the river Oka, roused in some places by Cossack bands and everywhere by the wildest rumours, the peasantry turned on their real or imaginary oppressors: government officials, money-lenders and merchants, landowners and priests, 'traitors and bloodsuckers' in Razin's terms. Some believed that Razin could fly, others that he was about to restore the tsar's eldest son, who had died in 1670 but was alleged to be in hiding.

The following account of Cossack banditry in the Ukraine in the reign of the last of the tsars, by a modern Russian writer, Konstantin Paustorsky, helps to recreate the world of fantasy and superstition in which the illiterate seventeenth-century Russian lived.

> Ever since the days of the Polish occupation there had been a colony of beggars at Mogilev on the Dnieper, many of them blind. They were known as 'the Old Men of Mogilev' and they had elders among them who were known as the Masters.... They scattered all over Polessye, Belorussia and the Ukraine but once a year gathered at some secret place – an isolated inn on the marshes.... They kept the peasants' anger alive by fanning it with their ballads about the wicked rule of the Polish landowners and the wretchedness of the village folk.... All that summer bandits had been infesting the province of Chernigov and the wooded region of the Polessye. They robbed the mails and trains and attacked isolated houses and farms. The most daring and elusive of the bands was that led by Andrey Gon.... Legends had already grown up about him. A student of Chernigov according to some, a village blacksmith according to others, he was thought to be a Robin Hood who attacked only the rich and protected the poor and oppressed.

Many of Razin's followers no doubt rose in some similar hope of release from the brutish servitude of their lives: they were promised freedom and loot. For a time Razin had controlled 800 miles of the Volga. But the risings were savagely repressed: Razin was captured and executed in June 1671, as were thousands of his followers, in specially constituted penal camps. Astrakhan was retaken in November.

'The one poetic figure in Russian history', in Pushkin's view, Razin had some political conceptions beyond mere pillage and the destruction of authority. Allegedly he proposed a general assembly of Cossacks. He offered loyalty to the tsar in return for a new social deal, the destruction of hereditary landowners and military governors (and with them labour dues and taxes) and their replacement by a democratic society of smallholders.

It was utopian, possibly cynical. *Kazak* was a Tartar word meaning a free warrior. The term could now be applied to anyone without a permanent home or definite occupation. Around the communities of the Cossack heartlands, living by stock-breeding, hunting, fishing and raiding, clustered a floating population of runaways and outcasts. As a vision of an alternative society, based upon freedom, in which every newcomer had to prove himself by his wits and courage and had to accept the rules of the assembly and his elected leaders, combined with the experience of peasant mobs and flaming barns, it remained a subversive force and a memory to haunt Russian rulers for a hundred years – until the Pugachev revolt of 1774 revived the danger in a new form. At the same time, the revolt indicates the extent to which the work of tsarist government had already progressed: great islands of settlement were being formed within the southern steppelands. Military colonists were given land to farm and to defend; monasteries were planted, as much outposts of colonization as houses of prayer. There was a constant trickle of runaway serfs from the more intensively farmed areas of old Russia to ensure that there was no shortage of labour. After the failure of Stenka Razin it was easier to employ and regulate such men. At the same time the strengthening of local government and garrisons consolidated the southward expansion of Russia which is not only one of the great themes of the seventeenth century, but is also the most important factor in the development of Russian absolution.

The Old Believers

Again and again in Russian history it happens that the idealism and constructive purpose of a young ruler, an 'enlightened' Catherine II, a liberal Alexander II, turns to disillusion as the theoretically omnipotent tsar encounters the realities of Russian society and government. Alexis spoke in terms that appear to have been consistent with his devout sense of divine authority and the austere practice of his own life when he urged that 'We great sovereign, and you boyars, with us, may in one mind govern this people justly and equally for all.' By contrast with Peter the Great it seems that he lacked will and energy, but when his authority was impugned he acted more like the jealous autocrat than the benevolent father figure. He was expected to use his authority. 'Thou, O Tsar,' ran a contemporary address, 'dost hold in thy hands the miraculous staff of Moses with which thou art able to work marvellous wonders in government. In thy hands there is full autocracy.' One is left with a sense of unresolved dilemmas. One such was that caused by the reforming zeal of Archbishop Nikon and the consequent revolt of the *Raskolniki*, Old Believers, which hardened into a permanent and damaging schism in Russian society.

Nikon, the strong man of the turbulent early years of Alexis's reign, was appointed patriarch in 1652. Another Becket in ability, comprehension of great issues, ambition and readiness to sacrifice himself for a principle, Nikon seems to have regarded himself, like Philaret before him, as co-sovereign; in 1654–6, when Alexis was campaigning in Poland, he was left in charge of the government. But unlike Philaret, grim and conservative, Nikon dared to look outside Holy Russia. One consequence of the Polish war was the revival of interest in the scholarship and churchmanship of Kiev and its famous academy, which had never lost contact with Greek Orthodoxy or subscribed to the typically arrogant Russian view that St Andrew had brought Christ's teaching direct to Muscovy without Greek mediation. The liturgical reforms of the 1650s look superficial: three fingers were to be used in making the sign of the cross, the frequency of singing of the word 'Hallelujah' in services was to be altered. But behind the externals of worship lay intensive study of original texts and significant corrections in the Russian versions. Nikon surrounded himself with Greek advisers. He was concerned, in the manner of his century, with Orthodoxy – but also with the authority of the church. He thought it essential to align Russian church teaching with that of the Balkan world. An isolated church, served by ignorant priests, could not, he said, defend itself against Roman Catholicism or western science: 'I am a Russian and the son of a Russian, but my faith and convictions are Greek.'

Ironically Nikon was destroyed by an atavistic reaction and fear of those very forces against which he sought to defend not the old Muscovy but a greater Russia. At first the tsar, who was interested in liturgy and aware of the practical problems arising out of the southward expansion of Russia, supported him. But he could not accept Nikon's philosophy without loss of status, for the patriarch taught that the priesthood was higher than the tsardom: 'Unction comes from God but it comes to the Tsar through the clergy.' Nikon's key idea, the independence of the clergy with regard to secular tribunals, ran counter to the absolutist trend of the age. However, his attempts to chisel off encrustrations of recent tradition were linked in people's minds with a policy of making the church an instrument of the state. For Russians, beliefs and ceremonies, spirit and matter, could not be separated; Aquinas, Luther, Descartes might never have existed: Russian Christianity had developed on its own, untouched by the great movements of western thought, unchallenged by secular ideas. Of 374 books published in Russia during the whole century only 19 were secular in content. Avvakum, leader of the conservatives, resisted apparently minute changes in ritual because he feared for the character of Muscovite life under the impact of 'western geometry'. He cherished therefore what Peter was so vehemently to attack – and for the same reasons, as signs of a whole way of thinking – the beards, long robes, the ceremonious sign of the cross of traditional Muscovy. Religion and national pride, as with the Spanish after centuries of war against the Moors, were wedded in the Russian mind: after the great advance into the Tartar khanates, Russia became 'Holy Russia' and the 'second Noah's Ark' – in which there was no place for foreign species!

Nikon, far-sighted but overbearing and impatient, roused a swarm of enemies. In 1658 he departed for his own monastery of New Jerusalem, whence he fulminated against all who opposed him. In 1666 he was condemned by the church assembly and deposed. The corrected books were, however, kept. If the government had expected resistance to die down with the removal of Nikon it was disappointed. To Solovesk, the famous monastery by the White Sea, whose inmates had declared that they would die rather than sully the purity of their faith, Alexis sent an army. After long hesitation and only after the garrison had renounced its allegiance to the tsar, it was taken by assault and its leaders hanged (1676). Avvakum was eventually burnt at the stake (1681). There were fanatical gestures, communal self-immolations in the northern forests: it has been estimated that between 1677 and 1691, 20,000 *Raskolniki* committed suicide. The mass hysteria died down but stolid, withdrawn, otherworldly conservatism remained.

It is difficult to measure the impact of the *Raskolniki* on Russian life or even to identify their political role because their resistance to the new church ordinances merged with a more general opposition to the crown. Communities of *Raskolniki*, secretive, cabalistic, but earnest, as dissenters tend to be when they are insecure in everything except their faith, provided natural centres of popular resistance. They were active among the supporters of Stenka Razin as of Pugachev a century later; at a different level they gave an ideological character to the otherwise selfish and anarchic resistance of the *streltsy* to Peter the Great. The secular policy of Peter confirmed their idea that the reformers had betrayed the church to the state; as for him, he was 'Antichrist', an imposter. The victory of the church had indeed only been obtained through the support of the civil power; the cost was the loss of moral authority to the church, not so much to the faith of ordinary people. For religion, in the words of one Russian, is 'like a nail – the harder you hit, the deeper it goes into the wood'. Bishops, enlightened as they might be, had lost touch with the bulk of their people. So the reforms which had been intended to strengthen the church, instead prepared the way for Peter's erastian reforms. When he instituted the office of procurator of the Holy Synod and abolished the patriarchate, the church hierarchy became an integral part of the state establishment.

Ordyn-Nashchokin

The phenomenon of the *Raskolniki* shows us one aspect of the pressure of the outside world. Peter's mission was to awaken Russians and their 'sleeping treasure house' (Pares) to the material advantages of western technology, to drill the people and to mobilize their resources so that he could achieve his strategic objectives. We have seen that the principles and structure of society and government differed fundamentally from those of western states. There was nothing barbaric about a culture which could create something like the 'pyramid' church of the Ascension at Kolomenskoe (compared by Berlioz to the cathedrals of Strasbourg and Milan). The Kremlin, that awe-inspiring complex of churches, government buildings and fortress, witnesses to the happy fusion of Italian and native styles. The Kremlin was essentially, by the end of the seventeenth century, as it is today: its latest building, the patriarch's palace, was completed in 1666. A man standing in the square of the cathedrals in the Kremlin does not feel himself to be out of civilization – but may be out of Europe! He may there reflect upon the edict of Tsar Alexis when he installed an ikon in the Tower of the Redeemer, that no man, even the tsar himself might pass through the gateway without dismounting and removing his hat.

As in early medieval Europe monasteries answered a deep-felt need. The monk's 'spirit of chastity, of humility, of patience and of love' (the prayer of St Ephraim) was in keeping with the submissive endurance of the Russian people during much of its history. But it was precisely this passive, rigid suspicious mentality that spelled backwardness to westerners in the age of the scientific revolution. Russia was less isolated, however, than is often thought. There were points of contact even before the Polish war. Because of the lack of demand in a natural economy of restricted local markets, foreign trade was most profitable. It was mostly in the hands of foreigners: English, Dutchmen, Germans or Danes. The country exported raw materials, wood, pitch, hemp, flax, potash, furs and hides. It imported manufactures, notably metal and textile goods. Fiscal requirements, as in other countries, but also the Russian emphasis upon state service, tended to fix the economy in a mould and to discourage initiative. For example, the upper class of the towns, the affluent merchants, *gosti*, were state officials. On the tsar's behalf they ran the customs and certain monopolies; they enjoyed tax privileges, but were answerable, with their property, for any losses they incurred. Below this élite, lesser trade organizations were similarly harnessed to the state machine. The government adopted 'mercantilist' measures to protect native traders. The statute of 1667, for example, restricted trade by foreigners to certain frontier points and exacted high dues for leave to take part in trade. In this way it hoped to draw in foreign currency. At the same time efforts were made to entice technicians from abroad. It was in the flourishing German quarter in Moscow that the young Peter learnt about compasses and clocks. He studied geography from a terrestrial globe which was a present from a Dutch ambassador to Tsar Alexis.

Alexis was served by some talented men. The career of Ordyn-Nashchokin, in charge of foreign affairs until 1671, suggests that the policy of Peter the Great was not inevitable, his methods not necessarily the best; that there was, between the extremes of isolationism and imperialism, a viable third course. He was primarily responsible for the combinations that led to the successful conclusion of the Polish war and the truce of Andrussovo. When, however, Alexis insisted on keeping Kiev after the limited period stipulated by Andrussovo he was scrupulous enough to resign and retired to a monastery. He was not a conservative but he saw a better future for Russia in alliance with Poland in a pan-Slav front than in an all-round aggression. He was indeed a pioneer builder of ships, an advocate of foreign trade, of streamlined ministries. Yet he was moderate enough to wish for progress by co-operation. When we think how nearly Peter the Great's designs ended in disaster – at Narva, or on the river Pruth – we can see the force of arguments for a moderate policy. Ordyn-Nashchokin was not the expansive favourite, the severe dictator or the single-minded bureaucrat – to take three familiar models of a statesman – but a man of a type which we may call distinctively Russian and which was to recur, though never perhaps so impressively, in her later history: a man of conscience, imaginative enough to appreciate both the parties that were forming around the deepening rift between old Slavonic, clannish, patriarchal Russia and the modernizers, so pragmatic and impatient with tradition. His maxim was 'There is no shame in borrowing what is good even from your enemies.' Klyuchevsky reckoned Ordyn-Nashchokin to be – with the possible exception of Alexander Speransky – the one statesman minister of Russian history. For all his talents, his grand aims, he was nearer to his master Alexis than to the artisan tsar who was to achieve much of what he advocated – but at a cost to the Russian people that would have appalled him. Clearly the authority of the 'sovereign and autocrat' was needed to carry out any but the most superficial changes.

Peter the Great: Child of Violence

Peter was the son of Alexis by his second wife Natalia Naryshkin. There were two sons by the first wife, Theodore and Ivan. Theodore became tsar on his father's death in 1676. His reign was a short one though it contained one important reform: the final abolition of the system of precedence among the nobles according to birth and service. When he died in 1682 Peter was proclaimed tsar, and Natalia regent, by the patriarch Joachim and a clique of boyars. The boyars sought to recover the influence that they had lost during the past century and a half. It was fortunate for the autocracy at this critical time that they lacked unified leadership and that the constitutional tradition had died with the old council of boyars. As it was, a power struggle ensued that threatened to produce a second Time of Troubles. Peter was 10, but tall and strong for his years, Ivan was timid and incapable. But

Sophia, one of Ivan's three sisters, a well-educated, somewhat masculine woman, was not disposed to accept the arrangement. She secured the support of the *streltsy*, the privileged but idle garrison troops, who saw themselves as standard-bearers of the old Russia; some of them were Old Believers; from the rulers' angle they were a dangerous anachronism. On the pretext that Natalia was ill-treating Ivan the *streltsy* stormed the palace and killed their commander Matveiev when he tried to restrain them. Peter, standing on the steps at the entrance to the Kremlin, watched their brutal rampage. He learnt a dramatic lesson in politics – and acquired a nervous facial twitch that troubled him for the rest of his life. Meanwhile he had to accept the outcome: with Sophia as regent, he and Ivan became joint-tsars (May 1682).

Sophia showed ability and spirit. When Hovansky, the officer who had organized the Kremlin *Putsch*, tried to exploit her favour she had him summarily executed. Her chief minister, Prince Basil Golitsyn, was a scholarly and capable politician: he planned to set up permanent embassies abroad and to send selected parties of young Russians abroad for training. Laws of this time improved the lot of women and beggars; he even considered the emancipation of serfs. He made a treaty with Poland and China and mounted expeditions against the Tartar khan of the Crimea. Sophia's government was not incompetent, but it was insecure so long as Peter's role remained undecided.

Peter was required to live with his mother in Preobrazhensky, a village near Moscow. Beyond reading, arithmetic and the liturgy of the Orthodox Church, he had little of formal education: he wrote clumsily and spelt badly for the rest of his life. Imaginative literature he despised as 'useless tales which waste time'. Always he was happiest when using his hands, designing a ship, tinkering with a watch or pulling out teeth. He drilled his friends and household staff in his own private 'Preobrazhensky army' – but first he went through the ranks himself, learning the duties of a soldier. To teach his regiment how to besiege a fortress he had one specially built. Much of his life was that of a wandering student who would eat and sleep wherever he happened to be. He spent a great deal of his time in the German suburb of Moscow, with acquaintances like the Scottish mercenary Gordon, the Dutchman Timmerman, both competent mentors. His friends generally were men who knew what he liked and could fit in with his restless but not purposeless life, the alternative spells of absorbed work and indolence or debauchery. To men like the semi-illiterate but capable bombardier Menshikov, perhaps his prime favourite, whom he promoted to prince, the first to hold that rank outside the appanage princes of the house of Rurik, the Genevan Lefort and Romodanovsky, a monstrous sot by all accounts, commander of the 'Preobrazhensky army' and virtual ruler of Russia during Peter's absence in the west, he gave a free hand – and the affection of an essentially lonely person. He was married in 1689 to Eudoxia Lopukhin, but it seemed that no woman could tame his temper or improve his manners. Sophia regarded him with misgiving and probably listened to suggestions that he should be removed. But Peter was acting on a false scare when he fled precipitately to the Trinity monastery. Starting with the advantage that no woman had yet ruled in Russia he made capital out of his situation. Number of boyars and *streltsy* deserted Sophia. Peter came to Moscow and dispatched her to a convent (September 1689). He had to deal at once with a weird case of treason. The nobleman Bezobrazov was tortured and executed when it was discovered that he had used a Moscow wizard to cast a spell on the new regime. Peter was learning lessons but he did not at once alter his way of life: he left the regency to his mother and Ivan remained co-tsar. Natalia died in 1694, Ivan in 1696. In that year Peter brought to a triumphant conclusion the siege of Azov which he had begun in 1695.

His first step on assuming sole power was to act on Lefort's advice and undertake a mission to Europe (1697–8) that was to prove of more than symbolic importance in his life. His political objective, the construction of a European alliance against the Turks, proved abortive. The Great Embassy was nevertheless a significant experience for Peter and the more perceptive of his entourage. There is something startlingly modern about the way in which the 'artisan tsar' trained himself for his work. Savage, crude, at best naive he may have seemed to diplomats who had to entertain him: staying with the diarist John Evelyn, sixteen Russians spoiled the house and celebrated garden by their drunken horseplay; 'right nasty,' said Evelyn's servant. But Peter acquired techniques and understanding. The shipyards of Zaandam, the garrisons of Königsberg and Woolwich, Dr Boerhaave's anatomical classes (where, to overcome the squeamishness of his entourage, Peter made them tear out the muscles with their teeth), the London Mint, were his 'open university'. In Holland he rented a room from a blacksmith and went to work as an ordinary carpenter. The red jacket and white canvas trousers of a Dutch shipwright could not conceal the identity of the huge tsar. In France he was impressed by the grandeur of Versailles but in England he attended a debate in the House of Lords and remarked that it was 'good to hear subjects speaking truthfully and openly to their king'. He realized the need for borrowing and for quick results; he was interested in government and political ideas but it was ships, guns, lathes and coins that filled his mind. He recruited a number of craftsmen for his own projected shipyards and ironworks. After Peter there was to be a regular two-way traffic, of Russians seeking education and of foreigners seeking their fortunes. In 1717 there were seventy Russians studying navigation in Amsterdam alone.

After visiting north Germany, Holland and England, Peter went to Vienna but returned hastily in July 1698 to deal with the *streltsy*. There seems to have been a plot afoot to depose him and reinstate Sophia. Peter took the opportunity to administer an unforgettable lesson in discipline and a warning to those who would obstruct reform. Thousands of the *streltsy* were executed, some after torture, to elicit information; the force was disbanded. Sophia was sent to a more distant convent while her sister Martha and Peter's wife Eudoxia, who had been involved in the plot, were also made to take the veil. Peter was never a man for half measures. He had grown up in an atmosphere of intrigue and feuding and had learned to fend for himself. Bestial drinking, a primitive respect for strength, tolerance of physical violence, a fatalistic outlook on life, an oriental submissiveness among women were among the features of Russian society. Peter, who was physically a giant – 6½ feet tall – and could drink any man under the table, earned awed respect, even affection, among the common people he encountered in his regular tours about the country. He wore homely dress, talked plainly, would put his hand to spade or chisel. He took seriously the need to promote the good of the people. Answering the plaudits of the senators on the conclusion of the peace of Nystad (1721), he declared, no doubt sincerely, that it was the sovereign's task to 'labour for the general benefit and profit'.

At the end of a war in which millions had endured unprecedentedly high taxes, had been driven like cattle to the army, to construction projects, mines and foundries, Peter could still convey a generous image. He drove others, but he also drove himself. 'What a Tsar!' said one peasant. 'He did not eat his bread for nothing but worked like a peasant!' Those who were nearer to the seat of power, the more sophisticated, those who were excluded from Peter's clique, particularly those who were sensitive about Russian traditions and civilities, were repelled by his boorish manners, the combination of shrewdness and savagery that suggested the devil's work, the brutal practical jokes, the buckets of corn brandy, the elaborate and childish blasphemies, above all an inconsistency of behaviour which suggests at least a mild schizophrenia. They saw that people, for Peter, were there to be used. His abnormalities of conduct, in particular his unnatural behaviour towards his family, notably to his son Alexis, with whom he never came to terms, may all be traced to his boyhood. He was the child of violence. This tsar who could bend a silver coin in his fingers meant to bend Russia to his will.

The First Russian Revolution

From the time when Peter led the untried Russian army, lacking in ships, engineers and adequate siege equipment, against the Turkish fortress of Azov between the lands of the Don Cossacks and the Black Sea, to almost the end of his reign, war and diplomacy were paramount in his mind. At Azov early failure was turned to triumph because he applied himself furiously to securing engineers and building war galleys. Peter was impulsive; his tendency to embark upon projects of every sort without measuring the consequences is his most serious failing as a statesman. Sometimes in the history of governments and reigns the first rash commitments determine the subsequent course of events. The example of Frederick the Great comes to mind. We need not then look for orderly unfolding of a grand design upon rational principles, or anything resembling controlled development. In 1700 Peter rashly committed himself to the alliance of Poland, Saxony and Denmark against Sweden when he would have done better to wait to see how it fared. The same day (in August 1700) that his envoys completed a treaty of peace with the Turks, Peter declared war on Sweden. He was exposed to the full brunt of the finest troops in northern Europe. His army of 40,000 was deployed against the Swedish fortress of Narva, a port between Estonia and Ingria; their position invited counter-attack. Peter was unlucky to draw the fire of the young Vasa king whom the world was now to acclaim as a military genius. When the Swedes attacked, in a blizzard that disconcerted the ill-trained Russians (November 1700), the latter were thrown into disorder and driven off the field by an army less than a third their size. They lost many generals and, what they could less well afford, nearly all their guns. The new infantry levies proved incompetent, the mercenaries unreliable; the guards fought hard but the cavalry contributed nothing. Peter admitted that it was a terrible setback and Russia was exposed to invasion before her army was in fit state to resist. Not for the last time the tsar was confronted by a crisis that was largely of his own making. By his superhuman efforts, his refusal to be bound by the decent conventions of government, especially by his willingness to learn from his mistakes, he survived. It should be added that he was lucky.[1]

In 1701 Peter's pride, the validity of his policies, even his throne, were in danger. Charles's advisers urged him to march on Moscow, to make contact with dissident groups, even to raise Sophia in Peter's place. Charles's refusal to follow up his victory and his decision to pursue the war with Poland was as serious a misjudgement as his later decision to invade Russia – in 1707, when Russia's army had been transformed. Peter made use of his respite to mobilize the resources of the country. The shadow of Narva darkened the lives of many Russians. They were made to pay, in labour, military service and taxes, for the tsar's ambition. Russia's trackless wastes, her vast distances, inhibited effective government. Peter was undaunted by the problem. He maintained, like King Frederick William I of Prussia, the simplest of courts, only a dozen companions, without any hierarchy of officials. He could not sit still for long and would retreat from fashionable gatherings to play a game of chess, puffing at a long Dutch pipe. He habitually walked so fast that others had to run to keep up. He travelled from Astrakhan to Derbent, from Archangel to Azov. An English engineer employed by him wrote that 'he has, I believe, for the proportion of time

[1] For an account of the Great Northern War from the Swedish angle, see also pp. 513–18.

I was in the country, travelled twenty times more than ever any prince in the world did before him'. He was at the centre of this first Russian revolution, the directing intelligence and the physical force. Stalin, whose own policies, designed to mobilize the resources of a country richer in people than in technology, could be called a monstrous imitation, even parody, of Peter, caught something of the abruptness of change when he wrote about Peter: 'he feverishly went about building factories and mills to supply his army and improve the defence of the country; it was a peculiar attempt to jump out of the framework of backwardness'. If a foreign policy which aimed concurrently at obtaining outlets to the Azov and Black Seas, conquering the Caspian shores, and establishing Russia on the Baltic, is set against the chronic weaknesses of administration and economy, with recurring revolts, especially in the Cossack lands, then his 'westernizing' measures assume perspective as a series of expedients. In general, Peter was only intensifying the earlier drives of the Muscovite state. Of course he was forced to compromise. But always amid the wreckage of the old and the scaffolding of new projects there was a vision of the future, sustained by what he had seen in the west: in economy another Holland, in government another Brandenburg, in war another Sweden.

The Russian army was not small. By the end of the Polish war Alexis had over 100,000 men under arms. The traditional levies supplied by the nobility had become a relatively small proportion of the whole. There were also *streltsy*, artillery men and Cossack fortress guards whose service was exacted in return for exceptional privileges. Other soldiers were provided by royal and ecclesiastical estates, according to the number of homesteads. Finally there were foreign mercenaries, with Scotsmen and Germans to the fore and most recently the formidable Cossacks. Although steps had been taken to establish a permanent officer corps and to introduce western-style drill, it can be said that the 'military revolution' of the west had passed Russia by. To enlarge his army Alexis had to raise new taxes – but his subjects hardly received value for money: the *streltsy* archers were of no use in war; the artillery were obsolete; mercenaries were both expensive and unreliable; nobles with their peasant levies were not amenable to regular training. War with the equally old-fashioned Polish army had engendered complacency. And so Peter had almost to start from scratch, to fashion a Swedish-style army and equip it with modern weapons, to provide commissariat and adequate artillery. He made his new army by selective conscription on a territorial basis: every province was to recruit, equip and pay for specified units. An average of 30,000 recruits was raised annually throughout the war. Many of them were peasants dragged off the land; others were priests' sons, fugitive serfs, or men who escaped classification and were therefore suitable material. The recruitment figures suggest that disease and desertion accounted for many more than casualties in battle. At a depot in the chief town of every recruiting district the 'immortals' were collected and trained – so called because for every man lost another had to be provided by his recruiting district. After 1712, every man recruited had a cross branded on his left hand; still the recruit, dragged to the depot in chains, deserted at the first opportunity, and robber bands, lurking in woods and marshes, terrorizing the roads, were part of the price of maintaining an army of 200,000 and placing Russia on equal terms with the great powers of Europe.

Slowly but surely the great Russian infantry tradition was being established. Artillery and engineering schools were created. The Guards regiments were used as training grounds for officers of line regiments. To ensure a proper supply of officers Peter completed the process of swamping the old nobility. Theodore had abolished the old books of precedence. Mindful perhaps of what he had seen in Brandenburg, but working on the basis of the existing Russian system, Peter formed a vast service class whose fourteen grades, as defined in the Table of Ranks (1722), in the three categories, military, civil and court, represented strictly the service that was provided. Those in the first eight grades, in the army all commissioned officers, automatically became *szlachta* (gentry). Adults had to serve in one category or other; for most this meant the army. They lost civil rights if they abstained. Their children were registered at the age of 10. Education was made obligatory for them; unless he could show a certificate of education a gentleman was not allowed to marry. The remodelling of the army radically altered the structure and functioning of society.

The building of the fleet was the tsar's most cherished project, and its *raison d'être* is plain. If Russia were to exploit Baltic conquests, to do more than simply peer through her 'window on the west', she must have ships to trade and fight. Yet the Russian navy was generally regarded by Peter's subjects as a great eccentricity. Peter loved the sea. He decided to build a fleet as early as 1690; Lefort was to be the first commander and the flagship was to be called the *Elephant*. But he had then only vague ideas as to where or how the fleet should be used. As so often, bold beginnings were made before any detailed assessment; experience and lasting results were bought at bitter cost. Ship-building was his main study on his western tour. He drew in foreign builders. He built St Petersburg at vast expense as a port and capital city: the port came first. The building of a new ship was celebrated like the birth of a baby. The navy continued to depend on Dutchmen, Scandinavians and British; Russians avoided naval service if they could. After Peter's death the navy soon fell into decay and was of little importance until later in the century. None the less it was an extraordinary achievement. Some of the ships were faulty in design and unserviceable. But when he died the fleet numbered 48 ships of the line, with 20 times as many small craft. In 1714 the Baltic squadron was able to defeat the Swedes at Gangut. For a brief spell Russia was one of the sea powers of Europe.

In a memorandum of 1734, drawing upon the experience of twenty-five years residence in Russia, Johann Vockerodt, the Prussian diplomat, wrote of Peter:

> Particularly, and with all his zeal, he sought to improve his military forces. At the same time the wars, which occupied his whole life, and the pacts he concluded with foreign powers in connection with these wars, compelled him to give attention to foreign affairs. In this, however, he relied in most part on his ministers and favourites.... His favourite and most pleasant occupations were shipbuilding and other activities related to navigation ... internal improvements in government, justice, economy, revenues and trade concerned him little or not at all during the first thirty years of his reign. He was content, provided his Admiralty and Army were adequately supplied with money, firewood, recruits, sailors, provisions and ammunition.

After 1714 his interests became more wide-ranging. The last ten years of the reign saw great reforms, reflecting, in Sumner's words, 'a broadening in Peter's outlook and a changing realization of the functions of the state, of the meaning of good government, and of the importance of institutions'. It is not necessary to accept the extreme view of Catherine the Great, who emerged from her first serious study of Peter's papers (for her own guidance) with the comment that 'He did not know himself what laws were necessary to the state.' The meticulous preparation of the Table of Ranks owed more to Ostermann than to the tsar. But it is characteristic that the main emphasis of his amendments was upon placing the military above the civil ranks at every stage. It is likely moreover that the constructive reorganization of the state was a secondary business, a means of the goal of power rather than the goal in itself.

Trying to build the superstructure of a great power on the base of an underdeveloped economy, Peter was always thwarted by want of money. The clumsy efforts of his predecessors had shown not that the tax-bearing capacity of the population was overstrained, but that an excessive levy on one commodity brought diminishing returns. For example, when in 1646 the salt tax was quadrupled, it actually produced a smaller amount. His efforts to remedy the situation show a fertile imagination at work. He carried out between 1698 and 1705 a profitable recoinage operation; he created numerous government monopolies such as those on tobacco, vodka, chess sets and cod-liver oil; and he initiated, after a national census, a direct *per capita* tax for all, 'excepting no one, from the aged to the very last babe' (1718). The last came to yield half the state revenue and remained the principal tax till 1886. Because Muscovite governments preferred to deal with communities rather than individuals, responsibility for payment of the tax was placed on the *mir*. They were thereby strengthened, though in other respects in decline, because of the growth of serfdom. The 'souls' tax would have been an incentive to peasants to abandon their holdings, but for a provision that the peasant who stayed and paid could increase his acreage without paying further tax. Some of Peter's taxes seem to have been instituted for their nuisance value, though the cumulative effect must have been more serious. The peasant who bought salt, required an oak coffin, used a river ferry or kept bees, paid a tax in each case. He could get away with wearing a beard (for which a merchant paid 100 roubles a year) so long as he did not enter a city; but if he did, he had to pay a kopeck. Shortage of cash explains Peter's action (1701) in placing monastic estates under government control; some were immensely wealthy, like Troitsa, which possessed 20,394 peasant houses. Taxes were tripled in Peter's reign; and the population fell by more than 10 per cent. It was the army that necessitated the 'souls' tax – and it was the army that collected it.

It is meaningless to label Peter a 'mercantilist'. The works of contemporary economists were not translated into Russian. Paternalist decrees did, however, abound, like that prohibiting the use of tar (a valuable export), or establishing a course for teaching craftsmen to process leather with whale oil. If Peter ever worked out a comprehensive economic policy there is no sign of it in his piecemeal acts; but it needed no theory to support a policy of state enterprise. As Peter wrote, 'Our state of Russia is richer than other countries in metals and minerals, which till this time have never been used.' But shortage of capital and of skilled labour, the absence of a sizeable middle class, and in all classes a timid aversion to change, produced a condition of inertia which only the state had the resources to tackle. Interestingly enough, Peter's most striking achievements were those which involved foreign technicians and native labour: notably the port of St Petersburg and the great canal systems, completed in 1732, which linked the great rivers and so provided a waterway from the Caspian to the Baltic. The labour could always be found somehow. One group of monastery estates sent peasantry for construction works in Novgorod and St Petersburg to build, to make saddlebars, to transport timber, to provide forage, and to supply thousands of horses and carts. It all imposed a burden on agriculture where already Peter had an uphill task. In large areas cultivation proceeded by the slashing and burning of a patch of forest, followed by cultivation of the cleared land for a few years; then it was abandoned and another patch of forest was tackled in the same way. Many peasants still used the primitive hook plough; in the steppelands the Cossacks prided themselves on never touching a plough at all. Government agents had a difficult task persuading peasants to adopt new methods, or crops like silk and flax. In a footnote to his detailed instruction to Prince Golitsyn, president of the college of the Treasury, ordering peasants to abandon the sickle and use the scythe, Peter wrote: 'though a thing be good and necessary, if it is new, our people will not do it unless forced to'. Another area of the economy proved more malleable: the war industries, iron and copper, flourished, above all in the Urals; they were based on abundant ores and timber for smelting, and forced labour – criminals, deserters or 'assigned peasants', who became their proprietors' hereditary serfs. In the eighteenth century nearly all industrial workers were slaves, living in barracks or settlements by the plant. Russia was a large exporter of iron by 1725. State or subsidized private enterprises included cotton, wool, silk and tobacco manufactories; a sail factory in Moscow employed over a thousand workers; a glass factory at St Petersburg is still in operation. Substantial capital was involved in enterprises, like Shapirov's silk company, which were subsidized rather than created by the Treasury. For a lucky few, among the more energetic of Peter's agents, the arms race spelt opportunity and riches. Nikita Demidov, originally a gunsmith, in class a state peasant, became an armaments tycoon, employing thousands and earning by the time of his death, in 1725, some 100,000 roubles a year – and he acquired a noble title. As during Russia's industrial revolution in the nineteenth century, foreign capital played a vital part. Latterly it became Peter's policy to transfer state factories to private ownership.

Peter tried to maintain the impetus of reform by repeated changes in the system of government; it is another expression of his utilitarian, engineering mentality. Until the later years, when a coherent shape emerged from the workshop, results were scrappy. He inherited the diversity of centuries of improvisation. The *Boyarskaya Duma* had become obsolete with the decline of the boyars and he allowed it to die. The *prikazy* (councils), more than forty of them, overlapped wastefully. Whenever the need had arisen, to deal for instance with the Cossacks, or the monasteries, or Siberia, a new *prikaz* had been set up. Their activity and authority depended upon the character of the boyar in charge; there was no hierarchy or co-ordinating authority among them. No less than twelve of them dealt with different aspects of military administration. The system was about as far removed as possible from that of Louis XIV's France, with its few specialized councils and network of trained officials. But France possessed a large, educated, ambitious bourgeoisie. Working almost in a vacuum, Peter at first relied upon small, intimate groups of his own associates. He created new *prikazy*: one for his fleet, of course, and also, less sinister in itself than in what it foreshadowed, the *Preobrazhensky prikaz*, one of whose duties was to eliminate opposition to the regime. The *Ratusha* (1699) played a central part in early reforms. It was set up to develop industry, to control the towns, to collect the taxes and to act as a treasury for the central government.

In 1708 the structure of provincial government was refashioned with the setting up of the *gubernii* (8 to start with, eventually 11). Till then administration in each district had been in the hands of *voivodes* (governors), usually a member of the service nobility, who had authority over the representatives of town and village. They could be replaced or overruled. It was despotism tempered by inefficiency, with an inherent tendency to corruption, and a danger, from the government's point of view, of a local *voivode* establishing a power base. Peter could not at a stroke instil new habits, let alone replace the aristocratic tradition by the values of a career bureaucracy. The bureaucracy he imposed upon the country had an alien look; it was German and military in character as the very titles suggest – *Oberkommandant*, *Oberprovientmeister*, *Landrichter*. The uniformed, meticulous official, rule book at hand, was to be the characteristic figure of St Petersburg government until the Revolution, and more imposing than the authority he represented. The strengthening of local government while maintaining central control was to remain a crucial Russian problem until the twentieth century and the establishment of a system based on totalitarian principles, aided by modern technology, and inevitably more oppressive than anything that any tsar could have conceived or desired. At no time did tsarist government forsake entirely the Christian paternalist tradition. In Peter's time, however, that tradition was overlaid by the tsar's conviction that Russians had to be driven and flogged for their own good. He had inherited the invaluable notion of the service state, and in his Table of Ranks he rationalized precedence and service in such a way as to ensure the survival of this system after his death. But with the system went an administrative paralysis that made a mockery of his rights and claims.

The *raison d'être* of the senate, a body of nine high officials instituted in 1711, was to provide oversight of government during Peter's frequent absences from the capital. It is significant that Peter felt it necessary to appoint an inspector-general (1715) to keep an eye on the senate; later the task of watching the watchdogs was assigned to the new office of procurator-general (1721). In 1715 an *Oberfiscal* was appointed to supervise finance, with 500 subordinate *fiscals*. Most important of all, in 1718, nine administrative colleges were founded to replace the *prikazy*. They were modelled on the theories of Leibnitz and the practice of Sweden; they were staffed largely by foreigners, or by Russians specially trained – in 1716 Peter sent forty civil servants to Berlin to learn German. There was a rational division of work, each college being responsible for a certain activity, for example the army or commerce, throughout the empire. It was still far removed from the spirit and methodical routines of a Scandinavian or German state, but Peter had taken some steps in that direction. The colleges were to provide a degree of continuity which – fortunately, as it was to turn out – reduced the importance of the individual tsar, minister or favourite in later reigns.

There will always be controversy, as there was among Peter's contemporaries, about the nature of Peter's achievement. For him it was a perpetual struggle against disillusionment, a labour of Sisyphus. He could make examples of individuals who offended. Prince Matthew Gagarin, governor of Siberia, was executed for corruption. Because he allowed himself to be – or was alleged to be – the figurehead of the conservatives, Peter's son Alexis was knouted to death (1718). The operations of government still depended upon human material and attitudes. The Russian did not wish to lose his beard because God wore a beard – and was not man formed in God's image? The peasant would not improve his soil because by time-honoured usage holdings were exchanged amongst villagers at regular intervals. Only 3 per cent of the population lived in towns, and the towns-man's state in such a society could only be a beleaguered one; after the *Ulozhenie* the townsman lived in a cage: for moving, even marrying outside his ward, he could be executed. Inevitably, enterprise and skills were provided by outsiders – but that was exactly what the vast majority of Russian gentry and clergy disliked. They suspected that the new deal was more German than Russian, an impression that was strengthened by the policy of Peter's successors, notably Anna (1730–41). 'There is no one among the nobility,' wrote the British ambassador in 1741, 'who would not wish St Petersburg at the bottom of the sea.'

St Petersburg, that modern capital built by the sweat and blood of conscript serfs, was the epitome of Peter's work and his lasting monument. It was begun in 1703, first fruit of the tsar's conquest of the Baltic provinces, on marshes around the mouth of the river Neva. Military outpost, administrative centre and port, it expressed at first in makeshift wooden buildings, later in severe but handsome architecture, the tsar's maritime and commercial ambitions: it represented progress to Peter and to the more advanced of his ministers – but to most Russians it was a white elephant. Peter's new colleges functioned in St Petersburg: that did not commend them, or the place, to his subjects. So inconveniently remote for a capital, so outrageous a defiance of Muscovite tradition and of geography – the capital was to remain outside the mainstream of Russian life, epitomizing the chasm that opened up with Peter between a westernized élite of office-holders and courtiers and the mass of Russians. 'We became citizens of the world,' wrote Karamzin in 1811, 'but we ceased in certain respects to be citizens of Russia. The fault is Peter's.'

Church and State

Peter believed that he was God's agent. His professions of duty to the church and the frequent citing of God in his letters have somehow to be reconciled with the decapitation of that church and the blasphemous idiocies of 'the most Drunken Synod', the club in which Peter and his cronies met to drink and scoff. He had grown up to respect the idea of Orthodoxy and to despise its representatives. The superstitions of the church invited ridicule; its wealth, according to Peter's philosophy, was unconstructively used. The Old Believers represented much that he disliked in Russian life, but the empire-building of Philaret and Nikon, followed by schism, had opened the way to state intervention. The faithful believed Peter to be Anti-christ, yet he was devout in his own way: he enjoyed reading the Epistles in the midst of the congregation. But like most rulers of the eighteenth century he had little regard for the church as a corporate body, with rules and aims separate from those of the state. He had three main concerns: to eliminate the possibility of political resistance, to use the church as an instrument of education in the ideas of the west, and to secure a proportion of the income of the church for the state. When the patriarch Joachim died in 1690, he left a testament in which he counselled Peter to repress religious novelties and to restrict the influence of foreigners, particularly in the church. Joachim's successor Adrian was similar in outlook. When Adrian died Peter appointed no successor; church property was placed under the control of a new department, *Monastyrskii prikaz*, which channelled a proportion of the monks' revenues to the tsar. In 1721 the Most Holy Directing Synod was set up. At first its members were churchmen; it enjoyed in theory the powers of the patriarch, but it was a department of state. The *Oberprokuror* was Peter's 'eye' and the instrument of the ruler's autocratic control with power to appoint and dismiss Synod members at discretion: they could not therefore be truly representative of the church. The Episcopate all accepted the new dispensation, while other patriarchs of the east were persuaded by the Russian ambassador to recognize the Holy Synod as 'their beloved brother in Christ'.

Explanations of the lack of resistance to Peter's iconoclasm must be sought in the history of the church in Russia. The tsars had long occupied a special position as guardians of the interests of the church, which was symbolized by the ceremony of Palm Sunday when the tsar led the ass ridden by the patriarch in a special procession through Moscow. A succession of tsars before Peter had been pious men, interested in ecclesiastical affairs, and it was assumed that future tsars would continue to support church traditions. Against the contingency that the tsar himself, the guardian of Orthodoxy, would attack the church, there was therefore no defence, no constitution or tradition round which to rally the faithful. Moreover the episcopacy was weak. The number of 17 dioceses had been regarded by the tsar Theodore as so inadequate that he proposed, at the council of 1682, to raise it to 70. More anxious for their incomes than for their flocks, the bishops turned down the proposal. Some leaders and many priests and laymen had recently challenged the reforms of Nikon. Some 20,000 people burnt themselves alive as a gesture of religious protest between 1667 and 1691. Why was there no comparable protest against Peter? The answer seems to be that Peter's reforms did not touch directly the rituals and beliefs which engaged the devotion of Russian Christians: they were relatively uninterested in organization. And so the church accepted its subordination. Though the clergy were better educated as the eighteenth century proceeded, their services were treated with disdain by many of the westernized upper classes as suitable only for simple boors. Allowed no voice in political and social matters, and subject to the enervating control of the bureaucracy, the church still did not lose its vitality. Everywhere in Europe the churches were fighting a rearguard action to preserve political influence. Those who point to the continued strength of monasticism despite Peter's heavy hand, to active missionary work, advances in theological study and the continuing devotion of the masses of ordinary Russians, argue a strong case. Peter did not alter at one stroke the character of Russian Orthodoxy, but he altered radically and permanently the framework within which the tradition of Orthodoxy could grow. In Zernov's words about the post-Revolution situation: 'The present conflict between the communist state and the Orthodox Church is rooted in those remote years when the new Empire sprang up on the shores of the Baltic Sea.'

From the day when Peter ordered his officials and gentry to shave their beards, to put aside their kaftans and to dress in western fashion (in 1698, immediately after the destruction of the *streltsy*), Russians were subjected to lecturing, bullying – through a stream of edicts – all to one end. Peter sought to transform a society based on custom into one that was drilled in conformity with precise regulations. In his own circle he seems to have encouraged free discussion. But he did not believe that 'English freedom' would work. In a country where he was met at all levels by the bland response, 'So it has been done from the days of our ancestors', he could see no way but coercion, and so he availed himself of every ounce of authority that pertained to the office of tsar. 'Police,' said Peter, 'is the soul of civil society and of all good order.' In the ordinance establishing a new administrative system for towns we find that his conception of police was all embracing. Instructions about criminal jurisdiction, pricing, regulation of markets, care for beggars, widows and orphans, recall the activities of the French *intendant*. In the founding of his School of Navigation and Mathematics in Moscow, and fifty mathematical schools in provincial towns; in his manual of deportment for young noblemen, the *Honourable Mirror of Youth*, in which they were adjured not to get drunk in daytime; in regulations about dress – men must wear a jacket in the French or Saxon style, a waistcoat, breeches, gaiters, boots and caps in the German style; or in instructions about the use of the Olonetsk medicinal springs which happened to have proved beneficial to the tsar's misused liver; in regulations about the building of houses down to the size of ovens and chimneys – in all these, it is possible to see a national principle at work, or at the very least one of nature's schoolmasters, with a passion for instruction. He did not believe in spoiling the young student. 'For the elimination of noise and lawlessness at the Naval Academy select good retired soldiers from the Guards and let one of them be present in each classroom during teaching with a whip in his hands, and if any pupils start to commit outrages, beat them, from whatever family they come.' 'Our people,' wrote this schoolmaster, 'are like children who never set about their ABC if they are not compelled to do it by the master.' As it were to children who are growing up and no longer responded only to unreasoning threats (the style of old edicts) he appended explanations to his regulations. 'In St. Petersburg, persons of all ranks are enjoined from allowing their cows, goats, pigs and other cattle out into the street without shepherds . . . as such cattle wandering in the streets and other places deface roads and spoil trees.'

Baltic Power, Eastern Approaches

It cannot be said that Peter had a foreign policy. There were several broad aims which can be simply defined by the names of the three seas which lay outside but within range of Russian power – the Baltic, Caspian and Black Seas. His motives were commercial, strategic and, more nebulous but perhaps important, imperialist: the prestige of the ruler and the advance of Orthodox Christianity were both factors in the drive into Persian and Tartar lands. When, however, we come to priorities and methods, all semblance to a policy disappears: there is a frenzy of activity, with thrusts in this or that direction; expeditions and campaigns suffering from inadequate intelligence and preparations; and Russia in a state of war for all but one year – 1724 – in the whole reign.

In 1696, after the capture of Azov, work was begun on the naval base of Taganrog. When Charles XII invaded Russia in 1707, he no doubt hoped to be able to repeat the victory of Narva. Particularly dangerous to Peter was the concurrent revolt of the *hetman* Ivan Mazeppa and his Cossacks. Charles XII was thwarted, however, by the defeat of his support army and the loss of its supply train, and further weakened by the ravages of a particularly severe winter (1708–9). Mazeppa proved an ineffective ally, while Peter wisely made his army tail the Swedes, rather than attack, until they were sufficiently exhausted. Poltava was a tough battle, none the less, but at the end of that July day in 1709 Peter had won what he called 'an unexpected victory', destroyed the Swedes and signalled to the expectant chancelleries of Europe a decisive shift in the balance of northern power. After a further twelve years of campaigning Russia secured from Sweden, by the treaty of Nystad (1721), a long stretch of land around the northern Baltic, with the provinces of Karelia, Ingria, Estonia and Livonia.

Meanwhile the Turks had declared war in 1710, at the behest of Charles XII, their distinguished but somewhat embarrassing guest. The ensuing sequence of events shows Peter at his most fallible. He mounted an offensive down the river Pruth and called upon Balkan Christians to rise and support him. They did not. He was surrounded by the Turks, and was fortunate to be able to buy himself out of trouble by the cession of Azov and his Black Sea settlement. In the last years of his reign, however, Peter conquered Derbent and Baku and the entire west and south coasts of the Caspian Sea, to prevent the decadent Persian kingdom from falling into Turkish hands, and to channel its silks and carpets into Russian waterways. Peter had sent an expedition to explore the Oxus valley (1714–17); it was trapped and destroyed, but not before sufficient information had been gleaned to compose an authoritative map for the French Academy. Expeditions to Siberia were less unfortunate, and in 1717 Omsk was founded. Thus the lines of expansion were drawn. It was already apparent that Russia would neither be short of space nor content with what she had.

Peter contracted a severe chill when in 1725 he waded into a November sea to rescue a sailor. He made it worse by insisting on attending the ceremony of blessing the waters. He died from it, with his last instructions incomplete. In 1722 he had caused a will to be drawn up, but leaving the name of his heir blank. In his last illness he was unable to name him, and so his successors were left to dispute the throne. Some of his work was to lapse. The navy was to rot at its moorings, but St Petersburg stood and remained the capital. It was to be embellished by his successors, embodying the resolution of the new monarchy. Russians continued to use the simplified alphabet which he had devised, to read the western books in Russian translation. Some native students joined the foreigners whom Peter had introduced to launch his new academies. Abroad, there were twenty permanent Russian embassies in foreign states, including Peking; their lavish spending and intrigues made them an increasingly important part of the diplomatic scene. Peter's successors did not abandon the gradiose policy of eastern dominion upon which he had embarked under the flag of liberator of Christians. The title of *imperator*, which he adopted in 1721 to the disgust of the Habsburgs, was no empty boast.

Further Reading

See the list at the end of chapter 16, pp. 598–600.

16

RUSSIA AFTER PETER

Peter's Legacy

After Peter there were six sovereigns in thirty-seven years. Three of them were women. In 1762 Catherine of Anhalt-Zerbst came to the throne with the army coup which deposed her husband: it was the third palace revolution of the period. With Catherine a degree of political stability returned to Russia. Her reforms only look insignificant when contrasted with the bold and 'enlightened' affirmations of her early years. She was apparently unable, however, or unwilling, to check the assertion of noble rights, and her reign saw the climax of the regressive movement which had set in since Peter's death. A measure of reaction was inevitable because of the radical and alien nature of Peter's reforms. How far did it go? How much was left of the spirit and substance of Peter's regime? Before those questions can be answered it must be stressed that by the end of Peter's reign the noble class as a whole was already consolidating its position, like its counterparts in other countries, in the expanding armed forces and government. Service to the tsar was having a centripetal influence, countering local loyalties: a man forgot his native Smolensk or Novgorod, remembering only that he was a councillor or a dragoon. There was a greater degree of administrative stability in the subsequent reigns than is indicated by periodic political upheavals. The 'aristocratic reaction' in Russia was more limited and superficial than the phrase suggests.

Peter had made the Russian army a force to be reckoned with, even by the great military powers; his successors maintained it. Frederick II thought that the Russians were more formidable adversaries in the Seven Years War than either French or Austrians. Behind that impressive fact was massed a population expanding at a faster rate than elsewhere in Europe. Less than half the increase of the eighteenth century, from 16 to 36 million, came from annexations. If life was more precarious, at least in the reign of Anna, for some politically minded members of the upper class, it was less so for the ordinary Russian, with less demand for labour gangs and scope for settlement in virgin lands. The economy began to show the benefits of Peter's dragooning. Internal costs remained high: the price of grain increased 1600 times on the journey from Kursk to St Petersburg. Credit facilities were primitive; until well into the eighteenth century money-lenders, charging between 12 per cent and 20 per cent, were the only source of credit. But the country was self-sufficient in timber, iron and copper, and nearly so in textiles. There remained large pockets of a closed natural economy – but there had been a vast expansion of foreign trade: in 1725 exports were worth 4.2 million roubles a year, imports only 2.1 million. The favourable balance, which was to continue throughout the century, is the more impressive because the figures include trade with the Middle East, in which the Russians were, in the main, importers. There was a healthy basis, therefore, for revenue: of 8.5 million roubles in 1725 more than half came from the poll tax which stimulated agriculture because the peasants cultivated more land to pay for it. The crucial difference between Russia and more developed western countries is that there was plenty of Russian land. Correspondingly, problems of government were more acute.

After the defeat of Mazeppa in 1709 the Ukraine had been brought more firmly under government control. By a process analogous to the Habsburgs' dealings with Hungary, massive land grants to Russians strengthened ties with the parent country. Until the appointment of Cyril Razumovsky in 1750, there was no *hetman* in the Ukraine and the vast area was ruled directly by a board in St Petersburg. Though a Cossack, Razumovsky had close connections with the court and maintained the policy of Russification which was to be one of the main themes of imperial history up to 1917. The Tartar and Finnish peoples of the middle Volga lands, and the Bashkirs of the Urals, were subjected to the harshest discipline, the latter now providing most of the serfs for the mines and foundries of their native hills. Of Russia's potential there could be no doubt. But Peter's work had been, in many aspects, superficial, depending for orderly development upon tough, single-minded rule. Inasmuch as he was a free agent he had chosen to concentrate upon enlarging the armed forces, leaving insufficient resources for the task of educating the people for progress. He was aware of the need; but learning could not be instilled simply by exhortation from the top. Together with the isolation and paucity of towns, and the lack of any body comparable to the middle class of the west, the lack of adequate schools remained crucial.

Within months of Peter's death, all but a handful of his secular schools were closed. Such education as there was, was provided, largely for its own purposes, by the church. A westernized élite of officials, imbued with Peter's spirit and proud to call themselves his 'fledglings', provided the mechanism of central detachments to assist in maintaining order. But the lack of educated rank-and-file officials meant that a system which looked neat on paper was both inefficient and corrupt; in the remoter districts it barely functioned at all. Peter's constant experiments indicate that he was dissatisfied with what he was achieving. After his death further adjustments reflected the changing relationships between rulers and their leading subjects rather than any altruistic or consistent designs of reform.

Lacking ideological commitment and unable to co-operate for long enough to present a solid front, the magnates failed to achieve a significant reversal in the political trend. They were thwarted by the sheer staying power of officials, loyal to the institution, if not to the person, of the ruler. Men like Ostermann and Münnich in the reign of Anna, and Ushakov, head of the Secret Chancellery, who continued in office after the coup which brought Elizabeth to power, ensured a degree of continuity in government which was to prove more important in the long run than the unsteady careers of some notably undistinguished sovereigns, or even their powerful favourites. Peter's failure to ensure a strong succession of heirs, the misfortunes of several of his successors, the lurid episodes and extravagant style which engaged the rapt, even horrified attention of foreign observers of court life, the periodic interventions of the army into politics, even the successive acts by which the nobility were released from their obligations to the state, thus fall into place in a pattern dominated by the central bureaucracy. The state was coming to be more important than its most privileged subjects. It is that which entitles Peter to a place in the select band of the greatest architects of absolute monarchy.

The unedifying history of rulers and courts can therefore be briefly told. The superstitious might regard it as heaven's judgement on Peter for his savage treatment of Alexis. When he killed his nervous son and heir, he ended the recurring nightmare of another palace coup such as he had known as a boy; but he failed to nominate another heir. His own law of succession had laid down that the successor would be chosen by the sovereign Peter. On his deathbed he asked for paper but could only write two words, 'Give all', before he sank into his final coma. His second wife, Catherine, had been crowned in the cathedral of the Assumption in the Kremlin in the previous year, ostensibly for her heroism during the battle of the river Pruth. The former peasant girl from Livonia had a bold spirit which appealed to the king; she was one of nature's camp followers but she could endure his fits and soothe his temper. Despite temporary disgrace over a bribery scandal, she had been restored to favour. She was also in league with Menshikov, who could be relied upon to perpetuate Peter's system. It is likely that he intended to nominate Catherine; the senate, assembled to decide the succession, assumed it, and voted for her. Two years later, however, she died and Peter, the 12-year-old son of Peter's half-brother Alexis, was raised to the throne. He was intended by the Dolgoruky faction to be a mere puppet behind whom they could dismantle the more objectionable features of Petrine autocracy: indeed they signalled change by moving government back to Moscow. But Peter II died of smallpox on the very day on which he was to have married Catherine Dolgoruky, destined to be the instrument of the family's supremacy. Menshikov, who had wished to marry the tsar to his own daughter, had already been elbowed out after an illness during which he lost control of his Guards regiments. The council, led by Dimitrii Golitsyn, offered the throne to 37-year-old Anna, daughter of Peter the Great's half-brother Ivan, but a widow since the first weeks of her marriage to the duke of Courland nineteen years earlier. She accepted the 'conditions' formulated by Golitsyn, which would have made her an instrument in the hands of the council. Demanding control over foreign and domestic policy, the army and important state appointments, Golitsyn was influenced, no doubt, by the current developments in Sweden, where the autocracy of Charles XII had been followed by a reversion to aristocratic government. The nobility, who had assembled in Moscow for Peter's wedding and stayed to hail the new sovereign, favoured a return to simple autocracy. They were suspicious of the motives of Golitsyn and his friends, and they sought social concessions which Anna was happy to give. Anna tore up the conditions, made some vague promise and was acclaimed absolute sovereign by sabre-rattling officers. She dismissed the councillors, except for the neutral vice-chancellor, Ostermann, set up her government at St Petersburg in token of her intention of returning to the principles of Peter the Great, and proceeded to rule in the wilful manner that Golitsyn had predicted and tried to prevent.

Anna (1730–40) abandoned Peter I's unpopular attempt to preserve estates by a law of entail which forbade subdivision between heirs, and allowed a reversion of traditional Muscovite succession law. She established a military academy at St Petersburg to enable young noblemen to enter the army as officers. Since increasing numbers of them found the service attractive, the relaxation, in 1736, of the principle of service, limiting it to twenty-five years and exempting one son (if a father had more than one) to enable him to look after the family estates, meant less than it seemed. The concessions marked the start of the process of entrenchment by the upper classes, in the privileged positions into which they were already settling by 1725. But they could also be seen as bones thrown to a dog that was expected to wag a loyal tail. For Anna showed from the start her preference for German officials. Land, office and the whimsical favours of an infatuated woman were showered upon the Courlander Bühren. She had built for him a special riding school and compelled nobles who attended it to wear a special dress of yellow buffalo skin, trimmed with silver galloon. Sounder principals in an increasingly ruthless regime were the veterans Ostermann and Münnich, in charge respectively of civil and military affairs. The Secret Chancellery was restored; it was responsible in ten years for at least 10,000 arrests. Through its spies and police, autocracy defended itself in ways that have become too familiar: the more precarious and isolated the regime, the more drastic the preventive purges, the more obsessive the surveillance, the more blatant, at the same time, the ostentation and propaganda. 'Your excellency cannot imagine how magnificent this court is since the present regime,' wrote the British envoy Lord Harrington, 'although there is not a shilling in the treasury and no one is paid.' Anna's taste for garish display, for dwarfs, freaks and cruel practical jokes, suggests more than the usual corruptions of power. But it is possible to discern a serious political purpose. Her entertainments might impress, even gratify her noble guests; they also helped to bankrupt them. Like Peter, Anna may have deliberately tried to humiliate grandees: Nikita Volkonsky was forced to sit in a specially constructed basket and made to cackle like a hen, Golitsyn to marry the ugliest girl Anna could find for him, and then spend his wedding night naked in a specially constructed ice house.

At the heart of this grotesque regime was the policy of subjecting the Russian upper class to a dependable, largely German, bureaucracy. It strengthened what was to prove an enduring feature of Russian life. The ineptitude of the magnates in 1730 suggests that James Keith may have been right when he wrote that 'the genius of the nation and the vast extent of the empire demands a souverain, and even an absolute one'. He might have added 'and people like myself to serve her'. One of those keen-eyed Scotsmen on whom historians have tended to rely for outside verdicts on the Russian regime, Keith may have been less than objective since one of Anna's first acts was to offer him command of a crack regiment. But he was only one of many foreigners who helped to ensure, through all vicissitudes, the continued vitality of the state. Most of them were Germans. The German Baltic lands were near and accessible. Peter had shown his partiality for German ways, and his children began the Romanov tradition of marriage into German courts. With Estonia and Livonia and his virtual protectorate over Courland, Peter had acquired a source of potential officials, keen to exchange their meagre homelands for the boundless opportunities of the Russian service in this century of expansion. They came to stay. They were an object of resentment to later generations of Slavophils, like Klyuchevsky, who wrote of them invading 'like chaff sprinkled from a leafy sack' so that 'they overran the court, besieged the throne and grabbed every sort of administrative post to which a salary attached'; no less to eighteenth-century nobles, yearning for the easier days of Russia before Peter. The Germans were loyal to the dynasty, but in a conservative, corporate fashion; they tended to stay apart, to keep their language and their

Lutheranism; they sought to perpetuate their power. The system was theirs, and they understood it.

Elizabeth and Peter III

Intending Bühren to rule in all but name after her death, Anna named her great-nephew Ivan, aged 4 months, as her heir. After a few weeks of his regency, on the initiative of Münnich, he was arrested and deported. Münnich and Ostermann wrestled for power; they would have done better to work together. In December 1741 Elizabeth Romanov was raised to the throne by a surge of anti-German feeling and a daring army coup. Ivan V was sent away to begin a tragic life of solitary confinement which would end only with his murder, in 1766, by the agents of Catherine II. Elizabeth was the daughter of Peter I and of Catherine; tall with lovely complexion and hair, regular features, and much admired blue eyes, she was sensuous and very vain. Her decision to call on the Guards to overthrow the German regime was out of character, for she was not easily roused. More interested in clothes than in politics, she spent much of her day dressing and undressing and was content to leave state affairs in the hands of her chancellor Bestuzhev and her lover Alexis Razumovsky, a Cossack, who had first attracted her by his singing in her chapel choir. After 1749, however, Razumovsky, and his brother Cyril, Grand *Hetman* of the Ukraine, began to lose ground to the Shuvalov family. Alexander Shuvalov was head of the secret police. More important was his brother, Peter, who had large, sensible ideas about the economy.

In 1754 all customs barriers within the empire were abolished. Shuvalov reformed the coinage and exploited commercial monopolies; from all of which he benefited immensely. The Seven Years War entailed extra expenditure but money could be found. Church revenues were diverted to the Treasury; merchants were made to pay more for the right to raise indirect taxes. The capital for his new Bank of the Nobility was raised initially from the profits of the state vodka monopoly. Loans were offered at 6 per cent on the security of noblemen's estates. Those who accepted assistance were letting themselves in for the genteel dependence that was to be the chronic condition of so many landed Russians. Eighty years later more than two-thirds of all the estates of the nobility had become mortgaged, without prospect of redemption. Some nobles were fortunate or clever enough to draw money from industrial undertakings, distilleries, tanneries, textile mills and timber yards. But for most the only way to raise funds was to get more from their land and serfs, in work, often as many as six days a week, and in dues which were increased wherever possible. Under such pressures more serfs ran away or rebelled. With the alarming increase of local disorder, unwilling or unable to create through their own agents an adequate law enforcement, which would have to include some measure of protection for serfs, government resorted to easier ways. Landowners were granted more powers to deal with their peasants. By 1762 they were allowed to sentence them to deportation or penal servitude, without referring them to public courts. It was the cycle of exploitation, resistance, repression and revolt which Catherine inherited and which, despite liberal pronouncements, she was unable to break.

It was the liaison of their nephew Ivan with the empress that first brought promotion to the Shuvalovs. He was not lacking in initiative. He prompted Elizabeth to found the University of Moscow and the Academy of Arts in St Petersburg. These years saw a strenuous effort by the Russian professors of the St Petersburg Academy of Science to oust foreigners from teaching posts. Little was left of Peter the Great's dream of an institution of European standing, attractive to the best minds of Germany and France. Besides the prejudice of Russian academics the reformers had to cope with the conservatism of Russian nobles. To induce them to attend the University of Moscow they were allowed to count years spent there as years of state service. Even so most preferred to attend the Military Academy, where a wide education was provided. Plays were performed there, a literary journal was produced; the first novels from abroad were printed there. They were translated into Russian, but French was coming to be used increasingly as the second language at court and in fashionable houses. Catherine's accession undoubtedly gave an impetus to the process of cultural westernization. But it had already begun under Elizabeth. Not that she made any contribution for she had no intellectual pretensions. She held that reading was positively injurious to the health. The English ambassador, Hanbury Williams, wrote of 'this lady's mortal backwardness in all sorts of business or anything that required one moment's thought or application'.

It was the object of Williams's diplomacy to secure the alliance of Russia in order to afford protection to Hanover, which the British believed was threatened by Prussia. After the treaty of Westminster (1756) between Britain and Prussia, Russia drew towards France; Williams conspired with Elizabeth's foreign minister, Bestuzhev, who had been in British pay since 1746; the details are uncertain since possibly incriminating documents were destroyed. It is probable that the object was to bind Russia to Britain by securing the accession of Peter, the young duke of Holstein, the son of Elizabeth's younger sister, the duchess of Holstein-Gottorp, noted for his pro-Prussian views; his wife Catherine was to be co-ruler. Elizabeth had a stroke in September 1757, but she lived till December 1761. Bestuzhev was arrested in February 1758, and Catherine was lucky that there was no evidence against her. She withdrew from the court and bided her time. Elizabeth had been sufficiently disturbed by the ambitions of Frederick the Great to join the coalition that led to the Seven Years War. She viewed the war, typically, in the light of a personal duel and would have fought to the bitter end – which it might well have been but for Frederick. At the start of 1761 the Russians were occupying East Prussia and part of Pomerania; Frederick contemplated suicide but he fought on. In December, Elizabeth died, leaving a wardrobe of 15,000 dresses and an heir whose first action was to recall the Russian army.

Elizabeth had made Peter her heir at the start of her reign, but his tutors found it an unrewarding task to train him for responsibility. Brutal treatment in childhood had shattered his nerves. A stiff manner and a shrill voice failed to impress. He spent hours playing with model soldiers. He was more than a little odd, but certainly not the moron that his wife came to depict. 'When he left the room,' wrote Catherine, 'even the dullest book was a delight.' One is left wondering what an older, more tactful, or simply less self-willed wife might have done for him. Catherine had been plucked out of her petty duchy of Anhalt-Zerbst, at 14, as the pretty girl of decided character and precocious tastes who might be expected to appeal to the duke and provide him with an heir. That she did; but claimed that Peter was not the father. If it is true, as was thought by some, that Saltykov, one of the first of Catherine's many lovers, was the father of the future Tsar Paul, there was no Romanov blood in the last seven tsars of Russia. But it was noticed that Tsar Paul resembled Peter in looks as in some aspects of character. Egocentric and impatient, Catherine resented Peter's indifference, despised his interests and feared his policies. With the energy and wit that were to make her such a formidable ruler, she was content to play neither the part of neglected wife, nor that of consort-in-waiting. For Peter was young and did not shrink from the responsibilities of rule. Even Catherine could not say that he was indecisive.

After concluding a peace with Prussia on terms considered derisory by patriotic Russians since Frederick regained all the land he lost, Peter issued a manifesto relieving the nobility of all forms of military or civil service. 'With this single act the monarchy created a large, privileged, westernised leisure class, such as Russia had never known before.' That is the view of Richard Pipes: it deserves careful examination. It should be recalled that, like the landed nobilities of other countries, the *dvoryanstvo* was far from a homogeneous class. Some 80 per cent of the serfs (designated 'souls', serfs were the usual measure of landed wealth in old Russia) were owned by 20 per cent of nobles. The 60 per cent who had less than 20 'souls' and altogether owned but 5 per cent of the total found state service essential if they were not to moulder in provincial poverty. The evidence suggests that it was attractive, too, to the better-off minority. That is why Peter's edict could be presented as generous recognition of a new spirit: 'We do not find that necessity for compulsion in service which was in effect up to this time.' Liberty was to be bestowed on the whole Russian nobility, not so that it could live in selfish sloth but to enable it to 'continue service both in Our Empire and in other European states allied to us'. The emphasis throughout is upon continuance of service and on educating children to be fit for it. The decree has been seen as Peter's attempt to consolidate his rule on the basis of a gratefully loyal *dvoryanstvo*, an attempt to emancipate himself from the confining, jealous circle of magnates; that some of them moved so quickly to destroy him lends support to this view. But should he also be denied a measure of higher statecraft, when he addressed himself to the facts and looked, like other sovereigns, for ways in which he could encourage the upper class to become a more useful class in a rapidly changing world? If that was an element in his thinking, then it is possible to speculate on what, if he had lived, his attitude to serfdom would have been.

He did not lack boldness. Indeed his chief fault may have been a naive lack of caution, even where his own security was at stake. He abolished the Secret Chancellery and provided safeguards against the denunciations leading to arbitrary arrests. He proposed to secularize church lands, then startled the Orthodox clergy by announcing that he was going to set up a Lutheran chapel for his servants; inevitably it was rumoured that he was about to revert to the religion that he had renounced when he became heir to the throne. It is hard not to see him as his own worst enemy, inviting unfavourable comparison with Catherine, who won friends by her amenable behaviour, contriving to seem the injured party when he announced that he would divorce her and marry his mistress. He made preliminary moves towards war against Denmark in the interest of Holstein. He spent hours on the parade ground in the uniform of a colonel of the Prussian Guards; he also made officers, even generals, take their turn at drill. Fatally, he dismissed the Preobrazhensky regiment from the guard duties which, he said, they had forfeited by their slackness. Did he hope to ward off danger by surrounding himself with loyal troops or was he simply unaware of the danger? It seems that he was badly advised; possibly Baron Korf, chief of police, was privy to the plot. A reading of recent Russian history might have instilled caution; yet even Russian court history offered no precedent for a wife conniving at the overthrow of her royal husband.

Catherine the Great

Contempt for her husband, pride in her lover Gregory Orlov, father of her 2-month-old son and a leading figure in the coup, were among Catherine's motives; she seems too to have respected the opinion of Count Panin, who represented an embryonic political élite based on the senate whose authority Peter, by reliance on his own henchmen, was clearly undermining. Significantly, Catherine's first action as sovereign was to restore the senate. It is unlikely that without the naked ambition to rule which Catherine took little trouble to conceal, the conspirators would have acted as promptly. In July 1762 she appeared before the Guards regiments and they acclaimed her empress. Dressed as an officer in the Guards she rode at the head of her soldiers to the palace of Oranienbaum where Peter had been waiting for her to attend his birthday celebration. Peter was seized and entrusted to the Orlovs. They subsequently claimed that he had been killed in a scuffle. There is little doubt that he was murdered: by issuing a manifesto stating that he had died of colic, suddenly, as 'evidence of God's divine intent', Catherine became accessory to the crime.

It was undoubtedly a conservative coup. Catherine was not expected by those who brought her to the throne to neglect their interest. She was to show that she had a mind of her own. She took herself sufficiently seriously as an intellectual to care about the opinion of the leaders of the western Enlightenment, who responded by expressing their delight at her accession at such a propitious time. By her measures, as well as by her pronouncements she sought to prove that they were right. But from the start too she was anxiously concerned about security: she knew that she could fall as suddenly as she had risen. Even when her personal position looked safe, she continued to be aware of the dangers that faced the regime: the Pugachev rising aroused the old fear of disintegration. Russia was already enormous, yet Catherine eagerly espoused policies of expansion, at the expense of Turks and Poles, which compounded the problem and necessitated drastic reforms in the structure of government. Such, briefly, were the themes of the reign.

Russia enjoyed the advantage that its neighbours were weak and that it was so far removed from the orbit of the great powers. Its remoteness was its strength, as Napoleon was to find. If, however, the ruler had been at odds with her leading subjects, or dominated by some narrow interest, if authority had been weak at the summit, Russian government would have been vulnerable, as it proved to be in the next century. In the restless contention for power Catherine managed to prevent any faction or individual from gaining a monopoly. Panin was checked, and with him the resurgence of the idea of a controlling oligarch, based on the senate. She even reined in the overwhelming Potemkin, her lover in the post-Orlov phase, and gave him scope only for projects which, like the conquest of the Crimea, enhanced her reputation. To her death, Catherine managed and disposed at will, the least restrained autocrat of her day. It was not only Russians who were dazzled by the conquests of her reign. But it is in political management, the area where her husband was so weak, that Catherine was a great ruler.

Successive coups witnessed to the dangerous lack of a fundamental law governing succession and to the powerful interests which could manipulate the situation for their own ends. Did the accession of Catherine now signal a change more fundamental than a transfer of personal sovereignty? An emancipated, cultivated woman, Russian only by adoption, she confidently embodied the values of the west. The style of rule was markedly different. But what of the substance? In important respects the continuity was more important than the novelty. The slow growth of Enlightenment ideas can be traced to the regime of the Shuvalovs; it was a logical development from the policies of Peter. Life for the mass of Russians in all classes went on as before – whether to serve, toil, malinger, rebel: the same questions, the same instincts. Trapped between the static yields of a primitive agriculture and mounting debts, the gentry looked to the government for support. Where there was growth in the economy, it was owing to measures taken by Catherine's predecessors to exploit Russia's rich natural resources. The bureaucracy was growing steadily and acquiring the possessive, conservative habits of its kind: established institutions were an obstacle to radical change. The paramount fact, however, was that Russia was unable to feed her rapidly growing population from the tired soils of the heartlands of old Muscovy. The ineluctable consequences can be measured in the force behind the drive for new lands. By conquest, at the expense of Poles, Turks and their tributary lands, the state created the opportunities; peasant colonists exploited them. The more Russian authority was extended, the more vulnerable it became. In this situation the economic and political interests of autocrat and landowners converged. Catherine came to appreciate it. She did not become less liberal so much as more realistic. A wholly determinist view of Catherine as the creature of circumstances largely beyond her control does less than justice to her achievement.

If Catherine were to survive, let alone impose her will, she had to ensure that no one faction dominated to the point of inciting some other faction to conspire. Balance was the aim. Her first move was to restore the senate. She then created the imperial council. As co-ordinator of national policy it met an important need in government; as intermediary between senate and tsarina it guarded, not only against the caprice of favourites, but also against the consolidation of those senators who had favoured Catherine's accession because they had hoped to rule themselves. On the advice of Panin, who did not lack personal ambition but seems also to have cared for the sound working of government, the senate's authority was further diffused and its role altered from executive to administrative by breaking it up into 6 departments, 4 in St Petersburg, 2 in Moscow. Without open assault, in a manner which recalls that other mistress of empirical statecraft, Maria Theresa, Catherine sought to divert to constructive purposes the energies of the emerging class of professional statesmen, self-constituted 'guardians' of an order that suited their interests. In the same spirit she established a Commission on the Freedom of the Nobility, to review and clarify Peter's decree. She could not abrogate the decree and may not have wished to, but it is significant that much of the Commission's work was concerned with the nature of a nobleman's duties in the armed forces bureaucracy and with his role as a landlord.

Meanwhile she travelled, observed and read. As a young woman, Russian by adoption in an alien court, Catherine had read widely for pleasure as well as for instruction. There had always been a strong didactic tendency: she liked to share ideas and advertise her learning. She did not abandon her intellectual pursuits when she became ruler. She remained an avid reader, a fluent writer. But inevitably her interests became more practical. The opportunity was immense, even unprecedented. It was what attracted the attention of the *philosophes* who, in some ways disappointed by Frederick the Great, saw Russia as the field of mission and Catherine as the prophet of Enlightenment. Catherine was easily flattered. But she was industrious and sincere in her wish to effect change. Her mind and pen were at the service of the state: it is the most admirable aspect of her reign. The perusal of such works as Voltaire's *Universal History* gave her a sense of historical perspective. Her mastery of the works of Montesquieu and Beccaria emboldened her to legislate. But she was too warm-blooded and observant to be dominated by theory. The process of political education which had begun when she came to Russia and adopted the Orthodox faith continued in the first dangerous years of power. She read Machiavelli, but she learnt more from Orlov and Panin.

There will always be debate about Catherine's motives in convoking in the summer of 1767 the Commission for the Composition of a Plan of a New Code of Laws. Was she, like Alexis in 1649, after the disturbances which had rocked his throne, seeking to assert legitimacy and evoke tradition, that of the *Zemskii Sobor*, by calling on representative Russians to give counsel? Was she reaching out for a larger audience, to remind the court magnates that they had no exclusive rights? Or was she seeking to wake the lethargic entrepreneurial spirit of commoners, or to call men from the outlying provinces to the centre, to impress upon them where their duty and interest lay? Or was it an exercise in propaganda, as much for *philosophes* as for benighted Russians? There is no need to exclude any of these interpretations.

As for Britain, France and Austria, the Seven Years War had been costly. The needs of the exchequer reinforced the lesson of her first essays into statecraft, that it was essential to strengthen local government. The disorder of Russia's laws offered a vast opportunity. She wanted to impress the pundits of the west through her own synthesis of their liberal ideas. She needed to keep the initiative in a situation in which some even of her own circle saw her as a caretaker till her son should come of age, while others resented her as a foreign usurper. All pointed to a positive legislative effort. She planned on a heroic scale. She composed a lengthy *Nakaz* or Instruction so that the representatives could study the views of western jurists. As she acknowledged, Montesquieu's *L'Esprit des lois* provided the basis for nearly half the treatise, Beccaria for other important sections, German cameralists for others again. It amounted to an argument for legal absolutism. Even if she had not been constrained by the advice of her serf-owning advisers it is hard to see that she would not have learnt from the character of an assembly in which nobles dominated and commoners, numerically in the majority, were apparently content with a passive role that an autocrat was required to direct a bureaucracy large enough to govern the Russian millions. Nor is it surprising that she avoided the issue of serfdom with the uncharacteristically vague comment that 'The Law may establish something useful for vesting property in slaves.'

The ineptitude and bemusement of the marshal of the Commission and others entrusted with the organization of the meetings, the laughably poor standard of debate and the confused messages that emerged from them, were reason enough for Catherine, after regular meetings in Moscow from July to December 1767 and less frequent meetings in St Petersburg after that, to adjourn the Commission in December 1768: officially it was because of the renewal of war against Turkey. She was probably relieved to be finished with the Commission. There was no sign that it was advancing the cause of legal reform. It had become a sounding board for those who had grievances to air. It had, moreover, already served a purpose. Like the *cahiers* which deputies brought with them to the French estates-general in 1789, the *nakazy* which the members brought for the attention of the commission provided valuable evidence for what Russians thought and wanted. No Russian ruler was so well informed as Catherine after the 'Great Commission'. It may not have been the chief purpose of the exercise but it was undoubtedly its chief value.

The Great Reform

From dreams of reform at home and conquest abroad, Catherine was rudely awakened by the revolt of Emelian Pugachev. She had carried out the partition of Poland and her armies were victorious against the Turks, when news of the revolt, spreading with terrifying rapidity, forced her to instruct her envoy to complete the treaty of Kutchuk-Kainardji on the best terms possible (1774). They were still favourable and it is because of its influence on Catherine's outlook, in particular with regard to questions of domestic government, that Pugachev's rising may be seen as a turning point in her reign. A combination of circumstances, inauspicious for Catherine's regime, conferred a brief greatness upon this bold fellow, who might have been shot for deserting from the Russian army but lived to command the allegiance of millions who never saw him, in an insurrection which shook the state.

The Yaik Cossacks, who resented the government's monopoly of salt-panning and fishing rights and killed the government inspector who was sent to investigate their grievances, were quicker than most to come to the boil, but they were representative of the alienated peoples for whom government spelt the rapacious presence of a colonizing power. The steppes had long sheltered the outcasts and runaways of the Russian countryside.

Latterly, they had experienced the full weight of *barshchina*, the system of payment by labour services, which was the usual form of serfdom in the lands of the middle and lower Volga. Working three days a week, from dawn to dusk, for landowners who cared little for traditional Cossack customs made them no more amenable to the compulsory military service exacted by government in preparation for the Turkish wars. The middle class of small proprietors, *odnodvortsy*, between *dvoryane* and serf dwelt nostalgically on the easier days when they paid no dues to lords, nor taxes to St Petersburg. Revolt might be better than the russification which Catherine advocated, so that they would 'cease to look like wolves of the forest'. Such men might not be taken in by Pugachev's claim to be Peter III. But many were, because they wanted to be. The pretender phenomenon is not easy to explain except in terms of deep hunger among deprived, alienated people for a just and merciful redeemer: 44 cases of such claims have been counted in eighteenth-century Russia, significantly twice the number of the seventeenth century, and mostly in the south-west. Peter's dark, secret end was a gift to a pretender. But the identity of the leader mattered less than the chance to muster, to assert traditional rights and to slay those who had usurped them.

When Pugachev failed in his prime military objective, the capture of the fortress of Orenburg, commanding the Don, he turned east and found more adherents, the Bashkirs of the Urals, especially those who worked the mines and factories, producing the ore and making arms for an ever growing market. These tribesmen were heirs to a distinctive culture, nearer to Turkey than to Muscovy, they were at the end of trading routes stretching to Asia Minor. They were camel-dealers, bee-keepers and wood-workers and they had only used the ore in which the foothills of the Urals were so fatally rich to make their simple implements. They had not been turned into industrial serfs without struggle: they rebelled six times in the eighteenth century. Now they made common cause with the Cossacks. By 1774 there were 30,000 men under arms, doomed to be suppressed when the government could deploy sufficient troops, but not before they had indulged in an orgy of pillage. The destruction was not wholly indiscriminate. Manorial records were sought out and burnt. In the most sinister phase of the risings, as the defeated Pugachev retired down the Volga, his end only a matter of time, peasants in hitherto peaceful regions began to take the law into their own hands, as they received garbled versions of the leader's edict. Pugachev, 'since with the authority of God's right hand our name flourishes in Russia', ordered peasants everywhere to 'hang the nobles and treat them in the same way as they, not having Christianity, have dealt with you, the peasants'. It was disturbing to the government to hear that some soldiers had gone over to Pugachev. When he was captured and executed, the danger of a bloody social war evaporated. But Pugachev's name lived on, in the stories and ballads of the common people and in the memories of landlords and officials and in their consciousness of limits and constraints. The whole affair sealed the knot that tied Catherine and her nobility in a way that was fervently expressed by the tsarina when she told the *dvoryanstvo* of Kazan that their security and well-being was 'indivisible with our own and our empire's security and well-being'.

It was this solid alliance of interests that informed the great reform of 1775. The changes envisaged by Catherine when she summoned the Great Commission, and prompted by the grievances and claims that emerged from the debates, became a matter of urgency in the aftermath of Pugachev. In preference to her edict Catherine declared her wish 'to furnish the empire with the institutions necessary and useful for the increase of order of every kind and for the smooth flow of justice'. In justice to Catherine her words could be taken as the text for her reign. The reform of government was carried out in a spirit some way removed from the pretentious language of the young student of philosophy or the academic models of Blackstone and Beccaria. But they represent something valuable, an effort to match the ideal to the real, as it was reported to her by trusted governors, like Volkonsky of Moscow and Jacob Sievers of Novgorod. She had no illusions about the obstacles. Of Blackstone she wrote, 'I do not make anything from what there is in the book but it is my yarn which I unwind in my own way.' In the 'institution' Catherine came to terms with the size of the empire, necessitating more manageable units, allowing for a measure of local initiative along with continuing central direction. The empire was divided into 50 *gubernia* of 800,000 inhabitants, each under a governor, further subdivided into counties or equivalent districts. Finance, local industries and services, hospitals, schools, provision for the poor, were made the responsibility of boards in each province. Another board assumed the responsibility for running civil and criminal justice; below it was planned a network of separate courts, dealing respectively with nobles, townspeople and peasants.

The reform had been thoughtfully, carefully prepared and the system was to be the basis of tsarist government up till the Revolution. It was roughly in line with what the *dvoryanstvo* wanted and could manage. It represented a considerable achievement on Catherine's part: in a decade she had earned a degree of trust and acceptance. It embodied the recognition of the separate identity of the nobility and accorded them corporate status. How far did it go to ceding them control of local government? Some posts were open to election. The official head of district administration, the *kapitan-ispravnik*, was an elective post; so was the marshal of the nobility, who spoke for them to the governor. Some high judicial posts were reserved for them. They were allowed to meet in assembly to formulate policy and elect their spokesman. But the governor did not have to accept him. Skilfully Catherine had presented her loyal *dvoryanstvo* with the semblance and some of the perquisites of government. When, ten years later, the Municipal Charter Act gave the appearance of self-government by creating six-man town councils which could then elect a mayor, the governor retained control since he managed the elections and used the council for collecting taxes. She preserved the real power of those whom she chose, the governors. Their position was analogous in some respects to that of the *intendants* of France. They were given almost unbounded powers, largely because they were mostly so far away that decisions had to be taken on the spot. But she alone appointed them and she knew whom she could trust; moreover, she had won sufficient authority by her spirit to be able to act independently: she was bounden to few, answerable to none. It was her main achievement. For the successes in war and diplomacy, culminating in the acquisition of the Crimea and of a substantial part of Poland, owed as much to the weakness of her opponents and to the strength of the Russian army as to her judgement and skill.

Supreme Between Europe and Asia

In the decade which saw France teetering towards bankruptcy, Britain lose her American colonies, even Prussia and Austria emerge without distinction from the futile 'potato war', foreign observers saw something inexorable about Russia's expansion. As early as 1776 a writer in the *Scots Magazine* wrote in fulsome terms of Russia: 'All her affairs are conducted upon a great and extensive system and all her acts are in a grand style. She sits supreme between Europe and Asia, and looks as if she intends to dictate to both.' The year before, at the peace of Kutchuk-Kainardji, Catherine had made a satisfactory end to a war which had begun in 1768 when the Turks arrested the Russian ambassador. Though the Turks had begun the war Catherine listened to the arguments mounted, by the brothers Orlov among others, that it would be to Russia's advantage to proclaim herself patron of the Orthodox communities in the Balkans and to work for the establishment there of independent states and the expulsion of the Turk from Christian Europe: it was the crusade in modern form, recognizing old traditions and new interests, tending to place Russia morally and strategically in the best position. Out of an army of about 400,000 Catherine's generals could call on about half for field service. The operations displayed the ability of commanders like Count Rumiantsev, who pushed the Turks beyond the Danube in 1769, and Admiral Spiridov, who with the Scotsmen Elphinstone and Greig destroyed the Turkish navy in a series of fights off the Anatolian coast. If Suvorov had had a free hand in 1773–4 Russian gains might have been even more spectacular. As it was, under the shadow of Pugachev, Russian negotiators were able to secure Kerch and Yenikale, with a lot of the coastline of the Black Sea from Bug to Dnieper, together with the right of free navigation in the Black Sea and into the Mediterranean. Thus Russian ships might pass under the guns of Constantinople; and so the 'eastern question' of the nineteenth century assumed its classical form:

who would be the heir to the manifestly crumbling empire of the Ottomans? Constantinople came within the sights of Russian diplomacy. Would Russia be the principal heir to Byzantium? Meanwhile there were more fruits to pick. The Crimea, contemptuously described by Potemkin as a 'pimple on Russia's nose', was left in nominal independence in 1774. In 1783, after secret negotiations with Austria to arrange for joint action, Russia acted unilaterally and annexed the whole region. Potemkin's easy victory cleared the way for the publication of the Charter of the Rights of the Nobility celebrating the glory of Russian arms, praising the 'judicious enterprise' of Field-Marshal Potemkin and linking him with no less deserving subjects in sumptuous panegyric: 'We praise you, descendants worthy of our forebears! these have been the foundations of Russia's majesty.' It was fortunate for Catherine that she could so invite her *dvoryane* to bask in reflected glory, rely on a mutual trust confirming the ties of reciprocal interest, and make concessions which sounded grand but really added little to the existing rights of the class. They should be noted, however, for they represent the highest point, anywhere in Europe, of the noble aspiration of privilege without obligation; that was only five years before the Revolution which was to damage beyond retrieval the concept of such privilege, so that where it survived, as in Russia, it became increasingly sterile and defensive.

Already it was the essential dependence of the class, economically as well as politically, that made it possible for autocracy to cede so much. The experience of the past ten years, during which increasing numbers of landowners had incurred crippling loans or mortgaged their estates, had shown that the local assemblies of nobles had generated no kind of political solidarity and therefore posed no threat to the regime. So it was now possible to define noble status more broadly: the law henceforth recognized equality in noble status between those of blood and those of service. The rights included security of person and property, monopoly of serf ownership, exemption from taxation, trial by peers and immunity from corporal punishment. Elected marshals were accorded the right to keep genealogical records. The nobleman was also allowed to travel abroad without permission. It was to be one way in which western ideas would infiltrate: appealing because they fell on cultural ground with little growth yet to show from Russian seed; insidious because they touched, for the most part, only the great families in whose circle of acquaintance one man's ideas quickly became another man's fashions; and, though Catherine could not be blamed for not foreseeing it, more dangerous because of the impending Revolution, which was to stir men of all classes, to think of liberties and rights which were derived not from the will of princes but the condition of nature, the common birthright.

That was what made Catherine think that she must act with the full forces of the state against dissidents like the unfortunate Radishchev. As a promising young nobleman he had been selected by Catherine for service as a court page and then for a special course at Leipzig University. Thirty years later he unburdened his conscience and wrote the *Diary of a Journey from Moscow to St Petersburg*. In it he denounced serfdom and wrote apocalyptically of the certainty of vengeance to come. He was not the only critic of the regime; nor was he, sentenced after commutation of the death penalty to life imprisonment, the only victim of a persecution which was, however, severe in the Russian context only by the relatively mild standards set by Catherine herself. The reign ended in an atmosphere of repression: the police burnt books, spied, interrogated and censored. The regime was firm to the end – but there was enough wild talk to justify Catherine's fears for her own security. She survived. In the 1790s in Russia, that was something in itself. But Catherine's achievement had been much greater. Russia was significantly stronger, better governed, under sounder laws than it had been in 1762. A higher proportion of a much higher number of Russian subjects were receiving education of some kind. There were more books in circulation. There were more factories in operation. All that depended upon the stability provided by Catherine's sure hand.

The bureaucracy grew steadily – there were 18,000 officials in 1775 – but did no more than keep pace with the rapid rise in population, from 23,250,000 in 1762 to 37,500,000 in 1795. More than half the rise was due to the acquisition of parts of Poland, and other lands; but the rate of natural increase was rapid too, even in the long-settled lands in the centre. It was sufficient to support a steadily growing army which, including garrison troops, numbered over 400,000 by the end of the reign. State income rose from 24 million roubles in 1769 to 56 million in 1795, with the percentage from direct taxes nearly half the total by then. But expenditure rose more steeply in the same period, from 23.5 million to 79 million roubles. The large deficit would have been more alarming had not the economy been showing striking growth in the later years of the reign. The government's inflationary policy of deficit finance may have done something to stimulate this growth. The liberal trading policies in force since the 1750s, when internal dues were abolished, also made a contribution. Most important was the insatiable demand in western Europe for Russia's raw materials, especially in wartime for iron ore, timber and naval supplies – hemp and tar. The French and British both imported from Russia more than they exported to her. Indeed Britain's imports were higher than from any other European power and it has been asserted that the industrial revolution would not have occurred without them. Admittedly making a case for his company before the House of Commons, the agent for the British Russia Company, Foster, argued that without this source of raw materials 'our navy, our commerce, our agriculture are at end'. A rise in the total value of exports, from 12,750,000 roubles in 1762 to 43,250,000 in 1793, supports the view of modern Russian historians that Russia's own industrial revolution was starting in these years. Making use of abundant serf labour, factory owners and state bailiffs were able to create surprisingly large concerns. No less important, since it effected noble incomes and so the level of demand in the high-spending sector of the economy, was the jump towards the end of the reign in the productivity of agriculture, after being more or less static for centuries. It reflects relatively quiet and settled times after the downfall of Pugachev; but owes more to the colonization of new lands, specially in the 'black earth' areas of the south-west, and more intensive cereal farming there; and something too to the initiatives of government, mainly through the agency of the Free Economic Society. The cultivation of cereals almost doubled in the last two decades of the century. Like the stirring deeds of Russian soldiers and the easy triumphal ride enjoyed by her diplomats, the surge in Russia's capacity to generate wealth cannot be attributed directly to Catherine. But it occurred within the framework of an ordered security and reflected her own intelligent concern for enterprise in economic affairs and, not least, the shameless opportunism that made her resist the temptation to meddle with the admitted abuses of serfdom, but led her to seize the opportunity to extend her lands at the expense of less fortunate neighbours.

Further Reading

In one respect the Revolution made little difference to Russian historical writing. It has always been strong on economy and society and specially so on the peasants who provide most of the material for social history. Conversely there is a dearth of good biographies. Political analysis can be expected to reflect the writer's philosophy, be it Slavophil, for example, or Marxist: in the latter case he may use evidence to support an ideological position which, as in the case of recent studies of Catherine the Great, can only have a distorting effect upon judgement. Such work is reviewed in C.E. Black (ed.), *Rewriting Russian History: Soviet Interpretations of Russia's Past* (New York, 1956). Fortunately for the student there is available work from the golden age of Russian historians, in the decades before the Revolution, while a number of fine foreign writers have recently made good use of the extensive archives.

With political overtones and the special interest created by the diaspora of émigrés, Russia more than any other country has tempted historians to write general histories. Among them, all entitled *History of Russia*, are those of J.D. Clarkson (New York, 1960), N.V. Risianovsky (2nd edn, 1969), L. Kochan (1962), S.F. Platonov (Bloomington, 1964) and G.V. Vernadsky (New Haven, 1961). The latter is among the editors of a valuable source of documents, *A Source Book for Russian History from Early Times to 1917* (3 vols, New Haven, 1972). A more ambitious book about Russia is that of M.T. Florinsky, *Russia, A History and an Interpretation* (2 vols, New York, 1953). There is much that is stimulating and revealing in the works of two English pioneers in the field: Bernard Pares, *A History of Russia* (3rd edn, 1955), and B.H. Sumner, *Survey of Russian History* (1961). Still invaluable is the masterpiece of V.O. Klyuchevsky, *A History of Russia*, still incomplete at his death in 1911 (5 vols, New York, 1960).

The section of Klyuchevsky's work on *The Rise of the Romanovs*, published separately under that title (translated and edited by Liliana Archibald, New York, 1969), and his *Peter the Great* (translated by L. Archibald, 1965) provide a vigorous introduction to Alexis and Peter. The latter may also be approached through Sumner's short biography, *Peter the Great and the Emergence of Russia* (1950). Sumner also wrote *Peter the Great and the Ottoman Empire* (1949). Marc Raeff edited and contributed to a collection of studies on the theme *Peter the Great, Reformer or Revolutionary?* (Boston, 1963). Among numerous recent lives, the most valuable to the student is perhaps that of M.S. Anderson (1978), who has also written a pamphlet *Peter the Great* (London, 1978).

Eighteenth-century Russia may be approached through A. Lentin, *Russia in the Eighteenth Century* (London, 1973), or through Jerome Blum, *Lord and Peasant in Russia from the 9th to the 19th Century* (1961), which is essential reading for the whole period but specially valuable as a basis for studying the noble reaction after Peter. In this context the relevant essay in A. Goodwin (ed.), *The European Nobility in the Eighteenth Century* (1953), should be read, as should R.E. Jones, *The Emancipation of the Russian Nobility, 1763–85* (Cambridge, 1973). While her immediate predecessors, perhaps not surprisingly, have been neglected (though Elizabeth has found a biographer: *Elizabeth, Empress of Russia*, by Tamara Talbot-Rice (London, 1970)), Catherine the Great has tempted numerous writers, for 'romantic interest', though few of the resulting biographies are of value to the historian. Gladys Scott Thompson's *Catherine the Great and the Expansion of Russia* (1947) is a helpful introduction by a judicious historian, as is the study of G.P. Gooch, whose understanding of diplomacy and the ways of courts makes his writing such an agreeable way into the eighteenth century; in this case, *Catherine the Great and Other Studies* (1954). Of wider significance than the title would suggest, because he deals with the central political issue, is Paul Dukes's fine *Catherine the Great and the Russian Nobility* (1967). A valuable collection of extracts, from older and more recent historians, edited by M. Raeff (1964), contains for example the most complete statement, by A.A. Kizevetter, of the view that Catherine was ruled by desire for fame. Two writers in a special series in *Canadian Slavic Studies*, 9 (1970), provide revaluations of Catherine's reign. In K.R. Morrison's view her reign 'created a civil administration such as had not previously existed in Russia'. J.A. Duran claims that after 1781 it was possible 'to submit the first meaningful budget in the history of Imperial Russia'. J.T. Alexander, *Autocratic Policies in a National Crisis* (1969), is an examination of policy-making during the Pugachev emergency. Towering over all, sympathetic to her subject but not blindly so, is Isobel de Madariaga, *Russia in the Age of Catherine the Great* (London, 1981).

From more specialist books and articles which may illuminate a wider subject than that which they ostensibly treat the following may be mentioned: R. Mousnier, *Peasant Uprisings in Seventeenth Century France, Russia and China* (London, 1971); R.O. Crummey, *The Old Believers and the World of Anti-Christ* (Madison, 1970); P. Avrich, *Russian Rebels 1660–1800* (New York, 1972); M. Raeff, *Origins of the Russian Intelligentsia* (1966); A. Kahan, 'Continuity in economic activity and policy during the post-Petrine period in Russia', *Journal of Economic History*, 25 (1965); A. Kahan, 'The costs of westernisation in Russia; the gentry and the economy in the eighteenth century', *Slavic Review*, 25 (1966); P. Dukes, 'Russia and the eighteenth century revolution', *History* (October 1971); L.R. Lewitter, 'Poland, the Ukraine and Russia in the seventeenth century', *Slavonic and East European Review*, 27 (1948–9); J.L.H. Keep, 'Decline of the Zemski Sobor', *Slavonic and East European Review*, 36 (1957).

In his memoirs, like so many twentieth-century travellers from the west, William Plomer describes his feelings of recognition of what had already become familiar through reading of Russian novels and memoirs. In this rich array nothing could be better for understanding late eighteenth-century society than Aksakhov's autobiographical trilogy, now available in paperback edition (Oxford, 1983). Among many studies of culture and society may be mentioned: R.E.F. Smith, *The Enserfment of the Russian Peasantry* (1968); James Billington, *The Icon and the Axe: an Interpretative History of Russia* (New York, 1965); L.R. Lewitter, 'Peter the Great, Poland and the westernisation of Russia', *Journal of the History of Ideas*, 19 (1958); and D.M. Lang, *The First Russian Radical: Alexander Radishchev, 1749–1802* (London, 1977).

17

THE OTTOMAN EMPIRE

A Tolerant Overlordship

In August 1648, while European diplomats were haggling over the final stages of the peace of Westphalia, after a series of wars which had diverted them for thirty years from the affairs of Turkey, mutinous janissaries, exasperated by his crazy, self-indulgent rule, and in particular by incompetent handling of the war against Venice, murdered Sultan Ibrahim and set in his place 7-year-old Mehmed IV. In one way or another, in Europe and Asia, he governed thirty million, more than any other ruler of his time. About half the people living round the Mediterranean were his subjects. The empire comprised altogether more than 32 provinces. Anatolia had seen the first consolidation of Ottoman power and it had the most disciplined and docile inhabitants. But Turks were not the most numerous element in the Empire. Along with them, Arabs, Kurds, Bosnians, Albanians, Circassians, Tartars and Caucasians made up the Muslim majority. There was a Christian minority of Serbs, Greeks, Magyars, Bulgars, Wallachians and Moldavians. South of the Danube were Thrace and Rumelia, corresponding to the European part of Turkey, and Bulgaria, today; also Greece, most of Yugoslavia and Albania as they are now. Most of Hungary, since Mohacs (1526), had been in Turkish hands, though crown and claims were Habsburg. Between the Danube and Dniester rivers, Moldavia and Wallachia were tributary principalities, though like the princes of Transylvania across the Carpathian mountains their rulers sought independence; meanwhile they found Ottoman suzerainty a useful card in dealings with their neighbours. The Tartar khan of the Crimea provided 20,000 men for the defence of the southern lands against the Cossacks of Dnieper and Don. In Dalmatia, where the Venetians maintained an uneasy frontier, Ragusa (modern Dubrovnik) bought independence with annual tribute. In Asia the Turks had relinquished their grip on Georgia, and after long costly wars on most of Persia, but they held Iraq. Egypt and Syria, first conquered in 1516–17 by Selim I, completed the barrier between Christendom and the Indian ocean. On the far side of the Mediterranean the 'regencies' of Barbary were useful clients and practised pirates – for the most part against Christian ships.

Established on well-tried principles, the Ottoman Empire retained much of the original vigour which made it so fearsome to the Christian powers. Uniquely among the great predatory empires, the Ottomans combined the conquering impulse with the organizing ability to enable them to survive. When they established authority over Anatolia they had been the first to offer a degree of coherence and stability in the tumultuous Muslim world of the Middle East; that remained their fundamental source of strength. They accepted the faith of Mohammed and adopted Islamic customs, but they were never completely absorbed by the fissiparous Muslim world, and so they stayed on top. Their impulse to go forward was indeed sanctified by the claims of religious duty. War against the infidel, *jihad*, was good, a holy undertaking. It had also been successful, however, because of superior techniques, discipline and weight of numbers. The warrior ethos of the arid steppe impelled the Turks in years of conquest and sustained them in years of retreat; it had as much to do with racial pride as with religious zeal.

Fortunate in their remoteness from the crippling pressures of Mogul invasions, dwelling advantageously near Byzantine lands, the Ottomans had been able to attract land-hungry exiles from less secure regions. The destruction of two great Christian states, Serbia in the late fourteenth century and Hungary in the early sixteenth, had brought subjects, lands and revenues within spheres of old authority that then enhanced the new. The acquisition of large old towns, notably Adrianople in 1354, further anchored the expanding state to orderly centres of administration and settled patterns of life. Their patronage of orthodox Sunnite Islam against the divergent, more loosely disciplined dervish elements among the zealous followers of the Prophet had several important consequences. In the Mosque schools were trained the *ulema*, a body of experts in Muslim law and theology from which emerged the rudiments of a civil service. It is an essential feature of Islam that there is no distinction between the priestly and the law-giving functions. Constricting orthodoxy widened the gap between Muslims and Christians till they became polarized, as they were for the two and a half centuries from the fall of Constantinople in 1453 to the treaty of Carlowitz in 1699. Within the Ottoman regime religious spirit was fortified by a battery of rules covering all aspects of life: business and hunting, duties of pilgrims and the treatment of slaves, manners at the dinner table and relations between the sexes.

Since, however, it was one of the tenets of orthodox Islam that there should be no forcible interference with the rights of other men's religion, there was steady restraint from the centre on the craving of warriors for war against the infidel. So had emerged one of the unique features of the Ottoman state: the survival, underneath a zealous Muslim regime, of docile Orthodox Christian communities, enjoying a large measure of autonomy in return for tribute. The Ottomans recognized the Greek synod and its right to elect the patriarch and other bishops, Orthodox monasteries were allowed to keep their property, and Turkish officials and troops were even instructed to enforce the collection of the church's own taxes. The Turkish conquest of the Byzantine Balkans had been for many a liberation from arbitrary, sometimes ferocious seigneurial regimes. Memories of oppression might still count for more with Christian peasants than the uncertain benefits of a second liberation. When in 1690 Serbs migrated in large numbers under the patriarch of Pec into the empty lands of southern Hungary the grand vizier Fazil Mustafa not only decreed that there should be no punishment but allowed the building of new churches and took measures to improve the lot of oppressed peasants. Such wise tolerance was to strengthen, not weaken Turkish overlordship. Long before the Reformation the ideological argument of crusading Christians had been weakened by the many differences between the Latin and Greek Orthodox systems. The great Christian powers, notably Austria, Poland and Venice, would have to show that they could defeat the Turk in battle before they could hope to appeal to the latent pride and faith of Christian communities and so begin the recovery of lands under Turkish control.

The acquisition of Constantinople in 1453 had guaranteed permanence to Ottoman conquests by securing the only base from which the Christian powers could deploy effectively against the Turk. Lying at the intersection of Europe and Asia, it was the natural capital for an empire of provinces in two continents. Constantinople's growth was to be phenomenal. It was three cities in one metropolis. Constantinople itself had a circumference of 23 kilometres (that of Venice was 13), 400 mosques with open spaces around them, and independent enclaves, like the Atbazar or horse market and the Seray, with its sumptuous palaces, kiosks and gardens; across the Golden Horn was Galata, port and arsenal, headquarters of the Admiralty, cosmopolitan city of shipwrights, merchants and shipping agents; on the Asian side, Scutari, terminus for the caravan routes from the east. With its pleasant waterfront suburbs the whole conurbation had grown from 80,000 inhabitants at the time of the conquest to 700,000 by the middle of the seventeenth century. The growth of states is accompanied by the concentration of money and resources; capital cities expand with that concentration, and some live by little else. Madrid, Seville, Rome, even Naples, were modest examples of such parasitic growth compared to Constantinople. Egypt, Anatolia and the Balkan states were exploited systematically to supply the metropolis with recruits for the army, taxes for government, above all food. The city consumed 400 tons of grain a day, 7 million sheep or lambs a year. It produced little except animal skins that was not for its own use. It commanded the wealth of the Black Sea trade in grain, timber, horses, fish, butter wrapped in freshly flayed skins, and the silks and spices that came across the mountains to Trebizond from Persia, Armenia and Mesopotamia. In his *Persian Travels* (1664) Tavernier gives an insight into the market forces that influenced the political patterns: Mingrelia was always on good terms with Turkey 'because the greatest part of the steel and iron that is spent in Turkie comes out of Mingrelia through the Black Sea'.

Until the Russians established themselves on the northern shore a century later, the Ottomans enjoyed a virtual monopoly, subjecting the trade to the meticulous control that was the hallmark of their government. Since the actual trading was held to be derogatory by Turks, it was largely carried out by Armenians, Greeks and Jews. The richest of them formed one of the several élites who exerted influence over affairs, along with the officials of the Seray and the harem, and the privileged establishments of army, government and Muslim law: respectively the janissaries, the divan and the *ulema*. Their separate, often conflicting interests produced dissension at the head of the Empire and could only be reconciled by a strong sultan or grand vizier. At the other end of the social scale, dock workers, sailors and artisans were all so numerous and tightly organized that their requirements meant continuous pressure, with demands for this or that action: threatening the stability of government by agitation in the bazaar and violence in the streets, they forced ministers and army commanders to find decisive, appealing ways of asserting their authority.

In Constantinople the Byzantine rulers had created a network of communications and administration which became the sinews of the Ottoman state. All was formally directed from the divan, the council chamber within the Sublime Porte, the seat of government. Customs duties on top of the agricultural surplus of Anatolia and the subject lands, land taxes, tithe from Muslims, poll taxes on Christians, special contributions from puppet rulers, windfalls from campaigns, all sustained the swelling city. Old imperial traditions and new needs imposed upon the Ottomans the apparent necessity to organize, plan and treat in western style. Like western states the Ottoman Empire experienced a great inflation of government. With competition for office went venality. The more officials there were, the harder they were to control. Like their Christian counterparts, Ottoman rulers went to war to promote their religion and to acquire new lands, beyond what was required for their security. When they could have continued the digging of the Suez canal that had been begun in 1529, or secured the lower Volga and reopened the silk route, they spent their strength in futile wars in the Mediterranean and Balkans. In the latter theatre it was only the weakness and distractions of the Christian powers that enabled them to hold on to their conquests until near the end of the seventeenth century. Thereafter, again, they survived in control of the southern Balkans, as much because of the rivalries of the contending powers as by their own tenacity.

Constantinople and Byzantium had, in a sense, overcome Islam. That faith, with its warring and irreconcilable sects does not lend itself to simple definition. But much of its character is summoned up in the phrase 'Islam is the desert', conveying the fierce, ascetic spirit and the tendency to mysticism that belongs to men who move and have their being in hot, parched and empty lands. Seen from that perspective the northern Islamic order of soldiers and horsemen that triumphed in the fourteenth and fifteenth centuries can also be said to have been betrayed by its very success. For they were uniquely successful in assimilation and exploitation. Fortified by the conviction that they stood at the centre of the world, they saw no need to learn more. Without a great stimulus towards progress at the centre, this most centralized of empires could only decay. For the only significant principle remained the essentially sterile one of conquest.

It was the periodically tough central direction, supported by a sophisticated apparatus of supply and control that put such weight behind Ottoman attacks; but it was often local initiatives and conditions that precipitated action. If the Hungarian barley harvest were poor there would be no Turkish attack that year for there would be no fodder for the *sipahi* horses. Pressure at a particular point along the immense land and the sea frontier was affected by wider strategic considerations. Priorities were determined by sultan or grand vizier, but they had to reckon not only with Christian attacks, as in the reign of Philip II, but also with dissident rebels, as during the unsettled years of Ibrahim. And so the pressure was not unrelenting, but for the frontier powers Poland, Austria and Venice there remained always the threat, with horrendous possibilities of destruction. For all the sophisticated governing skills it is misleading to think of the Empire simply in terms of structure. It is revealing that the word *sanjak*, used for a government district, meant the standard of an army unit, but can also be envisaged as a vast encampment periodically roused by the spirit of conquest that had been epitomized in the person of Suleiman the Magnificent (1520–66). Administering in the winter, campaigning in the summer, Suleiman had been like a medieval sovereign of the west, a Henry II for example, controlling the far-flung Angevin empire. When he made himself caliph, literally 'successor' to the Prophet, he formally assumed the guardianship of Islamic law whose master principle, sanctioning all its pronouncements in the name of Allah, was duty. Within the limits of a compendious theocratic system the ruler was able therefore to exert and expand the muscles of authority through his law-making role.

The sultan's authority was enhanced in a negative way by the absence of some of those vested interests and local areas of power and patronage where the greatest subjects could thwart the efforts of their rulers in Christian Europe. The fact that the *timars*, or fiefs, granted first to individual warriors, then to landowners in return for military service, were uninheritable, prevented the evolution of a territorial aristocracy: for a revealing comparison there is no need to go further than neighbouring Austria and Poland. In the corporate character of Turkish life there appears superficially to have been a resemblance to Christian Europe. At all levels, from street sweepers and artisans to the *ulema* itself, members were organized in Muslim 'mysteries': they were essentially spiritual in character and rule, under the religious authority, and therefore under the sultan. They did not therefore represent any permanent check on the ruler's will. On the contrary his absolute power was sanctified by the Muslim tradition which enjoined unqualified submission to the sultan. In his plenitude of power the sultan might appear to be more absolute than the most imposing of western sovereigns. But comparisons are unfruitful for he simply belonged to a different world from theirs. The theocratic regime imprisoned the sultan as much as it empowered him. In Islam there is no distinction between the law-giving and the priestly functions. Not only was the grand *mufti* chief spiritual authority; he was also guardian of the *Kanoun Namé*, the fundamental law promulgated after the capture of Constantinople; and it had become the tradition that the grand *mufti* had to be consulted before any important decision. If the sultan was a commanding, decisive figure, the grand *mufti* would be his ally. If, as was usual, he was ineffective, then the moral authority of the state was fragmented. Then, as in some Islamic countries today, religion inspired faction.

The *Kanoun Namé* also established the conciliar administration which was to last till the eighteenth century. Typically the mystic number of 4, rather than administrative requirements, determined the division of authority. Most powerful was the grand vizier, comparable to the chancellors of western Europe but endowed as of right with some of the special powers that might be entrusted to the *privado* or *premier ministre* of a king of Spain or France. Besides administrative functions he had oversight of foreign policy and it was his duty to lead the army in the field. When it seemed that faith, will and efficiency were hardening into a sterile conservatism, when the sultanate was falling into decadence, the authority of the grand vizier became crucial: Mehmed (1656–61) and Ahmed (1661–76) Köprülü were to show that fighting spirit could be roused by competent and masterful grand viziers; also what scope there was for adaptation and reform. But the grand vizier depended on the sultan. Most sultans after Suleiman preferred to remain behind the walls of the Seray, the palace. Like the *kazi-asker*, controller of the legal system, the *defterdar*, in charge of finance, and the *nichandji*, secretary of state, the grand vizier was nominated by the sultan which meant inevitably that the personalities of palace and harem, especially the Walide and Khasseki sultans, respectively mother and consorts of the ruler, enjoyed great influence. Osman II was brought to the throne, aged 14, in 1618, through the collusion of the *mufti*, the Kizlar Agasi, chief of the black eunuchs, and Mah Firuze, his slave mother.

It follows in such a state that there was no distinction in the provinces between the civil and military powers. The large cities or provinces were entrusted to a pasha. The title denoted membership of the divan or state council, and emphasized that his status came solely from the fact that he represented the sultan; he would normally be moved about regularly, and not always to a superior post. Osman Pasha for example, who became governor in turn of Syria, Anatolia and Egypt, was the son of a Bosnian shepherd, one Papovic. He had risen like so many of his countrymen through service to a local official before gaining, in 1672, the patronage of the grand vizier. Even his marriage to the daughter of Mustapha Kemal did not save him from being downgraded more than once. The government had to keep such pashas in their place: they relied on them, but in the remoter, more mountainous or desert districts they could not supervise them. The administrative efficiency of the Empire depended on a number of such men attached to the government in the profitable but precarious relationships of mutual dependence. The Balkan countries of relatively recent conquest were administered by *beglerbegs*, and the *sanjaks*, or military districts into which they were divided, by *begs*. The special arrangement was a concession to military necessity. The *begs* and their attendants were on the move continually, more like travelling garrisons than fixed agencies of government. Moreover tasks requiring specialized skills were carried out from the capital by teams of officials from the slave household furnished with special warrants. The most regular object of such commissions had long been the collection of *devshirme*, the child tribute which fed the slave ranks of government and the janissary corps of infantry.

By 1600 there were about 150,000 *sipahis*, the mounted cavalry sustained, except for those 15,000 of the Porte, by the *timars*. The more valuable the *sipahis* were, defending or extending the frontier, the more dangerous they became politically, remote from central control and rendered ambitious by conquest. To counterbalance *sipahi* turbulence the rulers had developed a loyal and pliable corps of slave administrators and soldiers on whom they could depend because they were raised, in Gibbon's words, as 'an artificial people ... by the discipline of education, to obey, to conquer and to command'. Wrenched by Tartar raiders from their Ukrainian or Podolian homelands the slaves might find themselves members of households whose prestige was weighted by their masters' display. But if they had been recruited from a Balkan village they would be trained to serve the state. Either class of slave was better off than the seaman or traveller seized probably by Moorish pirates and put to serve in the galleys. *Devshirme* became obsolete in the seventeenth century as more Albanians, Bosnians and Montenegrans found their way voluntarily into government service and janissaries were allowed to marry and produce their own recruits for the schools which trained their corps: they became less amenable to discipline and more concerned about their rights. But the Ottoman government continued to be profoundly affected by this unique kind of service, privileged but classless. It illustrates the Ottoman talent for creative response to the challenges of a society with a constant impulse towards conquest, together, however, with the disparate character of subject lands which had no organic unity such as might come from common tradition or race. The boy who entered the school of pages, the janissaries or the palace left behind a constricted rural world and glimpsed the antechambers of power. Set apart at an impressionable age such functionaries and soldiers tended still to be loyal to a regime to which they owed their status. Nor were they usually unsympathetic to the peasant peoples from whom they were sprung. Peasant communities could often rely on protection against rapacious landowners. The balance of power between bureaucracy and landed interest helped to secure the sultan's authority. In the last resort, however, all depended on the character of the sultan.

The achievement by successive sultans of a single authority over subjects for whom warfare brought profit and honour had enabled them to construct a war machine more formidable than any since the heyday of imperial Rome. But it was not a self-perpetuating process. Of the sultans who succeeded Suleiman the Magnificent only Murad IV (1623–40) did justice to his tremendous role. The rule by which a new sultan ordered the execution of all his brothers and male children could only be defended as the solution to the problem of combining the principle of heredity with the polygamous marriage customs of Islam. Those threatened with fratricide had the best possible reason for supporting the old sultan; but their intrigues and efforts to build up their own factions had an unsettling effect. Mehmed III, who in 1595 executed his nineteen brothers, was the last to celebrate his accession in that way. More significantly he was also the last to have been trained, like his predecessors, as governor of a province, being educated there by specialists in Ottoman culture and the theory and practice of government. The sultans of the seventeenth century were brought up in the effete, secluded world of the palace, surrounded by women and eunuchs trained to please. The throne now passed from brother to brother, then when one generation was exhausted to the eldest surviving son of the next generation. Thus on the death of Sultan Ibrahim his sons succeeded him in turn: Mehmed IV (1648–87), Suleiman II (1687–91) and Ahmed II (1691–5): only then did the throne go to Mehmed IV's son, Mustafa II.

Recessional

Before the reign of Murad IV there were signs that the expansion phase had passed a peak. The flexibility of Turkish organization, a design for conquest and depredation within a fluid area, was giving way to rigidity. The growth of population, with corresponding increase in the burden of taxes, provoked the peasants and encouraged artisans to emigrate to Persia. Between 1578 and 1606 civil war and two major foreign wars took place against a background of rampant inflation. The marches of Hungary and Dalmatia were particularly lawless regions but banditry was rife everywhere. The dream of an ordered Islamic state was fading. Murad was, however, an implacable ruler. He conquered Iraq and made a lasting peace and a firm frontier with Persia; he enforced discipline among the janissaries and *sipahis* of the Porte, recovered fiefs which had been abused and prepared a 'Book of Justice', defining their modest rights, for the peasants. In the Venetian envoy's judgement no ruler attained a more absolute domination of his empire. In his short reign disorder was stemmed, but its fundamental causes remained. *Sipahis* were finding war less profitable. Their opponents were better organized for attack and defence, while government maintained pressure on their fiefs. Friction between different parts of the army persisted, their feelings inflamed by sectarian religious passion. The ineptitude and extravagance of Murad's successor Ibrahim (1640–8) encouraged the factious. Court intrigue brought about the execution of the one efficient grand vizier Kara Mustafa (1644). With three-quarters of the revenue allotted to the army and navy, and a regular deficit, government was hamstrung as dissidents and fanatics raised their heads throughout Asia Minor. New taxes and a revaluation of the coinage roused popular frenzy. The corporate loyalties of the capital's tradesmen and craftsmen now menaced the stability which they normally ensured. In 1649 rebel Anatolians were marching on the capital before they were bought off by concessions. They were roused by fanatical sectarian Muslims, 'Shiite dogs', as the Ottomans called them. The fundamental difference between the Shiite Muslims of Persia and the Sunnite orthodoxy of the Ottoman Muslims would have been a major cause of war against Persia and continued to threaten the stability of the Asiatic provinces. Palace feuds encouraged militancy in the streets and workshops. The old Walide Kosem fought to preserve her influence after the deposition and death of her son Ibrahim. But the party of the new Walide Turkhan, mother of Mehmed IV, won the day and in 1651 Kosem was murdered.

A succession of grand viziers bobbed up and down, helpless rafts on this turbulent sea. In 1651 a rising of the tradesmen of Constantinople brought about the downfall of the grand vizier Melek Ahmed. The Venetians pressed their naval offensive and in 1656 destroyed the Ottoman fleet, captured Tenedos and Lemnos, and set up a blockade of the capital. With steeply rising prices and mutinous soldiers returned from Crete roaming the streets, the situation was sufficiently serious for a new grand vizier, Mehmed Köprülü, to be given authority by the notables for drastic measures. Disillusioned by the feuds of his servants and the anarchy of his capital, Mehmed IV moved his court to Adrianople, and devoted himself to hunting, with battues employing 10,000 beaters and vast slaughters of game, in grotesque parodies of the traditional role of sultan. With the departure of court and royal bodyguard there was less scope for disturbances among troops and townsfolk. The sultan was content to hunt and leave government to his grand vizier.

Eleventh to hold the office in eight years, the ferocious old Albanian took up the challenge with relish. No official was allowed to oppose him and he had a free hand in all appointments; all reports went through his hands. He scythed through the ranks of the incompetent and mutinous. The chief eunuch, chief treasurer, grand *mufti* and the commanders-in-chief of the navy and the janissaries figured among the 50,000 victims of Mehmed Köprülü's grand purge. Terror was calculated policy, a preparation for tighter government. From the records of one small Hungarian territory ceded by the Habsburgs in 1664 we can see the methodical spirit of the Köprülü regime. The old landowners were removed; new Muslim fief-holders replaced them. Taxes, dues and services were carefully itemized. Autocratic power was supported by vigilant control and bureaucratic order; it is impressive by any standard of the time, certainly by that of Habsburg administration. By prudent management Mehmed Köprülü found the means to pay regular wages and so secure the loyalty of the janissaries. Idle dockyard workers were stirred to fresh effort. More radical, lasting reforms would have been necessary to create a navy capable of sustaining Mediterranean power in the longer term. Since 1574 and the capture of Tunis the Turkish navy had gained no important success. Inactivity was always fatal. But Mehmed showed that demoralized sailors could be lashed into effective fighting. The islands of Lemnos and Tenedos were recaptured and the defences of the Dardanelles were strengthened. Mehmed was content, however, with stalemate in the Venetian war because his main aim was to restore imperial control in the Carpathian principalities. There amid dissolving patterns of allegiance the veteran princes of Wallachia and Moldavia took advantage of their suzerain's difficulties.

The ambitious young Calvinist prince George Rakoczy II of Transylvania, whose independence had been confirmed by the peace of Westphalia, sought to exercise his talents in a wider sphere. Opportunity for trouble-making had been provided initially by the fateful rebellion, in 1648, of Chmielnicki in the Ukraine. Initially that was a threat to the new King John Casimir of Poland, elected in the same year. The Tartars benefited from Polish weakness in the south while the Russians were not slow to take Chmielnicki under their wing. The eastern crisis acquired a new dimension when the Swedes invaded Poland in 1655. Chmielnicki meanwhile had sought to broaden his position by alliance with Moldavia: he married his son to the daughter of Basil 'the wolf'. But when Basil was overthrown by a palace revolution the alliance proved worthless. In the following year Matthew of Wallachia died and George of Transylvania intervened to support his successor Constantine. Because of their domestic troubles the Turks had been passive while the Russians established themselves on the Dnieper, and Cossack pirates preyed on the Black Sea trade routes. With Wallachia becoming a puppet of Transylvania two valuable dependants threatened to become one independent force. But George had no support from the Habsburgs and he overreached himself by allying with the Swedes: the Poles fought back strongly against Sweden and he was defeated. At that juncture, in 1657, Mehmed intervened. He appointed new rulers to Moldavia and Wallachia, then launched a series of attacks from his Danubian bases. He was able to exploit divisions within Transylvania. The great landowners there wanted to appease the Turks whom they had found tolerant overlords but the ordinary gentry, with less to lose, responded to George's patriotic appeal. In December 1660 George was killed as was his successor Janos Kemény in January 1662. With them died the cause of independent Transylvania. The Turks installed Michael Apafi as their puppet and kept the fortress.

The defeat of Transylvania exposed the flank of imperial Hungary to Turkish aggression and brought home to the Austrians that they could not hope to continue indefinitely on the old, comfortable basis: standing as it were back to back along the line that divided Hungary, each empire respecting the other's rule and free therefore to pursue its own objectives elsewhere. Turkey's own 'eastern question' was no longer pressing as Persia slid into decline, while the Habsburgs were to take a more realistic view of their prospects in western Europe. Behind the successes of Ottoman troops under more vigorous and single-minded leadership there were some disturbing reminders that Islam was on the march in more senses than one.

Along the military road, Constantinople – Sofia – Belgrade – Buda, new mosques, baths and schools witness to Muslim penetration along the strategic lines. A second deeper layer of conquest was maintained by preachers and teachers. There was the appeal of careers open to talent for the price of perhaps a nominal conversion; and undoubtedly the suspicion of the missionaries of the west, Franciscans and Jesuits seen as outriders of German-style government and landownership. It was significant that the Greek inhabitants of Crete accepted their invaders and often their religion even while the Venetian garrison of Candia was maintaining its epic resistance. Conversions were widespread in the mountains of Montenegro and Albania and the movement was influencing the Ottoman state at all levels, from the Köprülü viziers, whose austere statecraft made some of their predecessors look like weaklings or crude freebooters, to the peasant converts, who brought to army and government the toughness and the devotion of the *besa*, the traditional oath of friendship which bound men together in the age-long struggle for survival.

The ruthless purging of the old leadership and the recruitment of new men, proud of victory and expecting more, had transformed the army which Mehmed Köprülü bequeathed to his son Ahmed. In 1663 the Ottomans put 200,000 men into the field in a *razzia* of the traditional sort, a fast-moving, wide-ranging sweep. The Christian powers were roused at last. The veteran Raimondo Montecuccoli, who with a mere 9000 men had been a helpless spectator of the collapse of Transylvania, was now entrusted with a formidable army, strengthened by a contingent of French volunteers. At St Gotthard the Turks were decimated by the concentrated fire power of the Austrian army, cosmopolitan in composition but versed in techniques and tactics which the Turks had failed to learn. But the Emperor and his advisers were reluctant to commit themselves farther. The treaty of Vasvár (1664), virtually confirming the status quo, appeared to Hungarian patriots to be a betrayal, the more flattening because their hopes had soared. It also freed Turkish forces for other fronts.

Struggling against their Ukrainian rebels, Swedes and Russians, the embattled Poles had failed to rebuild the decayed strongholds or to maintain adequate garrisons in their southern lands. The government had no option but to leave the defence of the frontier to local magnates, like John Sobieski who made his name in the raids and skirmishes of these wide-open lands. For the most part Tartar and Cossack rode about Volhynia and Podolia unchallenged, seizing cattle and peasants, while the luckless inhabitants sought security in palisaded towns or the fortress villages of the chief landowners. In 1669, the year which also saw the surrender of Candia and with it complete control of Crete, the Cossack *hetman* Doroshenko, who had already thrown in his lot with the Tartars, acknowledged Ottoman suzerainty. At the same time Ahmed Köprülü appointed a new khan in the Crimea, Selim, talented poet and soldier. Forays into the heart of Poland, and the loss of the vital fortress of Kamenets, roused Sobieski to action. In a grand counter-attack in 1672 he recaptured strongholds and drove the raiders before him. In the same year, however, Louis XIV invaded Holland. For a decade there was to be no question of crusade against the Turks or co-operation between the western powers in simpler terms of self-interest. That by itself would account for Turkish success in the ensuing decade.

John Sobieski's lone effort merely had the effect of stirring the Turks to a more concerted effort under the sultan himself. The tides of war rolled back and forth, leaving wrack and waste. Sobieski's triumph at Chocim on the Dniester, coinciding with the death of King Michael (1673), strengthened his hand in the subsequent election. King John III Sobieski was able to bring more sustained pressure to bear on the Turks and their allies. He had some success in restoring the Polish position in the Ukraine but on this enormous front he could achieve nothing decisive. To win time to give to other concerns, constitutional and diplomatic, he made a truce in October 1676, ceding Podolia. Meanwhile the Russians, who had recently acquired Kiev, had been pressing on with the subjugation of the Ukraine. When in 1676, after a two-year siege, they captured Doroshenko's headquarters at Chigirin, on the Dnieper, Kara Mustafa, the new grand vizier took up the challenge. The main forces of the two empires, the Turks reinvigorated, the Russians committed to the expansionist course that she has never since abandoned, now stood face to face. The confrontation was portentous, though brief and indecisive. The place was remote and primitive; by the time the Turks had captured it in 1678 it was a ruin, apparently valueless. The area of future conflict was defined. But there was no immediate advantage to Russians in continuing a wasting war in such forsaken lands. At the peace, eventually ratified by the sultan at Adrianople in 1682, the Turks, confirmed in possession of Podolia, undertook not to garrison places between the Dnieper and Bug. The Zaporozhian Cossacks on the west bank of the Dnieper accepted Turkish sovereignty. With so much, Kara Mustafa was content to let go of the Ukraine and its *hetman*, to cede to Russia the Dnieper front and their Kiev bridgehead. He had something bigger in mind.

The treaty barred the way for the time being to the Christian people of the lower Danube. But they, Romanians and Serbs, had been encouraged to look to the tsar as their natural protector. For the frustrated warrior John Sobieski, as for the Venetians over Crete, Adrianople was unfinished business. So long as Hungary was in ferment there could be no stability. There Imre Thököly, a young nobleman whose grandfather had been executed for plotting rebellion against the Habsburgs in 1671, capitalized on the resentments of the Hungarian magnates against Habsburg officials and priests. But he was frustrated by well-timed concessions. In 1681 Leopold restored the old constitution of the kingdom and deprived Thököly of the support of the nobles who were already worried by the sultan's military preparations. The grand vizier reckoned, however, that Thököly would be able to provide a diversion on the Austrian flank; Thököly hoped to use the Turkish alliance to further his own plan of becoming king of an independent Hungary. Both men were so blinded by ambitions that they overestimated their strength and underrated their opponents' capacity to fight back.

The target of Kyzil Elma, or 'Red Apple' as Kara Mustafa called his grand design, was Vienna. For Mustafa statesmanship was aggression. Of the three tempting targets, Dalmatia, Cracow and Habsburg Hungary, the latter was most tempting: lines of communication would be shorter, Vienna was a prize to whet the appetites of his troops. They may not have numbered more than 150,000, including the contingent of Tartar horseman, the specialist units of artisans and tradesmen, sappers and gunners, but the pack animals and their grooms, servants and women accompanying the army gave it the appearance of a limitless horde. In the contrast between the soldiers of Anatolia and Albania, living on a handful of meal and, as Busbecq described them in 1555, drinking 'a kind of sour milk that they call Yoghurt', or a few grams of cheese, and the luxurious tented households of their leaders lay much of the history of the Ottoman Empire at war. It was holy war. Not for nothing was Kara Mustafa invested by the sultan with the robe of gold and standard of Mohammed. They provided the ultimate goal. Kara Mustafa, inflamed with self-importance, argued against Ibrahim Pasha, commander of Buda, who wanted the Turks first to concentrate upon reducing the fortresses of Gyor and Komarno: after Vienna's fall 'all the Christians would obey the Ottomans' and he would 'stable his horses in Venice'. He showed his ignorance of the western scene and of the way in which the military revolution of the past fifty years had altered the balance between Ottoman and Christian power. Yet it is understandable that he should have been confident that the powers would not combine effectively against him. In the event the emperor was slow to call on other sovereigns for aid. The relief of Vienna by the combined forces of John Sobieski and Charles of Lorraine came only as the Turks were preparing for a final assault to which Vienna would almost certainly have succumbed. On 12 September the allies launched their attack from the Kahlenberg heights. With superior artillery and tactics and the furious spirit of men who believed that they were engaged in a holy fight for Christendom Charles and Sobieski routed the Turks. They lost 10,000 men and retreated in panic leaving their encampment of 25,000 tents, with most of their supplies in the hands of the Polish cavalry.

After exalted hopes came demoralization. This time the Habsburgs did not hesitate to follow up their advantage. Secure in the west, after the truce of Ratisbon (1684), fighting under the banner of Pope Innocent XI's Holy League, which was formed at Linz in March 1684, the Habsburg armies drove deep into Hungary. John Sobieski was to be disappointed in his campaigns and could never mobilize sufficient forces to recover Podolia or annex Wallachia and Moldavia. The Venetians, the other principals in the League did, however, harry Turkish commerce in the Aegean and so added to the distress and anger in the capital which was to provide a turbulent background to the increasingly desperate efforts of grand viziers and generals to stem the Habsburg onslaught. In 1685 the Turks lost the great stronghold of Nove Zamky, and Ibrahim Pasha, the main army commander, parleyed for peace; he was executed for acting without the authority of the grand vizier, himself soon to be dismissed. Abdi Pasha defended Buda for 78 days against an army of 40,000. But with 'the shield of Islam', in September 1686, fell nearly all its defenders and the hopes of Thököly's independent Hungary. The following year saw Sobieski lunge deeply into Moldavia till forced to retreat before the formidable horsemen of Selim-Girei, khan of the Crimea, the Turks driven out of the Morea and the Venetian army, half-German in composition, occupy Athens; it was then that the Parthenon, used by the Turks as a magazine, was blown up by a

Venetian bomb. An attempt by the grand vizier Suleiman Pasha to recover Buda only brought disaster near the old battlefield of Mohacs: in August 1687 he was crushed, with the loss of 20,000 men. Mehmed 'the Hunter' long absorbed in his pleasures, indifferent to the mounting crisis, could no longer shield behind his unlucky servants. The *ulema* and the army combined to dethrone and replace him by his half-brother Suleiman II (1687–91). His first task was to deal with the janissaries. In one of the most outrageous episodes in their lurid history, they ruled the capital, appointed their own nominees to high office, swaggered and pillaged as if in a conquered city. After four months they were put down, but supplies had been cut off and the army's will to resist was sapped. First Eger, then Peterwardein were taken. In September 1688 Belgrade fell to the elector Max Emmanuel of Bavaria after a mere three weeks. Now Serbia and Bulgaria had come within range of the imperial troops. The sultan sued for peace but the Emperor stiffened his terms to include Transylvania; the Turks mustered their forces for a new campaign but to no avail: in September they lost Nish and Vidin to the margrave Lewis of Baden. Coming up with a large force of Tartars, Selim-Girei Khan covered Bulgaria, but some of Baden's cavalry penetrated Wallachia as far as Bucharest.

As in 1656, when the first Köprülü vizier came to power at a critical juncture, so in October 1689 his youngest son Fazil Mustafa Pasha was given sufficient authority to enable him to restore discipline in the army and order in government. For two years the Ottomans recovered lost ground, favoured by Louis's aggression in the Rhineland which led to the deployment of Habsburg troops in that area and in Italy, and the consequent weakening of their effort in the east. In October 1690 Fazil reoccupied Belgrade. The Ottomans' recovery of Serbia was marred by the extraordinary exodus of a host of Serbs, some 200,000, led by the patriarch of Pec, one of the holy places, into the near empty lands of southern Hungary. In the best tradition of Ottoman realism Fazil 'the Wise' prevented action being taken against them, allowed new churches to be built and even took positive steps to protect the Serbs living in these regions blighted by the passage of armies. He was maintained in office by the sultan Ahmed II who succeeded his half-brother Suleiman II in 1691. But he died fighting in the bloodbath of Zalankhamen. The imperialists won the battle (August 1691) but could thereafter do little more than hold their ground. Rivers and marshes hindered the movements of armies. Both sides asked too much for the British ambassador at the Porte, Lord Paget, to make the peace which the British so badly needed so that Austrian troops could be released for the western front. The Turks found encouragement in events in the Aegean, where the Venetian admiral Zeno had squandered precious troops on the occupation of Chios, only to lose it again in the following year, 1695. In that year a new and forceful sultan Mustafa II (1695–1703) took personal command of the army, won enough local victories to earn the title of *ghazi*, conqueror, and found new ways of raising money to put fresh armies into the field. But he was confronted by a new danger.

In 1696, undeterred by the failure of his first attempt, Tsar Peter took Azov. Beckoned by the prize of a warm-water port, encouraged by Serb, Romanian and Greek Christians who did not relish the prospect of liberation by German soldiers and Jesuit priests, Peter had now shown his hand. The Turks had to take seriously the defence of the Black Sea. It did not prevent Mustafa II from planning boldly for the recovery of Hungary. He had the misfortune to be opposed to Prince Eugène, newly released from operations in Italy. In the early evening of a September day in 1697 Eugène rounded off a brilliant forced march by an unexpected attack on the Turks as they were crossing the river Tisza, near Zenta. By nightfall the Turks had lost about 20,000 killed and another 10,000 drowned. While the furious janissaries killed their officers, Eugène drove on into Bosnia and sacked Sarajevo.

After Zenta the way was open to settlement under the auspices of English and Dutch mediators. It was completed at Carlowitz in January 1699. The Austrians were above all concerned by then with the imminent death of Charles II of Spain and attendant prospects and dangers. The Turks, acknowledging for the first time that they had been defeated and having conceded the principle of possession, could not avoid vast losses: Hungary and Transylvania, less the Banat of Temesvár; Dalmatia and the Montenegrin harbour of Cattaro; Morea and Aegina to Venice; Podolia, with Kamenets, to Poland. Russia, left to fight and treat by the allies, did not secure the straits of Kerch which they wanted. Peter made his own peace in 1700 after the outbreak of war in the north: he gained the Azov region, but still bore a grudge against the Habsburgs for what he saw as desertion. No less important for the future, in particular for the prestige of Russia in the Balkans, Russia was granted diplomatic representation at Constantinople, together with the right of pilgrimage to the Holy Land.

Carlowitz marked beyond dispute the end of the Turkish threat as it had existed, intermittently active, always present, since the first battle of Mohacs. The integrity of the much reduced Empire was in doubt. Could a regime which had grown by might in war rather than right of succession survive such a sequence of retreats and defeats? The Venetian fleet could strike at the Dardanelles. The Russians, moving into the northern Caucasus, were poised seemingly to move on: to the mouth of the Dnieper, to the Black Sea, and to the Crimea. In some parts the Ottoman government was unable to preserve order in the face of high grain prices, famine, beggary and brigandage. Yet Carlowitz was not to prove the beginning of the end. The Ottomans were helped by the fact that the Austrians were again heavily committed to a second, western front between 1701 and 1714. The Venetians were feeling the strain. They did not have a standing army but depended on hired troops and volunteers; and the Italian princes were less disposed to make a business out of soldiering than their predecessors. In tough and realistic reforms, in the stubborn rearguard action, with some effective counter-attacks, throughout the period up to the peace of Kutchuk-Kainardji in 1774, the Turks confounded prophets of doom. They showed the resilience of people fighting for a system which still offered good rewards to those ambitious and fortunate enough to achieve office. There were still exceptionally able men among them, like the grand vizier Ruseyn Pasha who toiled from 1697 to his resignation in 1702 to repair government and economy. He concentrated on aiding the Christian peasantry who had suffered specially from the breakdown of local government and the ravaging of armies who behaved without any of the restraints that gave a relatively civilized appearance to war in the west. He cancelled villages' long arrears of war contributions and did something to curb the excesses of fief-holders. The numbers of janissaries were reduced, fortresses were repaired, the navy was reformed, with greater emphasis on the construction of big ships, carrying fifty guns or more.

The sombre sultan Ahmed III (1703–30), a notable flower painter, combined sensitive appreciation of the finer sides of life with a ruthless pursuit of security, for himself and his country. After several unsatisfactory choices he found in Chörlülü Ali Pasha a statesmanlike grand vizier (1706–10) who had the intelligence to preserve neutrality against the strong temptation to take advantage of Peter's difficulties. By restraining the khan of the Crimea from joining the Swedes and Mazeppa he contributed to Peter's victory at Poltava in 1709, which meant such a big shift in the balance of power in north-east Europe. It suited the Turks to offer hospitality to the defeated Charles but he proved an unco-operative guest. Instead of accepting the safe conduct to Sweden which the Porte traded for Peter's agreement to demolish the small forts on the lower Dnieper, Charles intrigued with the khan, Mazeppa's successor Philip Orlik (the latter seeking to establish an independent Ukraine) and the chiefs of the *ulema*, for the overthrow of Chörlülü Ali and his policy of détente. A more militant vizier, Baltaji Mehmed Pasha found support for war. The provincial pashas were ordered to join the main army in the spring of 1711. Peter rose to the challenge. The banners of the Guards were inscribed with the Cross and the words 'Under this sign we conquer'. He proclaimed that his aim was to liberate the Balkan Christians from 'the yoke of the infidels'. He enjoyed the keen support of Serb churchmen and chieftains, notably Prince Bishop Daniel Petrovich in Montenegro and Michael Miloradovich in Herzegovina. Round the Black Mountain of Montenegro since 1702, Petrovich had been leading an insurrection, poorly armed but ferociously anti-Muslim. Peter could also count on Demetrius Cantemir, prince of Moldavia, who promised to provide forage for the invading Russians in return for recognition as hereditary prince. His rival Constantine Brancovan of Wallachia was also looking towards Russia, but cautiously withheld support till he knew the outcome of the war.

For Peter it was disastrous. By June 1711 the tsar's army had entered Moldavia, only to find that supplies were unobtainable because of drought and a plague of locusts. After an unexpectedly rapid Turkish advance and crossing of the river Pruth, the Russians found themselves trapped in a narrow plain, with the river behind them, a wide marsh on one side, and the Tartars blocking the road behind them. On 21 July 1711 Baltaji Mehmed was giving his orders for the great assault when the Russians surrendered. Exhausted and famished, they knew they faced annihilation. Charles XII expected that he would be rewarded for the plan which had worked so well by the return of his lost Baltic provinces. But Baltaji was in a hurry to get what he wanted: the return of Azov, Taganrog, the demolition of the new Dnieper fortresses. Peter conceded all, together with a promise of nonintervention in Polish affairs and an end to Russian representation at the Porte.

Charles, who had helped to engineer the victory received nothing from it. He continued to hold court among his friends at Bender, planning a grander future, not reconciled to exile but reluctant to move. In 1713 he was ejected, and with him went the last obstacle to a permanent peace. It was signed at Adrianople in June 1713. Peter's southern frontier was withdrawn to the river Orel and he was required to evacuate Poland whose king, Augustus II, was recognized by the Turks as ruler of the Polish Ukraine. Thus Orlik became another casualty, along with Petrovich and Demetrius Cantemir, of the Russian failure. All in all Adrianople was a sharp check to Peter's ambitions in the south. It was plain that the Russians could not yet do much for the Christian peoples of the Balkans. Able Greeks, like the Mavrogordatos and their like, known as Phanariots from the lighthouse or Phanar district in Athens where many of them lived, saw their best prospects for themselves and their faith to lie in serving the Turk in a privileged position in diplomacy and government. Intelligence, wide contacts and staying power enabled Alexander Mavrogordato to rise to the office of chief dragoman, or interpreter to the sultan, which he held from 1675 to 1700 and to provide a continuity which was specially valuable in those critical years. The advance of the Greek families in government reflected their dominant position in trade. It was accompanied by intellectual activity and spiritual revival in their church, protected but not emasculated by official patronage. The patriarch of Jerusalem had an inspiring success in 1672 when in defiance of Louis XIV's ambassador he secured the guardianship of the holy places. In the Danubian provinces in particular, where Greeks intermarried with the great Romanian families, monasteries flourished. In Bucharest Prince Serban Cantacuzene was a generous patron of Greek scholars.

The Greeks were one element in what, if not truly a revival, was at least a more resourceful and robust government in the years after Adrianople. Another was the emergence of a war party, led by Silahdar Ali Pasha, the sultan's son-in-law and favourite who, with the aid of the *mufti* and the Kizlar Agasi, had overthrown Baltaji Mehmed and became grand vizier in his place, in April 1713. Silahdar Ali had personal interests in the Morea, where Venetian officials and priests were proving predictably unpopular. The fractious Greeks had become used to the accommodating rule of the Ottomans and resented the efforts of Italians to improve agriculture and education. Claiming in justification that Venetian agents had assisted Montenegran rebels, in the summer of 1715, the Turks mounted a naval and military operation against Venice which threatened to bring the republic to its knees. As ever the Turks enjoyed the small-seeming but perhaps crucial advantages of the early start. Spring comes early to the Bosphorus. There are better sailing conditions in the Aegean than in the Adriatic. The fleet gave cover to the Turkish army as it captured Corinth and other Morean strongholds in a series of sieges, lightly resisted by the outnumbered Venetians. In July 1716 the Turkish navy moved on to Corfu, principal Venetian base in the area, but by then the Emperor, after efforts to mediate, had made a defensive alliance with Venice. Against the sober advice of some of the viziers, Siladhar Ali chose to regard the alliance as a breach of the terms of the treaty of Carlowitz (which he had already broken), invited Francis Rakoczy to proclaim himself King of Hungary, and directed an army of 120,000 to attack the frontier fortress of Peterwardein, north-west of Belgrade.

There in August 1717, by the river Drave, Eugène's massed cavalry, 180 squadrons, routed their opposite numbers and inflicted casualties, some 8000, which would have been even higher but for the stubborn resistance of the janissaries. As it was the grand vizier was killed along with other Turkish leaders and the Turks lost more than 100 guns. In October Eugène seized Temesvár, the fortress which controlled the Banat, sole remnant of Turkish Hungary. In the following summer he laid siege to Belgrade. With his friend and co-general Count Mercy he had put himself at risk, sandwiched between the formidable city, whose garrison outnumbered the besiegers, and the Turkish relieving force under the new grand vizier Halil Pasha. His inexperienced and faltering generalship and Eugène's boldness in attack brought the Habsburgs victory yet again, in confused fighting on a misty August morning. Two days later Belgrade surrendered.

Negotiations were difficult because the Turks wanted to keep Temesvár, Belgrade and the Morea, but the Venetians were fighting back strongly, and demands for peace were coming from within the divan as well as from the emperor Charles VI. He was concerned about the ambitious Italian schemes of the Spanish minister Alberoni and accepted the mediation of the British, Austria's ally in the Quadruple Alliance. The treaty of Passarowitz in July 1718 created a new frontier along the Save and Drina rivers, giving Austria the Banat, Little Wallachia and a fertile part of Serbia, including Belgrade. An accompanying commercial treaty conceded to the Austrians free trade throughout the Ottoman Empire. Through his new chartered company, operating from the port of Trieste, Charles also set out to develop trade in the Balkans. Finally Venice, her finances gravely impaired, her economy no longer buoyant, had to accept the loss of the Morea. But she kept her conquests in Dalmatia and regained Cerigo which was to be her advanced base between Ionia and the Aegean.

Further Reading

It may be inevitable that the European reader will see the Ottoman state largely in terms of its impact on Europe; in this period his view will be further coloured by the retreat of the Ottomans from some of their subject lands and by the arrival of 'the Eastern question'. He is well served in the way of introduction to these themes by D.M. Vaughan, *Europe and the Turk* (Liverpool, 1954) and P. Coles, *The Ottoman Impact on Europe* (1968), an illustrated survey. There remains a lacuna: there is no general history of the Ottoman state embodying the research and views of recent Turkish scholars. However, there is less excuse than formerly for ignorance of Muslim faith and institutions, to which H.A.R. Gibbs and H. Bowen provide a good introduction in *Islamic Society and The West* (1950), covering the confused situation in the southern fringe lands, Armenia, Georgia and Kurdistan. *The Emergence of Modern Turkey* (1961), by B. Lewis, is another sound account. Mention should be made of two good chapters in the *New Cambridge Modern History*, vols 5 and 6, by A.N. Kurat, and A.N. Kurat and J.S. Bromley, respectively. In the masterpiece of F. Braudel, *The Mediterranean and the Mediterranean World*, 2 vols (trans. S. Philipps, London 1972–3), there is material of interest and value relating to the Ottoman empire not confined to the sixteenth century with which the book nominally deals. Several particular topics have good books devoted to them: for example, *The Siege of Vienna*, by J.W. Stoye (1964), *Peter the Great and the Ottoman Empire*, by B.H. Sumner (Oxford, 1949), and *Europe's Steppe Frontier, 1500–1800*, by W.H. McNeill (Chicago, 1964). *The Great Church in Captivity* (Cambridge, 1968) by S. Runciman is a study of Orthodoxy under Turkish rule. A. Pallis, *In the Days of the Janissaries* (London, 1951) is an interesting collection, chosen from contemporary sources. In the *Journal of Lady Mary Wortley Montague* (London, 1965) there are fascinating descriptions of aspects of Ottoman life as viewed by the shrewd, if not entirely dispassionate wife of the British ambassador. M.A. Cook (ed.), *A History of the Ottoman Empire to 1730* (Cambridge, 1976), should also be read.

INDEX